The Bible and Disa   ~
A Commentary

Sarah J. Melcher
Mikeal C. Parsons
Amos Yong
Editors

scm press

© Sarah J. Melcher, Mikeal C. Parsons and Amos Yong 2018

Published in 2018 by SCM Press
Editorial office
3rd Floor, Invicta House,
108–114 Golden Lane,
London EC1Y 0TG, UK
www.scmpress.co.uk

SCM Press is an imprint of Hymns Ancient & Modern Ltd
(a registered charity)

Published in the United States in 2018 by Baylor University Press

Hymns Ancient & Modern® is a registered trademark of
Hymns Ancient & Modern Ltd
13A Hellesdon Park Road, Norwich,
Norfolk NR6 5DR, UK

British Library Cataloguing in Publication data

A catalogue record for this book is available
from the British Library

978 0 334 05686 7

Printed and bound by
CPI Group (UK) Ltd, Croydon

Contents

Foreword

The strange new world within the Bible:
Some reflections on the hermeneutics on disability

John Swinton

The Bible is a strange place, full of odd narratives and peculiar perspectives that speak to us of a paradoxical God who is both hidden (Isaiah 45:15) and revealed (John 6:37); weak (Philippians 2:5-11) and strong (Psalm 28:7); wholly divine (Isiah 45:5) and fully human (John 1:1). This God creates the world and loves it even unto death (John 3:16), but still asks us to wait with patience and perseverance (Romans 12:12) as redemption unfolds in the midst of suffering and joy (Romans 8:22). Through the words of Scripture, this strange paradoxical God reveals what Karl Barth has described as a strange new world.[1] As we allow the words of Scripture to illuminate and renew our minds (Romans 12:12) so we are enabled to view and comprehend the world differently. The new reality that is revealed to us in the Bible is not apart from the old reality that we have always seen and experienced. We just see, hear, feel and experience everything differently as the Spirit illuminates our imagination and helps us to see that which was previously unseen and indeed unseeable (Daniel 5:14).

WHY SCRIPTURE?

Precisely why this strange yet magnificent God chooses to reveal God's self specifically through text is a mystery. In many ways it would have been much easier if God had just sent angels and messengers directly to tell us the good news to each generation rather than leaving it to the unpredictable

---

[1] Karl Barth, *The Word of God and the Word of Man*, edited and translated by Douglas Horton (Pilgrim Press, 1928), pp. 28–50.

predilections of human interpretative actions to work it out over time! Of course, God did send angels and messengers to tell us the good news, but once their actions were written down the problems began. But for whatever reason, Scripture is the medium through which God has chosen to reveal God's self. The task of Scriptural hermeneutics in all of its diverse forms is therefore one of the most vital and one of the most Holy tasks of the Church. When we read and interpret the Bible we are participating in something profoundly important and something that has eternal significance. We can only approach such a task with our heads bowed in humility and hope.

A LIMITED HERMENEUTIC?

Reading the Bible is always and inevitably a complex hermeneutical event. Despite the fact that interpreting Scripture is fundamentally dependent on the illumination of the Holy Spirit (John 14:26), it remains a very human enterprise. That is why prayer and Scriptural interpretation are inextricably intertwined. We approach the Bible with certain conscious and unconscious prejudices, biases and presuppositions that influence, shape and form our interpretative practices. No matter how reflexive and knowledgeable we may think we are, we cannot escape from our cultural assumptions and internalised biases. One such assumption and potential is the temptation to read Scripture in our own image. By that I simply mean that the norms and assumptions that shape and form our personal and corporate worldviews impact deeply on how we read Scripture, what we think we see there, and how we respond to what we think we see in terms of knowledge development, personal behaviour and ecclesial practice.

One implicit norm that has been central to much biblical interpretation and theological construction relates to the issue of how we should interpret human diversity. If we approach Scripture with a hermeneutic that implicitly or explicitly assumes certain things about what is or is not "normal" in relation to human beings, those living with disabilities can very easily and very quickly become judged as "abnormal," both in terms of their bodily and their spiritual existence. We just need to glance at the everpresent controversies surrounding the healing of disabilities to see the ways in which certain interpretations deeply influenced by the assumptions of biomedical culture can become deeply oppressive to those who do not desire to be healed or for whom God in God's wisdom has chosen a different path.[2] The strange

---

[2] Obviously, God can heal whomsoever God chooses to heal. My point here is simply that whether we are healed or not healed is not a matter of human choice but of divine gift. For a further discussion on this point in relation to disability and the healing miracles, see Graham Monteith, *Deconstructing Miracles: From thoughtless indifference to honouring disabled people* (Covenanters, 2005).

new world within the Bible can become dangerously dissonant for those whom others decide are "not normal." When we choose to interpret the Bible in such ways, the richness of the strange new world is substituted for an understanding of the world that is guided by cultural norms which very often mask hidden prejudices and negative assumptions about the nature and origins of disability and the lived experiences of people with disabilities.

A DISABILITY HERMENEUTIC

The scholars who have gifted us the essays in this book take such observations very seriously. They all, in different ways, have come to recognise the ways in which the experience of people with disabilities has not been included in the standard Scriptural hermeneutic. This has meant that key questions about God, Church and the nature of humanness have not been adequately addressed. This is an omission that is not only to the detriment of people living with disabilities. It is also a profound loss for the Church. Without the hermeneutical voice of people living with disabilities, the revelation that God desires to impart to us remains lacking. The authors of this book push us to consider the necessity for a different hermeneutic: a disability hermeneutic.

Such a hermeneutic provides us with a way of interpreting Scripture that allows fresh, new and challenging questions to come to the fore in ways that are challenging and sometimes creatively dissonant and jarring. When this happens we are enabled to see things within texts that we were unable to see previously. Within this strange new world, human bodies and human disability are found to have meanings that stretch beyond simplistic bio-medical assumptions that we need to fix what is "broken" and normalise what some consider to be different. As we re-read the Bible in the light of human disability, old familiar passages take on new meanings. God chooses Moses, a person with a profound speech impediment, to speak to Pharaoh (Exodus 4:10-12). Through the thorn in his flesh – possibly depression, epilepsy, or scoliosis[3] – he finds God's strength not apart from but *through* his disabling condition (2 Corinthians 12:7b-10). In the disabled, pain wracked and deeply broken body of Christ on the Cross we encounter our redemp-tion. Even in the resurrection, Jesus' scars challenge standard assumptions about beauty, perfection and wholeness. Disabled human bodies can carry powerful messages of redemption just-as-they-are. To see such things we need to read Scripture in a quite particular way.

---

[3] For more on this see the essay by Adela Yarbro Collins, "Paul's Disability: The Thorn in His Flesh," in *Disability Studies and Biblical Literature*, edited by Candida R. Moss and Jeremy Schipper (Palgrave Macmillan, 2011), pp. 165–83.

READING THE CALL OF MOSES DIFFERENTLY

An example will help to make the point. One issue that people living with disability encounter in relation to the interpretations of Scripture is the tendency of some to use certain passages to try to explain why a person lives with a disability. One of the interesting things about modern people is our apparent inability to live with mystery and unanswered questions. We have a dangerous tendency to turn mystery into puzzles. Many of us feel most uncomfortable with things we don't understand. So we constantly try to name and explain things. If we can name and explain things we can, so we think, control them. So when faced with certain forms of human difference which raise questions that are difficult to answer, people often seek the simplest explanation. So, despite the fact that there are a variety of ways that we might describe human difference, some still insist on it being connected with sin or disobedience to God. Similarly, rather than reflecting on what it might look like for people to live well and live faithfully with their disabilities, there remains a tendency to look to healing as the "obvious solution" to human diversity. Either of these explanations can be deeply damaging for people, the basic assumption being that disability is the direct consequence of sin, and that someone cannot really fulfil their vocation unless their disability is taken from them. Within such interpretations disability is inevitably perceived as a profoundly negative thing that requires to be eradicated in order that a person can be freed to live well with God.

However, if we re-think these two assumptions in the light of the strange experience of Moses calling, new interpretative possibilities begin to emerge. In Exodus 4:10 we find this passage: "Moses said to the LORD, 'Pardon your servant, Lord. I have never been eloquent, neither in the past nor since you have spoken to your servant. I am slow of speech and tongue.'" Moses had a speech impediment that significantly impacted upon his ability to communicate. In this passage Moses is responding to God's giving him a key role in God's plan for the redemption of creation. Moses says that he can't do it because of his disability (note *Moses* says he can't do it because of his disability, not God). God *does not* respond with healing and the eradication of Moses disability. Basically he tells Moses to stop complaining and to do what he is told! It was not necessary for Moses' disability to be taken from him for him to fulfil a powerful deep calling from God. In like-manner to the experience of the Apostle Paul (2 Corinthians 12:9), God promised to be with Moses as he worked out his calling and in the midst of his perceived weakness, although of course his "weakness" was a human and not a divine ascription. Weakness and strength find quite different meanings within the Kingdom of God. Moses was called just as he was.

And even more mysteriously, God continues: "Who has made man's mouth? Or who makes him mute or deaf, or seeing or blind? Is it not I, the LORD?" (Exodus 4:11). The implications here are complicated and counterintuitive. What might it mean to say that God is responsible for disability? Well, at a minimum it casts significant doubt on those who would assert that disability is somehow the product of sin or a punishment from God. If God is the author of disability, then how could it be the product of sin? God does not indicate that these forms of disability are bad things; God simply says that he is responsible for their presence in the world. The creator God is in the midst of disabled lives, not simply as healer, but also as The Vocationer; the One who is calling *all* of God's people to participate in God's coming Kingdom just as they are.

Moses' story raises some fascinating issues in relation to what it might mean to interpret human difference from the perspective of human disability. When we allow our hermeneutic to be shaped and formed by the experiences of people living with disabilities, and when we allow that strange new world within the Bible to infiltrate and transform our minds, so we are led into fresh pastures, novel challenges, new possibilities for understanding and renewed options for faithful exegesis leading to more faithful practice. Healing and the ascription of sin may not be the best or the most faithful way to interpret disability. Within the Bible's strange world things look quite different.

I imagine that some readers are wrestling with counter-interpretations of the passage discussed above and others feel released to see the world differently. If that is the case, that is the point. A disability hermeneutic opens up new challenges, fresh conversations and different possibilities for faithful living. This important and challenging book offers a multi-perspective viewpoint on the ways in which a disability hermeneutic not only challenges, but often transforms the way in which we read and respond to Scripture. If we are serious about the power and significance of the strange new world within the Bible, then we should take the challenges in the pages that follow with both seriousness and anticipation. *Truth only emerges when we read Scripture together.* We can only truly be together when everyone has a valued seat at the table. This books sets a place for those whose voices are often overlooked, but whose contribution to the practice of knowing God is irreplaceable.

Preface

In 2011, upon successfully launching the Studies in Religion, Theology, and Disability series with Baylor University Press, the series editors (Melcher, a Hebrew Bible scholar, and Yong, a systematician) immediately began to discuss the possibility of the commentary you hold in your hands. Upon securing an additional set of perspectives (Parsons, a New Testament scholar), we wrestled with how to conceptualize the volume. A traditional verse-by-verse commentary seemed out of the question, even as it seemed impossible that we might be able to generate hermeneutical and methodological consensus on how to proceed given the diversity of subject positions, disciplinary expertise, ecclesial/religious commitments, and scholarly preferences that existed at the intersection where biblical studies and disability studies met. In the end we sought to combine some of the best features of existing perspectivally produced commentaries—for example, Carol A. Newsom, Sharon H. Ringe, and Jacqueline E. Lapsley, *The Women's Bible Commentary*, 3rd ed., revised and updated (Louisville, Ky.: Westminster John Knox, 2012), and Brian K. Blount et al., *True to Our Native Land: An African American New Testament Commentary* (Minneapolis: Fortress, 2007)—but yet to give our contributors the freedom, within certain parameters, to prosecute their task. That meant that we proceeded to invite biblical scholars trained in specific genres or certain segments of the scriptural traditions but who had already deployed disability studies perspective in their interpretive and exegetical work.

Our invitation stipulated that each contributor would have the opportunity to begin with an introduction that developed the specific hermeneutical approach to the assigned biblical books; be expected in general to engage in a thematic (rather than verse-by-verse) commentary not only on verses or passages that refer explicitly to disability but also on those that may otherwise also be relevant to disability experiences and perspectives; summarize and build upon the relevant literature at the interface of disability studies and biblical studies as such bears on the assigned section of the commentary; bring contemporary disability studies perspectives to bear on references to disability in their biblical books; interact with the latest biblical, historical, and theological scholarship on disability; provide literary, sociohistorical, and rhetorical perspectives that illuminate references to disability in their biblical books; as the opportunities arise, reread the biblical book(s) in light of central disability-related passages; and write throughout in a style that invites further research on religion and disability vis-à-vis the biblical literature being engaged. We are thrilled to have had such an enthusiastic set of responses to our original invitations. Although a small handful of those we approached were unable (initially or finally) to make a contribution to the following pages because of life—and disability-related, in some cases—circumstances and issues, we are pleased with the resulting product. This is not to be considered the final word on disability and the Bible, but an attempt to continue conversations that have been emerging over the course of the last few decades, and more specifically those precipitated by the founding of the Healthcare and Disability in the Ancient World Group in the Society of Biblical Literature and the Religion and Disability Studies Group in the American Academy of Religion in the last decade.

The introductory chapter will say more about why this commentary is valuable at this time and about how it has attempted to build bridges between two distinct areas of scholarship—biblical studies and disability studies—that work with very different presuppositions and commitments. The fact of the matter is that those of us without impairments are only what some in the disability community call "temporarily able-bodied" persons: we came into the world completely dependent on others and, if we are blessed to live long enough, we will exit the world increasingly, if not also completely, dependent on others. Disability and impairment are thus more intrinsic than incidental to the human condition than many of us would want to admit. This project proceeds from this realization to engagement with the Bible, one of the most important books in human history. Given this meeting of worlds—the biblical sphere and the disability domain—we invite you, our readers, to not only draw your own conclusions about how the Bible speaks to issues of impairment and disability, but perhaps also carve out alternative responses to those that we and our colleagues in this book have charted.

We are grateful to Hoon Jung (Yong's graduate assistant at Fuller Seminary), Jessica Cinefro (Melcher's graduate assistant at Xavier University), and Rebecca Poe Hays (Parsons' graduate assistant at Baylor University) for their assistance with various aspects of this book. Carey Newman at Baylor University Press has been an enthusiastic supporter of this volume and the series it appears in, for which we are thankful. The staff at Baylor University Press has been professional at every stage: from production through to publication and then marketing. All this support has been crucial to the appearance of this book; we now are hopeful that readers of the bestselling book in the world, the Bible, will be alerted to disability issues and perspectives in ways that allow both more critical and more faithful readings than have been possible before.

Introduction

Sarah J. Melcher

SETTING THE STAGE

The study of disability in the Bible has arisen as an important and integral part of the movement to engage in theological reflection through the lens of human disability. In the early stages of that movement, Nancy L. Eiesland's book *The Disabled God: Toward a Liberatory Theology of Disability* (1994) had an enormous impact. This book prompted theologians to reconsider religious texts, symbols, practices, and doctrines from the perspective of disability. Eiesland proposed the image of "the disabled God" as a liberating symbol that would bring the experience of disability to the center of theological reflection. Perhaps the most provocative image she offered of the disabled God was God in a "sip-puff wheelchair." The author reminds us that disability is a social construction shaped by particular historical contexts. Eiesland challenges common social conceptions of disability, aiding theologians in reformulating interpretations, symbols, practices, and doctrines that are both more realistic and emancipatory to people with disabilities. Essentially, *The Disabled God* has opened up a new area of theological conversations from the perspective of disability. Throughout the book Eiesland advocates in a persuasive way the full inclusion and participation of people with disabilities within the life of religious communities.

However, it was a later collection of essays edited by Eiesland and Don E. Saliers that explicitly included essays by biblical scholars who were reassessing biblical passages pertinent to the study of theology and disability

(*Human Disability and the Service of God: Reassessing Religious Practice*, 1998): Hector Avalos explored "Disability and Liturgy in Ancient and Modern Religious Traditions"; Colleen C. Grant reinterpreted the healing narratives in Christian Scriptures; Simon Horne wrote "'Those Who Are Blind See': Some New Testament Uses of Impairment, Inability, and Paradox"; while Sarah J. Melcher studied some Priestly passages in Leviticus and their conceptualization of disability. The framing question for these biblical studies was, "How does the participation of people with disabilities reframe biblical interpretation of the Hebrew Bible and the New Testament?" (Eiesland and Saliers 1998, 16).

Two very influential works in this nascent period in the study of disability in the Bible were Hector Avalos' *Illness and Health Care in the Ancient Near East: The Role of the Temple in Greece, Mesopotamia, and Israel* (1995) and his *Health Care and the Rise of Christianity* (1999). In the first, Avalos combines approaches from medical anthropology and critical biblical scholarship to compare holistically the health care systems in Greece, Mesopotamia, and Israel with a particular focus on the role of the temple within those health care systems. The author uses evidence from archaeology and from texts of various genres. His concern is to provide a socioreligious framework for understanding the respective health care systems. Important features of Avalos' first book are the emphasis on the systemic nature of health care and his use of appropriate methods for the comparison of health care systems. Avalos' work was carefully researched and documented and provided a resource for anyone interested in medicine and health care in the ancient Near East. As such, it became an important early resource for those who were studying the role of disability in ancient Near Eastern texts, including the Bible.

Avalos' second book, *Health Care and the Rise of Christianity*, continues the author's emhasis on medical anthropology and the study of ancient health care systems, but it focuses on the first and second centuries CE. The book compares the health care system reflected in early Christian texts with other contemporary health care systems in the ancient Near East. The author argues that the health care system promoted in early Christianity had much to do with Christianity's rapid rise as a socially desirable religion. Avalos examines canonical and noncanonical Christian literature, as well as texts from Jewish and Greco-Roman sources. Similar to his first book, the second book suggests the usefulness of medical anthropology for the study of disability in ancient Near Eastern texts. Biblical scholars and theologians alike have been influenced strongly by Avalos' emphasis on the socioreligious framework for understanding health care systems.

Another influential book in the early study of disability and the Bible within the more general conversation about theology and disability was John M. Hull's *In the Beginning There Was Darkness: A Blind Person's Conversations with the Bible* (2001). As a professor of religious education and as a person with a disability, Hull engages with numerous Scripture passages, exploring their meaning by calling upon his own experience in dialogue with these texts. His perspective introduces many new insights into the meaning of biblical passages. Hull describes the Bible as a book written for people with sight and as a collection of writings that envision God as sighted as well. While Hull notes this bias, he also concludes that God's knowledge extends beyond the limitations of sight and that an individual's faith needs to encompass a perspective that reaches beyond the conventional limitations of sight as well. Another suggestion that Hull offers is the idea that a person who is blind can readily identify with the sufferings of Christ. One of Hull's accomplishments with this early book is to suggest ways in which biblical scholars can use the lens of disability to discover new insights about biblical passages. Hull's book makes for fascinating reading, and he suggests new insights that biblical scholars can offer to theological reflection on the human experience of disability.

A turning point in the scholarly engagement between disability studies and biblical scholarship occurred in 2004 at the annual meeting for the Society of Biblical Literature, when the program unit "Biblical Scholarship and Disabilities" (Schipper 2006, 3) was initiated. The edited volume, *This Abled Body: Rethinking Disabilities in Biblical Studies*, was first conceived at one of the sessions for this program unit (Avalos, Melcher, and Schipper 2007). The name of the program unit is now "Healthcare and Disability in the Ancient World." With the birth of a program unit devoted to the study of health care and disability in the ancient world, the study of disability and the Bible reached a new level of focus within the scholarly guild of the Society of Biblical Literature.

OTHER IMPORTANT PRECURSORS TO THIS VOLUME

Before describing the expectations of the coeditors to this volume in regard to focus and approach, it is appropriate to review some of the preceding biblical scholarship about disability and the Bible. While the focus in this section will be on the content of these important precursors, I will also indicate at certain points how these scholars of disability and the Bible have raised important issues that shape this commentary.

Among the important precursors to this commentary is Jeremy Schipper's *Disability Studies and the Hebrew Bible: Figuring Mephibosheth in the*

David Story (2006). Schipper brings disability studies and biblical scholarship into dialogue in order to interpret Mephibosheth's role in the narrative
about King David. Schipper observes that, before his monograph, biblical
scholars exploring disability in the Hebrew Bible tended to focus on legal
materials rather than narratives. He notes as well that Mephibosheth is
the "only biblical character with a disability as a sustained character trait"
(3). Schipper's book establishes that Mephibosheth, as a character with a
disability, is part of an oppressed minority that is subjugated by dominant
"able-bodied ideologies encoded into larger social structures" (7). According to Schipper, the character of Mephibosheth is part of the David story's
complex depiction of disability imagery "as a subtle mode of narrating and
organizing various ideological positions regarding national identity" (4).
Within this framework, the character of Mephibosheth has considerable
impact on discourses presenting the motifs of kingship, Zion, and disability in an effort to mark insiders and outsiders.

One aspect of Schipper's approach to the topic is a review of the history of interpretation, in which Schipper outlines the tendency among
biblical scholars to assign a symbolic meaning to a physical trait in order
to uncover inner motives. Schipper's study challenges these approaches
because he demonstrates that disability was a "meaningful conceptual
category" (2006, 64) in ancient Near Eastern literature. Similar cultural
and political ideologies about physical difference are assumed by the
Bible when it constructs Mephibosheth's character. Of course, Schipper
also reveals that Mephibosheth's character is more complex than a simple
reflection of Near Eastern ideologies surrounding physical difference. The
presentation by the Deuteronomistic Historian is more nuanced than that.

In his conclusion Schipper notes that the Deuteronomistic History's
(DH) treatment of Israel's identity is complex and irreducible to one or
more abstract themes. Likewise, the treatment of Mephibosheth is complex. Indeed,

> his presence in the story questions the means by which the story distin-
> guishes between insiders and outsiders. Furthermore, the disability imagery
> surrounding his character participates in a larger rhetorical technique that
> heightens the irony of David and his dynasty's changing fortunes while also
> embodying Israel's possibilities and limitations. (2006, 128)

Schipper concludes that disability in the David story is a mode through
which the identity of Israel is reflected upon in all its intricacy and com-
plication. However, disability is an integral part of the DH. Since the DH
now advances, now frustrates particular viewpoints, it subverts monolithic
ideologies. Because the DH does this, Schipper suggests that it would be

useful to put the DH into dialogue with Deuteronomy or the Wisdom literature to "pose paradox and juxtaposition as a method of theological reflection" (2006, 130). Schipper calls biblical scholars to devote more time to the study of disability imagery in the DH.

Schipper's groundbreaking book offers a model for subsequent scholarship on disability and the Bible. His work brings disability studies into conversation with biblical scholarship on disability and at the same time observes standards long established by careful biblical scholarship in the past. His analysis pays very close attention to the literary aspects of the DH while it is informed by the most up-to-date findings of meticulous historical-critical method.

Saul Olyan's focus in his monograph *Disability in the Hebrew Bible: Interpreting Mental and Physical Differences* (2008) is disability as an analytic category in the literature of the Hebrew Bible. He attempts to reconstruct the Hebrew Bible's ideas of "what is disabling and the potential ramifications of those ideas" (xiii). Also, the author examines how biblical concepts about disability relate to ideas about disability in the greater west Asian cultural sphere, and he explores how ancient Jewish interpreters of the Bible perpetuate or transform biblical ideas and biblical models of disability.

The primary view of disability that drives Olyan's investigation is that of a social construction, which may or may not have a physical or mental basis. For that reason he focuses on the social dimension: "Thus, a primary goal of this study is to investigate the social dimensions of disability as it is represented, particularly the ways in which textual castings of disability function to realize and communicate patterns of social inequality" (2008, 3). Significantly, Olyan points out that it is difficult to say much about the lives of individuals or groups who have disabilities based on Israelite or Jewish history. Thus, the focus is on textual representations, which to some degree shaped social categories and differentiation in ancient Israel.

Olyan clearly shows how the biblical representations stigmatize and marginalize disabled persons, "contributing to social differentiation and inequality" (2008, 119). The author persuasively identifies several strategies employed by the biblical authors to devalue persons with disabilities. For example, a person with a disability that is associated with major pollution is cut off not only from the cult but from the community as well. Someone with a less polluting form of disability might be denied full access to the cult, but that person may participate fully in the community. According to Olyan, "The casting of persons with disabilities as despised, rejected by Yhwh, shamed, or cursed in biblical texts, could well have had the effect of causing others to avoid contact with them, leading to their social marginalization" (123). A primary impetus of Olyan's monograph is a concern to perceive how the biblical writers establish hierarchically significant difference and construct privilege for certain groups on the basis of physical or mental "wholeness" or "defect."

Olyan reveals that he has been unable to find any classifications of disability in the Hebrew Bible or in west Asian literature that resemble those in contemporary Western conceptions of disability, but he has discovered many passages that represent persons having various types of disability as somehow sharing underlying characteristics. "The basis for the association of the various disabilities does not appear to be an underlying notion of shared disability per se, but rather something else (e.g., shared somatic dysfunction, ignorance, helplessness, a shared threat to holiness)" (2008, 125).

The author suggests that the Hebrew Bible's passages reflect a variety of perspectives on the etiology of disabilities. Some suggest that YHWH is the ultimate source of all disabilities (e.g., Exod 4:11), others that God visits disabilities on humanity as a punishment for sin, but there are still others who indicate that disabilities may have been a typical occurrence in human life. Olyan (2008) offers examples of each of these perspectives. The biblical texts also offer a variety of perspectives on YHWH's attitude toward people with disabilities. These perspectives may reflect a range of cultural attitudes on the part of the biblical authors (126–27).

Several motivations for the biblical devaluation of persons with disabilities are posited by the author: the association of disability with ugliness and abomination, that they are not fully human, and that they "lack fundamental characteristics of the living" (Olyan 2008, 128). Olyan also notes that at times men with disabilities are feminized and that disabled groups are often associated with the marginalized—that is, the poor, the afflicted, and the alien, who share the characteristic of vulnerability.

Olyan's book makes important contributions to the discussion of disability in the Hebrew Bible. Olyan is especially astute in discerning underlying systems of thought and in making important comparisons among disparate biblical passages. Critically important, Olyan considers mental illness among the topics that he investigates. Olyan's reconstruction of the relationship among various types of disability and his clarification of the means used by the Hebrew Bible's authors to devalue, stigmatize, and marginalize certain classes of persons with disabilities is very useful. Olyan also begins the process of identifying the implicit overarching classifications that relate the types of disabilities to one another. Though Olyan is careful to represent these possible overarching categories as suggestive only, they offer insight into the organization of the Israelite conceptual domain related to disability.

In *Biblical Corpora: Representations of Disability in Hebrew Biblical Literature* (2008), Rebecca Raphael uses literary methods developed in disability studies to examine the representation of disability in the Hebrew Bible. The book explores not only the systematic ways that the Hebrew Bible represents disability but also how it relates to the other concepts in the corpus. In her study Raphael examines texts from all the major genres of the Hebrew Bible: law, narrative, wisdom, poetry, and prophecy. One of Raphael's innovations is that she asks how disability relates to some of the Hebrew Bible's major concerns: "holiness, ethics, historiography, exile, prophecy, wisdom, and God" (2). Raphael argues, "In order to discover deep structures of abled and disabled categories, we must survey a range of biblical material and investigate connections, both among the representations of disability, and across other categories such as power, election, and holiness" (3).

Throughout her carefully argued book, Raphael demonstrates what she summarizes in her concluding chapter: "Disability plays a significant, perhaps even indispensable role in the Hebrew Bible's articulation of God's power and holiness, and Israel's election. . . . Nor is disability an incidental thread in this tapestry: God's power depends, for its representation, on the disabled human figures" (2008, 132). She goes on in this vein to make the case that in Genesis "being chosen by God disables precisely because the human bodies must show God to be powerful" (132). In regard to the book of Isaiah and the other prophetic books, the implied narrative uses disability to represent sensory impairment and ruptured communication that is subsequently transformed to sensory restoration and resumed communication (133). Raphael notes the prophetic tendency to erase the existence of disability. In Job, God's control over human embodiment is represented in its extreme. God's power is demonstrated through the contrast with human physical weakness. Because of the book's excesses, the divine onslaught on Job's body almost undoes the concept that God's power is made manifest through people's bodies.

Raphael also argues that the Hebrew Bible constructs what is "normal" by means of its depictions of the human body. Notably, God is represented as physically normal. As Raphael explains it, a society's sense of the normal is an ideological construct, "not our colloquial sense of normal as what is roughly average or typical" (2008, 136). Because our society ideologically constructs what is considered normal for human beings, Raphael argues, "It should appear as no coincidence that those selections of human embodiment and experience favored by a given society are also attributed to that society's deity or deities. The Hebrew Bible represents God with the abilities it most values in the human (male) body" (136–37).

However, Raphael includes several insights in chapter 5, "Limping on Two Opinions," that are helpful to those of us engaging in the study of disability and the Bible. First, she reminds biblical scholars and other readers that when ignored or undervalued groups are present in a biblical passage, there is a prevailing tendency among interpreters to work at "Redeeming the Text" (2008, 137). That is, there is a tendency among biblical scholars to try to find something positive about such passages, even when the evidence does not support that. In reference to the Bible, Raphael states, "Small consolations are the most I expect to find with respect to disability. To read positively when this clearly violates what we can know about the text and its world strikes me as a breach of intellectual ethics for the sake of comfort, and in the long run, this is not even comfortable" (138). This last sentence is important for biblical scholars to keep in mind when doing research on disability and the Bible.

Important for the current project of a Bible commentary from the perspective of disability, Raphael maintains that "disability studies can contribute a critical mode to the Bible.... The standard biblical commentaries often do not give adequate attention to disability in the texts on which they comment, and when they do, fail to take a critical stance toward the text's constructions and attitudes" (2008, 138). She also observes that there is much critical work to be done in the history of interpretations.

Raphael offers us another set of observations related to her own experience as a person who is deaf. Her discussion of what a deaf-critical mode to interpreting the Bible might consist of is very informative. The editors of this volume are reminded by Raphael about the importance of taking the current human experience of disability into consideration when interpreting. It is the current editors' hope that contributors to this volume have taken the experience of persons with disabilities into consideration when writing their chapters.

In *Disability and Isaiah's Suffering Servant* (2011), Schipper demonstrates that the description of the "suffering servant" in Isa 52–53 reflects common language and imagery associated with disability in the Hebrew Bible and other ancient Near Eastern literature. However, Schipper argues that the history of interpretation erases disability from the picture and depicts the suffering servant as an otherwise able-bodied individual. Most often, interpreters focus on the theological issue of vicarious suffering rather than on disability per se. Schipper argues that using disability studies to reinterpret Isa 52–53 could help to provide a corrective to the previous neglect of the topic of disability. Happily, Schipper avoids the popular discussion of the servant's probable identity. He also does not attempt to reconstruct the original text or its redactions. According to the author, "There are so many differences between the Hebrew, Greek, Aramaic, and other ancient manuscripts of Isa 53 that it seems nearly impossible to recover the original text to begin with—much less speculate about how it developed through multiple but hypothetical editions or redactions" (5).

Well informed by disability studies, Schipper proceeds step by step to explore the disability imagery in Isa 52–53. He treats the text as a poem, not as a diagnostic text, nor as the biography of a historical person outside the passage. As Schipper says, "Poetic depictions of an experience of disability do not need to provide clear or developed descriptions of either the figure or the disability in order for readers to recognize it as describing a figure with disabilities" (2011, 5). Schipper argues that a scholar need not appeal to personal experience to study disability in the Bible. He maintains that any competent scholar should be able to make observations on the topic without direct personal knowledge of disability (9).

Significantly, Schipper argues that the manuscript evidence does not suggest that either the divine oracles (52:13-15 and 53:11b-12) or the psalm (53:1-11a) ever described the servant sans disability. Disability imagery is found in both genres in the passage.

The author is strongly influenced by the "cultural model" of disability, defining disability as *the social experience of persons with certain impairments*" (Schipper 2011, 18 [emphasis in original]). Schipper maintains that Isa 53 describes the social experience of a person with disabilities, thus making the cultural model particularly appropriate. In fact, Isa 53 focuses more on the social and political experience of disability than the nature of the impairments themselves. According to Schipper, Isa 53 comes much closer to the social or cultural model of disability than the medical model. In fact, as a poetic passage, the language is inexact so a precise diagnosis is virtually impossible. Yet in analyzing any passage through the lens of disability in the Bible, it is also crucial to explore how the Bible constructs able-bodiedness, since "able-bodied" is a marker of bodily difference in the same way that "disabled" is. Able-bodiedness is "not the default normal state of human experience from which disability deviates" (19).

In chapter 2 Schipper argues persuasively that the language of Isa 53 depicts the servant as having a disability, and he develops the argument that Isa 53 focuses on the servant's social and political experience. In fact, Schipper concludes that there is no evidence in the text that suggests that the disability has resulted from an attack by human hands. Rather, the text indicates that the servant was treated poorly socially because of the social ramifications of his disability. In chapter 3 the author traces the interpretive tendency to construe the servant as an able-bodied sufferer, rather than a person with a disability, back to the second century. In chapter 4 Schipper presents the tendency among interpreters of the modern period to focus so intently on discovering the original identity of the servant that the presence of disability imagery in association with the servant was overlooked. The concluding chapter explores some of the consequences resulting from the interpretation of the servant as an able-bodied sufferer. One implication of this reinterpretation is that it is difficult for a person with a disability to identify with the servant, since his disability has been removed in effect. As Schipper points out, the history of interpretation creates a servant who passes for able-bodied. Otherwise, the character might not have experienced such an interpretive afterlife: "Likewise, passing as able-bodied represents a dominant strategy for acceptance, if not survival, for many persons with disabilities in real-life situations" (2011, 110).

A collection of essays that is important to the study of disability and theology is Darla Schumm and Michael Stoltzus' *Disability in Judaism, Christianity, and Islam: Sacred Texts, Historical Traditions, and Social Analysis* (2011). Most relevant to our study here is the essay "Out of Darkness: Examining the Rhetoric of Blindness in the Gospel of John" by Jennifer L. Koosed and Darla Schumm. The authors contend that the metaphor of blindness in the Gospel of John functions in such a way as to exclude from the community both those with disabilities and those who are Jewish. Because of the combined function, the authors explore the intersection of the metaphor of blindness with these two exclusions in the Gospel of John.

Following the work of Adele Reinhartz, Koosed and Schumm attempt to "be friends with a text" in their approach to the Gospel of John, which entails engaging the book fully and honestly, making a commitment to face both positive and negative aspects of the text. Their friendship with the text is enhanced by the authors' friendship with one another. The question that Koosed and Schumm ask is, "Who do we become as we enter into relationship with the text of John?" (2011, 78).

The authors argue that darkness and light are "constitutive metaphors for John's cosmic system," which rise "to the level of macro-metaphor" (Koosed and Schumm 2011, 78). In other words, a cluster of metaphors surrounding the macro-metaphors of darkness and light are central in constructing John's world. If the reader accepts the world that John has created, then real-world exclusions are a possible result.

Koosed and Schumm are attentive to what the Gospel's metaphors may have meant in the original context, but they are also very concerned about the damage that these metaphors may have caused in the history of Jewish-Christian relations and in shaping communal attitudes toward persons with disabilities. The authors' treatment of these aspects is nuanced because they acknowledge that there are times in the Gospel of John "when the narrative undermines metaphors that equate spiritual wholeness with physical wholeness in ways consistent with Eiesland's shift to the disabled God" (2011, 90).

Another important precursor is the volume coedited by Candida R. Moss and Jeremy Schipper, *Disability Studies and Biblical Literature* (2011). The first goal of the book is for the study of disability in the Bible to be accomplished by professional biblical scholars. The book acknowledges the strides made in disability studies in recent years, with more nuanced models being developed for understanding disability as a social experience: "Often informed by recent critical theories of race, gender, and sexuality, these models consider how social, political, religious, environmental, and other structures contribute to the experience of disability" (2). Though most historically oriented biblical scholarship of the last century tended to assume a medical model in its approach to disability, the Moss and Schipper volume proposes to move beyond that in relating disability to larger social and cultural structures. According to the editors, scholarship "should also examine disability, medicine, and health care as cultural products intimately connected to the way we articulate various religious, political, cultural, social, and other ideological viewpoints" (3). Primarily, the volume adopts the cultural model, which "understands disability as a product of the ways that cultures use physical and cognitive differences to narrate, organize, and interpret their world. Whereas in the social model, disability refers to a type of social discrimination, in the cultural model descriptions of disability become one way by which we create or shape culture" (4).

Though the biblical scholarship in the volume is informed by disability studies in the humanities, it is still held to the same standards of critical biblical scholarship established over the centuries, which involve the method of argumentation, what constitutes acceptable evidence, citation of primary sources in their various original languages, and secondary sources recognizable to biblical scholars (Moss and Schipper 2011, 4). Moss and Schipper recommend that the study of disability in the Bible should be undertaken by specialists in biblical studies, though it is also advisable that biblical scholars benefit from cross-disciplinary work in disability studies or other fields.

At the time of this writing, there is no book that explores disability in the New Testament. This was also true at the time that Moss and Schipper published their volume (November 2011). In the coedited volume *This Abled Body: Rethinking Disabilities in Biblical Studies*, published several years before *Disability Studies and Biblical Literature*, of the ten essays only three address disability in the New Testament (Avalos, Melcher, and Schipper 2007). Moss and Schipper have achieved greater balance between the Hebrew Bible and New Testament essays in their 2011 volume.

The authors argue that biblical scholars can offer a more nuanced consideration of the history of discrimination toward persons with disabilities. Biblical scholars do not approach biblical passages in a monolithic fashion, according to Moss and Schipper, but see the Bible as a collection of texts that vary greatly in the ancient attitudes about disability as well as differing in cultural, sociological, and historical contexts.

Similar to *This Abled Body*, the essays in *Disability Studies and Biblical Literature* use a variety of methodologies. Several essays address the relationship of disability to gender in the Bible. Two of the essays examine the rhetorical function of disability in the prophetic literature. The New Testament essays all explore the relationship of the construction of disability to ancient medical theories and practices. Two essays look at how ancient Christianity viewed epilepsy. Another essay combines disability studies and postcolonial criticism to the Gospel of John.

Our intention in *The Bible and Disability: A Commentary* is to include a balanced representation of New Testament scholarship, commensurate with the division of material between the Hebrew Bible and the Christian Scriptures in the Bible itself. However, at this point I would like to include here some observations about the work of Candida R. Moss (2012, 320), who has used ancient medical theory as a "hermeneutical gaze" to examine 2 Cor 12:7-10 in order to suggest rhetorical functions for Paul's reference to his "thorn in the flesh." She reaches two major conclusions: first, the imagery of lancing recasts Paul's infirmity as a positive means to keep his puffed-up ego in check; second, through his rhetorical use of medical theories about weakness in the body and its subsequent permeability, Paul turns his weakness into Christ's power. Because of this greater permeability, Paul implies, the power of Christ resides within him. Though this article uses ancient medical theory, rather than disability studies per se, the article suggests the variety of approaches that can inform the study of disability and the Bible. It is also an example of a New Testament scholar who is pursuing this line of inquiry.

An earlier article by Moss, "The Man with the Flow of Power: Porous Bodies in Mark 5:25-34" (2010, 507), also explores the biblical passage in light of ancient medical theories of the weakness of bodies and their permeability. Moss outlines the medical theories about porosity of bodies and the implications porosity has, according to those theories, for a weak, vulnerable body. Moss' rereading of Mark 5:25-34 reverses some of these theories popular in the ancient world. The woman with the flow of blood is the personification of the theory of the porous body that is soft and wet, without maintaining proper bodily boundaries. Males usually are the model of the healthy body: dry, hard, and maintaining boundaries of the body that are impermeable. What is striking about the story of the healing of the woman with the twelve-year flow of blood is that she is healed because Jesus has a permeable body, one that leaks power. She takes on an assertive posture when she claims that healing. She becomes the faithful disciple who becomes dry, hard, and her boundaries impenetrable. These two articles, among others, demonstrate Moss' interest in the ancient New Testament writers' conception of illness and disability.

METHODOLOGICAL CONSIDERATIONS FOR THE CURRENT VOLUME

The essays in this commentary attempt to follow the best aspects of their predecessors. Although the work in this volume is informed by disability studies, the contributors to this volume are very attentive to historical and cultural contexts for the literature they study. Each individual contributor has been chosen because of his or her expertise in the block of literature in which he or she is working. In addition, each contributor has demonstrated an interest in the study of disability and the Bible. *The Bible and Disability: A Commentary* differs from some of the previous work in the field because of the more comprehensive nature of the volume. Much of the previous work in disability and the Bible has examined discrete passages, while this volume approaches blocks of literature because of the purpose to introduce the reader to a comprehensive look at the way disability is represented in the Bible as a whole.

The essays in this volume represent a variety of methodological approaches and a spectrum of attitudes and assumptions related to the nature and authority of Scripture. Since the editors of this volume wanted to include a wide representation of Scripture scholars working in the field of disability and the Bible, we have allowed much latitude in regard to personal commitment among our authors. Whatever their theological stance or religious commitments, all are biblical scholars with extensive training in biblical criticism. Their careful reading of texts, their awareness of historical, sociological, and cultural contexts, their knowledge of biblical languages, and their engagement with disability studies all offer grist for the theological mill, whatever the theological stance or personal commitments of the readers. We encourage the reader to read these essays thoughtfully, even though the reader may disagree with some of the assumptions or theological frameworks of the authors. The insights that are offered here are worth consideration to see if they can be applied, with possible revision, to the reader's own theological context. All the essays have a common concern to read the Bible through the lens of disability, informed by the experience of human beings with disabilities.

THE ESSAYS THAT FOLLOW AND THEIR CONTRIBUTORS

Chapter 1 opens our commentary on disability and the Bible with an exploration of "Disability in Genesis and Exodus" by Sarah J. Melcher. She begins, of course, with Genesis and a commentary on the creation of human beings in the "image and likeness" of God. Inspired by the work of Nancy L. Eiesland, Melcher asks what the implications for disability theology might be for the concept of the "image of God" in Gen 1:26-28, 5:1-3, 9:6. The author explores the physical side of "image" through the ancient rabbinical interpreters. Then, influenced by ancient Near Eastern studies of image through a Mesopotamian term that is cognate with the Hebrew from 1:26, she investigates broader possibilities for the concept of image. That term can include spiritual, relational, social, cultic, and physical aspects. The implications of a broader understanding of image in the biblical account for disability theology are outlined.

Later, Melcher offers an extended commentary on infertility as a disability in the lives of the matriarchs and patriarchs of Genesis. From the lengthy treatment of infertility in the Abraham and Sarah cycle through the overview of age, infertility, and disability in the stories of Isaac, Rebekah, Leah, Rachel, and Jacob, the biblical depiction of disability is nuanced and fascinating. Melcher examines related themes of God's sovereignty over reproduction and the role of reproduction in the establishment of a new nation.

As she moves on to the commentary on Exodus, Melcher spends some time unpacking the difficult passage in chapter 4 of Exodus. Exodus 4 brings up the issue of creation and whether God determines with intention who will have a disability and who will not. The commentary discusses an alternative possibility, that God creates humankind as occupying diverse positions on a spectrum of ability. Melcher goes on to scrutinize

God's responses to Moses' speech difficulties, where God seems to respond to Moses' impairment as an unsurprising aspect of his humanity. Later, the author attempts to view God's sovereignty through the lens of disability.

For David Tabb Stewart in chapter 2, Leviticus is arguably the most important book for understanding disability in the Hebrew Bible. Leviticus presents the main system of disability and ability to which the rest of biblical law (in Numbers and Deuteronomy) refers and amends. Like several of the chapters in this volume, this one attempts to explore both disability and ability in order to discern where disability fits within the larger context of physical categories established by the ancient society. In order to discern this system, Stewart investigates twenty-one topics related to disability and interprets the passages associated with these topics. Additionally, he discusses seven themes that relate to disability across the three biblical books. When he draws upon disability studies, Stewart emphasizes the point made by Rosemarie Garland-Thomson that disability is "a culturally fabricated narrative of the body" (2010, 356). Since Leviticus, Numbers, and Deuteronomy are cultural artifacts, this is a critical perspective.

Stewart is attentive to detail, including an analysis of the Hebrew terms that describe disability. The terminological study in chapter 2 gives us a glimpse of ancient Israel's evaluation of the body. The chapter delineates the differing standards for priests and lay Israelites, clarifying these distinctions in relationship to access to the worship space. In a very useful discussion, Stewart clarifies the role of the body in priestly holiness, offering the insight that "even the high priest's bodily (avail)ability is ultimately unstable and temporary" (83) because bodily purity discursively combines physical and ritual statuses. Stewart similarly illustrates the complexities of the physical/ritual status of the lay Israelite and the Nazirite. While he studies these features of the text, he also conceptualizes their impact for people with disabilities.

In chapter 3 Jeremy Schipper likewise takes a cultural approach to disability in the DH (Josh, Judg, 1 and 2 Sam, 1 and 2 Kgs) and Ruth. The author of this essay avoids imposing a unified disability theology on the passages covered, instead exploring disability on a case-by-case basis in distinctive passages. Schipper explores the various treatments of disability language and imagery within the appropriate passages in Joshua–2 Kings, seeking to contextualize these treatments within the narrative. This contextualization sometimes requires exploring the ancient Near Eastern background, employing grammar or philology, exploring language uses in other biblical passages, and drawing from the work of other biblical scholars.

Schipper's discourse remains consistent with his intentions as indicated at the beginning of the chapter. The books from Joshua through 2 Kings are diverse in their treatment of disability, and Schipper discusses each book in turn. The book of Joshua does not explicitly mention disability, and the chapter examines the implications of that. Though Judges includes some depictions of acquired disabilities (through war and conflict), it does not give us insight into the reality of lives lived with disabilities in ancient Israel. Instead, Schipper's study of Judges demonstrates how disability is used to make social and theological commentary, as well as how it functions as a structuring device.

Within the narrative of Ruth, Schipper explores whether fertility is considered to be the norm. He notes, "Reproductive capabilities were not taken for granted or considered the usual state of existence by default in the ancient Near East" (103). Indeed, within the Hebrew Bible, conception is enabled through divine help. The essay makes the point that there is little evidence in Ruth that suggests the ability to bear children is the default norm. In 1 and 2 Samuel, Schipper investigates how disability is used to mark a change in status for the various characters. For instance, Schipper suggests that Eli's dimming eyesight may be an indication that he did not possess the status of a prophet. Later, while studying 2 Samuel, Schipper makes the generalization that "disability imagery helps to characterize parties who present obstacles to David's political power and helps to contrast them with David's idealized royal family" (110). Also in the narrative about David's rise to power, disability marks the change of status—insiders to outsiders.

Ultimately, Schipper finds the deployment of disability imagery and language to be as diverse as life experience. This use of disability is a powerful means of expressing the gamut of Israelite experience from the entrance to the land to the fall of the monarchy in the Southern Kingdom.

Kerry H. Wynn's commentary in chapter 4 on Second Temple literature (Ezra, Neh, 1 and 2 Chr, and Esth) begins with the assumption of the scriptural character of this material. Wynn notes that one of the primary interests of the Chronicler is to construct a postexilic identity for the community that will be sustained even though the monarchy has not been restored. This corporate identity intends to transcend considerations of time and space. Another important goal of the Chronicler (CH) is to unite the Davidic and Mosaic covenants in such a way as to link worship in the temple with the cultic instructions of Moses. CH also attempts to legitimate the Aaronic priesthood and the Levitical offices. The consistent cultic separation of the monarchy and the priesthood shapes and reshapes the interpretation of disability in 1 and 2 Chronicles. Temple worship has become the basis of community identity in the postexilic era.

The chapter discusses the erasure of the story of Mephibosheth from CH's retelling of David's rise to power and subsequent reign. The character of Mephibosheth remains only as the brief genealogical reference to Meribaal. In addition, Wynn offers a plausible explanation of the absence of the story and for the missing adage from 2 Sam 5:6-10 in 1 Chr 11:4-9. Specifically, 2 Sam 5:8b makes a statement prohibiting the presence of some in the temple: "Therefore it is said, 'The blind and the lame shall not come into the house.'" However, since priests who have a disability are permitted in the temple precincts to eat the "most holy" offerings, then CH would be violating a tenet of the Mosaic Torah by including the adage from 2 Sam 5:8b. As Wynn observes, "While those offerings designated 'holy' may be eaten outside of the temple by both the priests and their households, those designated 'most holy' could only be eaten by males within the temple precincts themselves (Lev 7:1-6, 10:12-20, 22:10-14, 24:5-9; Num 18:9-13)" (125). Therefore if males of the priestly family are permitted to eat the "most holy," then they must be allowed into the temple precincts contrary to the maxim in 2 Sam 5:8b (Milgrom 2000, 1826). This is one important clarification offered by Wynn's essay.

Though punishment in 1 and 2 Chronicles has often been connected to nonnormate physicalities, Wynn makes it clear that this relationship is not monolithic. He points out that punishment is not always retributive, and nonnormate physicalities are not necessarily typical outcomes of that punishment. The author illustrates that punishment is manifested in many ways, sometimes as a means of discipline and sometimes for retribution, but death is a more typical retributive punishment than nonnormate physicalities.

For Ezra–Nehemiah Wynn explores loss and disability, the empirical gaze, and the social construction of models of disability. There are many connections between the loss the community experienced in and after exile and the sense of loss sometimes associated with disability. People with acquired disabilities might feel keenly the loss of function, or families might feel intensely the loss that a congenital disability may bring. For Esther the focus is on the idea of "passing," a concept of considerable significance for some of those people with disabilities. At Mordecai's advice, when Esther became a part of Ahasuerus' harem, she kept the identity of her kindred a secret. Wynn sees a connection between the independence and self-reliance of the character of Esther and the independent living movement for people with disabilities.

In chapter 5 Sarah J. Melcher scrutinizes the Wisdom literature (Prov, Eccl, and Job) through the lens of disability. Different concepts from disability studies fit the different books. For Proverbs Melcher analyzes the tendency for the book to establish physical norms. Proverbs links the acquisition of wisdom with bodily health and long life. The body is deeply involved with the pursuit of wisdom; the eyes, the ears, and the other body parts are to be used in acquiring wisdom. Yet in the final analysis, the efforts to gain wisdom are rewarded. The wise experience good health and long life, so the book constructs a world in which the pursuit of wisdom yields expected benefits for the body, including the heart. With the book of Proverbs, Melcher finds that Stanley Hauerwas' discussion of the "tyranny of normality" (2004, 37–43) resonates well with the issues raised by the biblical text.

In her discussion about Ecclesiastes, Melcher notes the emphasis on life as fleeting. Again and again, Qoheleth discusses the limitations that are woven into the fabric of life, including the limited nature of life itself. The frequent and strategic use of the term הבל (*hebel*, "breath, whiff, puff, steam") signifies life's transitory nature (Seow 1997, 47). Ecclesiastes makes the point that there is much in life that is beyond human control. All that is created by human hands is ephemeral. The only things that last are the works of God. For Ecclesiastes, Melcher weaves in the perspectives offered in Deborah Creamer's book *Disability and Christian Theology: Embodied Limits and Constructive Possibilities* (2009). Creamer's arguments and Ecclesiastes' observations about life have much in common that is useful in constructing a theology of disability.

When treating the book of Job, Melcher addresses some of the ethical issues raised by the prose framework for Job: "The wager and test of Job, including the death of Job's children, his servants, and the many animals under his care, raise some ethical issues from a disability perspective" (173). It is important to acknowledge the deity's role in the narrative as either the perpetrator of death and suffering or as a deity who steps aside to allow someone else to afflict pain on humans and animals. Melcher pursues this question in the analysis. The quality of life discussion from disability studies offers insights for thinking about the causation of death and physical suffering in the book of Job.

Melcher focuses on the extended description of Job's suffering in chapters 16, 17, and 19 of the book of Job. These sections of Job are very important because they represent the sufferer's own voice. The principle of listening to the voice and expressed experience of people with disabilities is emphasized repeatedly in disability studies. Of significance is Job's attribution of his suffering to God; he sees his suffering as a direct result of God's actions. The character of Job openly accuses God of abuse, and this language is explored in Melcher's chapter. The author interweaves insights from David R. Blumenthal's book *Facing the Abusing God: A Theology of Protest* (1993) in this chapter. It is his "theology of protest" that holds much promise for those with disabilities. Job's speeches challenge the moral view of traditional wisdom, so there is more from a disability perspective that can be gleaned from these chapters. The speeches of Job's friends present the viewpoints familiar from traditional wisdom. One aspect that is challenged from this worldview is the idea that people are rewarded or punished in life in orderly, expected ways. Job's speeches and, indeed, the book as a whole challenge traditional expectations of reward and retribution. These speeches, as presented by Melcher, also maintain that God is faithfully just in relationships with human beings. Of course, the friends are famous for suggesting that Job was guilty of some wrongdoing in order to deserve God's punishment. These issues are pursued at length in chapter 5 of this volume. The author also investigates ways of dealing with these in order to be sensitive to disability concerns. Finally, in the last section of the chapter, Melcher addresses the restoration of Job in the prose epilogue 42:7-17 and the implications of the fact that this passage is silent regarding his physical healing.

Jennifer Koosed argues in chapter 6 that the cultural model from disability studies has been the most fruitful in analyzing biblical texts, especially in the case of biblical poetry. She states, "Reading through the cultural model of disability allows the poems in Psalms, Lamentations, and Song of Songs to speak in all of their varied, even contradictory, voices" (190). In the Psalms she discerns three ways in which disability is incorporated. The Psalms often speak of forsakenness and punishment in metaphors of bodily pain, woundedness, and disability. Additionally, God is depicted as able-bodied in order to emphasize God's faithfulness and loyalty. Finally, disability is often associated with idol worship. The essay puts disability poetry, a distinct modern genre, into dialogue with the ancient psalms, and the results are evocative and insightful. Koosed concludes that the Psalms offer a varied understanding of embodiment, and these poems can draw upon a wide range of human experience. Not all representations of disability in the book of Psalms are stigmatizing.

The book of Lamentations raises some difficult questions of theodicy and the meaning of suffering. Koosed discusses these issues in light of the book, read through the lens of disability. She thoughtfully interweaves these considerations with insight from the modern genres of disability poetry and "crip music." The treatment of Song of Songs is at times in dialogue with Olyan's (2008) earlier work, but she challenges this earlier analysis of the book, in particular Olyan's theory that it represents love between two beautiful and physically whole individuals. Koosed notes the book's tendency to fragment different body parts in its poetic depiction. In this section of the essay, the author challenges the assumption that sex and love are the domain of the young, able-bodied, and beautiful people. The images and metaphors of Song of Songs challenge the conventional understandings of beauty. As the essay ends, Koosed notes the importance of these books in a liturgical context.

Like others in this commentary, J. Blake Couey's essay in chapter 7 explores the use of images and language of disability within the prophetic books (Major and Minor Prophets), but the author is particularly interested in the relationship between disability and divine power. In this essay Couey attempts to integrate literary and historical approaches to the text. Couey acknowledges that views of disability in the Hebrew Prophets have been culturally conditioned and that insights into that context could offer us understanding of our own culturally conditioned ideas about disability. Couey's essay examines numerous passages that deal with disability explicitly, but he also contends that "other texts that do not contain explicit representations of disability might nonetheless contribute to our understanding of the construction of disability in biblical prophetic literature or the intersection of this corpus with the concerns of contemporary disabled persons" (267). Indeed, Couey seeks to ground this study of images and language of disability within the treatment of embodiment by the prophets more generally.

While Couey's essay is in dialogue with other scholars who have written about disability and the prophetic literature, his approach is particularly nuanced, attempting to avoid any gratuitous stigmatization through portrayals of disability in prophetic texts. Generally speaking, the corpus of the Major and Minor Prophets is consistent in its portrayal of the divine causation of disability. These texts also draw a connection between sensory perception and religious experience. Indeed, the Hebrew Prophets stress the need for sight and hearing in order to receive prophecy. Of course, much of the corpus calls for heightened social justice. According to the essay, much of disability images and language serve to enhance YHWH's supremacy over the created order. In fact, most of the depictions of the body in the prophetic literature serve the same purpose—to make YHWH's supremacy apparent.

Candida R. Moss' essay on Matthew and Mark constitutes chapter 8, and the author draws upon various approaches and valuations of disability throughout the two Gospels. Some narratives receive more extensive attention in the commentary, such as the woman with the flow of blood, the saying on self-amputation, descriptions on eschatological bodies, and the eye as the lamp of the body. Moss' commentary makes "the common disability studies distinction between impairment (a physiological phenomenon) and disability (a social phenomenon)" (276). Although attentive to the historical context of the passages in Mark and Matthew, the commentary is eclectic in its methodological approach, employing perspectives from postcolonial theory, feminist studies, and literary criticism.

From the beginning of her analysis of Matthew, Moss illustrates the primary role played by fertility and infertility in these books of Christian Scripture. Drawing upon the unusual circumstances of Jesus' conception in this ancient document, Moss offers some insights for modern readers: "Joseph is Jesus' father apart from able-bodied procreation, and Jesus is God's son apart from able-bodied procreation. . . . For couples struggling with infertility, it is significant to note that Jesus is born into a family constructed according to love and duty, not biology and normative procreation" (279).

Moss investigates the relationship between sensory impairment and sin or moral deficiency in Matthew. This examination is nuanced and challenges a simple explanation for the correlation. The commentary also analyzes the healing narratives of the Gospel of Mark. One consistent theme that Moss sees in Mark is the equation of faith and physical wholeness. As Moss perceives it, people with disability are implicitly or explicitly cast out of the kingdom of God. Disability and illness are systematically removed from the world that Mark creates. In some detail Moss probes the connection that Mark makes between healing and the forgiveness of sin. In addition, the essay considers the implications of the stories of demonic possession and their interpretations, including the possible impact of these on people with disabilities.

Later in the chapter, Moss engages in a fascinating comparison of the porous body of Jesus and the woman with the flow of blood. According to the author, Jesus' power flows out of him much as the blood flows out from the woman; neither can control the flow. Moss also does detailed studies of the passion narrative. Both discussions are intriguing, and she suggests interpretations that defy expectations.

In chapter 9 David F. Watson employs social-scientific and historical perspectives in his study of disability in Luke and Acts. As a first topic,

Watson interprets the infertility of Elizabeth, comparing the situation to Hebrew Bible figures Sarah, Rachel, and Hannah. In addition to infertility, Watson explores the relationship between various disabilities and designations of purity and impurity. He stresses Jesus' tendency to ignore impurity boundaries constructed by society. Like Moss, Watson investigates the connection between healing and the forgiveness of sin. The author examines the story of the woman with a flow of blood, the impurity that was attributed to her, and the social alienation that was associated with this impurity. Later in the essay, Watson attempts to explain why Jesus heals on the Sabbath. Among other passages, Watson examines the story of Zacchaeus (Luke 19:1-10) from the perspective of disability, and the results are fascinating. One of these is the fact that Jesus does not attempt to heal him. A primary emphasis in the material on Luke is an analysis on the meaning of crucifixion as the ultimate disability.

Certainly, Watson's thorough study of Acts 8, the story of the Ethiopian eunuch, is a highlight of chapter 9. Ostracized from worship in the temple and devalued in society, the eunuch in this narrative is not healed of his condition but represents the kind of full inclusion represented in Isa 56. Watson points out that emphasis in Luke–Acts is on the relief of individual suffering rather than on restructuring the community. Relief is given, but on a case-by-case basis. But these passages do challenge the ancient practices regarding disability, demonstrating concern for those typically marginalized in society.

Disability in the Johannine literature (John, 1–3 John, Rev) is the topic for chapter 10. Jaime Clark-Soles also explores the link between demonic influence and disability. In this commentary of the Johannine literature, Clark-Soles wrestles with some deep theological questions. For the introductory verses of John 1, the author of the essay considers how people with disabilities fit into the scheme of creation. As other contributors do, Clark-Soles examines the connection among cure, sin, and forgiveness from the point of view of the Johannine literature: "Linking sin with impairment can be a dangerous, destructive habit. A connection may be possible in particular cases, but such is not inevitable. Similarly, tying salvation and forgiveness of sins to a 'cure' is also problematic" (344). The author's reading of the Gospel's first chapter affirms God's created order: "The whole created order reflects and symbolizes God's nature and activity (1:3)" (338). There is a very strong emphasis on the incarnation in the Gospel of John, according to the author, and she acknowledges a stress on physical touch throughout the Gospel.

Clark-Soles raises the issue in relation to John 5:1-18 that people with disabilities are sometimes treated as objects to make some other point. She draws on the work of David Mitchell and Sharon Snyder (2013) as Clark-Soles talks about the use of "narrative prosthesis" in the Gospel. In relationship to John 5, the author discusses how the politics of empire get mapped onto human bodies. In chapter 9 she makes good use of careful translation technique to resolve some issues about "who sinned." The clarification that the author makes is very helpful. Yet the commentary does not stop there but instead offers a full interpretation of the various scenes in the story. A perceptive treatment of John 11 stresses that "both disability and liberation are a communal project" (356), which is an insight derived from the story of Lazarus.

Clark-Soles' treatment of the Johannine letters focuses on five themes: (1) the role of the senses, (2) ethics and incarnation as expressed in embodied love, (3) hospitality, (4) the role of prayer, and (5) the "prosperity" gospel. Of course, 1 John emphasizes the important christological point that to be like Jesus is to love like him, with a love that is manifested by action. The essay maintains that the author of 1 John "claims epistemological authority based on sensory experiences" (361). At the end of this first letter, the author warns the reader against idolatry. Clark-Soles argues that ableism is a form of idolatry. In her interpretation of 2 John, Clark-Soles critiques the argument that those who hold different theological views should be denied physical hospitality. Importantly, 3 John deals with the relationship between physical health and spiritual health.

The author finds it helpful that the book of Revelation holds each person responsible for living the righteous life in spite of the pressures that the empire creates. This is a positive thing for people with disabilities because they can live righteously whatever the circumstances. At least, that is how the author understands the book of Revelation. The essay acknowledges that the book of Revelation is literature of protest and hope. It this way it can be liberative for people with disabilities. In other words, apocalyptic literature "emerges from communities that perceive themselves to be under severe stress and perhaps even physical danger. It is written for and by people on the margins who do not have access to political power" (368). Clark-Soles mentions that the book of Revelation is on "sensory overload" (369) because of the abundance of references to hearing, seeing, touching, tasting, and smelling. However, in the final analysis, the reader must repudiate the extreme violence of the empire and of Revelation itself while celebrating the nonviolent resistance that the book offers as an example. In the end, God's life-giving actions prevail. As she closes her essay, the author explores the value of suffering, especially as it is represented in the book of Revelation.

In chapter 11 Arthur J. Dewey and Anna C. Miller engage the authentic Pauline letters (1 Thessalonians, Galatians, 1 and 2 Corinthians, Philemon, Philippians, and Romans) and the later letters written in Paul's name (Colossians, Ephesians, Titus, 1 and 2 Timothy, and 2 Thessalonians). The authors note that disability is a modern conception that was not necessarily understood in the ancient world in binary terms (i.e., "disabled" vs. "non-disabled"). There was a broad range of terms in ancient Greco-Roman society to indicate many varying kinds of physical and mental impairments, but nothing resembling these binary categories. As a consequence, Dewey and Miller primarily employ the social and cultural models in their analysis, borrowing insights at times from the medical model. The authors respect the differences between ancient and modern constructions as they explore the role of disability in the letters attributed to Paul.

The essay by Dewey and Miller acknowledges the pervasive influence in the letters of the concept of God's full acceptance of the crucified one. The Christ figure, as interpreted by Pauline literature, is a person with a disability, someone deeply marginalized by society yet fully accepted by God. In Paul's address to his readers, he "urges them to become a community of sufferers that gives the greatest honor to its weakest members" (382). The authors explore the liberating potential of the perspective of the suffering community transformed through resurrection. As they explore this aspect of the letters, the essay also indicates a purpose for the authors' interpretation: "The task of the Pauline interpreter, then, is to see the tension in Paul's language, to see the utopian, liberating possibilities, while at the same time noting the ways in which Paul's choices of language and metaphor often subvert these possibilities by reinforcing standard power hierarchies that are deeply implicated in constructions of 'ability' and 'disability' in antiquity" (383).

According to Miller and Dewey, Paul's emphasis on valuing his own experience is particularly useful from a disability perspective because it encourages readers to value their experience as well. The authors encourage readers with disabilities to interrogate Paul and his "schools" through these letters in order to distinguish what is liberating from what is problematic or ambiguous in the letters. It is very important, according to the authors, that interpreters "identify and critique those elements that contribute to a logic of domination and injustice," so that the "liberative potential of these letters" (421) can be marshaled.

Martin Albl discusses three different models (medical, minority, and limits) to be used in chapter 12 to interpret Hebrews and the General Letters (Jas, 1 and 2 Pet, Jude). The chapter identifies some of the advantages and disadvantages in applying these models to reading Hebrews and the General Letters from a disability perspective. In applying the three models, Albl asks three major questions: "(1) Does the text refer to people with disabilities? (2) What attitudes or practices toward the disabled are evident? and (3) What assumptions regarding the cause of disabilities can be discerned in the text?" (430). Albl also employs a method of correlation: he identifies a theological theme of interest in a letter and then correlates it with a theme or themes in the disability studies literature.

In the interpretation of the Epistle of James, Albl engages in several Greek word studies to determine when the text may be referring to people with disabilities. In particular, the essay explores the connection between disability and poverty in the letter. It also investigates the role of the rich in the Epistle of James. Studying the Greek in depth again, Albl makes a link between disability and a trial, illustrating that this arises from the text of James. In addition, the book of James has a focus on "wholeness" that establishes a consistency between words and actions. These actions must demonstrate a concern for the poor and avoid any show of favoritism for the rich. The essay also investigates the social side of shame, humiliation, and degradation, which were experienced by Jesus in his crucifixion, and how that enables Jesus to identify with the marginalized and oppressed. One of the more important concepts discussed in the commentary on Hebrews is the idea that "there is no inherent contradiction between the divine nature of God and the weakness and limitations of the human condition. God's nature is not one that is eternally aloof, unconcerned with the weaknesses, suffering, and disabilities of the world" (450).

Though there is no direct reference to disability in 1 Peter, Albl argues that the social model from disability studies justifies the exploration of persecution and exclusion in the letter. Indeed, in Albl's words, "One could make the case that 1 Peter addresses a Christian minority group that suffers prejudice and exclusion" (451). Albl suggests that the early Christian communities saw themselves as oppressed minorities in a dominant Greco-Roman culture. As the author points out, there is direct evidence in the letter that these early Christians were persecuted by their pagan neighbors. There is also language that refers to the original audience's "trials." Certainly, these are aspects of 1 Peter with which people with disabilities can relate. In chapter 12 Albl also explores the meaning of passages in

1 Peter, 2 Peter, and Jude that refer to Christ as being "spotless" and "without blemish."

This collection of essays constitutes a comprehensive study of disability in the Hebrew Bible and Christian Scriptures. The essays are attentive to the biblical text itself, but they are also engaged with disability studies literature. The cross-disciplinary perspective is very helpful. We editors hope that this volume will encourage other scholars to pursue this cross-disciplinary approach to biblical literature, for there is much more to be discovered!

WORKS CITED

Avalos, Hector. 1999. *Health Care and the Rise of Christianity*. Peabody, Mass.: Hendrickson.

———. 1995. *Illness and Health Care in the Ancient Near East: The Role of the Temple in Greece, Mesopotamia, and Israel*. Harvard Semitic Monographs 54. Atlanta: Scholars.

Avalos, Hector, Sarah J. Melcher, and Jeremy Schipper, eds. 2007. *This Abled Body: Rethinking Disabilities in Biblical Studies*. Semeia Studies 55. Atlanta: Society of Biblical Literature.

Blumenthal, David R. 1993. *Facing the Abusing God: A Theology of Protest*. Louisville, Ky.: Westminster John Knox.

Creamer, Deborah Beth. 2009. *Disability and Christian Theology: Embodied Limits and Constructive Possibilities*. Oxford: Oxford University Press.

Eiesland, Nancy L. 1994. *The Disabled God: Toward a Liberatory Theology of Disability*. Nashville: Abingdon.

Eiesland, Nancy L., and Don E. Saliers, eds. 1998. *Human Disability and the Service of God: Reassessing Religious Practice*. Nashville: Abingdon.

Garland-Thomson, Rosemarie. 2010. "Integrating Disability, Transforming Feminist Theory." Pages 353–73 in *The Disability Studies Reader*. Edited by Lennard J. Davis. 3rd ed. New York: Routledge.

Hauerwas, Stanley. 2004. "Community and Diversity: The Tyranny of Normality." Pages 37–43 in *Critical Reflections on Stanley Hauerwas' Theology of Disability: Disabling Society, Enabling Theology*. Edited by John Swinton. Binghamton, N.Y.: Haworth Pastoral.

Hull, John M. 2001. *In the Beginning There Was Darkness: A Blind Person's Conversations with the Bible*. Harrisburg, Pa.: Trinity International.

Koosed, Jennifer L., and Darla Schumm. 2011. "Out of Darkness: Examining the Rhetoric of Blindness in the Gospel of John." Pages 77–92 in *Disability in Judaism, Christianity, and Islam: Sacred Texts, Historical Traditions, and Social Analysis*. Edited by D. Schumm and M. Stoltzfus. New York: Palgrave Macmillan.

Milgrom, Jacob. 2000. *Leviticus 17–22*. Anchor Bible 3A. Garden City, N.Y.: Doubleday.

Mitchell, David, and Sharon Snyder. 2013. "Narrative Prosthesis." Pages 222–35 in *The Disability Studies Reader*. Edited by Lennard J. Davis. New York: Routledge.

Moss, Candida R. 2012. "Christly Possession and Weakened Bodies: Reconsideration of the Function of Paul's Thorn in the Flesh (2 Cor. 12:7-10)." *Journal of Religion, Disability, and Health* 16, no. 4: 319–33.

———. 2010. "The Man with the Flow of Power: Porous Bodies in Mark 5:25-34." *Journal of Biblical Literature* 129, no. 3: 507–19.

Moss, Candida R., and Jeremy Schipper, eds. 2011. *Disability Studies and Biblical Literature*. New York: Palgrave Macmillan.

Olyan, Saul M. 2008. *Disability in the Hebrew Bible: Interpreting Mental and Physical Differences*. Cambridge: Cambridge University Press.

Raphael, Rebecca. 2008. *Biblical Corpora: Representations of Disability in Hebrew Biblical Literature*. New York: T&T Clark.

Schipper, Jeremy. 2011. *Disability and Isaiah's Suffering Servant*. Biblical Refigurations. Oxford: Oxford University Press.

———. 2006. *Disability Studies and the Hebrew Bible: Figuring Mephibosheth in the David Story*. New York: T&T Clark.

Seow, C. L. 1997. *Ecclesiastes: A New Translation with Introduction and Commentary*. Anchor Bible 18C. Garden City, N.Y.: Doubleday.

1

Genesis and Exodus

Sarah J. Melcher

This chapter examines the biblical text through the lens of disability. The primary method used is literary criticism, though the essay also draws on cultural criticism, when appropriate. Of course, the chapter studies passages that directly reference disability, but it is also concerned with how disability functions in more general literary and conceptual contexts. At times the cultural context for the passages in hand may imply that the authors and culture of the time had a different understanding of disability than those in more modern contexts.

Much of the commentary on Genesis addresses the disability of infertility. Though many modern readers would not consider infertility to be disabling, from an ancient Israelite perspective, it certainly was. If a physical, mental, or emotional condition significantly impairs a person's daily life, that condition is disabling (Raphael 2004, 401). As the biblical text construes it, infertility as a description of childlessness fits well with more modern definitions of disability (Moss and Baden 2015, 4). According to the field of disability studies, when certain conditions are identified as disabilities, this usually involves more than a medical diagnosis. Disability is a cultural construction that entails political, religious, sexual, and legal aspects and is dependent upon the particular social and cultural context in which human differences are located. Disability as this cultural product embraces perceptions of diverse social structures, institutions, and experiences (Moss and Baden 2015, 4–5). The cultural representations of infertility in Genesis and Exodus reflect this complicated social texture surrounding infertility, with connections to ideas about the family, marriage, gender, and nation building. The commentary in this chapter explores the biblical literature in Genesis that deals with some aspect of infertility. Yet the commentary also attempts to put biblical passages about infertility into a larger context that is concerned about reproduction more generally and about the desire to shape the next generation in a way that serves the greater interests of the community.

Other topics of Genesis that are treated in the commentary are the sovereignty of God and how that is reflected in God's control over reproduction. God's and the community's concerns with reproduction and a pure lineage are connected to the intention to establish a new nation, descended from the eponymous ancestor. Genesis is preoccupied with reproduction and the concern for a pure lineage. This commentary attempts to place the focus on infertility within these larger contexts, literary and cultural.

One of the most important and controversial passages to be discussed in the commentary is Exod 4, which implies that God is responsible for causing disability. Exodus 4 raises the issue of creation and whether God intentionally decides who will have a disability and who will not. The commentary discusses an alternative possibility, that God creates humankind as occupying diverse positions on a spectrum of ability. There are also implications that arise because of the way God treats Moses' speech disability. God acknowledges Moses' disability and finds means to address cultural attitudes about disability, but God ultimately treats Moses' disability in a matter-of-fact way, as an unsurprising feature of his humanity.

The passages of Exodus depict God as having sovereignty over human variation and over health and disability. The commentary explores the issue of divine sovereignty through the lens of disability. Exodus 9 depicts God as striking the Egyptians with plagues. The passage offers two rationales for God's actions: first, to show Pharaoh and the Egyptians that there is no one like God in all the earth (v. 14) and second, to reveal God's power and to make God famous everywhere (v. 16).

DISABILITY AND GENESIS

DISABILITY AND CREATION

The publication of Nancy L. Eiesland's *The Disabled God* (1994) raised some important ideas for those studying disability and theology. Though controversial for some, her suggestion for envisioning God with a disability that required a sip-puff wheelchair had profound ramifications for this field of study. Though the connection was not made directly in Eiesland's work, the idea that the concept of God could somehow include disability brings to mind Gen 1:26-27, where human beings are created according to the image of God. To pursue the implications raised by Eiesland's work, I will explore the meaning of Gen 1:26-27 in relation to disability.

The discussion of the phrase "the image of God" has been very important to modern readers of the Bible and to biblical interpreters, but it actually occurs rarely in the Hebrew Bible. In fact, only three passages in Gen 1–11 depict human beings as created in the image and/or likeness of God: Gen 1:26-28, 5:1-3, and 9:6 (Bosman 2013, 39). All three passages are widely regarded to be the work of the Priestly Source. Though modern interpreters have spilled a lot of ink over what the "image" (צלם, *tselem*) and "likeness" (דמות, *demut*) of God might mean in regard to the creation of humanity, it is not a major theme in the Hebrew Bible. Yet the creation of human beings in the image and likeness of God is a theme that has major implications for this study of disability in Genesis and Exodus.

Of course, the creation of human beings in the image and likeness of God means that humanity is similar to God in some fashion (Clines 1968, 53). According to Gen 1, the human being is the one creature in the created order that is like God, a matter of some significance. Of course, to be *like* God implies that human beings are also *unlike* God to an extent, with attendant limitations. Humans are not equivalent or synonymous with God; the representation or image of God to some degree is unlike the original (53–54).

For many ancient interpreters, to be made in the image and likeness of God is to physically resemble God. For instance, *Genesis Rabbah* 8 relates a charming story set at a time shortly after the first human being was created. After God had fashioned him, the first human resembled God so closely that the angels mistook him for God. As a consequence, God brought sleep upon the human so that all would know that the human being had limitations and was not divine (Neusner 1991, 63). The Babylonian Talmud also discusses a physical aspect of God's image in the human being, stating that any person who does not participate in the propagation of the human race diminishes the divine image (*b. Yebam.* 63b). These ancient interpretations of "image" carry implications for interpreting the language of the "image of God" in the midst of the genealogy of Seth in Gen 5. Classical rabbinic texts from the era bounded by the Mishnah at the beginning and the Talmud at the end are consistent in interpreting "image of God" as corresponding to the "physically embodied human being" (Weiss 2012, 24).

Ancient Near Eastern texts, which use a cognate term (*tsalmu*) to the Hebrew צלם (*tselem*), indicate a very broad understanding of the terminology for "image." The concept represented by the term *tsalmu* could relate to spiritual, social, interrelational, mental, and physical aspects. In light of the ancient Near Eastern evidence, Andreas Schüle elucidates its meaning in Gen 1–11 accordingly:

> First of all it becomes clear that the *imago dei* as the key concept in the anthropology of the priestly code is of all-embracing character. It is not limited to "religious" aspects of human existence—such as the participation in rituals or the spiritual encounter with God in prayer—, but relates to every instance of mental, physical, social and even sexual life. According to P, there is nothing that could possibly be said about Adam without referring to his being created in the image of God. (2005, 7; see also Herring 2008, 481)

Now we can see that the concept of the human being created in the "image of God" is broad, complex, and yet vague in Gen 1. However, the ancient Near Eastern study of the concept of cultic image suggests strongly that the image represents the divine presence on earth (Schüle 2005, 6). The cultic image in the ancient Near Eastern context serves as the medium for a god's presence and actions in the world; this is a full and complex understanding of the image as a god's representative. The meaning of the "image of God" in the priestly literature of the Hebrew Bible may reflect the larger context of the ancient Near Eastern construal of "image." The human being who is made in the "image of God" actually manifests God's presence and actions in the created world. In this sense, the first human beings participate in the divine life since they are designated as God's representatives in action and as God's physical medium for conveying the divine presence. The meaning of "image of God" in Gen 1 is thus both physical and spiritual in its essence.

There is ambiguity and overlap in the use of both צלם and דמות in verse 26, to be sure, but verse 27 emphasizes the importance of "image" over "likeness": "So God created humankind according to his image, in the image of God he created them; male and female he created them" (Gen 1:27). In verse 27 the Priestly source promotes the dignity of the whole of humankind by the use of the inclusive phrase "male and female he created them" (Bosman 2013, 45).

Genesis 5:1-3 reiterates the inclusiveness of the creation of humankind. The idea that humanity was created "in the image" and "according to the likeness" of someone is reaffirmed in 5:3, but the terms are reversed: בדמותו כצלמו (*bidmuto ketsalmo*, "in his likeness, according to his image"). In this case verse 3 refers to Adam fathering his son Seth in his own likeness and according to his image. However, the implication is clear (though not explicit) that the image and likeness of God is transmitted to each successive generation of human beings. The mention of humanity created as male and female in verse 2 is inclusive, but the subsequent genealogy in verses 4-32 makes no mention of any female descendants. In fact, only Seth is depicted as in the likeness and according to the image of his father (Bosman 2013, 45). The intention of these introductory verses in chapter 5 may be to indicate that all humanity throughout the generations serves as the representative image of God. Yet the intention is not made explicit, and because of the ambiguity in the passage, other interpretations are possible (e.g., Quine 2015, 296–306). However, the Babylonian Talmud sees any diminution of procreation as diminishing the "image of God," which means that these sages interpreted Seth's lineage as passing down the "image of God" to successive generations through procreation (*b. Yebam*. 63b).

Importantly, the Priestly writer reaffirms humanity being created according to the image of God in Gen 9:6: "Whoever sheds the blood of a human, by a human shall that person's blood be shed; for in his own image God made humankind." This reaffirmation is very important since it indicates that humanity still is the representative image of God, even after humanity's expulsion from the garden in Gen 3 and after the flood in Gen 9. In spite of humankind's flights into disobedience, it still bears the image of God, as God's representative on earth (Brueggemann 1997, 452). Genesis 9 is cited as well in the rabbinic arguments of *Yebamot* 63b.

The dominion (וירדו, *weyirdu*, "and let them have dominion") of humankind over the natural world appears to be a consequence of being created according to the image of God, as Gen 1:26 clarifies. In some ways, as God's representative, the human being reflects God's sovereignty over creation (Bosman 2013, 47). As the Priestly writer has established a connection between human beings and God, then, likewise, that connection between human beings and the rest of creation is set up (51). This rule over creation has a royal quality to it, raising the dignity of humankind to an even higher level. Ultimately, human beings are defined by their relationship to God and to other creatures (52; Towner 2005, 350).

God's creation of human beings according to the image of God means that God has created the human being in order to be in relationship (Brueggeman 1997, 453–54). This opens up the idea of a "relational theology of creation" (Fretheim 2010; Möller 2011, 6). Medieval interpreters and feminist theologians have also stressed the relational implications of creation in the image of God, indicating that human beings had the capacity to grow in that image to become more and more like God (Ross 1990, 102–3). That potentiality is represented by our ability to know and love. As we learn to love, we become more like God. According to Dorothee Sölle, this love manifests itself in a political way as the desire to pursue justice in the world (102–3).

At the beginning of this section, Nancy Eiesland's work *The Disabled God* was mentioned as raising the idea of God as a person with a disability who uses a sip-puff wheelchair. The idea that God encompasses disability in some fashion connects closely with the idea in Gen 1:26-28 that human beings are created according to the image of God. If human disability is an unsurprising aspect of being human, it could imply that God, too, shares that aspect of disability, since humanity represents the image of God. The reenvisioning that Eiesland engages in suggests a sharing of common traits between God and humanity, as these biblical interpretations argue. Humanity, as the representative image of God, has sometimes experienced disability. God includes disability. Though the representative image of God is not a perfect copy of God, possessing limitations as noted above, the possibility is implied that God shares in the experience of disability.

The relational nature of creation in the image of God has very positive potential for disability theology. The levels of relationship among God, humanity, and creation model the kind of relational support that can be very helpful for people with disabilities. All creation is interrelated, and gifts are shared among God's various creatures. The relationship among the various human beings—people with disabilities, caregivers, neighbors, and others—can look to Gen 1 as offering a model for interrelationship.

INFERTILITY, DISABILITY, THE MATRIARCHS, AND THE PATRIARCHS

Disability in the Abraham Cycle

Jeremy Schipper (2007, 105–7) provides important evidence that the Hebrew Bible regards infertility as a disability. As the author notes, "Biblical, comparative ancient Near Eastern, and early rabbinic material all contain examples of infertility treated as a disability or illness" (105). He cites several instances in which ancient writers categorized infertility "with other illnesses or impairments, such as deafness, lameness, or blindness" (105). Further, Schipper observes that the Hebrew Bible often portrays the woman as the cause of infertility. Moss and Baden (2015), Raphael (2008, 57–58), and Ackerman (2011) have all contributed to a scholarly understanding of infertility as a disability according to texts produced in ancient Israel.

The most extended treatment of infertility in Genesis is that of Sarah and Abraham. The Hebrew Bible is explicit in Sarah's case in making the woman the cause of the infertility, which is the tendency in most biblical cases (Moss and Baden 2015, 35–36). From the moment at which offspring are promised in Gen 12:2 until the end of the saga in 25:18, the primary driving theme of the Abraham cycle is whether God's promise of offspring would be fulfilled, establishing a great name for Abraham: "I will make of you a great nation, and I will bless you, and make your name great, so that you will be a blessing" (Gen 12:2). Sarah's infertility is the primary obstacle to the fulfillment of the promise and the main source of narrative tension in the Abraham cycle. In addition, Sarah's infertility is the foremost element of her character, as she is introduced in Gen 11:30 as barren (2015, 24–26). Yet chapter 12 affirms that there will be offspring and that they will have possession of the land: "Then the LORD appeared to Abram, and said, 'To your offspring I will give this land'" (v. 7a).

Later in chapter 12 (vv. 10-20), the promise is put at risk through the first of three "matriarch in danger" stories. In an effort to escape the effects of a famine, Abram and Sarai travel to Egypt. As they enter Egypt, Abram becomes frightened for his own survival. Because Sarai is beautiful, Abram is afraid that men will kill him in order to get access to his wife. He asks Sarai to say instead that she is his sister, so there will be no motive to hurt him. As Abram predicted, Sarai is found to be beautiful by the Egyptians, and she is taken into Pharaoh's house. If readers are not familiar with the story, they will wonder if the promise of offspring and land will be fulfilled. Will Abram be the father of Sarai's children or will it be Pharaoh? Will the children represent the beginning of the Israelite nation or will they be Egyptian (Sweeney 2009, 28)? A lot is riding on how the story is resolved.

God intercedes and strikes Pharaoh's house with "great plagues." At this occurrence Pharaoh confronts Abram, asking Abram why he did not tell people that Sarai was his wife. Pharaoh followed this by saying, "Why did you say, 'She is my sister,' so that I took her for my wife? Now then, here is your wife, take her, and be gone" (Gen 12:19). The implications are fairly obvious that Pharaoh intended to have sexual intercourse with Sarai. God prevented Sarai from becoming pregnant by afflicting Pharaoh's household with plagues so that he would know that something was awry. Once again, the narrative drives home the idea that God has oversight over reproduction. In this case God protects the interests of the preferred lineage, determining who shall be the recipients of the promise. God exercises control over the shape of the next generation, helping to establish the origins of the Israelite nation through the great ancestor Abram.

Though most of chapter 13 focuses on the land disputes between Abram and Lot, the promise of descendants is reaffirmed. Perhaps the reaffirmation was needed after the promise had been put at risk by the sojourn of Sarai in Pharaoh's household. The promise is reiterated in the following way:

> The LORD said to Abram, after Lot had separated from him, "Raise your eyes now, and look from the place where you are, northward and southward and eastward and westward; for all the land that you see I will give to you and to your offspring forever. I will make your offspring like the dust of the earth; so that if one can count the dust of the earth, your offspring also can be counted." (Gen 13:14-16)

Though Abram was prepared to give his wife into another's hands, God reassures him that he will be fertile, that he will father offspring as numerous as the dust of the earth. These myriad descendants will also possess the land, as far as Abram can see. The tension of the narrative is ratcheted up as the story moves from potential infertility to promised fertility.

Yet in Gen 15:2 Abram reminds God of the problem of barrenness, saying, "O Lord GOD, what will you give me, for I continue childless, and the heir of my house is Eliezer of Damascus." In the following verse, Abram restates the problem, the lack of fertility: "You have given me no offspring, and so a slave born in my house is to be my heir." God promises, to the contrary, that Abram's own offspring will be his heir. The promise is that Abram will ultimately be fertile. This time, in verse 5, God promises that Abram's descendants will be as numerous as the stars. Abram is seen as righteous because he believes in God's promise of eventual fertility. Abram will be a biological father. God will see to it.

Chapter 16 begins with Sarah's defining characteristic, her barrenness: "Now Sarai, Abram's wife, bore him no children" (Gen 16:1a). Famously, Sarai attributes her barrenness to God: "and Sarai said to Abram, 'You see that the LORD has prevented me from bearing children; go in to my slave-girl; it may be that I shall obtain children by her.' And Abram listened to the voice of Sarai" (Gen 16:2). Sarai attributes her barrenness to God's will, affirming the idea that reproduction is dependent on the divine will. Sarai comes up with a plan for a surrogate to provide a child for Abram, stating, "It may be that I shall obtain children by her" (16:2). The plan reflects what may have been expected on the part of a wife in the ancient Near East. A good wife who has been infertile for a length of time (over ten years, according to the biblical text; 11:30, 16:4) is expected to provide a fertile woman for her husband, who is able to give birth to an heir. This idea is supported by tablets found at an archaeological site at Nuzi. In Sarai's case, she asks Abram to have intercourse with her Egyptian slave, Hagar (16:2, 3). Abram goes along with the plan without dispute (according to the text), and Hagar becomes pregnant. It is certainly worth noting that Hagar is not asked whether she would like to serve the family with her reproductive potential. Sarai is using her slave as a means to an end, to serve the need to produce an heir.

Significantly, the biblical text in chapter 16 may reveal something of the social stigma attached to a woman's infertility. A barren woman "could be an object of scorn," and a woman who has not given birth could be perceived as the recipient of a curse (Baden 2011, 17). Once Hagar becomes pregnant with Abram's child, she does indeed perceive Sarai differently, seeing a shift of social status between the two women: "He went in to Hagar, and she conceived; and when she saw that she had conceived, she looked with contempt on her mistress" (Gen 16:4). In the following verse, Sarai confirms regarding Hagar that "she looked on me with contempt" (v. 5). A closer translation from the Hebrew emphasizes the change in status that occurs as a result of Hagar's pregnancy: "When she saw that she had conceived, I became slight in her eyes" (v. 5; see translation in Brett 2000, 58). The discomfort that Sarai experiences in her husband's relationship with Hagar is reflected in the blame she places on him. Abram relinquishes responsibility for Hagar's well-being to Sarai, who deals with Hagar harshly. Though Hagar runs away from Sarai's oppressive treatment, the solution proposed by God's messenger is for Hagar to return and to submit to the harsh treatment. The messenger then promises Hagar a fertile line of descendants, a promise compelling enough for Hagar to return to the site of her oppression. This is the power of the social pressure to bear children in this ancient context, and the authority of God's messenger, that a woman would accept oppression at the hands of her master and mistress. In fact, Hagar offers praise for her ability to see the divine and live (v. 13). So momentous is the occasion of the promise of descendants that Hagar is the recipient of an annunciation: "And the angel of the LORD said to her, 'Now you have conceived and shall bear a son; you shall call him Ishmael, for the LORD has given heed to your affliction" (Gen 16:11). God grants fertility, the blessing of children, to this person of low status. According to the worldview of the text, fertility ultimately lies in the hands of the deity. Following the messenger's instructions, Abram and Hagar name the child Ishmael at his birth. Hagar lives as a person of low status—as a slave—and she submits to the harsh treatment of Sarai, all because of the promise of many descendants.

As expected, because the promise of descendants through Sarai has been delayed and her potential fertility is put into question, the promise is reiterated in Gen 17:2, 4. The magnitude of the promise is made clear by God in verse 4: "As for me, this is my covenant with you: You shall be the ancestor of a multitude of nations." This passage adds the depth of covenant to the promise of fertility and many descendants. The covenant extends to Abram's descendants (17:7). There will be an everlasting bond between the covenant giver and his descendants. To reflect Abram's fertility, his name is changed to Abraham, and the rationale for the change is his future fatherhood to "a multitude of nations" (v. 5). Abraham's fertility is maximized for certain as God promises, "I will make you exceedingly fruitful; and I will make nations of you, and kings shall come from you" (17:6). His descendants will be great indeed, for some will become royalty. Chapter 17 also reiterates the promise of the land.

Chapter 17 of Genesis connects circumcision to the promise of descendants. As this chapter is constructed, it makes a fertility ritual mandatory for Abraham and his descendants—indeed, for all who belong to Abraham's house. Circumcision is a common fertility ritual in the ancient Near East, but the biblical text makes it a birth ritual rather than a rite of passage associated more typically with puberty. Circumcision, like fathering descendants, is connected to the covenant as a symbol and a stipulation. As a symbol of the covenant, "The practice has an intimate connection with the content of that covenant" (Eilberg-Schwartz 1990, 147). The centrality of this fertility ritual is emphasized because of the punishment associated with failure to comply, that punishment of "cutting off" from kinfolk (17:14). One of the possible meanings of the phrase ונכרתה הנפש ההוא (*wan-ikretah hanefesh hahiv'*, "and that person shall be cut off") is extirpation, the destruction of his lineage (Milgrom 1991, 459; cf. Eilberg-Schwartz 1990, 148). Those who fail to comply with the command to be circumcised (a fertility ritual) will not receive the blessing of a lasting lineage. The promise of descendants includes Sarai as well, and her name is changed to Sarah, so she is the explicitly named mother of the nations and kings who will be born to her and to her husband (17:16). Sarah and Abraham's ages are so advanced that it intensifies the tension of the narrative and makes the fulfillment of the promise more remarkable. It also emphasizes the message that God has sovereignty over reproduction. It is God who makes people fertile or infertile. God specifies that God will fulfill the promise through Sarah and provides the name for the offspring—that of Isaac. It is Isaac who represents the preferred lineage, but Ishmael is the recipient of an alternative promise/blessing: "As for Ishmael, I have heard you; I will bless him and make him fruitful and exceedingly numerous; he shall be the father of twelve princes, and I will make him a great nation" (17:20). It is worth noting that Ishmael will be circumcised as commanded in verse 23 in order to aid in the fulfillment of this promise (Eilberg-Schwartz 1990, 148). Yet Isaac's preferred status is evident in verse 21: "But my covenant I will establish with Isaac, whom Sarah shall bear to you at this season next year." This is the Priestly source's reaffirmation of the promise. Chapter 18 follows with the Yahwist's reiteration of the promise.

In Gen 18:1-15 three men come to Abraham and Sarah's tent, and one of them confirms the ancestral promise to Abraham (and indirectly to Sarah, who listens at the tent opening; 18:10). Susan Ackerman proposes that YHWH delivers the promise at first to Abraham in J because a barren woman may not have cultic interactions in the presence of the divine (2011, 36–37, 39). The Yahwist also emphasizes the miraculous nature of the promise by mentioning Sarah's menopause (v. 11). So farfetched is the idea that Sarah could engage in sex with her spouse and give birth that she laughs at the very notion. Yet the promise is clarified and confirmed again by one of the three men in verse 14. At a set time, God will return and a child will be born. Ackerman intimates that once the performative speech act of the divine announcement of pending birth is made, Sarah is no longer bound by the ban against cultic engagement. She will be pregnant soon, by divine decree (37).

So crucial is fertility and the founding of a lasting lineage that the concern is addressed again in Gen 19:30-38 as Lot's daughters consider their own fertility and how to capitalize upon it. After the near escape from Sodom and the trauma associated with its destruction, Lot decides to live in a cave with his two daughters. Living in a cave with their father does not make it easy to find suitable mates, so the daughters come up with an alternative plan:

> And the firstborn said to the younger, "Our father is old, and there is not a man on earth to come in to us after the manner of all the world. Come, let us make our father drink wine, and we will lie with him, so that we may preserve offspring through our father." (19:31-32)

When confronted with the possibility that they would not have the opportunity to give birth, the daughters plot to bear their father's children, without his consent. While it is true that the story may have been included to degrade Moab and Ammon, historical enemies of Israel, it does illustrate the pressure women were under to bear children in service to the lineage. Though we have no clear proof that there were prohibitions against incest in the era in which the text was composed, Israel had the tendency to be endogamous at the level of clan but to prohibit sexual intercourse with members of the בת אב (*bet 'ab*, "house of the father").

Once again the plot of the "matriarch in danger" story is repeated, just in time to put the Abrahamic promise of descendants at risk. Thus the larger narrative includes a story that puts Sarah in a position that makes the reader wonder if the promise of children through Sarah will be ful-filled. While sojourning in Gerar, Abraham tells the people of the land that Sarah is his sister. Abimelech, the king of Gerar, takes Sarah into his household, but he learns through God that she is a married woman. Though Gen 12:10-20 is ambiguous about whether anything sexual takes place between Pharaoh and Sarai, chapter 20 establishes definitively that nothing sexual occurred. Apparently God prevented Abimelech from hav-ing intercourse with Sarah (20:6). God then instructs Abimelech to restore her to her husband, Abraham, but threatens Abimelech and his loved ones with death if he does not follow God's will. The end of the saga once again establishes the theme that God has control over women's fertility:

> Then Abraham prayed to God; and God healed Abimelech, and also healed his wife and female slaves so that they bore children. For the LORD had closed fast all the wombs of the house of Abimelech because of Sarah, Abraham's wife. (Gen 20:17-18)

In a story often attributed to the Elohist, God protects the matriarch Sarah, though her husband Abraham does not. God somehow makes it impossible for Abimelech to have sexual intercourse with Sarah and goes further to make all the other women in the house of Abimelech infertile, so that Sarah remains untouched. Baden claims that this passage treats infertility as a curse (2011, 18). When Sarah is returned untouched to Abraham, then Abraham prays to God that the wombs in the house of Abimelech would be opened. God responds by making the women fertile once again. The saga strongly emphasizes two things: that the patriarch appeals to God through prayer to alleviate infertility and that God has complete control over reproduction. God is in control of the promise and removes obstacles to its fulfillment, but also has oversight over all wombs, not just Sarah's (cf. Baden 2011, 17–18).

Finally, the promise is fulfilled in chapter 21. God has overcome Sar-ah's infertility, and she gives birth to a son who is named Isaac, "at the time of which God had spoken to him" (v. 2). All comes to pass as God has predicted it. Abraham circumcises his son Isaac at eight days old as Gen 17 requires as a sign of the covenant. Thus Abraham follows the fertility ritual that is embedded in the covenant. Isaac grows and matures in chapter 21 until Sarah realizes that Ishmael could be a competitor with Isaac for Abraham's inheritance. She decides to banish Ishmael and Hagar, his mother, from the settlement. God cares for the boy and his mother in their banishment, and another nation develops from the descendants of Ishmael. However, Isaac represents the first in the preferred lineage of Abraham.

If the reader had experienced a sense of resolution with the birth of Isaac, the narrators again put the promise at risk through the near sacrifice or the binding of Isaac in chapter 22. The narrative puts the offspring of the preferred lineage at risk, but in the end Isaac is saved from death by God's provision of the ram as a sacrificial replacement for him. Predictably by now, the narrative reaffirms the promise after the obstacle to it in chapter 22 has been dealt with. Verse 17 indicates that God will make Abraham's descendants as numerous as the sands on the shore and the stars in the sky.

Chapter 24 is a long chapter that has much to tell us about the importance of fertility in the narrator's worldview. As mentioned above, the Hebrew people were largely endogamous within clan and tribal structures, in part to keep property within the clan or tribe. This longest chapter in Genesis reflects these endogamous structures as Abraham instructs his servant to find a wife for Isaac among his kinfolk in the city of Nahor in the region of Aram-naharaim. Rebekah appears as the appropriate mate for Isaac, one chosen by God. The passage designates her as a virgin (24:16), something that ensures that any child with Isaac would be of pure lineage. This would guarantee that Isaac would be the father. Abraham's servant assures Laban, Rebekah's brother, that Isaac is a man of some property.

Interestingly, Laban and other family members ask Rebekah for her opinion about going with Abraham's servant to become Isaac's wife. The purpose of the passage may be to inculcate in the female reader the tendency to serve clan interests as far as reproduction is concerned. The family's blessing is telling about cultural interests in reproduction:

> And they blessed Rebekah and said to her, "May you, our sister, become thousands of myriads; may your offspring gain possession of the gates of their foes." (Gen 24:60)

The most significant blessing possible, from the perspective of Rebekah's family, is to bless her with fertility, a stream of many descendants who are able to overpower their enemies. Rebekah serves as the model of the wife who will put the needs of the clan first and will lend her fertility willingly to establishing a pure lineage. Chapter 24 has a very happy ending because it describes Isaac taking Rebekah into his mother's tent, loving her, and finding comfort after his mother's death (24:67).

The sense of Abraham's fertility is enhanced by his fathering of children through his second wife, Keturah. The two of them produce six offspring (Gen 25:2).

Other Instances of Infertility in Genesis

The story of Rebekah continues after the end of the Abraham cycle. In Gen 25:21-28 we learn that Rebekah was infertile at one point. Isaac prays on Rebekah's behalf, God grants his prayer, and Rebekah becomes pregnant (25:21). The patriarch is the one to intercede with God, and once again God reveals control over women's wombs. God's answer to the prayer for fertility is so effective that Rebekah is carrying twins who are already in conflict within the womb. God predicts that the younger brother will eventually prevail (25:23). Unsurprisingly, the promise of descendants and land is extended to Isaac, and God affirms that Isaac's offspring will be a blessing to all the nations of the earth (26:3-4). Almost immediately after the promise is reiterated, a "matriarch in danger" story follows.

Because of a famine (Gen 26:1), Isaac and Rebekah leave Canaan and travel to Gerar, the kingdom of Abimelech. While there, Isaac tells those who inquire that Rebekah is his sister so that he will not be harmed when men of the country find Rebekah attractive. King Abimelech happens to see from his window Isaac fondling his wife Rebekah. The king enquires about why Isaac has told this lie. The worry was that someone else in Gerar might have had sexual intercourse with Rebekah: "Abimelech said, 'What is this you have done to us? One of the people might easily have lain with your wife, and you would have brought guilt upon us'" (Gen 26:10). Abimelech forbids the people of Gerar to cause any harm to Isaac and Rebekah. They prosper to the point where Abimelech asks them to move elsewhere.

This is the third time that the basic plot of the "matriarch in danger" story is told. In the first story in Gen 12:10-20, Abram and Sarai are in the land of Pharaoh; in the second story of Gen 20:1-18, the principal characters are Abraham and Sarah in the kingdom of Abimelech; in the third story of Gen 26:1-14, the protagonists are Isaac and Rebekah. The stories have some common concerns: concerns with threats to a pure lineage, with the problem of the founding of a new nation, with the guilt that comes from committing adultery (cf. Sweeney 2009, 23). The fact that the common story structure occurs three times in the book of Genesis may reflect shared cultural preoccupations.

People today may not view infertility in the same way as the ancient Israelite society. For instance, the founding of a nation is not a driving force behind the desire to bear children. It is also true that infertility is not widely considered to be a disability in the modern era. Nevertheless, a Centers for Disease Control website found it necessary to point out that both men and women may contribute to infertility for couples. The website mentions that many still assume that infertility is a woman's problem.[1]

Yet the Bible is still a very influential book that shapes how readers view matters related to reproduction and fertility. Some couples continue to feel great pressure to have children who are biologically related to them. It is possible that the Bible has contributed to the social pressure that people feel to conceive children. Thus, there are a few contrasts between how infertility was perceived in ancient Israel and how it is understood today, but there are some commonalities as well. Though many couples no longer feel the need to establish a lineage in service to the larger clan, there is still significant social pressure to produce biological children.

Age, Infertility, and Disability in the Stories of Isaac and Jacob

In Gen 27:1-40 Jacob uses Isaac's blindness to secure the blessing of the firstborn for himself, though Jacob's brother, Esau, was actually the firstborn. Isaac does not know the time of his eventual death, so he asks Esau to hunt for some game and prepare some savory food, and then Isaac will give Esau a blessing. Rebekah overhears the plan and plots with Jacob to take advantage of Isaac's blindness to obtain the blessing for Jacob. Through an elaborate scheme concocted by his mother, Jacob is able to impersonate Esau and receive the blessing for himself. The narrative itself does not pass negative judgment on Jacob or Rebekah for their duplicity, but it does result in Jacob's serious estrangement from his brother, Esau. The rift is so critical that Jacob must flee to Haran in order to preserve his own life (27:41-46). The narrative does not seem to cast Isaac in a negative light. There is nothing that indicates a negative assessment of his disability other than Jacob and Rebekah using his inability to their advantage.

It is noteworthy in chapter 28 that Jacob's father sends him away so that he will not marry one of the Canaanite women in the surrounding area (v. 1). His father instructs him to marry a daughter of Laban, his mother's

---

[1] Centers for Disease Control, "Infertility FAQs: What Is Infertility?," http://www.cdc .gov/reproductivehealth/infertility.

brother (v. 2). The concern is for Jacob to marry within the kinship group, as we saw for Isaac in Gen 24. Isaac gives a blessing to Jacob that is similar to the one Rebekah received in chapter 24: "May God Almighty bless you and make you fruitful and numerous, that you may become a company of peoples" (Gen 28:3). The most important purpose for Jacob is that he find a wife in his kinship group and that he establish a thriving lineage of descendants. Isaac clearly understands that it is God who can grant the blessing of children—God who controls reproduction. Possession of the land is obviously linked to the blessing of procreation by verse 4. On the way to Haran, Jacob received the ancestral promise from God:

> And the Lord stood beside him and said, "I am the Lord, the God of Abraham your father and the God of Isaac; the land on which you lie I will give to you and to your offspring; and your offspring shall be like the dust of the earth, and you shall spread abroad to the west and to the east and to the north and to the south; and all the families of the earth shall be blessed in you and in your offspring. Know that I am with you and will keep you wherever you go, and will bring you back to this land; for I will not leave you until I have done what I have promised you." (Gen 28:13-15)

So Jacob is thus strengthened for the journey, for he is reassured that the outcome will be successful.

In the discussion of the two daughters of Laban, Leah and Rachel, there has traditionally been the possibility that Leah has a disability, according to some interpreters. However, the NRSV has translated the phrase ועיני לאה רכות (we'ene leah rakkot, as "and Leah's eyes were lovely"). Traditionally, the phrase has been translated in a way that interpreted Leah's appearance in a negative light. Bill T. Arnold (2009, 266) has explored the meaning of the phrase in depth:

> Translations of the word "weak" to describe Leah's eyes should be reconsidered (e.g., rsv, njps, niv), because the word, rare as it is, more naturally means "delicate" or "soft" in this context. It seems unlikely that the matriarch of six of Israel's tribes should be described in unattractive terms. On the other hand, NRSV's "lovely" is probably too generous. More likely, Leah had "appealing" or "pleasant" eyes.

Hebrew lexicons support Arnold's approach to the translation of the phrase (see *BDB*, *HALOT*). In light of this development in the translation of the phrase ועיני לאה רכות, this commentary will not treat Leah as having a disability.

Once again we encounter the theme that God has control over women's reproductive potential:

When the LORD saw that Leah was unloved, he opened her womb; but Rachel was barren. Leah conceived and bore a son, and she named him Reuben; for she said, "Because the LORD has looked on my affliction; surely now my husband will love me." She conceived again and bore a son, and said, "Because the LORD has heard that I am hated, he has given me this son also"; and she named him Simeon. (Gen 29:31-33)

Perhaps God granted Leah children because Rachel was the favored one in order to compensate her for the differential treatment, but it is important to note that the text does not state that God caused Rachel's infertility per se. However, it is clear that God did not open Rachel's womb when Leah's was opened.

Chapter 30 reveals more information about the cultural attitudes about infertility that shaped the biblical passage. When Rachel comes to the realization that she is barren, she cries out to her husband, "Give me children, or I shall die" (30:1). Jacob reiterates a primary assumption that we have seen underlying these passages about infertility: "Jacob became very angry with Rachel and said, 'Am I in the place of God, who has withheld from you the fruit of the womb?'" (30:2). Similar to Sarai, Rachel finds a surrogate to produce children for Jacob—namely, Bilhah. Rachel uses a similar phrase to describe Bilhah contributing to the lineage in place of Rachel to that used by Sarai in a comparable situation: ואבנה גם־אנכי ממנה (we'ibaneh gam-'anoki mimmenah, "and I myself will be built up from her," 30:3; author trans.; cf. 16:2). Like Hagar for Sarai, Bilhah serves as a surrogate for Rachel, but the progeny are somehow credited to Rachel. Rachel has employed a practice to build a lineage that is permissible in her culture. Rachel's words in this instance may again reveal the reproductive pressures that she experiences because of cultural expectations: "Then Rachel said, 'God has judged me, and has also heard my voice and given me a son'; therefore she named him Dan" (30:6; cf. Westermann 1985, 475). The implication is that Rachel has been vindicated through Bilhah giving birth. She apparently needed this vindication since she had been unable to give birth to a biological child.

Later in the chapter, Rachel makes a deal for some mandrakes that belonged to Leah's son. Leah lets Rachel have them in exchange for a night alone with Jacob. Apparently, mandrakes had a quality that would increase fertility, and that was why Rachel wanted to acquire them. Finally, Rachel gets what her heart desires: "Then God remembered Rachel, and God heeded her and opened her womb. She conceived and bore a son, and said, 'God has taken away my reproach'" (30:22-23). Rachel is referring to the shame that her culture puts upon her for being infertile. Finally, she experiences relief because she has given birth to her own son.

Genesis 32 contains a passage about a potential disability, although it is unclear whether the injury in question is a temporary affliction or a permanent disability. As Jacob prepares to reenter the promised land and meet Esau, a man wrestles with him until daybreak. When it appears that Jacob is prevailing over his opponent, the man strikes him on the hip socket and puts his hip out of joint. Nevertheless, Jacob manages to hold his grasp on the man. The man decides to rename Jacob, saying, "You shall no longer be called Jacob, but Israel, for you have striven with God and with humans, and have prevailed" (32:28). Jacob interprets the injury as caused by God: "So Jacob called the place Peniel, saying, 'For I have seen God face to face, and yet my life is preserved'" (32:30). This, then, reprises the theme that we have seen repeatedly, that God has sovereignty over the state of the body. If someone has become disabled, God is the ultimate source of disability. Jacob retains at least some of the effects of the hip displacement as he limps past Penuel (32:31). Whether these effects are permanent is not clear from the biblical text.

Dinah is not identified as infertile, so Gen 34 is not directly related to disability. However, the passage does offer some features that may help explain how infertility fits into the larger picture of reproduction in Genesis. Many will be familiar with the story of Dinah and how she is raped. The interpretations offered by her brothers after her rape and their retaliation help us to see the bigger picture. In Gen 34:7 the brothers regard Shechem's actions as an outrage, but the passage refers to "lying with Jacob's daughter" as something that "ought not to be done." It does not refer directly to the forcible rape per se. The brothers develop an elaborate scheme to exact revenge against the city of Shechem. The rationale for their scheme is given in 34:13, "because he had defiled their sister Dinah." The defilement mentioned here may refer to the defilement of a pure lineage and the threat to the next generation, from which the new nation will come. It may also be a reflection of the expectation that marriage would be endogamous, within the kinship group. The reason the brothers plundered the city after killing all the males in the city is "because their sister had been defiled" (34:27).

After the threat to the matriarch in Gen 34, the promise is repeated to Jacob in the following chapter: "God said to him, 'I am God Almighty: be fruitful and multiply; a nation and a company of nations shall come from you, and kings shall spring from you. The land that I gave to Abraham and Isaac I will give to you, and I will give the land to your offspring after you.'" (35:11-12). This fits the pattern of a threat to the lineage followed by a reiteration of the promise. In chapter 36 an extensive genealogy is laid out that shows that the promise of fruitfulness was fulfilled.

Genesis 38 also illustrates the importance of endogamy and perpetuating the lineage. The character of Tamar demonstrates that she is willing to do anything to perpetuate the lineage. She attempts to follow the practice of levirate marriage in order to approximate the lineage contribution represented by her dead husband, Er. Eventually, she goes so far as to disguise herself as a prostitute and have sex with her father-in-law. Subsequently she bears twins for the sake of the kinship group.

This study of age, infertility, and disability in the narratives about Isaac and Jacob deepen our understanding of these concepts from what we learned in the Abraham cycle. Endogamous marriage is the rule, particularly marriage within the clan. Reproduction is of utmost importance in building up the lineages of the patriarchs. Infertility is a threat to the clan's hold on the land and to the establishment of a great nation. The various tales of the restoration of fertility to the matriarchs illustrate the divine's control over reproductive potential and God's ability to fulfill the promises extended to the ancestors. Although we learned that adultery was a threat to the promise in the Abraham cycle, the narratives about Isaac and Jacob clarify the importance of a pure lineage, in which the lineage extends in a clear succession from one patriarch to another in the next generation.

Also, the stories of Isaac and Jacob deepen our grasp of the effect of infertility on a woman's status. Women, too, were understood as contributing to a pure lineage. A family's greatest hope was that the wives and concubines would have great fertility and so produce a legacy of offspring for the following generations.

DISABILITY AND EXODUS

DISABILITY IN EXODUS 4

The first pertinent reference to disability in Exodus is in chapter 4, which is part of the call to Moses. In verse 6 God offers a sign that Moses can use to convince the Hebrew people that it was indeed the God of our ancestors who sent him. The sign is described in verses 6 and 7: "Again, the LORD said to him, 'Put your hand inside your cloak.' He put his hand into his cloak; and when he took it out, his hand was leprous, as white as snow. Then God said, 'Put your hand back into your cloak'—so he put his hand back into his cloak, and when he took it out, it was restored like the rest of his body" (Exod 4:6-7). God has chosen a disease that may be a kind of signature disease. The gods of the ancient Near East often struck people with various skin diseases, usually as a form of punishment. The skin disease צרעת (*tsara'at*, "leprous disease") was something associated with divine action (Lev 13–14; Num 12; etc.) and may have offered a means of identifying the God of the ancestors. At any rate, צרעת is a disabling disease, as several passages require ostracism from the community as part of the response to the disease. It is also considered ritually defiling to the person who is stricken with it. The ostracized person is not permitted to enter the tent of meeting or to engage in any sacred ritual. In Moses' case, of course, the affliction is only temporary, and Moses can restore his hand to be disease free by putting it back into his cloak.

More importantly, Moses does have a speech disability, according to Exod 4:10: "But Moses said to the LORD, 'O my Lord, I have never been eloquent, neither in the past nor even now that you have spoken to your servant; but I am slow of speech and slow of tongue.'" Moses hesitates to follow God's call to lead the Hebrew people out of Egypt because he has some problem that makes him slow of speech. A more literal translation from the Hebrew could render the pertinent phrase in verse 10 as "I am heavy of mouth and heavy of tongue," which many commentators have seen as a reference to a speech impediment (cf. Hamilton 2011, 72–73; contra Stuart 2006, 175). God's response to Moses reminds him of the scope of God's power and sovereignty: "Then the LORD said to him, 'Who gives speech to mortals? Who makes them mute or deaf, seeing or blind? Is it not I, the LORD?'" (Exod 4:11). In the following verse, God promises to be with Moses and to tell him what to say to God's people in Egypt. The idea is that Moses should trust in God's capacity to offer help in any way that is needed.

Nevertheless, Moses' anxiety gets the better of him, and he begs God to send someone else on this mission. God relents and arranges for Aaron to go with him as the one who will speak what Moses tells him. God clarifies this in verse 15: "You shall speak to him and put the words in his mouth; and I will be with your mouth and with his mouth, and will teach you what you shall do. He indeed shall speak for you to the people; he shall serve as a mouth for you, and you shall serve as God for him" (Exod 4:15-16). God does not remove or heal Moses' speech impediment. Rather, God makes accommodations for Moses, providing a partner who is a better speaker.

This passage raises some issues for those with a disability or their loved ones because of the assumption that has been underneath the passages we have explored. Exodus 4:16 confirms that God has sovereignty over health and disability. Some with disabilities would take issue with the idea that

God deliberately causes a disability to some while letting others be free of that disability. Yet others might find it comforting to know that God somehow intends for human beings to have diverse abilities. The suffering or pain that accompanies some disabilities makes this concept problematic. The passage is controversial, and a satisfactory solution to the interpretive problems has yet to be found.

One thing that the verse Exod 4:11 does is present a binary opposition between blindness and sight. Disability studies suggests to us that this binary opposition should be interrogated. "It is clearly more useful to think in terms of a spectrum of variation in terms of visual awareness or skill," writes Georgina Kleege (2013, 454). Kleege mentions that a "Hypothetical Blind Man" has often been used as a prop for "endless thought experiments where the experience of the world through four senses can be compared to the experience of the world through five" (447). While verse 11 sets up a binary opposition between blindness and sight, the greater emphasis is on God's role in human variations. This verse claims that God makes these choices deliberately. While this approach emphasizes God's dominion over all things human, the deliberateness implied here raises problems for our theological ruminations about the nature of God. Why would God make some human beings blind? Why not let all be sighted? Some of the implications arising from the passage are that the randomness of human variations in visual acuity is taken away. The idea that God might be responsible for creating a system of random variations on a spectrum of human sightedness is easier to come to terms with than the idea that God makes deliberate choices about which individual shall be sighted and which individual shall be limited in visual acuity. Hans S. Reinders makes a striking summary of the issues surrounding the question of divine providence in regard to disability: "For some there is great consolation in the belief that disability is part of divine purpose, which for others again is totally unacceptable" (2014, 1).

The ancient writers, in trying to make sense of disability, have tried to answer the question of why. In order to affirm their belief that everything has a divine purpose and that God's sovereignty means that all things in life come from God, these writers have attributed the statement "Who gives speech to mortals? Who makes them mute or deaf, seeing or blind? Is it not I, the LORD?" (Exod 4:11) to a God who controls an orderly universe.

There is one advantage to God's statement that all physical variation comes from God. The way this statement is phrased means that both hearing impairments and auditory capacity are unsurprising aspects of being human. Both speaking and being mute are unsurprising aspects of being human. Both seeing and being blind are unsurprising aspects of being human. It is all part of the spectrum of human variation. This apparent variety illustrated in Exod 4 works for an evolutionary framework, for instance, in which the variations that emerge are constrained within the creational forms.

Thus, the statement in Exod 4:11 reminds us that having a disability does not mean that we have either a curse or a blessing. It is not a "special condition," but part and parcel of all human experience. As Reinders points out,

> Whether a curse or a blessing, it is argued, the underlying assumption in both negative and positive responses is that disability is a *special* condition of human being. . . . One way or another, any view of disability as a special condition is to be criticized for being dependent on patterns of exclusion. Whether God has blessed you or punished you, in both cases you are set aside from his other creatures about whom such verdicts usually are not communicated. (2014, 12; emphasis in original)

Chapter 4 can be read in such a way as to say that God does not treat Moses any differently because of his speech disability. Rather, God simply finds another means of handling it. Moses remains God's primary actor and primary intermediary with God in the Exodus saga. However, his brother, Aaron, has been enlisted to speak to Pharaoh. The matter-of-fact way in which God handles it and the refusal to demote Moses to reduced status provide an alternative way to look at disability without resorting to the "special" designation.

Moses refers to his problems with speech (ערל שפתים, *'aral safatayim*, "uncircumcised lips") in later passages as well (Exod 6:12 and 6:30). In the first passage (Exod 6:12), Moses complains that the Israelites have not listened to him so why would Pharaoh do so: "But Moses spoke to the Lord, 'The Israelites have not listened to me; how then shall Pharaoah listen to me, poor speaker that I am?'" The JPS translation renders the last phrase as "a man of impeded speech." Nahum M. Sarna explains the last phrase as "the organ involved is, so to speak, obstructed by a 'foreskin' that blocks its proper functioning" (1991, 33). In the latter passage, Moses utters a similar complaint:

> On the day when the LORD spoke to Moses in the land of Egypt, he said to him, "I am the LORD; tell Pharaoh king of Egypt all that I am speaking to you." But Moses said in the LORD's presence, "Since I am a poor speaker, why would Pharaoh listen to me?" The LORD said to Moses, "See, I have made

you like God to Pharaoh, and your brother Aaron shall be your prophet. You shall speak all that I command you, and your brother Aaron shall tell Pharaoh to let the Israelites go out of his land." (Exod 6:28–7:2)

Moses is concerned because of his speech disability that he will lack credibility with Pharaoh. This may reflect cultural attitudes about speech disabilities. Though Moses assesses the situation to be unfavorable for him to be the spokesman, God again finds a way to adapt to Moses' condition by suggesting that Aaron can be the person to handle the contact with Pharaoh. Nevertheless, God never waivers in appointing Moses to be the person with whom God will deal. God adapts to the cultural attitude about speech disabilities, but Moses remains the primary person called by God. It is to Moses that God communicates the divine intention. Aaron serves in a secondary role, as an assistant to Moses. Moses will communicate God's will in these matters to Aaron, his brother.

Disability in Exodus Outside Chapter 4

Exodus 9:14-17, like other passages in Genesis and Exodus, reminds us that God has sovereignty over disease, injury, and disability. God instructs Moses to communicate to Pharaoh that if he does not release the Hebrew people to go to the wilderness to worship God, then God will strike Egypt with plagues:

> For this time I will send all my plagues upon you yourself, and upon your officials, and upon your people, so that you may know that there is no one like me in all the earth. For by now I could have stretched out my hand and struck you and your people with pestilence, and you would have been cut off from the earth. But this is why I have let you live: to show you my power, and to make my name resound through all the earth. You are still exalting yourself against my people, and will not let them go. (Exod 9:14-17)

God reminds Pharaoh (and also the reader) that God has oversight in regard to the human body, individually and corporately. If Pharaoh hinders God's will, God will send disease to afflict Pharaoh, his officials, and the common people. Two rationales are offered. First, in verse 14, God states that the purpose of these plagues is to prove to Pharaoh and the Egyptians that there is no one else like God in all the earth. The second rationale for God's deeds is stated in verse 16—so that God may manifest the divine power and make God's name known throughout the earth. Verse 17 describes Pharaoh as "exalting himself" against the people of God (see Sarna 1991, 244). Yet the issues arise more with the purposes given in verses 14 and 16. Those stricken with disease would find it disturbing that these afflictions serve the purpose of demonstrating God's power and enhancing God's renown. Some would be unhappy to be used as a foil to heighten God's reputation.

Also of interest to an interpretation through the lens of disability are the statutes about physical disability in Exod 21. In verses 18 and 19, the situation is covered in which two individuals quarrel and one strikes the other with a stone or fist (Houtman 2000, 154). Cornelis Houtman remarks that the meaning of *'egroph* is ambiguous (154). Whether the meaning is "fist" or "clod" or "club," the injured party is confined to bed initially but is able to get up later and walk with the aid of a staff. The statute then limits the perpetrator's liability to paying for the loss of time and "to arrange for full recovery" (21:19).

If people are fighting and a pregnant woman is injured by the fight and she miscarries but does not experience any additional injury, then the perpetrator shall be fined whatever the woman's husband demands (according to the judges' determination). However, if the woman experiences additional harm, the perpetrator will be punished "life for life, eye for eye, tooth for tooth, hand for hand, foot for foot, burn for burn, wound for wound, stripe for stripe" (see 21:22-25; cf. Lev 24:19-20; Deut 19:21; see Hamilton 2011, 386; Stuart 2006, 493). The premise of the case is that the woman was not initially a party to the fight but is injured in the concomitant melee (Houtman 2000, 161). The punishment for her injury is to be proportional to the harm that has been caused.

In the case of a slavehold striking his slave so that the slave's eye is destroyed, then the owner is to set the slave free. If the owner knocks out a tooth of a slave, the slave is to be set free. This is considered to be compensation for the damage to the slave.

These cases of injury recognize that those who are injured through another's violent act deserve some kind of compensation for this irresponsible act. It is encouraging that Exodus seeks to hold accountable anyone who would cause lasting injury to another person. For the person who must live with the physical consequences of a violent act, the fact that Exodus passages provided statutes for holding the perpetrator liable is comforting.

A passage later reflects the idea that God controls health and illness, implying that good health is dependent upon people's obedience to God's covenant: "You shall worship the Lord your God, and I will bless your bread and your water; and I will take sickness away from among you. No one shall miscarry or be barren in your land; I will fulfill the number of your days" (Exod 23:25-26). God promises that if people are obedient to

God's will, then God will keep them free from sickness, they will not have miscarriages, and no one will be infertile. People will live long lives. This raises controversy among those who are faithful and obedient to God yet experience illness, miscarriage, or infertility. This point of view illustrates the "normate" assumptions of an ancient society that illness, miscarriage, or infertility are a reflection of God's displeasure and a possible indication of wrongdoing on the part of the person afflicted with one of these conditions. While the book of Exodus is regarded as Scripture by some religious organizations, it is important to understand the implications for readers with a disability. Some religious groups allow for a reading of Scripture that makes distinctions between a sacred message and cultural influence. Certainly, a cultural remnant embedded in a biblical passage need not be accepted uncritically by those who read through the lens of disability.

CONCLUSION

Important for this chapter is the emphasis in Genesis on infertility as a disability (from an ancient perspective). In this chapter I have attempted to place infertility into the larger context of the role of reproduction in the establishment of a nascent nation. There was also an attempt to understand infertility as a threat to the formation of a new nation. Infertility was placed into a literary context as well, as it played a role in the ancestral promise of many descendants and possession of the land, creating narrative tension and heightening the drama of the eventual fulfillment of the ancestral promise.

The major conclusion reached is that further study needs to be done on the role of God's providence and sovereignty in the Hebrew Bible as it relates to disability. One major discovery of this chapter is how frequently the Hebrew Bible describes God as having control over issues of disability. Either God is depicted as having control over the disability of infertility or causing disability as the result of a wrestling match, or God has made disability an unsurprising aspect of creation. In any event, the question of God's providence as presented in the Hebrew Bible is a very important perspective that has influenced the biblical readers' understanding of disability and calls out for more extensive study in and of itself.

This chapter has been more focused on the final form of the biblical text, though it is perhaps appropriate to refer to the historical layers present in Genesis and Exodus, specifically as reflected in the pentateuchal sources of the Yahwist, the Elohist, and the Priestly sources. Biblical scholars are always conscious of the various sources that contributed to the final form of Genesis and Exodus, and it is important to acknowledge that

these sources originated in disparate historical and sociological circumstances. In some cases the sources may have originated in different locales
within Israel or in the diaspora created by the Babylonian exile. Nevertheless, some of the themes that have been emphasized in this study seem
to transcend the divisions acknowledged in source criticism. That is to
say, the concern for establishing a new nation and the interrelated themes
of reproduction, fertility/infertility, and God's sovereignty are common
to all the sources. The desire to establish a pure lineage, to reproduce to
serve the clan's needs, to tie the following generations permanently to the
ancestral lands, and to acknowledge God's sovereignty over reproduction
and disability are themes that are common to all the pentateuchal sources
in Genesis and Exodus. Though idiosyncratic use of style and language
are apparent among the various sources, they are all concerned to tell the
tale of the establishment of Israel. All the sources emphasize the interplay
between fertility and infertility and the promise to the ancestors, as well
as describing instances when the ancestors were afflicted with a disability.
It may be that these were concerns in the culture of ancient Israel across
multiple centuries.

WORKS CITED

Ackerman, Susan. 2011. "The Blind, the Lame, and the Barren Shall Not
Come into the House." Pages 29–45 in *Disability Studies and Biblical Literature*. Edited by Candida R. Moss and Jeremy Schipper. New York: Palgrave Macmillan.

Arnold, Bill T. 2009. *Genesis*. Cambridge: Cambridge University Press.

Baden, Joel. 2011. "The Nature of Barrenness in the Hebrew Bible." Pages
13–27 in *Disability Studies and Biblical Literature*. Edited by Candida R.
Moss and Jeremy Schipper. New York: Palgrave Macmillan.

Bosman, Hendrick. 2013. "Figuring God and Humankind: The *Imago Dei* in
View of Anthropologies in the Old Testament." Pages 39–56 in *Fragile
Dignity: Intercontextual Conversations on Scriptures, Family, and Violence*.
Edited by L. Juliana Claassens and Klaas Spronk. Atlanta: Society of Bib-
lical Literature.

Brett, Mark G. 2000. *Genesis: Procreation and the Politics of Identity*. Old Testament Readings. London: Routledge.

Brueggemann, Walter. 1997. *Theology of the Old Testament: Testimony, Dispute, Advocacy*. Minneapolis: Fortress.

Centers for Disease Control. "Infertility FAQs: What Is Infertility?," http://
www.cdc.gov/reproductivehealth/infertility.

Clines, D. J. A. 1968. "The Image of God in Man." *TynBul* 19: 53–103.

Eiesland, Nancy L. 1994. *The Disabled God: Toward a Liberatory Theology of Disability*. Nashville: Abingdon.

Eilberg-Schwartz, Howard. 1990. *The Savage in Judaism: An Anthropology of Israelite Religion and Ancient Judaism*. Bloomington: Indiana University Press.

Fretheim, Terence. 2010. *God and World in the Old Testament: A Relational Theology of Creation*. Nashville: Abingdon.

Hamilton, Victor P. 2011. *Exodus: An Exegetical Commentary*. Grand Rapids: Baker Academic.

Herring, Stephen L. 2008. "A 'Transubstantiated' Humanity: The Relationship between the Divine Image and the Presence of God in Genesis i 26f." *Vetus Testamentum* 58: 480–94.

Houtman, Cornelis. 2000. *Exodus*. Historical Commentary on the Old Testament 3. Leuven: Peeters.

Kleege, Georgina. 2013. "Blindness and Visual Culture: An Eyewitness Account." Pages 447–55 in *The Disability Studies Reader*. Edited by Lennard J. Davis. 4th ed. New York: Routledge.

Milgrom, Jacob. 1991. *Leviticus 1–16: A New Translation with Introduction and Commentary*. Anchor Bible 3. Garden City, N.Y.: Doubleday.

Möller, Karl. 2011. "Images of God and Creation in Genesis 1–2." Pages 3–29 in *A God of Faithfulness: Essays in Honour of J. Gordon McConville on His 60th Birthday*. Edited by Jamie A. Grant, Alison Lo, and Gordon J. Wenham. New York: T&T Clark.

Moss, Candida R., and Joel S. Baden. 2015. *Reconceiving Infertility: Biblical Perspectives on Procreation and Childlessness*. Princeton: Princeton University Press.

Neusner, Jacob. 1991. *Confronting Creation: How Judaism Reads Genesis. An Anthology of Genesis Rabbah*. Columbia: University of South Carolina Press.

Quine, Catherine. 2015. "Deutero-Isaiah, J and P: Who Is the Image and Likeness of God? Implications for אדם and Theologies of Creation." *Journal for the Study of the Old Testament* 29, no. 2: 296–306.

Raphael, Rebecca. 2004. "Things Too Wonderful: A Disabled Reading of Job." *Perspectives in Religious Studies* 31, no. 4: 399–424.

———. 2008. *Biblical Corpora: Representations of Disability in Hebrew Biblical Literature*. The Library of Hebrew Bible/Old Testament Studies 445. New York: T&T Clark.

Reinders, Hans S. 2014. *Disability, Providence, and Ethics: Bridging Gaps, Transforming Lives*. Studies in Religion, Theology, and Disability. Waco, Tex.: Baylor University Press.

Ross, Ellen M. 1990. "Human Persons as Images of the Divine: A Reconsideration." Pages 97–116 in *The Pleasure of Her Text: Feminist Readings of*

Biblical and Historical Texts. Edited by Alice Bach. Philadelphia: Trinity International.

Sarna, Nahum M. 1991. *The JPS Torah Commentary, Exodus*. Philadelphia: Jewish Publication Society.

Schipper, Jeremy. 2007. "Disabling Israelite Leadership: 2 Samuel 6:23 and Other Images of Disability in the Deuteronomistic History." Pages 103–13 in *This Abled Body: Rethinking Disabilities in Biblical Studies*. Edited by Hector Avalos, Sarah J. Melcher, and Jeremy Schipper. Semeia Studies 55. Atlanta: Society of Biblical Literature.

Schüle, Andreas. 2005. "Made in the 'Image of God': The Concepts of Divine Images in Gen 1–3." *Zeitschrift für die alttestamentliche Wissenschaft* 117: 1–20.

Stuart, Douglas K. 2006. *Exodus*. New American Commentary 2. Nashville: Broadman & Holman.

Sweeney, Marvin A. 2009. "Form Criticism: The Question of the Endangered Matriarchs in Genesis." Pages 17–38 in *Method Matters: Essays on the Interpretation of the Hebrew Bible in Honor of David L. Petersen*. Edited by Joel M. LeMon and Kent Harold Richards. Atlanta: Society of Biblical Literature.

Towner, W. Sibley. 2005. "Clones of God: Genesis 1:26-28 and the Image of God in the Hebrew Bible." *Interpretation* 50: 341–56.

Weiss, Daniel H. 2012. "Direct Divine Sanction, the Prohibition of Bloodshed, and the Individual as Image of God in Classical Rabbinic Literature." *Journal of the Society of Christian Ethics* 32, no. 2: 23–28.

Westermann, Claus. 1985. *Genesis 12–36: A Continental Commentary*. Translated by John J. Scullion, S.J. Minneapolis: Fortress.

2

Leviticus–Deuteronomy

David Tabb Stewart

INTRODUCTION: HERMENEUTICAL AND THEORETICAL APPROACHES

WHY INTERPRET?

Henri-Jacques Stiker, writing about Lev 21:16-24 in his book *A History of Disability*, startles the reader: "Legal uncleanness was attached to the disabled. . . . The disabled had the status of prostitutes or of women whom menstruation made unclean" (1999, 70). Could this possibly be true? The result heightens stigma associated with disability by giving it the color of biblical legitimacy. Stiker's view conflates two categories of biblical law—"ritual impairment," because of certain visible bodily conditions, with "ritual impurity," caused by normal bodily discharges or disease. Disabilities in the first category, called מומים (*mûmîm*, "visible physical blemishes") can permanently disqualify an Israelite priest from sanctuary service. But these "blemishes" do not prevent the approach of any other Israelite to the sacred or the "disabled" priest from eating from the sacred donations given to the temple. The second category, called טומאה (*ṭūmʾâ*, "impurity") covers menstruation, sexual emissions, and other discharges that arise from natural or disease processes. These temporarily impede Israelites and Israelite priests in their course of life. However, the two categories are *not the same* (Stewart 2011, 69–71). Perhaps Stiker meant to show what he thought was an oppressive absurdity. But the result is to obscure the text, fan social misunderstanding, and insult real people with disabilities by confusing biblical conceptions of "the disabled" with physical and moral impurity.

What I understand to be Stiker's misreading makes the study of Leviticus and biblical law on disability not just a corrective but also important to see how we and the biblical text begin from entirely different points of view. We are, after all, separated by more than 2,500 years from the writers. That the sky at dawn and dusk may appear to be the same disguises the fact that the earth turned and the sun traveled between them. The commentary that follows attempts to bring the two horizons together—the sunrise of Israelite understanding of disability with our sunset and evening, years later and miles distant.

Leviticus is arguably the most important book in the Hebrew Bible / Old Testament with respect to the study of disability, and certainly for the three books of biblical law considered here: Leviticus, Numbers, and Deuteronomy. Leviticus comprehends the main "system" of ability and disability within the Hebrew Bible / Old Testament to which the rest of biblical law mostly refers and amends and on which the rest of the Bible builds and supplements. Aside from the notion that disability is *part of the creation* (Exod 4:10-11), understanding disability in the biblical world begins here.

In what follows, I will use the composite term "(dis)ability" to signal that the discussion considers "disability" and "ability" at the same time. Writing (dis)ability this way helps remind one that disability as a category is constructed by social groups and cultures as they observe human bodies and try to understand them. Remarkably, from the divine perspective in Exod 4:11, ability is the same as disability. Bodies lacking *mûmîm* or *ṭûm'â*—apparently "able" bodies—must still be "enabled" by cutting (circumcision) or by adding something for them to do divine service or be part of the Israelite community.

WHAT LEVITICUS, NUMBERS, AND DEUTERONOMY SAY: TEXTS, TOPICS, AND THEMES

Twenty-One Topics

Most of the material on (dis)ability in these three biblical books and in all biblical law appears in Leviticus. The Mishnah tractate *Bekorot* ("Firstlings") and Babylonian Talmud tractate *Bekorot* that comments on the Mishnah text take up the disability materials in Leviticus and offer nearly the only commentary on them until the present era. So what is found in Leviticus, and also Numbers and Deuteronomy in their approximate order of presentation?

God calls out to Moses to speak to the Israelites (Lev 1:1). Yet we know from Exod 4:10 that Moses speaks with a "heavy mouth and tongue" (כבד־פה וכבד לשון, *kĕbad-pê ûkĕbad lāšôn*)—something YHWH did not see as impairing but for which he allows an accommodation: Aaron as spokesperson. At Lev 16:34 and elsewhere, the reader learns Moses *did* speak. Thus:

1. All of the Pentateuch in which Moses speaks contains the speech of the heavy-tongued, (dis)abled man.

The (dis)abled prophet of Exod 4:10, called upon to speak at Lev 1:1, raises twenty more *topics*:

2. The ritual enablement of the priests' bodies (Lev 8–9);
3. Ritual pollutions (scale disease, some discharges from the genitals) that disable priests and Israelites temporarily (Lev 12–13, 15);
4. The self-disenabling of the body (Lev 10:6, 19:27-28, 21:10);
5. Ritual restoration of the "person with scale disease" (מצרע, *mĕtsōrā'*; Lev 14);
6. Blemishes of priests and potentially sacrificeable animals (Lev 21–22, 24);
7. The problem of gendered laws for those with genital ambiguities (Lev 27:1-8);
8. Ethical laws concerning "disabilities" (Lev 19:14, 24:19-20).

Such ethical laws appear to be some of the first for people with disabilities. Among ancient legal materials, Leviticus alone features:

9. A law for the deaf.

Indeed, Leviticus may also hint at:

10. A priestly professional sign language.

Adding to the ritual of Lev 14, Numbers presents several passages that change the (dis)ability status of an Israelite:

11. The removal from the wilderness camp of *anyone* with scale disease or a discharge (Num 5:2). Removal for discharge is not found in Leviticus;
12. A ritual that disenables the woman suspected of adultery (סוטה, *sôṭâ*) through vaginal or uterine prolapse (Num 5:11-31);
13. A ritual that "enables" the body of a male or female Nazirite (Num 6:2-21).

To the disabling punishment of the *sôṭâ*, Numbers adds a parade example and further threats:

14. The story of Miriam portrays vividly the possibility that scale disease can be given as a divine punishment to a woman (Num 12:10-15), and

15. Scattered threats of punishment by plague (*makkâ*; Num 11:33).

Deuteronomy gives the least attention to issues of (dis)ability. However, besides additional disability-as-punishment threats, it offers some distinctions. Deuteronomy specifies:

16. Animal blindness and lameness as a "severe blemish" (מום רע, *mûm rā'*; Deut 15:21, 17:1).

Deuteronomy thus divides the category of *mûmîm* into two: severe and not-so.

17. Deut 19:21 follows the list of "disabling" injuries in Exod 21:24, omitting some items, and differs from the injury list in Lev 24:10.

18. Two examples of *ṭūm'â* ("impurity") are given further specification: nocturnal emissions in wartime result in time outside the camp (Deut 23:10-15); the skin affection of Miriam is diagnosed as צרעת (*ṣāra'at*, or "scale disease"; 24:8-9).

Perhaps the most important new law,

19. Excludes the complete eunuch from the congregation (Deut 23:2; v. 1 Eng.).

Both Isaiah, with his divine promises to eunuchs, and the author of Acts, with his story of the Ethiopian eunuch's conversion, seem to recognize this theme and ameliorate its consequences. In the nonlegal material of Deuteronomy, the cursing liturgy seems to add an additional ethical understanding to Lev 19:14:

20. A person who is blind should not be misdirected (Deut 27:18).

But in contrast to this cursing liturgy,

21. Blessed, abled, fertile bodies are promised (Deut 7:14) as fertile ones are at Lev 26:9.

Indeed, Moses himself continues to see undimmed—in contrast to his heavy tongue of Exodus (Deut 34:7).

If the disobedient body can be punished with disabilities in Numbers and Deuteronomy, the abled body—one speaking and walking—is held out as a metaphor for obedience to God. This last point feels "ableist" from a twenty-first century North American perspective. If those abled in certain ways are emblematic of obedience, are those disabled in the same ways disobedient? It is easy to invert the metaphor and so grow one's own internalized ableism.

Thus, there is a tension between Leviticus and Deuteronomy on this last point: on the one hand we have texts that speak in a nuanced way about ability where all stand "disabled" in some sense next to God. The material at the end of Deuteronomy overlooks this and begins to speak of the Israelite body norm as "abled" and the hero of the Torah, Moses, as not disabled. In this way Deuteronomy foreshadows a tension that will continue to appear in the biblical books that come after.

Themes across Leviticus, Numbers, and Deuteronomy

If we "reshuffle the deck" to look at *themes* across the three books, they present bodies that are socially, culturally, ritually, and divinely enabled, disabled, or presumed able. Bodies count as disabled because of natural bodily processes, congenital conditions, injuries, disease processes, social distinctions, or punishments (Lev 12, 13, and 15; 19:14; 21:16-23; 22:1-9, 10, 12; 24:19-20; Num 5:2-4; 12:10-15; and Deut 19:21; 23:10-15; 24:8-9; 27:18). The body with leaking genitals, for example, can be restored to ritual availability—that is, purity—by ritual action itself. But most of the conditions counted as disabling cannot. From the above, one can extract eight lists and three additional passages covering "disabling" conditions. Starting with the two most important:

1. Lev 21:18-20, disabilities that disqualify priests from sanctuary service;
2. Lev 22: 22-24, disabilities that prevent sacrificing an animal.

Because animals can sometimes allegorically stand in for humans, disability of animals available for sacrifice is also relevant (see also Lev 1:3, 10; 3:1, 6; 4:3, 23, 28, 32; Num 19:2; 28:3, 9, 11, 19, 30; 29:7, 13, 17, 20, 23, 26, 29, 32, 36; Deut 15:21; 17:1).

To these one can add three lists of impurities:

3. Lev 13 diagnoses the person with scale disease;
4. Lev 15 identifies four natural or dysfunctional genital discharges;
5. Num 5:2-4 summarizes sources of impurity;

along with short lists in ethical laws:

6–7. Lev 24:19-20 and Deut 19:21 identify compensable disabling injuries;
8.   Lev 19:14 offers the prime ethical law.

Two texts that add conditions not mentioned before:

9.   Deut 23:2 (v. 1 Eng.), the complete eunuch;
10. Num 5:11-31, the prolapse of reproductive organs in the סוטה (*sôṭâ*, the woman accused of adultery).

The last of the ten considers the parade example of Miriam's stigmatized body:

11. Num 12:10-15, Miriam's צרעת (*ṣāra'at*, or "scale disease").

These eleven key texts are discussed in detail below in the "Thematic Commentary": the first eight under the rubric of "The 'Disabled' Body" and the last three under "The Stigmatized Body."

The eleven texts, when inverted as if seen in a mirror, help us imagine bodies that ancient Israelite culture would presume able. However, not all the "able" are equal. Leviticus, Numbers, and Deuteronomy read the bodies of the high priest, ordinary priests, priestly families (including women and children), and lay Israelites at different ages in different ways. For instance, when considering the age factor, Lev 27:3 counts ages twenty through sixty as the prime years for socioeconomic ability; but ages thirty to fifty are privileged by Num 4:23.

Ritually enabled bodies include those of the high priest, ordinary priests, Nazirite men and women, the woman or man healed from "scale disease" (traditionally understood as "leprosy," but cf. Hulse 1975), and every Israelite male by circumcision (Lev 8:6-9, 12-13, 23-24, 26-27, 30; 12:3; 14:1-32, esp. vv. 8, 14, 17-18; Num 6:5-12, 18). By an elaborate ritual process in Lev 8, the priest's body is prepared for ordination. Once serving, priests must use their hands in rituals, and so the Bible describes a system of hand placements and gestures that may hint at a priestly, "professional" sign language (Lev 1:4; 3:2, 8, 13; 4:4, 29, 33-34; 7:30; 8:27-28; 9:21-22; 16:21; 24:14; Num 27:23). For example, when Lev 9:22 is read with Num 6:24-27, the words of the priestly blessing can be signified by a gesture. In contrast, the Nazirite keeps her (or his) body, when consecrated by a vow, by abstinence from haircutting and ingesting anything to do with grapes and by avoiding corpses. Completing the vow precipitates a status-changing ritual (Num 6:13-21).

The opposite of ritual enablement also exists: priestly bodies can be ritually disabled by rending one's garments, baring one's head, or going near a corpse (Lev 10:6, 21:10) or, for the Nazirite, likewise going near a corpse (Num 6:9-12). And for that matter, anybody can be socially disabled by self-inflicted wounds (gashing skin or cutting hair), injury, crime, or punishment (Lev 19:27-28, 21:5, 24:19-20; Deut 19:21, 23:2).

God's "body"—the epitome of ability—has a voice and so speaks directly to Moses, Aaron, and the non-Israelite prophet Balaam (Lev 1:1, 10:8; Num 23:4). God might divinely enable or protect bodies, making them fertile or preventing diseases (Exod 4:10-11; Lev 26:9; Num 8:19; Deut 7:14, 34:7). God can also divinely disable or punish bodies (Exod 4:10-11; Num 8:19, 11:33; 12:10-15; 17:11-15 [16:45-50 Eng.]; Deut 28:27-29, 35, 59; 29:21; 32:24; 33:11b).

The "Thematic Commentary," under the rubric of "The Enabled Body," colors in the picture of Moses' enablement by accommodation from Exod 4:10-17 and Lev 1:1-2—a case of (dis)ability. Aaron and his sons enabled as priests in Lev 8 offer a second example; and the Nazirite man or woman enabled in Num 6:2-21 shows the potential bodily enablement for divine service of any Israelite person. But the triumvirate of Israelite leaders in the exodus—Moses, Miriam, and Aaron—embody not just one but three positions that biblical law takes toward the body—disabling, stigmatizing, enabling. Their personal stories are a kind of "narrative prosthesis" (Mitchell and Snyder 2010, 278). That is, the overall exodus story "depends" on the disability and enablement accounts of its chief characters to clarify human disability and divine ability.

METHODS OF INTERPRETATION: DRAWING UPON DISABILITY STUDIES

If disability as a category emerged a long time before the contemporary political and cultural struggle over identity—where disability as an identity was solidified—the present moment has moved away from seeking some essential commonality among disabilities toward appreciating culturally diverse notions of disability. The ancient biblical writers and editors marked their notions of disability through the way they coined words and how they wrote texts. But the views of biblical writers are not precisely the same. Disability categories that are fairly well defined in one source (in the biblical Priestly literature, or "P") become fuzzier *across* sources (e.g., in comparison to the Deuteronomist, "D," Deut 12–26) though still exhibiting some "family resemblances" (Wittgenstein 1968, 1:66–67; see Stewart 2011, 71–75, 81).

Social constructivists would suggest that the category of disability is "constructed" by human communities through stigmatizing certain bodies (and esteeming others)—that is, disability is *not* a category of the natural world but a social and public category (Shakespeare 2010, 26–69). Social constructivists depend in some measure on medicine (and the medical model of disabilities) to define bodily impairments (Moss and Schipper 2011, 4). But there is no "correct" or "real" human genome (Davis 2010, 307); there is no one datum of the ideal body, only data of human variety. So locating impairment is also a process of social construction.

Recent efforts to "edit" the human genome illustrate this. CRISPR (i.e., "clustered, regularly interspaced short palindromic repeats") RNA "gene-drives" that target, cut out, and replace DNA sequences reflect the wish to reconstruct a perfect body physically. *Every* body has taken some problematic DNA from one parent when a better sequence existed in the other parent. Ergo, *every* body is "disabled" when it lacks the perfect DNA sequences available to it. Turning normalcy upside down, the use of tools to modify genes stigmatizes any natural human body as less than ideal. The "natural" becomes the "disabled." Any ethics of the body—even any discussion of the body—must begin now with "disabled" ones, something already understood by Lennard Davis (2010, 309).

In the cultural model, social and medical dimensions of disability are less important than understanding how disability develops "as a product of the ways cultures use physical . . . difference . . . to narrate, organize, and interpret their world" (Moss and Schipper 2011, 4; e.g., as a "synec-doche of all forms of the non-normative," Garland-Thomson 2010, 355). Thus disability can stand in for anything not thought normal. In Rosemarie Garland-Thomson's view, disability is a "cultural system that stigmatizes some bodily variations" (2010, 356). She argues further, "Disability, like femaleness, is not a natural state of corporeal inferiority, inadequacy, excess, or a stroke of misfortune. Rather, disability is a culturally fabricated narrative of the body" (2010, 356). That is, disability is a story told about bodies that makes sense inside a cultural/religious world. The (dis)ability "system produces subjects by differentiating and marking bodies" (2010, 356). How do notions of (dis)ability shape the biblical world and the worlds of biblical readers? How do biblical law and narrative mark bodies? To return to the figure of Moses, is he really abled, enabled, or disabled? If we find Moses "disabled," or "impaired" but not "disabled," how does it push us to rethink our settled biblical knowledge?

THEMATIC COMMENTARY

THE "DISABLED" BODY

Leviticus 1:1: The Bodies of God and Moses

Leviticus 1:1 begins with speaking and hearing: "The Lord called to Moses and spoke to him from the Tent of Meeting."[1] The Hebrew title of Leviticus, and its first word, ויקרא (*wayyiqrā'*, "he called"), points to YHWH's using a voice to speak to Moses from the portable shrine or tabernacle. YHWH spoke from the inner sanctum or holy of holies—presumably from the ark of the covenant. The lid of the ark together with the spread wings of the cherubim mounted on its lid marked out an empty space where a cult image might be placed. But here there was no image of a body, only empty space. Moses hears the voice tell him: "Speak to the Israelites and say to them" (v. 2). But Moses has a speech impediment. He is heavy-tongued. How is he to speak? Thus Leviticus begins with two bodily matters: Lev 1:1 reminds readers that God, without a visible body, speaks as if there were divine organs of speech; the disabled hero must repeat the message with impaired speech.

These first words point back to the creator God forming bodies in Gen 1–2 and to the explanation given to Moses about his speech organs (Exod 4:10-11). In Gen 1:27, האדם (*hā'ādām*, "the adam or human being") is famously made in "the image of God" (בצלם אלהים, *běṣelem 'elohîm*). The human body is an "image," a copy in a different medium of the divine "body." God's "body," at least analogously or metaphorically, has voice, a "hand," and a "back" (Exod 33:22). Moses is not allowed to see the "face" (v. 20). At the burning bush, Moses also hears a voice but sees fire (Exod 3:3-4). Thus human organs of sight show themselves inadequate to compose a comprehensible image of God's "body" (see Smith 2015). With respect to seeing God, Moses is also sight impaired, even though Deut 34:7 asserts the clarity of his physical sight at life's end.

Thus, when Moses protests his inability to speak, YHWH wittily answers with a play on words: "Moses said to YHWH: '. . . I am heavy-mouthed and heavy-tongued (כבד-פה וכבד לשון, *kěbad-pê ûkěbad-lāšôn*).' YHWH said to him, 'Who placed a mouth in the human, or who makes a person who is mute (אלם, *'illēm*), or deaf (חרש, *hērēš*), or perceiving (פקח, *piqqeāḥ*), or blind (עור, *'iwwēr*)? Is it not I myself, YHWH?'" (Exod 4:10-11; my trans.). "Mute," "deaf," "perceiving" (lit. "open"), and "blind" are all

---

[1] Translations are from the *Tanakh: A New Translation of the Holy Scriptures* (Philadelphia: Jewish Publication Society, 1985)—i.e., NJPS, unless otherwise specified.

iterations of the Hebrew (dis)ability noun form *qittēl* (Blau 1993, §40.19). Perceiving is paired with blind, suggesting "open-eyed." But it can also collect the antonyms of "mute" and "deaf," thus "open-mouthed" and "open-eared." Open-mouthed seems to answer to Moses' complaint. The joke here is that perception is treated as a disability. Perhaps compared to divine abilities, are open eyes not very different from blind ones and fluid tongues not so different from heavy ones?

In an ancient Hittite myth of Hurrian origin, there is also nascent perspectivism about (dis)ability. An exceptionally clever text from "The Sun God, the Cow, and the Fisherman" equates human two-leggedness with animal disability: "Cow [who has borne a human says]: '(My calf) should have four legs. Why have I borne this two-legged thing?'" (Hoffner 1998, 86). What constitutes bodily impairment for a cow is mapped onto a human. The very two-leggedness of a human being makes for animal disability. By humorously suggesting that all humanity shares disability, we have something akin to a modern debunking of ableism.

Lists of "Disabilities" in Biblical Law

Ancient evidence of disability as a category. Taking a historical, contextual approach, one ancient list of seven disabilities—perhaps the first—appears in the Sumerian "Birth of Man" (lines 58–59): palsied (?), blind, lame, deaf-mute or person with mental retardation (?), incontinent male, infertile woman, person without genitals (Jacobsen 1987, 159–61). The list of ten injuries spread over several laws of the Hittite Law Code (§§7, 9, 11, 13, 15; 74, 77b) constitutes another: blind, knocked-out tooth, battered head, broken hand or foot, bitten-off nose, torn-off ear, dehorned or lamed ox, blinded ox or horse (Hoffner 1997; Roth 1997, 218–19, 227). The twelfth-century-BCE Egyptian *Papyrus of Ani*, a version of the so-called *Egyptian Book of the Dead*, reveals a body map of twenty-one body parts that must be perfected by "deification"—identifying each with a god: "My hair is Nun; my face is Re; my eyes are Hathor . . ." (ch. 42; see Dassow 1998, 166–67 and plate 32). Such lists may have developed initially as folk taxonomies of ancient naturalists (Berlin 1972; Berlin, Breedlove, and Raven 1973) and found further impetus in the development of law and medicine. Egyptian medical texts, such as the papyri Kahun and Ebers, record various medical conditions, their diagnostic characteristics, and potential treatments (Strouhal, Vachala, and Vymazalová 2014; Nunn 2002; Morice, Josset, and Colau 1994; Stevens 1975).

The oldest "list" of disabilities in the Hebrew Bible can be constructed by taking a historical-linguistic approach. Early philologists noticed that disability terms often follow the Hebrew noun forms *qittēl* and *qattelet*, as one can see in table 1.

TABLE 1: DISABILITIES BASED ON MORPHOSEMANTIC FORMS
IN BIBLICAL HEBREW

Body Map	*Qittēl*	*Qattelet*
Head	עור (*'iwwēr*, "blind") חרש (*ḥērēš*, "deaf") אלם (*'illēm*, "mute") פקח (*piqqēaḥ*, "perceiving")	עורת (*'awweret*, "blind")
Limbs	פסח (*pissēaḥ*, "lame")	
Trunk	גבן (*gibbēn*, "hunchbacked")	
Skin and hair	חרס (*ḥērēs*, "itch; scabies") גבח (*gibbēaḥ*, "forehead baldness") קרח (*qērēaḥ*, "crown baldness")	יבלת (*yabbelet*, "wart") ילפת (*yallepet*, "scab(?) / tetter(?)") צרעת (*ṣāra'at*, "scaly affection / skin disease") ספחת (*sappaḥat*, "rash")

Leviticus 21:18-20 and 22:22-24. The Bible gives us three large lists of "disabilities" and five small ones: four in the Holiness Code (Lev 17–26; or "H"), two in the Purity Code (Lev 11–15), and one each in Numbers and Deuteronomy. Five of these lists (1–5) have something to do with Israelite religion and ritual but not with things moral (cf. Peckruhn's "moral/religious" model of disability [2014, 102]). The sixth, seventh, and eighth lists deal with things moral and include the "measure-for-measure" laws of Lev 24:19-20 and Deut 19:21 (6 and 7) and the "categorical" moral laws in Lev 19:14 (8).

The first long list collects disabilities that disqualify priests from altar service, and the second surveys blemishes disqualifying animals from sacrifice. That both lists in Lev 21:18-20 (1) and Lev 22:22-24 (2) contain twelve items in rough parallelism suggests an attempt to match human and animal disability (see table 2 below):

Leviticus 21:18-20:

כי כל־איש אשר־בו מום לא יקרב איש עור או פסח או חרם או שרוע
או איש אשר־יהיה בו שבר רגל או שבר יד
או־גבן או־דק או תבלל בעינו או גרב או ילפת או מרוח אשך

(v. 18)   *kî kol-'îš 'ašer-bô mûm lo' yiqrāb 'îš 'iwwēr 'ô pissēaḥ 'ô ḥārum 'ô śārûaʿ*

(v. 19)   *'ô 'îš 'ašer-yiheyê bô šeber rāgel 'ô šeber yād*

(v. 20)   *'ô-gibbēn 'ô-daq 'ô teballul beʿênô 'ô gārāb 'ô yallepet 'ô měrôaḥ 'āšek*

(v. 18)   No one who has a blemish (מום, *mûm*), shall be qualified [to function as a priest], neither a blind person (עור, *'iwwēr*), nor lame (פסח, *pissēaḥ*), nor one with a split nose(?) / stunted limb(?) (חרם, *ḥārum*), nor one with an overgrown limb (שרוע, *śārûaʿ*),

(v. 19)   nor one who has a broken leg or arm איש אשר־יהיה בו שבר רגל או שבר יד, *'îš 'ašer-yiheyê bô šeber rāgel 'ô šeber yād*),

(v. 20)   nor one hunchbacked (גבן, *gibbēn*), nor one small of stature(?) / having a cataract(?) (דק, *daq*), nor one with a growth(?)/discoloration(?) in the eye (תבלל בעינו, *teballul beʿênô*), nor a (boil) scar (גרב, *gārāb*), nor scab(?) (ילפת, *yallepet*), nor a crushed testicle (מרוח אשך, *měrôaḥ 'āšek*) (my trans.).

Leviticus 22:22-24:

עורת או שבור או־חרוץ או־יבלת או גרב או ילפת לא־תקריבו אלה ליהוה
ואשה לא־תתנו מהם על־המזבח ליהוה
ושור ושה שרוע וקלוט נדבה תעשה אתו ולנדר לא ירצה
ומעוך וכתות ונתוק וכרות לא תקריבו ליהוה

(v. 22)   *'awweret 'ô šābûr 'ô-ḥārûṣ 'ô-yabbelet 'ô gārāb 'ô yallepet lō'-taqrîbû 'ēllê l-*YHWH *weʾiššê lō'-titnû mēhem ʿal-hammizbēaḥ l-*YHWH.

(v. 23)   *wešôr wāśê śārûaʿ weqālûṭ nedābâ taăśeh 'otô ûlnēder lō' yērāṣê.*

(v. 24a)   *ûmāʿûk wekātût wenātûq wekārût lō' tiqrîbû l-*YHWH . . .

(v. 22)   Blind (עורת, *'awweret*), or broken limbed (שבור, *šābûr*), or maimed (חרוץ, *ḥārûṣ*), or having a wart (יבלת, *yabbelet*), or a scar (גרב, *gārāb*), or a tetter(?) (ילפת, *yallepet*), such you shall not present to the LORD; as a food-gift you shall not put any of them on the altar for the LORD.

(v. 23)   A herd- or flock-animal with an overgrown or short limb (שרוע, *śārûaʿ* or קלוט, *qālûṭ*), you may sacrifice as a freewill offering, though as a vow it will not be accepted.

(v. 24a)   But one with bruised (מעוך, *māʿûk*), crushed (כתות, *kātût*), torn (נתוק, *nātûq*), or cut-off (כרות, *kārût*) testicles you shall not present to the LORD (my trans.).

Note that there are two levels of disqualification: an animal with an overgrown or short limb (*śārûaʿ*; *qālûṭ*) can be offered on the altar for limited purposes; all other blemishes completely disqualify. The priest with *śārûaʿ* does not get a break. Table 2 collects and compares the disabilities of priests and sacrificeable animals from Lev 21–22.

TABLE 2: Priests' and Animal Bodies in Parallel

Body Map	Priests' *mûmîm*	Sacrificeable Animal *mûmîm*
Head	Blind (עוּר, *'iwwēr*) Cataract? (דק, *daq*) Growth in eye (תבלל בעינו, *teballul be'ênô*) Split nose? (*ḥārum*)	Blind (עורת, *'awweret*)
Limbs	Lame (פסח, *pissēaḥ*) Stunted limb? (*ḥārum*) Broken leg or arm (*šeber*) Limb too long or too short (שרוע, *śārûa'*)	Maimed (חרוץ, *ḥārûṣ*) Broken limbed (שבור, *šābûr*) Overgrown or foreshortened limb (שרוע, *śārûa'*; קלוט, *qālûṭ*)
Trunk	Hunchbacked (גבן, *gibbēn*) Small of stature/dwarf? (דק, *daq*)	
Skin or hide	(Boil) scar (גרב, *gārāb*) Scab? (ילפת, *yallepet*)	Scar (גרב, *gārāb*) Tetter? (ילפת, *yallepet*) Wart (יבלת, *yabbelet*)
Genitals	Crushed testicles (מרוח אשך, *mĕrôaḥ 'āšek*)	Bruised, crushed, torn, or cut-off [testicles] (מעוך, *mā'ûk*; כתות, *kātût*; נתוק, *nātûq*; כרות, *kārût*)

Both lists begin with blindness, then proceed to impaired limbs, followed by skin anomalies other than the impure *ṣāra'at* (צרעת) and finally damage to the genitals. The human list has two or three eye impairments; six to eight of limbs, locomotion, and stature (depending on the reading of *ḥārum* and *daq*); two skin anomalies; and one concerning testicles. The animal list includes one sort of blindness (possibly different from the two or three human eye impairments), four blemishes that affect limbs and locomotion, two anomalies of animal hides, and four genital injuries read as damage to the testicles in light of the priests' list.

Mishnah *Bekorot*, commenting on these passages, fans the twelve disabilities of priests into sixty-three more permutations (*m. Bek.* 7) and adds to it the expanded list of forty-seven animal blemishes from Mishnah tractate *Bekorot* 6 (*m. Bek.* 7:1), making a hundred and ten human *mûmîm*. Thus early Jewish interpreters worked out all possible permutations of bodily disqualifications of priests after the destruction of the Jerusalem temple. The lists in Leviticus and tractate *Bekoroth* are ultimately diagnostic for ritual purposes and not medical.

Leviticus 13. A third list of twelve conditions is scattered throughout Lev 13 and concerns all Israelites, including the priests:

1. שאת (śĕ'ēt, "swelling"; v. 2);
2. ספחת (sappaḥat, "rash"; v. 2);
3. בהרת (baheret, "discoloration"; vv. 2, 38);
4. נגע צרעת (nēga' ṣāra'at, "a scaly affection"; v. 2);
5. מספחת (mispaḥat, "rash"; v. 8; see v. 2 for same root);
6. שחין (šĕḥîn, "inflammation"; v. 18);
7. נתק (neteq, "scall"; v. 30);
8. בהק (bōhaq, "tetter(?)"; v. 39);
9. קרח (qērēaḥ, "crown baldness"; v. 40);
10. גבח (gibbēaḥ, "forehead baldness"; v. 41);
11. פרחת (pōraḥat, "eruption" or "wild growth"; vv. 42, 57);
12. ממארת (mam'eret, "malignant eruption"; v. 51 mentioned in cloth only).

We do not know the precise medical term to match with all these conditions. "Tetter" is supplied by translators who choose from an English thesaurus of skin conditions but are unable to identify its precise biological correlation. Likewise, two kinds of "rashes" make use of the same root. Most of the conditions in this third list represent potential precursor conditions to ṣāra'at, or "scale disease" (not leprosy), with the exception of the two types of baldness. Priests used this list to determine a person's exclusion from the community or readiness for reentrance ritual after healing (Lev 14), but this does not record any medical intervention.

Leviticus 15. A fourth list of four conditions in Lev 15 covers זובים (zôbîm, "discharges") that affect all Israelites, including priests:

1. זב (zāb, "male genital discharges including semen emission, but especially gonorrheal"; v. 2);
2. שכבת-זרע (šikbat-zāra', "semen emission"; v. 16);
3. זבה (zābâ, "female genital discharges including menstrual and lochial [postpartum in Lev 12], but especially dysmenorrheal or hypermenorrheal discharges"; vv. 19, 25ff; Stewart 2008, 71–72);
4. נדה (niddâ, "menstruant; menstrual flow"; v. 26).

Genital discharges and ṣāra'at are natural body processes or medical conditions that cause one to become ritually polluted and unable to approach the holy. Most healthy human beings between puberty and menopause are subject to at least one of these "pollutions" unless their genitals or reproductive organs are injured or removed. Those who are "polluted" by discharges are taken out of social intercourse temporarily, as in the case of nocturnal emissions in wartime (Deut 23:10-15); for ṣāra'at one may have to leave the community as Miriam does in Num 12.

Numbers 5:2. A fifth list gives a summary of polluting condition and legislates removal from the community:

Numbers 5:2:

צו את־בני ישראל וישלחו מן־המחנה כל־צרוע וכל־זב וכל טמא לנפש

(v. 2) *ṣaw ʾet-bnê yiśrāʾēl wîšallĕḥû min-hammaḥănê kol-ṣārûaʿ wĕkol-zāb wĕkol ṭāmēʾ lānāpeš*

(v. 2) Instruct the Israelites to remove from the camp anyone with any scaly affection (כל־צרוע, *kol-ṣārûaʿ*), or any discharge (כל־זב, *kol-zāb*), and anyone polluted (טמא, *ṭāmēʾ*) by a corpse (my trans.).

The Emergence of Disability Law

Leviticus 24:19-20: Compensation for injuries. A sixth short list of three items appears at the center of an elaborate chiastic structure in Lev 24:13-23. Milgrom (2004, 295–96) identifies verse 20a, the "talion" or "law of the claw," as the exact center:

Leviticus 24:19-20:

ואיש כי־יתן מום בעמיתו כאשר עשה כן יעשה לו
שבר תחת שבר עין תחת עין שן תחת שן
כאשר יתן מום באדם כן ינתן בו

(v. 19) *wĕʾîš kî-yittēn mûm baʿămîtô kåăšer ʿāśâ kēn yēʿāśê lô*
(v. 20a) *šeber taḥat šeber ʿayin taḥat ʿayin šēn taḥat šēn*
(v. 20b) *kåăšer yittēn mûm bāʾādām kēn yinnāten bô*

(v. 19) If anyone maims (יתן מום, *yittēn mûm*) his fellow, as he has done so shall it be done to him.
(v. 20a) Fracture for fracture (שבר, *šeber*); eye for eye (עין, *ʿayin*); tooth for tooth (שן, *šēn*).
(v. 20b) The injury he inflicted (יתן מום, *yittēn mûm*) on another shall be inflicted on him.

The purpose of chiastic structures, apart from pleasing the hearer/reader and serving as mnemonic devices, appears to be emphasis: what is central *is* central. The first item, *šeber*, resonates with *šeber rāgel ʾô šeber yād* ("broken leg/foot or broken arm/hand") in Lev 21:19, both by repetition of the critical term and by its central position. Leviticus 24:19-20 also picks up two other leading terms: *mûm* (21:18) and *ʿênô* (21:20; i.e., *ʿayin* with a possessive suffix). These three repeated terms, coupled with the centralizing position of *šeber*, suggest that Lev 24:20a is citing (or at least alluding to) Lev 21:18-20. Two limb conditions and two eye conditions, whether by birth, disease process, or injury, disqualify priests from service in Lev 21. A broken tooth does not—though Mishnah tractate *Bekorot* adds this to the list of disqualifiers in the Tannaitic period, along with the loss of one eye. But Lev 24:19-20 is not about disqualifying priests. Rather, it concerns all Israelites (and presumably resident aliens, too).

Leviticus 24:20a identifies three *mûmîm*-by-injury, whether accidental or intentional, that have a moral consequence. Injured persons must be compensated in a commensurable way: a broken limb with the value of a broken limb (not by breaking the perpetrator's limb); an eye with the value of an eye; a tooth with the value of a tooth.

Deuteronomy 19:21 in its version of the talion law includes injuries to hand (יד, *yād*) and foot (רגל, *regel*), following Exod 21:24-25—a seventh list. However, Deuteronomy's version is shorter, omitting "burn" (כויה, *kĕwîyâ*), "wound" (פצע, *peṣaʿ*), and "bruise" (חבורה, *ḥabbûrâ*). In light of these two talion laws, Lev 24:20a has a distinction—the broken limb. But this last is not an innovation, as it shows up in a more ancient legal code. The Code of Hammurabi compensates victims for broken bones and accidental or intentional eye loss at the hand of a free person (§§196–99; see Roth 1997, 121).

Leviticus 19:14: Protections for people with disabilities. Leviticus 19:14 is the key verse in all of biblical law concerning disability (and the eighth of the disability lists considered here). It is found in a significant chapter that functions as a mini-Torah (i.e., a compendium for more than seventy-five laws that evokes key legal texts from throughout the Torah, including various versions of the Ten Commandments; Stewart 2015). In this respect it shows itself as a negative instantiation of the golden rule at Lev 19:18 and 34: "Love your fellow Israelite as yourself; you shall love [the resident alien] as yourself." Thus,

Leviticus 19:14:

לא־תקלל חרש ולפני עור לא תתן מכשל ויראת מאלהיך אני יהוה

(v. 14)   *lōʾ-tĕqallēl ḥērēš wĕlipnē ʿiwwēr lōʾ tittēn mikšōl wĕyārēʾtā mēʾĕl-ōhêkā ănî* YHWH

(v. 14)   You shall not curse/insult (תקלל, *tĕqallēl*) a deaf person (חרש, *ḥērēš*) or place (תתן, *tittēn*) a stumbling block (מכשל, *mikšōl*) before one who is blind (עור, *ʿiwwēr*). You shall fear your God. I am the LORD (my trans.).

So we might say, "If you don't like to be cursed when you can hear, don't curse people who cannot hear; if you don't like to be stumbled when you have seeing eyes, don't stumble people who do not have sight."

Tĕqallēl. The *pi'el* use of the verbal root √*qll* in *tĕqallēl* is simultaneously declarative and factitive. That is, in this case it simultaneously *"declares* someone insignificant" and *makes it happen.* When a governor says, "I declare this highway open" while cutting the ribbon, he or she makes it so. Within the Holiness Code, father and mother are "marked as cursed" (Lev 20:9) using the same *pi'el* root; at Lev 24:15 when a man "blasphemes" his God, the same form of the root indicates simultaneous word and action.

Milgrom (2000, 1639) prefers to think of the verb in its more diffuse sense of "insult." He takes the verb to mean here "carrying out a cruel practical joke to belittle a deaf person." One could be tempted to read back the Egyptian Instruction of Amenemope from the Ramesside period: "Do not laugh at a blind man and do not tease a dwarf" (xxiv: 9). However, I think the sense of Lev 19:14 goes beyond practical joking or teasing.

The מקלל (*mĕqallēl,* "blasphemer") at Lev 24:14 is taken out to be stoned because he belittled the divine name (v. 11). The *mĕqallēl* implied at Lev 19:14, the "insulter" or "curser," may well have belittled the name of the deaf person in a way that causes it to stink in the community. The action that simultaneously happens with the declaration suggests an effect more long lasting, less transitory.

Word pair ḥērēš + 'iwwēr. Avishur (1984) identifies "word pairs" as a particular Semitic literary figure or pragmatic linguistic strategy. In this regard word pairs can function as an A-to-Z merismus or a quick way to sum up things that make a category. Three biblical word pairs in *qiṭṭēl*-form related to "disability" are of interest: "blind and lame" (*'iwwēr + pissēaḥ*), which occurs in Lev 21:18 and is inverted in Deut 15:21 (see Job 29:15; Isa 35:5a, 6a; 2 Sam 5:6, 8); "deaf and mute" (*ḥērēš + 'illēm*), which unfortunately resonates with abandoned pejorative language in English (see Isa 35:5b, 6b and its inverse in Exod 4:11); and "blind and deaf" (*'iwwēr + ḥērēš*), which occurs at Isa 35:5 and its inverse in Lev 19:14. Elsewhere I argue for two Israelite categories of disability that comprehend impairments that are *mûmîm* and impairments not-*mûmîm*, as illustrated in table 3 below (Stewart 2011, 69–71). If we take the pair "blind and lame" to cover *mûmîm* (as they are part of the same class) and "deaf and mute" to cover non-*mûmîm*, what do "blind and deaf" or "deaf and blind" conjure? "Blind" stands as the leading word for *mûmîm*, "deaf" as the leading word for non-*mûmîm*. The word pair pulls together both categories at once: *mûmîm* and non-*mûmîm* that are nonpolluting (Lev 13 and 15 point to impairments that pollute, a third category). That is, "deaf and blind" stands in for an abstract category we might label "disability," as there is no single term for it in biblical Hebrew.

"Deaf and blind," in precisely this order, appears uniquely at Lev 19:14. Similarly, of all places where the word pair "father and mother" are used, Lev 19:3 (in the same chapter) sets "mother" first for obvious emphasis. Thus, "deaf" before "blind" betrays more than artfulness. It appears significant in the light that "deaf" stands in for disabilities that do not disqualify priests. It stands out because both "blindness" and "respect for father" receive more stress than "deafness" and "respect for mother" in biblical law.

Mikšōl. "Placing a stumbling block (*mikšōl*) in the way of the blind" is cruelly ironic and evokes something concrete, as in the phrase סור מכשל (*ṣûr mikšōl*, "stumble stone"; Isa 8:14). Yet the Deuteronomic "Cursing Liturgy" seems to understand this law in a broader, less concrete way as "misdirection": "Cursed be (ארור, *'ārûr*) he who misdirects a blind person ('*iwwēr*) on his way" (Deut 27:18a). Note that this curse stands as one of twelve against idolatry, dishonoring parents, murder, and incest, and thus underlines the seriousness of the behavior. Perhaps it is not a surprise, then, that Ezekiel takes *mikšōl* metaphorically for "stumbling block of sin" (Ezek 3:20). If we take the three texts together, the sense of *mikšōl* can range from physical and verbal blockages to moral. But to whatever degree the laws of Lev 19:14 may be generalized, they begin with specific behaviors.

Wěyārē'tā mē'ĕlōhêkā. The command to fear/revere God at Lev 19:14bα acts like a fence to prevent or warn one from trespassing against the Divine Name (in v. 14bβ). Indeed, the very same verb, √ירא (*yr'*), used at Lev 19:3a to revere/fear mother and father, precedes the clause *ănî* YHWH *ĕlōhêkem*. Leviticus 20:9 forbids one from cursing (יקלל, *yĕqallēl*) one's father and mother. Leviticus 18–20 are part of a larger literary structure and should be read together (Stewart 2015). Reading Lev 19:3 and 20:9b (one reveres mother and father; one does not curse father and mother) together with Lev 19:14 (one does not curse the deaf; one reveres God), cursing the deaf and cursing one's parents partake of the same cloth.

Ănî YHWH. The "motive" clause at Lev 19:14bβ, אני יהוה (*ănî* YHWH), recollects the first commandment in Exod 20:2 and Deut 5:6 and resonates with the fifteen other uses of the phrase in Lev 19. In a sense it folds the Lev 19:14 command into Lev 19's first commandment frame. It suggests that the motivation to keep this law should be found in the being and nature of God—a motivation of love. But the structure of Lev 19 suggests a second motivation in the command to fear/respect God. The first clause in verse 14bα parallels Lev 19:32b, ויראת מאלהיך אני יהוה (wĕyārēʾtā mēʾĕlōhêkā ʾănî YHWH, "you shall revere your God. I am the LORD"). Leviticus 19:32 calls for deference to the aged. Likewise, the partial parallel with verse 19:3 concerning תראו . . . אני יהוה אלהכם (tîrāʾû . . . ʾănî YHWH ĕlōhêkem, "You shall revere . . . I the LORD am your God") uses the same verb and reshuffles the divine names for its command to revere parents. The artful parallels allow us to think about parents, the aged, and persons who are deaf and blind at the same time. One can assume that in ancient Israel parents were not revered, the aged not deferred to, those deaf were insulted or cursed, and blind people were stumbled. Laws are not usually made to forbid things that have not been done. Thus, Lev 19:14b and its parallels in the same chapter provide a double motivation to keep the law: love and fear.

Leviticus 19:13-14 as a unit. Gewalt (1985), Milgrom (2004, 229–30), and others make the argument that Lev 19:14 represents the larger purpose of protecting the poor and helpless. Contextually, verse 14 is part of a unit with verse 13, set off by the clause *ʾănî* YHWH at the end of verses 12 and 14, that includes a command concerning the poor: "You shall not extort your Israelite neighbor and you shall not plunder; you shall not let the earned wages of a wage-laborer stay overnight with you until morning" (Lev 19:13). This juxtaposition forms the case for thinking of persons deaf or blind together with wage-laborers and robbery victims now impoverished.

Gewalt's (1985) reasoning runs this way: there is a wisdom tradition in the ancient Near East that urges protection of the poor. Persons who are blind or deaf are fungible with the class of the "poor and weak." The curse is a great travesty because the person who is deaf could not "hear" the curse and so could not make a defense. Therefore such a person should be protected. Indeed, there *is* something ironic in the choice of the bully's weapon. But a person who is deaf is not necessarily blind: he or she can see the gestures of others, their faces, their postures, their movements, and their actions. The factitive sense of the *piʿel* verb form in this case assures us that the deaf person would have something to see. So the question might be asked: Is this a command to protect a class of people with disabilities as a subclass of all that are weak?

Gewalt (1985) notes further *the uniqueness of the command* "You shall not curse a deaf person" in the literature of the ancient world. For him it is an accident of transmission history that the command survived, as the

wisdom tradition of protecting the blind is much stronger. Despite its survival, Gewalt gives the command little significance, as "deaf" and "blind"
are shills, in his view, for the "poor." This is where an earlier, paternalistic
approach to disability shipwrecks: Gewalt steps on his own observation.
"You shall not curse a deaf person" is a command unique to the Bible as far
as we know. It functions as a command in its own right.

Laws protecting people with disabilities are conspicuously absent in
the ancient Near East. The Code of Hammurabi allows compensation for
accidental eye loss or broken bones at the hand of a free man (§§196–99):
"In Israel the law has moved beyond compensation for injury (Exod 21:23-
25; Lev 24:19-20; Deut 19:21) . . . to nonmonetary, ethical protections for
a class" (Stewart, quoted in Milgrom 2000, 1641). The Holiness Code has
done this by equating the two classes of disability signified by "deaf and
blind" with two respected classes, parents and the aged, and linking them
with (but not subsuming them under) the YHWH-protected poor. Laws
affirming the dignity of people with disabilities begin here.

THE STIGMATIZED BODY

Deuteronomy 23:2: Gender Anomalies

A text from the Deuteronomic source, Deut 23:2 (v. 1 Eng.) takes us
beyond the disabling of a priest or the disqualification of a sacrifice because
of partially damaged genitals to something new: complete exclusion from
the Israelite congregation:

Deuteronomy 23:2:

לא־יבא פצוע־דכא וכרות שפכה בקהל יהוה

(v. 2)   *lōʾ yābōʾ pĕṣûaʿ-dakāʾ ûkarût šāpĕkâ biqhal* YHWH

(v. 2)   A person with crushed testicles (פצוע־דכא, *pĕṣûaʿ-dakā*), or a cut-off
penis (כרות שפכה, *karût šāpĕkâ*) shall not enter into the congregation
of YHWH (v. 1 Eng.; my trans.).

Thus, a castrated person—either one who has completely lost the func-
tionality of his testicles or his penis—is excluded from the community
altogether. This may be because the evidence of circumcision has been
lost or because the biological evidence for "male" gender has been erased.
Whether by accident or by intention, this eunuch was made by human
action (crushing or cutting), either a סריס אדם (*sārîs ʾādām*, "eunuch emasculated by men"; *m. Yebam.* 8:4) or perhaps a סריס ממש (*sārîs mammāš*,
"a real, tangible castrate"), as Rav asserts about Hananiah, Mishael, and

Azariah (*b. Sanh.* 93b; cf. Dan 1:1-7 with Isa 39:7) where there is visible evidence but the castrator is not specified. *Not in view here* is the congenitally castrated person, סריס חמה (*sārîs ḥammâ*, "a eunuch from the time of seeing the sun—i.e., a natural eunuch born with a penis but without visible testicles or without other signs of sexual maturity by age 20"; *m. Yebam.* 8:4; *b. Yebam.* 80a).

These three kinds of *castrates* could be conceived as different genders, a notion not alien to the early rabbis who had to interpret laws that specifically applied only to males or females—as do those about vowing a person (Lev 27:1-8). The rabbis were well aware of the 1.7 percent of humanity that is intersexed (though their categories do not precisely comport with modern medical intersex terminology) because of the observations made when males were circumcised shortly after birth. They reserved three more terms for such: אנדרוגנוס (*'anděrôgînôs*, "androgyne") with both male and female characteristics (*m. Bik.* 1:5); טומטום (*tûmṭûm*, "person of indeterminate gender; a person whose genitals are hidden or undeveloped"; *m. 'Arak.* 1:1); and אילונית (*'aylônît*, "a woman like a ram; barren, wombless woman incapable of conception"; *m. Yebam.* 8:5; *b. Ketub.* 11a). All such Israelites, whose visible biological sex is neither male nor female, could not be the subjects of vows (as was, in contrast, Samuel by his mother, Hannah).

Numbers 5:11-31: Disability by Curse but Ability from Blessing

A P text portrays a condition induced by a ritual self-curse, and directed by a priest, that would lead to female infertility. The ritual occurs at the demand of a husband suspicious that his wife has committed adultery—the ritual of the suspected *sôṭâ*.

Numbers 5:22a:

ובאו המים המאררים האלה במעיך לצבות בטן ולנפל ירך

(v. 22)   *ûbā'û hammayim ham'arrîm hā'ēllê běmē'ayik laṣěbbôt beṭen wělaněppil yārēk*

(v. 22)   May this cursed water come into your innards causing your womb to prolapse and genitals to sag out (my trans.).

The ritual result proving infidelity causes the womb to prolapse (lit. "distend") (לצבות בטן, *laṣěbbôt beṭen*) and the genitals (lit. "thigh") to sag out (לנפל ירך, *laněppil yārēk*). *Yārēk* can function as a euphemism for genitals on the principle that linguistic substitutions are made for unmentionable body parts from nearby anatomy. The implications of this passage range from miscarriage (possibly by induced abortion) to prolapse of any of the reproductive organs (Frymer-Kensky 1987; cf. Magdalene 1992). The uterus or other pelvic organs can bulge into the vaginal wall and potentially protrude into the vaginal area, causing the vagina itself to extend outside the body. In the most extreme case, the entire uterus can extend outside the body (Stenchever and Fenner 2001, 576–79). Knowledge of uterine prolapse is found in a sixteenth-century BCE Egyptian medical text, the Ebers Papyrus (no. 789; Morice, Josset, and Colau 1994, 135) but is not treated here as a medical condition.

The negative result of the self-cursing ritual is not only the effect on the body but also the effect on the woman's reputation—she herself becomes a curse among her people (Num 5:21, 27). Such a woman could be spoken of as having a רחם משכיל (reḥem maškîl, "miscarrying womb"; Hos 9:14) or as a שכלה (šikkĕlâ, "mother who has lost children including through miscarriage"; Lev 26:22; Isa 49:20) or an אילונית (ʾaylônît, "wombless woman")—but none of these terms are used here. If the ritual fails to undo her, she is counted as pure (Num 5:11-31, esp. 21-22, 27-29) and retains her reproductive capacity; she has not made herself impure (נטמאה, niṭmĕʾâ; Num 5:28).

The complete inverse of this is the promise at Deut 7:14: "You shall be blessed above all other peoples: there shall be no sterile male (עקר, ʾāqār), nor female (עקרה, ʾaqārâ), among you or your livestock." Levine (1989, 342) argues that ʾaqārâ means "one deprived of a root": "It describes a woman whose womb is closed so that male seed could not enter." A similar blessing in Deut 30:9 promises "fruit of the womb" (פרי בטן, prî beṭen). Likewise, Lev 26:9 promises this blessing if one follows the laws: "I will make you fertile, (והפריתי, wehiprêtî)." Why are there multiple promises of fertility? Tigay asserts that "human sterility was regarded as one of the greatest personal tragedies" in the biblical world (1996, 89), as the stories of Abraham and Sarah, Rachel and Jacob, and Hannah and Elkanah attest. One should note that Deut 7:14 calls out male infertility, unlike Exod 23:26. Deuteronomy does not label these disabilities as mûmîm (as it does blindness and lameness). The genitals are not visibly damaged, cut-off, or distended. Infertility is hidden until it "appears" by the absence of conception.

The addition of the above two cases, the person with cut-off genitals and the woman with ritually induced prolapse of her reproductive organs, calls for a modification of table 2. Table 3 below shows the division of representative disabilities into four categories: mûmîm, non-mûmîm (both nonpolluting), ṭûmʾâ (polluting conditions), and conditions that permanently exclude from the community.

TABLE 3: Body Map by Representative Disabilities

Body Map	*Mûmîm*	Non-*mûm* Non-*ṭūm'â*	*Ṭūm'â*	Permanent exclusion from community
Eyes and Nose	Blindness (*'iwwēr*); split nose? (*ḥārum*)			
Ears and mouth	Broken tooth	Deaf (*ḥērēš*); heavy tongue		
Limbs and trunk	Lameness (*pissēaḥ*); hunchback (*gibbēn*)			
Genitals	Damaged testes	Infertility (*'āqār(â)*)	Discharge (*zôb*); prolapse	Castrate (*sārîs*); uncircumcised
Skin and hair	Scar (*gārāb*); *yallepet*; *yabbelet*	Baldness; skin anomalies that are not yet *ṣāra'at*	*Scale disease (ṣāra'at)*; Nazirite's hair after vow broken (Num 6:11)	

Numbers 12:10-15: Miriam's Punishment

Numbers 12:10:

והענן סר מעל האהל והנה מרים מצרעת כשלג ויפן אהרן
אל־מרים והנה מצרעת

(v. 10a)   *wĕheʿānān sār mēʿal hāʾohel wĕhinnê miryām mĕṣōrāʿat kaššāleg*

(v. 10b)   *wayyipen ʾahărōn ʾel-miryām wĕhinnê mĕṣōrāʿat*

(v. 10)   When the cloud retreated from above the Tent [of Meeting], there was Miriam scaly as snow (מצרעת כשלג, *mĕṣōrāʿat ḳaššāleg*). When Aaron turned toward Miriam she had scale disease (מצרעת, *mĕṣōrāʿat*) (my trans.).

Traditional rabbinic interpretation assigns to Miriam the crime of defaming or slandering Moses (Milgrom 1990, 97). This version of נגע צרעת (*nēgaʿ-ṣāraʿat*, "scale disease") is similar to the symptoms of whitened skin in Lev 13:3 or verses 9-11 (Stewart 2008, 66–68). The first passage points to deep white skin patches; the second diagnoses white skin swellings: "So she was shut out of camp seven days" (Num 12:15a). The effects are dramatic but only temporary, and not resolved ritually as in Lev 14.

Thus, it is important to remember that Num 12 is not usually assigned to the Priestly literature but classically assigned to the Elohist (E), and Noth assigns it to the Jahwist (J) (1980, 273). Just as the resolution of Miriam's condition is not Priestly (P), neither is the "theology." Where P does not associate ṣāra'at with sin, Num 12 does (Baden and Moss 2011, 660). When Deut 24:8-9 makes it explicit that nēga'-ṣāra'at was Miriam's condition, exhorting the reader to "remember" and "to do exactly as the levitical priests instruct you" (v. 8), it appears to interpret JE—perhaps through the lens of Leviticus.

Threatened, promised, and actual blows against Israelites include נגף (negep, "affliction") on those who impinge on the holy precincts or rebel (Num 8:19, 17:11-15); מכה (makkâ, "plague") for rejecting manna (Num 11:33) and repeated disobedience (Deut 28:59, 29:21); רשף (rešep) and קטב (ḳeṭeb, "plague and smallpox"; Deut 32:24) for neglecting God; also, שחין (šĕḥîn, "inflammation"); עפלים (ŏpōlîm, "hemorrhoids"); גרב (gārāb, "boilscar"), which is a mûm; חרס (ḥerēs, "rash; scabies"), a mûm; עורון ('iw-wārôn, "blindness"); and lameness by inflammation of knees and thighs (Deut 28:27-28). Moses sings in his blessing for Levi that God will smite the hands of Levi's enemies (Deut 33:11b). All of these texts fall outside the Priestly source; they reflect a different theology where disease and disability reflect punishment for sin.

While the various "plagues" sometimes represent God's personified wrath in the form of disease or injury, these plagues also include mûmîm and polluting conditions like ṣāra'at as punishments. These punishments set the stage for use of the term mûm to cover moral blemishes (Deut 32:5) and for the confusion of ritual pollution with moral pollution in the history of the reception of these texts. Ironically, metaphors of obedience, relying on abilities such as speaking and walking (Deut 30:14-15), also can affect readers' views of the "disabled other." Yet Moses, the hero of Leviticus, Numbers, and Deuteronomy, who cannot speak well, loses his ability to move around with age (Deut 31:2).

THE "ENABLED" BODY

As Peckruhn notes, the biblical treatment of disability is not confined to individuals with apparent disabilities but extends to "the social, political, and cultural . . . attitudes that take a 'normal' body as the ideal" (2014, 102). What is that "normal" and "whole" body, or, biblically speaking, the body that is תמים (tāmîm), an abstract plural term meaning "whole/able/acceptable" (see Olyan 2008, 18)?

Leviticus 8: The Bodies of Aaron and the Priests

If Moses' disability is not much different from ability, what of Aaron, his brother, as the high priest—the epitome of the "abled" priest? "What is the idealized or 'whole' priestly body?" Reading in a mirror Lev 21:16-21 on disqualifying blemishes, chapter 13 on scale disease, and chapter 15 on discharges, the inverted image yields a priest that sees clearly—neither blind nor partially blind; one who can ambulate without the problems caused by short or broken legs, hunchback, or lame feet; one who has "usable" arms, neither short nor broken, nor disproportionate to the trunk as in the case of a dwarf; one whose skin barrier is intact, not having certain suppurating sores, nor boil scars, nor scale disease and skin, hair, or beard discolorations (exhaustively defined in Lev 13); and one whose genitals are intact and not leaking reproductive fluids (Lev 15:2-18). So the eyes, nose, legs, arms, skin, hair, and genitals are without troubles, whole and functional.

Cut, imperfect, and washed. However, such a body described above is not actually "whole" or "acceptable"—that is, *tāmîm*. The foreskin must actually be cut off the male genitals. Circumcision, it is said, makes the male body more like God's (Avot de Rabbi Natan, A2:58; *Gen. Rab.* 54–55). Moreover, the priest *may be* deaf, have a heavy mouth or tongue, be bald, have nondisqualifying marks on his skin, be infertile, and the like. That is, a *wabi-sabi* aesthetic allows for small asymmetries, asperities, and suggestions of natural aging such as age spots on the skin. The priest's body was also washed to clear the effects of any prior impure discharges (Lev 8:6). The very washing reminds one of the impermanence of ritual purity. The need to wash will return; ritual purity is an ongoing process.

Not beautiful nor naked. Nor is the priest's body idealized like Solomon's: clear skinned and ruddy, with curled black locks, hands like rods, belly like a tablet, legs like marble pillars; in all, a body "stately as cedars" (Song 6:10-16). Nor is the priest's body to be appreciated naked. "Uncovering nakedness" is a metaphor for incest and sex with the *niddâ* (Lev 18:6-16, 20:18; Stewart 2006, 98). Rather, "The priest who is exalted above his fellows, on whose head the anointing oil has been poured and who has been ordained to wear the vestments, shall not bare his head nor rend his vestments" (Lev 21:10). The properly anointed and ordained priest is not naked, nor can he make himself naked while officiating, even when hearing of or seeing the death of his kin (Lev 21:1-4; Num 5:1-3). For Aaron and his sons Eleazar and Ithamar were told by Moses after the death of Nadab and Abihu in the sanctuary—that is, Aaron's sons and Eleazar and Ithamar's brothers—"Do not bare your heads and do not rend your clothes

lest you die and anger strike the whole community'' (Lev 10:6). Howard Eilberg-Schwartz suggests that later rabbinic Judaism had "a general
inclination to keep the naked and the sacred apart" such that one is not to
be naked during prayer (1994, 209).

Covered and anointed. Though some nondisqualifying anomalies of skin
and hair are allowed—including baldness—the vestments now make
this a moot point. The skin and head hair are all covered by the tunic,
sash, robe, ephod, breastplate, and headdress (Lev 8:7-9, 13). Exodus 39,
in the account of the making of vestments, adds special shoulder pieces
and breeches (vv. 20, 28) and a diadem with the engraved words "Holy to
the LORD" (v. 30). Moreover, certain exposed parts of the body must also
be covered by oil and blood. First, Aaron's head was anointed with oil
(Lev 8:12) that famously dripped down to his beard in one of the Songs of
Ascent (Ps 133:2). With the blood from the אשם (ʾašām, "offering of ordination"), Moses placed blood on the ridges (or antihelices) of Aaron's and
his sons' right ears, the thumbs of their right hands, and their right big toes
(Lev 8:23-24). (They must have all these body parts intact.) In their naked
palms were placed open-faced sandwiches (made with unleavened bread,
oil bread, thin wafers, suet, and the right mutton thigh from the sacrifice)
for an elevation offering (vv. 26-27). The priests' bodies were thus mostly
covered by vestments, smeared and dappled with oil and blood, and, at one
point, holding sacrificed food.

Purity is neither holiness nor completeness. Thus, in the search for the nature
of bodies *tāmîm*, the priestly body is acceptable (though still imperfect)
when it can functionally perform in the sanctuary, when it has been made
ritually pure after cyclic impurity, when it has been properly ritually initiated, including circumcised, and when it has been vested to minister.
A priest's body that has not been aspersed with blood and oil at ordination can be "pure" but not "holy"—incomplete but retaining an inchoate
potential to act. The priestly body must be made "able" by ritual action.

Ritual liminality and the insufficiency of vestments. Anointing with oil and
blood is a liminal ritual. The healed *mĕtsōrāʿ* (or person with "scale disease"
or certain hair anomalies—formerly translated "leper") is like the inchoate
priest. They both stand at the portal between two ways of being. The rite
of ordination for the priest and the rite of cleansing and reentrance into
the community for the *mĕtsōrāʿ* do have several differences; the *mĕtsōrāʿ* is
completely shaved for one, like the Nazirite at the end of his or her vow
(Lev 14:8; Num 6:16). But the striking and oft-remarked similarity to the
priest's ordination comes with the placing of blood from the *ʾašām*-sacrifice

(the so-called guilt offering) on the right ear ridge (i.e., antihelix, or, alter-natively, the earlobe), right thumb, and right big toe of the *mĕtsōrā'* and the ordinand (Lev 14:14; 8:23-24). For the *mĕtsōrā'* this is followed by an appli-cation of oil to the same protuberances (14:17) with the balance of the oil poured on the head (14:18), just as some of the oil is also poured on Aaron's head at ordination (8:12). But differing from the *mĕtsōrā'*, the vestments of Aaron and his sons are aspersed at ordination. That is, in some sense, the priestly clothes, too, are insufficient to cover the priest. Moses sprinkles them with oil and blood from the altar (Lev 8:30): "Thus he consecrated Aaron *and his vestments*, and also his sons *and their vestments*" (v. 31).

Bodily "wholeness" cannot be characteristic of the priest's holiness because holiness is a composite of bodily conditions and ritual treatment. As shown by the ritually and temporarily abled priest above, "ability" to serve is unstable. This is so not only because accidental injury or aging unravel "wholeness" but also because ritual errors in bodily preparation destabilize the priest's "ability." Further, natural vicissitudes that betray "purity"—scale disease, skin anomalies, molds in the warp and woof of garments, bodily discharges, and deaths of near kin—undermine the priest's "wholeness" throughout life. No priest, including the high priest, can remain "whole" or "abled" for long.

Indeed, because even the high priest's bodily (avail)ability is ultimately unstable and temporary, his ability cannot be physical and not just ritual, but it in the end must be "discursive." That is, having done all that is ritu-ally required, he must still have *words* sewn onto his turban: "Holy to the LORD." To say that the priest is "able" does not refer to something "natu-ral" but to a construction. In ancient Israel the abled high priest's body is ritually and culturally—through words—put together.

The bodies of Israelites

An ordinary male Israelite must have circumcised genitals that are other-wise fully and obviously intact (Deut 23:2; v. 1 Eng.). Likewise, the woman must have her organs of reproduction intact (Num 5:12-31) and be fertile (as in Gen). However, women were not circumcised in ancient Israel. Both men and women in their ideal state must be free of genital discharges—the men from seminal or gonorrheal flows, the women from menstrual, dysmenorrheal, or lochial flows (the last after childbirth). Both men and women must be free of the stated list of skin and hair anomalies of Lev 13—but baldness is not among them. The Deuteronomistic literature (Dtr), especially 1 and 2 Samuel, paints a more elaborate picture of the ideal Israelite body in the person of the king (Schipper 2006), as does the Song of Songs. But here in Leviticus, Numbers, and Deuteronomy, the Israelite abled and ideal body has many fewer prescriptions than that of the priest or high priest. However, the purity rules in Lev 11–15 also mean that an Israelite's ritual ability is temporary. And on a practical level, other disabilities are acknowledged—both blindness and deafness (Lev 19:14) and injuries to limbs and teeth (Lev 24:19-20). Thus the abled Israelite has intact eyes, ears, limbs, and teeth, but these have no effect on his or her ritual status.

Numbers 6:2-21: The bodies of Nazirites. The vow of a Nazirite confers on him or *her*—because both Israelite men *and* women can take this vow (Num 6:2)—a special status that could be analogized to a lay religious order. A vow can be made for oneself, or one can vow another person (as by the mother for Samuel and Samson; see also Lev 27:1-8). The conditions of the vow include following a restricted food regimen (no grape products or any intoxicant; Num 6:3-4) beyond that required of all Israelites (no blood, no meat from "impure" animals or improperly slaughtered carcasses; Lev 11 and 17:13-16); no cutting hair (Num 6:5); and no coming near to a person who is dead or going inside where a corpse is located (Num 6:6-7). The reason given for the last is that the "hair set apart for his God is upon his head" (Num 6:7b). If someone dies near the Nazirite, he or she must bring to the priest the requisite supplies for both a purgation offering and a burnt offering and shave hair—because his or her "consecrated hair was defiled" (Num 6:11).

At the end of the vow, he or she must bring a complete well-being sacrifice to the priest: "The Nazirite shall then shave his consecrated hair, at the entrance of the Tent of Meeting, and take the locks of his consecrated hair and put them on the fire that is under the sacrifice of well-being" (Num 6:18). Thus there are controls on what the Nazirite's body can ingest, where the body can be with respect to corpses, and when hair can be cut. The Nazirite becomes "enabled" by following the bodily restrictions but desanctified and so "disabled" if willfully, or even accidentally, breaking them. At the end of the vow's term, one must undergo a liminal ritual to end the vow—to disenable oneself and so return to common Israelite status. In the ritual a body part is cut and burned on the altar, placed there by the Nazirite who imitates a priestly action.

There are many fewer bodily restrictions to becoming a Nazirite—only those that socially exclude one from the Israelite community: uncircumcision and complete castration in males, probably *ṣāraʿat* in skin or hair for males and females, and possibly prolapse of reproductive organs in females. That is, neither any of the twelve conditions that disqualify a priest, such as blindness, nor any genital discharges that make either man or woman temporarily impure, nor having a body that is otherwise functionally impaired can prevent one from taking the vow. Logically, though, complete baldness would "disable" or prevent one from vowing in this case—a social and religious disability because hair loss prevents the required rituals. Although Mishnah tractate *Bekorot* 7:2 does assert that baldness disqualifies a priest for temple service, the *Gemara* (the commentary in *b. Bek.*) cites Raba, who says, "This meant only where he has not a line of hair from ear to ear in the hinder part, but he has it in the front" (*b. Bek.* 43b). That is, although rear baldness disqualifies, Raba understands crown and forehead baldness as exempted. This may also be the case for Nazirites.

Thus it appears that "abled" bodies are scaled according to "social" class—high priest, serving priests, nonserving priests and their wives and children, then Nazirites and Israelites. Those excluded from the community are, by definition, not abled. The more elite the class, the more socially disabling conditions exist. And though we have no capital *D* Deaf cultural communities in view, deafness and speech impairments are counted as ritually able in this system of idealized bodies.

CONCLUSIONS

Leviticus, Numbers, and Deuteronomy cover a large amount of material related to (dis)ability, the full richness of which can only be sketched here. The discussion above has focused on fifteen key texts: eight with a lens on disability (Lev 13; 15; 19:14; 21:18-20; 22:22-24; 24:20; Num 5:2; Deut 19:21), three that evidence stigma (Deut 23:2 [v. 1 Eng.]; Num 5:11-31; 12:10-15), and four that illustrate the body enabled (Exod 4:10-11 and Lev 1:1-2; Lev 8; Num 6). Of these fifteen, I would argue that Lev 1:1-2, 19:14, and Num 6:2-20 are the most significant of all.

One movement in biblical law appears to destabilize "ableism." Starting with the passage at Exod 4:10-11 that equates perception and nonperception, all ability is shown as relative in comparison to God. The irony of God "speaking" without a visible body and Moses physically repeating God's words with a heavy tongue and heavy mouth undermines "ableism" yet further. Indeed, Moses and his siblings are shown as "disabled." Aaron's body must be washed, vested, anointed, and ritually prepared to enter the sanctuary. Like a cyborg, he is not able to act without these appliances and processes. Miriam, after her slander of Moses, suffers *ṣāraʿat* for seven days. Leviticus, Numbers, and Deuteronomy feature "disabled" characters. They are not fully able; they are not *ṭāmîm*.

Moses, Aaron, and Miriam carry the narrative of the three books. As their stories exhibit disability, stigma, and enablement, and the narrative itself depends on them, they function as a "prosthesis." The very way the biblical story is told becomes iconic of disability. Moses' heavy tongue, and his accommodation through Aaron, is a thematic structure holding the entire narrative arc of Exodus through Deuteronomy. With respect to that story, Moses' disabled and enabled body is held in tension with the ideal, able, and hidden "body" of God.

A taxonomy of disabilities is among the greatest achievements of biblical law. Arising out of observations of nature and natural body processes, circumcision practice, legal practice, and ritual needs, concrete listmaking provided the working materials for developing the abstract concept "disability." On the other hand, an anomalous category—the one that stands out from all other disabilities—is the complete castration of a eunuch. Alone of all, Deuteronomy calls for permanent exclusion from the community of this person. Not until Isaiah will a countermove emerge.

One of the surprises about biblical disabilities is that they are correlated with social class. The severest consequence for any disability is to be placed outside the community; this is reserved for uncircumcised males (whose genitals have not been cut) and those that lost the mark of circumcision by too much cutting. It is not clear whether the woman who loses her reproductive organs by prolapse remains in the community, but she is under a curse. Beyond the outsider, elite priests and the high priest suffer the most social restrictions because of bodily impairment. Another surprise—deaf priests are not specifically restricted from their sacerdotal duties in biblical literature (though they are in later Mishnaic literature). Indeed, in the "sanctuary of silence" it may be an advantage. A second sacerdotal class, the Nazirites, is not impeded in keeping its special vow by any bodily impairments except the complete lack of head hair. For the average Israelite, the former and latter prophets show everyday stigma for blindness, lameness, and infertility. But in biblical law this only appears in divine threats of judgment.

To the achievements of taxonomic description and first-level abstraction for disability, we can add the ethical laws. Leviticus 19:14 protects persons deaf and blind specifically, deaf and blind generically, all the species of disability in these two phyla, and as the supercategory "deaf and blind," all Israelites with "permanent disabilities." This law protects not just their persons but also their dignity as a negative instantiation of the golden rule.

Biblical law also takes up the principle of commensurable compensation for injury in its several talion laws still embodied in life and liability insurance policies today.

Despite all that is above, God as creator of (dis)ability comports with the idea of God as punisher by disability. And we find that God can punish by blindness and lameness and scale disease, among other conditions. In particular, stigma is attached to Miriam's skin disease and the woman-suspected-of-adultery's prolapse of reproductive organs, both divine punishments.

It is also possible for a Nazirite to break his or her vow, and it is possible for a priest to unravel his sanctity by devesting when mourning or otherwise. The *sôṭâ* can curse herself such that she suffers a prolapse. A man can make himself a *sārîs*. If there are rituals to enable Nazirite, priest, and Israelite, these are antirituals that disenable oneself. It is a short step from these to create new homologies: disability (especially self-created disability) is like sin, just as ability is like righteousness. This last idea does appear in the end matter of Deuteronomy. Righteousness is equated there with the ability to speak and walk.

Thus, there is something to be wary of here, as Stiker suspected. It is not that the text is generally handicappist (though the stigma cases feel that way). It is not just that readers can make the text handicappist if they wish. It is not just that the end of Deuteronomy seems to take a turn toward ableism. It is that the homologies can be turned around into equations: if sins can be punished by disability, all disability is evidence of unrighteousness. But it is not.

One explanation for the various tensions between biblical texts observed above can be found in the Priestly and non-Priestly theologies expressed in their "sources." P (found primarily in Lev 1:1 through Num 10:10 in Lev, Num, and Deut) details *mûmîm* and things that ritually pollute; enables the disabled Moses to speak; ritually enables the priests, persons healed of scale disease, and Nazirites; ritually disenables the woman accused of adultery; ritually marks the end of the Nazirite vow with a hair sacrifice; protects and dignifies the two categories of disability subsumed under deaf and blind; and compensates three representative injuries. In P we find the first law for the deaf.

In the non-P material (JE, D, Dtr) found in Exodus and the rest of Numbers and Deuteronomy, God announces disability as part of the creation and punishes with disability. The non-P material expels Miriam for her skin disease and expels the complete eunuch. It offers a few further specifications: severe *mûmîm* distinguished from minor, placing a stumbling block before the blind abstracted as "misdirection," and so forth. Avoidance of disability comes by divine blessing.

If the non-P texts show a sovereign that creates, judges, punishes, and blesses, the P texts begin with the implicit understanding that disability is the normal bodily state of affairs. It is true that one can imagine an "able" body by mirror reading all the impairing conditions. But P makes clear that any such able-state is unstable and impermanent. Rather, P takes steps to enable, protect, and dignify.

Bodies must be ritually enabled to do divine service by circumcision, ordination, vesting, or the Nazirite protocol. All bodies must be ritually reenabled after particular genital discharges, after healing from scale disease, and after breaking the Nazirite vow. There is no starting or resting state where sacral ability is normal.

If sacral ability is supported by various prosthetic measures, the Nazirite vow is an open door to religious and social enablement. Any Israelite of any gender can potentially take the vow and keep its rule no matter what his or her bodily state (with the exception of complete baldness). The significance of their vow appears with the offering of their hair on the altar when they exit their liminal status. Acting as a lay priest, they burn their hair in the same place an acceptable animal offering would be burned, thus completing the homology between sacrificeable animal and priest. They are priest and sacrifice in the symbol of their hair. They can offer their hair on the altar whether they have *mûmîm* or not. This is a surprise workaround to the whole problem of disqualification by physical blemish, gender, or gender anomalies.

WORKS CITED

Avishur, Yitzhak. 1984. *Stylistic Studies of Word-Pairs in Biblical and Ancient Semitic Languages*. Alter Orient und Altes Testament. Neukirchen-Vluyn: Neukirchener Verlag.

Baden, Joel S., and Candida R. Moss. 2011. "The Origin and Interpretation of *ṣāraʿat* in Leviticus 13–14." *Journal of Biblical Literature* 130: 643–62.

Berlin, Brent. 1972. "Speculations on the Growth of Ethno-botanical Nomenclature." *Language in Society* 1: 51–86.

Berlin, Brent, Dennis E. Breedlove, and Peter H. Raven. 1973. "General Principles of Classification and Nomenclature in Folk Biology." *American Anthropologist* 75: 214–42.

Blau, Joshua. 1993. *A Grammar of Biblical Hebrew*. 2nd amended ed. Porta Linguarum Orientalium NS 12. Wiesbaden: Otto Harrassowitz.

Dassow, Eva von, ed. 1998. *Egyptian Book of the Dead: The Book of Going Forth by Day Being the Papyrus of Ani*. Translated by Raymond O. Faulkner. 2nd rev. ed. San Francisco: Chronicle.

Davis, Lennard J. 2010. "The End of Identity Politics: On Disability as an Unstable Category." Pages 301–15 in *The Disability Studies Reader*. Edited by Lennard J. Davis. 3rd ed. New York: Routledge.

Eilberg-Schwartz, Howard. 1994. *God's Phallus and Other Problems for Men and Monotheism*. Boston: Beacon.

Frymer-Kensky, Tikva. 1987. "The Strange Case of the Suspected Sotah (Numbers V 11-31)." *Vetus Testamentum* 34: 11–26.

Garland-Thomson, Rosemarie. 2010. "Integrating Disability, Transforming Feminist Theory." Pages 353–73 in *The Disability Studies Reader*. Edited by Lennard J. Davis. 3rd ed. New York: Routledge.

Gewalt, Dietfried. 1985. "Taube und Blinde nach Levitikus 19,14." *Dielheimer Blätter zum Alten Testament* 22: 119–39.

Hoffner, Harry A., Jr. 1997. *The Laws of the Hittites: A Critical Edition*. Documenta et Monumenta Orientis Antiqui 23. Leiden: Brill.

———. 1998. *Hittite Myths*. Society of Biblical Literature Writings from the Ancient World 2. 2nd ed. Atlanta: Scholars.

Hulse, E. V. 1975. "The Nature of Biblical 'Leprosy' and the Use of Alternative Medical Terms in Modern Translations of the Bible." *Palestine Exploration Quarterly* 107: 87–105.

Jacobsen, Thorkild. 1987. *The Harps that Once . . . : Sumerian Poetry in Translation*. New Haven: Yale University Press.

Levine, Baruch A. 1989. *The JPS Torah Commentary: Leviticus*. Philadelphia: Jewish Publication Society.

Magdalene, F. Rachel. 1992. "Abortion: ANE and HB/OT." Pages 1–3 in vol. 1 of *The Anchor Bible Dictionary*. Edited by David Noel Freedman. Garden City, N.Y.: Doubleday.

Milgrom, Jacob. 1990. *The JPS Torah Commentary: Numbers*. Philadelphia: Jewish Publication Society.

———. 2000. *Leviticus 17–22*. Anchor Bible 3A. Garden City, N.Y.: Doubleday.

———. 2004. *Leviticus: A Continental Commentary*. Minneapolis: Fortress.

Mitchell, David, and Sharon Snyder. 2010. "Narrative Prosthesis." Pages 274–87 in *The Disability Studies Reader*. Edited by Lennard J. Davis. 3rd ed. New York: Routledge.

Morice, P., P. Josset, and J. C. Colau. 1994. "La gynécologie et l'obstétrique en Egypte antique." *Journal de gynécologie, obstétrique et biologie de la reproduction* 23: 131–36.

Moss, Candida R., and Jeremy Schipper, eds. 2011. "Introduction." Pages 1–11 in *Disability Studies and Biblical Literature*. New York: Palgrave Macmillan.

Noth, Martin. 1980. *A History of Pentateuchal Traditions*. Translated and with an introduction by Bernhard W. Anderson. Chico, Calif.: Scholars.

Nunn, J. F. 2002. *Ancient Egyptian Medicine*. Norman: University of Oklahoma Press.

Olyan, Saul M. 2008. *Disability in the Hebrew Bible: Interpreting Mental and Physical Differences*. Cambridge: Cambridge University Press.

Peckruhn, Heike. 2014. "Disability Studies." Pages 101–11 in vol. 1 of *The Oxford Encyclopedia of the Bible and Gender Studies*. Edited by Julia M. O'Brien. Oxford: Oxford University Press.

Roth, Martha T. 1997. *Law Collections from Mesopotamia and Asia Minor*. Society of Biblical Literature Writings from the Ancient World 6. 2nd ed. Atlanta: Scholars.

Schipper, Jeremy. 2006. *Disability Studies and the Hebrew Bible: Figuring Mephibosheth in the David Story*. New York: T&T Clark.

Shakespeare, Tom. 2010. "The Social Model of Disability." Pages 266–73 in *The Disability Studies Reader*. Edited by Lennard J. Davis. 3rd ed. New York: Routledge.

Smith, Mark S. 2015. "The Three Bodies of God in the Hebrew Bible." *Journal of Biblical Literature* 134: 471–88.

Stenchever, M. A., and D. E. Fenner. 2001. "Anatomic Defects of the Abdominal Wall and Pelvic Floor." Pages 565–606 in *Comprehensive Gynecology*. Edited by M. A. Stenchever et al. 4th ed. St. Louis: Mosby.

Stevens, J. M. 1975. "Gynaecology from Ancient Egypt: The Papyrus Kahun: A Translation of the Oldest Treatise on Gynaecology That Has Survived from the Ancient World." *Medical Journal of Australia* 2: 949–52.

Stewart, David Tabb. 2006. "Leviticus." Pages 77–104 in *The Queer Bible Commentary*. Edited by P. D. Guest et al. London: SCM Press.

———. 2008. "Does the Priestly Purity Code Domesticate Women?" Pages 65–73 in *Perspectives on Purity and Purification in the Bible*. Edited by Baruch J. Schwartz et al. New York: Oxford University Press.

———. 2011. "Sexual Disabilities in the Hebrew Bible." Pages 67–87 in *Disability Studies and Biblical Literature*. Edited by Candida R. Moss and Jeremy Schipper. New York: Palgrave Macmillan.

———. 2015. "Leviticus 19 as Mini-Torah." Pages 299-323 in *Current Issues in Priestly and Related Literature: The Legacy of Jacob Milgrom and Beyond*. Edited by Roy E. Gane and Ada Taggar-Cohen. Resources for Biblical Study. Atlanta: Society of Biblical Literature.

Stiker, Henri-Jacques. 1999. *A History of Disability*. Translated by William Sayers. Ann Arbor: University of Michigan Press.

Strouhal, Eugen, Břetislav Vachala, and Hana Vymazalová. 2014. *Surgery, Gynecology, Obstetrics, and Pediatrics*. Vol. 1 of *The Medicine of the Ancient Egyptians*. Edited by Eugen Strouhal, Břetislav Vachala, and Hana Vymazalová. Cairo: American University in Cairo Press.

Tigay, Jeffrey H. 1996. *The JPS Torah Commentary: Deuteronomy*. Philadelphia: Jewish Publication Society.

Wittgenstein, Ludwig. 1968. *Philosophical Investigations*. Translated by G. E. M. Anscombe. 3rd ed. New York: Macmillan.

3

Joshua–Second Kings

Jeremy Schipper

The books of Joshua, Judges, Ruth, 1 and 2 Samuel, and 1 and 2 Kings tell a story of Israel from the people's emergence in the land of Canaan until the Babylonians conquer Jerusalem over six hundred years later. Some refer to these books as the "Former Prophets," as their authorship is attributed to various prophets according to a rabbinic tradition (*b. B. Bat.* 14b; cf. 1 Chr 29:29). The Former Prophets, however, do not include Ruth because in standard Masoretic Hebrew Texts (MT), Ruth is placed among the "Scrolls." The Scrolls are a collection of books that also include Song of Songs, Lamentations, Ecclesiastes, and Esther. Many contemporary biblical scholars claim that, with the exception of Ruth, Joshua–2 Kings were edited together in ways that show the legal and theological influence of Deuteronomy. Thus they refer to these books as the Deuteronomistic History (DH). At the same time, ongoing debate exists among scholars over the details of this theory. For example, among other issues, scholars hold different positions on the number of editions of DH that existed over time and how many persons or groups were responsible for its contents (for a detailed review of such arguments, see Hutton 2009, 79–156).

In Christian Scriptures, Ruth comes after Judges and before 1 Samuel based on the order of the books in Greek texts. At the request of this volume's editors, the present commentary follows this ordering. Therefore, I will discuss Ruth within my commentary on Joshua–2 Kings. In the fourth century CE, the Christian bishop Athanasius referred to the seven books that I will discuss in this commentary along with five others (1 and 2 Chr, Ezra, Neh, and Esth) as "histories." Thus, all twelve books are often referred to as the "Historical Books." Regardless of the order in which these books occur, various religious and scholarly traditions acknowledge that they were compiled over a long period by multiple authors or editors.

With or without Ruth, the complicated history of Joshua–2 Kings' composition makes it difficult to identity one unifying purpose or theme. This difficulty also applies to the use of disability imagery and language within these books. These books do not reflect a unified approach or "theology" of disability. Rather, various texts throughout these books, composed or edited by multiple parties over time, use disability imagery to express a wide variety of ideas and positions on a wide variety of topics. One should not try to reduce the diverse use of disability language and imagery in these texts to a unified theological system. Thus, this commentary addresses both disability and nondisability imagery in each book on a case-by-case basis.

In terms of methodology, this commentary will not offer a comprehensive survey of the contents or compositional history of these books because oflimited space. Rather, it will focus on the many uses of disability language and imagery throughout these books and contextualize them within their narrative settings. At points, this contextualization process will involve explaining the ancient Near Eastern background for a particular image, exploring particular grammatical or philological nuances of the language used to describe human difference, drawing connections between an image in one passage and its use in other biblical texts, or engaging the analysis of an image by other biblical scholars. The specific method of contextualization in this commentary will vary from text to text depending on the particular image, language, or setting under discussion.

This commentary focuses on a variety of interpretive issues related to the critical study of disability in Joshua–2 Kings. Such issues include, but are not limited to, attention to various meanings that are mapped onto disability imagery in these texts, reconsiderations of whether nondisability is considered the norm and disability as a deviation from that norm, whether disability is considered a form of divine punishment in these texts, the use of disability as a structuring device and a way of organizing and expressing multiple perspectives on a variety of theological or ideological positions, the influence of contemporary medical models of disability on interpretations of disability in these texts, and how texts or their interpretations often use disability imagery to discuss topics unrelated to persons with disabilities themselves. As we will discover, disability imagery and language serve as a major form of cultural expression in Joshua–2 Kings. Biblical scholars have often focused on subjects such as Zion, kingship, or Deuteronomic law in order to gain a more critical and comprehensive understanding of the material in these texts and the cultures that produced these texts. Yet, until recently, scholars have not studied the frequent use of disability imagery and language in these texts in a similar fashion. Nevertheless, along with study of royal or legal language and imagery, the study of disability imagery allows for a more complete understanding of various perspectives presented in Joshua–2 Kings. Many scholars correctly assume one cannot claim to have a thorough understanding of the theological or ideological landscapes in Joshua–2 Kings without critically analyzing the Zion or Deuteronomic language and imagery. Yet scholars should make a similar assumption regarding the disability language and imagery in these texts.

The ways that disability is conceptualized in Joshua–2 Kings provides significant insight into how these texts discuss a variety of the ideologies, themes, and worldviews unrelated to persons with disabilities that have traditionally preoccupied scholars specializing in Joshua–2 Kings. In this sense, the importance of critically analyzing the use of disability in these texts is not limited to scholars specializing in disability studies, (self-)advocates for persons with disabilities, or those who identify as both scholars and advocates. Rather, as with much of the Hebrew Bible, the critical study of disability in Joshua–2 Kings is relevant to anyone claiming competency in these texts.[1]

THE BOOK OF JOSHUA

The book of Joshua tells the story of the Israelites' entrance into the land of Canaan. The generation that participated in the covenant at Sinai after Moses led the Israelites out of Egypt had died in the wilderness (5:6; cf. Num 14:1-39, 32:10-13). Thus Joshua leads a new generation into Canaan and the LORD renews the covenant with them at the culmination of the book (Josh 23–24; cf. 8:30-35). The book concludes by noting that the generation that entered the land served the LORD during the lifetimes of Joshua and the elders who outlived him (24:31).

This book does not describe any members of this new generation as having a disability, illness, or disease. In fact, unlike most other books in the Hebrew Bible, this book never uses any disability imagery explicitly. Rather, it assumes the Israelites' ability to walk, talk, hear, and see as it

---

[1]All biblical quotations come from the New Revised Standard Version (NSRV) and follow its versification even when it differs from the versification in the MT. Any differences in wording from the NRSV reflect my own translations.

narrates Israel's entry into the land and renewal of the covenant. Whereas some biblical texts use images of disability as metaphors for Israel collectively after the people are exiled from Canaan (for references, consult the discussion of 2 Kgs 25:27-30 below), Joshua depicts the faithful generation that enters and occupies Canaan as collectively nondisabled.

In Joshua nondisability does not describe a universally recognized "normal" state of human existence from which disability deviates. Nor is it passively expressed by the absence of explicit disability imagery. Rather, nondisability imagery actively expresses what Israelite obedience to the LORD looks like. Throughout the book the Israelites demonstrate their obedience by following commands to look, hear, walk, and shout. For example, as they prepare to cross the Jordan, the commanders instruct the people to follow the priests when they "see the ark of the covenant of the LORD your God being carried by the Levitical priests" (3:3). A few verses later, Joshua commands the Israelites to "hear the words of the LORD your God" (3:9). In contrast, 5:6 uses images of "not hearing" and "not seeing" to describe the disobedience and punishment of the older generation of Israelites who died in the wilderness.

Once the people enter Canaan, the plan for conquering Jericho requires the people to shout (6:10, 20), which assumes their ability to speak. The renewal of the covenant also requires Joshua to speak and assumes the people's ability to hear. After Joshua gathers all the assembly of Israel together, he reads the entire law of Moses (8:35). The book of Joshua reinforces the importance of hearing as an element of entering into the covenant during the ceremony at Shechem in the book's final chapter. Having reminded the people that "your eyes saw [what the LORD] did to Egypt" (24:7), Joshua erects a stone monument (24:26) that serves as an anthropomorphized witness against them if they break the covenant because the monument "has heard all the words of the LORD that he spoke to us" (24:27).

The people's ability to cross the Jordan rests on the priests' ability to walk. The waters of the river part only when "the soles of the feet of the priests who bear the ark of the LORD, the Lord of all the earth, rest in the waters of the Jordan" (3:13; cf. 3:15; 4:3, 9). The Jordan returns to its normal flow as soon as the soles of the priests' feet touch dry ground again (4:18). The ability to walk is not only important for a successful entry into Canaan but also provides a central image for divine promises regarding the people's occupation of it. The book opens with the LORD promising Joshua that "every place that the sole of your foot will tread upon I have given to you [Israel], as I promised to Moses" (1:3; cf. Deut 11:24). Later, Caleb cites this promise when he claims that the LORD sustained him during Israel's journey though the wilderness (Josh 14:9). He references his retention of his physical strength into old age as evidence that the LORD blessed him (14:11). For Caleb, his physical ability represents a divine blessing for his faithfulness.

The lack of disability in the book of Joshua's descriptions of the new generation is striking considering that the story takes place against the backdrop of intense warfare, especially in Josh 6–12. Although warfare on the scale discussed in Joshua would certainly have resulted in many acquired disabilities in the ancient Near East, disabilities are not included in the world narrated in this book. Other books include at least sporadic acknowledgments of this reality (Judg 1:7, 16:21; 1 Sam 11:2; 2 Sam 4:4; 2 Kgs 25:7, among others). Yet although thousands of people are said to have died in the battles depicted in Joshua, fatal injuries do not qualify as disabilities. Remarkably, Joshua does not record any acquired disabilities despite its many military conflicts.

In fact, the book only describes bodily alterations that enhance rather than disable the Israelites' social and cultic status. Joshua contains no physical descriptions of Israelite bodies aside from the fact that the males were circumcised. In order to observe the law properly (1:7-8, 8:32-35, 23:6, 24:26), males were required to undergo this permanent bodily alteration. The ideal Israelite male body in Joshua is not a biologically whole or complete body as opposed to a body with disabilities. Instead, it is a body that is properly altered by circumcision and not improperly altered by acquired disabilities. Joshua circumcises the new generation of Israelite males immediately after they cross the Jordan and enter Canaan (5:2-9). This allows them to keep the Passover (cf. Exod 12:43-44, 48).

After their circumcision, the LORD declares, "Today I have rolled away from you the disgrace of Egypt" (Josh 5:9). This "proper" bodily alteration removes disgrace, whereas Zeph 3:18-19 associates certain disabilities with the word "disgrace" (Olyan 2008, 37). Yet the reason(s) one bodily alteration removes disgrace while another bodily alteration, such as certain disabilities, is associated with disgrace depends on cultural context rather than inherent biological properties. Joshua depicts Israel as collectively nondisabled with only socially enhancing bodily alterations. This contrasts sharply with final image of an Israelite in the land in 2 Kgs 25. Yet, as we will discover, such bodily alterations and contrasts will repeatedly help to mark the shifting statuses of "insiders" and "outsiders" as the story of Israel in Canaan unfolds in the books that follow.

THE BOOK OF JUDGES

Often, scholars comment that the book of Judges contains a more complex and less idealized narrative of Israel's occupation of Canaan than in Joshua (e.g., cf. Josh 10:40-43 with Judg 1:8-36). Likewise, Judges is less idealized regarding nonfatal causalities of war. Whereas Joshua portrays the occupation of Canaan without including any acquired disabilities as a by-product of this violence, Judges acknowledges this reality from its opening verses. In the first battle against the Canaanites, the tribe of Judah captures Adoni-bezek at Bezek. The warriors of Judah cut off his thumbs and big toes before bringing him to Jerusalem, where he dies (1:5-7). Adoni-bezek may have died as a result of this mutilation, although it remains unclear how long he lived after his mutilation. In 1:7, however, Adoni-bezek says, "Seventy kings with their thumbs and big toes cut off used to pick up scraps under my table; as I have done, so God has paid me back." He implies that the seventy kings under his table lived with the disabilities that they acquired as the result of war. His statement creates associations between acquired disabilities and warfare and captivity from the very beginning of the book of Judges (cf. 16:21-30; 2 Kgs 25:7).

This does not mean that Judges includes these disabilities simply to present a more complete depiction of the cost of warfare. One should not confuse the presence of acquired disabilities in the book of Judges for a reliable portrayal of life with a disability in ancient Israel. Even if Judges acknowledges the reality of disability in its narratives, it shows little, if any, interest in providing a realistic sense of what it may have been like to live with acquired disabilities. Judges includes disabilities as a literary device that helps to flesh out its themes and its structures rather than out of a concern for historical accuracy or realism. Bodily images help signal the introduction and conclusion of the wars in the book as Israel moves from a unified community (Judg 1:1-2) to one fractured by infighting (Judg 20–21) and ultimately chaos (21:25). Such bodily images give shape and structure to themes that run throughout Judges' depiction of the way the world operates in its narratives.

Along these lines, the supposed meaning that Adoni-bezek ascribes to physical impairments fits with what David Mitchell and Sharon Snyder observe when they write, "To give an abstraction a literal body allows the idea to simulate a foothold in the material world that it would otherwise fail to procure" (2000, 62–63). For example, in 1:7 the bodily imagery allows Adoni-bezek to articulate this ideological or theological abstraction. Adoni-bezek's interpretation of impairments introduces a particular ideological or theological idea of God as one who operates according to a principle of *lex talionis*, in which the punishment fits the crime (cf. Exod 21:23-25; Lev 24:19-20; Deut 19:21).

A similar use of bodily imagery occurs toward the end of the book. In Judg 19 the sexual assault and death of a Levite's unnamed concubine serves as a catalyst for infighting among the tribes (Judg 20–21) and a state of social chaos (17:6, 21:25). Following the assault of the concubine, the Levite chops her into twelve pieces and uses her mutilated body to provide a social commentary on the current state of the Israelite society. According to 19:29-30, the Levite "took a knife, and grasping his concubine he cut her into twelve pieces, limb by limb, and sent her throughout all the territory of Israel. Then he commanded the men whom he sent, saying, 'Thus shall you say to all the Israelites, "Has such a thing ever happened since the day that the Israelites came up from the land of Egypt until this day? Consider it, take counsel, and speak out." ' "

A few verses later, the Levite claims to have mutilated the concubine postmortem (20:5-6), but the narrator does not actually confirm whether the concubine was alive or dead when she was mutilated (19:29). It is possible that, as with mutilations in 1:6-7, the concubine's body is mutilated before she dies. To be clear, the concubine's fatal or postmortem mutilation does not qualify as an acquired disability. Nevertheless, whether they result in physical disabilities (1:7) or death (19:29), characters such as Adoni-bezek and the unnamed Levite use mutilated bodies as resources for social or theological commentary. Additionally, these bodies provide a structuring device in the current form of Judges. The mutilations in 1:6-7 and 19:29 serve as the respective consequence of and catalyst for the first and last battles in the book.

Likewise, images of disability help to structure the narrative and articulate certain theological perspectives in the story of Samson (Judg 13–16). As a structuring device, a divine granting of conception to an infertile woman (13:2) and Samson's desire for revenge for his acquired disability after he loses his eyesight (16:28) serve as the respective catalysts for Samson's birth and his death. Other texts from antiquity also associate infertility with various disabilities, including blindness (*Gen. Rab.* 53:8; *COS* 1.159:518). In 13:2-3 both the narrator and an angel of the LORD note that Manoah's unnamed wife is infertile. Nevertheless, the angel declares that she will have a son. The angel's statement comes to fruition later in the chapter when Manoah's wife gives birth to a son, whom she names Samson (13:24). Although the text does not indicate that she had other children explicitly, the presence of Samson's brothers in 16:31 may hint that she remained fertile beyond Samson's birth. Unlike Adoni-bezek's mutilation, this woman's infertility is not discussed as a form of divine retribution. Although 13:1 claims that the Israelites did evil in the eyes of the LORD, 13:2 does not conceive of her infertility as form of divine punishment. In fact, infertility is never conceived of as a divine punishment in Joshua–2 Kings. Rather, Samson's mother's infertility provides an opportunity for the LORD to demonstrate control over mundane events (cf. 14:4).

In addition to studying the use of disability for narrative structure or theological commentary, Judges provides an opportunity to examine how various meanings have been mapped onto images of disability throughout the history of biblical interpretation and scholarship. For example, Samson has captured the imagination of countless generations of readers, scholars, artists, and poets. He is one of the most complex and enigmatic characters in the Hebrew Bible. Interpreters have used a wide range of reading strategies to access his inner motives. Over the centuries he has been depicted as a national hero, a terrorist, an antihero, a shallow womanizer, a folkloric wild man or trickster, a tragic figure, and everything in between. Likewise, interpreters have struggled to find a central point or moral to his story. They have often used Samson's blindness as a window into his soul and as a way to map moral coherence onto his story. Yet connections between blindness and Samson's inner life or moral state do not emerge from obvious textual evidence in Judg 13–16. Instead, these connections become naturalized over time through repeated efforts to find a coherent character or moral in these chapters (Moulton 2014).

Unlike his mother's infertility, some interpreters have understood Samson's blindness as a form of punishment or at least poetic justice. In 14:3 Samson tells his parents to get a Philistine woman to be his wife "because she is pleasing in my eyes." After the Philistines capture and blind him, he asks for God to strengthen him one final time stating, "So that with this one act of revenge I may pay back the Philistines for my two eyes" (16:28b). A talmudic tradition (*b. Sotah* 9b) interprets the loss of Samson's eyesight as punishment for his relationship with a prostitute whom he "saw" in Gaza (16:1; cf. 14:1). Thus he ends up blinded and imprisoned in Gaza (16:21). Such interpretations project a moral meaning onto Samson's disability even though the text never connects his blindness to his relationships with his wife or the prostitute in Gaza. In fact, in the ancient Near East, captors often forcibly blinded their victims as a way of physically marking their status as captives (e.g., 2 Kgs 25:7; Isa 42:19; Ps 146:7b-8; cf. van der Toorn 1986). Within an ancient Near Eastern context, the association of his blinding and his captivity may have made more sense than an understanding of his blinding as a moment full of moral significance.

Others have interpreted Samson's blindness as a catalyst for Samson to take inventory of his lifestyle and paradoxically "see clearly" his faults and his mission (e.g., Galpaz-Feller 2006, 201–18). This type of interpretation, popular since at least John Milton's *Samson Agonistes*, uses Samson's blindness as a point of entry into Samson's inner life. It reflects the myth that people with disabilities gain some type of sensory or moral compensation for their disabilities (Mitchell and Snyder 2000). Against this tendency one should note that Samson makes statements about revenge on the Philistines before and after his loss of eyesight (Judg 15:3, 7; 16:20, 28). This raises questions about whether his blindness signals any change in his inner character at all.

As one method of finding narrative coherence in the Samson story, some scholars debate whether Judg 13–16 follows a comic or tragic pattern. While arguing that the overall structure of the story is a comedy, J. Cheryl Exum (1998) explains how she came to understand Samson as a tragic figure after seeing Lovis Corinth's painting *Blinded Samson*. Confronted with this visual image of Samson after he is blinded, Exum concludes, "If the Samson story in Judges 13–16 had been told in the first person by Samson, it would have been a tragedy, not a comedy" (424). Yet as Exum acknowledges, one could also interpret the painting as depicting grit and perseverance in the face of his captors' abuse. Exum's conclusion that Samson, having acquired a disability, would recount his life story as a tragedy may be based more on cultural stereotypes about one's quality of life with a disability than on either Corinth's painting or the biblical text. In an earlier publication, Exum astutely critiqued scholars' and artists' tendency to objectify Bathsheba's body by viewing her through a "male gaze" (1996, 19–53). Yet Exum's earlier critique regarding objectified bodies seems applicable to her own reading of Samson's disabled body. The supposed association of disability with tragedy becomes amplified when the disabled body is objectified through a nondisabled stare or gaze (on the nondisabled stare, see Garland-Thomson 2009).

This brief study of Judges and its interpretations shows how one can map a variety of meanings onto biblical images of disability, including, but not limited to, punishment, tragedy, narrative structures, and other theological or ideological abstractions. Nonetheless, one should remember that many, if not all, of these supposed meanings do not reflect the everyday lives of actual persons with disabilities. Commenting on literature more broadly, David Mitchell and Sharon Snyder (1997, 12) note that disability is rarely "explored as a condition or experience in its own right; disability's psychological and bodily variations have been used to metaphorize nearly every social conflict outside its own ignoble predicament in culture." The Hebrew Bible often uses imagery and language associated with disability to discuss topics other than the everyday experiences of people with disabilities. One should try to identify the actual topic(s) under discussion when one comes across disability terminology or imagery in biblical texts and scholarship.

THE BOOK OF RUTH

As in Joshua, the book of Ruth does not include any disability language or imagery explicitly. Yet the lack of explicit disability imagery in Ruth does not necessarily mean that it portrays its characters as nondisabled. Often we assume nondisability as the norm unless biblical texts explicitly indicate otherwise. We might unreflectively map nondisability onto biblical texts instead of pausing to ask what in the text indicates that a given character is nondisabled. For example, Genesis does not indicate whether the hip injury that Jacob sustains in a wrestling match was only temporary or resulted in a permanent limp (Gen 32:25). Comparative evidence from other biblical texts associates leg injuries with lifelong disabilities rather than a temporary condition (2 Sam 9:3, 13; 19:26; Schipper 2011, 24–25). Nevertheless, as Kerry Wynn documents, scholars often assume Jacob's limp was temporary without citing evidence from the text to support this assumption (2007, 99).

The following discussion of Ruth will focus on issues of fertility to show how nondisability is mapped onto characters rather than indicated by the text (much of this discussion comes from Schipper 2016). To be clear, the book never indicates directly that any character is infertile. Thus, I will not try to prove that a particular character in Ruth is portrayed as infertile or as having a disability. Instead, my point is that the book raises questions about whether fertility is portrayed as the unwritten norm and infertility is portrayed as a deviation in Ruth. If the text does not support the assumption that fertility is normal unless indicated otherwise, one may question whether one should map fertility onto the characters.

Outside Ruth, infertility is often, but not always, identified with the Hebrew root ʿpr (Gen 11:30, 25:21, 29:31; Exod 23:26; Deut 7:14; Judg 13:2-3; 1 Sam 2:5; Isa 54:1; Job 24:21). Yet the use of the root ʿpr to indicate infertility does not mean that one should assume fertility unless the text uses this root. Several texts indicate short-term or long-term infertility without using ʿpr (Gen 16:2, 20:17-18; 1 Sam 1:5-6; Isa 66:9; also possibly 2 Sam 6:23; 2 Kgs 4:14). The absence of ʿpr in Ruth does not necessarily mean that one should assume the characters are fertile. According to Ruth 1:4, both Orpah and Ruth were married for "about ten years" without any indication that they had children. Some scholars compare these ten-year marriages to the statement in Gen 16:3 that after "ten years" Sarai gave Hagar to Abram because she claims "the LORD has prevented me from bearing children" (16:2; cf. Sasson 1995, 21). For example, Robert Hubbard (1988, 95) makes this comparison and refers to Orpah and Ruth as "infertile daughters-in-law," although the lack of children could just as easily have resulted from their husbands' sterility since the Hebrew Bible does acknowledge male sterility as well as female infertility (e.g., Gen 20:17; Deut 7:14; possibly 2 Kgs 4:14). At any rate, questions concerning Ruth's possible infertility have existed since very early in the history of interpretation. According to a rabbinic tradition, Ruth did not have a uterus until "the LORD made her conceive" (4:13; cf. *Ruth Rab.* 7:14).

The fertility of Ruth (as well as Boaz) remains inconclusive before 4:13. This should caution us against mapping fertility onto the characters. Reproductive capabilities were not taken for granted or considered the usual state of existence in the ancient Near East. Certain Mesopotamian texts imply that some humans were created infertile (e.g., *Epic of Atra-Hasis*, COS 1.130:452; *Enki and Ninmah*, COS 1.159:518). Moreover, while the assumption across ancient Israelite literature seems to be that most humans were created with the capacity to conceive within the appropriate age range, this does not mean that successful reproduction was guaranteed. Rather, the assumption was that all humans still depended on divine action to have children. Multiple texts depict successful conception and reproduction under any circumstance as a divine blessing. Even if one is created with the necessary biological equipment, it requires a divine blessing to activate successful conception and reproduction. For example, although both Eve and Leah had given birth previously and thus their reproductive potential was not in question, they acknowledge the LORD's continued aid in their ability to reproduce (cf. Gen 4:25 and 29:33, respectively). Other texts assume that, if not for an extremely unusual divine blessing, at least some fertile women will miscarry under normal circumstances (Exod 23:26; Deut 7:13, 28:11; Ps 127:3; Baden 2011, 14–17).

Likewise, there is very little textual evidence in Ruth to suggest that successful reproduction was considered the default norm. Instead, it is the result of divine blessing, as the narrator makes clear: "So Boaz took Ruth and she became his wife. When they came together, the LORD made her conceive, and she bore a son" (4:13). As scholars often note, this is the only action that the narrator explicitly attributes to the LORD in the entire book. (The narrator acknowledges but does not verify the rumor of the LORD's action in 1:6.) The attribution of conception to a divine blessing in Ruth is in keeping with other ancient Near Eastern texts. In a text from Ugarit, the god El blesses Kirta and promises that his bride will bear eight sons (Parker 1976, 26).

In Gen 24:60, when Rebekah leaves home to become Isaac's wife, her mother and brother bless her with a prayer that she will have thousands of descendants. The following chapter attributes her conception to divine involvement: "Isaac prayed to the LORD for his wife, because she was barren; and the LORD granted his prayer, and his wife Rebekah conceived" (25:21). Similarly, Ruth only has a child after an explicit divine intervention following the townspeople's appeal to God (4:11-12). Moreover, when the townspeople bless her marriage, they compare Ruth specifically to Rachel and Leah (4:11). In Genesis God "opens" the wombs of Leah and Rachel so they can produce children (Gen 29:31 and 30:22, respectively) just as God "opens" a donkey's mouth so it can speak (Num 22:28) or "opens" a rock (Ps 105:41) so that it produces water. Yet ancient Israelites would not consider speaking donkeys or water-producing rocks as normal (Baden 2011, 14–17).

Even if human fertility occurred frequently, several biblical texts suggest that fertility was a divine blessing rather than a given. The notion of fertility as a blessing is very different from a contemporary understanding of fertility as normal and infertility as a deviation from this norm. The assumption that fertility in Ruth represents a normative state of existence often reflects contemporary nondisabled privilege rather than textual evidence.

THE BOOK OF FIRST SAMUEL

The books of Samuel tell the story of Israel's transition from a system of leadership organized around various judges to the leadership of the Davidic monarchy. This transition involves constant shifts among various characters or households from "insiders" to "outsiders" and vice versa. My discussion of 1 and 2 Samuel focuses on how these books use imagery of disability and idealized bodies to mark such shifts in status.

Samson is the last judge discussed in the book of Judges. The early chapters of 1 Samuel continue the discussion of judges with the stories of Eli and Samuel, both of whom served as judges over Israel (1 Sam 4:18 and 7:15-16, respectively). As noted earlier, imagery of disability helps to structure the narrative and articulate certain theological ideas in the story of Samson. First Samuel uses similar techniques as it narrates the conclusion of the period of leadership by judges. Although 1 Samuel uses different terms for infertility and blindness than those in Judg 13–16, a divine granting of conception to an infertile woman (1 Sam 1:5, 19-20; cf. Judg 13:2) and Eli's inability to see (1 Sam 4:14-18; cf. Judg 16:28) help to introduce and conclude the story involving the leadership of Eli's priestly household.

The book of 1 Samuel begins with the story of Hannah. Unlike the infertility of Samson's unnamed mother, the narrative explicitly attributes Hannah's infertility to divine causation: "The LORD had closed [Hannah's] womb" (1:5; cf. 1:6; Job 3:10). Yet as with Samson's mother, the text does not provide any motivation for this divine intervention. We have no reason to associate infertility with divine punishment simply because it is attributed to divine causation. Instead, as in Judg 13, Hannah's infertility provides an opportunity for the LORD to demonstrate control over mundane matters. Toward the end of 1 Sam 1, Hannah becomes fertile because "the LORD remembered her. In due time, Hannah conceived and bore a son. She named him Samuel, for she said, 'I have asked him of the LORD'" (1:19b-20; cf. Gen 30:22-23).

Hannah's story also introduces the use of disability imagery to mark shifts in status among characters. Although many scholars doubt that the poem in 1 Sam 2:1b-10 was originally composed in reference to Hannah (McCarter 1980, 75–76), it is attributed to her in the current form of the story. Hannah's song praises God for orchestrating a variety of reversals in status, including an example involving infertility: "The barren has borne seven, but she who has many children is forlorn" (2:5b). Disability imagery and language will articulate these types of reversals throughout 1 and 2 Samuel.

Samuel is the son to whom Hannah gives birth in 1 Sam 1. Eventually, Samuel replaces Eli as a judge over Israel. In 1 Sam 2–3, the LORD revokes the divine promise of a long-lasting, if not permanent, priesthood for Eli's household. First, an unnamed prophet announces this divine judgment to Eli (2:30-36). Second, Samuel receives divine word that this judgment is eminent and he relays this message to Eli (3:11-18). In the midst of these two announcements, the narrator states that "the word of the LORD was rare in those days; visions were not widespread. At that time Eli, whose eyesight had begun to grow dim so that he could not see, was lying down in his room; the lamp of God had not yet gone out" (3:1-3a). In the MT, the word translated as "dim" (כהה, *kēhê*) is spelled according to a pattern used for Hebrew nouns expressing various physical differences, including disabilities that are often grouped together such as "deaf," "mute," "lame," or "blind" (Exod 4:11; Lev 19:14; 2 Sam 5:8; Isa 29:18, 35:5-6, 43:8, 56:10; Jer 31:8; Mal 1:8; Job 29:15).

The Hebrew root for the word "dim" also describes Moses' eyesight at the end of his life in Deut 34:7. Yet this verse reads, "[Moses'] eyesight had not dimmed." The physical depiction of Eli contrasts sharply with that of Moses, who is praised as an unparalleled prophet at the end of his life (34:10-12). Unlike Moses, Eli must rely on others to receive rare prophetic messages from the LORD, which were not widespread in his lifetime (1 Sam 2:27, 3:17-18). In fact, Eli would presumably not be able to see the LORD, who not only speaks to Samuel but also appears to him. As noted in 3:10, "The LORD came and stood there, calling as before, 'Samuel! Samuel!'" To be clear, the inability to see does not necessarily disqualify one from functioning as a prophet (e.g., Ahijah in 1 Kgs 14, discussed below). Nevertheless, the contrast between Eli's and Moses' eyesight reinforces the fact that Eli was never a prophet in the first place. Eli may be a judge and a non-Aaronide priest (contrast Lev 21:16-23), but he is never a prophet. One may also use 1 Sam 3:1-3 to contrast Eli's dimmed eyesight with another important leader in Israel's history. These verses contrast Eli's inability to see with "the lamp of God." Other texts associate the image of a "lamp" with the LORD's promise of fidelity to the Davidic dynasty (2 Sam 21:7, 22:29; 1 Kgs 11:36, 15:4; 2 Kgs 8:19; Polzin 1989, 49–54). After Eli's death, Samuel facilitates the transition between the eras of the judges and the Davidic monarchy. He anoints both Saul and David as Israel's first two kings (1 Sam 10:1 and 16:13, respectively). Eventually, the Davidic dynasty will solidify the replacement of judges with kings as the primary form of leadership in Israel.

This transition from judges to kings involves multiple images of disability. Soon after Samuel anoints Saul, Nahash the Ammonite attacks Jabesh-Gilead and threatens to disable the men of Jabesh when he tells them, "On this condition I will make a treaty with you, namely that I gouge out everyone's right eye, and thus put disgrace upon all Israel" (11:2; cf. Num 16:14; Judg 16:21). When Saul hears of Nahash's conditions for a treaty, he leads Israel in battle against Nahash and defeats him (1 Sam 11:4-11). After this victory the people recognize Saul as king (11:12-15). Whereas diminished eyesight helped to mark the end of Eli's authority, preventing diminished eyesight serves as the catalyst for the recognition of Saul's authority.

The stories of Saul's rise to power describe him as not only nondisabled but also as physically idealized. In 9:2 the narrator says that Saul was "a handsome young man. There was not a man among the people of Israel more handsome than he; he stood head and shoulders above everyone else" (cf. 10:23-24). As will be explained in more detail below, such physical idealization will later describe David and members of his family. Nevertheless, despite Saul's physical idealization, God tells Samuel that when choosing a king, humans "look on the outward appearance, but the LORD looks on the heart" (16:7). Regarding a king's heart, just after Samuel anoints Saul as king of Israel, the narrator states, "As he turned away to leave Samuel, God gave him another heart" (10:9; cf. 1 Kgs 3:9, 12). Yet when the LORD decides to replace Saul with another king, Samuel tells Saul, "The LORD has sought out a man after his own heart" (13:14). A few chapters later, Samuel anoints David as king (16:13). In the very next verse, the narrator states, "Now the spirit of the LORD departed from Saul, and an evil spirit from the LORD tormented him" (16:14). This evil spirit will continue to torment Saul and affect his behavior over the next several chapters (16:23, 18:10, 19:9).

A number of scholars equate Saul's torment with some type of cognitive or emotional disability. Some have offered diagnoses using contemporary medical terminology. For example, Robert Alter describes Saul as having "fits of depression later accompanied by paranoia" (1999, 98; cf. McCarter 1980, 280–81). Philip Esler suggests that a plausible diagnosis "is that Saul suffers from anxiety disorder featuring panic attacks" (1998, 249). Such diagnostic speculation may give the impression of a historical explanation for what the text depicts as the activity of an evil spirit. Yet such explanations do not represent historically responsible scholarship. Instead, they interpret these verses according to a modern medical model for understanding cognitive and/or emotional disabilities that is foreign to the ancient Near Eastern culture that produced these verses. Read within an ancient Near Eastern historical context, these verses identify the spiritual agent that tormented Saul but show no concern for explaining it with the diagnostic approaches that have preoccupied many scholars.

In general, the Hebrew Bible does not use disability imagery to provide diagnostic explanations of physical or cognitive differences among humans. Rather, disability imagery often helps to develop certain literary themes in biblical literature. For example, Saul's behavior is attributed to a spiritual manipulation beyond his control. One may contrast his behavior with David's feigned behavior in 21:10-15. In this passage, David hides from Saul in Gath, which was Goliath's hometown (17:4). Residents of Gath identify David, which causes him to fear Achish, the king of Gath. In 21:13-15 the narrator explains how David gets out of this difficult situation: "So he changed his behavior before them; he pretended to be mad when in their presence. He scratched marks on the doors of the gate, and let his spittle run down his beard. Achish said to his servants, 'Look, you see the man is mad; why then have you brought him to me? Do I lack madmen that you have brought this fellow to play the madman in my presence? Shall this fellow come into my house?'" (cf. 2 Kgs 9:11, discussed later).

Saul Olyan provides a detailed analysis of the Hebrew terminology used to describe David's behavior in these verses. He concludes, "Behaviors that constitute 'madness' . . . suggest a real or perceived loss of self-control, whether due to severe mental retardation [!], drunkenness, extreme anguish, rage or shock, excessive risk taking, or some form of perceived or actual mental disturbance" (2008, 69–70). To be clear, not all of Olyan's descriptions accord with contemporary understandings of disability, and one should avoid offering exact diagnoses of the condition that David feigns. Nevertheless, whether or not the residents of Gath thought David's supposed "madness" resulted from a disability, they understood it as a loss of self-control. Yet David does not actually lose self-control but only fakes it to get out of a dangerous situation. By contrast, Saul does not fake his behavior in the surrounding chapters. The text notes repeatedly that an evil spirit controls his behavior. At one point the spirit of the LORD prevents Saul from capturing David by sending Saul into a prophetic frenzy, causing him to lay naked all day and night (1 Sam 19:18-24; cf. 10:10-13). Over the last several chapters of 1 Samuel, David emerges as more poised and in control than Saul. Imagery that one could associate with unspecified disabilities helps to narrate the shift in status and power from Saul to David.

THE BOOK OF SECOND SAMUEL

David continues to consolidate his power in 2 Samuel. In order to do so, David distances himself politically from a variety of parties that represent diverse groups. These parties do not represent a monolithic group. Instead, they include Joab and his household, the inhabitants of Jerusalem, and various members of Saul's household. Nonetheless, the opening chapters of 2 Samuel lump these diverse parties into a unified "other" by characterizing them all with disability or impurity imagery.

One reason that David must distance himself from certain parties is that some people suspected David was behind several of the murders of his political rivals. David had publicly condemned those who murdered Saul and his sons (2 Sam 1:1-16, 4:4-12). Yet, several chapters later, as David flees Jerusalem during Absalom's coup, a member of Saul's family named Shimei curses him, shouting "Out! Out! Murderer! Scoundrel! The LORD has avenged on all of you the blood of the house of Saul, in whose place you have reigned" (16:7b-8a). David also publicly condemned Joab when Joab murdered Saul's general, Abner. David even publicly mourned Abner's death (3:27-39). Afterward, the narrator states, "So all the people and all Israel understood that day that the king had no part in the killing of Abner son of Ner" (3:37). This statement assumes that before David's mourning over Abner, some people had suspected his involvement in Abner's murder.

When David condemns Joab, he states, "May the house of Joab never be without one who has an unusual genital discharge, or who has a skin disease, or who holds a spindle, or who falls by the sword, or who lacks food" (3:29). To be clear, this curse includes perpetual ritual impurities but not disabilities. Other biblical texts discuss both unusual genital discharges and skin diseases, mistranslated as leprosy in the NRSV since it is actually unrelated to Hansen's disease (Avalos 1995, 311–16), as sources of ritual impurity (Lev 13–15; Num 5:2). Both conditions disqualify a priest from eating the sacred food (Lev 22:4). Yet a few verses earlier, priests with blemishes, which include visual and mobility impairments among others, are explicitly permitted to eat sacred food (21:22). This implies that such disabilities were not sources of ritual impurity. In Samuel and Kings, ritual impurities may function as a curse or a divine punishment (consult the discussion below of Amaziah and Gehazi in the books of Kings). By contrast, these books do not discuss disabilities as a form of divinely induced curses or punishments, even if disability imagery helps to mark certain changes in a character's or group's status.

In 2 Sam 4 the text uses disability imagery to characterize members of Saul's family. When Saul's son Ishbaal hears of Abner's death, the text describes his reaction with the idiom "his hands became feeble" (4:1). Although this is an idiom for a loss of courage, the imagery involves physical weakness (Num 13:18). Three verses later, the text introduces Mephibosheth, Saul's grandson, and immediately notes his disability: "Saul's son Jonathan had a son who was crippled in his feet. He was five years old when the news about Saul and Jonathan came from Jezreel. His nurse picked him up and fled; and, in her haste to flee, it happened that he fell and became lame. His name was Mephibosheth" (2 Sam 4:4). The opening verses of 2 Sam 4 characterize Saul's heirs as having enfeebled hands and impaired feet. After Ishbaal is murdered in 4:7, the narrative continues to connect hand and foot imagery when David has Ishbaal's assassins killed and their hands and feet cut off (4:12).

After Ishbaal dies David becomes king over all Israel (5:1-5) and immediately conquers Jerusalem. When he attacks the city, the text uses disability imagery to characterize his opposition. The words "blind" and "lame" occur three times each in 5:6-8. In v. 8 the terms "lame" and "blind" describe the parties whom David "hates." In 6:16 the text uses the verb "hated" to describe Michal's reaction to David when he danced as he brought the ark into Jerusalem. A few verses later, the narrator states, "Michal the daughter of Saul had no child to the day of her death" (6:23). Although this verse does not use the Hebrew root *'pr* (consult the discussion of infertility in the section on Ruth), this verse could imply Michal's infertility (Schipper 2007, 105–7). As noted earlier during the discussion of Samson, infertility was associated with various disabilities, including visual and mobility impairments, in other biblical and ancient Near Eastern texts.

The first verse in 2 Sam 7 states that "the LORD had given [David] rest from all his enemies around him." At this point, the only viable remaining heir to the throne from Saul's household is Mephibosheth, whose disability is mentioned repeatedly in the subsequent chapters (9:3, 13; 19:26).

The use of disability imagery to characterize David's opposition contrasts sharply with the physical idealization of David himself, who is described as having "beautiful eyes and a handsome appearance" (1 Sam 16:12). Even members of David's family who do not become king are often physically idealized. For example, like Saul, David's brother Eliab is tall (16:7). David's sons Absalom and Adonijah are handsome (2 Sam 14:25 and 1 Kgs 1:6, respectively), and his daughter and granddaughter, both named Tamar, are beautiful (2 Sam 13:1 and 14:27, respectively). David's wives Abigail and Bathsheba, who have children with him and thus continue the royal bloodline, are also described as beautiful (1 Sam 25:3 and 2 Sam 11:2, respectively). By contrast, Saul's daughter Michal, whom David marries but never impregnates, is never described as beautiful. Disability imagery helps to characterize parties who present obstacles to David's political power and helps to contrast them with David's idealized royal family.

At the same time, disability imagery helps to mark shifts in status. For example, 5:6-8 indicates that Jerusalem's residents included "the blind and the lame" before David establishes the city as his capital. In 5:6 the residents of Jerusalem say, "David cannot come in here." Yet when David conquers the city, he declares his hatred for the blind and the lame (5:8). The same verse explains, "Therefore it is said, 'The blind and the lame shall not come into the house.'" This passage uses persons with disabilities, who had been in Jerusalem while David was outside the city, to represent those on the outside once David takes over. Regarding access to Jerusalem, the contrast between David and persons with disabilities helps to signal changes among insiders and outsiders.

This contrast continues over the next several chapters. In 9:4-5 David summons Mephibosheth, who enters Jerusalem despite the earlier prohibition against "the lame" coming into the city. After David and Mephibosheth talk, the story ends with the statement "Mephibosheth lived in Jerusalem, for he always ate at the king's table. Now he was lame in both his feet" (9:13). This verse states explicitly that Mephibosheth now dwells in Jerusalem *and* that he was lame (cf. 4:4, 9:3). A few chapters later, David must flee Jerusalem and his rebellious son Absalom enters the city (15:14-37). At this point David is on the outside. While exiled from Jerusalem, a man named Ziba tells David that Mephibosheth still "lives in Jerusalem for [Mephibosheth] said, 'Today the house of Israel will give me back my grandfather's kingdom'" (16:3). One should note that the narrative indicates David's reversal of fortune through not only the loss of his capital city but also a reminder that persons with disabilities once again dwell in Jerusalem (cf. 5:6). After Absalom's defeat, Mephibosheth contests Ziba's report (19:24-30). While scholars debate whether this conversation happens in or outside Jerusalem (Schipper 2006, 52 n. 56), it is possible that Mephibosheth speaks to David when the king returns to Jerusalem, whereas previously David had spoken to Mephibosheth when the king first summoned him to Jerusalem in 2 Sam 9.

During David's exile from Jerusalem, he is described with imagery that had characterized members of Saul's family during David's rise to power. For example, the narrator described Ishbaal's hands as feeble shortly before David replaced him as king (4:1). During David's exile, Ahithophel tells Absalom that David "is weary and his hands are feeble" (17:2). In 17:29 David and his troops are described as "hungry, weary and thirsty in the wilderness." A man named Machir is listed among those who provide them with food while they are outside Jerusalem (17:27-28). Previously, Machir provided for Mephibosheth while he lived outside Jerusalem before David brings him into the city (9:4-5). Although David is described as physically depleted rather than disabled (cf. 16:14, 21:15), the physical imagery once again reinforces a change in his status during his exile. Imagery toward the end of 2 Samuel continues to develop themes of reversals in status that were introduced during Hannah's song in 1 Sam 2.

THE BOOK OF FIRST KINGS

First Kings continues the story of the monarchic period. The opening chapters narrate the transition of the kingship from David to Solomon. The book begins when David is old and too sick to warm himself even with coverings (1:1). His servants find a beautiful woman to lay with him for warmth (1:2; cf. Eccl 4:11). The text does not indicate whether this plan works. Instead, it only notes that David does not have sexual relations with her. This contrasts with his procreative success when he first became king (2 Sam 3:2-5, 5:13-16). Immediately after the story of David's sickness, his son Adonijah tries to claim his father's throne (1 Kgs 1:5-10) but loses out to his brother Solomon, who ultimately succeeds David (2:24). As with the disability imagery in Samuel, the imagery of sickness helps to mark a transition in leadership.

Although Solomon has a long and prosperous reign, the prophet Ahijah tells a man named Jeroboam that he will rule over ten of Israel's tribes because Solomon worshipped gods other than the LORD (11:31-39). Solomon tries to kill Jeroboam, but he flees to Egypt until after Solomon's death (11:40). When Solomon's son Rehoboam becomes king, Jeroboam returns from Egypt. He requests that the new king "lighten the hard service of your father and his heavy yoke that he placed on us" (12:4). When Rehoboam refuses this request, Jeroboam leads ten tribes in seceding from Judah and forming the northern nation of Israel (12:15-20). At first Jeroboam resembles a new "Moses." Although the parallels are not exact, the text associates Jeroboam with Egypt. He confronts a king regarding the forced labor imposed upon the Israelites (5:13-18; cf. Exod 1:11). The king threatens to increase the Israelites' oppression (1 Kgs 12:13-14; cf. Exod 5:7-9), but Jeroboam leads the Israelites to freedom and establishes a new nation. Yet the comparison to Moses breaks down when Jeroboam makes a golden calf in Dan and another one in Bethel and proclaims, "Here are your gods, O Israel, who brought you up out of the land of Egypt" (1 Kgs 12:28). This is almost exactly what Aaron says when he makes the golden calf at Sinai: "These are your gods, O Israel, who brought you up out of the land of Egypt" (Exod 32:4; cf. v. 8). Although this incident still resembles the Exodus story, Jeroboam begins to resemble Moses less and less.

In 1 Kgs 13 an unnamed prophet confronts Jeroboam at the altar at Bethel. He announces that the altar will be desecrated and torn down by the future king Josiah (13:2-3; cf. 2 Kgs 23:15-16). When he hears this announcement, Jeroboam "stretched out his hand from the altar, saying, 'Seize him!' But the hand that he stretched out against him withered" (1 Kgs 13:4). As with Moses' hand with a skin disease, Jeroboam's hand is restored in the following verses (13:6; cf. Exod 4:6-7). Nevertheless, as with Eli's dimmed eyesight, Jeroboam's withered hand reinforces a contrast between Moses and him. According to Deut 34:7, not only had Moses' eyesight not dimmed at the time of his death, but he also remained

"moist." The NRSV incorrectly translates the Hebrew word for moisture as "vigor." Yet Moses' retention of his "moisture" probably refers to
his unwrinkled or unwithered skin even at the age of 120 (Tigay 1995).
Remarkably, Moses had the eyesight and appearance of a much younger
person. As with the word "moist," the Hebrew word "withered" describes
one's skin or body in some biblical texts (Lam 4:8). The word "withered"
can represent the opposite of "moist." For example, Nazirites are not
allowed to "eat grapes, moist or withered" (Num 6:3). Jeroboam's hand
contrasts with Moses' youthful appearance and reinforces the idea that
ultimately Jeroboam is no Moses.

In 1 Kgs 14 Jeroboam's son and presumably the heir to his throne
becomes sick and dies (14:1, 5, 17). Elsewhere, a son's sickness may serve
as a divine punishment for a king's transgression. For example, although
the text uses a different word for sickness, David's unnamed son becomes
sick and dies as a divine punishment for David's actions regarding Uriah
and Bathsheba (2 Sam 12:14-19). Yet, like ritual impurity and disability,
the Hebrew Bible does not use sickness and disability interchangeably.
Although the prophet Malachi discusses sick animals along with animals
that are blind or lame (Mal 1:8, 13), the term that describes Jeroboam's
son's condition often describes a fatal or nonfatal illness or injury usually in
reference to otherwise nondisabled persons (e.g., 1 Sam 19:14; 2 Sam 13:5-
6; 1 Kgs 17:17, 22:34; 2 Kgs 1:2, 8:7, 13:14; 2 Chr 22:6; Ezek 34:4). For this
reason, one should not interpret Hezekiah, who is otherwise nondisabled,
as having a disability just because he becomes sick (1 Kgs 20:1-11; cf. Isa
38). A healthy person with a disability or a nondisabled person who is sick
is not an oxymoron.

When Jeroboam's son becomes sick, his unnamed wife disguises herself and consults the prophet Ahijah in Shiloh (14:2-3). The text notes,
"Now Ahijah could not see, for his eyes were set because of his age" (14:4).
Ahijah's blindness is described with nearly the exact same phrase as 1 Sam
4:15 uses to describe Eli's blindness. Moreover, both Eli and Ahijah are
from Shiloh (1:9 and 1 Kgs 11:29, respectively). The difference between
Eli and Abijah is that the former must rely on others to receive divine messages whereas the latter receives the message that he delivers to Jeroboam's
wife directly from the LORD (14:7-14). As discussed earlier, Eli functions
as a priest and a judge but never a prophet. In either case, the inability
to see does not disqualify them from serving in their respective offices.
Eli retains his authority as priest in Shiloh during his lifetime. Likewise,
Ahijah retains his authority as a prophet in Shiloh. In fact, the narrator

refers back to Ahijah's prophecy regarding the fall of Jeroboam's household explicitly when this household comes to an end in the next chapter (15:27-30).

While 1 Kgs 15 narrates the demise of Jeroboam's potential dynasty, it also reiterates the LORD's commitment to the Davidic dynasty (15:4; cf. 1 Sam 3:3, discussed above). Unlike the Israelite king Jeroboam, disability or disease imagery is not associated with the end of the Davidic dynasty at this point. For example, regarding King Asa of Judah, the narrator states, "But in his old age he was diseased in his feet" (1 Kgs 15:23). This comment occurs after the narrator heavily praises Asa and notes that he reigned for forty-one years, which is among the longest reigns of any king of Judah or Israel (15:10-11). Although the text does not indicate Asa's age when he began to reign (contrast 14:21, 22:42), it is quite possible that his long reign lasted well into what would be considered old age in ancient Israel. If so, there is no reason to assume that Asa did not remain king for many years after he acquired this disease. Asa's reign partially overlaps with Jeroboam's reign (15:9). Yet in contrast to Jeroboam's withered hand, Asa's diseased feet are unrelated to a change in his authority.

In 1 Kgs 16 Ahab becomes king over Israel (16:29). Most of the remaining chapters in 1 Kgs focus on his reign. Ahab worshipped Baal and built a temple for this god (16:31-32). According to 16:33, he provoked the LORD's anger more than all the previous kings of Israel (cf. 22:53). During Ahab's reign, the Israelites' loyalty waffles between Baal and the LORD. The prophet Elijah confronts the people, saying, "How long will you go limping with two different opinions? If the LORD is God, walk after him; but if Baal, then walk after him" (18:21). Elijah uses imagery of disability (limping) and nondisability (walking after) to contrast the Israelites' indecisive behavior with the loyalty that they should demonstrate. A few verses later, the narrator returns to the same disability imagery. When the prophets of Baal attempt to evoke a response from Baal, the narrator states, "They limped about the altar that they had made" (18:26). The narrator uses mobility impairment imagery (cf. 2 Sam 4:4) when describing unsuccessful attempts at divine communication. By contrast, after Elijah defeats the prophets of Baal, the narrator describes Elijah with divinely enhanced mobility when he outruns Ahab's chariot (1 Kgs 18:46).

THE BOOK OF SECOND KINGS

Shortly before Elijah ascends to heaven (2 Kgs 2:11), the prophet Elisha requests a "double share" of Elijah's spirit (2:9). Over the next several chapters, Elisha performs a series of miracles, several involving disability imagery, which help to verify his prophetic authority. In 2:19, when Elisha is told that a city's water is bad and its land miscarries, he pours salt into the water and declares, "Thus says the LORD, I have made this water wholesome; from now on neither death nor miscarriage shall come from it" (2:21). Elisha also demonstrates control over human fertility when he is told about a woman who has no son and her husband is old (4:14), which could imply infertility on either the wife's or husband's part. Elisha announces that she will have a son, and his prophecy is fulfilled shortly thereafter (4:16-17).

Elisha exhibits divinely endorsed control over skin diseases in 2 Kgs 5. An Aramean officer named Naaman has a skin disease but is healed when he follows Elisha's instructions to wash in the Jordan (5:1-14). Afterward, Elisha's servant Gehazi lies to Naaman to get money from him. As punishment, Elisha brings Naaman's skin disease onto Gehazi, declaring that "the skin disease of Naaman shall cling to you, and your descendants forever" (5:27; cf. David's curse of Joab, discussed above). Permanent skin diseases serve as a form of divine punishment elsewhere in 2 Kings. In 15:4-5 the narrator states that during King Azariah's reign over Judah, "The high places were not taken away; the people still sacrificed and made offerings on the high places. The LORD struck the king, so that he had a skin disease to the day of his death, and lived in a separate house" (cf. 2 Chr 26:16-21). Nevertheless, as discussed earlier (consult the discussion of 2 Sam 3:29), skin diseases were not considered disabilities. As in 2 Samuel, 1 and 2 Kings does not conceive of disabilities as a form of divine punishment.

During the wars between Aram and Israel, Elisha's miracles and prophecies involve not only skin diseases but also blindness. When the Arameans attack Israel, Elisha prays, "Strike this people, please, with blindness" (2 Kgs 6:18). Then, Elisha delivers the now-blinded army to the king of Israel in the capital city of Samaria. Once in the city, Elisha prays for their eyesight to return (6:20). Elisha's control over the Arameans' eyesight reinforces his prophetic authority. When the Arameans attack again, they surround Samaria and try to starve the Israelites out (6:24-25). During the siege, Elisha prophesies that the Israelites will have abundant food the next day (7:1). That night, four men who are outside the city gate with skin diseases (cf. Lev 13:46; Num 5:2-3) go to the Aramean camp. These four men discover the camp abandoned except for food, gold, silver, and clothing (2 Kgs 7:8). The narrator explains that the Arameans had fled because God "had caused the Aramean army to hear the sound of chariots, and of horses, the sound of a great army" (7:6). The narrator explicitly confirms the fulfillment of Elisha's prophecy when the Israelites plunder food from the abandoned camp (7:16). While Elisha's prophecy does not involve skin diseases directly, people with skin diseases become the catalyst for its fulfillment.

Often we imagine persons with disabilities as the ones who are healed or the recipients of miracles rather than as those capable of performing healings or miracles. Yet the only physical description of Elisha himself occurs when, as he travels to Bethel, "some small boys came out of the city and jeered at him, saying 'Go away, baldhead! Go away, baldhead'" (2:23). A possible, although uncertain, connection between baldness and disability exists in the MT. The word "baldhead" is spelled according to a pattern used to spell Hebrew nouns for various physical differences, including disabilities (consult the discussion of Eli's "dim" eyesight above). Moreover, Lev 13:40 specifies that baldness, like other disabilities, is not a source of impurity. While a contemporary audience might not connect baldness with disabilities, this connection points to how notions of disability are culturally situated rather than universally inherent Elisha's appalling reaction to the boys' jeers provides another confirmation of the prophetic authority that he inherited from Elijah. A bear mauls forty-two of the boys after Elisha curses them in the name of the LORD (2 Kgs 2:24). Rather than reinforcing a romantic stereotype of supposedly noble persons with disabilities as always virtuous, patient, or gracious, this horrific scene provides a cautionary tale against mocking persons with disabilities (cf. Lev 19:14; Deut 27:18).

Another possible, but uncertain, use of disability imagery during Elisha's prophetic career occurs when he instructs another prophet to anoint Jehu as king over Israel (2 Kgs 9:1-3; cf. 1 Kgs 19:16-17). This prophet does so and tells Jehu that he will overthrow Israel's current royal household (2 Kgs 9:8-10; cf. 9:14–10:17). Afterward, the other army officers ask Jehu, "Why did that madman come to you?" (9:11). Other texts characterize prophets as "madmen," possibly due to a perceived loss of self-control during prophetic activity (Jer 29:26; Hos 9:7). The term also describes David's behavior in Gath, which may suggest an unspecified cognitive or emotional disability (consult the earlier discussion of 1 Sam 21:10-15). In other words, imagery that could be associated with disabilities once again occurs in passages dealing with shifts in leadership. Yet unlike the use of disability imagery to mark outsiders during leadership changes in Samuel, possible use of such imagery in this passage and elsewhere in Kings marks the one who announces a leadership change. As discussed earlier, the prophet Ahijah announces the fall of Jeroboam's household after he becomes blind (1 Kgs 14:1-17).

The final chapter of 2 Kings revisits imagery of disability from earlier books when narrating the climactic shifts in leadership when the Babylonians capture Jerusalem. In 24:15-17 the Babylonians imprison the Judean king Jehoiachin and establish Zedekiah as king in his place. After Zedekiah rebels and then flees Jerusalem, the Babylonians capture him on the plains of Jericho. They gouge Zedekiah's eyes out, bind him in bronze shackles, and take him to Babylon (25:5-7; cf. Jer 39:5-7, 52:8-11). His fate is strikingly similar to Samson's fate when the Philistines gouge out his eyes and bind him in bronze shackles (Judg 16:21).

Zedekiah's fate also recalls language from Joshua and Samuel. Outside 2 Kgs 25:5, the only biblical references to the plains of Jericho occur when the Israelites successfully enter Canaan and the males are circumcised at the "plains of Jericho" (Josh 4:13, 5:10). Like the Israelites in Joshua, Zedekiah experiences a physical alteration after reaching the plains of Jericho. Yet after he unsuccessfully attempts to escape from Canaan, Zedekiah's physical alteration is socially disabling rather than enhancing. Physical alterations with contrasting social significance mark Israel's entry into and exit from Canaan. Moreover, when David first conquers Jerusalem, the narrator states that the "blind and the lame" were prohibited from entering the "house," which refers either to the temple, David's palace, or Jerusalem (2 Sam 5:8). In 2 Kgs 25 the last Davidic descendant to rule in Jerusalem ends up blind and imprisoned far outside the city. By revisiting the physical imagery used to narrate Israelite entries into the land and into the capital city, Zedekiah's fate marks a grim reversal of fortunes.

Yet the story does not end with Zedekiah. In the final verses of 2 Kings, the Babylonian king releases Jehoiachin from prison but never restores him to his throne. Rather, according to 25:29, "Every day of [Jehoichin's] life he always ate in the king's presence." While this verse does not include any disability imagery, it recalls the fate of Saul's grandson Mephibosheth after his household lost the throne. While Mephibosheth, who had a disability, never won back his grandfather's throne from David, "he always ate at the king's table. Now he was lame in both his feet" (2 Sam 9:13). The final scene in Joshua–2 Kings depicts an exiled Israelite using imagery previously associated with arguably the most prominent character with a disability in any of these books.

CONCLUSIONS

As we have discovered in this brief survey of images of disability in Joshua–2 Kings, the deployment of imagery of disability and what it may represent is as varied as the many ways that disability manifests itself within human experience. Rather than trying to reduce these images in Joshua–2 Kings to transparent or stable meanings—be they theological, political, or otherwise—these books serve as a prime example of how biblical authors employed disability as a powerful means of expressing the rich diversity and complexity of our lived experience. Indeed, as the story of Israel continues beyond Joshua–2 Kings, imagery of disability will become one of the most dominant metaphors for Israel's collective experience in the post-monarchic period (Isa 42:19, 52:13–53:12; Jer 31:6-8; Mic 4:6-7; Zeph 3:16-20).

WORKS CITED

Alter, Robert. 1999. *The David Story: A Translation with Commentary of 1 and 2 Samuel*. New York: W. W. Norton.

Avalos, Hector. 1995. *Illness and Health Care in the Ancient Near East: The Role of the Temple in Greece, Mesopotamia, and Israel*. Harvard Semitic Monographs 54. Atlanta: Scholars.

Baden, Joel S. 2011. "The Nature of Barrenness in the Hebrew Bible." Pages 13–27 in *Disability Studies and Biblical Literature*. Edited by Candida R. Moss and Jeremy Schipper. New York: Palgrave Macmillan.

Esler, Philip F. 1998. "The Madness of King Saul: A Cultural Reading of 1 Samuel 8–31." Pages 220–62 in *Biblical Studies—Cultural Studies: The Third Sheffield Colloquium*. Edited by J. Cheryl Exum and Stephen D. Moore. Sheffield: Sheffield Academic.

Exum, J. Cheryl. 1996. *Plotted, Shot, and Painted: Cultural Representations of Biblical Women*. Journal for the Study of the Old Testament Supplement Series 215. Sheffield: Sheffield Academic.

———. 1998. "Lovis Corinth's 'Blinded Samson.'" *Biblical Illustrator* 6: 410–25.

Galpaz-Feller, Pnina. 2006. *Samson: The Legend and the Man: The Story of Samson (Judges 13–16)*. Bern: Peter Lang.

Garland-Thomson, Rosemarie. 2009. *Staring: How We Look*. New York: Oxford University Press.

Hallo, William W., ed. 1997. *Canonical Compositions from the Biblical World*. Vol. 1 of *The Context of Scripture*. Leiden: Brill. [= COS]

Hubbard, Robert L. 1988. *The Book of Ruth*. New International Commentary on the Old Testament. Grand Rapids: Eerdmans.

Hutton, Jeremy M. 2009. *The Transjordanian Palimpsest: The Overwritten Texts of Personal Exile and Transformation in the Deuteronomistic History*. Beihefte zur Zeitschrift für die altestamentliche Wissenschaft 396. New York: de Gruyter.

McCarter, P. Kyle. 1980. *I Samuel: A New Translation with Introduction and Commentary*. Anchor Bible 8. Garden City, N.Y.: Doubleday.

Mitchell, David T., and Sharon L. Snyder. 1997. "Introduction: Disability Studies and the Double Bind of Representation." Pages 1–31 in *The Body and Physical Difference: Discourses of Disability*. Edited by Mitchell and Snyder. Ann Arbor: University of Michigan Press.

———. 2000. *Narrative Prosthesis: Disability and the Dependencies of Discourse*. Ann Arbor: University of Michigan Press.

Moulton, Vincent. 2014. "Sight and Sightlessness: An Evaluation of the Exegetical Diversity of Samson's Blindness." Paper presented at the annual meeting of the Society of Biblical Literature. San Diego, Calif., November 25.

Olyan, Saul M. 2008. *Disability in the Hebrew Bible: Interpreting Mental and Physical Differences*. New York: Cambridge University Press.

Parker, Simon B. 1976. "The Marriage Blessing in Israelite and Ugaritic Literature." *Journal of Biblical Literature* 95: 23–30.

Polzin, Robert. 1989. *Samuel and the Deuteronomist: A Literary Study of the Deuteronomic History*. Part 2, *1 Samuel*. San Francisco: Harper & Row.

Sasson, Jack M. 1995. *Ruth: A New Translation with a Philological Commentary and a Formalist-Folklorist Interpretation*. 2nd ed. Biblical Seminar 10. Sheffield: Sheffield Academic.

Schipper, Jeremy. 2006. *Disability Studies and the Hebrew Bible: Figuring Mephibosheth in the David Story*. New York: T&T Clark.

———. 2007. "Disabling Israelite Leadership: 2 Samuel 6:23 and Other Images of Disability in the Deuteronomistic History." Pages 103–13 in *This Abled Body: Rethinking Disability and Biblical Studies*. Edited by Hector Avalos, Sarah Melcher, and Jeremy Schipper. Semeia Studies 55. Atlanta: Society of Biblical Literature.

———. 2011. *Disability and Isaiah's Suffering Servant*. Oxford: Oxford University Press.

———. 2016. *Ruth: A New Translation with Introduction and Commentary*. Anchor Yale Bible. New Haven: Yale University Press.

Tigay, Jeffrey H. 1995. "*lo ʾnasleho*, 'He Had Not Become Wrinkled' (Deut. 34:7)." Pages 345–50 in *Solving Riddles and Untying Knots: Biblical, Epigraphic, and Semitic Studies in Honor of Jonas C. Greenfield*. Edited by Ziony Zevit, Seymour Gitin, and Michael Sokoloff. Winona Lake, Ind.: Eisenbrauns.

van der Toorn, Karel. 1986. "Judges XVI 21 in the Light of Akkadian Sources." *Vetus Testamentum* 36: 248–53.

Wynn, Kerry. 2007. "The Normate Hermeneutic and Interpretations of Disability in Yahwistic Narratives." Pages 91–101 in *This Abled Body: Rethinking Disability and Biblical Studies*. Edited by Hector Avalos, Sarah Melcher, and Jeremy Schipper. Semeia Studies 55. Atlanta: Society of Biblical Literature.

First and Second Chronicles–Esther

Kerry H. Wynn

The five books that will be examined here are found in the third section of the Hebrew canon, the Ketuvim or Writings, and within the Historical Books of the Christian canon. While all five books share a common concern with Jewish identity after the exile, 1 and 2 Chronicles are set within preexilic Judah, Ezra–Nehemiah within the community of the return from exile, and Esther within the exilic community itself. When we turn to the task of relating these five books to disability, the range of the material found in these five books becomes rather problematic, for only 1 and 2 Chronicles make direct reference to physical diversity.

METHODOLOGIES

Within the following commentary, disability will determine methodology, and it is assumed that Scripture "is redemptive for the experience of disability" (Yong 2011, 6–7). Indeed, if Scripture is not good news for people with disabilities, it is not good news for anyone. The methodologies used in the following discussion will be eclectic and will be adapted to address disability and the good news.

Chronicles contains ample material related to disability. This material becomes more extensive when we examine how the Chronicler redacted the Pentateuch and the Deuteronomic History, the Chronicler's primary sources, in rewriting Israel's monarchical and cultic history. The Chronicler dealt with Deuteronomistic disabilities through retention, revision, expansion, and erasure (Jonker 2008, 713–14). The Chronicler's shaping of this history reveals his understanding of disability within his context.

In Ezra–Nehemiah and Esther, on the other hand, where disability is virtually nonexistent, a historical-critical examination of disability is no longer possible. Thus the text must be mined for parallels to the contemporary experience of disability. In Ezra–Nehemiah we find an analogy between Jerusalem—the disabled city—and the contemporary experience of disability. This parallel can shed analogical light on the biblical narrative. While Esther has no direct reference to disability, it provides an opportunity for intertextual analysis through the survival of two Greek recensions in addition to the Masoretic Text (MT). Esther's experience raises the issues of passing, dependence, and independence, which are key disability concerns in the modern world.

FIRST AND SECOND CHRONICLES

The Chronicler's History (CH) provided a postexilic reinterpretation of the preexilic history of Israel differing from the one found in the earlier Deuteronomic History (DH). "First and foremost in the Chronicler's presentation is his understanding of the identity of the postexilic community" (Jonker 2008, 714). The goal of the Chronicler was to enable the Jewish community returning to Jerusalem to retain a sense of corporate identity in the absence of the Davidic monarchy—an identity that transcended time and space. The Chronicler focused on the two institutions of the Zion covenant, the throne and the temple, as of central concern. This does not mean that the covenants with Abraham and Moses are not foundational to the Chronicler's project. Hahn notes that 2 Chr 3:1 is the only place in the Hebrew Bible where the Temple Mount is identified with Mount Moriah, the sight of the binding of Isaac (Gen 22:1-14). This "serves to bind the Davidic covenant with the Abrahamic covenant, as well as the worship of the patriarchs with the sacrifices of the temple" (Hahn 2012, 30). Turning to the Mosaic covenant, Hahn asserts that, for the Chronicler, "David and Solomon are exalted as the ideal kings, but their kingship and kingdom are premised on the Sinai covenant and serve to fulfill that covenant, not supersede it" (50). This foundational role of the Sinai covenant applies to the cult as well as the monarchy, for the author "presents the Davidic temple liturgy as an authentic development of the tradition of worship established by Moses on Sinai" (126). Japhet identifies a two-stage process for this development: "First, the Law, with its precepts and the details of the sacrificial cult, was given through Moses; then the place of worship, its order and organization were established as permanent institutions by David and achieved their complete realization under Solomon" (1993,

45). The chief task of the Davidic monarchy for the Chronicler was to build the Jerusalem temple and to establish the Aaronic priesthood and the Levitical offices in line with the Mosaic law. CH reshapes DH to bring it into greater conformity with the Pentateuch, which became authoritative Scripture in the postexilic community (Neh 8).

Myers notes, however, that for the Chronicler "the Davidic line had come to an end in the eclipse of Zerubbabel," and "political control was largely in the hands of the priesthood who guided the affairs of the little community until the time of Nehemiah" (1965, xxvii). Nehemiah, however, was a Persian appointee and not a Davidic monarch. Thus, "the political aspect of the Davidic line had come to an end," and "hope for Israel lay in the fortification of the religious institutions that survived the tragic experiences of 587 BC and the long years of Exile" (xxx). Thus, CH establishes a three-stage process rather than Japhet's two. The worship of the Jerusalem community may have been designed by Moses and established by David, but it is administered by the Aaronic priesthood and the Levitical offices. When a king offers sacrifices in CH, he, like any other member of the community, presents the offering to the priests, who administer the sacrifice as set forth in Leviticus. A king can give a royal blessing, but only a priest can give a priestly blessing. This distinction between priest and king is central to the Chronicler's theology of the survival of the Jerusalem community apart from the Davidic monarchy, a distinction that determines the Chronicler's use of disability. That the Davidic monarchs present sacrifices at the Jerusalem temple at times of dedication and rededication is a reflection of their role as the ones who establish worship, not as the ones who administer worship.

Mount Moriah and Mount Sinai are united to Mount Zion, and all three covenants are actualized through temple worship. Sacramentally, the physical presence of the Davidic monarch is no more essential than are the presence of Abraham and Moses for Israel to live within this triad of covenants. The Chronicler is open to a possible return of the Davidic monarchy, but as Klein notes, "The Chronicler nowhere explicitly advocates the reestablishment of the Davidic monarchy," for the author "seems relatively content with life under Persian suzerainty, provided that the worship at the temple in Jerusalem is able to continue without restraint" (2006, 47). It is temple worship that has become the basis of the community's identity. "The postexilic community," concludes Jonker, "is therefore first and foremost understood to be a religious community, not a political one" (2008, 715). The Davidic kingdom has been transformed into what Hahn has so aptly called a "liturgical empire."

These theological concerns are the basis for the representation of disability and nonnormate physicalities that we find in CH. While non-normative physicalities may be used to describe the prowess of military allies (1 Chr 12:2, 8; 2 Chr 15:7) or foes (1 Chr 11:23, 20:4-8), it is primarily these key concerns for throne and temple, identity and community, that underpin the Chronicler's shaping and reshaping of physical conditions—whether disease or disability, wound or so-called "leprosy"—that deviate from normate standards.

Erasures

The most obvious erasure of disability within CH is the erasure of Mephibosheth, the son of Jonathan and grandson of Saul (2 Sam 9, etc.). He is only retained as "Meribbaal" (1 Chr 8:34, 9:40) within the extensive genealogical material that the Chronicler uses to link the pre- and postexilic communities in order to establish continuity within Israel. Mephibosheth's story is erased because it has no value for the author's theological agenda.

Of greater significance is the erasure of disability found when moving from 2 Sam 5:6-10 to 1 Chr 11:4-9. Reasons given for this erasure range from the assertion that David's hatred of people with disabilities went counter to the Chronicler's intent to exalt David as the ideal king to the suggestion that this account of disability in DH was too obscure for the Chronicler to include (Klein 2006, 300, 301 n. 31). When the Chronicler's historical context and theological concerns are taken into consideration, however, this erasure becomes understandable.

The Chronicler's issue lies with the proverbial edict in 2 Sam 5:8b: "Therefore it is said, 'The blind and the lame shall not come into the house.'" While there is some uncertainty as to how "the house" is to be understood, it is likely that the Chronicler understood it as a reference to the Jerusalem temple, as did the translators of the LXX, who translate the simple Hebrew "the house" (הַבָּיִת, habbāyit) as "the house of the Lord" (οἶκον κυρίου, oikon kyriou) with the Vulgate reading "the temple" (templum) (McCarter 1984, 140; Brueggemann 1990, 240; cf. Schipper 2006, 105 n. 10). While this maxim is not attributed to David himself, a Davidic origin seems to be implied. The Chronicler does not have just his DH Vorlage before him but also the now-canonical Pentateuch. This prohibition is in direct conflict with the passage on blemished priests in Lev 21:16-24. While a blemished priest, including "one who is blind or lame" (21:18), "shall not come near to offer the food of his God" (21:21)—that is, to serve at the altar—such a priest "may eat the food of his God, of the most holy as well as of the holy" (21:22). While those offerings designated "holy" may be eaten outside the temple by both the priests and their households, those designated "most holy" could only be eaten by males within the temple precincts themselves (Lev 7:1-6, 10:12-20, 22:10-14, 24:5-9; Num 18:9-13). Therefore, if males of the priestly family are permitted to eat the "most holy," then they must be allowed into the temple precincts contrary to the maxim in 2 Sam 5:8b (Milgrom 2000, 1826). While the Chronicler may have David expand on the Mosaic legislation in order to implement the cult, he cannot allow him to establish a practice that is independent of, much less contrary to, the Mosaic Torah. Thus the prohibition in 2 Sam 5:8b must go.

The establishment of Jerusalem as the City of David is central to the Chronicler's project. Thus, unlike the story of Mephibosheth, the account of David's conquest of the city cannot be erased in its entirety. Indeed, as Japhet has noted, the Chronicler has violated both chronology and literary structure to give the conquest of Jerusalem a central role within the account of David's accession to the throne (1993, 233–34). The Chronicler also revised the identification of David's forces, which are no longer David's private mercenary army, "the king and his men," but are now "David and all Israel." Thus David is established as king, and simultaneously Jerusalem becomes the center of the religious and political life of all Israel (239; Myers 1965, 85). The identification of Jerusalem as "the City of David" no longer means that the city is the personal property of the Davidic monarchy but that it is the center of the Davidic establishment of Israel's worship. Within this context, the erasure of DH's references to people with disabilities enhances the harmonious nature of the Chronicler's portrait of the unity and continuity of the triune covenant promised to Abraham, defined by Moses, established by David, and actualized by the priests and Levites through temple worship. The erasure is not related to any view held regarding disability but serves to harmonize Mosaic legislation with Davidic practice.

Retentions

The simplest erasures of nonnormate physicalities are those embedded in DH's history of the Northern Kingdom, which is virtually written out of CH, save where it affects the Southern Kingdom or the Davidic monarchy or is merged into "all Israel." Where such physical conditions are retained, such as the fatal wounds of Ahab in 2 Chr 18:33-34 (1 Kgs 9:16) and Joram in 2 Chr 22:6 (2 Kgs 9:15), they bear directly upon the history of the Southern Kingdom and the Davidic monarchy. These particular incidents reveal how the etiology of such physical conditions was viewed by the Chronicler. The wounding of Ahab is the result of a very human action, an arrow in battle, but it is attributed to God as the fulfillment of prophecy. The wounding of Joram, on the other hand, is presented as one of the natural and inevitable outcomes of war with no divine or demonic etiology implied. This is the way of the world among mortals. It may be governed by the divine order, but it is not presented as a direct divine action against Joram. God's judgment on Joram comes with his death at the hands of Jehu.

The verb חָלָה (ḥālâ) is used to describe the conditions of both Ahab and Joram in DH and CH. In addition to the use of חָלָה (ḥālâ) in 2 Chr 18:33 and 2 Chr 22:6, the Chronicler uses the term in both 2 Chr 32:24 and 35:23 in relation to the two kings of Judah who are only surpassed by David himself, Hezekiah and Josiah, respectively. Second Chronicles brings ḥālâ over from 2 Kgs 20:1, but 2 Chr 35:23 introduces the term into a quote from Josiah, where no parallel quote appears in DH. In the case of Hezekiah the term refers to a natural illness, while in the case of Josiah it refers to a fatal battle wound. We will look at the two Davidic kings more closely when we examine revisions. Here we would note that the physical "weakness," the ḥālâ in these passages, covers very disparate etiologies and morphologies. We only have clear divine retribution in the case of Ahab where retribution does not take the form of disability or disease but death.

Klein maintains that "the doctrine of rewards and punishments takes on a special form in Chronicles" where "these rewards/punishments are more immediate and individual" (2006, 46). What role disability, disease, and death play in this paradigm will need to be examined throughout the following discussion. Here it should be noted that retribution is not synonymous with punishment. There are two forms of punishment to be found in CH: retribution, yes, but also discipline. We will find no monolithic view of reward and punishment, however, within the Chronicler's understanding of nonnormate physicalities.

EXPANSIONS

Pestilence and Plague

David's census is one of the few accounts found in DH (2 Sam 24) retained by CH (1 Chr 21:1–22:1) that presents David in a negative light. The Chronicler's concern for David centers on his role as the one who, with his son Solomon, established the temple cultus (Myers 1965, 146). This passage becomes important to the Chronicler because it presents David at worship. What is more important is that through the addition of 1 Chr 22:1 to the DH account, the Chronicler shows David establishing the site of the Jerusalem temple. The abatement of the plague sets the precedent for what the Chronicler sees as a key function of the temple as well (2 Chr 6:28-31, 7:12-14, 20:9).

While the Chronicler shifts the responsibility for inciting David to take the census from God in DH to "Satan" or "an adversary" in 1 Chr 21:1, the nature of David's transgression remains elusive. There is no biblical prohibition of such a census. Indeed, the book of Numbers (1:1-47) opens with God commanding Moses to take just such a census as the one taken by David. Only the tribe of Levi is exempted from Moses' military census (Num 1:48-49). While there is no stated exemption of the tribe of Levi in David's census in DH, the Chronicler reports that Joab took it upon himself to omit not only the tribe of Levi from the census but also the tribe of Benjamin (1 Chr 21:6). The ban on the counting of Levi applies only to a military census, for it is permitted to count the Levites for cultic purposes (Num 3–4). CH reports David undertaking just such a census without penalty in 1 Chr 23. The only warning regarding such a census is found in Exod 30:11-16 (Johnstone 1997, 227–29). Here a half-shekel offering is required from everyone registered "so that no plague may come upon them" (30:12). No mention is made in CH regarding this "ransom," however, and if this were the central problem, we would expect Joab to have offered the collection of this payment rather than opposing the census itself. While this link is tenuous, it implies far less than the usual attempts to psychologize David conjecturing an improper attitude on the king's part, an attitude for which the text gives no evidence. The link between census, plague, and worship site, which is central to the Chronicler, is also central to Exod 30:11-16.

The warning in Exod 30:11-16 falls within the description of the tabernacle and is preceded by the description of the altar of incense (30:1-10) and followed by the description of the bronze basin for washing (30:17-21). The link appears to lie in 30:10 with its prescription for the "rite of atonement" (וְכִפֶּר, wĕkipper), which precedes the command in 30:11-16 that those who are registered "shall give a ransom (כֹּפֶר, kōper) for their lives to the Lord" in order "to make atonement" (לְכַפֵּר, lĕkappēr). The "atonement (הַכִּפֻּרִים, hakkippurîm) money" was to be "for the service of the tent of meeting" and a remembrance "of the ransom (לְכַפֵּר, lĕkappēr) given for your lives." This link embeds 30:11-16 within the guidelines for the establishment of the tabernacle, guidelines that the Chronicler will adapt as both David's preparations for the temple in 1 Chr 22:2-5 and his guidelines for Solomon in 1 Chr 28:11-19. Johnstone concludes, "David's neglect of these necessary preliminaries to the muster of the host of Israel, with the involvement of the Levites," is what "lies at the heart of his offence" and "will bring the penalty not just on himself but on Israel" (1997, 229).

Thus the danger of a "plague" (נֶגֶף, *negep*) is linked to the taking of a census in Exod 30:12. While the noun *negep* does not appear in the account in 1 Chr 21, the more common cognate מַגֵּפָה (*maggēpâ*) is found in this chapter (Johnstone 1997, 229). Both words share the common verbal root נָגַף (*nāgap*, to "strike" or "smite"). The Chronicler uses the term in 1 Chr 21:17, where David pleads with God, declaring, "Do not let your people be plagued (*maggēpâ*)!" and in 21:22 when he tells Ornan to sell him his threshing floor "so the plague (*maggēpâ*) may be averted from the people" (2 Sam 24:22; cf. 25). The term *maggēpâ*, however, does not necessarily imply a form of disease but could also be used of slaughter in battle (1 Sam 4:17; 2 Sam 17:9), and it is likely that famine could be categorized as *maggēpâ* as well. "Plague," whether *negep* or *maggēpâ*, should be understood as a variety of calamities that might fall on a community, and thus all three items on the menu Gad presents to David would be considered as "plagues," not just pestilence alone.

The Chronicler has not only adopted but has also adapted the triad of plagues presented to David in 2 Sam 24:13. The Chronicler lists famine (רָעָב, *rāāv*), the sword (חֶרֶב, *herev*) of David's enemies; and pestilence (דֶּבֶר, *dever*), identified as "the sword of the Lord" in 1 Chr 21:12. DH makes no mention of either the sword of the enemy or the sword of the Lord. The Chronicler's reference to "the sword of your enemies" makes the fatal nature of this judgment more specific than DH's "while they pursue you." It also brings the terminology he uses into alignment with the classical triple-threat formula as seen particularly in Jeremiah and Ezekiel. The triad of threats in these prophets is not a menu but a progression describing God's judgment in the form of foreign invasion and deportation (Ezek 7:15). The invasion by Babylon incorporates all three threats. Thus, the order used by these two prophets varies from the order found in DH and CH. There the dominant order is sword, famine, pestilence (Jer 14:12; Ezek 6:11; etc). The invader attacks with the sword; devastates the land, leaving famine in his wake; and lays siege to the city, where pestilence will inevitably break out (Morschauser 2010, 299–300). While both prophets vary the order (Jer 34:17; Ezek 5:12), only a few preclude this tripartite image of war (Jer 21:6-7).

While the Chronicler adopts the standardized terminology of the prophetic imagery, he retains DH's use of the terminology as a menu of curses.

This menu is also found in the prayer of Solomon in 2 Chr 6:28, where CH adopts its *Vorlage* in 1 Kgs 8:37 verbatim. This treatment of the list as three independent curses does not necessarily negate the tripartite single image of war and destruction. Johnstone (1997, 232) observes that the "choice of only one of the three is a measure of the divine leniency." Rightfully, the entire package should have befallen David and all Israel.

The term *dever*, usually translated "pestilence," is always communal, almost always punishment for sin, and always fatal. Indeed, where LXX reads *dever* in its Hebrew *Vorlage*, it consistently translates *dever* with θάνατος (*thanatos*, "death") itself. It is generally directed at human beings, but on a few occasions at animals (Exod 9:3; Jer 21:7; Ezek 14:19, 21). This LXX tripartite image of war is expanded into the Four Horsemen of the Apocalypse in Rev 6:1-8, with "Death" as the final rider. In the final analysis, pestilence is neither disease nor disability but death itself.

Neither crime nor punishment is the Chronicler's primary concern in this account of pestilence. The primary role of this plague is constructive rather than destructive. The Chronicler is relating the story of how God is building up his priestly kingdom, and the plagues are tools to be used by God in that construction. Again, the addition of 1 Chr 22:1 moves beyond the account in DH by identifying this event with the establishment of the temple site. "The centre of gravity of the chapter," Japhet observes, "is the concluding passage added by Chronicles to the original narrative, relating the dedication of the altar and the assignment of the sacred precinct as the future site of the Temple" (1993, 372).

Gad relays the angelic command to David, instructing him to build an altar at Ornan's threshing floor (1 Chr 21:18), which David understands is necessary "so that the plague may be averted from the people" (1 Chr 21:22). If the transgression of the census is to be related to Exod 30:11-16, we would expect that the solution to the plague would be to pay the per capita ransom "for the service of the tent of meeting." Here the Chronicler adds 1 Chr 21:29-30 to DH to explain that David could not go to the tabernacle in Gibeon "for he was afraid of the sword of the angel of the Lord."

David is thus cut off from the "tent of meeting," which he has failed to serve according to the Mosaic law. So "when David saw that the Lord answered him at the threshing floor of Ornan the Jebusite, he made his sacrifices there" (1 Chr 21:28). Indeed in 1 Chr 22:1, David transfers all the functions of the tabernacle now at Gibeon to the new site of "the house of the Lord." While 1 Chr 21:25 multiples the price of the field found in 2 Sam 24:24 twelvefold, perhaps symbolizing the ransom of the twelve tribes (Myers 1965, 149; Klein 2006, 428), as well as changing silver to gold, this sum still falls short of Israel's requisite half shekel per capita atonement. Once David transfers the role of the "tent of meeting" to "the house of the Lord," he immediately begins to collect resources for the "service" of this new cultic site in 1 Chr 22:2-5, resources that would most likely exceed the ransom or atonement price due from the census (cf. 1 Chr 22:14). The plague becomes the tool by which God leads David to the temple site and begins the preparations for its erection.

This identification of the new site of "the house of the Lord" with the site where David "called upon the Lord, and he answered him with fire from heaven on the altar of burnt offering" (1 Chr 21:26) sets the stage for the future role of the temple. While 2 Sam 24:25 makes no mention of fire from heaven, its role in 1 Chr 21:26 is to link the event to the sacrifices at the dedication of the temple in 2 Chr 7:1 immediately following Solomon's dedicatory prayer beseeching God to answer prayers in times of famine, pestilence, war, and other traumas (2 Chr 6:28-31). Japhet notes that the prayer "reveals a special degree of sensitivity to human suffering" (1993, 596–97). This is evident in the fact that "the distinct features of the retribution cycle, 'because they have sinned against thee' and 'acknowledgment of thy name,' are omitted." Solomon prays that God will "forgive, and render to all whose heart you know, according to all their ways, for only you know the human heart" (2 Chr 6:30). God will need to "forgive" some and simply "render" or "give" to others in relieving these plagues. The Psalms reflect that the temple cult provided for the restoration of the health of both those who were innocent (Ps 31) and those who had transgressed (Ps 39). There is no cause-and-effect relationship between plague and punishment within Solomon's prayer or in Jehoshaphat's reiteration of the prayer in 2 Chr 20:9, where only "judgment" by its very nature would imply guilt. It is only when we turn to God's response to Solomon's prayer in 2 Chr 7:12-14 that we find "pestilence" initiated directly by God and the proviso that Israel must "turn from their wicked ways" if God is to "forgive their sin and heal their land." Plague and pestilence may or may not be punishment, but what is assured, in either case, is if God's people turn to the temple with prayer and sacrifice, they will be delivered. The assurance of this lies in the fact that God has already provided such deliverance for David at this very site, even before the temple was ever built.

There is an ancillary proactive role for this plague. While 1 Chr 21:5 reports that the census counted only those "who drew the sword," 1 Chr 21:14 reports "seventy thousand persons fell in Israel," a total not limited to those who were of military age and ability. The mortality figure cannot simply be subtracted from the census figure to establish a new count of military strength. The plague has erased the census, for all practical purposes returning Israel to its precensus status.

While the Chronicler's constructive cultic concerns are primary, it remains true that the plague of pestilence is presented as a punishment. What is not totally clear is who is being punished and thus whether this punishment should be considered discipline or retribution. David clearly maintains the sin to be his alone (1 Chr 21:17) and the pestilence imposed on Israel is not just for "these sheep," of whom David asks, "What have they done?" Japhet notes, however, citing the Chronicler's expansion of Joab's speech in 1 Chr 21:3, that CH "sees the census as a cause of 'guilt,'" concluding that "by his decision David makes transgressors of the people as well, for to submit to a census is itself a sin!" (1993, 377). Such corporate guilt would appear more just if each citizen had failed to pay the required ransom for the census. Johnstone asserts that David "has compromised his status as God's representative and has implicated God's people," for "he has infringed the sphere of the holy" (1997, 231). Thus pestilence, which is always death, is retribution on those in Israel who die in the plague but discipline for David, who does not die.

While David offered the sacrifices in this account, it is not likely he performed the sacrifices himself. Johnstone suggests "a consequence of David's guilt" is that "a paradigm shift has taken place in the mode of Israel's realization of itself as the people of God," with the result that there is "a new balance in the respective roles of king and priesthood" (1997, 237). This new balance between king and priest will prove essential for an understanding of disease and disability within CH.

Asa

Two individual rulers, Asa and Uzziah, provide examples of the Chronicler's expansion of divergent physicalities for theological purposes. The Chronicler expands the brief statement on Asa's physical condition in 1 Kgs 15:23, which simply states that "in his old age he was diseased in his feet," setting it in the thirty-ninth year of his reign and reporting that "his disease became severe; yet even in his disease he did not seek the Lord, but sought help from physicians" (2 Chr 16:12). DH identifies Asa's condition using the verb חָלָה (ḥālâ), which we have already seen can refer to a wound in battle, as in the case of Ahab, Joram, and Josiah, or illness, as in the case of Hezekiah. CH uses a variant form of the verb and the derivative noun חֳלִי (ḥŏlî) to describe Asa's condition. The range of possibilities for the etiology of his condition is therefore broader than what is usually associated with the English term "disease." It is likely, however, that Asa's condition is not a mobility impairment at all. Recent scholarship suggests that Asa's physical condition was a form of genital dysfunction employing the common biblical metaphor "feet" for genitalia (Exod 4:24-26; Ruth 3; 1 Sam 24:3; 2 Sam 11:8; Prov 7:10-11; Isa 6:2; Ezek 16:23-29) (Schipper 2009, 643–48).

Etiology is more important than diagnosis for understanding the Chronicler's expansion on Asa's physical otherness, however. Jeremy Schipper asserts, "One should take into account the (largely Deuteronomic) theological standards by which Dtr evaluates Asa" in understanding the cause of Asa's condition in DH (2009, 644–45), while Japhet maintains that within "the Chronicler's philosophy of history, every misfortune is regarded as a chastisement" and thus Asa "surely deserved whatever ill befell him" (1993, 737). Schipper suggests that Asa's sin is his failure to exempt the newly married from the forced labor in 1 Kgs 15:22 in light of their exemption from military service in Deut 24:5 (2009, 643–48). Japhet suggests, "Asa's present illness must be due to another specific error," pointing to "his treatment of the prophet" (1993, 737). Yet if one is seeking a clear etiology from DH or CH, one must conclude that if punishment was the authorial understanding of Asa's condition, the authors have made every effort possible to obscure the fact and hide it from their readers. DH presents only one logical etiology for Asa's condition, and that is his age. The idea that disability and disease can be part of the natural aging process apart from divine intervention is clearly accepted by biblical authors, as seen in the case of Isaac's waning vision (Gen 27:1). Asa's age is the only etiology supported by the text.

The Chronicler, unlike DH, provides Asa's condition with a theological interpretation. The Chronicler suggests a progression in Asa's condition, noting that "his disease became severe" and his prognosis did not improve because "even in his disease he did not seek the Lord, but sought help from physicians." Here the Chronicler is returning to Solomon's prayer in 1 Chr 6:28-31, for one seeks the Lord by turning to the temple "whatever sickness there is." The Chronicler expands the account of Asa's condition in order to reinforce the central role of the Jerusalem cult. God will answer the prayers of those who turn to God rather than other sources, and to turn to God is to turn to God's temple and its worship.

We find no interest in punishment, neither retribution nor discipline, in this passage. What we do find is a concern for the maintenance of cultic boundaries. The etiological source of Asa's condition is the natural aging process, but even this natural aging process can be mitigated by turning to the temple cult. The Chronicler makes a concerted effort to show that kings must subject themselves to the cultus just like everyone else. The center of the life and hope of Israel is the Jerusalem temple and the Jerusalem temple alone.

Uzziah

The boundary between priest and king is more markedly laid out in the Chronicler's expanded account of the "leprosy" of Uzziah, DH's Azariah (2 Chr 26:16-23). DH simply reports that God "struck the king, so that he was leprous to the day of his death, and lived in a separate house" (2 Kgs 15:5). The NRSV, as almost all English translations, has followed the tradition established by the LXX in translating מְצֹרָע (*mĕṣōrāʿ*), from the verb צָרַע (*ṣāraʿ*), as "leprosy" (λελεπρωμένος; λεπρός) in 2 Kgs 15:5 and 2 Chr 26:20, 21. The noun צָרַעַת (*ṣāraʿat*) in 2 Chr 26:19 is likewise translated as "a leprous disease" (λέπρα). While both the Hebrew and Greek terms refer to a range of dermatological symptoms, the contemporary use of leprosy is usually applied to Hansen's disease. The following discussion will retain the Hebrew *ṣāraʿat* to emphasize that this is a collection of symptoms, more like a syndrome than a disease.

The assertion that YHWH "struck" (נָגַע, *nagaʿ*) Azariah with *ṣāraʿat* in 2 Kgs 15:5 is retained in 2 Chr 26:20. Melcher notes that the cognate noun נֶגַע (*negaʿ*) is used in the phrase *negaʿ ṣāraʿat* (ASV: "plague of leprosy") in Lev 13–14. She notes that *negaʿ* often "designates a 'stroke' inflicted by someone" and "God is the usual initiator," and thus "*negaʿ* is a form of divine punishment" (1998, 61). We have already encountered *negaʿ* in Solomon's prayer in 2 Chr 6:28, 30, however, where there is little indication that it is to be considered as punishment. Baden and Moss argue convincingly that *ṣāraʿat*, in the Priestly presentation, carries no religious or moral guilt, is not associated with any kind of sin, but is rather a simple fact of human existence, one that, like many others, has cultic and ritual implications" (2011, 645). Indeed, "*ṣāraʿat* according to the Priestly writings is a natural phenomenon" (652).

Baden and Moss maintain, "The non-Priestly narratives involving *ṣāraʿat* are generally in agreement that the affliction is the direct result of sinful behavior of some sort" (2011, 643). This assertion, however, does not hold true. In addition to Uzziah, these "non-Priestly narratives" include the *ṣāraʿat* of Miriam (Num 12), of Naaman, and of Gehazi (2 Kg 5), and the curse of David on the house of Joab (2 Sam 3:29). Baden and Moss note that in the case of Naaman, *ṣāraʿat* "is not explicitly from YHWH" and, it should be added, no sin is ever identified in his case (644). Indeed, while we might identify sin on the part of Gehazi and Joab, ṣāraʿat in these two cases is "not explicitly from YHWH" either but reflects curses from human sources.

Although 2 Kgs 15:5 explicitly states that Azariah's ṣāraʿat was an act of YHWH, there is no sin stated to justify an assertion of punishment. "We are misunderstanding Israelite religion anachronistically," write Baden and Moss, "if we draw a sharp distinction between natural phenomena and the work of YHWH." Furthermore, "Although not everything that comes from YHWH is necessarily punishment, everything does come from YHWH" (2011, 652).

Baden and Moss observe that the account in DH "does not make an explicit connection between ṣāraʿat and sin," even though it is reported that YHWH is the source of Azariah's extraordinary physical condition. Thus, "The notice in 2 Kgs 15:5 seems to be simply an annalistic comment on the health of the king rather than a judgment." They maintain that CH "transforms this brief comment into the scheme of sin and punishment that we see in other narratives" (2011, 644).

The Chronicler modifies DH's account of Azariah's ṣāraʿat to advance the view that throne and temple are the central institutions of Jewish identity and, more important, to set the boundaries between the two institutions. The only other passage of Scripture where God is the direct cause of ṣāraʿat is Num 12. Here Miriam becomes covered with ṣāraʿat when she and Aaron try to transgress the boundaries of Moses' divinely established authority and office. God reestablishes those boundaries by setting Miriam outside the community by means of ṣāraʿat. While Budd may be right in asserting that one cannot find any "clear signs that for the Yahwist Aaron represents priestly interests" in Num 12 and that "the activity of Aaron is not peculiarly or necessarily priestly" in this particular passage (1984, 138), it does not mean that the Chronicler would not have read this account with priestly concerns in mind. For the Chronicler, Aaron may have been exempted from ṣāraʿat so he would not be "excluded from the house of the Lord" (2 Chr 26:21) like Uzziah. Such an exclusion of the high priest would have been a punishment on all Israel and not Aaron alone. CH maintains that Uzziah's ṣāraʿat is given by God as a means of reestablishing the boundaries between throne and temple just as it had reestablished the boundaries between the role of Miriam and the office of Moses. The curses of ṣāraʿat on Gehazi and Joab are also related to their violation of the boundaries of another's office. Where Uzziah differs from Miriam is that while Miriam humbles herself and accepts her period of expulsion from the community, Uzziah retains his hubris, isolating himself within the community rather than accepting the requisite expulsion (Lev 13:45-46). Thus, whereas Miriam recovers, Uzziah retains his *ṣāraʿat* until the day of his death (2 Chr 26:21). The role of *ṣāraʿat* as punishment has a disciplinary role. Miriam learned her lesson and the punishment was removed. Uzziah never learned his lesson, and so the discipline had no end save in his death.

The Chronicler does not automatically assume that God imposes *ṣāraʿat* as punishment but sees it as a tool that God uses to achieve God's own ends. In the case of Uzziah, God's use of *ṣāraʿat* is proactive not reactive, creative not destructive. God does not use *ṣāraʿat* solely for punishment but mainly for the restoration of the separate roles of priest and king. Jonker concludes that the "religio-cultic personnel . . . occupied a position of dominance in the Second Temple society as reflected in the Chronicler's perception" and that "in the narrative about Uzziah," we find "that political leaders should not transgress in this domain" (2008, 718).

Josiah

CH's expanded account of the death of Josiah introduces Josiah's acknowledgment of his fatal wounding (חָלָה, *ḥālâ*) in 2 Chr 35:23. DH relates this event in one brief verse (2 Kgs 23:29), and the reader is led to believe that this is neither a punishment nor the simple vagaries of war but an act of divine mercy in light of the words of the prophetess Huldah (2 Kgs 22:18-20). While CH retains these words of the prophetess, the expanded account in 2 Chr 35:20-25 removes Josiah's death from the realm of divine mercy and places the responsibility for his death on Josiah himself. Ironically, the death of Josiah, one of the best Davidic kings of Judah, appears to be shaped by the death of Ahab, the worst of the apostate kings of Israel. Like Ahab, Josiah refuses to heed the divine word; like Ahab, Josiah goes disguised into battle; like Ahab, Josiah is struck by a stray arrow; and like Ahab, he is carried away in his chariot at his own request when he is fatally wounded (2 Chr 18).

Whereas Ahab's fate was announced by the prophet Micaiah, the divine warning to Josiah comes from Neco of Egypt. "The Chronicler," observes Jonker, "turns at least two foreign kings into conveyors of Yahweh's message," and thus "the Chronicler, although acknowledging the political and military power of these foreign monarchs, portrays them as being under Yahweh's dominion" (2008, 717). These two kings are Neco and Cyrus. Within the closing verses of the book in 2 Chr 36:22-23, Cyrus asserts, "The God of heaven . . . has charged me to build him a house at Jerusalem." The purpose of political power for Israel, whether Davidic or foreign, serves one purpose: the establishment and maintenance of the temple, the priesthood, the Levites, and worship. Cyrus only speaks when "the Lord stirred up the spirit of King Cyrus." Thus the Lord was with Cyrus, and it would seem likely this is what the Chronicler meant when he has Neco speak of "God, who is with me" (2 Chr 25:21). Neco and Cyrus "are not portrayed as antagonists in history," Jonker asserts, "but rather as those characters who are acting out Yahweh's plan with history" (717).

Josiah has just celebrated the Passover in 2 Chr 35:1-19. Hahn notes, "Neco's warning deliberately evokes the night of the first Passover" (2012, 184). Now, however, it is Pharaoh who brings the word of God to the leader of God's people, and it is the leader of God's people whose heart is hardened to his own destruction. Thus, Josiah is wounded and dies like Ahab. By reworking the role of Neco in paradox with the first Passover, the Chronicler sets the stage for the great reversal that occurs in the following chapter, where God calls the gentile Cyrus to fulfill the Davidic role in establishing the Jerusalem cultus. "Foreign monarchs are acknowledged for their role in history," Jonker concludes, "but they are included within the Chronicler's religio-cultic frame of reference" (2008, 717).

The parallels between the deaths of Ahab and Josiah serve to highlight the final contrast between the two monarchs. Of Ahab 1 Kgs 22:37 reports, "The king died, and was brought to Samaria; they buried the king in Samaria." Likewise, 2 Kgs 23:30 reports that Josiah's "servants carried him dead in a chariot from Megiddo, brought him to Jerusalem, and buried him in his own tomb." For the Chronicler, however, so great a Davidic monarch and cultic reformer should not die away from Zion and the city of David, and thus he revises Josiah's death so that they "brought him to Jerusalem" and it was "there he died, and was buried in the tombs of his ancestors" (2 Chr 35:24). As for Ahab, "They washed the chariot by the pool of Samaria; the dogs licked up his blood, and the prostitutes washed themselves in it" (1 Kgs 22:38). On the other hand:

> All Judah and Jerusalem mourned for Josiah. Jeremiah also uttered a lament for Josiah, and all the singing men and singing women have spoken of Josiah in their laments to this day. They made these a custom in Israel; they are recorded in the Laments. (2 Chr 35:24-25)

Regardless of the similarities reported regarding their deaths, the two monarchs could not have been more different.

REVISIONS

Jehoram

While the CH account of Jehoram is more expansive than 2 Kgs 8:16-24, the report of his extraordinary physical condition in 2 Chr 21:11-20 is an addition not found in DH. DH relates Jeroham's death in Jerusalem without any indication of how he died. CH introduces the nature of his death.

Jehoram presents a clear case of punishment as retribution. This is made abundantly clear by the unusual introduction of an oracle from a prophet of the Northern Kingdom by means of a letter. Japhet asserts that the "gravity of Jehoram's sins demands a prophetic figure of Elijah's caliber, and the Chronicler is not deterred by the geographical or political borders between the two kingdoms" (1993, 812). The Chronicler judges Jehoram because "he made high places in the hill country of Judah, and led the inhabitants of Jerusalem into unfaithfulness" (2 Chr 21:11). Jehoram has transgressed the Chronicler's primary concern—the centrality of the temple and its cult within Jerusalem. It is appropriate that Elijah condemn Jehoram, for he accuses him of walking "in the way of the kings of Israel," the judgment for which Elijah has a special expertise. For the Chronicler, the "way of the kings of Israel" is set forth in 2 Chr 11:13-17, which records Jeroboam's rejection of the Aaronic priesthood, the Levites, the Jerusalem temple, and his establishment of "his own priests for the high places, and for the goat-demons, and for the calves that he had made" (v. 15). Such idolatry is the heart of Elijah's accusation that Jehoram had "led Judah and the inhabitants of Jerusalem into unfaithfulness, as the house of Ahab," Jehoram's grandfather and Elijah's personal nemesis, had "led Israel into unfaithfulness" (2 Chr 21:13). Elijah identifies the Lord as "the God of your father David," which, for the Chronicler, points directly to the role of David and his house as the ones who establish and preserve the Jerusalem temple and its worship. Jehoram, however, has not "walked in the ways of your father Jehoshaphat" who had reasserted the central role of the Jerusalem temple. He has not even "walked in the ways of King Asa of Judah" who had neglected the temple (2 Chr 21:12). For the Chronicler there can be no greater sin or failing on the part of a Davidic monarch.

Elijah wrote, "The Lord will bring a great plague (מַגֵּפָה, *maggēpâ*) on your people, your children, your wives, and all your possessions" (2 Chr 21:14). Here the "plague" is the enemy's sword, that of the Philistines and Arabs (2 Chr 21:16-17). Retribution in the form of physical condition is reserved for Jehoram alone. Elijah wrote, "and you yourself will have a severe sickness (חֳלִי, *ḥŏlî*) with a disease (מַחֲלָה, *maḥălâ*) of your bowels, until your bowels come out, day after day, because of the disease" (2 Chr 21:15). The Chronicler reports that after the "plague" upon his family, "the Lord struck (נָגַף, *nāgap*) Jehoram with an incurable disease (חֳלִי, *ḥŏlî*)" so that "at the end of two years, his bowels came out because of the disease (חֳלִי, *ḥŏlî*) and he died in great agony" (2 Chr 21:18-19). This heaping up of terms for nonnormate physicalities emphasizes the most extreme case of physical retribution encountered in CH. Once again retribution takes the form of death, not disability. This is the only example of retribution where death is prolonged through two years of intense suffering. The Chronicler reserves this punishment for the most apostate of the kings of Judah.

Joash

DH reports Joash's death by assassination in 2 Kgs 12:19-21. This report does not include the wounding of Joash before his assassination and the cause of the assassination plot recorded in 2 Chr 24:25-26. CH reports that Joash had been "severely wounded" (מַחֲלָה, *maḥălâ*) by the army of Aram and that "his servants conspired against him because of the blood of the son of the priest Jehoiada, and they killed him on his bed." The military defeat that left Joash wounded is presented as God's judgment (2 Chr 24:24). During the life of Jehoiada, Joash had been the ideal king, the Davidic monarch who gave first place to the Aaronic priesthood, the Levites, and the Jerusalem temple (2 Chr 24:4-14). When the priest Jehoiada died, however, Joash followed counsel of "the officials of Judah" and, like Jehoram, "abandoned the house of the Lord" and "served the sacred poles and the idols" (2 Chr 24:18). The Davidic monarch had done well under the guidance of the Aaronic priesthood but had floundered when following secular politicians. Because Joash abandoned God and the temple, "wrath (קֶצֶף, *qeṣep*) came upon Judah and Jerusalem."

Addressing the sole occurrence of *qeṣep* in DH (2 Kgs 3:27), Scott Morschauser observes "that קֶצֶף, while certainly denoting divine anger in general, does sometimes refer to conditions that were frighteningly tangible" (2010, 299–300). Noting the case of Jer 21:5 and "the outbreak of pestilence in Jerusalem, as the city suffers under the duress of a Babylonian siege," he concludes *qeṣep* "is not as imprecise as often regarded, but is to be linked specifically to the unexpected raging of sickness in the Israelite camp" (301). This identification of *qeṣep* with pestilence is found in 1 Chr 27:24, referring to the aftermath of the Davidic census in 1 Chr 21. While *qeṣep* appears only once in DH, it appears quite frequently in CH, where it reflects "divine anger in general" in a number of cases (2 Chr 19:2, 34:21,

36:16), but in other occurrences it seems more "tangible" (1 Chr 27:24; 2 Chr 19:10, 29:8, 34:25). Of these tangible occurrences, some refer to the sword (2 Chr 29:8) and others to pestilence (1 Chr 27:24). Thus *qeṣep* can represent the same range of manifestations as *negep* and *maggēpâ*. We find no clear indication that *qeṣep* is tangible in 2 Chr 24:18. Still some form of "plague" may be implied. We will return to *qeṣep* when we examine the case of Hezekiah in 2 Chr 32:24-26.

Whether or not God's *qeṣep* was made tangible, the sending of prophets provides a fresh opportunity for Joash to transgress. Zechariah, the son of Jehoiada and thus himself a priest, begins to prophesy and is assassinated within the temple precincts at Joash's instigation (2 Chr 24:20-22). This was a profanation of the temple, which Jehoiada had been careful to avoid when he had Athaliah led to the gate of the king's house before her execution (2 Chr 23:14). "The particular effect of stoning is first and foremost in its public character," writes Japhet; indeed, "It is always executed by a crowd" (1993, 849). The fact that this is carried out at Joash's command makes his turning the people away from the Jerusalem temple and its priesthood quite concrete. While the Chronicler singles out Joash's ingratitude, his assassination of Zechariah illustrates how he has "abandoned the house of the Lord" (2 Chr 24:18).

At first glance Joash's defeat by Aram appears as divine judgment, while Joash's death at the hands of the conspirators appears as human rather than divine retribution. Japhet notes that the DH and CH accounts of Joash's encounter with Aram and his death "share nothing but the general topic" (1993, 851). In 2 Kgs 12:17-18, there is also an invasion by Aram, but Joash buys Hazael off with the temple treasuries and he returns home. There is no indication that this invasion is an act of divine judgment. This is immediately followed by the summation of Joash's reign (2 Kgs 12:19). It is only after this summation that DH reports the conspiracy that led to Joash's assassination without identifying any cause for the uprising (2 Kgs 12:20-21). CH, however, identifies the Aramean encounter as a divine judgment ending in military defeat (2 Chr 24:23-24). The Chronicler moves the account of the conspiracy to immediately follow the Aramean invasion in 2 Chr 24:25-26. It is only after the conspiracy that the Chronicler provides a very different summation of Joash's reign, joining two unrelated DH events into one CH account (2 Chr 24:27). This realignment is drawn together by CH's reference to Joash's severe *maḥălâ*. The military defeat plus the disabling wound of the king embolden his assassins to do the deed. The judgment of defeat for the general desertion of the house of the Lord and its priesthood is linked to the judgment for the specific illustrative assassination of a priest within the house of the Lord itself. The conspirators are merely completing the divine judgment initiated by the military defeat. Joash's wound becomes the means by which the two events are merged into one divine judgment. As always in Chronicles, divine retribution takes the form of death.

Hezekiah

The illness (חָלָה, ḥālâ) of Hezekiah in 2 Chr 32:24-26 greatly abbreviates 2 Kgs 20:1-11. The Chronicler has not only erased Isaiah's death announcement, Hezekiah's actual prayer, and Isaiah's sign, but he has also removed Isaiah the prophet completely. The Chronicler cites only the opening announcement from its *Vorlage* and briefly states that Hezekiah prayed and God gave him a sign. The Chronicler, however, adds a new element in 2 Chr 32:25, asserting, "Hezekiah did not respond according to the benefit done to him, for his heart was proud," so that "wrath (קֶצֶף, qeṣep) came upon him and upon Judah and Jerusalem." When Hezekiah and "the inhabitants of Jerusalem" corporately humbled themselves, however, "the wrath of the Lord did not come upon them in the days of Hezekiah" (2 Chr 32:26).

Japhet maintains that the erasure of Isaiah is "intentional in itself" so that "the communication between Hezekiah and the Lord is direct, with no need of an intermediary" (1993, 992). When we contrast Hezekiah's experience with that of Asa, however, it is likely that the Chronicler saw a different intermediary. Both Asa and Hezekiah become ill without any divine causation. The focus in each account is on the monarch's reaction to the illness. Asa had "sought the help of physicians" and "did not seek the Lord," so "his disease became severe" (2 Chr 16:12). Here, Hezekiah "prayed to the Lord, and he answered him and gave him a sign" (2 Chr 32:24). Again, Asa should have gone to "seek the Lord" at the Jerusalem temple. By erasing Isaiah's bedside visitation found in DH, the Chronicler provides a contrasting account to that of Asa where the king is healed when he does seek the Lord through the temple cultus as prescribed in 2 Chr 6:28-31. Hezekiah's shortcoming was that he "did not respond according to the benefit done to him" (2 Chr 32:25). The NRSV reading "respond" misses the sense of הֵשִׁיב (hēšîb) in the Hebrew text—literally, "cause to return," which can have the sense of "pay, repay, or give." While Hezekiah had turned to the temple for healing, it appears he failed to fulfill any vows he had made in the process or to give appropriate thanksgiving offerings once he had been healed. This failure was the sign of his arrogance.

Japhet observes that the nature of the *qeṣep* that befell Hezekiah and Jerusalem "all remains as vague generalities" (1993, 993). She suggests it "could be understood as a constant waiving of the still impending Assyrian threat," which would be an instance of *qeṣep* brought about by the sword (994). The Chronicler seems almost contradictory in asserting that "wrath came upon him and upon Judah and Jerusalem" in one verse and "that the wrath of the Lord did not come upon them in the days of Hezekiah" in the very next verse (2 Chr 32:25-26). The threat of the return of Assyria could be perceived as *qeṣep* come upon king and community, which is delayed when the right response diverts the wrath. This would not be the case with pestilence or famine, whose approach is unannounced and which cannot be turned back before it arrives unless it is understood as the inevitable result of war. That the deliverance from this *qeṣep* was not achieved by Hezekiah humbling himself alone but included "the inhabitants of Jerusalem" would indicate a corporate worship service at the temple. Thus, the Chronicler shows that kings are subject to the temple cultus in all its aspects and must comply with all its requirements.

CONCLUSION

While punishment is often linked with nonnormate physicalities in CH, there is no monolithic generalization regarding this relationship. The assertion that the Chronicler holds that such a condition "implies the existence of sin, while healing demands that the sin was forgiven" (Japhet, 1993, 993) ignores the etiological diversity found in CH. Any attempt to invent sins for hypothetical punishments gives this presupposition precedence over the text itself. Punishment usually occurs in the form of retribution, but occasionally as discipline. Retribution usually takes the form of eminent death rather than disability or chronic illness, although retributive death is prolonged in the case of Jehoram. The *ṣāraʿat* experienced by Uzziah is disciplinary. Uzziah's *ṣāraʿat* is never removed. He never seems to have learned the lesson of the discipline by humbling himself and following the Torah, which would have sent him outside the community rather than isolating himself within the royal precincts. One person's retribution may be another's discipline, as was the pestilence that killed many but served to discipline David. The Chronicler's understanding of punishment is diverse and complex.

The view of nonnormate physicalities held by the Chronicler, and by the world of the Hebrew Bible, is best represented by an earlier text found in Exod 4:11: "Who gives speech to mortals? Who makes them mute or deaf, seeing or blind? Is it not I, the Lord?" Physical variation is part of the created order. God as creator creates not only normate bodies but also physical variations. For the Chronicler, physical variation is a multipur-pose tool that God deftly uses to work out his plan in establishing Israel as a priestly nation focused on the Jerusalem temple, the priesthood, the Levites, and proper worship.

The Chronicler sees God using the pestilence sent on Israel after David's census to establish the location for the temple. Here God also establishes the site of David's sacrifice as the sacred space where Israel is to turn when "there is famine in the land, if there is plague, blight, mildew, locust, or caterpillar; if their enemies besiege them in any of the settle-ments of the lands; whatever suffering, whatever sickness there is" so that God will hear and address their suffering (2 Chr 6:28-30). Even kings such as Asa must turn to God at this site rather than to human knowledge for healing. Kings such as Hezekiah, who do turn to God and this site for healing, are not exempt from the mandates of the Jerusalem cultus. There is no hope, however, for kings such as Jehoram and Joash, who turn from this site and from God. Uzziah's ṣāraʿat was the means by which God rees-tablished the boundaries between throne and temple. "The one distinction that is upheld," observes Jonker, "is the distinction between the political leader and the priesthood" (2008, 716).

EZRA–NEHEMIAH

There are no direct references to nonnormate physicalities in Ezra-Nehemiah, and so a different approach is required. Here the narrative and the lived experience of disability present analogical parallels. Nancy Eiesland identifies two difficulties encountered by people with disabilities: "living our ordinary, but difficult lives, and changing structures, beliefs, and attitudes that prevent us from living ordinarily" (1994, 13). These are two problems faced by the postexilic Jerusalem community as well. We will look at three aspects of the disabled experience: loss and disability, the empirical gaze (i.e, the treatment of the human subject as objective specimen through medical or scientific examination), and the social con-struction of models of identity.

LOSS AND DISABILITY

Nehemiah was well aware that a trauma had occurred. How else would he have found himself "in Susa the capital" (Neh 1:1)? Yet he had held out hope for Jerusalem until his brother arrived to tell him that those "who escaped captivity are in great trouble and shame," for "the wall of Jerusalem is broken down, and its gates have been destroyed by fire" (1:3). Now Nehemiah was confronted with the reality of the disabled city and he "sat down and wept, and mourned for days, fasting and praying before the God of heaven" (1:4). Such loss can be the experience not only of the person with a disability but, of their families and communities also. Indeed, in the case of a congenital or early-onset disability, it may be felt as a greater loss by one's family and community than by the person with the disability. Like those newly acquiring a disability, who with friends, family, and the medical community hope that the condition will be temporary and reversible, Nehemiah waited for a word of well-being from his native city. The day finally comes for Nehemiah, like it does for those experiencing disability, when reality can no longer be denied and hope gives way to grief.

Nehemiah's immediate response to his sense of loss is one of guilt, as he prayed "confessing the sins of the people Israel" and declaring that "I and my family have sinned" (1:6). Beatrice Wright notes that the person with a disability "may ascribe the source of suffering to wrongdoing in himself or in someone else," while "hardly a parent of a child who has a disability can escape the conviction that in some way avoidable mismanagement was a contributing cause if not *the* cause of the disability" (1960, 258). Nehemiah is not simply subject to a normate worldview in his sense of guilt, however. While not all disability can be attributed to "wrongdoing," there are instances where this is the case. The motorcyclist who has been continuously warned of the need to wear a helmet and sustains a head injury must take at least partial responsibility for his or her disability. Smokers who have constantly ignored the labels on cigarette packages must accept their accountability for their lung cancer. Nehemiah knows that Israel has been warned time and again that "failing to keep the commandments" that God had delivered on Sinai would lead to their dispersion among the nations (1:7-8), leaving Jerusalem desolate. Nehemiah is aware that he and his community bear responsibility for the disabling of Jerusalem.

Nehemiah's sense of loss is regarding not simply the physical defense of the disabled city but also the loss of identity that accompanies that newfound vulnerability. For the Jewish community in exile, Jerusalem remained the center of their identity as much as it did for the community of the return. While a similar sense of loss of identity is common among those with acquired disabilities, the actual impact of disability on self-identity varies greatly depending on the person, the context, and the nature of the disability.

Ezra 3 records the preparations for the rebuilding of the Jerusalem temple by the postexilic community. The laying of the foundations of the temple is undertaken in a liturgical fashion reminiscent of Chronicles. When the foundation had been laid, "old people who had seen the first house on its foundations, wept with a loud voice" while the younger generation "shouted aloud for joy" (3:11b-12). These two disparate reactions are directly linked to each individual's experience with the now-destroyed Solomonic temple (cf. Hag 2:3). Williamson notes that the elders link the new temple with its predecessor, but these elders "clearly found the comparison bitterly disappointing" (1985, 48–49).

The sense of loss for many people who acquire disabilities, and for their families and their communities, often depends on their prior experience with a more normate social positioning and physicality. For people who acquire a disability later in life the sense of loss of both function and identity can be great. Wright observes "that a disability incurred after the self-concept has already achieved some structure requires that the new state be integrated within old notions about the self" (1960, 155). For persons with congenital or early-onset disabilities, the sense of loss may be minimal. While societal factors have an impact on the self-identity of a person with such a disability, there is less a sense of loss where normate biases have not already taken root. When the person with a late-onset disability begins to regain minimal or compensatory function, they, like the elders who knew the Solomonic temple, may mourn the loss of their former abilities. Those who have no memory of a more normate body, like those who had no memory of the Solomonic temple, may perceive every new level of functioning as gain rather than loss, and thus rejoice. The families of this latter group, having experience of the lost functions, may mourn a loss not shared by the person with the disabilities.

THE EMPIRICAL GAZE

Nothing has been so dominant in defining today's understanding of disability as the birth of modern medicine. "Medical rationality" observes Michel Foucault, "plunges into the marvelous density of perception," where "the experiment seems to be identified with the domain of the careful gaze, and of an empirical vigilance receptive only to the evidence of visible contents" (1973, xiii). By the means of the empirical gaze, the individual acquired the "status of object" and thus one's "particular quality" (xiv). Foucault notes that for modern medicine "certainty is based not on the *completely observed individuality* but on the *completely scanned multiplicity of individual facts*" and thus such "knowledge will gain its certainty only in relation to the number of cases examined" (101; emphasis in original). Through the power of "the gaze," Leonard Cassuto observes, "clinical medicine quickly standardized and quantified this objectifying, 'calculating' practice" and thus creating "a quantifiable idea of the normal" (2002, 120). There is but one example of the "gaze" scanning "a multiplicity of individual facts" and thus gaining increased certainty by the "number of cases examined" in Ezra–Nehemiah. This is found in Ezra 10:16-17, where those appointed by Ezra "examine the matter" of foreign marriages. Ezra 10:18-44 lists all the individual cases that supported the generalization that this was a problem. While the "empirical" gaze with its stress on the "quantifiable" would have to await the Enlightenment, we find an earlier form of the diagnostic gaze in Ezra–Nehemiah.

The "gaze" can be expressed in various ways and be brought to bear by various subjects upon multiple objects within Ezra–Nehemiah. As those who had been able to "see" (רָאָה, rāʾah) the first temple wept at the sight of the new temple, so Nehemiah was able to "see" those prepared for battle (Neh 4:14 [Heb. 4:8]), those who violated the Sabbath (13:15), and those who married foreign wives (13:23). As those appointed by Ezra in Ezra 10:16-17 could "examine" (דָּרַשׁ, dāraš) this same issue, so could Ezra himself "examine" the Scriptures (7:10). Those who come to Ezra in Neh 8:13, however, are said to "study" or "ponder" (שָׂכַל, śākal) the law. The Persian officials "searched" (בְּקַר, běqar) their records and "discovered" (שְׁכַח, šěkaḥ) what the king required (Ezra 4:19, 6:1-2). The king brought a diagnostic "gaze" to bear on Nehemiah himself (Neh 2:1-2). Ezra "reviewed" (בִּין, bîn) the people and priests (Ezra 8:15) and "found" (מָצָא, māṣaʾ) no Levites, a group "sought out" (בָּקַשׁ, bāqaš) (Neh 12:27). Nehemiah "inspected" (שָׂבַר, śābar) the walls of Jerusalem (Neh 2:13-15) and "perceived" (נָכַר, nākar) and "saw" or "beheld" (הִנֵּה, hinnēh) the treachery of Shemaiah (6:12). He also "discovered" (בִּין, bîn) the misuse of temple resources (Neh 13:7) and "found" or came to "know" (יָדַע, yādah) the inappropriate use of temple resources (13:10). The opponents of both Ezra and Nehemiah bring the "gaze" to bear by "hearing" (שָׁמַע, šāmaʿ) (Ezra 4:1; Neh 2:10, 19; 4:1 [Heb. 3:34], 7 [Heb. 4:1], 15 [Heb. 9]; 6:1, 16), thus their "gaze" is secondhand.

The medical "case study" serves as "a discourse that has medicalized disability and frequently objectifies disabled people," Cassuto asserts, for it has become "the vehicle by which rationally based medical science turned the disabled person into a medical narrative" (2002, 118–19). In a similar fashion, the "gaze" in Ezra–Nehemiah creates a narrative based on the presuppositions of the observer that shapes the image of the object observed.

Occasionally, the "gaze" will lead directly to diagnosis and treatment, as does Nehemiah's inspection of the walls of Jerusalem (Neh 2:11-17) and the subsequent rebuilding of the walls with the results that, according to the NJPS translation, "healing (אֲרוּכָה, *ărûkâ*) had come to the walls of Jerusalem" (4:7 [Heb. 4:1]). As nowhere else in Scripture, the written records—whether the letters exchanged between the province Beyond the River and the royal court, the royal Persian archives, or the book of the law that Ezra brings back from Babylon—become the primary form of narrative that determines the image, status, and identity of the postexilic community.

Cassuto notes that the "case study arises from the relation in medicine between the individual and the general" (2002, 123). The compilation of individual case studies provides "the number of cases examined" (Foucault 1973, 101) that will be the means by which medical "knowledge will gain its certainty." A second type of medical genre, the individual "medical record," may never become part of the generalization process but serves to bring the results of multiple generalizations to bear on the individual. With the case study, "The individual becomes subordinated to the general," and "the patient becomes little more than a vessel for the condition being studied" (Cassuto 2002, 124). The individual medical record can become a self-fulfilling narrative as it shapes all future diagnosis and treatment. Both medical case studies and medical records serve to narrate the lives of people with disabilities through the means of the medical gaze. No other narrative in contemporary society is more authoritative than the medical narrative. "The most stringent power we have over another," writes Stanley Hauerwas, "is not physical coercion but the ability to have the other accept our definition of them" (2004a, 40). The same movement between the general and the individual is found in the written records in Ezra–Nehemiah. While there is always a latent threat of physical coercion in these books, the main struggle is the struggle to determine who will get to narrate the postexilic community.

The most common written genre within Ezra–Nehemiah is the letter. The first letters are the one by the leaders of the people of the land (Ezra 4:11-16) and its royal response (4:17-22). Then there is letter of Tattenai, the governor of the province Beyond the River (5:7-17), with its royal response as well (6:2-12). General royal letters are given to both Ezra (Ezra 7:11-26) and Nehemiah (Neh 1:7-9).

The first four letters make reference to the royal archives in Babylon and Ecbatana. The archive at Ecbatana contained the official text of the royal edict of Cyrus (Ezra 1:2-4), summarized in the letter to Tattenai

(6:2-5). The letter of "the adversaries of Judah and Benjamin" (4:1) and the letter of Tattenai function as diagnostic assessments of Judah and call for an objective evaluation in light of Judah's medical history stored in these royal archives. These letters in turn become part of the medical record of Judah and thus will shape all future assessments of the postexilic community. The first diagnostic assessment appeals to the clinical gaze (4:12) and makes a prognosis (4:13) based on Judah's medical history (4:15-16), referencing the medical records in the royal archives. No treatment plan is stated, but one certainly is inferred. Despite the illusion of objectivity, the reader knows the assessment reflects the experience, the biases, and the presuppositions of those making the assessment (4:1-6). Tattenai, on the other hand, does not make his assessment based solely on the clinical gaze but interviews Judah (5:10-11) and incorporates Judah's self-report within his diagnostic assessment (5:11-16). Tattenai makes no prognosis and suggests no treatment plan before the medical history can be examined and consultation made with the king (5:17). The royal responses to each letter reveal that the diagnostic assessment itself shaped how the medical history was read and what parts of the medical records were accessed. When the case summary found in Ezra 4:15-16 was verified in the archives of Babylon (4:19-20), no further search was made, and a treatment plan was developed based solely on the partial records and the diagnostic assessment (4:21-22). When Tattenai reports a case history missing from the medical records stored in Babylon, however, an additional search is made at Ecbatana and a fuller medical history is established (6:2), leading to a totally divergent treatment plan (6:6-12).

The Persians, however, are not the only ones who have archives of written records. Such records would include the written genealogies of the exiles (i.e., Ezra 2:62). These serve a diagnostic function as people are included and excluded from positions within the community based on these genealogical records. Artaxerxes' letter given to Ezra makes reference to Ezra as "the scribe of the law of the God of heaven" (Ezra 7:12) and to "the law of your God, which is in your hand" (7:14). This law is a written document (7:10-11) that serves as the medical textbook by which foreign wives and children are excised from the community (Neh 13; Ezra 9–10). This action, however, is not solely based on a textbook application of a divine decree but is also backed up by appeal to a case study—namely, the case of Solomon (Neh 13:26). Indeed, Solomon represents a collection of case studies in DH that serve as the means by which "knowledge will gain certainty" (Foucault 1973, 101). Ezra's book of the law becomes the central documentation for communal identity in Neh 8.

Constructing Models of Identity

"The case study is one of the most powerful tools of the Western medical profession," Cassuto observes, one which "helped turn the doctor into an authority on such narratives," enabling physicians to script "a corporate authority built on laypeople's deference to their expertise and an institutional dependence on their services" (2002, 119). While Simi Linton affirms "medical treatments that have increased the well-being and vitality of many disabled people, indeed have saved people's lives," she laments that "the medicalization of disability casts human variation as deviance from the norm, as pathological condition, as deficit, and significantly, as an individual burden and personal tragedy" (1998, 11). This perspective is known as the medical model of disability. The medical model focuses on medical treatment, rehabilitation, education, and training. Disability studies has proposed an alternative model, "a social model," which maintains that society "disables" people with physical impairments by marginalizing them and limiting their inclusion in the broader society (Barnes, Mercer, and Shakespeare 1999, 28). This model of disability focuses on physical accessibility and political action. Ezra–Nehemiah presents two competing models for defining the postexilic community as well.

The model advocated by Zerubbabel, Jeshua, Ezra, and Nehemiah was long in construction. Its roots lie in the life and history of preexilic Israel; it was honed in the crucible of the exile and was now presented as an overarching narrative accompanied by related practices. Central to this model is the understanding that the ongoing exile and subjection of Judah was due to the failure of their ancestors to keep strict adherence to the law of God (Neh 1:4-11; 9:16-17, 26-30, 33-35). Thus, strict adherence to the law was the means by which the contemporary postexilic community guaranteed that things had changed and God should deliver the community and ensure its ongoing existence.

Nehemiah 8 sets "the book of the law of Moses" as the definitive authority for both narrative and practice. This narrative is expanded in the recitation of the salvation history in Neh 9:6-37 within Ezra's prayer and the vow of the people (10:28-39). The expanded salvation history covers the time from Moses to the contemporary community, whose leaders confirm this recitation with a written document (9:38–10:27). The Mosaic model is further developed in a mosaic of narratives, including the report of Tattenai (Ezra 5:11-16), the prayer of Nehemiah (Neh 1:4-11), and brief comments such as Nehemiah's in Neh 2:20.

The practices of the model include the enforcement of the boundaries on the community (Ezra 4:1-3 [Heb. 3:33-35], 10-13; Neh 13:1-3, 23-30), the prohibition on usury (Neh 5:1-13), the study of Torah and the observance of Sukkot (8:13-18), tithes and offerings (10:32-39), the organization of temple worship (Neh 12–13), and Sabbath observance (13:15-22). As with models of disability, narrative and practice are woven into one fabric.

For the modern reader who sees the "good society" as democratic, inclusive, and diverse, Zerubbabel's rejection of the offer of the people of the land to assist in rebuilding the temple (Ezra 4:1-3) and the exclusion of foreign wives and their children appears harsh. The Mosaic model seems to be imposed by the elite minority on the majority. This Mosaic model, however, serves to guarantee the survival of the community that is not free but subject to the whims of the Persian overlord (Neh 9:36-37).

The competing model begins with this rejection of assistance in rebuilding the temple (Ezra 4:1). The model's narrative is set forth in the letter to Artaxerxes, which declares "that this is a rebellious city, hurtful to kings and provinces, and that sedition was stirred up in it from long ago" (4:15). While this narrative shares some of the same "facts" as the Mosaic model, these "facts" are interpreted in a significantly different way. This model of rebellion is advanced by the mocking comment of Sanballat, Tobiah, and Geshem in Neh 2:19. The conversation of Sanballat and Tobiah (4:1-3 [Heb. 3:33-35]) portrays the Jewish community as incompetent workmen in terms of disability when Sanballat calls them "feeble (אֲמֵלָל, *ămēlāl*) Jews." This model holds that the Jewish community should not maintain a separate identity but should be incorporated into the social, political, and economic network of both the region and the empire.

This narrative leads to certain practices. Those prohibited from joining in the reconstruction of the temple send their letter to Artaxerxes, and they ensure that the work on the temple ceases (Ezra 4:23-24). When the work on the wall challenges Sanballat and Tobiah's portrayal of the Jerusalem laborers as "feeble Jews," they "plotted together to come and fight against Jerusalem and to cause confusion in it" (Neh 4:8 [Heb. 4:2]; cf. Neh 6). The prophet Noadiah's participation in such a plot (6:10-14), the priest Eliashib maintaining a familial relationship with Tobiah and supplying him with a room within the temple (13:4-9), the widespread practice of intermarriage and violation of the Sabbath (13:15-22), and the failure to implement the required cultic practices all reflect just how dominant this integrationist model was within the Jewish community itself. Those advancing the Mosaic model were struggling against an alternative model already engrained in the imagination of the postexilic community.

These two models of identity stood in tension with each other as the medical and social models of disability do today. They were not the only two models in play in Ezra–Nehemiah, however. Both of these models were subject to the Persian model of empire. What should be noted about the model advanced by Ezra–Nehemiah is that it is advanced by prayer and the public reading of the Scriptures in worship. Ezra–Nehemiah itself would have been read within the communal context. Thus, like Chronicles, Ezra–Nehemiah turns to liturgy to establish the "liturgical empire" (Hahn 2012).

ESTHER

Esther, like Ezra–Nehemiah, has no direct reference to extraordinary physical conditions, and we will once again turn to analogy with the experience of disability. This time, however, our analogy will not be based on the final redaction of the narrative. There are three extant recensions of Esther: the Hebrew version of the MT and two Greek translations, Greek A and Greek B, the latter serving as the Esther of LXX. We will draw on the historical concerns that gave rise to these variant recensions. We will focus on "passing" and "dependence/independence," which were concerns for the communities that gave rise to MT and LXX Esthers, which are concerns for people with disabilities today.[1]

PASSING

When Esther was taken into the harem of Ahasuerus, "Esther did not reveal her people or kindred, for Mordecai had charged her not to tell" (MT 2:10). This point is reiterated chiastically for emphasis in MT 2:20: "Esther had not revealed her kindred or her people" (Moore 1971, 22). Thus Mordecai instructed Esther to "pass" as a gentile. Erving Goffman defined "passing" as the "management of undisclosed discrediting information about self" (cited in Barnes, Mercer, and Shakespeare 1999, 44). "Disabled people, if they are able to conceal their impairment or confine their activities to those that do not reveal their disability, have been known to pass," observes Simi Linton (1998, 19–20). Such "passing may be a deliberate effort to avoid discrimination or ostracism," she writes, "or it may be an almost unconscious, Herculean effort to deny to oneself the reality of one's racial history, sexual feelings, or bodily state." Goldman maintains Mordecai must have thought that if Esther was Ahauserus' choice, "it can only be because God desires to make her the instrument of His purpose,"

---

[1] References for the LXX Additions to Esther follow those adopted by the NRSV Apocrypha from the Vulgate.

and thus if Esther "reveals the fact that she is a Jewess, and therefore a member of a subject people, she will prejudice her choice, and thereby the possibility of becoming God's instrument" (1984, 147–48). Thus "discrediting information" is hidden and justified by appeal to the greater good—indeed, to the will of God. Carey Moore notes, "*Everyone* had a good impression of Esther," and "to have accomplished this must have involved some 'compromises' in the area of religion" (1971, 28); emphasis in original). Moore suggests that "to have concealed her ethnic and religious identity . . . in the harem, she must have eaten . . . , dressed, and lived like a Persian rather than an observant Jewess." LXX 2:20, however, protests that "she was to fear God and keep his laws, just as she had done when she was with him," and "thus Esther did not change her mode of life" (cf. Day 1995, 40). According to R. Abraham ibn Ezra, Esther hid her Jewish identity in order that "she might observe her religious obligations secretly," for had "she declared her faith, she would be forced to transgress" (Goldman 1984, 148).

MT presents Esther as one who is deft and comfortable with the task of passing. Linda Day asserts that MT Esther "is extremely level headed, and even unemotional" (1995, 177). She suggests, "There are a few instances in the MT text when the reader can infer that Esther feels a certain confidence" and gives the impression that she is "certain that what she is doing is correct and will yield the results she desires." MT only presents the façade that Esther created in order to pass. Linton observes that when people with disabilities "pass for nondisabled," however, "the emotional toll it takes is enormous" (1998, 20). The emotional cost of passing becomes evident in the image of Esther in LXX. Day observes that LXX "characterizes Esther with three particular emotions: fear, loneliness, and concern for the Jewish people" (1995, 176). Day maintains LXX Esther "is more afraid and lonely than in the other texts, and these emotions are interpreted particularly within her relationship to God, as is evident especially in her prayer" (LXX 14:1-19). This prayer is where Esther's façade is exposed.

"Some people must be avoided" when one is passing, Harlan Lane observes, "especially similarly stigmatized people—while accomplices must be recruited" (1999, 98). This is the situation in which Esther finds herself in MT 4:9-17. Mordecai has been open about his Jewish identity, and it has brought him and the Jewish people to the brink of disaster at the hands of Haman. Esther's Jewish status is hidden from Haman, however. Enabled by Esther's enclosure within the royal household, her secret is maintained since she has no direct contact with Mordecai or the Jewish people. Esther's "accomplices" are her maids and her eunuchs, particularly Hathach, who report Mordecai's status to her and serve as intermediaries between Esther and Mordecai. Mordecai becomes the intermediary between Esther and the Jewish people in turn (4:16). While MT Esther shows fear at approaching the king, it is not because of her stigmatized status as a Jew but because of the law prohibiting appearing before the king unbidden on the threat of death. Once MT Esther's resolve is set, however, she moves confidently and decisively.

Here enters Esther's prayer in LXX 14:1-19. LXX Esther cries out to God, "Help me, who am alone and have no helper but you" (14:3), and again, "Save us by your hand, and help me, who am alone and have no helper but you, O Lord" (14:14). Here we see Esther's loneliness and sense of isolation. In the intervening verses, however, she recounts the story of the Jewish people and their relationship to "the God of Israel"; thus, "Esther expresses a sense of connection with the Jews" (Day 1995, 69). Moore observes, "Esther's prayer is not a self-centered prayer in which her personal safety is primary and her people's secondary," for "she first prayed extensively for her people . . . , *and then* prayed at lesser length for herself" (1977, 213; emphasis in original). The reader senses the loss Esther must have felt at her separation from the Jewish community. Similarly, Linton asserts such "loss of community, the anxiety, and the self-doubt that inevitably accompany this ambiguous social position and the ambivalent personal state are the enormous cost of declaring disability unacceptable" (1998, 21). It is in the second part of Esther's prayer, however, where the real personal cost of passing comes to the surface (LXX 14:15-18). Vashti had been dethroned, divorced, and exiled because "she refused to come to the king's command conveyed by the eunuchs" (MT 1:12). MT Esther feared appearing before Ahasuerus unbidden; how much more stressful must LXX Esther's avoidance of the tables of Haman and the king, no less than the religious libations, have been for her? She certainly feels she has compromised the command in Deut 7:3 even though the Persian king is not from one of the prohibited seven nations. Little wonder that she finally cries, "Save me from my fear!" (4:19). "Passing can be exhausting," writes Lane, "each situation requires its own brand of cunning and contains its own threats of disclosure" (1999, 98). Esther's prayer supports ibn Ezra's assertion that Esther passed in order to secretly keep the Torah. We can only imagine what "cunning" and "threats of disclosure" such attempts would present.

Both MT and LXX Esther seem reluctant to reveal their identity. Her stigmatized status plays no role in her dangerous encounter with the king.

Indeed, it requires two dinner parties where she has been empowered by serving as the host to bring her to the place where she can blurt out, "If I have won your favor, O king, and if it pleases the king, let my life be given me—that is my petition—and the lives of my people—that is my request" (MT 7:3). It is at this point that the tide turns, Haman is destroyed, and Esther, Mordecai, and the Jewish people are empowered. "Shame and fear are personal burdens," writes Linton, "but if these tales are told, we can demonstrate how the personal is indeed political" (1998, 22). Esther is only led to reveal her Jewish identity because of the threat to her and her people's lives, and Esther and Mordecai's political actions once they are empowered are solely shaped by the genocide planned by Haman. Lane warns that while members of the minority group may insist that the one who is passing should stop "trying to be like the oppressor" and "should take a militant stand," whether passing or opposing, "his behavior is determined by the oppression" (1999, 98).

DEPENDENCY

Esther's prayer reveals another aspect of the experience of disability. While MT Esther's words before presenting herself to the king are strong and resolute—"if I perish, I perish" (4:16)—LXX Esther goes on to pray, "Help me, who am alone and have no helper but you" (14:3) and finally, "Save me from my fear!" Day notes LXX "Esther is significantly more passive" than either A Text or MT Esther (1995, 174). LXX Esther "expects others to save her," Day observes, "to change Artaxerxes' temper" and "to decide how the Jews should act in defense" (175). Such concerns regarding passivity and activity, weakness and strength, and dependency and independency are central to the contemporary experience of disability.

These concerns are not limited to the portrayals of Esther alone but are characteristic of the two divergent books as a whole. One of the most noted characteristics of MT is the complete absence of any reference to God. By contrast, God appears not only in the additions in LXX but also throughout the narrative as a whole. Mordecai expresses dependence on God in his prayer in LXX 13:8-17 and in LXX 10:4-13. Mordecai asserts that salvation has come to the Jews solely by the intervention of God. Even Haman's wife no longer simply asserts that if Mordecai "is of the Jewish people, you will not prevail against him," but now she and his friends add that Haman will fail "because the living God is with him" (LXX 7:13). It is not only the characters within the story that reflect reliance on God; it is the entire book itself.

This polarization of dependency and independency represents a central concern of the two communities that gave rise to the two diverging texts. The original story probably emerged within the diaspora no earlier than 400 BCE (Moore 1971, lix). Its arrival within the postexilic community "would have been shortly before the arrival of Alexander's forces on their way to conquer Egypt in 332 B.C.E." (Wynn 1990, 162). The earliest form of Esther "served the upper strata of the Jewish Diaspora," for whom the story "provided a means for passive resistance and preservation of the group identity" (158). Soon after the Esther story arrived in Jerusalem, the role of foreign domination shifted from the Persians to the Hellenic rulers of Seleucid Syria and Ptolemaic Egypt. The Esther story was adapted to serve as propaganda for opposing Judean parties over the next two centuries, first for opposing parties of separatists and assimilationists during Hellenistic domination (164–74), then for militant nationalists over against nonmilitant pietists during the Maccabean revolt (178–201), and finally between those supporting and those opposing the Hasmonean dynasty (202–18). For the militant nationalists and the independent Hasmonean state, it was beneficial to erase "the divine name and elements" from the Esther narrative, for this "limitation on the role of the divine within the text serves to focus the attention of the reader on the necessity of human action on the part of the Jewish community in order to ensure their own survival" (206). This is the recension of the text preserved in MT. LXX was developed by the pietists, who leaned toward passive resistance and later provided "an attempt to resolve the differences between the pious concerns of the Pharisees and the nationalistic concerns" of the Hasmoneans, for "Esther was now a pious and observant Jew." More important, "Esther declared that in truth God alone is king" (217). MT calls for action, independence, and strength. LXX calls for waiting for God to act, dependence upon God, and acknowledgment of human weakness in light of divine strength.

The self-reliance of MT Esther is a characteristic greatly valued in Western culture and has undergirded the vocational rehabilitation and independent living movements as they address disability. Cull and Hardy saw the vocational rehabilitation movement as arising out of "the public's growing recognition of a social obligation to help disabled people move toward their independence and self-sufficiency and at the same time the increasing realization of the economic benefits that come as a result of the rehabilitation process" (1972, 6). The independent living movement went a step further. "Independence was measured not by tasks one could perform without assistance," writes Joseph Shapiro, "but by the quality of one's life with help" (1993, 51).

As with MT Esther, these two movements represent a process moving from dependence to independence. MT Esther starts from a position of obedient dependence. "Esther did not reveal her people or kindred, for Mordecai had charged her not to tell" (2:10). Mordecai advanced this dependency, for he "would walk around in front of the court or harem, to learn how Esther was and how she fared." Addressing dependency between Deaf people and service providers, Lane observes, "The more the provider plays the parental role, the more the recipient is encouraged to play the dependent role" (1999, 75). MT 2:15 shows a transfer of dependency as Esther moves away from her life in Mordecai's home to her role at court, for she now asks "for nothing except what Hegai the king's eunuch, who had charge of the women, advised." Those with disabilities within the vocational rehabilitation process likewise transfer their dependence from family or medical community to rehabilitation professionals and those within educational or vocational training programs. Those who journey toward independent living transfer dependence from familial or custodial care to self-help and advocacy organizations and independent living programs (Shapiro 1993, 50–58). Esther finds her peer support from her maids and the eunuchs—those who share the margins as powerless and physically other and become coconspirators in her passing. As the role of the one depended upon becomes "unmasked," Lane observes, "dependence is no longer tolerable," and a "dependent's inferior standing seems a gross injustice" (1999, 98). MT Esther confronts her inferior status when she enters before the king in MT 5. She is the one who intercedes with the king in MT 7–9. She appears equal with Mordecai in MT 7:7-8 and 9:29-32. Like the rehabilitation client who has succeeded in job placement or the person with disability who has gained control over the hiring and supervision of his or her personal-care attendant, MT Esther appears to have achieved full independence.

Such independence remains illusory, however. While Cull and Hardy's goal is for people with disabilities to "move toward their independence and self-sufficiency," the whole movement is dependent on "a social obligation to help disabled people" (1972, 6). Furthermore, "Regardless of their qualifications," Eiesland writes, "people with disabilities are regularly denied opportunities for employment because of attitudinal and architectural barriers" (1994, 52). While the independent living movement, by contrast, asserted that people with disabilities "knew better than doctors and professionals what they needed for daily living," the goal of enhancing "the quality of one's life" was still advanced "with help" (Shapiro 1993, 51–52). Such assistance usually relies on financial resources subject to the whims of the political system. MT Esther may become independent from Mordecai, but her power, well-being, and success remain dependent on the whims of the king. Indeed, independence is illusory for all people, with or without disabilities. Susan Wendell reminds us that "most industrialized societies give non-disabled people . . . a lot of help in the form of education, training, social support, public communication and transportation," to name a few (1996, 40–41). "The help that non-disabled people receive tends to be taken for granted and not considered help but entitlement." She continues, "It is only when people need a different kind or amount of help than that given to 'paradigm' citizens that it is "considered help at all, and they are considered socially dependent." Stanley Hauerwas states that people with developmental disabilities "need help, which is but a reminder that that is who we are—creatures who need help," for all people "desperately need one another, but if we forget or deny such need," "we cannot help but become less than we were meant to be" (2004b, 193).

Surprisingly, LXX Esther with her dependence on a faithful and reliable God is less dependent than the self-reliant MT Esther who remains dependent on the whims of an unpredictable monarch. With LXX's theological call to "wait upon the Lord," the focus of events shifts. When Esther appeared before the king, she had not "won his favor" (MT 5:2) by her own merits, but "he looked at her in fierce anger," which is only assuaged when "God changed the spirit of the king to gentleness" (LXX 15:7-8). It is no longer by chance that "the king could not sleep," but now "the Lord took sleep from the king" (6:1) when he was read his debt to Mordecai. Mordecai concludes, "God remembered his people and vindicated his inheritance" (LXX 10:12). Deliverance no longer comes from the king, nor even from Mordecai and Esther, but from God alone. Kings have no freedom to follow their whims, for these too are subject to the will of God. Through dependence and weakness, LXX transforms the defense of a demographic group identity, often seen as a tale of reversal in ethnic group dominance and oppression, into a call to relationship with God.

WORKS CITED

Baden, Joel, and Candida R. Moss. 2011. "The Origin and Interpretation of ṣāraʿat in Leviticus 12–14." *Journal of Biblical Literature* 130: 643–62.

Barnes, Colin, Geof Mercer, and Tom Shakespeare. 1999. *Exploring Disability: A Sociological Introduction*. Cambridge: Polity.

Brueggemann, Walter. 1990. *First and Second Samuel*. Interpretation. Louisville, Ky.: John Knox.

Budd, Philip J. 1984. *Numbers*. Word Biblical Commentary 5. Waco, Tex.: Word.

Cassuto, Leonard. 2002. "Oliver Sacks and the Medical Case Narrative." Pages 118–30 in *Disability Studies: Enabling the Humanities*. Edited by Sharon L. Snyder, Brenda Jo Brueggemann, and Rosemarie Garland-Thomson. New York: Modern Language Association of America.

Cull, John G., and Richard E. Hardy. 1972. *Vocational Rehabilitation: Profession and Process*. Springfield, Ill.: Charles C. Thomas.

Day, Linda. 1995. *Three Faces of a Queen: Characterization in the Books of Esther*. Journal for the Study of the Old Testament Supplement Series 186. Sheffield: Sheffield Academic.

Eiesland, Nancy L. 1994. *The Disabled God: Toward a Liberatory Theology of Disability*. Nashville: Abingdon.

Foucault, Michel. 1973. *The Birth of the Clinic: An Archaeology of Medical Perception*. Translated by A. M. Sheridan Smith. New York: Vintage.

Goldman, S. 1984. "The Book of Esther." Pages 119–88 in *The Five Megilloth*. The Soncino Books of the Bible. Edited by A. Cohen and revised and expanded by A. J. Rosenberg. New York: Soncino.

Hahn, Scott W. 2012. *The Kingdom of God as Liturgical Empire: A Theological Commentary on 1–2 Chronicles*. Grand Rapids: Baker Academic.

Hauerwas, Stanley. 2004a. "Community and Diversity: The Tyranny of Normality." Pages 37–44 in *Critical Reflections on Stanley Hauerwas' Theology of Disability: Disabling Society, Enabling Theology*. Edited by John Swinton. Binghamton, N.Y.: Haworth Pastoral.

———. 2004b. "Reflections on Dependency: A Response to Responses to My Essays on Disability." Pages 191–97 in *Critical Reflections on Stanley Hauerwas' Theology of Disability: Disabling Society, Enabling Theology*. Edited by John Swinton. Binghamton, N.Y.: Haworth Pastoral.

Japhet, Sara. 1993. *I & II Chronicles*. Old Testament Library. Louisville, Ky.: Westminster John Knox.

Johnstone, William. 1997. *1 Chronicles 1–2 Chronicles 9: Israel's Place among the Nations*. Vol. 1 of *1 and 2 Chronicles*. Journal for the Study of the Old Testament Supplement Series. Sheffield: Sheffield Academic.

Jonker, Louis. 2008. "Who Constitutes Society? Yehud's Self-Understanding in the Late Persian Era as Reflected in the Books of Chronicles." *Journal of Biblical Literature* 127: 703–24.

Klein, Ralph W. 2006. *1 Chronicles*. Hermeneia. Minneapolis: Fortress.

Lane, Harlan. 1999. *The Mask of Benevolence: Disabling the Deaf Community*. San Diego: DawnSignPress.

Linton, Simi. 1998. *Claiming Disability: Knowledge and Identity*. New York: New York University Press.

McCarter, P. Kyle. 1984. *II Samuel*. Anchor Bible 9. Garden City, N.Y.: Doubleday.

Melcher, Sarah J. 1998. "Visualizing the Perfect Cult: The Priestly Rational for Exclusion." Pages 55–71 in *Human Disability and the Service of God: Reassessing Religious Practice*. Edited by Nancy L. Eiesland and Don E. Saliers. Nashville: Abingdon.

Milgrom, Jacob. 2000. *Leviticus 17–22*. Anchor Bible 3A. New Haven: Yale University Press.

Moore, Carey A. 1971. *Esther*. Anchor Bible 7B. Garden City, N.Y.: Doubleday.

———. 1977. *Daniel, Esther, and Jeremiah: The Additions*. Anchor Bible 44. Garden City, N.Y.: Doubleday.

Morschauser, Scott. 2010. "A 'Diagnostic' Note on the 'Great Wrath upon Israel' in 2 Kings 3:27." *Journal of Biblical Literature* 129: 299–302.

Myers, Jacob M. 1965. *I Chronicles*. Anchor Bible 12. Garden City, N.Y.: Doubleday.

Schipper, Jeremy. 2006. *Disability Studies and the Hebrew Bible: Figuring Mephibosheth in the David Story*. Library of Hebrew Bible/Old Testament Studies 441. New York: T&T Clark.

———. 2009. "Deuteronomy 24:5 and King Asa's Foot Disease in 1 Kings 15:23b." *Journal of Biblical Literature* 128: 643–48.

Shapiro, Joseph P. 1993. *No Pity: People with Disabilities Forging a New Civil Rights Movement*. New York: Random House.

Wendell, Susan. 1996. *The Rejected Body: Feminist Philosophical Reflections on Disability*. New York: Routledge.

Williamson, H. G. M. 1985. *Ezra, Nehemiah*. Word Biblical Commentary 16. Waco, Tex: Word.

Wright, Beatrice A. 1960. *Physical Disability—A Psychological Approach*. New York: Harper & Row.

Wynn, Kerry H. 1990. "The Socio-historical Contexts of the Recensions of Esther." Ph.D. diss., Southern Baptist Theological Seminary.

Yong, Amos. 2011. *The Bible, Disability, and the Church: A New Vision of the People of God*. Grand Rapids: Eerdmans.

5

Job, Proverbs, and Ecclesiastes

Sarah J. Melcher

INTRODUCTION

Darla Schumm and Michael Stoltzfus make the case that religious teachings and practices help to establish physical norms and standards in cultural representation: "It is widely recognized that religious teachings and practices across the globe help establish cultural representations for what is deemed normal human physical and mental behavior and in establishing typical standards for measuring conventional health and wellbeing" (2016, 1). For example, Proverbs is a biblical book that intends to establish standards for the role of the body in the search for wisdom. The body is depicted as deeply involved in the pursuit of wisdom, and the book presents acquired wisdom as residing deep within the body. Proverbs also makes the case that achieving wisdom plays a role in the body's health and well-being. Long life and good health are seen as the inevitable consequence of following wisdom's path. The focus of the first section will be on Proverbs' attempt to shape a multifaceted, but distinctive, way of understanding the body and physical well-being. This focus, however, is very important to understand the biblical Wisdom literature through the lens of disability. It is widely acknowledged in the field of disability studies that it is important to explore how a culture conceives of embodiment in general to understand the role of disability within that conception (Garland-Thomson 1997, 5–9).

Rosemarie Garland-Thomson argues that the representation of disability in culture is part of a larger cultural project of establishing a hierarchy of corporeal difference, where some bodies are valued as superlative or ordinary while others are devalued as deviating from these standards:

Therefore, I focus here on how disability operates in culture and on how the discourses of disability, race, gender, and sexuality intermingle to create figures of otherness from the raw materials of bodily variation, specifically at sites of representation such as the freak show, sentimental fiction, and black women's liberatory novels. Such an analysis furthers our collective understanding of the complex processes by which *all* forms of corporeal diversity acquire the cultural meanings undergirding a hierarchy of bodily traits that determines the distribution of privilege, status, and power. (1997, 6; emphasis in original)

This chapter will focus on disability in biblical Wisdom literature but will also attempt to follow Garland-Thomson's example and will deal with those passages that hint at superlative and normative models for corporeal standards in culture. Thus, the chapter will focus on disability itself, when the biblical text makes a direct reference, but it will also look at references that seem relevant to cultural standards for corporeal existence.

DISABILITY AND PROVERBS

The book of Proverbs addresses disability in only the most fleeting manner. In fact, of the few direct references to disability, one is found in Prov 26:7: "The legs of a disabled person hang limp; so does a proverb in the mouth of a fool."[1] Here the intent is to construct the figure of speech known as an asyndeton. An asyndeton constructs a relationship between two things simply by placing them side by side. In this asyndeton a comparison is constructed between the two cola in the verse, where in the Hebrew the comparison is accomplished by a simple *waw* "and" (Martin 1995, 67). The implication that is made through this construction is to say that a proverb in the mouth of a fool lacks power in the same way that the legs of a person with a mobility impairment may lack power. Of course, such a comparison with the speaking fool reflects unfavorably upon the person with a disability of the legs. The language used for "fool" or "dullard" in this case is כסיל (kĕsîl). In fact, the word כסיל (kĕsîl) refers to people "with morally deficient characters that prompt their irrational behavior" (Waltke 2014, 112). Proverbs uses the term frequently in contrast to the wise or prudent person (see, e.g., 3:35, 10:1, 14:16, 14:24, etc.).

THE PHYSICALITY OF PROVERBS

In Proverbs the search for wisdom involves the whole person. The body figures prominently in following the path to wisdom.

[1] All translations are the author's.

For example, learning how to live wisely involves the ear, in the practice of active listening, as in Prov 2:2, where the reader is advised about "making your ear attentive to wisdom and inclining your heart to understanding." The active involvement of the ear is also emphasized in 4:20: "My child, be attentive to my words; incline your ear to my sayings." Proverbs 5:1, in its call to attention, makes it clear that the full engagement of the ear is crucial to the pursuit of wisdom: "My child, be attentive to my wisdom; incline your ear to my understanding" (Yoder 2009, 61). In one case, in chapter 5, the speaker places blame for his or her ruin on the failure to incline the ear: "I did not listen to the voice of my teachers or incline my ear to my instructors. Now I am at the point of utter ruin in the public assembly" (vv. 13-14).

In a metaphorical way, wisdom is depicted as an adornment to the body, as something that enhances the body's attractiveness. For example, Prov 1:8-9 both stresses the active involvement of the ear in acquiring instruction and suggests that instruction in wisdom serves as an adornment for the wise one: "Hear, my child, your father's discipline, and do not reject your mother's instruction; for they are a graceful wreath upon your head, and pendants for your neck."

Another feature that emphasizes the physicality of Proverbs and the acquiring of wisdom is the inculcated image of the wise one "walking wisdom's path." Of course, as Proverbs offers a positive image of walking a path to wisdom, it often brings out its opposite, "walking the path toward evil." An example of each of these is found in 4:26-27: "Keep straight the path of your feet, and all your ways will be established. Do not swerve to the right or to the left; turn your foot away from evil." Proverbs 10:9 also uses that contrasting parallelism for which the book is known: "Whoever walks in integrity walks securely, but whoever follows perverse ways will be found out." This verse, too, pictures the pursuit of wisdom as a walking journey along a path but acknowledges the possibility of following a path toward evil (cf. Murphy 1998, 73). Verse 17 in that chapter makes a similar argument for walking the right path: "Whoever heeds training is on the path to life, but one who rejects a rebuke goes astray."

Of course, the capable woman is portrayed substantially by what her hands accomplish:

She seeks wool and flax, and works her hands with delight. . . . She considers a field and buys it; with the fruit of her hands she plants a vineyard. She girds herself with strength, and makes her arms strong. . . . She puts her hands to the distaff, and her hands grasp the spindle. She opens her hand to the poor, and reaches out her hands to the needy. (Prov 31:13, 16-17, 19-20)

Her hands are strong, and they are involved with supporting her household and showing solidarity to the poor. With her hands she demonstrates her own initiative in acquiring land. She makes clothing with some skill; her hands are a symbol of her capability. Hands serve the quest for a wise and honorable life. The passage concludes by offering her a reward for using her strong and capable hands wisely: "Give her a share in the fruit of her hands, and let her works praise her in the city gates" (Prov 31:31).

As Proverbs constructs it, wisdom resides deep within a person's body, most often in the heart. The heart is deeply involved in the pursuit of wisdom: "My child, give me your heart, and let your eyes observe my ways" (23:26). Also, 23:12 shows the involvement of the heart: "Apply your heart to discipline and your ear to words of knowledge." The innermost part of the body is involved in acquiring knowledge: "The heart of the discerning one acquires knowledge, and the ear of the wise seeks knowledge" (18:15). The heart influences other parts of the body and helps the wise one to behave well: "The heart of the wise makes their speech judicious, and adds learning to their lips" (16:23).

The most startling physical aspect of the book of Proverbs is the promise of long life as a consequence of living a life in pursuit of wisdom. The book constructs a relationship between walking the path of wisdom and living to a ripe old age. A major emphasis in Proverbs is to encourage the reader to see the consequences of living the life of wisdom. Wisdom herself contrasts the consequences of two different ways of life: "For waywardness kills the simple, and the complacency of fools destroys them; but those who listen to me will dwell securely and at ease, without dread of disaster" (Prov 1:32-33).

Of course, Proverbs also advocates for solidarity for those who are vulnerable. Proverbs 31:8-9 is an interesting example: "Speak out for those who cannot speak, for the rights of all the destitute. Speak out, judge righteously, defend the rights of the poor and needy."

An underlying assumption of the book of Proverbs is that leading a life in the pursuit of wisdom and in the practice of prudence will result in long life, health, and prosperity. An example of this can be found in Prov 3:1-2: "My child, do not forget my teaching, but let your heart keep my commandments; for length of days and years of life and abundant welfare they will give you." As Leo G. Perdue describes these two verses, "The motive clauses that follow in the succeeding couplet are two of the chief values of the wisdom tradition: long life (3:16; 4:10) and well-being (3:17)" (2000, 96). A second assumption is that the avoidance of evil deeds and walking God's path will lead also to long life, health, and prosperity.

Chapter 4 (vv. 11, 12) goes so far as to say this: "I have taught you the way of wisdom; I have led you in the paths of uprightness. When you walk, your step will not be hampered; and if you run, you will not stumble." Though verse 12 may be intended as metaphorical, the implication is that following the path of righteousness will keep one fully mobile.

A reading from a disability perspective challenges these underlying assumptions. People with disabilities and the people who love them have long known that the occurrence of disability has nothing to do with sin or transgression, nor can disability be avoided by pursuing wisdom or acting with prudence. For the most part, disability is a random occurrence, though according to a U.S. Census report in 2010, 56.7 million people in the United States, or 19 percent of the population, had a disability.

Yet it is the underlying assumptions that are most troubling from a disability studies perspective—those assumptions that make a link between following wisdom and health, prosperity, and long life. The link that is constructed suggests that following wisdom leads inevitably to a life lived without disability. These underlying assumptions are oppressive to those who have a disability. In a sense, Proverbs is stating that the path to wisdom provides a way to maintain one's bodily health. The book of Proverbs suggests that the pursuit of wisdom results in "normal bodies"—that is, bodies without a serious impairment. All who acquire wisdom, according to Proverbs' worldview, will live a long life free of physical impairment. Of course, as the book of Proverbs defines a standard for embodiment, it also establishes the bodily traits that lie outside the standard. In addition, Proverbs implies that the person whose body does not fit the standard has not acquired the requisite amount or kind of wisdom necessary to ensure physical well-being. A body outside the normal implies a person who is not wise.

Stanley Hauerwas discusses the "tyranny of normality" in an early essay where he states, "The most stringent power we have over another is not physical coercion but the ability to have the other accept our definition of them" (2004, 40). Proverbs defines some as worthy of a vibrant physicality and others as unworthy. Hauerwas advocates for "a community of diversity that enhances differences" (40). He speaks against the kind of tyranny that defines, on the one hand, some bodies as acceptable and as indicators of a life lived prudently and, on the other hand, some bodies as below standard and as indicators of a life devoid of wisdom.

Proverbs does imply that some bodies are deemed outside the norm. In the words of Douglas Baynton, "The natural and the normal are both ways of establishing the universal, unquestionable good and right. Both are also ways of establishing social hierarchies that justify the denial of legitimacy and certain rights to individuals or groups" (2013, 18). In Proverbs the wise are established as the elite and at the top of the social ladder, as those who are rewarded physically for their possession of wisdom. Those who do not belong to this group are regarded as lower in the social hierarchy, and their physical nature reflects their lower status. In the final analysis, it seems clear that the book of Proverbs can foster ableist perspectives.

DISABILITY AND ECCLESIASTES

The Wisdom literature provides diverse perspectives vis-à-vis disability, and the transition from Proverbs to Ecclesiastes is one of stark contrast. Proverbs constructs a well-ordered life in which the pursuit of wisdom provides the expectation of a peaceful life with physical well-being. Ecclesiastes, on the other hand, emphasizes that the benefits from the pursuit of wisdom are limited. In Ecclesiastes wisdom does not guarantee a full life with all the physical benefits.

Physical life itself is ephemeral, according to Ecclesiastes. Length of life, even for the righteous, is not a stable category. Life can be fleeting, even for the wise. James L. Crenshaw suggests that the preoccupation with death is the book's primary emphasis:

> The arbitrariness of death troubles Qohelet more than anything else. His predecessors believed in a positive correlation between virtue (or lack of it) and the timing and manner of one's death. They explained rare instances of incongruity by appeal to family or community influence. Qohelet denies any pattern at all in death's timing and choice of victims. (1987, 25)

While Crenshaw has a point, I think that Qoheleth's concern is broader throughout the book, meaning that he is focused on human limitations more generally. The author(s) stresses many of life's limitations, including the transience of life itself. These various limitations will be the focus here. I have been strongly influenced in this approach by two books: *Coping with Transience: Ecclesiastes on Brevity in Life* by Daniel Fredericks (1993) and *Disability and Christian Theology: Embodied Limits and Constructive Possibilities* by Deborah Creamer (2009).

Perhaps Qoheleth's view of life's fleeting nature is reflected in the frequent and strategic use of the Hebrew term הבל (*hebel*). The word appears thirty-nine times in the book of Ecclesiastes (Seow 2000). Literally, the meaning is "breath, whiff, puff, steam":

> It refers to anything that is superficial, ephemeral, insubstantial, incomprehensible, enigmatic, inconsistent, or contradictory. Something that is *hebel*

cannot be grasped or controlled. It may refer to something that one encounters or experiences for only a moment, but it cannot be grasped—neither physically nor intellectually. (Seow 1997, 47)

For the most part, the word הבל (*hebel*) appears in two key phrases in Ecclesiastes: "all is breath" and "this (also) is breath." The word is used frequently to convey the idea that nothing in human life is truly permanent. Only the earth (1:4) and some other works of God are permanent: "I know that whatever God does endures forever; nothing can be added to it, nor anything taken from it; God has done this, so that all should stand in awe before him" (Eccl 3:14). In contrast, the works of humanity are ephemeral are fleeting.

Seow makes a very good case for understanding הבל (*hebel*) as a key to the meaning of the book of Ecclesiastes as a whole (2000, 1). This is also the position of Fredericks, who states, "The whole meaning of Ecclesiastes depends on this somewhat ambiguous metaphor, 'breath'" (1993, 11–12). Seow argues convincingly that the uses of the term הבל (*hebel*), whether employed on the literal end of the spectrum or on the metaphorical, never departs from the root sense of "breath" or "vapor," stressing the ephemeral nature of life itself and of life's activities. For Fredericks, the very pronunciation of the term הבל (*hebel*) reflects its meaning, suggesting that the etymology is onomatopoeic; "that is, it is *aspirated* initially by 'h' and continued by the *spirant* 'v' sound, thus spoken by the exhalation of breath that the word itself denotes. The pronunciation is itself a direct illustration of what the word means" (1993, 12). In his conclusion Fredericks emphasizes Qoheleth's focus on what is temporary in life. He translates the final phrase using several occurrences of the word הבל (*hebel*) as "temporary, temporary; *total* temporariness" (92; Eccl 12:8).

Ecclesiastes focuses considerable attention on the limits of physical life. Ecclesiastes 1:15 may reflect this sense of limits: "What is crooked cannot be made straight, and what is lacking cannot be counted." Though there is likely to be a metaphorical element to the statement, at the basis of all metaphor is a rootedness in the physical world (Lakoff and Johnson 1999). According to Ecclesiastes, there is much in life that is beyond human control. It may also reflect a certain level of pessimism that a physical blow may leave a mark that cannot be remedied.

Deborah Creamer's book *Disability and Christian Theology*, read in conjunction with the book of Ecclesiastes, provides insight into Qoheleth's worldview. Qoheleth seems depressed or saddened by humanity's limits while Creamer views this through a more positive lens, but both Creamer and Qoheleth see limits as inherent and unsurprising aspects of human life:

I begin with the claim that limits are a common and unsurprising aspect of being human. We may already know this, but it is also something we tend to forget or reject. In common usage, the word "limited" comes with a particular connotation, signifying a lack or absence and emphasizing what cannot be done. It highlights barriers and constraints—one *is* limited. I propose an understanding of limits that more positively connotes a quality of being. It emphasizes a characteristic of humanity—one *has* limits. This proposal suggests that limits, rather than being an array of unfortunate alternatives to omnipotence, are an unsurprising characteristic of human nature. (2009, 93–94)

Creamer highlights three "significant religious claims" that are central to the limits model and that resonate with Christian tradition (2009, 94). First, having limits is an unsurprising aspect of being human; that is, human beings are clearly different from God and dependent upon God. A second claim is that having limits is intrinsic, that it is part of what it means to be human. The third is that limits are good (94). This makes sense since humanity was part of God's good creation from the beginning and humans had limits from the beginning. In fact, Creamer argues that the limits model "explores how limits constitute our self-understandings and our relationality with others. It leads to an ethic of how we should act toward others" (95).

Creamer maintains that society tends to view disability through a "deficit model," which sees disability as having a lack, rather than seeing limits as part of a good creation. The limits model offers us a new paradigm for thinking about disability—a paradigm that views limits in a positive way. The limits model also helps with the porous category of "disability." Because those people with disabilities may share little in common with others in the same category, it is difficult to find common ground. On the other hand, all persons have an understanding of the category of "limits," since that is a part of every person's experience. Finally, Creamer offers the following insight: "The limits model challenges the deficit model, suggesting that disability is not something that exists solely as a negative experience of limitation but rather that it is an intrinsic, unsurprising, and valuable element of human limit-ness" (2009, 96).

Of course, for Qoheleth, the most obvious physical limit that all persons share is the ephemeral nature of life itself. No matter how much honor a person attains in life, or how much success one achieves, or how much fame one experiences, in the end it does not matter, for humans will not be remembered by the generations that follow: "The people of long ago are not remembered, nor will there be any remembrance of people yet to come by those who come after them" (Eccl 1:11). All humans meet the same end. Death is inevitable and reflects a common limitation for all humanity. The theme occurs again in chapter 2: "The wise have eyes in their head, but fools walk in darkness. Yet I perceived that the same fate befalls all of them" (2:14).

Qoheleth emphasizes the joy that can come in life, and since life is fleeting, the reader is encouraged to pursue joy and grasp it when possible. The body is deeply involved in the pursuit of joy: "Whatever my eyes desired I did not keep from them; I kept my heart from no pleasure, for my heart found pleasure in all my toil, and this was my reward for all my toil" (Eccl 2:10). The most frequent source of joy is toil, according to Qoheleth.

However, Qoheleth expresses the limits of joy and pleasure by stating that "all things are wearisome; more than one can express; the eye is not satisfied with seeing, or the ear filled with hearing" (Eccl 1:8). Not surprisingly, this limit is expressed in physical terms as insatiable human desires that cannot be fulfilled through any aspect of the body, including sight and hearing. In essence, the human body cannot satisfy the desires within the human person. If a person should find satisfaction for their desires through toil or through pleasures, this ultimately is fleeting as well: "Whatever my eyes desired I did not keep from them; I kept my heart from no pleasure, for my heart found pleasure in all my toil, and this was my reward for all my toil. Then I considered all that my hands had done and the toil I had spent in doing it, and again, all was vapor and a chasing after wind, and there was no advantage under the sun" (2:10-11).

In spite of pleasure's limitations, Ecclesiastes advocates that human beings enjoy life when possible, as it is a gift from God: "Moreover, it is God's gift that all should eat and drink and take pleasure in all their toil" (Eccl 3:13). In particular, one should pursue and experience pleasure, because there is no way to know what will come later: "So I saw that there is nothing better than that all should enjoy their work, for that is their lot; who can bring them to see what will be after them?" (3:22).

Qoheleth recognizes that there are limits to human knowledge. Human beings lack the ability to grasp all that is important in life. Full knowledge of God and the patterns of life seem just out of reach. The pursuit of wisdom can be like vapor; the full grasp of it is elusive.

One of life's limits is humanity's inability to make sense of existence. As the poem in chapter 3 indicates, there is a rhythm to life, and it is possible that God has an organized plan, but it is impossible for human beings to discern the divine pattern: "He has made everything suitable for its time; moreover he has put a sense of past and future into their minds, yet they cannot find out what God has done from the beginning to the end" (Eccl 3:11). Human beings can sense that nature reflects patterns instilled by the divine, but people do not have the capacity to recognize those patterns fully. According to Qoheleth, the accomplishments of life are fleeting, indeed:

> I applied my mind to seek and to search out by wisdom all that is done under heaven; it is an unhappy business that God has given to human beings to be busy with. I saw all the deeds that are done under the sun; and see, all is vapor and a chasing after wind. (1:14)

Chapter 1 of Ecclesiastes sets the tone for the rest of the book. The notion that true wisdom is beyond the grasp of humankind is a theme that crops up in many places in Ecclesiastes. In the author's perspective, whoever we are in life and whatever we humans build here on earth will not last: "The people of long ago are not remembered, nor will there be any remembrance of people yet to come by those who come after them" (1:11).

ECCLESIASTES 2

In chapter 2 Qoheleth provides a list of his many accomplishments and the things that have brought him pleasure (2:1-10), but his conclusion is that this is הבל (*hebel*): "Then I considered all that my hands had done and the toil I had spent in doing it, and again, all was vapor and a chasing after wind, and there was no advantage under the sun" (2:11). Chapter 2 is a pivotal chapter in Ecclesiastes for two reasons: first, Qoheleth makes it clear that a list of accomplishments, no matter how impressive, does not solve the fundamental problem of the brevity of life; and second, both the wise and the foolish meet the same end. In the first section of chapter 2 (vv. 1-10), Qoheleth describes the experiments he attempted in order to discern life's meaning. At the top of the list, Qoheleth indicates that he experimented with pleasure: "I said to myself, 'Come now, I will make a test of pleasure; enjoy yourself.' But again, this also was vapor" (2:1). Laughter and pleasure did not provide a lasting benefit, nor did wine or folly. Qoheleth states his own purpose in exploring these, "until I might see what was good for mortals to do under heaven during the few days of their life" (2:3). Though he pursues pleasure in order to find meaning, Qoheleth conducts this search with constant knowledge of the brevity of life.

As part of his search for meaning, Qoheleth used his wealth to build some impressive works, including gardens and parks (2:5). He acquired many possessions, including some very luxurious items—"treasures of kings" (v. 8). In fact, he claimed that he accumulated more wealth than anyone else in Jerusalem. Qoheleth did find pleasure in all his toil, but in the end he concluded that it had no lasting value: "Then I considered all that my hands had done and the toil I had spent in doing it, and again, all was vapor and a chasing after wind, and there was nothing to be gained under the sun" (2:11). The value of pleasure, wealth, and other accomplishments is fleeting.

Even the pursuit of wisdom has limits, as Qoheleth discovered during his quest. Wisdom is one of life's goods, dramatically excelling folly (2:13), and the wise have better behavior than the fool: "The wise have eyes in their head, but fools walk in darkness. Yet I perceived that the same fate befalls all of them" (2:14). Indeed, Qoheleth wonders if there was any point in cultivating wisdom, since both the wise and the fools meet the same fate: "Then I said to myself, 'What happens to the fool will happen to me also; why then have I been so very wise?' And I said to myself that this also is vapor" (2:15). The benefits of wisdom, though pleasing in themselves, are fleeting and last only through one lifetime. Neither the wise one nor the fool is remembered after death (v. 16).

It is because of the fleeting nature of life and because of the elusive nature of life's benefits that Qoheleth concludes, "There is nothing better for mortals than to eat and drink, and find enjoyment in their toil. This also, I saw, is from the hand of God" (2:24). Qoheleth recommends eating, drinking, and finding enjoyment where and when one can. Such enjoyment certainly will not last. Indeed, one cannot achieve any permanent benefit from what one does. In fact, all will face death, whatever one does.

ECCLESIASTES 3

Chapter 3 of Ecclesiastes affirms the idea that there is a pattern in time to created life on earth. The very famous poem of verses 1-8 presents a seasonal polarity, in which a balance is constructed between the contrasting ends of a spectrum: "a time to be born, and a time to die; a time to plant, and a time to pluck up what is planted . . ." (3:2).

However, after affirming this seasonal pattern, Qoheleth then expresses the limits inherent in this pattern: "He has made everything suitable for its time; moreover he has put a sense of past and future into their minds, yet they cannot find out what God has done from the beginning to the end" (3:11). In other words, God has embedded time-structured patterns within created life, patterns that human beings can discern. In addition, people have instilled within them a sense of the past and the future.

But they are unable to know all the acts of God from beginning to end, indicating their limits in contrast to what God can do. (Eccl 11:5 offers a similar perspective: "Just as you do not know how the breath comes to the bones in the mother's womb, so you do not know the work of God, who makes everything." In other words, there are limits to human wisdom.) As he does elsewhere, Qoheleth extols the greatness of God: "I know that whatever God does endures forever; nothing can be added to it, nor anything taken from it; God has done this, so that all should stand in awe before him" (3:14). God is not constrained by limits, since the acts of God "endure forever." Though it does not state so explicitly, verse 14 suggests that God endures forever as well, that God is not subject to a fleeting life as human beings are.

Given the limits that human beings experience, Qoheleth recommends that people eat, drink, and find enjoyment where they can (cf. Eccl 11:9). Specifically, he suggests that work is a place where enjoyment can be found (3:13). Yet after making these recommendations, Qoheleth raises another irony in human limitations: human beings will meet the same fate as animals (v. 19); both will meet death. This irony is characterized as הבל (hebel, "vapor"). Life for both animals and humans is fleeting, like vapor (cf. 11:10).

Ecclesiates 4

Though life is fleeting, generally speaking Qoheleth affirms life itself and recommends enjoyment of pleasure (as he does in chapters 2 and 3), when possible, but there are some exceptions to this in the book. A striking exception is found in chapter 4:

> Again I saw all the oppressions that are practiced under the sun. Look, the tears of the oppressed—with no one to comfort them! On the side of their oppressors there was power—with no one to comfort them. And I thought the dead, who have already died, more fortunate than the living, who are still alive; but better than both is the one who has not yet been, and has not seen the evil deeds that are done under the sun. (4:1-3)

In the case of human oppression, Qoheleth argues that those who have died already or those who were never born are better off than those living human beings who must endure or witness evil oppression under the sun (cf. 7:1-4, where Qoheleth contends that the day of death is better than the day of birth and the house of mourning better than the house of mirth). Though Qoheleth does take this difficult stance in 4:1-3, he is generally affirming of life and advises others to enjoy life's pleasures.

Nevertheless, this position is not helpful from a disability perspective. Qoheleth takes the stance that it is better to be dead so as not to witness evil, particularly in this literary context of human oppression. Certainly, people with disabilities and their allies have witnessed oppression, and people with disabilities have sometimes experienced oppression. Qoheleth's viewpoint here raises quality-of-life issues. Hopefully we will move to the point where decisions surrounding quality of life will be made by those who witness or experience oppression themselves, not by an implied author who wishes to state more generally that there are some circumstances in which life cannot be affirmed. In contrast to Eccl 4:1-3, it is worth noting that life is strongly affirmed in 9:4-6:

> But whoever is joined with all the living has hope, for a living dog is better than a dead lion. The living know that they will die, but the dead know nothing; they have no more reward, and even the memory of them is lost. Their love and their hate and their envy have already perished; never again will they have any share in all that happens under the sun.

A very helpful perspective in chapter 4 is found in verses 9-12:

> Two are better than one, because they have a good reward for their labor. For if they fall, one will lift up the other; but woe to one who is alone and falls and does not have another to help lift up. Again, if two lie together, they keep warm; but how can one keep warm alone? And though one might overpower another, two will withstand one. A threefold cord is not quickly broken.

This brief statement advocates for people to rely upon one another. It suggests that relationships are positive and that two people together may lift one another up when support is necessary. Disability studies maintain that healthy, mutual relationships are beneficial for people with disabilities. In some cases people with disabilities may successfully join together in order to advocate for social change (Shakespeare 2013, 215–17). Elsewhere, Qoheleth recommends the enjoyment of life with one's spouse: "Enjoy life with the wife whom you love, all the days of your fleeting life that are given you under the sun—all your fleeting days—it is your portion in life and your toil at which you labor under the sun" (Eccl 9:9). Thus, he urges the reader to enjoy that relationship.

In conclusion, then, the book of Ecclesiastes offers a useful perspective through a disability lens because of its emphasis on the limits of human life. The author of Ecclesiastes has come to accept the idea that human limitations are an expected and inevitable aspect of life. We modern readers can adopt this acceptance to our benefit. This could serve as a counternarrative to the modern notion that disability represents a deviation from what is "normal." Qoheleth recognizes that all human beings are subject to limits. He acknowledges that limits can become more pronounced or noticeable as a person ages:

> Remember your creator in the days of your youth, before the difficult days come, and the years approach when you will say, "I have no pleasure in them"; before the sun and the light and the moon and the stars grow dark and the gloomy clouds return with the rain; in the day when the guards of the house tremble, and the strong men are bent, and the women who grind cease working because they are few, and those who look through the windows see dimly; when the doors on the street are shut, and the sound of the hand mill is low, and one rises up at the sound of a bird, and all the daughters of song are brought low; when one is afraid of heights, and terrors are in the road; the almond tree blossoms, the grasshopper drags itself along and the caper berry fails; because all must go to their eternal home, and the mourners will go about the streets; before the silver cord is snapped, and the golden bowl is broken, and the pitcher is broken at the fountain, and the wheel crushed at the cistern, and the dust returns to the earth as it was, and the breath returns to God who gave it. (12:1-7)

Ecclesiastes 12:1-7 depicts life as people age, when vision becomes impaired and people are otherwise physically affected. It acknowledges that as we age, we develop greater physical limits. All human beings, then, if they live long enough, will experience disability as they grow older.

DISABILITY AND JOB

THE PROSE FRAMEWORK OF JOB: JOB 1–2; 42:7-17

One of the most problematic sections of Job, from the perspective of disability and the Bible, is the prose framework. The prose framework, of course, sets up a kind of wager between God and השׂתן (*hasatan*, "the Adversary"). The Adversary examines individuals to see if they are genuinely pious toward God or if they are neglecting pious activity. This work of examination is apparently acceptable to God and expected from the Adversary. In light of the Adversary's vocation, God offers up Job as an example for the Adversary to consider: "The LORD said to the Adversary, 'Have you considered my servant Job? There is no one like him on the earth, a blameless and upright man who fears God and turns away from evil'" (Job 1:8). The Adversary argues that Job's faithfulness has much to do with God's preferential treatment of him, protecting him from harm and making him prosperous (vv. 9-10): "But stretch out your hand now, and touch all that he has, and he will curse you to your face" (1:11). God takes the Adversary's challenge and grants permission for the Adversary to strike anything of Job's, but not to injure Job directly (1:12).

Of course, the results of the Adversary's first round of strikes against "all that he has" are horrendous. Oxen, donkeys, sheep, camels, servants, sons, and daughters are all killed through the actions of the Adversary (vv. 13-19). In the epilogue (42:7-17), Job's fortunes are restored and he fathers a new set of children:

> The LORD blessed the latter days of Job more than his beginning; and he had fourteen thousand sheep, six thousand camels, a thousand yoke of oxen, and a thousand donkeys.
>
> He also had seven sons and three daughters. He named the first Jemimah, the second Keziah, and the third Keren-happuch. In all the land there were no women so beautiful as Job's daughters; and their father gave them an inheritance along with their brothers. After this Job lived one hundred and forty years, and saw his children, and his children's children, four generations. And Job died, old and full of days. (42:12-17)

At the risk of being a "naïve reader," the wager and test of Job, including the death of Job's children, his servants, and the many animals under his care, raise some ethical issues from a disability perspective (for this sense of a "naïve" reading, see Newsom 2003, 36). Carol Newsom discusses the work of Adam Zachary Newton, who "focuses on the act of narrating as a site of ethical inquiry" (36). Newton's work helps the reader to clarify whether it is appropriate or naïve to be upset over the test of Job and the death of his children. Newton argues for the transformative power of narrative:

> As we know from Coleridge, the sheer experience of narrating or witnessing stories can transform persons in ways they often cannot control. Indeed, the mere representation of another, the translation of human "background" into fictional form, is fraught with ethical tensions. (1995, 291)

The ancient authors and compilers may have intended that the reader focus on the ethical integrity of Job, but the (perhaps) unintended result of the prose framework of Job is that it engenders dismay in some of its current readers. As Newton argues, a representation of a person's physical being "calls its perceivers and fabricators to account" (1995, 291). When reading from a "disability and the Bible" perspective, the arbitrary death of servants and offspring presents an ethical tension worthy of discussion.

Of course, one of the important ethical issues that the prose narrative framework raises is the idea that God has caused or allowed extreme hardship. According to the narrative setup, God has permitted השׂטן (hasatan, "the Adversary") to inflict extreme hardship on Job directly. Some commentators have argued that this very setup is preposterous. This preposterous nature of the narrative setup has influenced some commentators to dismiss God's role in Job's suffering as beside the point. The argument is that God's behavior is so implausible that the reader then must focus on Job's disinterested piety. However, through the lens of disability theology, the role of the deity in human suffering must be acknowledged. Of course, one possible way to view the issue of theodicy in the prose framework is to note that Job represents the kinds of "vulnerabilities and contingencies" to which human life is subject (Clifton 2015, 30).

An important issue in disability studies and theology is the value of human life. Often in disability studies arguments are given for the high value of life itself. The prose framework of Job argues against the high valuation of human beings through the early annihilation of the servants and offspring, then through the subsequent replacement of children in the epilogue (42:7-17). Quality-of-life conversations can be very controversial. However, in disability studies the primary movement is to affirm the quality of all human life. Scholars in disability studies point to the value of life as evidenced in the daily interactions with people with disabilities. In the words of Martha Saxton,

> Many who resist selective abortion insist that there is something deeply valuable and profoundly human (though difficult to articulate in the sound bites of contemporary thought) in meeting or loving a child or adult with a severe disability. (2013, 90)

In any event, the depiction of almost every relative and close associate of Job being wiped out is disturbing to many, and with some readers it raises a question about God, God's intentions, and God's sense of justice. A reading through the lens of disability might want to read against the grain in this case.

Job's Physical and Social Suffering in Chapters 16, 17, and 19

Chapters 16, 17 and 19 are important from a disability theology perspective because they represent Job's own voice describing his physical suffering and social alienation. He also discusses God's violence and injustice throughout (see also Newsom 2003, 124). Though Job's physical afflictions are temporary and he is restored to health in the epilogue, Job's condition fits the concept of disability rather well. As Hebrew Bible scholar Rebecca Raphael argues, Job's condition fits the category of disability since the effects of his unnamed skin disease "significantly impair his daily life"

(2004, 3). Job's descriptions of his disability in 30:16-19 contrast significantly with his former status in 29:15-16. He seems confined to his home
without any travel outside the immediate vicinity, and he experiences
notable social estrangement as a result of his disease (3). As disability activists have argued time and again, it is crucial in disability studies to listen
carefully to the voice and expressed experience of people with disabilities.
The slogan "Nothing about us without us" exemplifies one of the most
important precepts of disability studies—that people with disabilities and
their perspectives should be "included in accounts of disability and the
formation of disability policy" (Lukin 2013, 313). The closest we can come
to listening to Job's voice about his experience of disability is to attend to
Job 16, 17, and 19.

Job attributes his predicament to God. Of course, the reader of the
prologue (Job 1:1–2:13) is under the impression that השׂטן (hasatan, "the
Adversary") is directly responsible for afflicting Job with skin disease. The
premise of the prologue, however, indicates that God allows the Adversary
to afflict Job (2:6; though 2:3 implies that God is complicit in the attack).
As we have seen, Job sees all life as subject to God's sovereignty; that is, Job
attributes both good and bad things to God: "He said, 'Naked I came from
my mother's womb, and naked shall I return there; the LORD gave, and the
LORD has taken away; blessed be the name of the LORD'" (Job 1:21).

In Job 16:7-17 Job describes his situation as the result of divine action
against him. In verse 7 Job accuses God of wearing him out and devastating all his closest family and friends: "Surely now God has worn me out;
he has made desolate all my company" (16:7) (for the meaning of עדתי
['adati, "my company"], see Hartley 1988, 259). God's actions are so severe
that it gives Job's friends reason to accuse him of wrongdoing: "And he
has shriveled me up, which is a witness against me; my leanness has risen
up against me, and it testifies to my face" (Job 16:8). In spite of his innocence, Job states that the community will assume that he is guilty of the
most egregious, deliberate sin because he has been visibly and physically
stricken by God.

The language in verses 9-14 describes God as Job's adversary. According to these verses, God has launched a violent attack against Job, though
aided frequently by human enemies. Indeed, God has turned Job over to
these human enemies to be mistreated in the extreme:

> He has torn me in his wrath, and hated me; he has gnashed his teeth at me;
> my adversary sharpens his eyes against me. They have opened their mouths
> at me; they have struck me reproachfully on the cheek; they mass themselves
> together against me. God gives me up to the ungodly, and casts me into the

hands of the wicked. I was at ease, and he broke me in two; he seized me by the neck and dashed me to pieces; he set me up as his target; his archers surround me. He slashes open my kidneys, and shows no mercy; he pours out my gall on the ground. He bursts upon me again and again; he rushes at me like a warrior.

The rhetoric of verses 9-14 implies that God is abusive. Some of the Hebrew verbal forms denote repetitive or continuing behavior on God's part. For instance, S. R. Driver and G. B. Gray (1921) suggest the translation of "hate actively" for the form וישטמני (vayistmeni). The sense of the imperfect in the case is continuous action, indicating that God continued to "hate Job actively" (Hartley 1988, 260). In verse 9 God is depicted as tearing Job in wrath, gnashing his teeth at him, and "sharpening the eyes"—that is, glaring at him.

The same kind of abusive treatment comes from human beings as well, for in verse 10 the people stare at him with their mouths open, strike him on the cheek, and gather together against him. In verse 11 Job interprets the abuse from human beings as a result of God handing Job over to the ungodly and casting him into the hands of the wicked.

God's deliberate violence toward Job intensifies in verse 12: "I was at ease, and he broke me in two; he seized me by the neck and dashed me to pieces; he set me up as his target" (16:12). The description of violence is extreme, depicting God as doing more than attacking. God breaks Job in two and dashes him to pieces. Of course, verses 13 and 14 heighten the impression of God as abuser, as God is portrayed as slashing open kidneys without mercy and bursting upon Job again and again.

Chapter 16 raises the issue clearly of God as abusive. This can have some relevance in reading Scripture from the perspective of disability. Because of Job's intense suffering, it is no wonder that he would see God as abusive. In *Facing the Abusing God*, David Blumenthal (1993; see also Pfau and Blumenthal 2001) references Job in his search for biblical examples of protest against God's harmful actions. It may be that some people with disabilities have seen God as abusive. However, it is also the case that Job serves as an example of someone who protested God's treatment of him. The book of Job is extremely important to interpretation from a disability perspective because Job is someone who was in dialogue with God (Blumenthal 1993, 251). Job and some traditional interpretations of the book offer the reader permission to argue with God (Laytner 1990). Blumenthal eloquently notes the role of the book of Job in empowering a theology of protest:

The theology of protest goes back to the Bible and is present most forcefully in the Book of Job. The central figure in that text, Job, never questions God's existence, nor God's power to do what God is doing. Rather, Job questions God's justification, God's morality, God's justice. Throughout, Job rejects the moral panaceas and theological rationalizations of his friends, as does God in the end. No pat answers; rather the repeated assertion of his innocence and the recurrent questioning of God's justice. No easy resolutions; rather, the repeated assertion of loyalty to God and the recurrent accusation of injustice. (1993, 251)

A theology of protest can be a very important and cathartic outlet for people with disabilities and for those who love them. One should remember as well that the biblical record indicates that God can be moved by protest and dialogue, as in Gen 18:16-33, where Abraham challenges God, saying,

Then Abraham came near and said, "Will you indeed sweep away the righteous with the wicked? Suppose there are fifty righteous within the city; will you then sweep away the place and not forgive it for the fifty righteous who are in it? Far be it from you to do such a thing, to slay the righteous with the wicked, so that the righteous fare as the wicked! Far be that from you! Shall not the Judge of all the earth do what is just?" (Gen 18:23-25)

Yet for all the talk of abuse, Job turns ironically to God to exonerate him. "Even now, in fact, my witness is in heaven, and he that vouches for me is on high" (Job 16:19). The implication is that God knows the truth about Job's innocence, which Job has just proclaimed again in verse 17. Since God can testify as a witness, Job makes an appeal to God in spite of his perspective that God is his abuser. In Job's judicial world, God functions as accuser, as well as witness and arbitrator: "that he would maintain the right of a mortal with God, as one does for a neighbor" (16:21). God is the only one who can confirm Job's innocence, so with tears Job turns to God to arbitrate on Job's behalf (contra Gray 2010, 255).

In the tradition of the complaint psalms, Job continues in chapter 17 to recount his painful experience. Job begins by stating, "My spirit is broken; my days are extinguished; the graveyard is ready for me" (17:1). The character of Job continues by relating that people are mocking him and provoking him. Yet in verses 3 and 4, Job appeals to God to "make a pledge" with God; that is, the deity would make a pledge on Job's behalf with the deity (Gray 2010, 258). Job asks God to be the one "to give surety for me" (v. 3)—that is, provide a bond or deposit to guarantee Job's innocence in this matter. He petitions God not to let the mockers prevail (v. 4). Job suggests that friends have denounced him in order to benefit from his property. His social alienation is deep. Indeed, Job's sense of being abused by God may be related to his experience of being abused by his friends and by society's conventions. In other words, Job's protest is ultimately based in his sense of social alienation, and his only recourse is to cry out to or against God.

In the tradition of a true lament, Job lists the problems that beset him: "My eye has grown dim from grief, and all my members are like a shadow" (Job 17:7). Righteous and pure people are disturbed by his physical state, probably in the presumption that Job is guilty of wrongdoing (v. 8). Yet Job affirms that a righteous person stays on the right path and that those who are innocent grow stronger and stronger (v. 9). Job invites those who have deserted him back, proclaiming their lack of wisdom. However, he thinks that his days are at an end and his deepest desires and plans are thwarted. Toward the end of chapter 17, Job anticipates that he is facing his impending death, so that he will soon be in the company of worms in the pit, in Sheol (vv. 13-14). Job ends his speech in chapter 17 by asking from where the hope for his future would come: "Where then is my hope? Who will see my hope? Will it go down to the bars of Sheol? Shall we descend together into the dust?" (vv. 15-16).

Job again wonders whether his current suffering will end in death. He is so distraught because of his grief and his physical condition that he wonders if there is any hope for him or whether he will end up in Sheol. His questions about his future end the chapter, and Bildad's response in chapter 18 follows immediately.

After Bildad presents a predictable world in which the wicked experience punishment for their misdeeds, in chapter 19 Job discusses his situation. He makes the point that his friends assume that he is guilty of wrongdoing (19:3-5). Beginning with verse 6, Job takes the position that God has "put me in the wrong." Though Job cries out to God, he complains that there is no justice. God has stripped Job of his good status and of his hope (vv. 9-10). Verses 11 and 12 portray God as Job's enemy and God as having a battalion that enacts violence on God's behalf. In verses 13-19 Job describes his sense of social alienation, which is clearly very deep:

> He has put my family far from me, and my acquaintances are wholly
>   estranged from me.
> My relatives and my close friends have forgotten me;
> the guests in my house have forgotten me; my serving girls count me as
>   a stranger; I have become a foreigner in their eyes.
> I call to my servant, but he gives me no answer; with my own mouth I
>   plead with him.
> My breath is repulsive to my wife; I am loathsome to my own family.

> Even young children despise me; when I rise, they talk against me.
> All my intimate friends abhor me, and those whom I loved have turned against me.

Chapters 16, 17, and 19 depict a deep sense of isolation for Job in conjunction with his experience of physical illness—an experience that resonates with some people with disabilities. Job's description of his treatment at others' hands suggests that his friends and acquaintances made assumptions about his guilt. Some individuals with a disability have had people make these same theological assumptions about guilt or innocence. An assumption that disability may stem from sinful behavior on the part of the person with a disability or on the part of his or her ancestors is a fairly common assumption. The speeches of Job in chapters 16, 17, and 19 challenge these assumptions. The book of Job is consistent in presenting Job as free of significant guilt. He does admit to the possibility of some error (19:4), but nothing that would justify a punishment of chronic and severe illness such as that afflicting Job.

Job challenges more than the assumptions about a connection between illness and guilt. As Carol A. Newsom points out, "Job's words are an attack on the reality of the entire moral world" (2003, 124). A reading of the speeches attributed to Job's friends make clear that the book of Job challenges traditional wisdom's confidence in an orderly universe in which righteousness is rewarded and wickedness is punished.

THE SPEECHES OF JOB'S FRIENDS: JOB 4–5, 8, 11, 15, 18, 20, 22, 25, 32–37

The speeches of Job's friends are very important because they illustrate the very worldview that the book is challenging. The book of Job is at root a dialogic discourse, and the friends' speeches represent the traditional wisdom that the book is calling into question.

The first speech of Eliphaz the Temanite firmly argues for a world in which the divine maintains an orderly and reliable system of reward and retribution. In the words of Eliphaz: "Remember now, who that was innocent ever perished? Or where were the upright cut off?" (4:7). In his world the righteous are rewarded and the guilty are punished. However, at the same time, he argues that all human beings fall short before God:

> Can mortals be righteous before God? Can human beings be pure before their maker? Even in his servants he puts no trust, and his angels he charges with error; how much more those who live in houses of clay, whose foundation is in the dust, who are crushed like a moth. (4:17-19)

Though Eliphaz argues that God provides reward and retribution in a predictable way so that the righteous are rewarded and the wicked are punished, he maintains at the same time that no human can be truly righteous before God. Before the divine, no one can be totally innocent.

Given Job's predicament, Eliphaz advises him to turn to God and to plead his case (5:8) because God keeps those who mourn safe (5:11). Finally, Eliphaz counsels Job to submit to God's discipline because then Job will be restored to good health and prosperity: "How happy is the one whom God reproves; therefore do not despise the discipline of the Almighty. For he wounds, but he binds up; he strikes, but his hands heal" (5:17-18). If Job submits to God's punishments knowing that it is all part of God's discipline, then afterward Job will live a closely protected life (vv. 19-24), he will have numerous descendants (v. 25), and he will live to a ripe old age (v. 26).

In Bildad the Shuhite's first speech (Job 8), he staunchly defends God's practice of justice: "Does God pervert justice? Or does the Almighty pervert the right?" (8:3). Then, Bildad uses Job's children as an example. He reasons that Job's children must have been guilty and that they were killed for their transgressions. Like Eliphaz, Bildad recommends that Job entreat God to acknowledge his innocence and "he will . . . restore to you your rightful place. Though your beginning was small, your latter days will grow very great" (8:6b). Bildad, like Eliphaz, indicates his faith that God will restore Job's great prosperity. At the end of chapter 8, Bildad strongly contends that God maintains justice: "See, God will not reject a blameless person, nor grasp the hand of evildoers. He will yet fill your mouth with laughter, and your lips with shouts of joy. Those who hate you will be clothed with shame, and the tent of the wicked will be no more" (vv. 20-22).

In Zophar the Naamathite's first address, he goes so far as to declare Job guilty in no uncertain terms: "Know then that God exacts of you less than your guilt deserves" (Job 11:6b). In an argument not dissimilar to the ones from Eliphaz and Bildad, Zophar urges Job to put iniquity away and to eschew wickedness (11:14). Zophar states that if Job avoids sin, all will be great in his future, his life "will be brighter than the noonday" (11:17a).

In chapter 15 Eliphaz repeats his insight in verses 14-16 that humans cannot be innocent or righteous before God. Since God cannot fully trust "his holy ones," then how can God completely trust human beings (vv. 15-16). He also reiterates his view of the world as a place where the wicked receive the punishment they deserve (vv. 20-35). In an extended poem, Bildad emphasizes again that the wicked will get the expected punishment

(18:5-21). Zophar follows with another long poem (20:5-29) that assures his listeners that the wicked will get their just deserts. It is extremely important to the friends to convince Job (and themselves) that there is justice for the righteous and suitable punishment for the wicked. Much space is devoted to this subject in the discourse of the friends.

Eliphaz is convinced of Job's guilt, and he puts it in the strongest terms: "Is it because of your piety that he reproves you, and enters into judgment with you? Is not your wickedness great? There is no end to your iniquities" (Job 22:4-5). Friend Eliphaz attributes Job's guilt to his supposed failure to give drink to the weary, bread to the hungry, support to the widow, and protection to the orphan. He cautions Job against following the way of the wicked. In the latter part of chapter 22, Eliphaz advises Job to make his will conform to God's and to avoid evil deeds. This implies that Eliphaz believes that Job needs to repent of sin and to turn again to God.

Elihu emphasizes the futility of "contending" with God, describing the fearful repercussions that people experience if they do not accept God's approach to things. However, Elihu also depicts the marvelous restoration that people undergo when they turn again to God and reject sinful practices: "Then he prays to God, and is accepted by him, he comes into his presence with joy, and God repays him for his righteousness" (Job 33:26). Like others before him, Elihu defends God's sense of justice:

> Therefore, hear me, you who have sense, far be it from God that he should do wickedness, and from the Almighty that he should do wrong. For according to their deeds he will repay them, and according to their ways he will make it befall them. (34:10-11)

Elihu fosters the worldview that God promotes a just and predictable system of reward and retribution. Indeed, God does not "pervert justice" (v. 12b). He stresses God's sovereignty over all creation (vv. 13-15). Indeed, if God were to withdraw God's breath from creatures (including human beings), they would perish. Elihu reassures his listeners that surely the wicked will be punished.

In summary, the speeches of Job's friends strive to maintain a world in which one can expect an orderly and reliable system of reward and retribution. Those who are righteous will be rewarded and those who are wicked will be punished. The innocent will not be punished and the wicked will not receive a reward. Eventually, all will be judged according to their deeds, and subsequently their fates will be impacted by how well they lived up to God's expectations. Yet the friends argue that all human beings, however righteous they may be, fall short before God. So human efforts to be righteous will only take one so far.

The friends encourage Job to turn again to God and to repent of wrongdoing. So the assumption is that Job could commit himself more completely to following God's way. The friends are convinced that the causes of Job's predicament lie with him. Somehow along the way, he failed to follow fully God's path. They maintain that if Job turns again to God, he will have relief. His circumstances will improve, and he will be restored to his former status.

The worldview of the friends is problematic for a disability reading of the Bible. People with disabilities understand that the world does not conform to a system of justice that is predictable and reliable. To a great extent, disability has little or nothing to do with justice, except the justice that respects a person with disabilities and accords her or him full rights. Disability is most often a random, unsurprising aspect of human life. It is oppressive for people to attribute guilt to those who have a disability or to their families.

People with disabilities sometimes have the experience that they cannot find justice. For the friends to maintain that God always protects justice, rewarding the righteous and punishing the wicked, causes a stark disconnect between what tradition maintains and what a person with a disability has come to expect. Job's speeches are more sensitive to varied experiences among human beings and perhaps more reflective of reality. The book of Job calls into question a worldview that sees God's justice as unfailingly reliable. The speeches of Job recognize that justice isn't always available in the world, that the innocent suffer, and that God does not inevitably rescue the righteous.

A very positive aspect to the book of Job is its encouragement of a theology of protest. The book affirms God's availability to the person who is experiencing the world's injustice. In Job's case, God was willing to hear Job's complaint and to appear to him. Though Job accused God of abuse, though Job called into question God's justice, God came in the whirlwind. Whether God provides a reasonable answer to Job (from Job's perspective), God does make an appearance and answers Job's concerns (chs. 38–42). In the epilogue (42:7-17), God affirms Job's perspective on reality, *not* the friends' defense of traditional wisdom:

> After the Lord had spoken these words to Job, the LORD said to Eliphaz the Temanite: "My wrath is kindled against you and against your two friends; for you have not spoken of me what is right, as my servant Job has. Now therefore take seven bulls and seven rams, and go to my servant Job, and offer up for yourselves a burnt offering; and my servant Job shall pray for you, for I will accept his prayer not to deal with you according to your folly; for you

have not spoken of me what is established, as my servant Job has done." So Eliphaz the Temanite and Bildad the Shuhite and Zophar the Naamathite went and did what the Lord had told them; and the Lord accepted Job's prayer. (42:7-9)

The book of Job does not resolve some of the ethical issues that it raises. In the final analysis, it does not offer reassurance that God is just. It does not explain satisfactorily why the righteous suffer, though it does affirm in the end that disinterested piety is possible. Job remains faithful throughout. He turns to protest as a traditionally acceptable way to express concern to God. Though one can protest that the book does not value the lives of Job's servants and children appropriately, it does affirm eventually Job's experience and his righteousness. In the process it demonstrates God's availability and God's commitment to truth telling.

The Epilogue of Job (42:7-17) Revisited

The epilogue to the book of Job provides a very encouraging conclusion to the book because it does not include Job's healing from skin disease in his remarkable restoration. This may seem counterintuitive, but it actually can be very affirming to those with a disability who do not feel a need to be healed or who have not experienced healing. The biblical text does not mention any physical healing for Job, though it does indicate a long life for Job after his restoration: "After this, Job lived one hundred and forty years. He saw four generations of his children and his children's children!" (Job 42:16). This suggests that many people can live a flourishing and long life with a disability.

Jeremy Schipper points out that very few modern biblical scholars have emphasized the lack of healing in the epilogue (2010, 18). Schipper notes that ancient authors addressed this absence in different ways. Nevertheless, Job's skin disease serves as a catalyst for the friends' speeches. Both Job and his friends reference the skin disease numerous times throughout the book. The friends see Job's affliction as proof of his sinfulness, while Job uses it as a means to express his pain (19–20). There is a strong emphasis on Job's skin disease in his own speeches and those of his friends, yet the emphasis disappears in the epilogue.[2] As Schipper argues, "God's

[2] For a perspective on Job's skin disease that is in contrast to Schipper's viewpoint, please see David Wolfers' monograph (1995). Wolfers argues that the book of Job has frequently been mistranslated, and he systematically treats many passages to make his point. One of the implications of his work is that he disputes that the Masoretic Text represents Job as having a skin disease (119–34). He examines every passage that has traditionally been

silence regarding the skin diseases in the epilogue undermines the friends' repeated connection between disease and wrongdoing in the dialogues" (22). In fact, the book of Job challenges the idea that innocence results in physical wholeness, as Proverbs would have us believe. The character of Job, his conduct, and his comments are vindicated by God at the end, but he is not healed. The upshot is that Job is found worthy and righteous by God, but that worthiness is not dependent upon physical wholeness. Job demonstrates that the person with a disability can be fully worthy and fully righteous as well as favored by God.

CONCLUSION

The three wisdom books treated here each offer a very different perspective in respect to disability. With the book of Proverbs, we see an example of how society may seek to establish a social hierarchy that denigrates physical impairment. This construction is not uncommon among various cultures, but the acknowledgment of this problem in Proverbs may help us to find a way to counter these perspectives.

---

understood as making a reference to skin disease. In each case Wolfers determines that the Hebrew does not refer to skin disease: "One thing is certain. There is no reference in the poem of Job to any disease of the skin" (131). He stresses the metaphorical meaning rather than an explicit reference to skin disease. These passages refer to Israel, the nation, and the suffering of its people, not to the individual Job, according to Wolfers' argument. Even Job 2:7 is not a direct reference to Job's skin disease, but "Job's illness is a metaphor for the ravaging of his country and community, and Job 2:7 is a true quotation of Deuteronomy 28:35" (132).

Due to the limitations of space, it is not possible to address each of Wolfers' arguments about translation in these multiple passages. Yet a major implication of his book is that this point of view erases the experience of an individual with a chronic disability. Whether one accepts Wolfers' translations, Job has traditionally been understood as a book that discusses the experience of a man stricken with skin disease. Most readers of the biblical book understand Job's apparent suffering and pain to be related to the skin disease on his body. To erase the skin disease would invalidate centuries of tradition related to the book. It also affects the relevance of the book for readers who have a disability. For this chapter I have chosen to accept the representation of Job's skin disease as part of an individual human being's experience.

Wolfers' contention that the book of Job reflects the experience of the community in a particular time and place is a difficult premise to accept. On the face of it, the book addresses the concerns of individuals: Job, his wife, his children, his servants, and his friends. If we accept the historical context for the book as Wolfers has delineated it, it would require us to accept the particulars of time and place. The authorship, provenance, and date of origin have been the subject of much debate over the centuries. My preference is to accept the representation of the book and its focus on the individual Job and his friends as intentional.

The view in Ecclesiastes about disability is very different. Ecclesiastes acknowledges that all human life is subject to limitations. All human activities have inherent limitations, including the pursuit of wisdom itself. In regard to disability, this is a very helpful point of view. If all human life has limitations, then this outlook has an equalizing aspect. The perspective of Ecclesiastes stresses the features of life that give commonality to all human beings.

The book of Job helps the reader to understand that the world does not always provide justice for the deserving. The righteous may experience suffering, no matter how pious or committed they are to following wisdom's path. However, the book of Job gives the suffering person the right of protest. It encourages the reader to trust in one's own vision of life and to persist in one's innocence before God. In the case of Job, God responds favorably to protest, affirming Job's analysis of the situation and defending his perspective over against that of his friends. The reader is encouraged to turn to God in suffering and to learn that God will be present.

Finally, the epilogue demonstrates Job's righteousness, and he experiences vindication from God, the redeemer. However, the epilogue undermines the friends' view of physical disease as punishment for wrongdoing. Rather, the epilogue maintains that a person can have a disability yet be fully worthy and righteous before God.

WORKS CITED

Baynton, Douglas C. 2013. "Disability and the Justification of Inequality in American History." Pages 17–33 in *The Disability Studies Reader*. Edited by Lennard J. Davis. 4th ed. New York: Routledge.

Blumenthal, David R. 1993. *Facing the Abusing God: A Theology of Protest*. Louisville, Ky.: Westminster John Knox.

Clifton, Shane. 2015. "Disability, Theodicy, and Fragility." *Theological Studies* 76, no. 4: 765–84.

Creamer, Deborah Beth. 2009. *Disability and Christian Theology: Embodied Limits and Constructive Possibilities*. Oxford: Oxford University Press.

Crenshaw, James L. 1987. *Ecclesiastes: A Commentary*. The Old Testament Library. Philadelphia: Westminster.

Driver, S. R., and G. B. Gray. 1921. *A Critical and Exegetical Commentary on the Book of Job*. New York: Scribner's Sons.

Fredericks, Daniel C. 1993. *Coping with Transience: Ecclesiastes on Brevity in Life*. The Biblical Seminar 18. Sheffield: Sheffield Academic.

Garland-Thomson, Rosemarie. 1997. *Extraordinary Bodies: Figuring Physical Disability in American Culture and Literature*. New York: Columbia University Press.

Gray, John. 2010. *The Book of Job*. The Text of the Hebrew Bible 1. Edited by David J. A. Clines. Sheffield: Sheffield Phoenix.

Hartley, John E. 1988. *The Book of Job*. New International Biblical Commentary on the Old Testament. Grand Rapids: Eerdmans.

Hauerwas, Stanley. 2004. "Community and Diversity: The Tyranny of Normality." Pages 37–43 in *Critical Reflections on Stanley Hauerwas' Theology of Disability: Disabling Society, Enabling Theology*. Edited by John Swinton. Binghamton, N.Y.: Haworth Pastoral.

Lakoff, George, and Mark Johnson. 1999. *Philosophy in the Flesh: The Embodied Mind and Its Challenge to Western Thought*. New York: Basic.

Laytner, Anson. 1990. *Arguing with God: A Jewish Tradition*. Northvale, N.J.: Jason Aronson.

Lukin, Josh. 2013. "Disability and Blackness." Pages 308–15 in *The Disability Studies Reader*. Edited by Lennard J. Davis. 4th ed. New York: Routledge.

Martin, James D. 1995. *Proverbs*. Old Testament Guides. Sheffield: Sheffield Academic.

Murphy, Roland E. 1998. *Proverbs*. Word Biblical Commentary 22. Nashville: Thomas Nelson.

Newsom, Carol A. 2003. *The Book of Job: A Contest of Moral Imaginations*. Oxford: Oxford University Press.

Newton, Adam Zachary. 1995. *Narrative Ethics*. Cambridge, Mass.: Harvard University Press.

Perdue, Leo G. 2000. *Proverbs*. Interpretation. Louisville, Ky.: John Knox.

Pfau, Julie Shoshana, and David R. Blumenthal. 2001. "The Violence of God." *CrossCurrents* 51, no. 2: 177–200.

Raphael, Rebecca. 2004. "Things Too Wonderful: A Disabled Reading of Job." *Perspectives in Religious Studies* 31, no. 4: 399–424.

Saxton, Martha. 2013. "Disability Rights and Selective Abortion." Pages 87–99 in *The Disability Studies Reader*. Edited by Lennard J. Davis. 4th ed. New York: Routledge.

Schipper, Jeremy. 2010. "Healing and Silence in the Epilogue of Job." *Word & World* 30: 16–22.

Schumm, Darla, and Michael Stoltzfus, eds. 2016. *World Religions and Disability: An Introduction*. Waco, Tex.: Baylor University Press.

Seow, C. L. 1997. *Ecclesiastes: A New Translation with Introduction and Commentary*. Anchor Bible 18C. Garden City, N.Y.: Doubleday.

———. 2000. "Beyond Mortal Grasp: The Usage of *hebel* in Ecclesiastes." *Australian Biblical Review* 48: 1–16.

Shakespeare, Tom. 2013. "The Social Model of Disability." Pages 214–21 in *The Disability Studies Reader*. Edited by Lennard J. Davis. 4th ed. New York: Routledge.

United States Census Bureau. 2010. "Nearly 1 in 5 People Have a Disability in the U.S., Census Bureau Reports." https://www.census.gov/newsroom/releases/archives/miscellaneous/cb12-134.html.

Waltke, Bruce K. 2014. *The Book of Proverbs: Chapters 1–15*. New International Commentary on the Old Testament. Grand Rapids: Eerdmans.

Wolfers, David. 1995. *Deep Things Out of Darkness: The Book of Job, Essays, and a New English Translation*. Grand Rapids: Eerdmans.

Yoder, Christine Roy. 2009. *Proverbs*. Abingdon Old Testament Commentaries. Nashville: Abingdon.

6

Psalms, Lamentations, and Song of Songs

Jennifer L. Koosed

INTRODUCTION

The poetical books of the Hebrew Bible (Pss, Lam, and Song) differ in content and structure, context and style. As *poetical* books, however, they share the primary feature of Hebrew poetry—parallelism—and many of the qualities of poetry in general—imagery, symbolism, metaphor, assonance, consonance. As collections of poems, they are among the most complex and evocative of biblical texts and thus can be explored from a disability perspective in equally complex and evocative ways.

Disability studies offers not so much an exegetical method with a series of steps but a subject matter examined with the aid of various models or analytical lenses. The subject of disability studies is bodies that have somatic or psychic features defined as deviating from the norm. Disabilities can be physical (blindness, paralysis), intellectual (dyslexia, Down syndrome), or mental (bipolar, schizophrenia). Disability studies have examined disability through three different lenses: the medical model, the social model, and the cultural model. In the medical model, disability is defined in terms of medical diagnosis. The disability is described in terms of bodily limitations, deficiencies, and differences. In the social model, a distinction is made between disability and impairment. The impairment may be located in the individual's body, but the disability is located in society's response to the body. This response includes negative attitudes, stereotypes, and prejudices toward people with bodies that function differently from what is defined as the "norm"; in the social model, the disability is also located in structural issues (e.g., someone in a wheelchair is only disabled insofar as buildings are not constructed with adequate ramps and elevators).

189

Noting limitations to both these ways of understanding and analyzing disability, a third approach called the cultural model has emerged as a corrective. As Nyasha Junior and Jeremy Schipper explain,

> According to the cultural model, we cannot define disability by just one factor such as the medical condition of an individual body (medical model) or social discrimination against people with impairments (social model). Unlike the social model, the cultural model does not differentiate impairments from disabilities in a way that might artificially distance the social experiences of people with disabilities from their biological realities. Instead, disability is made up of a complex variety of cultural factors, which might include medical issues and social discrimination, but is not limited to these factors. (2013, 23)

The problems with the first two models are even more acute when working with biblical texts. Not only did biblical authors lack the type of medical knowledge we have today, they were also not interested in chronicling symptoms for symptoms' sake. Biblical writers were not concerned with diagnosis. Without a body to diagnose (or at least accurate medical records for reference), it becomes impossible to separate out impairment from societal attitudes toward that impairment. In this way, both the medical model and the social model fail when reading biblical text. The Bible is, however, a cultural record that expresses a range of ideas and values. As a model that approaches the question of disability in ways both more holistic and complex than the other two models, in biblical studies the cultural model has proven the most fruitful (Junior and Schipper 2013, 24–25; see also Moss and Schipper 2011, 2–4).

The cultural model is especially productive for the reading of biblical poetry. Poems are concentrated packets of signification; they convey meaning through content, structure, and sound. Poems layer meaning upon meaning; they are polyvocal. Biblical poetry in particular is not trying to convey historical realities as much as emotional experiences. Even with Lamentations, which is the most explicitly tied to a historical event (the siege and then capture of Jerusalem by the Babylonians in 586 BCE), the poems are written to evoke emotion, not to communicate facts. Reading through the cultural model of disability allows the poems in Psalms, Lamentations, and Song of Songs to speak in all their varied, even contradictory, voices.

Although poetry as a genre has lost much of its influence in the twentieth and twenty-first centuries, it still contains an unrivaled power to connect and explore the deepest questions of human existence. Poetry that focuses on the complex emotions, atypical bodies, and difficult social interactions experienced by those with disabilities emerged as a recognizable subgenre in 1986 with the publication of the anthology *Towards Solomon's Mountain*, edited by A. J. Baird (Bartlett, Black, and Northen 2011, 18). Since this first work, many anthologies and single-author works of "disability poetry" have followed. In addition, disability-focused magazines and journals regularly publish poetry, and the journal *Wordgathering* is dedicated exclusively to disability poetry.

Whereas disability poetry covers a wide range of topics, emotions, and perspectives (just like "disability" itself is a diverse and constantly shifting category), some disability poets do attempt to define a core sensibility. Jim Ferris, for example, not only writes poetry but has also written several seminal essays theorizing the subgenre of disability poetry. For Ferris, "Disability poetry can be recognized by several characteristics: challenge to stereotypes and an insistence on self-definition; foregrounding of the perspective of people with disabilities; an emphasis on embodiment, especially atypical embodiment; and alternative techniques and poetics" (as cited in Bartlett, Black, and Northen 2011, 22). Biblical authors are anonymous, and therefore their physical capacities are unknown. Given the realities of bodily variation, however, it would be surprising if there were no disabled writers, singers, or storytellers who contributed to the formation of the biblical text. Given the ways in which artists can tap into aspects of human existence through imagination and empathy, it would be surprising if the Bible did not reflect deep thinking about disability even if the poets were not themselves disabled. Although there is no way of identifying authors, readers today can certainly examine the body of the text with an eye toward discerning perspectives that are resonant with disability poetics, including issues of stereotyping and atypical embodiment, and an ear toward hearing alternative techniques of structure and form. As many biblical scholars working on disability in the ancient world and in sacred texts have noted, the Bible certainly does employ negative stereotypes about disability, but these are not the only voices that speak out through Hebrew poetry.

Further discussing and defining disability poetry in the introduction of a recent anthology, Jennifer Bartlett concludes,

> Part of what is so energizing about considering the current landscape of disability poetry is the degree to which thinking about disability enlists or engages viscerally many concerns animating other current poetry movements. . . . Much of human consideration of time and mortality hinges around the body—how it ages, changes, gains and loses capacities. Questions of how, why, whether this is in fact necessary, go to the deepest center of what it means to be human. (Bartlett, Black, and Northen 2011, 17)

As cultural products created to express some of the deepest human feelings, sentiments, and sensations, poetry reaches deep within us but also stretches out through time and across culture. Insofar as Hebrew poetry can challenge our thinking, express the vicissitudes of embodiment, and even employ alternative poetic techniques, it can enter into conversation with contemporary disability poetry and even become disability poetry itself.

The books of Psalms, Lamentations, and the Song of Songs do not contain characters that are disabled. All three poetical books do, however, have passages where disability is a part of the metaphor, image, or structure of the text. In addition to literary considerations, all three poetical books have effects upon contemporary ethics, theologies, and liturgies. In the Jewish ordering of the canon, the three books are a part of the Ketuvim (or Writings). Psalms is, in fact, the first book of the Ketuvim; Lamentations and the Song of Songs are both books in the Megillot, the five "Scrolls" that are read in their entirety on specific Jewish holidays. All three books are extensively used in Jewish liturgy. In the Christian Old Testament, Psalms and Song of Songs appear after the Historical Books and before the prophets; Lamentations is found immediately after Jeremiah because of the tradition that Jeremiah is its author. Like in Judaism, the Psalms are an important part of the liturgical tradition in Christianity; unlike Judaism, neither Lamentations nor Song of Songs has a significant role in Christian liturgy. In each of the sections below, I will briefly address the historical considerations of each book, but then move into a literary analysis of disability, and finally end with some considerations concerning ethics, theology, and liturgy.

PSALMS

One of the primary religious impulses is the desire to reach out to the divine through prayer and song. "Sing to the LORD a new song" commands Ps 96 (v. 1) and all the psalms respond, exemplifying this yearning for connection and communication. The psalms, however, are not *new* songs, and therein lies their power. They are ancient and they are familiar; they allow a reader to enter into and connect not only with the divine but also with the community of worshippers that stretch back through time. The psalms, even the individual laments and thanksgivings, are ultimately collective experiences. They are set, formal prayers that are always waiting for a worshipper to pick up and enter. They cover a wide array of emotions and experiences: happiness, despair, gratitude, rage. There is a tension between the wild feelings of one experiencing great pain or great joy and the structured script of a psalm. But that is the point. The psalms allow worshippers to channel and express the full range of human emotion within a highly structured (and therefore safe, even comfortable) worship environment. There are a number of ways in which the psalms explicitly engage metaphors of ability and disability. In addition, a focus on the feelings evoked by these songs uncovers a deeper level at which psalms can resonate with the experience of disability.

The title "Psalms" is derived from the Greek name of the book in the Septuagint. It is a word possibly derived from the Hebrew מזמור (*mizmor*), which means "song." The Hebrew name for the book is תהלים (*tehillim*, "hymns"; Craigie and Tate 2004, 31). In both cases—Hebrew and Greek—the essential component of music is underscored. The psalms are not just prayers; they are musical prayers. Most, perhaps all, of these poetical pieces were composed to be sung, as indicated by the musical notations and terms that appear in many of the superscriptions and throughout the poems. Music reaches places that words alone may miss; embodied in song, psalms can become even more memorable and emotionally resonant.

Psalms is an anthology consisting of five separate collections, perhaps modeled after the five books of the Torah, for a total of 150 individual songs. Between each collection is a doxology (words of praise), and the entire anthology ends with an extended doxology, Ps 150. The first book of psalms (1–41) is characterized by ascription to David in the superscription (all in this first collection, save four) and the use of the personal divine name YHWH. The second collection (42–72) uses the word "Elohim" to refer to God, and the ascriptions are various, including David, Asaph, the sons of Korah, and even Solomon. The third book (73–89) also uses primarily Elohim to name the divine, and again names a number of men in the superscriptions (David, Asaph, Korah, Ethan). Book 4 (90–106) and book 5 (107–150) contain psalms that have few common characteristics and are perhaps grouped together simply because they did not fit within the previous collections (Dahood 1966, xxxi–ii).

Both Jewish and Christian tradition attributes the psalms to David, as author and composer. Most of the psalms, however, do not themselves indicate Davidic authorship, and those that are associated with David use a term that is not clearly an attribution of authorship. A number of psalms are לדוד (*l-David*), but the preposition ל (*l-*) has a wide range of meaning and can be translated as "to," "of," "concerning," "about." In fact, "by" is not the most common translation of ל (*l-*) in any circumstance (Craigie and Tate 2004, 33–35). Davidic authorship cannot be ascribed with certainty to any of the psalms, and other historical and literary considerations militate against this traditional understanding of psalmic authorship. Internal evidence suggests that the psalms were written over a period of several hundred years, beginning sometime in the period of the Judean monarchy (see, e.g., the psalms that discuss temple and kingship, like Ps 20 and 21) and ending sometime after the Babylonian destruction (see, e.g., Ps 137). If not songs penned in Jerusalem by the great king David, what, then, is the context of the psalms? Currently, the most common way of reading the Psalms is through the method of form criticism. Pioneered by Hermann Gunkel, form criticism identifies particular psalmic genres and then assigns the genre to a *Sitz im Leben*, or "Setting-in-life." Through form critical analysis, Gunkel and his student Sigmund Mowinckel first suggested that these pieces be understood as liturgical and that the book of Psalms as a whole should be situated in the Second Temple period, as something like the "hymnal" of the second temple (Craigie and Tate 2004, 45–46).

Like any anthology that includes material written over the course of centuries, the psalms cover a wide range of topics and perspectives. Like any biblical book, Psalms has had a long and layered history of interpretation. It is complex, diverse, even contradictory as it addresses many topics, especially the topic of disability. Hector Avalos, Sarah J. Melcher, and Jeremy Schipper open their groundbreaking work at the intersection of disability and biblical studies with a moment in the history of interpretation that illustrates how psalms engage some of the deepest questions of human existence through reflection on disability. They begin *This Abled Body* with a rabbinic midrash on Ps 34 that cites Ps 104:

> How manifold are Thy works, O Lord! All those which Thou hast made in wisdom (Ps 104:24), David meant: Thou hast made all in wisdom, and hast made well, except for madness. And David said to the Holy One, blessed be He: "Master of the Universe, what profit is there for the world in madness? . . . is this beautiful in Thine eyes?" (2007, 1)

In this citation, one can see several of the themes in disabilities studies in general, and the study of the psalms in particular. One of the major psalmic themes is creation—Israel's God is the creator God. Yet there are aspects of this world that are puzzling at best and promote human suffering at worst. How are these features to be understood within the basic framework of creation theology? Questions of theodicy and providence, then, immediately arise. This midrash specifically singles out mental disability as, perhaps, counter to God's ordered world, and yet the midrash is alluding to an episode in David's life where he became mad in order to elude capture by the Philistines (1 Sam 21:10–22:1). In this story madness is not oversight or error or punishment; rather, cognitive disability is a "means of divine deliverance for David" (Avalos, Melcher, and Schipper 2007, 1). Disability is not just about pain and suffering but can and does contribute to human flourishing. There is no single way to approach the conditions of disability, and there is no single way to approach the texts of disability in the Bible and its history of interpretation.

Like the midrash on Ps 34, many of the ways in which the book of Psalms addresses the themes and metaphors of disability engage them in ways that are complicated and move across different interpretive possibilities. In Psalms the larger themes of theodicy and providence are ever present. In addition, there are three ways in which the psalms engage issues of disability more specifically and explicitly. First, many psalms discuss forsakenness and even punishment through metaphors of bodily pain, woundedness, and disability. Second, God is portrayed as able-bodied, and the psalms employ parallelism to create a matrix of metaphors that associate God's able-bodiedness with intangible divine attributes like faithfulness and loyalty. Finally, some psalms discuss idols as disabled and associate the sin of idol worship with physical impairment. Although these three ways that disability is engaged in the Psalms express negative attitudes and perpetuate stereotypes, some of these very same passages also disrupt stereotypes and can provide new perspectives on the experience of disability. As songs that express a wide array of human experiences and emotions, they also intersect with contemporary disability poetry itself, poetry that sometimes expresses negative feelings about disability. Discussing her own embodied existence and the poetry that results, Lisa Gill writes,

> I listen to the traffic and train whistles. The church bells and disembodied "fuck yous" that rise through my window.
> I feel safe. I feel happy. I feel sad.
> I write it all down. (Bartlett, Black, and Northen 2011, 246)

Those who sung the psalms listened, and felt, and wrote it all down as well.

The psalms often portray being forsaken or punished by God as a disabled condition; the prayer to return to God is a petition not only for spiritual healing but also for physical restoration. Such associations are particularly evident in the lament psalms, the genre designation of most of the psalms in the book. Psalm 38, for example, employs a number of different images of woundedness and disability: "There is no soundness in my flesh because of your indignation; there is no health in my bones because of my sin. . . . My wounds grow foul and fester because of my foolishness. . . . For my loins are filled with burning, and there is no soundness in my flesh" (38:3, 5, 7). Sin is manifest in the body and God's rejection is evident in its wounds. In later verses, the speaker in the psalm also connects his own suffering with the suffering of people with definable disabilities: "But I am like the deaf, I do not hear; like the mute, who cannot speak" (38:13). Here, spiritual and emotional suffering is connected to physical disability.

Built through poetic parallelism, there are also associations between those with disabilities and other "marginal" groups like the poor. As Saul Olyan notes, "The weakness and vulnerability of the petitioner, a common enough theme in Psalms of individual complaint, is asserted here [in Ps 38] vividly through comparison with the helplessness of deaf or mute persons before their accusers in court" (2008, 52). From the perspective of the biblical authors, the disabled, the poor, and the forsaken are all marked by their lack of agency and their need for protection. The psalmist does urge those who can to defend those who cannot; however, the disabled are always and already understood to be in need of such protection: "The association of disabled persons with marginal groups such as the poor and the afflicted is a taxonomic move that functions to stigmatize them as marginal, weak, vulnerable, and dependent. They are further stigmatized when texts represent them as needing special protection from the strong and the able" (53). There is a similar association in Ps 146:7-9 (6–7).

On the one hand, as clearly and forcibly argued by Olyan, these associations certainly can reinforce negative attitudes about people with disabilities. On the other hand, people with disabilities do sometimes feel vulnerable and in need, forsaken and forgotten. Asking if he is a nobody in the poem "Deaf Blind: Three Squared Cinquain," John Lee Clark writes, "I am sorry to disappoint, / but I am." Even worse, the Nobodies ultimately exclude him, too. He is rejected by them, even when he catches "a bus of stinking Nobodies" (Bartlett, Black, and Northen 2011, 160). As a form of disability poetry, many of the lament psalms express such despair as well. In addition, the psalms that categorize the disabled with the vulnerable do acknowledge a reality: people with disabilities often do need additional aid from other people. Denying the need may be just as harmful as defining people only in terms of the need. Even further, the equation between bodily impairment and sin in this psalm is not stable (Raphael 2008, 111). Subjecting the poem to a close reading that focuses especially on the dynamics between the speaker and his two implied audiences (his enemies and God), Rebecca Raphael concludes that the psalm is about power: "The speaker's powerlessness opens up the space in which God is to manifest God's power. Self-abasement before God, then, is paradoxically powerful: the speaker's weakness calls out God's power against the enemies. Thus the speaker's power with respect to both God and the enemies lies in his/her weakness, as represented by images of illness and disability" (113). Psalm 38 thereby locates the power to call upon God in the impairment of the body. Raphael reads Ps 94 in a similar way (114–16).

A second way that the book of Psalms engages disability is in the descriptions of God's body. Despite the biblical understanding that God is incorporeal, the psalms occasionally use physical descriptions of God's body in order to depict God's character. In these psalms, God has a super-human, able body. Psalm 89 exemplifies the interconnections between the ideas of God as faithful and loving with his possession of a strong arm. The psalm opens with its theme: "I will sing of your steadfast love, O LORD, forever; with my mouth I will proclaim your faithfulness to all generations" (89:1). The psalm then moves to recounting God's greatness; the polytheistic background of the biblical text is evident in this psalm as it proclaims God greater than all other supernatural beings, conquering them all: "You crushed Rahab like a carcass; you scattered your enemies with your mighty arm" (89:10). Attention to the use of Hebrew parallelism makes the equations between faithfulness with the strong arm even more evident: "You have a mighty arm; strong is your hand, high your right hand" (89:13). Here the three lines are synonymous and the three adjectives are equated: "mighty," "strong," and "high" are the words that describe God's limbs. The next line also employs synonymous parallelism: "Righteousness and justice are the foundation of your throne; steadfast love and faithfulness go before you" (89:14). Thus, the writer is associating God's mighty arm with God's righteousness, justice, steadfast love, and faithfulness. God's strong and able body becomes a metaphor for God's positive intangible attributes.

While not explicit, the metaphor certainly implies the converse: unrighteousness and unfaithfulness are associated with physical weakness. The psalm relies on negative understandings of the physically disabled body to express confidence in God. Yet much like the analysis of Ps 38, different interpretive possibilities emerge on closer and more comprehensive examination. Strong arms are not just attributes of abled bodies. Some people who have lost their legs or the use of their legs also have very muscular arms. In fact, many disability sports depend upon the strong arms of the otherwise disabled body; examples include wheelchair rugby (also known as "murderball," an indication of the aggression and strength displayed on the fields of play), various aquatic sports, and wheelchair hockey. God is portrayed as having a body, at least metaphorically, but that body is not whole. It is fragmented—an arm here, a hand there; never is a full image of an able-bodied God presented in the book of Psalms. Readers may fill in the gaps by imagining a full and abled body, but that image is a result of the readers' own preconceived notions. It is the reader that has assumed that strong arms are only on the bodies of the abled. God's body in Ps 89 may be more like a Paralympic powerlifter than a paragon of the normative body.

Not only may God's fragmented body be disabled, but some psalms also explicitly invoke the possibility of impairment in God's body, especially deafness and muteness (see, e.g., Pss 35, 50, 83, 109), in order to provoke response in God. Asking God not to be deaf but to hear the petitioner or not to be mute but to respond to the petition is a question that only works if God's deafness and muteness are real possibilities. The fact that God has the power in these poems to *choose* disability in ways that most people cannot does not detract from the image of the disabled God, as it is rhetorically deployed. In Raphael's analysis, these images of disability are used "not simply to depict a state that is valued negatively, but as representations of a whole range of communicative options, in which the terms actively elicit some responses and seek to repress others" (2008, 119). The rhetoric of petition engages metaphors and images that associate the divine body with definable disabilities.

Related images of divine ability and disability cluster around the polemic against idolatry. For example, in Ps 115 God is portrayed as able-bodied and the competing idols as impaired in various ways. The psalm declares, "Our God is in the heavens; he does whatever he pleases. Their idols are silver and gold, the work of human hands. They have mouths, but do not speak; eyes, but do not see. They have ears, but do not hear; noses, but do not smell. They have hands, but do not feel; feet, but do not walk; they make no sound in their throats" (115:3-7). The pagan images of the divine are deaf, blind, mute. They lack the ability to smell or to use their hands and legs. The medical diagnoses pile up: anosmia, quadriplegia. And all are put in antithetical parallel structure to the abilities of the God of Israel. As Olyan writes,

> The fact that polemicists such as the author of Jer 10:5 and Ps 115:5-8 have chosen to focus their attacks on the physical disabilities of the "idols," rather than on other qualities such as the materials out of which "idols" are manufactured, how they are made, or who made them, reveals the degree to which such somatic dysfunctions are stigmatized and devalued. (2008, 52; see also Olyan 2009)

The contrast between God's abled body and the disabled bodies of the icons in Ps 115 is far more comprehensive than the image of God's body present in Ps 89. Even more disturbing, the deeper meaning of this psalm is that the God in Israel is alive and real and that the gods of the surrounding cultures are not. Do disabilities make one somehow less alive, even less real, than someone who does not have these physical impairments? The metaphor that censures idolatry by connecting pagan icons to disability relies upon the society's negative evaluation of disability in order to convey its meaning.

These three primary ways in which Psalms employ metaphors and images of disability demonstrate that disability is stigmatized—associated with abandonment by and punishment from God, and with sinfulness in general and idolatry in particular. However, in Psalms, disability images move across several interpretive possibilities, the negative associations are not always stable, and these songs are not without their power. There is a thriving community of people who write about their lives with a disability in poems, essays, memoir, and song. Writing not only allows an individual to express his or her thoughts and feelings, but writing actually aids in the organization and articulation of these thoughts and feelings; writing engenders understanding and self-understanding. Poetry especially taps the deepest wells of emotion, beyond rational thought and critical analysis. As Jill Alexander Essbaum exclaims, *"poets were purposed to drink life deeply and to share their intoxication with the world through their poems"* (Bartlett, Black, and Northen 2011, 50; emphasis in original). And that includes both negative and positive emotions, both negative and positive experiences.

When we pray the psalms, we put ourselves in the position of the speaker, and we are both writer and reader. As such, the psalms allow us to articulate, organize, express, communicate, and therefore feel empathy with a wide array of emotions and conditions. Disability is a fluid category, encompassing different somatic and psychic attributes for different cultures at different times. However defined, most people move in and out of disabling conditions, for bodies are in a constant state of change. Some are born with the condition. Some genetic conditions manifest immediately; some not until years (even decades) later. Some become disabled through injury or illness. Those who live long enough become disabled through old age. Even though there are commonalities, each body is different, and each person experiences his or her body differently. As one experiences and reflects upon one's body, a range of ideas and emotions emerge, not in any linear manner (moving from anger to acceptance, for example) but in the messy, tangled way we all live. Even though some of the specific ways in which psalms employ metaphors of disability rely on negative attitudes and stereotypes, the psalms do allow a full range of human emotion to be expressed. As human beings in this world, we experience joys and sorrows, we are helped and we are hindered, we dance in our bodies and we are limited by them as well. Those experiencing disability may be angry, regretful, guilty, sorrowful, joyful, strong, and resentful. Sometimes they long for an abled body and sometimes they enjoy their own unique embodied experience. And they may feel these emotions and have these attitudes all at the same time. An early voice in the poetry of disability, Vassar Miller, wove together in psalms of her own her deep faith and her experiences living with cerebral palsy:

> Except ourselves, we have no other prayer;
> Our needs are sores upon our nakedness.
> We do not have to name them; we are here. (2000, 152)

The Psalms give us, in all our differently abled bodies, the words to sing out and be heard.

LAMENTATIONS

The book of Lamentations is a howl of pain. Written sometime after the Babylonian siege and then destruction of Jerusalem, the poem throbs with the horrors experienced and the suffering felt. The body has been shattered. Individual bodies were destroyed and lives were ended; individual bodies were wounded and thus fated to bear the mark of the Babylonian onslaught. The social and political body was also shattered—parts destroyed, parts maimed and wounded. The book of Lamentations is about this wounding—emotional and physical, individual and political— but it does not focus on disabled characters, nor does it employ metaphors of disability. Rather, the book embodies disability in its very rhythm and form. Lamentations does not have characters who are disabled; Lamentations itself is disabled.

The book of Lamentations is a series of five poems. The poems appear to be written by a single hand sometime after the Babylonian conquest and subsequent exile (after 586 BCE). Because of the vivid descriptions and the powerful emotions, some commentators have attributed the poems to someone who actually experienced the destruction; however, these attributes of poetry are the consequence of literary artistry, not necessarily personal experience. The only fact that can be said with certainty about the author is that he or she was well acquainted with the event, whether through personal experience, written accounts, or oral testimonies. Traditionally the poems have been ascribed to Jeremiah, but like the tradition that associates David with the Psalms, the evidence points away from the prophet (Hillers 1972, xxi–ii).

Because the disability of the book of Lamentations is seen in its form and heard in its rhythm, it is most evident in Hebrew. Each of the five poems that constitute the book of Lamentations engages the Hebrew alphabet in some way. Four of the poems are acrostic, meaning that each successive line or stanza begins with a letter of the alphabet, from א (*aleph*) to ת (*tav*). The fifth and last poem does not follow the acrostic formula but does have twenty-two lines, equal to the number of letters in the Hebrew alphabet. The acrostic form is exacting and quite limiting to a writer. As scholars have noted, acrostics are better used in the exercises of schoolchildren than in serious poems of mourning. Other biblical acrostics are often dismissed as being "the pious practice of a modest art" (Hermann Gunkel as quoted in Hillers 1972, xxvi), and scholars have asked why the author would choose to submit to such a constraint. Most note that to write such poems successfully (and Lamentations is a powerful piece of writing), an author must be highly creative and have a prodigious vocabulary. Acrostic poetry is a display of artistry and linguistic dexterity (Hillers 1972, xxvi; Garrett and House 2004, 306–7). But to reduce the acrostics in Lamentations to a kind of "showing off" does not do justice to the many effects of the form on those who read and hear the poem, and the many ways in which this form contributes to meaning. From a disability perspective, the acrostic structure can be understood as a brace, strict and hard and unyielding. The brace of the acrostic wraps around and holds up the wounded body of the text itself.

However, the brace does not cover over the disability even as it enables the body to move more freely; the acrostic structure does not suppress the disordering nature of the grief even as it gives a certain articulateness to its expression. The woundedness of the body is still evident, not just in content (as will be explored below) but also in rhythm. Jim Ferris has suggested that disability poetry is marked by certain types of experimentation with structure and form. Concerning his own poetry (and responding to A. R. Ammon's characterization of a poem as "a walk"), Ferris notes, "When I walk, I aim to get somewhere. If my meters are sprung, if my feet are uneven, if my path is irregular, that's just how I walk. And how I write" (Bartlett, Black, and Northen 2011, 353). Unlike other forms of biblical poetry, Lamentations adheres to an identifiable meter. The meter of the poems is a *qinah* meter (3+2)—in other words, a "limping" meter (Garrett and House 2004, 308–10). The poem skips a stress; even with their brace, the words walk with a limp.

As Delbert R. Hillers notes, "In Lamentations, the impression is of a boundless grief, an overflowing emotion, whose expression benefits from the limits imposed by a confining acrostic form, as from the rather tightly fixed metrical pattern" (1972, xxvii). Not only does the text express emotion, but it also seeks to construct meaning in the face of the tragedy. And meaning is found even in the letters. The alphabet is one of the first lessons learned in literate society. When children learn their ABCs, they develop their powers of memorization and their ability to think in order. The order of the letters, the structure of the alphabet itself, is the foundation for all other types of linguistic order, pattern, structure, and therefore meaning. It is the desire to make meaning in the midst of our pain that propels us to reach out through language. In Lamentations, suffering strips the people of almost everything, and they reach back and down to cling to the alphabet. Stripped down to nothing, the writer begins by simply repeating the letters over and over again, hoping that they will later reorder into words and thus reorder the world.

Yet the acrostic structure "stumbles" a few times, as if the limp is embedded even here. The first acrostic poem in chapter 1 follows the order of the alphabet exactly. But in the second, third, and fourth acrostic poems, there is a "minor peculiarity"; two letters are out of order (Hillers 1972, xxvii). In these three poems, the ע (*ayin*) and the פ (*pe*) are reversed (2:16 and 17; 3:46-48 and 49-51; 4:16 and 17). Whereas it has been suggested that the order of these two letters were not yet fixed, there is no evidence to support such a contention (xxvii). Rather than a historical reason, a literary interpretation emerges when read through the methodological lens of disability. One begins to make meaning by simply reciting the alphabet, but meaning falters even at this foundational level because ultimately there is no clear and straightforward sense to be made out of such tragedies.

Lamentations is, after all, asking one of the most vexing questions of human existence: Why do we suffer? There is a dominant perspective present in Lamentations that is in line with much of biblical Scripture: the national catastrophe that befell Judah in 586 BCE was the result of God's punishing wrath. The people of Judah sinned, and God responded by allowing Babylon to destroy them: "Jerusalem sinned grievously, so she has become a mockery; all who honored her despise her, for they have seen her nakedness; she herself groans, and turns her face away" (Lam 1:8). However, at the level of the individual body, under the full weight of the assault, this dominant perspective breaks down: "Look, O LORD, and consider! To whom have you done this? Should women eat their offspring, the children they have borne? Should priest and prophet be killed in the sanctuary of the LORD? The young and the old are lying on the ground in the streets; my young women and my young men have fallen by the sword; in the day of your anger you have killed them, slaughtering without mercy" (2:20-21). There is no ready response, no appeal to divine justice that makes sense when holding a dead child.

As Darla Schumm and Michael Stoltzfus write in their introduction to *Disability in Judaism, Christianity, and Islam*, "There is a persistent tendency to associate disability with individual sin" (2011, xiv). Such perspectives, whether explicit or implicit, are damaging: "For people with disabilities, such explanations can lead to spiritual anxiety in the private sphere and alienation from religious association in the public sphere" (xiv). The problem of theodicy—why there is evil and suffering in the world—confounds people of faith and is at the heart of much biblical interpretation and theological reflection in disability studies. Understanding suffering as a result of sin is common both in and out of the Bible, but as Lamentations alone demonstrates, no theodicy is without its problems and no theodicy is without its critics. Exploring the question of theodicy from a theological and philosophical perspective, Amos Yong notes that "there are problems across the theodicy spectrum and that these are further intensified when assessed in disability perspective" (207).

Individual disability challenges all the models that have arisen, in part because disability challenges the very distinction between "natural" and "moral" evil (Schumm and Stoltzfus 2011, 211), much like understandings of disability challenge the distinction between the biological and the social. Certainly, many disabilities are a result of natural bodily processes and natural psychic, somatic, and genetic variability. Yet with attention to the social model, much of the suffering that is a result of disability is a product not of the medical condition itself but of systems of exclusion both structural and attitudinal. Where, then, does the sin lie? Who bears the brunt of the punishment? These are the precise questions raised by Lamentations; there may be sin in Jerusalem, but not every inhabitant of Jerusalem is equally responsible. And as the afflictions experienced by individuals inhabiting a city under siege and beset by a political enemy vary, disability has an extraordinarily wide range of causes and manifestations, all of which interact differently with the question of theodicy (211). Famine and genetic mutation, disease and accident, the sword and the bullet strike indiscriminately, without distinction and without regard. But in some of these scenarios the chaos is released by human agency, and in some of these scenarios human response contributes to the suffering involved. As the cultural model of disability affirms, the natural and the social interact in complex ways that are not easily disentangled. Reading Lamentations while asking questions of theodicy and questions of disability leads not to any answer but rather to increasingly more complex questions.

Why are people born with bodies that function differently, or why do accidents happen that permanently alter bodies? How do people get caught in wider political and military conflicts over which they have no control? The situations addressed in disability studies are different from the ones described in the book of Lamentations, but the same questions around the reason and purpose of suffering still arise. Much like Psalms, the poetry of Lamentations can give expression to a wide range of responses to those questions without necessarily resting in any one answer. It expresses regret and repentance but also anger and defiance; it expresses fear in the face of chaos but also a deeply felt human need to order the world, and a deeply felt hope: "Restore us to yourself, O LORD, that we may be restored; renew our days as of old—unless you have utterly rejected us, and are angry with us beyond measure" (Lam 5:21-22). Following Yong's concluding reflections, in the end the only adequate responses to questions of evil and suffering from a disability perspective are those that reorient us toward action, particularly acts of justice and inclusion (Schumm and Stoltzfus 2011, 220). The only liberation is one that begins by becoming "more deeply sensitized to the ultimate issues of human suffering, meaning-making, and hope" (221). Listen to Lamentations, read its words, hear its voices calling out in their pain across time and place.

Lamentations is not just a howl of pain; it is also a stunningly beautiful song. With its limping meter and haunting melody, with its complex presentation of experience and emotion, Lamentations is an example of "crip music" as defined by poet Petra Kuppers. Listening to her own unique walk, her own particular music of movement, she writes, "with the crutch cane stick beat / the cripple who ripples across / the street" (Bartlett, Black, and Northen 2011, 116). Limping bodies sound different, and the notes do not just sing tragedy. In Kuppers' poem the tune is mournful (v. 4), but the song also lifts (v. 27), and even a giggle is found at its center (v. 11). Such comingling of sadness and celebration can be found in much disability poetry. In her groundbreaking theology of disability, Nancy Eiesland writes, "Most people with disabilities see our bodies not as signs of deviance or deformity, but as images of beauty and wholeness. We discern in our bodies, not only the ravages of injustice and pain, but also the reality of surviving with dignity" (1994, 115). Lamentations as a disabled body is mournful, but it also lifts; it expresses all Eiesland names here: injustice, pain, survival, dignity, beauty. According to both Tod Linafelt and Chip Dobbs-Allsopp, the hope of Lamentations is located in its very expression of survival, a difficult survival but a dignified one nevertheless (Garrett and House 2004, 321–22). The poems hold together the complex experiences and emotions, questions and responses of being wounded, of being disabled.

SONG OF SONGS

What does it mean to be beautiful? What kinds of bodies fall in love? Who is sexy and desirable, and to whom? The Song of Solomon, also called the Song of Songs, is a series of love poems. The work is traditionally ascribed to Solomon; however, internal evidence suggests that the poems were written in the Persian period, some five hundred years after Solomon's reign (Fox 1985, 186–91). The poems unabashedly celebrate emotional passion and physical desire. The two characters in the Song are clearly not married (hence their constant longing and searching for one another), yet they are just as clearly exploring and enjoying each other's bodies. Even though the poem does express some fear of censure—there seems to be some reason why the two lovers cannot be united—there is no reference to biblical law or sexual ethics. The picture is counter to most people's understanding of what the Bible teaches about proper sexual conduct between unmarried people. The poems also contain no reference to God. Taken together, these aspects of the Song often prompt the question, What is a book like this doing in the Bible?

The connection between the Song of Songs and disability perspectives may be equally as perplexing at first, in part because the sexuality of people with disabilities is not often explored. They are assumed to be either nonsexual, undesirable, or both. Robert McRuer and Anna Mollow open their collection of essays, *Sex and Disability*, exploring the dissonance of their title and their topic:

> The title of this book unites two terms that are, if not antithetical in the popular imagination, then certainly incongruous. The assertion that able-bodiedness is the foundation of sexiness might seem self-evident. After all, the sexiest people are healthy, fit, and active: lanky models, buff athletes, trim gym members brimming with energy. Rarely are disabled people regarded as either desiring subjects or objects of desire. And when sex and disability are linked in contemporary American cultures, the conjunction is most often the occasion for marginalization or marveling: the sexuality of disabled people is typically depicted in terms of either tragic deficiency or freakish excess. Pity or fear . . . But what if disability were sexy? And what if disabled people were understood to be both subjects and objects of a multiplicity of erotic desires and practices? (2012, 1)

The seventeen essays that then follow explore the conjunction of sex and disability from a variety of perspectives—analysis and advocacy, race and gender, autobiography and history. The burgeoning movements in art, memoir, and poetry by people with disabilities also frequently address their personal perspectives on sex and love. The puzzlement around the conjunction between sex and disability mirrors the puzzlement around sex and the sacred. However, as an integral aspect of being human, sexuality is entwined with the sacred just as it is entangled with somatic and psychic variability, and the Song can be a site of confluence among all three.

Saul Olyan is the only biblical scholar, reading through the methodological lens of disability studies, who does turn to the poetry of the Song. He does not find disability perspectives reflected in the Song; rather, he discovers a book that reinforces the divide between sex and disability. Olyan argues that the Song of Songs bears witness to ancient Israelite standards of beauty and that these standards extol bodies without blemish or impairment; therefore, beauty must have been associated with whole bodies and not those that were disabled. In the poetry of the Song, physical beauty includes "plumpness; thick hair on the head; ruddy, clear skin; beautiful eyes; symmetrical teeth and breasts; significant height; quickness and agility of movement; and physical strength" (2008, 18). In addition, the repeated descriptions of the woman dancing (6:13) and the man leaping and bounding (2:8-9) assume legs that work without a limp.

However, are the bodies described in the Song of Songs as beautifully and perfectly abled as Olyan contends? Olyan is certainly correct to note that the man and the woman do appear to have bodies that move without issue. "My lover is like a gazelle" (2:9) sings the woman, and the image certainly implies strength and agility. The woman runs out into the night searching for him (3:2); she dances. Both can stand and move on their legs. But ability in one limb does not imply ability in all, nor does it take two unimpaired legs to walk and leap. Physical wholeness should not be assumed from a poetic collection of lines that linger on one body part and then another, never really forming the whole. The category of disability covers a very wide range of bodily variability. Even the disabled can dance.

The conventional beauty of the man and woman in the Song of Songs is also questionable. The Song contains numerous descriptions of the two lovers' bodies, and there are four poems in particular that focus on the body (Song 4:1-5, 6:4-7, 5:10-16, and 7:1-10). Like Olyan, most readers proceed from the assumption that the lovers are both beautiful and able. Yet this assumption is built upon a number of prejudices of contemporary society. Young people in love and desiring each other's bodies are usually imagined as beautiful, and sex is the exclusive domain of the abled. As Tobin Siebers notes, "The preference for ability permeates almost every aspect of human culture, including the ability to have sex. In fact, sex may be the privileged domain of ability. . . . As a result, sex and human ability are both ideologically and inextricably linked" (McRuer and Mollow 2012, 40–41). After all, the lovers do call each other "beautiful." The woman says about herself, "I am black and beautiful" (1:5), and her lover echoes her assessment, "Ah, you are beautiful my beloved, truly lovely" (1:16). She calls him "radiant and ruddy" (5:10) and "altogether desirable" (5:16). But closer reading reveals images and physical descriptions that do not necessarily fit within a conventional understanding of the beautiful—at least not without a whole lot of interpretive work. Fiona Black highlights the strangeness of the images and metaphors employed to describe the bodies of the lovers: "At their best, the images are playful, maybe comic or the subject of teasing. At worst, they take on an unsettling quality, making the body ridiculous, conflicted, even alienating" (2009, 2). Black, then, deploys the category of the "grotesque" through which to read the body as presented in the Song of Songs.

Black does not engage disability studies or perspectives in her interpretation of the Song, instead focusing on literary theory and feminist hermeneutics, but there are implications in her readings for disability studies. She underscores the strangeness of the bodily images in the Song. They are discordant couplings of human body parts with animals, rocks, architectural elements, and martial objects. She is compared to doves, ewes, goats, towers, shields, army banners, big bowls, palm trees, flowers, and mounds of spices (see esp. 4:1-15, 6:4-10, 7:1-8). She has both a big belly (7:2) and a big nose (7:4). He is compared to doves and ravens, gold and sapphires, columns and the entire country of Lebanon (see esp. 5:11-15). There are many ways of understanding the strange images, but these bodies are certainly not described as beautiful in any straightforward way. Those who interpret these images in terms of conventional standards of beauty are doing so based upon their own expectations and biases, according to what Black (2009, 25) calls a "hermeneutic of compliment." Olyan's critique (2008) appears to be more about the standard interpretations of the Song—as a heterosexual love affair between two perfectly formed and beautiful people—than what the words on the page say themselves.

In contradistinction to a hermeneutic of compliment, Black proposes using the grotesque as the interpretive lens through which to read the imagery of the body (2009, 64). The "grotesque" is a term that is difficult to define with simple precision. Black summarizes,

> The grotesque body is the body in process, the body undergoing change. There is a particular emphasis on its mechanics, that is, its digestive, excretory and sexual/reproductive workings. . . . It is often represented as hybridized, a mixture of a variety of natural and human-fashioned elements. Mixing, too, can sometimes refer to the combination or confusion of gender. The grotesque body is meant to be viewed; it is itemized, consumed, and sometimes, thus, fetishized. In this capacity, there are attendant, pressing issues to be considered, issues about the objectification and autonomy of the lookers and the bodies being looked at. The spirit behind grotesque bodily figuration is, moreover, as mixed as the bodies themselves. The grotesque body can be inherently playful and comical, but as we have seen, it may also develop into the repulsive, that which is transgressive, alien and vile. In light of its status as spectacle, it carries also the potential for unease and discomfort in viewer and body. (120)

The bodies in the Song are comic, repulsive, unruly, and uncompliant, especially uncompliant in conforming to norms and regulations. The bodies change, they are hybridized with both animals and artifacts; one body part comes to the fore and then another, without the reader ever seeing the whole (122). Such descriptions can describe the disabled body, too. The disabled body is experienced and viewed as unruly and sometimes repulsive. Discussing her desirability, Vassar Miller highlights her own grotesque body by commenting that she is regarded as "a monster / in search of a horror movie to be in" (Bartlett, Black, and Northen 2011, 53). In some ways the disabled body brings into sharp relief the unpredictability and mutability of all bodies, the "monstrous" in us all. Perhaps that is why the disabled are often feared.

And yet the bodies of the Song are also desirable, sexy, alluring and intriguing, not despite but *because* of their strangeness, hybridization, and lack of compliance with conventional categories. The grotesque encompasses it all and breaks down the boundaries established between beauty, sex, and disability. In the poem "What You Mourn," Sheila Black describes the medical obsession with "fixing" her body, with special attention to operations performed so that she could become marriageable. Opposed to what "you" may see and mourn, she experiences her body as something desirable as it is: "that body / they tried so hard to fix, straighten was simply mine, / and I loved it as you love your own country" (Bartlett, Black, and Northen 2011, 212). Black reads the notion of the grotesque alongside the Song to help provide her opportunities to read the bodies in the Song "in light of a heuristic that privileges the unexpected, variability and difference" (2009, 124). I read the grotesque in the Song alongside disability to provide us all with opportunities to rethink our very notions of sex and beauty. The disabled body foregrounds the incongruous, variable, different, unexpected. This too is sexy and beautiful and desirable.

The poetry anthology *Beauty Is a Verb* already challenges static definitions of beauty in its very title. Many of the poets in the collection continue this challenge by exploring their own bodies and standard definitions of the beautiful. For example, Kenny Fries' poem "Beauty and Variations" opens with the question, "What is it like to be beautiful?" The verses that follow explore the contrast between his lover's normative body and his disabled one:

> Beauty, at birth applied, does not transfer
> to my hands. But every night, your hands
> touch my scars, raise my twisted limbs to
> graze against your lips. Lips that never
> form the words—*you are beautiful*—transform
> my deformed bones into—*what?*—if not beauty.
>
> (Bartlett, Black, and Northen 2011, 107;
> emphasis in original)

He ends his reflection: "So each night, naked on the bed, my body / doesn't want repair, but longs for innocence. If / innocent, despite the flaws I wear, I am beautiful" (109). Beauty is about becoming; it is about relationship. Beauty is not about conforming to some fixed standard. The Song of Songs sings to such dynamic notions of beauty and difference, and where beauty and difference converge, the sacred emerges.

CONCLUSION

The Song of Songs celebrates love and desire, and Lamentations mourns war and death. Besides beautiful and evocative poetry, little seems to connect these two biblical books. Yet as two scrolls in the Megillot, two scrolls incorporated into the Jewish holiday cycle, additional levels of meaning open up in the ritual context. As read in the synagogue as part of Jewish liturgy, the texts are resignified in ways that further link them together and invite additional engagement with disability perspectives.

The Song is read during the holiday of Passover, the commemoration of Israel's exodus from Egypt. As such, the Song is not about the desire of two young people. Instead of reading at a literal level, the Song is understood allegorically to express the love God and Israel have for one another.

Rabbinic exegesis knits the Song of Songs together with the Passover experience in particular by interweaving passages from the Song with verses from Exodus. This interweaving is seen most extensively in *Song of Songs Rabbah*; here, the two books are almost a call and response to each other. Read alongside Exodus, the Song of Songs is about the joy of liberation and the religious ecstasy experienced when Israel draws near to her God. Subsequent rabbinic interpretations link the Song of Songs more broadly to exile and return—not just the single event of the exodus but the entire Israelite and Jewish history of being cast out of the land and then coming home. Rashi, for example, understands the Song as Solomon foreseeing the repeated exiles of Israel, including the Babylonian exile, and that "in exile they would lament their former glory and remember the former love which God had shown them above all other nations" (Pope 1977, 102). Rashbam interprets the text in similar ways (103). In these rabbinic readings, then, Lamentations is the first cry of distress in the moment of exile, the Song of Songs the second cry, reflecting back nostalgically on the love that had been lost.

Love and loss, exodus and exile, Song of Songs and Lamentations: as moments in sacred time, the two come together. Liturgy also brings them into conversation around issues of disability, specifically impairment of mobility. As liturgical texts, both biblical books limp—Lamentations in how it sounds as read on Tisha b'Av and Song of Songs as it is connected to Passover. In Hebrew the name of the holiday also means "to limp."

The limp is the most obvious in Lamentations. When canted out loud in the Hebrew, the acrostic brace and its *qinah* meter, its limping rhythm, is evident to the eye and ear. In the biblical text, disability in general but lameness in particular is not just an aspect of a body considered ugly and undesirable. Lameness is also a "metaphor for divine rejection" (Olyan 2008, 89). The destruction of Jerusalem by the Babylonians does not just result in physical suffering; the destruction of Jerusalem is a sign of God's rejection, and it is that sense of spiritual anguish that imbues the melody with its mournful limp. Not just in Lamentations but in multiple prophetic texts—Isaiah, Jeremiah, Micah, and Zephaniah—the Judeans who were sent into exile were driven away limping. The images of Micah and Zephaniah also evoke the metaphor of sheep and shepherd; the lame, limping Judeans are injured sheep, and God as their shepherd has cast them out. The association with animality deepens the sense of rejection because lame sheep are precisely the animals prohibited from being used in sacrificial rituals in the temple (see Deut 15:21).

Such animals are also described as "ugly" and "an abomination" (see Deut 17:1; Olyan 2008, 90).

As lameness is a metaphor for divine rejection, the hope of redemption is expressed through YHWH's ability to heal disabilities. In Isaiah especially, the liberated Judeans have been transformed from being lame to being able to "leap like a gazelle" (35:6; see also Jer 31:7-9), the exact same language used to describe the male lover's athleticism in the Song of Songs. The ability to transform a lame person into someone who can "leap" is emblematic of the power of YHWH to liberate. So in these examples, limping and leaping are the antithesis of one another, both in terms of a description of physical ability and as an indication of spiritual health. Israel limps away rejected in Lamentations and leaps in love and redemption in the Song. Yet the distinctions between limping and leaping are not as firm and stable as the preceding analysis might suggest, and it is Passover itself that breaks down the distinctions. The verb "passover" (*pasah*) means literally "to pass over," "to spring over," "to leap." Yet, as stated above, the word also means "to be lame," "to limp." What is Passover about? Do the Israelites leap or limp into freedom? Later, do the Judeans leap or limp into exile? Is the Passover, the leap/limp, about rejection or redemption?

Lameness is certainly considered a "defect" in the biblical text, often associated with other "somatic deficiencies" like blindness. As a condition, difficulty in walking can result in "weakness, vulnerability, and dependence" (Olyan 2008, 52). There is no denying that mobility disabilities are inconvenient at best. However, disabilities are not only regarded in negative terms, and impaired bodies are not only invested with suffering. A disabled person does not always experience his or her body in terms of tragedy and pain, nor does the Bible always associate disability with tragedy and pain. In fact, one of the most central texts about Israel's identity and Israel's relationship to God is a text about a wounded leg, a text about becoming lame.

In Gen 32 Jacob wrestles with an angel. As they are struggling together in the deep of the night, when God "saw that he did not prevail against him, he struck him on the hip socket; and Jacob's hip was put out of joint" (32:25). Even so, he continues to wrestle into the dawn of the day, and the divine man cannot defeat him. Despite a common interpretation of this story that sees Jacob as a "cripple" and a "tragic hero" because of the crippling (Avalos, Melcher, and Schipper 2007, 97), there is nothing negative in the story itself. In fact, Jacob's wound is a sign of his power, his strength, and his victory. There is no indication in the biblical text that he is ever disadvantaged later on because of it. Rather, as Kerry Wynn notes, "The disability was Jacob's sign of the covenant" (Avalos, Melcher, and Schipper 2007, 101). Israel as a name means "one who wrestles with God." But since the change from Jacob to Israel also involves a wounding, Israel is also the one who is lamed by God, who carries this wound as a mark, not of ugliness and rejection but as a sign of the covenant, a sign of divine favor, a sign of relationship.

Laurie Clements Lambeth, a contemporary poet diagnosed with multiple sclerosis as a teenager, writes how those two identities are inextricably intertwined: her disease "is indeed the blessing-wound that changed my thinking and brought me to poetry" (Bartlett, Black, and Northen 2011, 174). Further,

> Fitting form to the poem, lending it shape and order, granted me a tremendous sense of power—not to change my physical condition at all (why would I want to change?), but to relay its essence and create a thing of beauty that speaks simultaneously about the individual and a more universal sense of alienation, all of us trapped in chaotic bodies, the potential of unrest ever-present in every body, which I hope, if the poem's shaped well and the reader willing to follow, will foster empathy, not sympathy, for the blessing-wound. (176–77)

The blessing-wound shapes her engagement with the world and generates her very identity. It gives her poetry and thus puts her into relationship with the world.

The limp is also a leap. The wound, while painful, is also productive. The blessing-wound is what transforms Jacob and his sons into Israel with its twelve tribes. The blessing-wound is what transforms various collections of national stories, legends, songs, laws, and rituals into sacred Scripture, into the Hebrew Bible. The blessing-wound is what transforms Judah, a small and insignificant nation, into Judaism, the first monotheistic world religion. In all these poems and stories of disability, whether biblical or contemporary, we see people wresting meaning out of their wounds. By reading Lamentations and Song of Songs together as part of the Megillot and through the analytical lens of disability, both become reflections on the experience of exile and return, both become about gladness and sorrow, both are steps in this divine dance where we limp and leap and limp again.

WORKS CITED

Avalos, Hector, Sarah J. Melcher, and Jeremy Schipper, eds. 2007. *This Abled Body: Rethinking Disabilities in Biblical Studies*. Semeia Studies 55. Atlanta: Society of Biblical Literature.

Bartlett, Jennifer, Sheila Black, and Michael Northen, eds. 2011. *Beauty Is a Verb: The New Poetry of Disability*. El Paso, Tex.: Cinco Puntos.

Black, Fiona C. 2009. *The Artifice of Love: Grotesque Bodies in the Song of Songs*. New York: T&T Clark.

Craigie, Peter C., and Marvin E. Tate. 2004. *Psalms 1–50*. Word Biblical Commentary. Nashville: Thomas Nelson.

Dahood, Mitchell. 1966. *Psalms I:1-50*. Anchor Bible 16. Garden City, N.Y.: Doubleday.

Eiesland, Nancy L. 1994. *The Disabled God: Toward a Liberatory Theology of Disability*. Nashville: Abingdon.

Fox, Michael V. 1985. *The Song of Songs and the Ancient Egyptian Love Songs*. Madison: University of Wisconsin Press.

Garrett, Duane, and Paul R. House. 2004. *Song of Songs/Lamentations*. Word Biblical Commentary. Nashville: Thomas Nelson.

Hillers, Delbert R. 1972. *Lamentations*. Anchor Bible 7A. Garden City, N.Y.: Doubleday.

Junior, Nyasha, and Jeremy Schipper. 2013. "Disability Studies and the Bible." Pages 21–37 in *New Meanings for Ancient Texts: Recent Approaches to Biblical Criticisms and Their Applications*. Edited by Steven L. McKenzie and John Kaltner. Louisville, Ky.: Westminster John Knox.

McRuer, Robert, and Anna Mollow, eds. 2012. *Sex and Disability*. Durham, N.C.: Duke University Press.

Miller, Vassar. 2000. "Without Ceremony." *Literature and Medicine* 19, no. 2: 152.

Moss, Candida R., and Jeremy Schipper, eds. 2011. *Disability Studies and Biblical Literature*. New York: Palgrave Macmillan.

Olyan, Saul M. 2008. *Disability in the Hebrew Bible: Interpreting Mental and Physical Differences*. New York: Cambridge University Press.

———. 2009. "The Ascription of Physical Disability as a Stigmatizing Strategy in Biblical Iconic Polemics." *Journal of Hebrew Scriptures* 9: 1–15.

Pope, Marvin H. 1977. *Song of Songs*. Anchor Bible 7C. Garden City, N.Y.: Doubleday.

Raphael, Rebecca. 2008. *Biblical Corpora: Representations of Disability in Hebrew Bible Literature*. New York: T&T Clark.

Schumm, Darla, and Michael Stoltzfus, eds. 2011. *Disability in Judaism, Christianity, and Islam: Sacred Texts, Historical Traditions, and Social Analysis*. New York: Palgrave Macmillan.

Yong, Amos. 2011. *The Bible, Disability, and the Church*. Grand Rapids: Eerdmans.

7

Isaiah, Jeremiah, Ezekiel, Daniel, and the Twelve

J. Blake Couey

In ancient Near Eastern religions, prophets functioned as intermediaries between the divine and human worlds, relaying verbal messages from the former to the latter. Along with astrologers and diviners, they were regarded as the primary mechanism by which the demands of deities were made known. The Hebrew Bible contains a series of fifteen or sixteen books that are putatively named for ancient Israelite and Judahite prophets, depending on whether one counts the book of Daniel, which appears in different places in the Jewish and Christian canons. It is reasonable to assume that the activity of historical prophets lies behind some of the books in this corpus, but they were supplemented and edited over a period of many centuries. In their final forms, they reflect the concerns of the Judahite scribes who produced them during the Babylonian and Persian periods. The prophetic books are set between approximately 750 and 450 BCE, a time when the kingdoms of Israel and Judah were successively subjugated to Assyrian, Babylonian, and Persian control. During this turbulent period, Israel was conquered by Assyria, and Judah was conquered by Babylon. The Babylonians destroyed the city of Jerusalem and the temple to YHWH, and they deported many citizens of Jerusalem to Babylon. Some descendants of these exiles returned to their ancestral homeland under Persian rule, and the city and temple were eventually rebuilt. The prophetic books depict these sociopolitical upheavals as the work of YHWH to punish the sins of Israel and Judah or deliver them from their adversaries. As a result, these books are particularly concerned with the interplay between doom and hope, and disability language features prominently in the portrayal of both.

The representation of disabled and other non-"normal" bodies plays a critical role in prophetic discourse about embodiment, which intersects with other significant themes in these books such as divine and human nature, gender, forced migration, worship, and ecology. For this reason, attention to the portrayals of disability in prophetic literature pays interpretive dividends not simply for a specific set of ideological concerns—although those are by no means trivial—but also because these images, even if few in number, serve important functions in the text. This chapter offers close readings of prophetic texts that contain language or images associated with disability, with special attention to the relationship between disability and divine power. In addition, I will consider how other texts might inform one's understanding of disability in this corpus or be relevant to the concerns of disabled persons. I rely heavily on seminal studies of disability in prophetic literature by Saul Olyan (2008, 78–92), Sarah Melcher (2007, 115–29), Rebecca Raphael (2008, 119–30), and Jeremy Schipper (2015, 319–33), although I offer different interpretations of some key texts and discuss others that receive little notice in their work. In a few cases, I have found more nuanced portrayals of disability in texts that they read quite negatively—although I hasten to add that few if any depict disability in unambiguously positive terms. My approach to these texts seeks to integrate literary and historical methods of interpretation. Like all literary works, the biblical prophetic books create an imaginative world that must be understood on its own terms, which requires an appreciation for the artistic devices that generate and enhance meaning. Images of disability exist within this literary world and derive their significance from their place in it. They seldom refer to actual disabled persons; rather, they stand in for a variety of other concepts, projecting onto them attributes associated with disability. At the same time, prophetic texts were composed by historical persons for historical audiences with particular rhetorical aims. Although contemporary interpreters can only imperfectly approximate the concerns of the original producers and consumers of these texts, the attempt to do so has great value for this project. Currently favored models in disability studies hold that views and evaluations of disability are culturally conditioned. By understanding the similarities and differences between ancient and contemporary perspectives, we will better appreciate the constructed character of our own understandings of disability.

DISABILITY IMAGERY AND LANGUAGE
IN THE PROPHETIC BOOKS

Disability is an aspect of embodiment. It will be helpful, then, to ground this treatment of disability in the prophetic books in the larger context of their discourse about bodies more generally. One should note that this discourse is not limited to humans; disabled animals (Jer 14:6; Mic 4:6; Zech 12:4; Mal 1:8) and idols (Isa 46:7; Jer 10:5; Hab 2:18-19) also appear in the prophetic corpus. It is striking how many of the bodies portrayed in this corpus deviate from generally accepted standards for so-called whole or normal bodies—often quite gruesomely so. Along with a number of attributes commonly perceived today as disabilities, one finds bodies with crushed, burned, or stripped bones (Jer 8:1-2; Amos 2:1; Mic 3:3). Corpses appear everywhere, often in great quantities (Isa 5:25; Jer 34:18-20; Ezek 6:5; Amos 8:3; Nah 3:3). Female bodies are subject to mutilation (Ezek 23:25; Hos 13:16; Amos 1:13). When cities or nations are given metaphorical bodies—an ancient variation on the idea of the "body politic"—they are almost invariably wounded (Isa 1:5-6; Jer 14:17, 30:12-13; Hos 5:13; Nah 3:19). Even the implied authors of these texts do not possess stereotypically normal bodies. Prophets are beset by involuntary tremors (Isa 21:4; Jer 23:9; Hab 3:16) and depicted as mentally ill (Jer 29:26; Hos 9:7), with visible signs of self-mutilation (Zech 13:6). All these bodies inhabit an environment that is itself diseased or devastated (Hos 4:3; Joel 1:7-13; Amos 8:8; Zeph 1:3, 18). The overwhelming number of deviant bodies likely reflects the traumatic disturbances of the centuries during which these texts were created, mapping social, political, and religious upheavals onto bodies and landscapes.

Perhaps surprisingly, the body of YHWH is also depicted as abnormal in the Prophets, but in ways that highlight its extreme size and strength. In an extended hymnic description of YHWH's appearance in Hab 3, the divine body is as bright as the sun, horns extend from the divine hands, and the divine gaze causes earthquakes (Hab 3:3-4, 6, 10). Ezekiel compares the appearance of the divine body to fire, gleaming metal or gemstones, and a rainbow (Ezek 1:26-28). Other texts depict mountains or clouds beneath YHWH's feet, indicating the deity's enormous stature (Mic 1:3-4; Nah 1:3; Zech 14:4). In Isa 6:1 YHWH sits upon a giant throne, and the mere hem of the deity's robe fills the temple; similarly, Isa 40 imagines that the primordial waters can fit in the divine hand (40:12) and declares that humans are as puny as grasshoppers in proportion to the deity (40:22). Zechariah 4:10

depicts YHWH with seven eyes "that roam about all the earth."[1] In addition to the unusual number, the latter detail suggests that the divine eyes are detachable and mobile. To be sure, many of these details are not meant to be taken literally; Hos 11:9 suggests that the authors of the prophetic books understood their descriptions of God as metaphorical. Nonetheless, the contrast between portrayals of the divine body, which consistently emphasize its power, and other bodies, which generally emphasize their weakness, is instructive. This dynamic is in play in almost every instance of disability language or imagery in the corpus. Such imagery heightens the impression of divine power by demonstrating YHWH's capacity to cause disability, by depicting YHWH's care for disabled persons, or by using disability as a foil to demonstrate YHWH's superiority over other entities. Other interpreters make similar claims about biblical narratives or the Hebrew Bible as a whole (Olyan 2008, 9–10; Raphael 2008, 26).

The following survey is not quite exhaustive, but it covers many significant references to and representations of disability in the biblical prophetic books. Although several common themes emerge from this survey, such as the association between exile and disability or the attribution of disability to images of foreign deities, the texts ultimately display greater variety than homogeneity. Each text, moreover, derives much of its meaning from a specific context in a particular book. For this reason, the survey proceeds mostly by order of occurrence, although occasionally a group of thematically similar texts in relatively close proximity may be treated together for the sake of convenience.

ISAIAH

The book of Isaiah is the largest of the biblical prophetic books and the most influential in Judaism and Christianity. Like other prophetic books, it is a mixture of harsh denunciations of human sin and graphic warnings of divine judgment on the one hand and deeply comforting words of reassurance and promises of restoration on the other. As depicted within his namesake book, Isaiah was a prophet in Jerusalem from approximately 740–700 BCE, and he was especially concerned with social injustice, the fate of the royal Davidic dynasty, and the increasing power of Assyria. Only some texts from Isa 1–39 can be plausibly associated with the historical prophet, however. Since the turn of the twentieth century, biblical scholars have argued that Isa 40–55, which are concerned with the return

---

[1] Unless otherwise indicated, biblical translations in this chapter are my own.

of exiled Judahites from Babylon, date to the late sixth century BCE. The material in Isa 56–66 seems to come from an even later period, reflecting the challenges of life in Jerusalem under Persian rule. These three sections are often called First Isaiah (or Proto-Isaiah), Second Isaiah (or Deutero-Isaiah), and Third Isaiah (or Trito-Isaiah). Although the development of the book was probably much more complex, this tripartite division remains broadly useful for thinking about its structure.

Isaiah contains more references to disability than any other book in the prophetic corpus, and the imagery of blindness and deafness features especially prominently in its discourse about the divine-human relationship. Attention to this imagery has played an important part in recent discussions about the formation of the book. Prior to the 1970s, there was broad agreement that the major sections of Isaiah developed independently and were combined later with little care. That consensus has shifted, however, and many scholars now hold that the book grew organically in ways that established meaningful overarching themes, including the interplay among disability images in its different sections (Clements 1985, 101–4; Clements 1988, 189–200; Williamson 1994, 47–50). In Isa 6:9-10 YHWH imposes a state of spiritual imperceptiveness on the people of Judah, which is described metaphorically as the inability to see or hear; this theme is developed in other preexilic texts such as 29:9-10 and perhaps 32:3-4. Isaiah 40–55 describes the people's spiritual blindness and deafness as an existing state (e.g., 42:16, 18-19; 43:8) in ways that seem to presuppose and respond to these earlier passages. Notably, the material from Second Isaiah uses the explicit disability terms "blind" (עִוֵּר, ʿiwwēr) and "deaf" (חֵרֵשׁ, ḥērēš), which do not appear in the preexilic texts. Related disability imagery in 29:18 and 35:5, which depict the future healing of disabled bodies, likely represents even later development of these themes, although these passages precede Isa 40–55 in the final form of the book.

Over the past decade, biblical scholars with interests in disability studies have returned to these texts from Isaiah. Raphael (2008, 120–28) connects the shifting disability imagery to the book's portrayal of the breakdown and restoration of communication between the deity and the people (cf. Carroll 1997, 87; Olyan 2008, 7, 35). She concludes, "Blindness and deafness thus draw their local value from relational terms, a value that depends on what kind of communication is held up as the model, and what kind is deplored" (Raphael 2008, 124). Combining approaches from disability studies and narratology, Simeon Chavel (2014) also explores the interface between disability and communication, with a focus on Isa 40–48. In these chapters he maintains that references to bodily impairment denote "disability when it comes to storytelling." The manufacturers of idols and the Judahite exiles both appear as disabled because they cannot adequately narrate Yhwh's role in world events (2014, 23–25). Finally, Jeremy Schipper (2015, 319–33) argues that the uniquely Isaianic motif of healing from disability forms part of a larger rhetorical strategy in the book, in which the postexilic restoration of Jerusalem is associated with exaggeratedly idealized human bodies that are no longer subject to conventional physical limitations.

For the sake of convenience in arrangement, the following treatment of disability imagery in Isaiah examines the three major sections of the book separately. Nonetheless, there is both thematic continuity across these divisions and thematic tension within each section.

Isaiah 1–39

The image of a collective body of the people of Judah first appears in the opening chapter of Isaiah, which many interpreters regard as a thematic introduction to the book as a whole. Isaiah 1:5-6 describes how Yhwh has repeatedly struck the people as a punishment for their rebellion against the deity, leaving their metaphorical body so disfigured that its entire exterior surface is nothing but abrasions. The image is grotesque to the point of absurdity (Raphael 2008, 121). Although it is difficult to imagine that a body so severely injured would not be permanently impaired, these verses do not use explicit disability language. Nonetheless, the metaphor of the body and the association between bodily injuries and divine punishments anticipate much of the disability imagery in the following chapters, including the depiction of the nation's lame body in Isa 3:1-8. Verse 1 announces the imminent removal of Jerusalem and Judah's "staff and stay" (משען ומשענה, *maš'ēn ûmaš'ēnâ*), identified in verses 2-3 as their political and religious leaders.[2] These words do not occur elsewhere in the Hebrew Bible. Many interpreters assume that they are abstract terms for support, but they are better understood as references to support technology for persons with limited mobility. A related term משענת (*miš'enet*) designates a crutch or walking stick (Exod 21:19; 2 Kgs 18:21 = Isa 36:6; Zech 8:4). Isaiah 3:8 predicts that, without their "staff and stay," Jerusalem and Judah will "stumble" and "fall." Together then, 3:1 and 8 depict the nation as a lame person and its leaders as its crutch (Couey 2014, 95–97, 101–3). When those leaders are removed for abusing their authority (vv. 12-15),

---

[2] The translation "staff and stay" follows KJV, which nicely reflects the alliteration of the Hebrew.

the nation experiences difficulty walking. In support of this reading, the verb כשל (kšl, "stumble"), which occurs in verse 8, specifically denotes lameness in Isa 35:3, Jer 31:9, Zech 12:8, Job 4:4, and 2 Chr 28:15.

Unlike later Isaianic texts that depict disabled bodies as aberrations that require healing, Isa 3:1 and 8 associate disability with a seemingly normal state of affairs—human dependence on just leadership. The focus on support technology in Isa 3:1 and 8 is also unusual among prophetic texts with disability. It implies an understanding of disability as a complex interaction between a body and its environment and not merely a flaw located in the body, which resonates with contemporary social or cultural models of disability rather than medical ones (Couey 2014, 104–6, 108–9). Among other prophetic texts that depict disability, only a few like Isa 56:3-5 and Jer 31:8-9 similarly consider the interaction between bodies and their social or physical environments, as will be discussed later in this chapter.

One of the most important passages in the book of Isaiah is the first-person narrative account of the prophet's commission in Isa 6. The episode is set in the temple, where Isaiah sees a vision of the enthroned deity surrounded by heavenly attendants (vv. 1-4). Reflecting a common motif in such narratives, the prophet responds by lamenting his unworthiness, which he expresses in bodily terms: "I am a man with unclean lips, and I dwell among a people with unclean lips; yet the king, YHWH of hosts, my eyes have seen!" (v. 5). This characterization is consistent with the frequent tendency in prophetic literature to describe human sinfulness with somatic language. In response to this confession, one of the deity's attendants purifies Isaiah by searing his lips with a coal from the altar (vv. 6-7). This fiery purgation anticipates the similar purification of the people, as depicted throughout the book (Isa 1:7, 25; 5:24; 33:14). Ironically, this action that should have severely injured his mouth instead makes it possible for him to speak as a prophet on behalf of YHWH, whose commission he enthusiastically accepts in verse 8. Although the narrative has not yet directly evoked the theme of disability, it already suggests that the prophetic vocation transforms and potentially impairs the prophet's own body, a theme that will appear in even more pronounced fashion with Jeremiah and Ezekiel.

Following the prophet's assent to YHWH's call to service, the deity gives him disturbing instructions:

> Go and say to this people:
> "Listen intently, but do not comprehend!
> See carefully, but do not know!"
> Make the heart of this people sluggish,

and weigh down their ears, and shut their eyes,
lest they see with their eyes, hear with their ears,
and perceive with their hearts
and repent and be healed. (Isa 6:9-10)

These verses have a number of disturbing theological implications, but for the purposes of this commentary, the disability imagery holds the most interest. Although it does not use explicit disability terms like "deaf" (חרש, ḥrš) or "blind" (עור, 'wr), the passage depicts the interruption of the Judahite people's collective faculties of sight, hearing, and perception. As indicated by the final line of verse 10, this impairment is a metaphor for the inability of presumably able-bodied Judahites to receive communication from the deity, the intended result of which is their destruction. Whereas the prophet identified himself with the people in terms of their sinful lips in verse 5, now he is clearly distinguished from them. His "eyes" clearly witnessed the magnificence of the deity, but the people's eyes are now prevented from seeing or understanding divine revelation. Indeed, Isaiah himself is the agent of—and thus complicit in—this hardening, a shocking reversal of the prophet's typical role as the communicator of the divine will (Carroll 1997, 83). The prophet protests the harsh assignment by asking, "How long, my Lord?"—a familiar plaint from psalms of lament—in verse 11.

Raphael argues that the "divinely afflicted impairment" in Isa 6:9-10 responds to the people's own "self-inflicted impairment"—namely, that "powerful humans have refused to see or hear their oppressed fellows or the divine demands for justice" (2008, 121–22). YHWH's response to this willful disregard in the book of Isaiah is twofold, according to Raphael. The deity may respond in kind by refusing to see or hear the people, thus adopting "a temporary or selective disability," as in 1:15 (cf. 37:17, 57:11, and 58:3, which Raphael does not cite). The more sustained response, however, is to impose disability upon the people. Repeated refusal to see, hear, or perceive thus leads to inability to see, hear, or perceive in a kind of poetic justice that one frequently finds in prophetic literature. This largely convincing reading offers a helpful scheme for thinking about the extensive discourse surrounding disability in Isaiah—in particular, the failure of sight or hearing.[3] Other texts throughout the book revisit this motif from

---

[3] Raphael's case would be stronger if other texts in Isaiah used the language of seeing or hearing to depict the flouting of divine expectations for justice. The closest it comes is describing the people's general unwillingness to "see" YHWH's purpose and align their actions with it (5:12, 22:11).

6:9-10 to describe further breakdown in divine-human communication or its future restoration (e.g., 29:9-10, 18; 32:3-4; 35:5; 42:16, 18-19; 43:8).

A prophetic speaker in Isa 21:1-9 reports bodily distress accompanying a vision of the fall of Babylon. Scholars disagree over the date of the composition of the chapter and whether any of it is attributable to Isaiah of Jerusalem (Blenkinsopp 2000, 325–27; Roberts 2015, 274–75), but readers or hearers of the book will naturally connect the first-person speaking voice with the literary figure of Isaiah. In response to his vision, the prophet experiences severe emotional, mental, and physical disturbance, including temporary disability. In verse 3 he describes himself as "too doubled over to hear" and "too overwhelmed to see," and he complains about the upheaval of his "heart" in verse 4. Ironically, then, the prophetic speaker himself briefly suffers the fate that he is commanded to make happen to the people in 6:10, undergoing disruptions of sight, hearing, and perception. Elsewhere in Isaiah, a prophetic speaker expresses dismay or experiences somatic disturbance in response to threats against Judah (22:4) and even Moab (16:9-11). These texts extend the discourse of Isaiah's commission account in chapter 6, which highlights the effects of the experience on the prophet's own body.

Disability language occurs repeatedly in Isa 29:9-24, a passage containing two or three originally independent units that themselves developed in multiple stages (Blenkinsopp 2000, 403–4, 407–8). In verse 9 the prophet commands the people to "shut your eyes and be blind," using two different forms of the verb שׁעע (šʿʿ), which is unique to Isaiah and also appears in 6:10. There, the prophet was commanded to impede the people's sight on behalf of the deity; here, he commands them to blind themselves, likely with sarcastic intent. In 29:10, however, YHWH directly causes the people's blindness, having "poured upon you . . . a spirit of deep sleep." The verse goes on to explain the cause of the people's blindness: "He has closed your eyes, the prophets."[4] Not unlike Isa 3:1 and 8, this verse represents the people of Judah as a body and their prophets as its eyes. By taking away the prophets' visionary powers, the deity effectively renders the people spiritually blind (cf. 1 Sam 3:1; Mic 3:6-7; Ps 74:9). Once more, tension emerges between this text, in which spiritual blindness results from prophets' inability to carry out their tasks, and Isa 6:9-10, in which it results from Isaiah's successful execution of his prophetic vocation. The identification of

[4] It is possible to take "prophets" in this line and "seers" in the next as vocatives instead of appositives (so NRSV: "he has closed your eyes, you prophets, / and covered your heads, you seers"); see Roberts 2000, 368.

Y<small>HWH</small> as the one responsible for the situation further conflicts with 30:10, in which the people themselves "say to the seers: do not see!" (Carroll 1997: 85). As these examples demonstrate, although the use of sight and blindness as metaphors for divine-human communication recurs throughout Isaiah, the details of its deployment are frequently inconsistent.

The imagery changes in 29:11-12, which compares a "vision" to a "sealed scroll." It is inaccessible both to the literate, because it is sealed, and to the illiterate, because they cannot read. The term for "vision" (חזות, ḥāzût) is associated with prophecy in 21:2, and a related term with the same meaning (חזון, ḥāzôn) designates the book of Isaiah itself in 1:1. Isaiah 29:11-12 thus seems to have prophetic visions in mind, perhaps even a collection of the prophecies of Isaiah (cf. 30:8). The passage depicts a scenario much closer to that of 6:9-10, in which the people have access to prophecy but cannot comprehend it. Because 29:11-12 appears in prose rather than poetry, most scholars think these verses were not originally part of this chapter, and it is tempting to imagine that a later editor added them to mitigate the tension between 29:9-10 and 6:9-10. In any case, the shift from images of sight and blindness to images of reading and illiteracy creatively develops the discourse about the interaction between sight and spiritual perception (Carroll 1997, 81–82).

Isaiah 29:15 opens a new section in the chapter and denounces political schemes that run counter to God's will:

> Hey, you who hide a plan too deep for Y<small>HWH</small>,
> and whose work is in a dark place,
> who say, "Who sees us? Who knows about us?"

The verse uses a cluster of roots associated with sightlessness in Isaiah: חשך (ḥšk, "dark"), ראה (rʾh, "see"), and ידע (ydʿ, "know"). Judah's leaders think their actions will escape divine notice because they believe Y<small>HWH</small>'s sensory capacities are limited, a motif that occurs in other prophetic texts (Jer 12:4; Ezek 8:12). From the perspective of Isaiah, this view is fundamentally mistaken. Other texts in the book make clear that the failure of sight lies not with the deity but with humans, who "do not look to the action of Y<small>HWH</small> / and do not see (ראו, rāʾû) the work of his hands" (Isa 5:12; cf. 5:19, 22:11, 31:1). As Carroll (1997, 85) observes, "They are a people who cannot see and who imagine that (therefore) they cannot be seen." Later in the book, ironically, the people will lament that Y<small>HWH</small> does not seem to notice them (40:27), the very state of affairs over which they boast in 29:15.

The tone shifts from denunciation to promise in 29:17-24, which almost all scholars date to the exilic or postexilic periods. Following the description of a transformed landscape in verse 17, verse 18 depicts the future reversal of disability:

> The deaf ones will hear, on that day, the words of a scroll,
> and without murkiness or darkness the eyes of the blind ones will see.

The verse incorporates motifs from earlier in the chapter. "Scroll" looks back to verses 11-12, while the roots for "dark" (חשך, ḥšk) and "see" (ראה, r'h) recall verse 15. Contemporary readers from highly literate societies, who primarily correlate access to a written document with eyesight, may find the first half of verse 18 odd. In an ancient society with restricted literacy and limited text production, however, one would typically encounter the contents of a document by hearing it read aloud (cf. Exod 24:7; 2 Kgs 23:2; Neh 8:3). Deafness would thus prevent access to performances of texts. The link between blindness and darkness, by contrast, apparently seemed as natural to an ancient audience as to a modern one (cf. Deut 28:29; Isa 42:16; Acts 13:11), even if it more accurately reflects the stereotypes of sighted persons than the lived experiences of blind persons. The word translated here as "murkiness" (אפל, 'ōpel) denotes a particularly intense darkness (cf. Job 3:6, 10:22, 28:3; Ps 91:6), further differentiating blindness from a sighted person's experience of the absence of light.

Because verse 18 uses explicit terms for disability (חרשים, ḥērĕšîm, "deaf ones"; עורים, 'iwrîm, "blind ones"), one might plausibly read it as a straightforward depiction of the transformation of disabled bodies. Along with the reinvented landscape of verse 17, this transformation demonstrates Yhwh's remarkable, world-altering power (Melcher 2007, 122–23; Olyan 2008, 86–89). On the other hand, there are good reasons to interpret the language metaphorically. The "scroll" in verse 18 is likely a collection of prophecies attributed to Isaiah (cf. 29:11, 30:8), in which case the deaf ones are humans who had been previously unwilling or unable to comprehend divine revelation, but whom God has now given the power to do so (Blenkinsopp 2000, 402, 409; Raphael 2008, 125–26). The imagery of darkness and blindness in the second half of the verse would then represent the former absence of prophetic revelation, as in 29:10 (cf. 8:19-22).[5] Isaiah 29:18 thus reverses 6:9-10, in which Isaiah's audience is described as unsighted and unhearing as a result of their divinely imposed inability to comprehend the prophet's message. This understanding of the verse

---

[5] Raphael suggests instead that it indicates idolatry (2006, 126). It is also possible, given the reference to the end of tyranny in Isa 29:20, that the darkness symbolizes oppression (cf. Isa 9:1 [Eng. 9:2]).

explains why the reversal of disability is paralleled by the reversal of ignorance and obstinacy in 29:24. The surrounding verses also associate these
reversals with the fructification of Lebanon (v. 17) and the exultation of
the "humble" and the "poorest of humans," further casting disability in a
negative light (Melcher 2007, 121–22; Olyan 2008, 87–89).

Regardless of whether the images are understood literally or metaphorically, the verse is one of several Isaianic texts depicting the future
healing of disabled bodies, most of which probably come from the exilic
or postexilic periods (cf. 32:3-4; 35:5-6; 42:7, 16, 18). They promote a view
of disability as an anomaly or deficiency, and their vivid imagery and carefully constructed poetry make their ideology all the more persuasive. As
Olyan explains, "Although utopian texts function to exalt YHWH through
his saving and transformative acts, they also tend to stigmatize disabled
persons . . . by eliminating their disabilities entirely in the envisioned utopia, suggesting that disabilities have no place in a model world" (2008,
79). If anything, these texts become more problematic if one understands
them as metaphorical; then they not only stigmatize disability but also
appropriate its imagery to describe the experiences of able-bodied persons,
with little concern for actual disabled persons (Raphael 2008, 127–29). The
motif of the healing of disabilities does not explicitly appear in other prophetic texts, and other Isaianic depictions of the future contain disability
imagery without depicting its healing.[6] One should not treat it, then, as
the normative view within prophetic literature. Rather, as Jeremy Schipper has argued, it should be understood as part of a rhetorical strategy
within some texts in Isaiah to depict inhabitants of the glorified future city
of Jerusalem with dramatically enhanced bodily capacities (2015, 327–33).
This rhetoric includes able-bodied persons as well who experience supernatural speed (40:28-31), dramatically enhanced life spans (65:17-20), and
instantaneous and painless childbirths (66:7-8).

The vision of a future righteous ruler in Isa 32:1-8 contains additional
imagery of the removal of disability. Although most scholars think that
32:1-8 belongs to later stages of the book's development (Blenkinsopp
2000, 430–31; Wildberger 2002, 234–36), a few argue that it derives from
the eighth-century prophet Isaiah of Jerusalem or from a possible seventh-
century edition of the book (Roberts 2015, 408; Williamson 1994, 48).
Following a generalized description of the ruler in verses 1-2, the poem
announces the radical changes that will mark his reign:

---

[6] The motif reappears in the New Testament in the accounts of Jesus' healings in the
Gospels, which have almost certainly been influenced by texts from Isaiah, esp. Isa 35:5-6
(Blenkinsopp 2000, 409; Clements 1988, 190–91, 199).

> And the eyes of those who see will not be shut,
> and the ears of those who hear will pay attention;
> and the hearts of the rash ones will perceive knowledge,
> and the tongues of stammerers will hurry to speak distinctly. (vv. 3-4)

These reversals characterize the transformed world over which the future ruler will govern, much like the reordered animal kingdom in the similar royal vision of Isa 11:1-10. The text may also be informed by the expectation that just rulers offer care to disabled persons along with other vulnerable classes, as reflected in Ezek 34:4 and Zech 12:16. (See the discussion of these texts later in this chapter.) If so, this vision far transcends what one might reasonably expect of most rulers!

Isaiah 32:3-4 contains both textual and linguistic problems. In the first line of verse 3, the Masoretic Hebrew Text (MT) reads "gaze," from the root שעה (šʿh), which makes little sense here. The original reading was almost certainly "shut," from the similar root שעע (šʿ)—the same verb that appears in Isaiah's commission in 6:10 (Blenkinsopp 2000, 429; Roberts 2015, 409; Wildberger 2002, 231). Verse 4 contains the only appearance of the term עלגים (ʿillĕgîm) in the Hebrew Bible. Because the term appears in the qittēl noun pattern associated with perceived human defects, it likely denotes some kind of disability, which would fit the larger context. The similar root לעג (lʿg), which means "jeer" in most contexts, depicts the sound of foreign languages in Isa 28:11, Isa 33:19, and Hos 7:16, suggesting that it could be used for unintelligible speech. Most likely, the term in Isa 32:4 comes from this root—hence the translation "stammerers"—but with the first two letters swapped. J. J. M. Roberts (2015, 408 n. 4) suggests that the transposed letters play on the idea of a speech impediment.

Isaiah 32:3 does not explicitly describe the transformation of disabled bodies. Instead, it envisions the ongoing perception of persons who can already see and hear, confirming that disability language in Isaiah may represent the spiritual deficiencies of able-bodied persons (Raphael 2008, 126). Especially given the likely occurrence of the rare verb "shut" (שעע, šʿ), almost all commentators understand the verse as a reversal of the hardening passage in 6:9-10, proclaiming a future in which the people of Judah experience unhindered access to YHWH (Blenkinsopp 2000, 430; Clements 1988, 196; Wildberger 2002, 238). Its explicit reference to able-bodied persons notwithstanding, Raphael deems 32:3 one of the clearest depictions of "the non-existence of disability in the eschatological future . . . in keeping with the belief that God was the sole etiology of disease, disability, and healing" (2008, 127–28). Moreover, verse 4 clearly depicts the erasure of disability. The second line imagines the healing of persons with speech impediments (Schipper 2015, 330). The term "rash ones" (נמהרים, *nimhārîm*) in the first line comes from a root meaning "hurried," indicating rushed, unclear thinking. It possibly denotes a cognitive disability; a similar phrase refers to anxiety in 35:4. Alternatively, the "rash ones" may be willfully ignorant or closed-minded persons, and this line identifies the target of the metaphorical language of the surrounding lines, much like the juxtaposition of disability with lack of knowledge in 29:18 and 24. The restored ability of their "hearts" (לבב, *lēbab*) to "perceive knowledge" (יבין לדעת, *yābîn lādā'at*) further recalls and reverses the language of 6:10.

Isaiah 33 is also a vision of future redemption, emphasizing the restoration of Zion. Unlike 32:1-8, it has little place for a human ruler in its imagined future, emphasizing rather the kingship of YHWH (33:17, 22). Isaiah 33:15 lists six characteristic behaviors of people who may live with YHWH in the future Jerusalem, culminating in a pair of lines that use the language of temporary disability:

> those who plug their ears from hearing bloodshed
> and shut their eyes from seeing evil.

In addition to the tight parallelism, the lines contain the rhyming verbs אטם (*ōṭēm*, "plug") and עצם (*ōṣēm*, "shut"), enhancing the aesthetic appeal of the verse and thus the kind of ethical life that it commends. The first verb is directly linked with deafness in Ps 58:5 (Eng. 58:4), while the second only occurs here and in Isa 29:10, where it is used of shut eyes. In isolation, these lines could perhaps describe a willful ignorance of the plight of victims of injustice (cf. Prov 21:13; 28:27), as in the English idiom "turn a blind eye," but in the context of Isa 33 they designate rather a principled refusal to assent to or participate in wrongdoing. In a kind of poetic justice, as Carroll (1997, 89–90) observes, the poem goes on to describe in verses 17 and 20 how the one who does not see evil will see YHWH the divine king and the restored city of Jerusalem. This positive use of disability language hardly balances the negative portrayals of disability in Isaiah, but it reveals the complex variety of the book's rhetoric of disability, cautioning against overbroad generalizations.

Later, the poem depicts a repulsed invasion of the future Jerusalem by enemy ships (vv. 21-23a). In its aftermath disabled persons join warriors in dividing spoil from battle:

> Then loot and spoil will be divided abundantly;
> the lame will plunder greatly. (Isa 33:23b)

As it stands, the MT makes poor sense in the first line of the couplet: "Then it will be divided until (עַד־, *'ad-*) spoil abundantly." Instead of a preposition, it is possible that עַד is a rare noun meaning "loot," found in Gen 49:27 (cf. NRSV; Roberts 2015, 421), as reflected in the translation above. Alternatively, some interpreters modify the secondary vowels on the verb to make it an active form and emend עַד to עִוֵּר (*'iwwēr*, "blind"): "Then the blind will divide spoil abundantly" (Blenkinsopp 2000, 445; Olyan 2008, 155 n. 7; Wildberger 2002, 297). Although the term "blind" is typically paired with "deaf" in Isaiah (29:18, 35:5, 42:18-19, 43:8), "blind" and "lame" occur together in Lev 21:18, 2 Sam 5:6-8, Jer 31:8, Mal 1:8, and Job 29:15. Clements (1988, 194–96) even suggests that 2 Sam 5:6-8 influenced the composer of Isa 33:23. Ultimately, both understandings of the verse are plausible, but the first involves less change to the received text and is preferred here.

In either case, the verse includes disabled persons in an activity typically reserved for presumably able-bodied soldiers—although some soldiers no doubt acquired disabilities as a result of injuries in battle. To appreciate the surprisingness of this scenario, one might compare 2 Sam 5:6, which presents military action by blind and lame persons as an absurd hypothetical possibility. Their participation in the division of plunder in Isa 33:23b suggests that the failed invasion of Jerusalem resulted in large amounts of spoil that the soldiers could not handle alone. The disability imagery thus illustrates the security and inviolability of Jerusalem (v. 20). Still, the verse is notable for the absence of any suggestion of transformation of disability (Blenkinsopp 2000, 46; Olyan 2008, 84), which is all the more striking given that surrounding chapters contain vivid depictions of such transformation (32:3-4, 34:5-6). Here, instead, the lame retain their present condition. Olyan observes that access to plunder makes it possible for them to support themselves and their families, leaving them less reliant on others for survival. He also argues that, despite its otherwise empowering portrayal, the text "stigmatizes" disabled persons by presenting them as dependent upon "YHWH's special intervention" (2008, 84). While this may be true of other passages, Isa 33:23 does not explicitly attribute the enhanced status of the lame to particular divine action, although it is possible, as Jeremy Schipper has insightfully suggested, that פִּסְחִים (*pishîm*) in Isa 33:23 is a wordplay "to describe Zion's inhabitants as those who are both spared and disabled" (2015, 324). In addition to denoting "lameness," the root may also mean "spare" or "pass by." It has this meaning in Exod 12:13 and 23—from which the noun פֶּסַח (*pesaḥ*, "Passover") is derived— and Isa 31:5, which also refers to the divine protection of Jerusalem.

Surprisingly, the very next verse returns to the imagery of eschatological healing. The first line of 33:24 declares, "No inhabitant will say, 'I am sick (חליתי, ḥālîtî).'" Although the root חלה refers more generally to illness and not necessarily to disability, it also occurs in conjunction with lameness in Mal 1:8 and 13. At the very least, verse 24 undercuts the vision of future inclusion of disabled persons in verse 23. The contrast is so stark that Joseph Blenkinsopp suggests that verse 24 might be the work of a later editor, who wanted to correct the view of verse 23 in line with other Isaianic visions of a future without disability (2000, 446; cf. Roberts 2015, 430). The second line of verse 24 refers to forgiveness of sins, suggesting that the language of sickness is metaphorical. Even so, the tension between the two verses underscores the diversity of Isaiah's rhetoric concerning disability, which is so pervasive that one finds conflicting perspectives even within the same poem.

Isaiah 35 is a richly imaginative poem that joins landscape and disability imagery to depict the return of exiles to Judah. Because it draws upon themes from both chapters 1–33 and 40–55, most scholars think that it was composed to bridge the two collections (Blenkinsopp 2000, 450–51; Clements 1988, 192). Language of bodily infirmity appears in verses 3-4 of the poem as the speaker calls for "weak hands" and "stumbling knees" to be strengthened and "anxious hearts" to be reassured. The most extensive depiction of the eschatological healing of disability in the book of Isaiah follows in verses 5-6a:

> Then opened will be the eyes of the blind,
> and the ears of the deaf will be cleared.
> Then the lame will leap like a gazelle,
> and the tongue of the mute will shout for joy.

Verse 5 is a tightly composed poetic couplet. The lines are arranged chiastically so that the beginning of the first line mirrors the end of the second line and vice versa, and the two verbs rhyme and share almost all the same consonants: תפקחנה (tippāqaḥnâ, "opened") and תפתחנה (tippātaḥnâ, "cleared"). Both verses contain a high concentration of explicit disability language, including a sequence of four nouns in the qittēl pattern, which is associated with disabilities and other perceived defects: "blind" (עורים, ʿiwrîm), "deaf" (חרשים, ḥērěšîm), "lame" (פסח, pisseaḥ), and "mute" (אלם, ʾillēm). In addition, the verb פקח (pqḥ, "open") is used almost exclusively of eyes, and specifically of reversing blindness in Exod 4:11 and 23:8, Ps 146:8, and Isa 42:7; it also occurs in conjunction with deafness in Isa 42:19-20. As with some previously discussed texts, interpreters dispute whether

35:5-6 refers to actual disabled exiles or uses disability as a metaphor for YHWH's transformative power (contrast Blenkinsopp 2000, 409, 456; Clements 1988, 192, 198; Olyan 2008, 86; Raphael 2008, 127).

Like Isa 29:18 and 32:4, 35:4-5 depicts the future transformation of disabled bodies. While verse 4 simply reports the removal of disability, verse 5a depicts the formerly disabled persons performing actions that would previously have been impossible. In fact, as Olyan observes, the lame receive superhuman ability; they do not simply walk with their changed bodies, but they "leap like a gazelle" (2008, 87). This detail is further evidence of the rhetoric of physical idealization in certain texts in Isaiah (Schipper 2015, 331). Notably, in three of the four lines of verses 4-5a, the text specifically identifies the body part associated with the disability ("eyes," "ears," "tongue"). This anatomical focus suggests an understanding of disability as located solely within human bodies, known in disability studies as the medical model. Such a view is not surprising in a passage that portrays the healing of disability, but it differs from other prophetic texts that portray disability as a complex social experience shaped by interactions with other people and one's environment. For instance, in Jer 31:8-9, YHWH creates a "level road" that can more easily be used by disabled persons, as will be discussed later in this chapter. Isaiah 35 also goes on to describe a highway for the returned exiles in verses 8-9 (cf. 40:3, 49:11, 62:10), but there is no indication that it has been designed with the needs of disabled persons in mind—especially since disability has been eliminated by the time anyone travels on it (Couey 2014, 107).

The next six lines (Isa 35:6b-7) describe the transformation of different kinds of barren landscapes into lush and well-watered ones, echoing similar language at the beginning of the poem (vv. 1-2; cf. 41:18-19, 43:19-20, 51:3). The two halves of verse 6 are connected by the causative particle כִּי (kî), suggesting that the removal of disabilities occurs because of the changes in the natural world. The reversals of disabled humans and arid environments function alike as signs of divine power, as was also true in 29:17-18. Their comparability is demonstrated by the use of the same verb, "shout for joy" (רנן, rnn), for the desert in verse 2 and the mute in verse 6 (Raphael 2008, 127). Olyan describes the implications of this comparison: "For just as a desert is arid, unproductive, and limited with respect to the life it supports, the author appears to be suggesting something comparable for the blind, the lame, the deaf, and the mute through his implicit comparison" (2008, 87–88). Both represent an affront to YHWH's desired order that must be eliminated in an ideal future world.

Isaiah 40–55

Disability imagery occurs throughout Isa 40–55, the so-called Second Isaiah. As noted earlier, the language of blindness and deafness in these chapters seems to be connected to similar language in Isa 1–39. Three different
entities are described as disabled in Second Isaiah: the Judahite exiles, who
are typically called "Jacob" or "Israel"; the enigmatic poetic figure known
as Yhwh's "servant"; and the images of foreign deities, along with their
manufacturers and worshippers. In all three cases, the disability language
enhances the portrayal of divine omnipotence. It indicates the exiles' reliance upon Yhwh for deliverance from Babylon, it demonstrates the servant's exemplary reliance upon Yhwh for support and vindication, and
it differentiates the weak and ineffectual deities of Mesopotamia from
Yhwh. These contrasts are consistent with the depiction of the deity as
incomparably super-abled throughout these chapters, which contain one
of the most dramatic portrayals of divine sovereignty in the entire Hebrew
Bible (Chavel 2014, 24). Among other claims of Yhwh's unrivaled supremacy, these chapters repeatedly identify the deity as the only effective divine
power in the universe (43:11, 44:6-8, 45:5-6, 46:9).

Scattered references to Yhwh's servant appear throughout Isa 40–55,
and more extensive portrayals of a figure with this title appear in Isa 42:1-
9, 49:1-11, 50:4-10, and 52:1–53:12. These four poems have been the subject
of intense critical inquiry for over a century, with particular interest in the
servant's identity, although little consensus has been reached (Blenkinsopp
2002, 76–80, 118–20; Schipper 2011, 32–35). Only in the past decade has the
scholarly discussion taken note of the repeated association of the servant
with disability, especially in the first and last of the servant poems (Raphael
2008, 122–25; Schipper 2011, 2–112; Schipper 2015, 324–26). In Isa 42:3-4,
the servant is identified as the agent of Yhwh's justice. In this capacity, he
will defend the vulnerable and oppressed, described metaphorically as "a
crushed reed" and a "faint wick."[7] The root for "faint" (כהה, *khh*) is used of
loss of eyesight in Gen 27:1, 1 Sam 3:2, Job 17:7, and Zech 11:17. Although
this is not the only sense of the term, it at least suggests that the servant's
protection of the oppressed includes disabled persons. This impression
is confirmed by Isa 42:7, in which Yhwh proclaims that the servant has
been appointed

---

[7] For an alternative interpretation, see Paul (2012, 185–86), who takes these phrases as
references to the servant's weakness.

to open blind eyes,
to bring captives out of prison,
those who dwell in darkness from the dungeon.

This verse depicts prisoners whose eyesight has been impaired by prolonged confinement in dark cells (cf. Ps 146:7-8). Imprisonment is almost certainly a metaphor for exile here (Paul 2012, 190; Schipper 2015, 324; cf. Isa 42:22, 49:9; Ps 107:10-14). Isaiah 42:7 thus depicts the servant's role in the liberation of exiles using characteristically Isaianic language of restoring sight to blind persons.

Similar disability language appears later in the chapter in a speech by YHWH:

I will make the blind walk on a road they don't know;
On paths they don't know I will cause them to travel.
I will make the darkness light before them,
And the uneven ground level. (Isa 42:16)

Like other exilic and postexilic texts in Isaiah, this verse depicts a highway by which the displaced Judahites will return to Jerusalem (cf. 40:3, 49:11, 62:10). Similar to Isa 35:8-9, the exiles are figuratively portrayed as blind, heightening the impression of their dependence on YHWH. The language also recalls Isa 6:9-10, suggesting that the Judahites' spiritual imperceptiveness has persisted from the time of the prophet Isaiah through the exile (Clements 1985, 101–3; Paul 2012, 198). Isaiah 42:16 describes the deity's assistance to these metaphorically disabled exiles in conflicting ways. On the one hand, the verse seems to indicate that they remain blind, since YHWH leads them and makes the road "level" for them—a detail that could suggest environmental modifications to accommodate disability (Paul 2012, 197; cf. Jer 31:9). On the other hand, "make the darkness light" could refer to the miraculous healing of blindness, as in Isa 29:18, and other references to level highways in Second Isaiah have nothing to do with disabled persons; they are simply examples of God's power to flatten mountains or raise valleys (Isa 40:4, 45:2). The inconsistency likely reflects the nonliteral character of the language as a metaphor for exile. This association between exile and disability appears in several other prophetic texts (Isa 35:5; 42:7, 16; 43:8; Jer 31:8-9; Mic 4:6-7; Zeph 3:19). This correlation likely reflects the historical experience of forced migration. As Raphael explains, the experience is "disabling" in that it disrupts prior ways of functioning, and the accompanying military violence would have left some Judahites actually disabled (2008, 129). More generally, the disability imagery emphasizes the helplessness and dependency of the exiles, thereby suggesting that their repatriation depends entirely on YHWH's power and compassion (Olyan 2008, 82–83). The repeated characterization of the exiles in Isa 40–48 as "blind" also denotes their confusion about YHWH's roles in world events, including their own impending liberation (Chavel 2014, 25).

Both Isa 42:7 and 16 thus associate exile with disability and use the healing motif to describe the deliverance of exiles, either directly by YHWH or through the agency of YHWH's servant. Somewhat surprisingly, then, the servant himself is also portrayed as disabled in the chapter. Isaiah 42:18 addresses persons who are "blind" and "deaf," paradoxically ordering them to "listen" and "look and see." Further commands to "give ear," "pay attention," and "listen" appear in verse 23. The addressees of verse 18 are almost certainly the exiles, who were depicted as blind in verse 16, and the assumption that they in fact can see and hear demonstrates the figurative character of the disability language. In verse 19 YHWH then turns to the figure of the servant, who is also "blind" and "deaf." As if to emphasize this point, the word "blind" is repeated three times in the verse. Verse 20 clarifies that the servant's blindness and deafness is also metaphorical, describing him as "seeing much" and "open of ears," yet neither "watching" nor "hearing." These verses are difficult to interpret, in no small part because the relationship between the blindness and deafness of the exiles and that of the servant is never explained. Many scholars identify the servant as a collective or idealized representation of Israel (cf. Isa 41:8-9, 44:1-2, 45:4), in which case all the disability language in 42:18-20 refers to the exiles' spiritual malaise (Paul 2012, 198–202). This interpretation is consistent with the further identification of the Judahite exiles as "blind but having eyes" and "deaf but having ears" in 43:8. Later in that passage, YHWH calls the exiles "my servant, whom I have chosen" and declares that they will "know (ידע, yd ') . . . and perceive (בין, byn)" the deity's power, despite their limited capacities (43:10). The verbs "know" and "perceive" also appear in Isa 6:10, and their occurrence in 43:10 anticipates the reversal of the earlier imposition of spiritual blindness and deafness upon the people.

Alternatively, one may identify the disabled servant in 42:18-20 as a separate figure from the disabled exiles. This passage thus ironically demands that a group of figuratively blind and deaf persons make use of their capacities to see and hear, even as it commends to them another entity who is figuratively blind and deaf because he refuses to see or hear. Offering similar explanations for this conundrum, Chavel (2014, 36–42) and Raphael (2008, 122–24) both identify the servant as a prophetic figure, and they compare his portrayal as blind and deaf with other texts that associate prophecy with disability. In support of this identification, note God's designation of the servant as "my messenger, whom I send" in Isa 42:19 (cf. 44:26), which may echo 6:8. According to Chavel, Yhwh draws attention to the servant's disability in 42:19 to buttress the authenticity of his proclamation: "None is as impaired as my herald, yet he hears and transmits the truth" (2014, 42; cf. Carroll 1997, 88). One might compare 50:10, which declares that the servant "walks in darkness and has no light" yet remains faithful to Yhwh. Raphael argues that the servant's blindness and deafness signify his avoidance of the images of foreign deities, the worship of which had been denounced earlier in 42:17. Practically anywhere else in Isaiah—33:15 is a notable exception, as noted above—such willful refusal to see or hear is castigated as spiritual recalcitrance, but in this case it becomes commendable. This interplay demonstrates the flexibility of disability imagery in prophetic texts. Its presentation may vary greatly depending upon the subject, object, and context (Raphael 2008, 122, 124). Significantly, the text never directly depicts the servant being healed from his own disabilities following 42:19-20, despite having used such language to describe the servant's liberation of others in 42:7 (Schipper 2015, 324).

Both Paul (2012, 199) and Raphael (2008, 124) note that, ironically, the servant's blindness and deafness makes him similar to the images of foreign deities, who are portrayed as blind or deaf elsewhere in the Hebrew Bible. A number of texts in Isa 40–48 denounce the veneration of these divine images or, in more pejorative language, idols (40:19-20; 41:7, 21-29; 42:8, 17; 44:9-20; 45:16, 20; 46:1-7; 48:5). Similar polemics appear in Deuteronomy, Psalms, Jeremiah, and Habakkuk. Among other common features, these texts deride divine images, their manufacturers, and/or their worshippers, typically emphasizing the material construction of the images and denying their power or effectiveness. Several of the polemics employ disability motifs, stressing that the images lack such bodily capacities as sight, hearing, touch, taste, or motion (Deut 4:28; Isa 46:7; Jer 10:5; Ps 115:5-7, 135:16). The use of these motifs underscores the lifelessness of the idols, and it may also project onto them some of the stigma associated with disabled humans or animals in other biblical texts (Olyan 2011, 91–98; Raphael 2008, 41–43). Olyan argues the emphasis on the images' inertness responds directly to certain Mesopotamian rituals that were intended to bring the images to life (2011, 93). In all these texts, the impotence and ineffectiveness of the images of foreign deities is contrasted, at least implicitly, with the power and effectiveness of Judah's deity. The flip side of attributing disability to idols, consequently, is the construction of an able-bodied Yhwh.

Disability imagery appears in two idol polemics in Isa 40–48: 44:9-20 and 46:1-7. The first uses familiar Isaianic language of sightlessness to deride the manufacturers and worshippers of images. The polemic opens in the first half of 44:9 by calling the manufacturers "empty," a term that refers to the images themselves in Isa 41:29. The second half of 44:9 is difficult to understand, possibly due to textual corruption. A possible translation is "their own witnesses do not see (יראו, *yir'û*) or know (ידעו, *yēdĕ'û*)." The link between sight and knowledge—or lack thereof—is characteristically Isaianic (Williamson 1994, 49–50). Most likely, the "witnesses" in this verse are the devotees of idols (Blenkinsopp 2002, 239). In the previous chapter, foreign nations had been challenged to "present their witnesses" (43:9), who could confirm the power of their deities to predict future events. The claim in 44:9 that these witnesses lack vision and perception discredits any testimony they might provide on behalf of their deities. By contrast, the Judahite exiles function as YHWH's witnesses in 43:10, 12, and 44:8, despite their own blindness. Isaiah 44:9 thus participates in the complex discourse in Second Isaiah that associates witnessing with sight and blindness. At the same time, the language of not seeing is used elsewhere in idol polemics of divine images, emphasizing their mere materiality and powerlessness (Deut 4:28; Pss 115:5-7, 135:16). In this way, the two halves of Isa 44:9 respectively attribute to the makers and worshippers of images characteristics that are elsewhere associated with the images themselves (cf. Pss 115:8, 135:18).

The poem uses disability imagery again in Isa 44:18 to make a similar rhetorical move:

> They neither know nor perceive;
> For their eyes are too plastered over to see,
> Their minds to discern.

An extensive cluster of vocabulary in this verse recalls the hardening passage in Isa 6:9-10: "know" (ידע, *yd'*), "perceive" (בין, *byn*), "eyes" (עינים, *'ênayim*), "see" (ראה, *r'h*), and "mind" (לב, *lēb*; lit. "heart"). In this way the denunciation of idolatry is connected to one of the most prominent lines of discourse in Isaiah (Clements 1985, 102; Williamson 1994, 49–50). Initially, it is unclear whether 44:18 attributes a lack of perception to the images or their makers, but verses 19-20 make clear that it is the latter. The manufacturers are mocked for failing to recognize that they construct idols from the same material that they burn to cook their food. Chavel points out the irony of ascribing disability to these highly skilled craftspersons: "Such artisans, physically unimpaired and technically capable, malfunction cognitively and religiously" (2014, 24). They have become as torpid as the images they construct (Blenkinsopp 2002, 242).

The idol polemic in Isa 46:1-7 emphasizes the immobility of divine images, in particular those of the powerful Babylonian deities Marduk ("Bel") and Nabu ("Nebo"), whom some exiled Judahites may have begun to worship. Ironically, the first line of the poem depicts them in motion, albeit the degrading movements of obeisance: "Bel bows, Nebo bends down" (46:1). These movements, however, turn out to be illusory. The inert images are being transported by weary pack animals, who stoop beneath the weight of their loads and thus cause the images to appear to move. Not only are they incapable of movement, these deities are incapable of preventing their own capture in verse 2, presumably by Cyrus of Persia upon his defeat of Babylon in 539 BCE (Blenkinsopp 2002, 266–67; Levtow 2008, 68–69; Paul 2012, 276). Verses 3-5 contrast the impotence of these idols with the power and agency of the true god, Yнwн. While Marduk and Nabu must be "carried" and "borne" by animals, Yнwн "carries" and "bears" Israel; while they are unable to "rescue" themselves, Yнwн "rescues" Israel. Language of immobility appears again in verse 7, which stresses that worshippers must carry an idol from one place to another because it is incapable of movement on its own (Olyan 2011, 92). This inability to move parallels the image's inability to answer its worshippers, with possible implications of muteness, or rescue them from distress. Although the poem does not explicitly ascribe lameness to divine images, it depicts their dependence and helplessness in much the same way as texts about persons with ambulatory disabilities.

The figure of Yнwн's servant appears again in Isa 52:13–53:12. This poem emphasizes the suffering endured by the servant with language associated with disability in other biblical texts, as Schipper has argued at great length (2011, 31–110). For example, Isa 53:4 and 8 use the root נגע (ng', "stricken") to describe the harsh treatment of the servant; in Lev 13, נגע repeatedly refers to the symptoms of a disfiguring skin disease (vv. 2, 4-6, 9, 12-13, etc.). Isaiah 53:8 also uses the root גזר (gzr, "cut off"), and these two roots only appear together elsewhere in 2 Chr 26:20-21, which describes the isolation of King Uzziah due to his skin disease (cf. 2 Kgs 15:5). The terms "disfigured" (משחת, mišḥat; Isa 52:14) and "sickness" (חלי, ḥŏlî; 53:3-4) are related to terms describing blind, lame, and diseased animals that are unacceptable for sacrifice in Mal 1:8 and 13-14, a text that will be discussed later in this chapter. Comparing the servant to a sheep that does not protest its shearing, Isa 53:7 uses a root that is frequently associated with muteness (אלם, 'lm; cf. Exod 4:11; Ps 38:14; Isa 35:6; Hab 2:18).

Finally, the ostracization of the servant described in Isa 53:2, 4, and 8-9 is consistent with the experiences of disabled persons elsewhere in the Bible, underscoring the social dimensions of disability (Schipper 2011, 36–42; cf. Lev 13:46; Num 12:10-15; 2 Kgs 15:5; etc.). Based on some of these textual details, the nineteenth-century Isaiah scholar Bernhard Duhm, who first identified the four servant poems as a distinct collection within Isaiah, argued that the servant suffered from a skin anomaly (Schipper 2011, 32–33). Such a precise diagnosis goes much further than the textual data allow. Nonetheless, one may conclude from these details that Isa 52:13–53:12 depicts YHWH's servant as disabled. Although 53:5 describes the healing effects of the servant's suffering for others, the text never indicates that he receives healing for his own disability (Schipper 2015, 326; cf. Isa 42:7, 19-20). Despite occasional acknowledgments to this end, most biblical scholars imagine the servant as an able-bodied person who suffers injury and perhaps death, and many of them insist upon identifying him with able-bodied literary or historical figures (Schipper 2011, 42–59, 80–106).

ISAIAH 56–66

Third Isaiah (Isa 56–66) opens with one of the most distinctive texts about disability in the prophetic corpus. In Isa 56:3b-5 YHWH offers a permanent memorial to devout eunuchs to compensate for their lack of offspring:

> Let not the eunuch say,
> "Look, I am a dried tree."
> For thus says YHWH:
> To the eunuchs who keep my Sabbaths
> and choose what I desire
> and hold fast to my covenant,
> I will give them, within my house and my walls,
> a memorial and a name better than sons and daughters.
> An everlasting name I will give them
> that will not be cut off.

This word of reassurance to eunuchs is bracketed by a promise of temple access to pious foreigners in verses 3a and 6-7. For this reason, many interpreters argue that Isa 56:3-7 directly subverts Deut 23:2-9 (Eng. 23:1-8), which forbids or restricts temple access to men with crushed testicles and various foreign ethnic groups (Blenkinsopp 2003, 138; Olyan 2008, 85; Paul 2012, 453), although Jacob L. Wright and Michael J. Chan have recently questioned this connection (2012, 100–102). Whether or not they are connected, both texts reflect the cultural stigmatization of eunuchs.

Although individual eunuchs could occupy positions of considerable power in the ancient world, as a group "this population was often stigmatized and represented as being morally and sexually distorted" (2012, 117). Like barren women, eunuchs would have been considered disabled in the ancient world because they lacked the capacity to procreate (Lemos 2011, 49–52; Olyan 2008, 10–12, 28–29, 84–85; Raphael 2008, 54–55; cf. Lev 21:20, 22:24).

Isaiah 56:3 imagines a eunuch referring specifically to his disabled status by lamenting that he is "a dried tree." This metaphor for diminished reproductive capacities recalls the common Isaianic comparison between barren landscapes and disabled bodies, almost as if the eunuch has internalized the book's demeaning rhetoric. Unlike other texts in Isaiah that depict the healing of disabled bodies, though, this passage does not directly promise that the deity will restore the eunuch's reproductive capabilities. Verse 5 seems to pun on this possibility; the Hebrew word here translated "memorial" (יָד, yād; lit. "hand") is a euphemism for penis in other biblical texts like Isa 57:8, 10, and Song 5:4, as well as Ugaritic and Dead Sea Scroll texts (Blenkinsopp 2003, 139; Lemos 2011, 51; Paul 2012, 454). The implied recovery of the eunuch's genitalia, however, exists only at the level of double entendre, as the poem goes on to address the social consequences of the lack of progeny, not the biological conditions that caused it. In particular, Isa 56 is concerned with the endurance of the eunuch's "name" (שֵׁם, šēm)—that is, his memory and influence. Reflecting a largely communal sense of identity, one's progeny is the primary mechanism by which one's name is preserved into the future in the Hebrew Bible; consequently, a lack of progeny means that one's name would be lost following death—a fate analogous to permanent nonexistence (Num 27:4; Deut 25:6-7; Ruth 4:10; Levenson 2006, 114–21).

In response to this threat, Yʜᴡʜ offers to preserve the eunuch's name on a monument in the Jerusalem temple in verse 5 ("within my house and my walls"). By guaranteeing the public endurance of his memory, the monument provides a concrete substitute for children (Blenkinsopp 2003, 139; Levenson 2006, 121; Paul 2012, 453). In this way it functions as a kind of accommodation for the eunuch's disability (Couey 2014, 107–8). This strategy was not unprecedented. In 2 Sam 18:18, Absalom erects a pillar for himself because he lacked offspring "to cause [his] name to be remembered"; the narrator claims that the monument remained standing long after Absalom's death, implying the successful fulfillment of its purpose. In addition, Wright and Chan note that memorial inscriptions or monuments were commonly placed in ancient temples (2012, 102–3).

This eunuch's case is unique in that the deity makes the provision for his memorial. For this reason, Olyan's claim that the eunuch does not "require YHWH's special intervention to make his disability less marginalizing" seems overstated (2008, 85). Moreover, YHWH promises in Isa 56:5 that the eunuch's "everlasting name . . . will not be cut off" (לא יכרת, lōʾ yikkārēt). In addition to the obvious play on the notion of castration (Lemos 2011, 51; Paul 2012, 454–55; Wright and Chan 2012, 101), this promise alludes to the common biblical threat that one's descendants will be "cut off" by an enemy (e.g., 1 Sam 24:21-22; Isa 14:22; Ps 109:13, 15). The eunuch thus receives greater security than reproductively able-bodied persons, who have no guarantee of the permanent survival of their descendants, making his memorial "better than sons and daughters" (Isa 56:5).

The final examples of disability imagery in Isaiah both use blindness as a metaphor for social disruption. Although neither appears to allude specifically to earlier Isaianic texts, both passages are consistent with the rhetorical tendencies of the book. Isaiah 56:10a describes the nation's "sentinels" (צפים, ṣōpîm) as "blind" (עורים, ʿiwrîm). "Sentinel" usually denotes a military lookout (1 Sam 14:16; 2 Sam 13:34; 2 Kgs 9:17-20), but it is used metaphorically of prophets in Ezek 3:17, Ezek 33:7, and perhaps Hos 9:8 (cf. Hab 2:1). Although the critique in Isa 56:10 may extend to other kinds of leaders in the postexilic Jewish community, it likely has prophets specifically in mind. The unusual term הזים (hōzîm) later in the verse, which probably means "dream," seems to pun on the prophetic title חזה (hōzeh, "visionary"; Blenkinsopp 2003, 146–47). If this interpretation is correct, then the verse uses blindness as a metaphor for the spiritual imperceptiveness of failed prophets in much the same way as 29:10. Isaiah 56:10b further compares the ineffective leaders to useless watchdogs who sleep on the job and are "mute" (אלמים, ʾillĕmîm) because they "cannot bark." The verse thus uses a pair of explicit disability terms to critique ineffective leadership.

Isaiah 59:9-15 is a communal lament to YHWH, as indicated by the "we" language. The people metaphorically equate this absence of social justice with "darkness" (חשך, ḥōšek) and "gloom" (אפלות, ʾăpēlôt) in verse 9. A pair of related nouns appears in Isa 29:18 in conjunction with blindness, and the next verse in Isa 59 exploits this stereotypical association to extend the comparison between injustice and darkness:

> We grope like the blind (עורים, ʿiwrîm) along a wall;
> like those without eyes we grope.
> We stumble at noon like twilight,
> and among the vigorous like the dead. (Isa 59:10)

The language recalls Deut 28:29, in which Yhwh threatens Israel with blindness for breaking their covenant with the deity. Both texts contain the motif of experiencing darkness "at noon" and use related verbs meaning "grope." Similar language appears in Zeph 1:17, which will be discussed later in this chapter. Isaiah 59:10 enhances this traditional curse language with the striking and apparently novel image of someone feeling their way along a wall in the darkness. As Raphael (2008, 14n32) points out, all these texts construct blindness "primarily as a mobility impairment," as made clear in Isa 59:10 by the verbs "grope" (גשש, *gšš*), which also describes drunken staggering in Job 12:25, and "stumble" (כשל, *kšl*). This might seem odd to contemporary readers in literate, technologically advanced societies, where sight has many uses that would have been uncommon or nonexistent in antiquity. These contrasting perspectives demonstrate the culturally conditioned character of conceptions of disability.

As made clear by the fourfold repetition of "like" (כ, *k-*), the blindness imagery in Isa 59:10 is a simile. Like most prophetic texts with disability imagery, then, the verse has little to do with actual disabled persons. If anything, its description of limited mobility resulting from darkness seems more appropriate for sighted persons than for blind persons, who frequently need only modest accommodations at best to move about without impediment (cf. Blenkinsopp 2003, 193). Job 5:14 even uses similar language to describe persons without permanent vision impairments. Nonetheless, Isa 59:10 rhetorically denigrates disability in several ways. First, it uses blindness as a metaphor for social ills, characterized as the result of human sinfulness in verse 12. Second, like other biblical texts, it presents disability as foil to Yhwh's power. As described in verses 15-20, the sorry state of the postexilic Jewish community can only be alleviated by intervention from the divine warrior. Finally, verse 10 equates blindness with death, suggesting that disabled persons lead diminished lives; note the progression of similes across the four lines of the verse: "like the blind," "like those without eyes," "like twilight," and "like the dead."

JEREMIAH

The book of Jeremiah depicts the tumultuous decades immediately before and after the fall of Jerusalem to the Babylonians in 587 BCE, a period during which Judah suffered multiple invasions and deportations. The chaos and trauma of that period may be reflected in the very organization—or, rather, disorganization—of the book, which is a chronologically jumbled mishmash of genres (O'Connor 2011, 29–34). To a much greater degree than other prophetic books, the prophet Jeremiah himself plays a substantial role in the collection that bears his name. It contains extensive narratives about the prophet, and many of the poems feature a highly developed first-person voice. Although it is sometimes difficult to determine whether this voice belongs to the deity or the prophet, in many cases it is clearly Jeremiah's (e.g., 12:1-4, 15:15-18, 20:7-18). These texts may preserve some genuine memories about the historical prophet. Recent scholarship has been less interested in reconstructing a biography of Jeremiah, however, and more interested in appreciating the literary and theological effects of these texts (O'Connor 2011, 69–70).

Many of these texts focus upon the experience of being a prophet, which is often depicted in terms of Jeremiah's body. In the account of Jeremiah's commissioning, YHWH "touched" (נגע, ng‘) the prophet's mouth in order to place the divine word inside the prophet's body (Jer 1:9; cf. Isa 6:6-7). The verb sometimes has violent connotations (e.g., Gen 32:26; Isa 53:4, 8; Ps 104:32), and so it might better be translated "struck" here (Lundbom 1999, 235). The presence of the divine inside Jeremiah's body causes intense somatic distress. He describes it as a "burning fire" in his heart and bones (Jer 20:9; cf. 5:14, 23:29), and he complains that his heart is "shattered" and his bones "flutter" as a result (23:9). His prophetic activity leaves him with "unending pain" and an "incurable, unhealable wound" (15:18). The prophet even loses control over his actions, finding himself unable to control the content of his speech and forced to speak against his will (6:11, 20:8-9). Two passages explicitly associate Jeremiah's exercise of his prophetic vocation with disability motifs. In Jer 16:1-4 the prophet is commanded not to marry or have a wife. His lack of family portends the widespread bereavement that will result from the Babylonian invasion of Jerusalem. As noted in the discussion of Isa 56:4-5 earlier in the chapter, childlessness carried considerable social stigma in the ancient world, and the physical conditions that frequently caused it, such as infertility or damaged genitals, were regarded as disabilities. In Jer 29:26-27 one of Jeremiah's opponents calls him "a lunatic who pretends to prophesy" (משגע ומתנבא, mešuggā‘ ûmitnabbē’). Second Kings 9:11 and Hos 9:7 similarly associate prophecy with mental disability, perhaps because of the bizarre actions of many prophets (Chavel 2014, 38–40; Olyan 2008, 69; Raphael 2008, 122–23). Neither Jer 16:1-4 nor 29:26-27 suggest that Jeremiah was actually disabled. Rather, the texts uses disability as a point of comparison for the experience of being a prophet, suggesting that he was regarded by his contemporaries with some of the same stigma as disabled persons.

Jeremiah's prophecies often contain evocative somatic language. Reminiscent of Isa 1:5-6, passages about the suffering of Judah frequently refer to the nation as wounded or bruised (6:14, 8:11, 14:17-19, 30:12-13; cf. 46:11, 51:8-9). In a bizarre metaphorical combination of body parts, the prophet accuses the people of Judah of having "ears with foreskins" in Jer 6:10. Like Isa 6:9-10, the text associates rejection of the prophetic word with deafness. Bodily imagery appears in another prophetic critique in Jer 5:21, with suggestive intertextual connections. Each of the three poetic lines in this verse attributes an impaired physical capacity to the audience:

> Hear this, foolish and mindless [lit. "heartless"] people—
> They have eyes but don't see;
> they have ears but don't hear.

Ironically, the verse opens with a command to the people to "hear," but it closes with a statement that they are incapable of doing so (Allen 2008, 80). The association between religious failings and blindness and deafness may reflect the influence of the Isaianic tradition (cf. Isa 6:9-10; Williamson 1994, 50). Even more striking, identical or nearly identical couplets appear in idol polemics in Pss 115:5 and 135:16 (cf. Deut 4:28). Lundbom (1999, 402–3) even suggests that Jeremiah has turned briefly from his critique of the people to denounce the worship of images, noting the contrast between the second- and third-person address in the respective halves of Jer 5:21. It is not unusual in prophetic texts for direct address to include third-person pronouns and verbs, however, and the verse reads much more smoothly as a single reference to the people (Allen 2008, 80). The people have become so resistant to YHWH that they might as well be lifeless statues. Olyan suggests that the evocation of idol polemics directly connects the people's rejection of YHWH with their worship of foreign deities (2011, 97; cf. Jer 5:19). If so, the verse may be another example of the motif of idol worshippers becoming like idols, as discussed above with Isa 44:9 (cf. Pss 115:8, 135:18).

Corroborating the possibility of such an allusion, a lengthy idol polemic appears in Jer 10:1-16 with such recognizable themes as the material construction of divine images (vv. 3-4, 9) and the shared imperceptiveness of idols and their worshippers (vv. 8, 14). Verse 5a describes the diminished faculties of the images in terms reminiscent of disability:

> Like a scarecrow in a cucumber patch, they do not speak.
> They must surely be carried, for they do not stride.

The emphasis on the images' immobility recalls Isa 46:7 (cf. Ps 115:7), and other idol polemics similarly note that images lack the capacity for speech (Hab 2:18; Pss 115:5, 135:16). According to Olyan, in fact, muteness is the most common disability attributed to divine images in polemical texts (2011, 94). The "scarecrow" simile in Jer 10:5 captures the grotesque tension between the human form and utter lifelessness of divine images (92). Similarly, verse 14 describes their inertness in terms reminiscent of a dead body: "There is no breath in them." The second half of verse 5 argues that idols are unworthy of reverence because they can neither "do evil" nor "good," suggesting that they are completely incapable of action (McKane 1986–1996, 1: 221–22; cf. Isa 41:23-24; Zeph 1:12). The upshot of this polemic is the contrast between the ineffectiveness of foreign deities and the power of YHWH, as made clear by the alternating denunciations of idols and hymns of praise to YHWH (vv. 6-7, 10, 12-13, 16; Levtow 2008, 50–55). In particular, the idols' muteness (v. 5) is juxtaposed to YHWH's capacity for speech that has devastating effects (v. 13: "at his giving voice, there is a roar of waters in the heavens").

Despite this contrast, the prophet reports in Jer 12:4 that the people ascribe disability to the deity. Jeremiah 12:1-4 is one of several poems in which Jeremiah complains to YHWH about the difficulties of the prophetic calling and his mistreatment by his contemporaries and even by the deity. The complaint focuses on injustice in the world, expressing dismay that God allows the wicked to prosper (cf. Hab 1:2-4). This perceived lack of consequences leads the wicked to conclude, as Jeremiah reports it, "He [YHWH] does not see our future" (Jer 12:4).[8] This claim echoes the critique of the people in 5:21, which itself echoed the language of idol polemics. In other words, the wicked in Jer 12:4 speak of YHWH in the same way that one might speak of idols. Their claim is directly reversed in Jer 16:17:

> For my eyes are upon all their ways.
> They are not hidden from my face,
> and their iniquity is not concealed from my eyes.

The repetition of "eyes" in the first and last lines, which forms an *inclusio* around the verse, emphasizes the deity's ability to see the sins of the people, despite their attempts to hide them (cf. Isa 29:15).

Many of the Jeremianic texts discussed so far use disability imagery to depict divine judgment. Jeremiah 31:8-9b, by contrast, includes blind and lame persons in its portrayal of the restoration of Israelite exiles:

---

[8] The NRSV loosely translates the Hebrew phrase לא יראה (*lōʾ yirʾeh*, "he does not see") as "he is blind," although the typical Hebrew root for blindness (עור, *ʿwr*) does not appear in the verse. This translation creates the impression that the disability language is more explicit than is actually the case. The NRSV also follows the Septuagint by reading the final words of the verse as "our ways" instead of "our future," as the Hebrew MT reads. The variant reading strengthens the connection between Jer 12:4 and 16:17.

> I will soon bring them from the land of the north,
> And gather them from the ends of the earth.
> Among them the blind and the lame,
> The pregnant woman and the woman in labor together—
> A great assembly will return here. . . .
> I will lead them to streams of water
> On a level road on which they will not stumble.

Jeremiah 31:8-9 is especially similar to Mic 4:6-7 and Zeph 3:19, which also use lameness imagery. At the same time, Jer 31 stands out among prophetic texts that associate disability with exile. In most such texts, the disability language is figurative (e.g., Isa 42:7; Mic 4:6; Zeph 3:19), but Jer 31:8 refers to blind and lame persons "among" the exiles, for whom—along with women in later stages of pregnancy—the journey back to Jerusalem would be especially challenging (Allen 2008, 347; McKane 1986–1996, 2:790). At the same time, the larger context emphasizes that all the exiles require special divine intervention in order to return home, suggesting that the disabled exiles are a synecdoche for the larger group. In further contrast with some texts from Isaiah, Jer 31 is notable because it does not depict the healing of blind and lame exiles (contra Lundbom 2004a, 424). Instead, YHWH creates for them "a level road on which they will not stumble." Rather than transformed human bodies, the text imagines transformed circumstances in which disability is less of an impediment to movement. To a greater degree than perhaps any other biblical text, it resonates with contemporary understandings of disability that emphasize the interaction between bodies and their physical environments. Raphael remarks, "If anyone wants a proof-text for universal design, here it is" (2008, 129; cf. Olyan 2008, 82; Schipper 2015, 321–22). The motif of a highway for the returning exiles also occurs in Isaiah, but there disabled persons are healed before they ever travel it (Isa 35:5-10, 42:16). Despite its less negative portrayal of disabled bodies, however, Jer 31:8 still emphasizes the vulnerability of the blind and lame exiles, as evidenced by the parallel reference to "the pregnant woman and the woman in labor" in the next line. This juxtaposition may also call into question the masculinity of blind and lame men, at least from the perspective of an ancient patriarchal society (Olyan 2008, 83). That certainly seems to be the case with texts in Jeremiah that compare male warriors to women (48:41, 49:22, 50:37, 51:30). Even so, by comparing blindness and lameness to pregnancy, Jer 31:8 remarkably associates disability with a physical state that occurs naturally and is generally regarded positively.

The extensive narrative sections in the book of Jeremiah include two accounts of the Babylonian invasion of Jerusalem in 587 BCE. Jeremiah 52, which forms an epilogue to the book, is identical with 2 Kgs 24:18–25:30, and an alternative account in Jer 39:1-10 contains many of the same details. Both narrate the capture of King Zedekiah of Judah, the slaughter of his children, the mutilation of his eyes, and his imprisonment in Babylon (39:6-7, 52:10-11). His punishment is horrific. By slaughtering Zedekiah's offspring, King Nebuchadrezzar of Babylon effectively denies him any possibility of postmortem existence, and the subsequent loss of his eyes means that the violent deaths of his children were likely the last thing he ever saw (Lundbom 2004b, 88). The text emphasizes this by repeating the word "eyes": "And the king of Babylon slaughtered the sons of Zedekiah before his eyes . . . and the eyes of Zedekiah he blinded" (Jer 52:10-11; cf. 39:6-7). Mutilation was a common practice in ancient Near Eastern warfare (cf. Judg 16:21; 1 Sam 10:27), and it would have been a significant source of noncongenital disabilities among men (Olyan 2008, 39–45). In the case of Zedekiah, who was a vassal of Nebuchadrezzar and had even been placed on the throne by him (2 Kgs 24:17; Jer 37:1), the mutilation would serve as recognizable punishment for rebellion. Deuteronomy 28:28-29 includes blindness in a long list of calamities that will befall Israel should they break their covenant with YHWH, and similar curses appear in surviving ancient Near Eastern treaties (Lundbom 2004b, 88). By punishing Zedekiah so harshly, Nebuchadrezzar both inflicts severe pain upon him in retaliation for his betrayal and makes an example of him to deter other vassals from rebelling.

Jeremiah is likely dependent on 2 Kings for its account of Zedekiah's fate, which has particular resonances within the larger narrative of Joshua–2 Kings. (See the discussion by Jeremy Schipper in the chapter on Joshua–2 Kings in this commentary.) Even so, the episode fits effectively within the prophetic book as well. Zedekiah is a prominent character who appears in multiple prophecies and narratives in the middle chapters of Jeremiah (e.g., Jer 21:1-10, 34:1-7, 38:14-28), and the account of his fate completes this narrative trajectory. Further, given the repeated emphasis in Jeremiah on Zedekiah's rejection of the divine order to surrender to the Babylonians (Jer 21:9; 27:11-13; 38:17-18, 20-23) and the portrayal of Nebuchadrezzar as YHWH's servant who carries out the divine will (Jer 25:9, 27:6, 43:10), the blinding of Zedekiah is cast much more strongly as a divine punishment than in 2 Kings. Other Jeremianic texts in which YHWH's judgment takes the form of disability include Jer 14:6, in which donkeys go blind from lack of water during a divinely imposed drought, and Jer 25:16, in which Yнwн subjects the nations to staggering and mental disability.

EZEKIEL

Like Jeremiah, the book of Ezekiel also unfolds against the backdrop of the Judahite exile. According to Ezek 1:1-3, the prophet Ezekiel was a priest who had been deported following the Babylonian subjugation of Jerusalem in 598 BCE, and he was active as a prophet for nearly twenty years (1:2, 29:17), during which time he both announced and received word of the destruction of Jerusalem (24:21-24, 33:21). Set primarily in Babylon, the book contains prophecies of judgment against Judah (chs. 1–24), prophecies of judgment against foreign nations (chs. 25–32), and prophecies of hope for Judah (chs. 33–48). Although most prophetic books contain violent and disturbing imagery, Ezekiel seems to have more than its fair share, especially when it comes to human bodies. Repeatedly, readers encounter landscapes littered with dead bodies (6:3-14, 9:1-7, 35:6-8, 37:1-2); the book's climactic battle produces so many corpses that it takes seven months to bury them (39:12-14) and wild animals are summoned to feast upon them (39:17-20). Other aberrant bodies include an infant flailing in its own blood (16:4-6), foreign men with abnormally large genitalia (23:20), and a woman whose face is horrifically mutilated (23:24). Fantastic composite creatures with multiple wings and faces attend the deity (1:5-14, 10:15-20). The Egyptian pharaoh becomes a monstrous sea creature (29:3-5, 32:2-6). Despite this proliferation of bodies that deviate from culturally accepted norms, however, the book of Ezekiel contains relatively little explicit disability language. Such language is used repeatedly to characterize Ezekiel's exercise of his prophetic calling; beyond that, a few scattered references to disability are minimally elaborated and barely differentiable from other biblical texts.

Consistent with the exaggerated tone of much of the book, Ezekiel's prophetic activity seems extreme in comparison to other biblical prophets. He receives longer and more lurid visions (1:1-28, 8:1–11:24, 37:1-14, 40:1–48:35), and he performs more—and more bizarre—symbolic actions (4:1-5:4, 12:1-20, 24:15-27, 37:15–28). As an explanation for his unusual behavior, some interpreters have proposed that Ezekiel suffered from a mental disorder like schizophrenia (see the summaries of research by Garber 2015, 25; Zimmerli 1979, 17–18). Along similar lines, noting that some of Ezekiel's symbolic actions entail immobility (4:4-8) and trembling (12:18), Walther Zimmerli suggests that Ezekiel actually suffered from some "bodily weakness" that "became an element of his message"

(1979, 20). While Zimmerli acknowledges the impossibility of diagnosing the specific condition, his proposal still exceeds what the textual evidence seems to allow. Such interpretations of Ezekiel reflect a medical model of disability, which understands disability exclusively as a physical condition located within the body. More recent studies have treated the book as a product of the collective trauma experienced by Judahite exiles in the sixth century BCE (Garber 2015, 26), which is more amenable to social or cultural models of disability.

While it is speculative to claim that Ezekiel himself was mentally disabled, the book does use explicit disability language to describe his work as a prophet. Like Isaiah and Jeremiah, but to a much greater degree, Ezekiel experiences bodily disruption as a result of his vocation. During his commissioning, a divine spirit repeatedly takes over his body and moves him involuntarily (2:2; 3:12, 14), an experience that leaves him "dumbfounded" for seven days (3:15). His prophetic activity requires him to remain immobile for longs periods of time, in ways suggestive of paralysis (3:25, 4:4-8). Perhaps most strikingly, Yhwh takes control of Ezekiel's speech organs in 3:26-27 and refuses to let him speak; this debilitating condition apparently continues until the destruction of Jerusalem by the Babylonians over seven years later (24:27, 33:21-22; cf. 29:21). This divinely imposed silence is repeatedly described with the verb "be mute" (אלם, ʾlm; 3:26, 24:27, 33:22), which is related to the biblical Hebrew term for muteness (אלם, ʾillēm; Exod 4:11; Ps 38:14; Isa 35:6; Hab 2:18). The phrase "cause the tongue to cling to the palate" in Ezek 3:26 may also be an idiom for disability (cf. Ps 137:6).

The depiction of Ezekiel's silence raises several interpretive problems, including the apparent contradiction between Ezek 3:17-21 and 26-27 and the fact that he speaks in 11:25, 14:4, and 20:3. It is possible that Yhwh lets him talk only when delivering prophetic oracles, which is a plausible interpretation of 3:27 (Greenberg 1983, 103). However one resolves those tensions, Ezekiel is perhaps the clearest example of the association between prophecy and disability in the Bible (Chavel 2014, 40). In ceding his entire body to the service of Yhwh, he loses physical autonomy in ways for which disability is the closest analogy. Interestingly, the phrase פתחון פה (pithôn peh; "opening of the mouth") in 29:21, which describes Ezekiel's recovery of speech, echoes the name of a Mesopotamian dedication ceremony for divine images. During this ceremony, the appropriate deity was believed to enter and animate the image. By alluding to this ritual practice, according to James M. Kennedy, the text "portray[s] Ezekiel as a kind of living idol. Like the idol, he is deaf and mute until the deity moves to speak through him" (1991, 235). As discussed above, the use of blindness and deafness imagery in Isa 40–55 likewise results in unexpected similarities between the portrayals of the servant of YHWH and idols.

Other references to disability in Ezekiel are less developed and largely similar to those in other biblical books. Ezekiel 3:5-6 describes non-Hebrew speakers as "deep lipped and heavy tongued." The latter phrase (כבדי לשון, *kibdê lāšôn*) also describes Moses' stuttering in Exod 4:10, suggesting that foreign languages could be viewed as a kind of speech impediment (cf. Isa 33:19). As in Isa 29:15 and Jer 12:4, the people of Judah imagine that YHWH cannot see their wicked deeds in Ezek 8:12, a notion of which the deity violently disabuses them in 9:9-10. Ezekiel 12:2 metaphorically describes the spiritual failures of the people of Jerusalem as the inability to see or hear (Melcher 2007, 124–25). Like Jer 5:21 the language of this verse recalls the attribution of disability to idols in Pss 115:5 and 135:16; this connection is especially ironic given that Ezekiel elsewhere blames idolatry on the ability to see (Ezek 6:9; 18:6, 12, 15; 20:7-8, 24; 33:25). References to King Zedekiah's blindness appear in Ezek 12:12-13. Using a common ancient Near Eastern metaphor, Ezek 34 criticizes the failed rulers of Judah by depicting them as shepherds who do not provide adequately for their flock, including "sick" (חולה, *hôlâ*) and "maimed" (נשברת, *nišberet*) sheep (34:4). Both terms are associated elsewhere with animals that are unfit for sacrifice because of their perceived imperfections (Lev 22:22; Mal 1:8, 13). In contrast to the neglectful shepherds, YHWH promises to "bind" the disabling injuries of these sheep in Ezek 34:16. This passage articulates a standard of beneficent governance that includes care for disabled persons (Melcher 2007, 123; cf. Zech 11:16). Finally, as part of a lengthy vision of the future temple in the restored Jerusalem following the exile, Ezekiel restates prohibitions against sacrificing animals with "blemishes," a category that includes some disabilities, for certain kinds of offerings (Ezek 43:22-25; 45:18, 23; 46:4-6, 13; cf. Lev 22:18-25; Deut 15:19-23; 17:1; Mal 1:7-8, 12-14; etc.). Comparable restrictions on the service of priests with blemishes (Lev 21:17-23) are not repeated in this section of Ezekiel, but earlier chapters may display awareness of these regulations, insofar as God demands that Ezekiel mar his body in ways that disqualify him from priestly service (Lapsley 2012, 232–35).

THE MINOR PROPHETS

The twelve short prophetic books of Hosea–Malachi were typically written on a single scroll in antiquity. Together, they are comparable in length to Isaiah, Jeremiah, or Ezekiel. (The descriptor "minor" in Minor Prophets refers to their relative size, not to their content or importance.)

These books span a slightly longer period than the book of Isaiah, with books set from the mid-eighth century BCE (Hos and Amos) to the mid-fifth century BCE (Mal), thus covering the respective rises to power of the Assyrian, Babylonian, and Persian empires and the losses of political independence by Israel and Judah. Recently, some biblical scholars have proposed that the Minor Prophets are meant to be read from beginning to end as a unified work, calling attention to recurring motifs in the corpus and apparent editorial activity bridging the seams between books (e.g., Joel 4:16, 18 [Eng. 3:16, 18] and Amos 1:2; 9:13; see Nogalski 2011, 1–17). Others, however, view the Minor Prophets as an anthology of twelve discrete prophetic works, arguing that any common themes do not overcome the sense of separation between them (Ben Zvi 2009, 47–96). The depiction of disability provides a common thread among some of these books, but the claims made in this chapter do not require a particular view of the unity of the corpus as a whole. The following survey explores representations of disability in five of the twelve books of the Minor Prophets: Micah, Habakkuk, Zephaniah, Zechariah, and Malachi.

MICAH

The book of Micah is attributed to Micah of Moresheth, a Judahite prophet in the late eighth century BCE (Mic 1:1; cf. Jer. 26:18). In its present form, the book is a complex pastiche of warnings of divine judgment (e.g., 1:2–2:11, 6:9-16), promises of future restoration (e.g., 2:12-13, 4:1–5:8 [Eng. 5:9]), ethical admonition (6:1-6), and psalmic material (7:1-20). Most scholars only associate some of the announcements of judgment, if anything, with the historical prophet for whom the book is named. More hopeful texts are typically dated to the exilic or postexilic periods, including two with disability imagery: Mic 4:6-7 and 7:16.

Micah 4 depicts the restoration and vindication of Jerusalem, whose destruction had been threatened at the end of the previous chapter. Verses 6-7 use lameness as a metaphor for exiled Judahites whom YHWH will bring back to Jerusalem, much like Jer 31:8-9 and Zeph 3:19.[9] The context suggests that these verses in Micah have the Babylonian exile in mind (cf. Mic 4:10), although the utopian language would have been meaningful in

---

[9] The Targum, an ancient Aramaic translation of the Hebrew Bible, makes this clear by translating "limping one" as "exiles" in Mic 4:6-7 and Zeph 3:19 (Melcher 2007, 123 n. 5, citing Evans 1997, 81–92). James Nogalski argues unconvincingly that "limping one" in these verses only refers to those who remained in the land of Judah following the Babylonian invasions in 598 and 587 BCE (2011, 750).

multiple historical settings (Ben Zvi 2000, 110–11). Verse 6 names three groups on whose behalf YHWH promises to act:

> I will assemble the limping one,
> And the displaced one I will gather,
> And the one whom I harmed.

In light of similar texts like Isa 40:11, Jer 23:3, and Mic 2:12, most interpreters think that this verse depicts YHWH as a shepherd, reassembling a dispersed flock. Note the apparent cultural expectation that shepherds would extend special care to injured or disabled sheep in Ezek 34:4 and Zech 11:16. "Limping" (צלעה, ṣōlēʿâ) designates sheep with limited mobility in Mic 4:6, while "displaced" refers to sheep who have wandered away (cf. Deut 22:1; Ezek 34:4).[10] The alternation of subject and verb in these two lines emphasizes YHWH's action by placing it at the beginning and end of the segment. The verb "whom I harmed" in the third line could refer to an additional group whom the deity rescues, separate from the "limping" and "displaced," but more likely it describes those groups, implying that YHWH made them limp and drove them away (McKane 1998, 128). Insofar as it refers to sheep, not humans, and is a metaphor for exiled Judahites, the reference to lameness in Mic 4:6 is two steps removed from actual disabled persons. The returning exiles may have included persons with disabilities, but their concerns are not at the forefront of the text.

The metaphor of exile as disability in Mic 4:6 projects upon exiled persons the qualities of helplessness and dependency, associated with disabled persons in both the ancient and contemporary worlds. Lameness especially fits this context because of the restricted mobility of exiles, who have been forcibly removed and cannot change locations of their own volition. Only YHWH can bring them home; the text thus affirms the power of the deity (Olyan 2008, 91). The disability imagery in the verse is coupled with feminine imagery, which reinforces the connotations of helplessness (O'Brien 2006, 156). "Limping" and "banished" are both feminine participles, a detail that may reflect either grammatical or literary convention (see Ben Zvi 2000, 112; McKane 1998, 127; Sweeney 2000, 382; Wolff 1990, 124). Several texts from the Hebrew Bible suggest a cultural association between femininity and weakness (e.g., Isa 19:16; Jer 51:30; Nah 3:13), and other

---

[10] William McKane (1998, 128) argues that צלע does not denote a permanent condition in Mic 4:6 but simply describes "sore feet as a consequence of a long march." The use of the term to describe Jacob's injury in Gen 32:32 (Eng. 32:31), however, suggests a more serious condition. Further, Jer 31:8 uses the more common Biblical Hebrew term for lameness (פסח, pissēaḥ) in a nearly identical context.

prophetic texts similarly use feminine language to characterize refugees or exiles (e.g., Isa 11:12, 16:2). Note especially Jer 31:8, in which disability and pregnancy are paired as metaphors for returning exiles, as discussed earlier in the chapter.[11] Notably, the next verse in Mic 4 switches to masculine grammatical forms (e.g., עֲלֵיהֶם, ʿălêhem, "over them") to refer to the exiles after they have returned to Jerusalem, as Ben Zvi (2000, 112) observes.

Micah 4:7 describes the subsequent transformation of the exiles into a populous and powerful nation. It claims that the "limping one" from verse 6 will become a "remnant," a small subset of survivors who are the basis for future restoration (cf. Isa 37:32; Jer 23:3; etc.). In this way, the nation's new start marks a return to its origins. The ancestral figure Jacob is described as "limping" (צֹלֵעַ) following his wrestling match with YHWH in Gen 32:32 (Eng. 32:31), after which he was renamed "Israel." Given the rarity of this verb, which only occurs elsewhere in Zeph 3:19, it seems likely that Mic 4:6-7 intentionally alludes to that episode, especially given the reference to the exiles as the "remnant of Jacob" later in Micah (5:6-7 [Eng. 5:7-8]; Sweeney 2000, 382; Wolff 1990, 123). The subsequent depiction of the nation as "mighty" (עָצוּם, ʿāṣûm) somewhat minimizes its figuratively lame past. The most common meaning of the adjective is numerical magnitude (e.g., Deut 26:5; Joel 1:6; Prov 7:26), but it also refers to physical strength (e.g., Deut 11:23; Isa 53:12; Prov 18:18), which presumably excludes limping. It may be, however, that the lameness metaphor has become "unsustainable" and is no longer assumed at this point in the poem (Raphael 2008, 130). Certainly, unlike texts from Isaiah that imagine the healing of disability in an idealized future (e.g., Isa 35:5-6), Micah does not explicitly erase disability from the restored Jerusalem (Olyan 2008, 91; Raphael 2008, 129–30; Schipper 2015, 321–22).

In short, conflicting constructions of disability lie behind Mic 4:6-7. Lameness is a metaphor for the traumatic experience of exile, and the associations upon which the metaphor depends—weakness and dependence—are largely negative. The text connects these qualities with femininity, reinforcing other harmful ideologies. The last line of verse 6 ("those whom I harmed") also characterizes disability as a divine punishment. On the other hand, one should not overstate the harmful effects of the metaphor. Olyan argues that the disability image implies divine rejection, based on the unsuitability of lame sheep for sacrifice in Deut 15:21 and Mal 1:8 (2008, 90). Not all references to sheep necessarily have cultic overtones, however.

---

[11] For more on the interplay between femininity and disability, see Fontaine 2007, 62–69; Olyan 2008, 83, 121–22, 128.

The majority of sheep in ancient Israel and Judah were raised for purposes other than burnt offerings, and the sheep imagery in these verses is implicit and underdeveloped to begin with. By comparison with the similar text in Zeph 3:19, Mic 4:6-7 largely avoids gratuitous stigmatization of disability. For better or for worse, it shows little interest in historically real lame persons but rather appropriates their experience for other purposes, as is frequently the case in the Hebrew Bible and Western literature.

Additional disability language occurs in the final unit of Micah, a prayer for the vindication of Jerusalem (Mic 7:8-20). The prayer anticipates the restoration of Jerusalem following the exile and the concomitant humiliation of its enemies, and the speaker wants these events to be visually perceptible to both Jerusalem and its enemies, appealing to the exodus as a precedent (Mic 7:15; cf. Exod 15:14-16; Josh 2:9-11; Isa 40:5; etc.). Ironically, this visual experience results in the loss of other sensory capacities in Mic 7:16. The enemy nations "will put hand over mouth," and "their ears will become deaf" (אזניהם תחרשנה, 'oznêhem teḥĕrašnâ). According to McKane, these actions signal their "inability to take in the scale of the experience which has overtaken them" (1998, 231). Similar bodily reactions are depicted in the Hebrew Bible as natural responses to overwhelming experiences; in fact, the exact phrase "put hand over mouth" describes the reaction to Job's disfigurement in Job 21:5. This is especially true of sensory encounters of divine power, as illustrated by the theophanic hymn in Hab 3. There, the mountains "see" YHWH and "tremble" in 3:10, while the speaker "hears" and experiences considerable somatic distress in 3:16, including the "trembling" of his innards and his steps. The same verb "tremble" (רגז, rgz) describes the abasement of the enemy nations in Mic 7:17. In short, encounters with YHWH can be disabling, as is the case for Jacob in Gen 32, further demonstrating the deity's power over humans (Raphael 2008, 132). One might also note Zechariah's muteness and Saul's blindness in the New Testament (Luke 1:20; Acts 9:8).

While it is possible to understand the disability imagery in Mic 7:16 as the expected outcome of an encounter with a divine being, other elements suggest a more negative interpretation. Wolff understands the nations' loss of speech as the punishment for their taunting speech in 7:10, a kind of poetic justice frequently evoked in prophetic literature (1990, 227). Their further actions in 7:16-17 establish a trajectory of increasing degradation. Before losing their speech and hearing, the nations become "ashamed," a quality similarly associated with disability in Zeph 3:19. In Mic 7:17 they "lick dust like a snake." The echo of the curse against the serpent in Gen 3:14 further suggests that the humiliation is a calculated punishment, and the connection between disability and bestialization represents disability as a dehumanizing condition. The book of Micah thus draws to a close by depicting the infliction of disability upon the nations who participated in Jerusalem's destruction and exile, even as it had earlier imagined the exile itself as a disability requiring special care from YHWH.

HABAKKUK

Although assembled from diverse textual materials, the book of Habakkuk displays a high degree of order in its present form, in contrast to many other prophetic books. Habakkuk 1:1–2:3 is a dialogue between Habakkuk and YHWH in which the prophet complains about injustice while the deity delights in the violent prowess of the approaching Babylonian armies. A series of short pronouncements in Hab 2:4-20 criticize ill-gotten wealth, violence, and deception. Although their target is not clearly identified, they develop the prophet's criticisms of the Babylonians. Finally, Hab 3 contains a psalm attributed to the prophet, which includes a vision of YHWH as divine warrior in verses 3-15. The book concludes with Habakkuk's stated intent to wait patiently for divine justice and the vindication of his people (3:16-19).

Disability imagery appears in the last of the prophetic pronouncements in chapter 2. Habakkuk 2:18-20 is a brief idol polemic with familiar motifs, including the mundane construction of divine images and the futility of worshipping them. Although the occurrence of disability motifs in such contexts is hardly unique—see the discussions of Isa 44:9-20, Isa 46:1-7, and Jer 10:1-16 above—Hab 2:18 connects idols and disability even more explicitly than other passages by using the adjective "mute" (אלם, 'illēm), which appears in the Hebrew word pattern associated with disability. The striking soundplay in the Hebrew phrase אלילים אלמים ('ĕlîlîm 'illĕmîm, "mute idols"), created by the repetition of the sounds ', l, m, and i, is especially ironic in the context of the inability to speak. Verse 19 develops this categorization further, referring to the raw material for the idol as "silent stone" and rhetorically asking, "Can it teach?" As noted earlier, muteness is the most common disability assigned to idols in polemical texts (Olyan 2011, 94). It contrasts with YHWH's ability to communicate with humans through various divinatory and revelatory channels, such as prophecy (cf. Isa 44:6-8). In support of this connection, recall that Ezekiel's divinely imposed inability to speak is described with a verb related to the root for muteness (Ezek 3:26, 24:27, 33:22). This contrast may explain the enigmatic phrase "teacher of falsehood" in Hab 2:18, which J. J. M.

Roberts connects to the use of images to solicit oracles (1991, 126). It is also implicit in the genre of Habakkuk as prophecy; the very existence of this text demonstrates that YHWH can do what mute idols cannot. Thus Hab 2:18 posits the existence of an able-bodied YHWH by emphasizing the disability of idols.

Verse 20 develops the contrast between YHWH and idols in a different direction. The first half of the verse affirms YHWH's presence "in his holy temple." Ancient Judahites viewed the temple in Jerusalem as the location from which YHWH ruled the world and would march forth in battle, as vividly described in the next chapter of Habakkuk. The temple thus signifies YHWH's power, and according to the second half of the verse, the proper response to this power is silence: "Be silent before him, all the earth" (cf. Zeph 1:7; Zech 2:17 [Eng. 2:13]). In the future imagined by Habakkuk, then, idols are not the only mute entities. All created beings finally fall silent before YHWH, who alone retains the capacity for speech and thus becomes the only truly able-bodied being. This claim anticipates Habakkuk's own experience of bodily disruptions in response to his vision of divine power in Hab 3:16.

ZEPHANIAH

The book of Zephaniah also has a clearer structure than most prophetic books. Its three chapters consist respectively of prophecies of judgment against Judah and Jerusalem, prophecies of judgment against other nations, and prophecies of salvation and restoration. The superscription in Zeph 1:1 dates the prophet's activity to the reign of King Josiah of Judah (640–609 BCE), but the texts themselves contain no clear references to specific events from that time. As with other prophetic books, many scholars date much of the material later, especially the hopeful texts in Zeph 3 (but see Sweeney 2003 for a Josianic date for the entire book). Like Micah, Zephaniah uses disability imagery in both contexts of judgment (Zeph 1:3, 17) and restoration (3:16, 19).

Zephaniah 1 contains one of the most chilling depictions of divine judgment in the Hebrew Bible. A repeated motif in this chapter is the "day of YHWH" (1:7, 14-16), a phrase referring to future, although not necessarily eschatological, divine acts of retribution. References to the day of YHWH appear throughout the Minor Prophets (Nogalski 2011, 11–12; cf. Joel 1:15, 2:1; Amos 5:18; Obad 1:15; etc.). Twice the poem uses disability language to describe this coming judgment. In 1:3a the deity threatens to eliminate humans, birds, fish, and the enigmatic phrase והמכשלות את־הרשעים

(wĕhammakšēlôt ʾet-hārĕšāʿîm), woodenly translated "the ones causing the wicked to stumble." Although the root translated "stumble" (כשל, kšl) may designate a momentary loss of mobility, it frequently denotes disability in other biblical texts (lameness in Isa 35:3; Jer 31:9; 2 Chr 28:15; etc.; blindness in Lev 19:14; Isa 59:10). Most scholars regard the phrase in Zeph 1:3 as a later addition to the text. It may refer to the animals named earlier in the verse, taking them as zoomorphic idols whose worship angers YHWH (Roberts 1991, 167), or it may designate Judahites who encourage the misdeeds of their fellow citizens (Sweeney 2003, 64–65). In either case, "stumbling" stands for religious or ethical shortcomings, an image that occurs in other prophetic books (Jer 6:21; 18:15; 20:10; Ezek 7:19; 14:3-4, 7; 44:12; Hos 4:5; 5:5; 14:2, 10 [Eng. 14:1, 9]; Mal 2:8; cf. Prov 4:19; 24:16). The image plays upon the common metaphor of proper conduct as a path in which one walks (e.g., Hos 14:10 [Eng. 14:9]; Ps 119:9; Prov 3:6). Alternatively, one might emend the first word of the phrase to the *hipʿil* perfect הכשלתי (hikšaltî, "I will cause to stumble"; cf. NJPS, NRSV). On this reading, "stumbling" refers to the effects of YHWH's punishment, much like blindness later in the chapter (Zeph 1:17).

The second occurrence of disability language in the chapter is Zeph 1:17, a poetic triplet in which YHWH speaks:

> I will bring distress upon humans,
> And they will walk like blind people,
> For they have sinned against YHWH.

The relationship between the first two lines is likely one of cause and effect (Vlaardingerbroek 1999, 111). The third line casts these actions as YHWH's response to human sin, perhaps the same religious failures criticized in 1:4-6, 8-9. It is not obvious from the context what it means to "walk like blind people," save that it is regarded as negative, but other biblical texts fill this gap. Drawing upon a common ancient Near Eastern curse for treaty violations, Deut 28:28-29 and Isa 59:9-10 use similar language to equate sightlessness with darkness and unsteady movement. This connection explains how the blindness imagery fits in Zeph 1, where four terms for darkness are used to describe the day of YHWH (1:15). One of these terms (אפלה, ăpēlâ, "deep darkness") also occurs in Deut 28:29 and Isa 59:9.

Zephaniah 1:17a thus imagines that victims of YHWH's judgment will become confused and disoriented, and it associates these qualities with blindness. It is worth noting that the text has able-bodied persons in view, as indicated by the use of simile ("*like* blind people"). Further, the staggering associated with blindness is not itself the punishment depicted in the text.

That punishment takes the form of military destruction (1:14, 16-17), while staggering is the reaction to the severity and magnitude of that punishment. Thus Zeph 1:17 stops short of identifying actual blindness as a divine punishment. Even so, it associates it with sinfulness and divine displeasure, contributing to the negative perception of disability (Olyan 2008, 34; Melcher 2007, 125). The assumptions about blindness are also problematic. As in Isa 59:10, the confusion and disorientation evoked by the text better fit the experience of unexpected darkness by sighted persons. Johannes Vlaardingerbroek questions the cogency of the simile in Zeph 1:17 on such grounds: "This comparison stems from people who do see and do not know how the blind live" (1999, 111). Vlaardingerbroek's comments are worth quoting because of their exceptional concern for the lived experiences of disabled persons. At best, most conventional biblical commentaries do not consider the perspectives of disabled persons when interpreting passages about disability, and at worst they explicitly validate the ableist assumptions and negative constructions of disability in the text (Raphael 2008, 138).

Additional references to disability in Zephaniah occur in the book's final unit, Zeph 3:14-20. This poem ends the book on a stirring note of hope, in contrast to the strains of judgment that dominated the preceding chapters. Verse 15 alludes to earlier "judgments" suffered by Jerusalem, but the prophet promises a future free from trauma, as the city's exiled inhabitants will be brought home (v. 20). In verse 16 the personified city is commanded, "Do not fear . . . do not let your hands grow weak." "Weak hands" is a well-attested designation in the Hebrew Bible for lack of courage or resolve (e.g., 2 Sam 4:1; Ezek 21:12; Neh 6:9). It occurs in conjunction with "stumbling knees" and "anxious hearts" in Isa 35:3-4, part of a poem that similarly depicts the return of exiled Judahites. Although one should not make too much of the expression, given its idiomatic nature, it does equate a negative state with a temporary experience of physical weakness. Its occurrence here associates physical weakness with Jerusalem's difficult past and calls for it to be left behind in order to enter the glorious future.

The first couplet of Zeph 3:19b is almost identical to Mic 4:6:

> And I will save the limping one
> And the displaced one I will assemble.

Notably, both passages use the rare verb צלע (ṣlʿ, "limp"), only attested otherwise in Gen 32:32 (Eng. 32:31). There is almost certainly some literary relationship between the texts in Micah and Zephaniah, although it is unclear whether one is dependent upon the other or both are dependent upon another source (Nogalski 2011, 750; Sweeney 2003, 206; Wolff 1990, 154). The only substantive difference is the opening verb; whereas Micah has "gather" (אספה, *ʾōsĕpâ*), Zephaniah has "save" (והושעתי, *wĕhôšaʿtî*). This difference points to the more negative evaluation of disability in Zephaniah. Although it implies dependence upon others, "gather" stays within the domain of impaired mobility. "Save," by contrast, suggests a more extensive state of vulnerability and hopelessness, requiring more dramatic intervention, and the surrounding lines of poetry reinforce this stigmatization. Zephaniah 3:18 had referred already to the "disgrace" (חרפה, *ḥerpâ*) of Jerusalem, which anticipates the disability language in the next verse, as חרפה is associated with disability or physical duress in other texts (1 Sam 11:2; Pss 31:12 [Eng. 31:11], 109:25; etc.). Then, in the second couplet in verse 19b, YHWH promises to change the "shame" of the limping, displaced exiles into "praise and fame." To be sure, the text's real concern is the national disgrace that results from conquest and loss of land, but it takes for granted that the audience attributes similar stigma to disability. The metaphor would not work otherwise (Melcher 2007, 122).

Zephaniah 3:20 repeats much of the vocabulary of verse 19 ("at that time," "assemble," "praise," etc.). The disability metaphor gives way to nonfigurative language, and even the pretense of addressing "the limping one" is dropped, as evidenced by the second-person masculine plural pronouns. YHWH promises to rehabilitate Jerusalem's reputation "among all the peoples of the earth" and restore its previous state "in your eyes"— that is, in Jerusalem's own estimation. Some interpreters plausibly emend the text to read "their eyes," referring to the other nations, which would reflect the same concern as Mic 7:15-16 that YHWH's actions be obvious to all (e.g., Roberts 1991, 221–22). In either case, the reference to functioning eyes marks a striking contrast to Zeph 1:17, where divine wrath had left human beings virtually sightless.

ZECHARIAH

According to Zech 1:1, 7, and 7:1, the prophet Zechariah was active early in the reign of the Persian ruler Darius I, around 520 BCE. In its present form, the book of Zechariah seems to reflect at least two different historical settings, although some scholars have questioned this neat division (e.g., Sweeney 2000, 526–27). Zechariah 1–8 contains eight visions attributed to Zechariah that address challenges facing the recently returned exiles, including the reconstruction of the temple and the city of Jerusalem (e.g., Zech 1:16-17, 4:9, 6:12-13). While acknowledging the difficulties of the exile and its aftermath, these texts portray the future optimistically. By contrast, chapters 9–14 anticipate a more violent and dangerous future, although they ultimately maintain hope for the vindication of Jerusalem. Most scholars think these chapters were written later than Zech 1–8, likely during the late Persian period (e.g., Meyers and Meyers 1993, 26–27; Redditt 2012, 29). Perhaps not surprisingly, given that it is the longest book in the corpus, Zechariah contains the most references to disability in the Minor Prophets. Blindness is especially frequent, as humans or animals lose their sight in violent fashion on three different occasions (11:17, 12:4, 14:12). Indeed, the book of Zechariah displays a curious interest—bordering on obsession—in eyes and eyesight, a motif that bridges both sections of the book (Meyers and Meyers 1993, 321–22). Variations of the phrase "lift your/my eyes" often introduce vision reports (2:1, 5 [Eng. 1:18, 2:1]; 5:1, 5, 9; 6:1). References to YHWH's eyes denote the deity's care for Jerusalem in 2:12 (Eng. 2:8), 9:8, and 12:4, and the contrast between human and divine eyes establishes YHWH's limitless power in 8:6. In an especially grotesque turn, 4:10 describes the deity as having seven eyes "that roam about all the earth." Meyers and Meyers take this as a reference to YHWH's "omniscience and omnipresence" (1987, 254), while Petersen argues that it symbolizes "divine beneficence" (1984, 227–28). This detail anticipates descriptions of multi-eyed divine beings in later Jewish literature (Holden 1991, 124–26).

The first instance of disability language in Zechariah reprises a theme from Isaiah—rebellion against God as willful deafness. Zechariah 7:11 describes the actions of the audience's ancestors: "They refused to pay attention, and turned a stubborn shoulder, and made their ears too dull to hear" (ואזניהם הכבידו משמוע, wĕʾoznêhem hikbîdû miššĕmôaʿ). The last clause recalls Isa 6:10, in which the prophet Isaiah is commissioned to "stop the ears" (ואזניו הכבד, wĕʾoznāyw hakbēd) of the people, "lest they hear" (ישמע, yišmāʿ). Intentional allusion seems likely, as these are the only texts in which that verb and object occur together. In addition, Zech 7 contains several echoes of Jer 7 (Nurmela 2003, 250–51). Allusion to earlier prophetic texts proves quite effective in this setting, which recalls the rejection of the words of "the former prophets" (Zech 7:7) by preexilic Jerusalemites. In an ironic turn, YHWH responds to the people's refusal to hear the divine word by refusing to hear their prayers and sentencing them to exile (7:13-14; cf. Isa 1:15; Jer 7:16; etc.). Zechariah 7:11 thus establishes yet another link between disability and divine punishment. Whereas many other texts imagine disability as the form of punishment, however, this one uses it to characterize the behavior that is punished.

Even as Zech 7 recalls the trauma of exile, Zech 8 offers hope to the newly returned exiles. It begins with a vision of the restoration of Jerusalem, set early in the Persian period when Jerusalem remained underpopulated and only partially rebuilt. The description of the future city begins with an idyllic but ordinary scene: "Once more will old men and old women sit in the plazas of Jerusalem, each with their cane in hand because of advanced age. And the plazas of the city will be full of boys and girls, playing in its plazas" (Zech 8:4-5). Marking the beginning and end of the life cycle, this pairing of elderly persons and children encompasses the entire population, and the reference to both genders underscores this comprehensiveness (Meyers and Meyers 1987, 416; Petersen 1984, 300). Children and elderly persons were especially vulnerable to the deprivations of siege warfare (2 Kgs 6:24-29; Lam 2:21). Their untroubled leisure thus implies safety from military threats. It also means that their labor is not required for agriculture, suggesting an abundance of food (Meyers and Meyers 1987, 415; Petersen 1984, 300). While depictions of Jerusalem's glorious future appear throughout the prophetic corpus, the closest parallel to Zech 8:1-8 is Isa 65:18-25. It, too, highlights the presence of infants and elderly persons in the restored city, but like other utopian texts from Isaiah, it depicts them in a miraculously transformed fashion (Schipper 2015, 332). In Isa 65:20 infant mortality is eliminated and human life spans are drastically extended, redefining the very concept of old age. By contrast, the picture in Zech 8 is unremarkable on its own terms. It seems miraculous only because of its contrast with the present reality of Jerusalem (Nogalski 2011, 892). Even so, Zech 8:6 takes this transformation as an opportunity to praise the deity's all-surpassing power.

It has become axiomatic in discussions of disability to observe that any person who lives long enough will experience diminished bodily capacities. Reflecting this truism, Zech 8:4 describes elderly persons sitting with "their cane in hand." Disability thus has a place in Zechariah's vision of human flourishing, in which needing a cane is as ordinary as children "playing," the parallel action in 8:5. Modest though it may be, this is one of the only unambiguously positive representations of disability in the prophetic books. Old age is generally regarded highly in the Hebrew Bible, despite the increased occurrence of bodily impairments that accompany it (e.g., Gen 25:8; Lev 19:32). It is unclear whether these impairments would have been regarded as disabilities in the ancient world (Schipper 2011, 20–23). Even so, texts depicting disabled elderly persons sometimes employ negative stereotypes associated with those disabilities in other contexts. In 1 Sam 2–3, for instance, the blindness of the elderly priest Eli accompanies his poor judgment about his sons. Moses' and Caleb's lack of impairments at the end of their long lives is depicted positively in Deut 34:7 and Josh 14:10-11, which implies that such impairments would have carried disgrace even in their old age. No such stigma appears in Zech 8:4, where impaired mobility is presented as a natural form of embodiment for elderly persons. In fact, its presence has become a sign of hope for the future.

Additional disability imagery appears in the symbolic action report in Zech 11:4-17, in which the prophetic speaker becomes the shepherd of "a flock for slaughter" (11:4). This notoriously difficult text has occasioned much discussion but little consensus. Drawing upon a conventional ancient metaphor of leaders as shepherds (e.g., Num 27:17; 2 Sam 5:1-2), it develops earlier prophetic critiques of Judahite leadership in Jer 23:1-4; 25:34-38; and Ezek 34:1-23 (Redditt 2012, 89–91; Sweeney 2000, 677). Unlike those precursors, however, Zech 11 offers no hope for future benevolent leadership, which perhaps reflects the growing disillusionment of Judahites in the late Persian period (Petersen 1995, 90). Commentators disagree on the identification of the intended target of the passage, with proposals ranging from Persian rulers (Sweeney 2000, 677–78), to Judah's native governors and priests (Redditt 2012, 83–84), to false prophets (Meyers and Meyers 1993, 250–51, 264–65). It is not clear that this text even lends itself to such identifications, and they are not important for understanding the disability language in its final verses.

After commanding the prophet to resume his role as shepherd in Zech 11:15, Yʜwʜ announces the imminent arrival of a new, abusive shepherd in verse 16. Four successive clauses describe how this shepherd will neglect his responsibilities to different kinds of sheep. As in Ezek 34:4, which probably influenced this passage, one of the terms for sheep with special needs is "maimed" (הנשברת, *hanniš̌beret*). The word is a passive form of a verb meaning "break," which likely refers to animals with broken bones (cf. Exod 22:9, 13 [Eng. 22:10, 14]); the same root appears in Lev 22:22 in a list of defects that make animals unsuitable for sacrifice. The fact that the shepherd makes no effort to "heal" such animals indicts him as "worthless" (Zech 11:17). This criticism suggests that the audience would have expected shepherds to show special care for sheep with physical limitations. Insofar as the shepherd is a metaphor for political or religious leaders, it suggests a comparable expectation of them as well, thus making an important contribution to the Hebrew Bible's otherwise limited demand for social justice for disabled persons (Melcher 2007, 123). At the same time, Zech 11:16 belongs to a category of texts that, as Olyan explains, "may have been intended to challenge negative representations of the blind and other dependent sufferers by suggesting that such persons are of special interest to the powerful . . . [but] nonetheless affirm their weakness, vulnerability, dependence, and lack of agency, thereby stigmatizing them" (2008, 7).

The next verse contains a curse against the ineffective shepherd. It is not clear whether the speaker is the prophet (Petersen 1995, 100) or YHWH (Redditt 2012, 88; Sweeney 2000, 682). It seems odd for YHWH to curse the shepherd for doing what the deity intended, but there is no indication that the speaker changes between verses 16 and 17. In any event, the curse calls for a sword to strike the shepherd's "arm" and "right eye," which will "completely wither" and "completely dim." The latter verb (כהה, *khh*) denotes blindness in Gen 27:1, Deut 34:7, and 1 Sam 3:2. Even though it does not use the same language as the preceding verse, one is tempted to find a certain poetic justice in the curse in Zech 11:17. The incompetent shepherd did not adequately care for maimed sheep, and so he becomes maimed as a result. Once more, divine punishment takes the form of physical impairment (Melcher 2007, 125). Several interpreters note the effects that these injuries will have on the shepherd, such as making it impossible for him to continue working as a shepherd (Nogalski 2011, 938; Redditt 2012, 88). For Meyers and Meyers, the shepherd's arm and eye are metonyms for his "physical and mental abilities," and so the curse ultimately takes away his "autonomy" (1993, 291–92). If the shepherd represents the high priest, as Redditt argues—although this is far from certain—then his injuries would render him unfit for temple service (2012, 88; cf. Lev 21:18).

Zechariah 12 describes a cataclysmic battle in which other nations attack Jerusalem and Judah, only to be repelled by YHWH. The chapter contains several references to injury and disability. In verse 4 YHWH promises to protect Judah from its enemies:

> I will strike every horse with panic (תמהון, *timmāhôn*)
> And its rider with madness (שגעון, *šiggā'ôn*).
> And upon the house of Judah I will open my eye,
> But every horse of the peoples I will strike with blindness (עורון,
>   *'iwwārôn*).

The rhyming nouns "panic," "madness," and "blindness" recall the curse in Deut 28:28-29, in which YHWH threatens Israel with punishment for covenant violations. Here the curse is enacted against an enemy army for Judah's benefit, but it still casts both cognitive and physical disabilities as divine punishment. By generating panic and madness among the cavalry, YHWH disrupts their military capacities. Note the use of the term "madness" to describe erratic horse riding in 2 Kgs 9:20 (cf. Jer 46:9; Nah

2:5 [Eng. 2:4]). The deity then promises to "open my eye" upon Judah, an expression that signals divine protection. Divine favor is similarly linked to the deity's eyes elsewhere in Zechariah (cf. Zech 2:12 [Eng. 2:8]; 9:8). YHWH finally causes the horses of the invading armies to go blind, rendering them incapable of participating in battle. Ostensibly, these lines contrast the blinded horses with "the house of Judah," which enjoys divine favor. The reference to the divine eye also distinguishes YHWH from the blinded horses (Petersen 1995, 114; Redditt 2012, 105). Once more in this corpus, disability functions as a foil to enhance the portrayal of the able-bodied deity. As noted above, YHWH is not merely sighted but supersighted in the book of Zechariah (4:10).

Following additional promises of victory for Jerusalem and Judah, Zech 12:8 envisions a radical restructuring of Judahite society: "The feeblest among them (הנכשל בהם, hanniḵšāl bāhem) on that day will be like David, and the house of David like God, like the angel of YHWH before them." In the first stage of this transformation, disabled citizens of Jerusalem are elevated to a status like that of King David. It is possible, given the military context, that the root כשל (kšl) refers to soldiers who trip during battle or retreat (cf. Lev 26:37; Jer 46:12; Nah 3:5). As noted in earlier discussions, however, it frequently denotes disability, and this seems more likely here given the connection to David. Images of disability, especially lameness, appear frequently in stories about David's reign in 2 Samuel. He engages the Jebusites in a series of taunts that include belittling references to "the lame" (פסח, pissēaḥ) in 2 Sam 5:6-8, and he houses and provides for Mephibosheth, the lame grandson of King Saul, in 2 Sam 9:1-13. To be sure, Zech 12:8 does not use the same vocabulary for disability, but it seems plausible that the author has these texts in mind. Zechariah 9–12 contains a wealth of connections to other biblical texts, and the comparison between the house of David and "the angel of YHWH" later in verse 8 likely alludes to Mephibosheth's flattery of David in 2 Sam 19:27: "My lord the king is like an angel of God" (Redditt 2012, 101; cf. 2 Sam 14:17).

The verse seems to contrast the perceived weakness of the "feeble" with the strength associated with David, perhaps with fitness for battle especially in mind. As Jeremy Schipper has argued, many texts in 2 Samuel use disability imagery to discredit David's opponents and establish the legitimacy of his rule. At the same time, other texts in 2 Samuel associate disability with David himself and thereby minimize the difference between David and his rivals (Schipper 2005, 424–34). Zechariah 12:8 completes this trajectory by eliminating all sense of difference between David and persons with ambulatory disabilities. It also affirms, in a new context, the hyperbolic boast of the Jebusites in 2 Sam 5:6 that even the lame could defend Jerusalem. But what exactly does Zech 12:8 imagine? It seems to stop short of the miraculous removal of disability, a possibility that is familiar from Isaiah but never explicitly broached in the Minor Prophets. Perhaps the disabled gain exceptional physical capacities to compensate for their impairment (cf. 1 Sam 2:4). Redditt takes the verse to mean "that the Davidides in the future would protect the feeblest members of the city, as God does" (2012, 101). On this reading, Zech 12:8 endorses a view of ideal leadership that includes special care for the disabled, similar to 11:16, and it would seem to critique the lack of such leadership at the time that the text was written. Redditt's proposal is not entirely convincing, however; if lame persons have indeed experienced an elevation of status in the world imagined by the text, then it is unclear what protection they would still need. The imagery in Zech 12:8 may also be metaphorical. Sweeney suggests that it promises the restoration of Judah, reversing earlier texts that depict the nation's punishment as stumbling (2000, 687). The enigmatic imagery precludes certainty.

MALACHI

Although the book of Malachi does not refer to specific historical events, its presupposition of a completed second temple (Mal 1:10) and its use of the term "governor" (1:8) suggest a date in the mid- to late-Persian period, perhaps a century or so after Zechariah. The word "Malachi" means "my messenger" (מלאכי, malʾāḵî), and it is generally understood as a title rather than a name, perhaps taken from 3:1 (Sweeney 2000, 714). It is possible that the book consists entirely of scribal prophecy and does not reflect the public activity of a particular prophet. Malachi deals with a wide range of issues, including proper worship and priestly duties (1:6–2:9, 3:8-15), divorce (2:10-17), and the coming day of YHWH (Mal 3:1-5, 19-24 [Eng. 3:1-5; 4:1-6]). Many units in the book take the form of a rhetorical disputation between YHWH and the addressees (e.g., Mal 1:2-5, 6-9; 3:6-15).

Malachi 1:6-14 denounces the offering of disabled animals as sacrifices in the second temple, depicting the practice as an affront to YHWH. It is addressed to "priests who despise [YHWH's] name" in 1:6, although the critique includes worshippers who bring unacceptable offerings in verses 13-14. The unacceptable offerings are described in verse 8 as "blind" (עור, ʿiwwēr), "lame" (פסח, pissēaḥ), or "sick" (חלה, ḥōleh). The first two adjectives are explicit terms for disability, employing the associated Hebrew word pattern; the third is a more general term for illness or injury that is

associated with lameness in Isa 33:23-24. This passage from Malachi extensively and explicitly denigrates disabled bodies to an even greater degree
than most other prophetic texts. For instance, Mal 1:8 assumes as a matter of course that the Persian-appointed governor would not accept such
animals as gifts. Sacrificing them is equated with theft in 1:13 and broken
religious vows in 1:14, associating disability and illness with moral shortcoming. Perhaps most shocking of all, 1:10 declares that a closed temple
with an unused altar would be better than one in which such animals were
sacrificed—a poignant statement coming perhaps only a century after the
temple had been rebuilt around 515 BCE.

The cultic restrictions in Malachi also seem stricter than those in legal
texts from the Torah that prohibit sacrificing animals with perceived
defects (Lev 22:18-25; Deut 15:19-23, 17:1). Common vocabulary, such as
the root רצה (rṣh, "acceptable"; Lev 22:19-20, 23-24; Mal 1:8) and the participle משחת (mošḥāt, "ruined"; Lev 22:25; Mal 1:14), suggests that Malachi
draws upon the same traditions as these texts, although it is difficult to
demonstrate a direct literary connection (see Nogalski 2011, 1020; Petersen
1995, 180). Unlike Malachi, however, neither Leviticus nor Deuteronomy
prohibits the sacrifice of sick animals, although some defects in Lev 22
could be symptoms of disease (Nogalski 2011, 1020). Further, Lev 22:23
permits sacrifices of animals with elongated or stunted limbs as freewill
offerings but not votive offerings. Although Mal 1:14 also refers to the fulfillment of religious vows, the earlier verses seem to exclude such animals
from all kinds of sacrifice. Finally, Malachi appears to regard disabled
animals as ritually impure, unlike Leviticus and Deuteronomy, which
never use language of impurity to justify their prohibitions (Schipper and
Stackert 2013, 466–67). Malachi 1:7 and 12 call the unacceptable sacrifices
"polluted" (מגאל, mĕgōʾāl), a term used in exilic and postexilic texts for
priests without proper pedigrees (Ezra 2:62; Neh 7:64, 13:28-29), unclean
food (Dan 1:8), and contact with blood (Isa 59:3; Lam 4:14; cf. Isa 63:3).
YHWH boasts of receiving "pure" offerings in other nations in Mal 1:11,
implying that the unacceptable offerings in Jerusalem are impure. Because
they pollute "the table of the Lord" (1:12)—that is, the altar—these sacrifices risk spreading ritual impurity to other worshippers and thus threaten
the well-being of the entire community (cf. Hag 2:11-13). Olyan argues
that the threat of ritual contamination imagined here also accounts for the
stringent restrictions on disabled persons in 2 Sam 5:8, which he takes to
prohibit blind and lame persons from entering the temple, and the Temple
Scroll from Qumran (11Q19 45:14–15), which bans blind persons from
Jerusalem (2008, 30–31, 104–5). The phrase "polluted food" in Mal 1:7

may even suggest that Malachi disapproves of eating blind or lame animals under any circumstances, in contrast to Deut 15:22, which allows for their consumption outside the temple precincts.

This threat notwithstanding, the more pressing problem for Malachi is the perceived slight to Yhwh's honor, as indicated by the repetition of "name" in Mal 1:6, 11, and 14. The deity complains repeatedly about receiving less respect than human authorities, such as fathers or slavehold (1:6). In 1:14 Yhwh claims to be a "great king," a phrase that mimics the titles of Assyrian, Babylonian, and Persian rulers (Sweeney 2000, 728). According to 1:8, however, the priests have more respect for a mere provincial governor, to whom they would not dare present a blind, lame, or sick animal. Suspicious readers might wonder whether these emphatic protestations reveal insecurity on the part of deity, or even overcompensation for perceived insufficiency. Among other reasons, disabled sacrificial animals were an affront to Yhwh because they had less perceived economic value than able-bodied animals. Malachi 1:14 accuses worshippers who offered "ruined" animals of withholding more valuable animals, which may have been motivated by the economic duress of the Persian period (Nogalski 2011, 1018). By presenting animals whose worth was not commensurate with the deity's status, priests and worshippers publicly insulted Yhwh. Additionally, Jeremy Schipper and Jeffrey Stackert (2013, 465, 468–70) argue that restrictions on disabled priests in Lev 21:17-23 reflect a common expectation in the ancient Near East that members of the royal court be able-bodied (cf. Dan 1:4). Given the emphasis on Yhwh's kingship in Mal 1:14, it is plausible that similar royal disdain for disability is operative here.

Even if the ultimate target of Mal 1:6-14 is the disrespectful attitude of priests and worshippers, the portrayal of disability in these verses is incredibly demeaning, ascribing impurity to it and declaring that its mere presence diminishes Yhwh's status. Because Mal 1 only deals with sacrificial animals, one should not automatically assume that its view of disability applies to humans as well, as Olyan (2007, 35) recognizes. At least some overlap seems likely, however, given the similar restrictions on priestly service in Lev 21:17-23. Once again, the text uses disability to enhance its portrayal of Yhwh, but it does so even more negatively than usual. In other examples from the Minor Prophets, disability serves as a foil for divine power in ways that require at least some proximity between the deity and disability. Here, Yhwh cannot even tolerate its presence.

OTHER THEMES RELATING TO DISABILITY IN THE PROPHETS

In addition to the passages treated above, other texts that do not contain explicit representations of disability might nonetheless contribute to our understanding of the construction of disability in biblical prophetic literature or the intersection of this corpus with the concerns of contemporary disabled persons. Three prominent themes are especially relevant: divine causation, the sensory character of religious experience, and social justice.

As discussed throughout this chapter, some texts from the prophetic books present disability as the result of divine activity, frequently as punishment for wrongdoing (e.g., Isa 6:9-10; Zeph 1:17; Zech 11:17, 12:4). Others depict the exile as a metaphorical disability (e.g., Isa 42:7; Mic 4:6; Zeph 3:19); elsewhere in the prophetic books, exile is understood as divine judgment (e.g., Isa 5:13; Jer 29:1, 4, 14; Ezek 39:28; Amos 5:5, 27; Mic 2:4). Such texts might be taken to imply that all disabilities are directly caused by God, or even that all disabilities are divine punishments for human sin. Both views are expressed elsewhere in the Bible (e.g., Exod 4:11; John 9:2). The prophetic books do not contain any explicit statement of either view, but the corpus as a whole consistently expresses a high view of divine causality. The most elaborate expression of this view is a poem in Amos 3:3-8 that unfolds a series of scenarios in which one action clearly causes another. The series culminates with a rhetorical question: "Does disaster happen in a city / that Yhwh did not do?" (3:6). Second Isaiah claims that Yhwh, as the sole effective power in the universe, is responsible for "creating light and darkness / making peace and creating evil" (Isa 45:7). The upshot is clear—all events, especially those with harmful effects, are caused by God. It follows that within the world imagined in the prophetic books, disability must inevitably result from divine activity. This need not mean that all disabilities should be regarded as punishments, but this seems to be the case at least some of the time. In addition to specific claims to this effect, one should note that Yhwh's judgment frequently takes the form of military activity in these texts (e.g., Isa 10:5-6; Jer 21:7; Hos 10:9-10; Mic 1:15). For much of human history, war has been the primary cause of noncongenital disability. At the very least, then, many disabilities would be direct consequences of events understood in prophetic literature as divine punishments.

A second relevant theme is the frequent correlation of sensory perception and religious experience. Two common means by which humans receive knowledge about God in prophetic literature are sight (e.g., Isa 40:5; Jer 2:10; Amos 6:2; Zech 10:7; Mal 1:5) and hearing (e.g., Isa 40:21, 28;

Jer 28:7; Hos 5:1; Hab 3:2; Zech 8:23). Sight and hearing are especially closely associated with the prophetic reception and transmission of the divine word. Prophets frequently encounter the deity through visions (e.g., Ezek 8:3-4; Hos 12:11 [Eng. 12:10]; Joel 3:1 [Eng. 2:28]; Hab 2:1-3; Zech 2:1 [1:18], 5:1). The entire books of Isaiah, Obadiah, and Nahum are designated as "visions" in their superscriptions (Isa 1:1; Obad 1; Nah 1:1). Similarly, the opening lines of many prophetic speeches include some variation of the phrase "hear the word of YHWH" (e.g., Isa 28:14; Jer 2:4; Hos 4:1; Amos 7:16; Mic 6:1). Amos 8:11 even describes the cessation of prophecy as "a famine . . . of hearing the words of YHWH." In short, prophetic books consistently assume that the capacities to see and hear are necessary for religious enlightenment. Indeed, before the relatively recent development of tactile communication technologies like Braille, the very existence of the prophetic books as texts presumed an audience that could see their words or hear them read aloud, as made clear in Isa 29:18 and Hab 2:2. Needless to say, these assumptions exclude blind and deaf persons from full religious participation, and nowhere do these books even acknowledge this problem, much less propose accommodations for it. To be fair, all sensory perceptions ultimately prove inadequate for perceiving the divine in the prophetic corpus. Ezekiel 3:15, Mic 7:16-17, and Hab 3:16 describe the incapacitating effects of encounters with the deity upon human senses, suggesting that all humans have limited faculties for apprehending divine reality, which at least partially relativizes the distinction between disability and ability. Such cases, however, are exceptional. For most conventional forms of religious experience, disability proves to be a disadvantage in prophetic literature.

Finally, a number of prophetic texts harshly condemn structural oppression or demand social justice. This is especially true of First Isaiah, Amos, and Micah, although similar texts may be found in other books as well. Denunciations of unjust activities typically focus on economic exploitation (e.g., Isa 3:14, 5:8-9; Amos 2:6-8, 5:11, 8:4-6; Mic 2:2) or legal corruption (e.g., Isa 10:1-2; Amos 5:10, 12; Mic 3:11; Hab 1:4). Amos 5:21-24 famously makes social justice a prerequisite for acceptable worship (cf. Isa 1:16-17), while Mic 3:8 identifies advocacy for justice as a distinguishing characteristic of true prophecy. Zechariah 7:9-10 recognizes four categories of vulnerable persons who require special social protections: widows, orphans, refugees, and the poor. None of these passages explicitly include disabled persons in their purview; although rare, such texts do exist in other parts of the Hebrew Bible (e.g., Lev 19:14; Deut 27:18; Ps 146:7-8; see Olyan 2008, 10–11). The only prophetic texts that seem to recognize the reality of injustice against disabled persons are Ezek 34:4 and Zech 11:16, which assume that responsible social leadership includes attention to their particular needs. The absence of explicit calls for justice for disabled persons alongside victims of economic oppression constitutes a deficiency in the ethical discourse of the prophetic books, especially since these texts do not hesitate on other occasions to exploit disability as a source for metaphors for other concerns.[12] This fact does not preclude the possibility that prophetic texts could offer a theological rationale or motivation for advocacy for disabled persons (cf. Melcher 2007, 127–28; Sanderson 1998, 222). It must be recognized, though, that such advocacy would extend the call for justice in these books in a direction that their producers or original audiences do not seem to have anticipated.

By way of conclusion, the prophetic books offer a diverse range of textual representations of disability while broaching other issues that implicitly pertain to the concerns of disabled persons. The portrayals of disability in these texts are part of a broader discourse about bodies and embodiment that ultimately serves to magnify claims of Yhwh's supremacy over the created order. They seldom have actual disabled persons, or even humans at all, in view; rather, they use disability as a literary motif to explore the nature of divine judgment and deliverance against the backdrop of Assyrian, Babylonian, and Persian supremacy over Israel and Judah. Most if not all of these images presume and perpetuate the negative evaluation of disability. At the same time, many details of these representations demonstrate their culturally conditioned character, revealing that disability was more a matter of social construction than biological reality in the ancient world, just as it is today. Although they are relatively few in number, careful attention to these images is crucial for informed interpretation of prophetic books, as they are connected to some of the most prominent literary and theological themes of the corpus.

WORKS CITED

Allen, Leslie C. 2008. *Jeremiah: A Commentary*. Louisville, Ky.: Westminster John Knox.

Ben Zvi, Ehud. 2000. *Micah*. Forms of the Old Testament Literature 21B. Grand Rapids: Eerdmans.

———. 2009. "Is the Twelve Hypothesis Likely from an Ancient Readers' Perspective?" Pages 47–96 in *Two Sides of a Coin: Juxtaposing Views on*

---

[12] For a critique of a comparable double standard in Amos' treatment of women, see Sanderson 1998, 219.

Interpreting the Book of the Twelve/the Twelve Prophetic Books. Edited by Ehud Ben Zvi and James D. Nogalski. Analecta Gorgiana 201. Piscataway, N.J.: Gorgias.

Blenkinsopp, Joseph. 2000. *Isaiah 1–39: A New Translation with Introduction and Commentary*. Anchor Bible 19. Garden City, N.Y.: Doubleday.

———. 2002. *Isaiah 40–55: A New Translation with Introduction and Commentary*. Anchor Bible 19A. Garden City, N.Y.: Doubleday.

———. 2003. *Isaiah 56–66: A New Translation with Introduction and Commentary*. Anchor Bible 19B. Garden City, N.Y.: Doubleday.

Carroll, Robert P. 1997. "Blindsight and the Vision Thing: Blindness and Insight in the Book of Isaiah." Pages 79–93 in vol. 1 of *Writing & Reading the Scroll of Isaiah: Studies of an Interpretive Tradition*. Edited by Craig C. Broyles and Craig A. Evans. Supplements to Vetus Testamentum 70. Formation and Interpretation of Old Testament Literature 1. Leiden: Brill.

Chavel, Simeon. 2014. "Prophetic Imagination in the Light of Narratology and Disability Studies in Isaiah 40–48." *Journal of Hebrew Scriptures* 14: art. 3. http://www.jhsonline.org/Articles/article_197.pdf.

Clements, Ronald E. 1985. "Beyond Tradition History: Deutero-Isaianic Development of First Isaiah's Themes." *Journal for the Study of the Old Testament* 31: 95–113.

———. 1988. "Patterns in the Prophetic Canon: Healing the Blind and Lame." Pages 189–200 in *Canon, Theology, and Old Testament Interpretation: Essays in Honor of Brevard S. Childs*. Edited by Gene M. Tucker, David L. Petersen, and Robert R. Wilson. Philadelphia: Fortress.

Couey, J. Blake. 2014. "The Disabled Body Politic in Isa 3:1, 8." *Journal of Biblical Literature* 133: 95–109.

Evans, Craig A. 1997. "A Note on Targum 2 Samuel 5.8 and Jesus' Ministry to the 'Maimed, Halt, and Blind.'" *Journal for the Study of the Pseudepigrapha* 15: 79–82.

Fontaine, Carol. 2007. "'Be Men, O Philistines!' (1 Samuel 4:9): Iconographic Representations and Reflections on Female Gender as Disability in the Ancient World." Pages 61–72 in *This Abled Body: Rethinking Disabilities in Biblical Studies*. Edited by Hector Avalos, Sarah J. Melcher, and Jeremy Schipper. Semeia Studies 55. Atlanta: Society of Biblical Literature.

Garber, David G., Jr. 2015. "Trauma Theory and Biblical Studies." *Currents in Biblical Research* 14: 24–44.

Greenberg, Moshe. 1983. *Ezekiel 1–20: A New Translation with Introduction and Commentary*. Anchor Bible 22. Garden City, N.Y.: Doubleday.

Holden, Lynn. 1991. *Forms of Deformity*. Journal for the Study of the Old Testament Supplement Series 131. Sheffield: JSOT Press.

Kennedy, James M. 1991. "Hebrew *piṯḥôn peh* in the Book of Ezekiel." *Vetus Testamentum* 41: 233–35.

Lapsley, Jacqueline E. 2012. "Body Piercings: The Priestly Body and the 'Body' of the Temple in Ezekiel." *Hebrew Bible and Ancient Israel* 1: 231–45.

Lemos, T. M. 2011. "'Like the Eunuch Who Does Not Beget': Gender, Mutilation, and Negotiated Status in the Ancient Near East." Pages 47–66 in *Disability Studies and Biblical Literature*. Edited by Candida R. Moss and Jeremy Schipper. New York: Palgrave Macmillan.

Levenson, Jon D. 2006. *Resurrection and the Restoration of Israel: The Ultimate Victory of the God of Life*. New Haven, Conn.: Yale University Press.

Levtow, Nathaniel B. 2008. *Images of Others: Iconic Politics in Ancient Israel*. Biblical and Judaic Studies from the University of California San Diego 11. Winona Lake, Ind.: Eisenbrauns.

Lundbom, Jack R. 1999. *Jeremiah 1–20: A New Translation with Introduction and Commentary*. Anchor Bible 21A. New York: Doubleday.

———. 2004a. *Jeremiah 21–36: A New Translation with Introduction and Commentary*. Anchor Bible 21B. Garden City, N.Y.: Doubleday.

———. 2004b. *Jeremiah 37–51: A New Translation with Introduction and Commentary*. Anchor Bible 21C. Garden City, N.Y.: Doubleday.

McKane, William. 1986–1996. *A Critical and Exegetical Commentary on Jeremiah*. 2 vols. International Critical Commentary. Edinburgh: T&T Clark.

———. 1998. *The Book of Micah: Introduction and Commentary*. Edinburgh: T&T Clark.

Melcher, Sarah J. 2007. "With Whom Do the Disabled Associate? Metaphorical Interplay in the Latter Prophets." Pages 115–29 in *This Abled Body: Rethinking Disabilities in Biblical Studies*. Edited by Hector Avalos, Sarah J. Melcher, and Jeremy Schipper. Semeia Studies 55. Atlanta: Society of Biblical Literature.

Meyers, Carol L., and Eric M. Meyers. 1987. *Haggai and Zechariah 1–8: A New Translation with Introduction and Commentary*. Anchor Bible 25B. Garden City, N.Y.: Doubleday.

———. 1993. *Zechariah 9–14: A New Translation with Introduction and Commentary*. Anchor Bible 25C. Garden City, N.Y.: Doubleday.

Nogalski, James D. 2011. *The Book of the Twelve*. 2 vols. Smyth & Helwys Bible Commentary. Macon, Ga.: Smyth & Helwys.

Nurmela, Risto. 2003. "The Growth of the Book of Isaiah Illustrated by the Allusions in Zechariah." Pages 245–59 in *Bringing Out the Treasure: Inner Biblical Allusion in Zechariah 9–14*. Edited by Mark J. Boda and Michael H. Floyd. Journal for the Study of the Old Testament Supplement Series 370. London: Sheffield Academic.

O'Brien, Julia M. 2006. "Once and Future Gender: Gender and the Future in the Twelve." Pages 144–59 in *Utopia and Dystopia in Prophetic Literature*. Edited by Ehud Ben Zvi. Publications of the Finnish Exegetical Society

92. Helsinki: Finnish Exegetical Society; Göttingen: Vandenhoeck & Ruprecht.

O'Connor, Kathleen M. 2011. *Jeremiah: Pain and Promise*. Minneapolis: Fortress.

Olyan, Saul. 2008. *Disability and the Hebrew Bible: Interpreting Mental and Physical Differences*. New York: Cambridge University Press.

———. 2011. "The Ascription of Physical Disability as a Stigmatizing Strategy in Biblical Iconic Polemics." Pages 89–102 in *Disability Studies and Biblical Literature*. Edited by Candida R. Moss and Jeremy Schipper. New York: Palgrave Macmillan.

Paul, Shalom. 2012. *Isaiah 40–66*. Eerdmans Critical Commentary. Grand Rapids: Eerdmans.

Petersen, David L. 1984. *Haggai and Zechariah 1–8: A Commentary*. Old Testament Library. Philadelphia: Westminster.

———. 1995. *Zechariah 9–14 and Malachi: A Commentary*. Old Testament Library. Louisville, Ky.: Westminster John Knox.

Raphael, Rebecca. 2008. *Biblical Corpora: Representations of Disability in Hebrew Biblical Literature*. Library of Hebrew Bible/Old Testament Studies 445. New York: T&T Clark.

Redditt, Paul L. 2012. *Zechariah 9–14*. International Exegetical Commentary on the Old Testament. Stuttgart: W. Kohlhammer.

Roberts, J. J. M. 1991. *Nahum, Habakkuk, and Zephaniah: A Commentary*. Old Testament Library. Louisville, Ky.: Westminster John Knox.

———. 2015. *First Isaiah*. Hermeneia. Minneapolis: Fortress.

Sanderson, Judith E. 1998. "Amos." Pages 216–23 in *Women's Bible Commentary*. Edited by Carol A. Newsom and Sharon H. Ringe. 2nd ed. Louisville, Ky.: Westminster John Knox.

Schipper, Jeremy. 2005. "Reconsidering the Imagery of Disability in 2 Samuel 5:8b." *Catholic Biblical Quarterly* 67: 422–34.

———. 2011. *Disability and Isaiah's Suffering Servant*. Biblical Refigurations. New York: Oxford University Press.

———. 2015. "Why Does Imagery of Disability Include Healing in Isaiah?" *Journal for the Study of the Old Testament* 39: 319–33.

Schipper, Jeremy, and Jeffrey Stackert. 2013. "Blemishes, Camouflage, and Sanctuary Service: The Priestly Deity and His Attendants." *Hebrew Bible and Ancient Israel* 2: 458–78.

Sweeney, Marvin A. 2000. *The Twelve Prophets*. 2 vols. Berit Olam. Collegeville, Minn.: Liturgical.

———. 2003. *Zephaniah: A Commentary*. Hermeneia. Minneapolis: Fortress.

Vlaardingerbroek, Johannes. 1999. *Zephaniah*. Historical Commentary on the Old Testament. Leuven: Peeters.

Wildberger, Hans. 2002. *Isaiah 28–39*. Translated by Thomas H. Trapp. Continental Commentaries. Minneapolis: Fortress.

Williamson, H. G. M. 1994. *The Book Called Isaiah: Deutero-Isaiah's Role in Composition and Redaction*. Oxford: Clarendon.

Wolff, Hans Walter. 1990. *Micah: A Commentary*. Translated by Gary Stansell. Continental Commentaries. Minneapolis: Fortress.

Wright, Jacob L., and Michael J. Chan. 2012. "King and Eunuch: Isaiah 56:1-8 in Light of Honorific Royal Burial Practices." *Journal of Biblical Literature* 131: 99–119.

Zimmerli, Walther. 1979. *Ezekiel 1: A Commentary on the Book of the Prophet Ezekiel, Chapters 1–24*. Hermeneia. Minneapolis: Fortress.

8

Mark and Matthew

Candida R. Moss

The Gospels of Matthew and Mark are commonly known as the "First" and "Second" Gospel. Their order in the canon and the traditional association of Matthew with the tax collector Levi seem to suggest that Matthew is the older and more reliable tradition. In actual fact, the overwhelming majority of scholars would agree that the Gospel of Mark was written first (ca. 70 CE) and was used as a source for the author of the Gospel of Matthew, who wrote anywhere from ten to twenty years later. The close literary relationship between the two narratives means that there is a great deal of duplication—especially of miracle stories and parables—between the two accounts. At the same time, each gospel has its own particular message and stance on the identity, teachings, and ministry of Jesus. The authors share a commitment to the idea that Jesus was the Son of God but use varying imagery to explicate this idea and, arguably, hold different notions of how or what parts of this identity is important. Thus, while a great deal of the material pertaining to disability is the same in both texts, the framing of these stories occasionally differs.

Broadly speaking, disability appears in the Gospels in one of three ways: (1) in the miracle or so-called healing stories in which an impaired individual is "cured" by Jesus; (2) as a metaphor for sin, ignorance, obstinacy, stubbornness, or other moral failing; and (3) in moments of silence in which traditional readings have tended to overlook the presence of disability or assume able-bodiedness in the text. As a number of scholars have noted, the Gospel of Mark and religious literature in general tend to associate impairment with sinfulness. This idea—commonly known among disability studies theorists as the "religious model of disability"—is present in Matthew and Mark and will receive treatment in the section on Mark. Because this line of interpretation has dominated theological and historical commentaries on the subject, it will not receive its fullest exposition here. Rather than hammering home every problematic association of bodily difference and sin, I will attempt to draw out the variety of approaches and valuations of disability in the Gospels of Matthew and Mark. For the purposes of this commentary, material that appears in both Matthew and Mark will be treated in the Gospel of Mark, analysis of sensory imagery will appear in Matthew, and certain stories (the woman with the flow of blood, the saying on self-amputation [the removal of hand, foot or eye by the patient him or herself], descriptions of eschatological bodies, and the description of the eye as the lamp of the body) will receive more extensive treatment.

This commentary will employ the common disability studies distinction between impairment (a physiological phenomenon) and disability (a social phenomenon). Various forms of bodies are essentially neutral and are only disabled in social contexts that restrict access, benefits, political power, social capital, and so forth. It is important to remember that physiological phenomena are interpreted differently in different contexts, especially across time and space (Kelley 2007, 31–45). The physiological condition known as epilepsy today seems to have been interpreted as the "Sacred Disease" in the ancient world because it conferred special precognitive powers and an association with the god Apollo (205–7). While epilepsy might seem to have no positive connotations in the context of the modern hospital and medical models of disability, it had a particular spiritual significance in the ancient world. Conversely, physiological conditions that we might consider "normal" or even desirable may have been disabling in the ancient world.

In analyzing the Gospels of Matthew and Mark, we will try to understand these accounts in their own historical context without anachronistically supplying modern ableist notions of the texts. I will also ask, from a disability perspective, what do these texts allow us to see and what does the text not allow us to see? How can the Gospels constrain and how can they liberate? Historical approaches to disability in the Bible have sometimes been accused of failing to address the issues or concerns of those with disabilities who read the text (e.g., by Lawrence 2013, 23–24). Ironically, this accusation is leveled against disabled historians whose disabilities are erased in the leveling of this critique. This argument, therefore, seems to rehearse ableist discourse that silences and then seeks to speak *for* the disabled.

Demonstrating that in its own time and in its composition the Bible does not unequivocally endorse ableism is, to my mind, an important project. If historical readings of the Bible are (rightly or wrongly) regnant in biblical scholarship today, then it is important to show that disability criticism is not a marginal issue but one of central importance.

In addition to historical readings, this commentary will also draw on methods from postcolonial theory, feminist studies, and literary criticism. It is eclectic and (arguably) methodologically incoherent. This seems to me to mirror the accusations of "disordered" perspective levied against disabled activists in general. It is possible to recognize that disability is a construction, to appreciate the variegated experience of disability, and to seek treatments and accommodations that might mitigate certain aspects of that condition. Eclecticism, which embraces historically antithetical approaches, seems to me to mirror this experience—a set of experience, I should add, that I myself share.

THE GOSPEL OF MATTHEW

The Gospel of Matthew appears to have been written after the destruction of the Jerusalem temple by an author familiar with biblical prophecies about the Messiah and interested in presenting its protagonist as a kind of new Moses. Like the Gospel of Mark, it depicts Jesus engaging in numerous cures and healings. It develops and expands the association of sensory perception and knowledge found in the Gospel of Mark in discussions of ethics, action, and moral conduct. Unlike Mark, it supplies an origins story for Jesus in the form of a genealogy and larger infancy narrative, which raises questions about fertility and familial arrangement in the holy family.

THE INFANCY NARRATIVES (MATT 1:1–2:19)

The Genealogy (Matt 1:1-17)

Matthew begins with a biblically styled genealogy. The structure of the genealogy focuses on God's promises to the ancient Israelites: the list begins with Abraham and traverses the history of God's people via David and Solomon. One interesting aspect of the genealogy is the insertion of four women's names into the account. The women mentioned are Tamar (Matt 1:3), who disguises herself and plays the prostitute with her father-in-law, Judah; Rahab (1:5a), the prostitute who facilitates the fall of Jericho; Bathsheba (1:6), the "widow of Uriah," who committed adultery with David; and Ruth (1:5b), David's grandmother, who snuck into the threshing floor at night and "uncovered [Boaz's] feet." All these women have scandalous reputations.

While a variety of explanations for this scene have been offered, it seems appropriate to focus on the issue of procreation in general. This is, after all, a genealogy. In the case of the first woman, Tamar, her story introduces the biblical theme of infertility and childlessness into the book. Tamar was forced to "play the prostitute" because she had married her brother-in-law after her husband had died without issue. In the absence of biological offspring, Tamar was compelled by Levirate law to raise up children on behalf of her husband with her husband's brother. That her brother-in-law was noncomplicit in this practice may make her famous, but the occasion for her story is the childlessness of her first marriage and the issue of procreation. Already, then, in the genealogy the issue of childlessness, infertility, and progeny is raised. Infertility, the preeminent disability in the Hebrew Bible (Baden 2011, 13–15) provides the context for the genealogy of Jesus. And the unusual mechanics by which the divine family is composed is highlighted by these genealogical abnormalities.

The Birth of Jesus (Matt 1:18-25)

Throughout the infancy narrative, Matthew's focus is firmly planted on Joseph, Jesus' assumed stepfather (to use modern terminology). Not only does the genealogy trace Jesus' lineage back through Joseph, but it is Joseph's response to the annunciation that takes center stage. Jesus is presented as Joseph's child, and the unusual dual-patrilineage of Jesus plays an important role in establishing how it is that Jesus is both Son of God and Son of David.

According to both Matthew and Luke, Mary was betrothed to Joseph when she conceived Jesus. As a social status, betrothal was one that under ordinary conditions would have granted Joseph sexual privileges. That being the case, both evangelists are clear that Joseph and Mary had not had sexual relations. In Matthew, Joseph's angry response and resolution to have her "quietly put away" is evidence that he is convinced that the child is not his. This is not ordinary procreation.

Joseph's role is maximized throughout the Matthean infancy narrative. It is to Joseph that divine revelations are given. Joseph is alerted to the divine origins of the child in a dream and is instructed to relocate the family, first to Egypt to avoid Herod's slaughter of the innocents, and finally to Nazareth. While we might assume, on the basis of the Gospel of

Luke, that Mary had received her own divine revelations, especially upon realizing that she was pregnant, Matthew does not mention this. Instead, he preserves the same structure found in the story of Abraham and Sarah, and Isaac and Rebekah, in which the male head of the household communicates with divine intermediaries and notifies his wife of the divine plan. Matthew's focus on Joseph indicates that while Joseph is very much not the biological father, he is not the emasculated cuckold, either.

In reconciling divine and human parentage, the majority of commentators have assumed that Jesus was Joseph's son by adoption or—to use quasi-modern terminology—his stepson (Levin 2006, 422). By marrying Mary, Joseph adopted Jesus and raised him as his own (Matt 1:24-25). It was, after all, Joseph who circumcised and named Jesus and presented him in the temple (Luke 2:21-24) and taught him a vocation (Matt 13:55).

Whatever miraculous mechanisms lie behind the virgin birth, Matthew is clear on two points: that Jesus was conceived apart from sexual intercourse, and that Joseph is the father of Jesus in some very real sense. The paradox is more striking to modern readers accustomed to the hard and fast rules of genetic testing. But even as Matthew labors to construct a vision of Jesus' conception and paternity that makes Jesus unquestionably both Son of God and Son of David, he undercuts that vision from the start. Joseph is Jesus' father apart from able-bodied procreation, and Jesus is God's son apart from able-bodied procreation. In modern medical terms we might judge Mary as a surrogate, but however the infancy narrative is interpreted, it is clear that "normal" procreation is not operative here (Moss and Baden 2015). For couples struggling with infertility, it is significant to note that Jesus is born into a family constructed according to love and duty, not biology and normative procreation.

Sermon on the Mount (Matt 5–7)

Amputation and Salvation (Matt 5:28-30, 38-42)

Much of what can be written about autoamputation and salvation can be found in the analysis of the original saying about autoamputation in Mark (see below). But it is worth noting that Matthew explicitly ties the notion of autoamputation to salvation and the *lex talionis*. In 5:38-42, eight verses after instructing his listeners to remove offending bodily parts from their bodies, Jesus explicitly refers to the rule "an eye for an eye and a tooth for a tooth." Yet in this instance Jesus exhorts his audience to do otherwise, instructing them to "turn the other cheek" and "give over one's coat." The effect of this instruction is to undercut the traditional idea that bodily members must be extracted as payment for sins committed against another party. Instead, says Jesus, we should forgive.

The positioning of this passage close on the heels of the instruction to autoamputate and self-blind in verses 28-30 has an effect on how we read the experience of bodily mutilation and blinding in Matthew. It suggests that these impairments should not be read as implementations of the principle of the *lex talionis* but rather as piety in practice. For further discussion, see the treatment of this issue in Mark below.

Hypocrisy, Almsgiving, and Proprioception (Matt 6:2-4)

One tendency derived from the Bible and found in biblical scholarship (and ableist perspectives in general) is to use language and imagery of disability as metaphors for ignorance, stubbornness, and moral failure. Disability is coded negatively and interpreted as symbols of larger negative truths. We can see this in Matthean use of sensory imagery, which is often—although not in this volume—seen as harmless theological embellishment.

Interestingly, however, the opposite phenomenon rarely occurs. It is almost unheard of for a bodily image that correlates to a positive ethical injunction to be interpreted as symbol of a disability. To retort that there are no instances of this in the Bible would be to commit what Lennard Davis calls a "sin of omission," common when "participating in ableist discourse" (1995, 6). One example of this line of interpretation can be found in Matt 6:2-4, the well-known statement about hypocrisy in which Jesus instructs his followers that "when you give alms, do not let your left hand know what your right hand is doing." The statement is part of the injunction about almsgiving, but it envisions a highly specific embodied activity and state. The state of embodiment envisioned here is one in which an individual is unaware of the activity and spatial movement of parts of his or her body.

To some readers this bodily state may seem purely hypothetical, but to those familiar with proprioceptive deficits, it is clear that there are individuals whose bodies already operate in this way. Proprioception is an awareness of movement, posture, and orientation in space. Among other medical diagnoses, it is often associated with tethered cord syndrome. A former student of mine, Lisa, described her experience of this impairment to me as a lack of awareness about her body's position and movement. Lisa's body would, therefore, already encode the values endorsed by Matt 6:2-4. While the passage might be focused on almsgiving, her body is already prepared for and oriented toward almsgiving by virtue of her impairment. In the way that broad shoulders and long arms may give a person an advantage in the swimming pool, proprioceptive deficits are embodied examples of a moral advantage when it comes to almsgiving.

The Eye Is the Lamp of the Body (Matt 6:22-23)

In Matthew there are a number of references to sensory perception and cognition, which are repeatedly linked to the nature of the heart, ethical behavior, and eschatological judgment. There is a clear-cut distinction between those who truly see and hear and those others who "see but do not hear." The ability to see is in turn linked to understanding; thus the disciples are those who are blessed (*makarioi*) because their eyes see and their ears hear (Matt 13:16). Set in contrast to the disciples are those who "seeing they do not perceive, and hearing they do not listen, nor do they understand" (Matt 13:13; cf. the exhortations to those who "have" ears and eyes in 11:15, 13:9, 15:10). The inability to see and hear is connected in Matt 13:15 to a kind of lethargy that has afflicted the eyes, ears, and hearts of the people and as a result they are unable to perceive or understand. The severity of the situation is such that they are in need of deliverance and yet are unable to ask for a cure because they themselves do not understand the predicament they are in (Moss 2011; Lawrence 2013).

Underlying Matthew's discussion of salvation is the generally held idea that unethical behavior or failure to obey the commandments is both the cause of sensory malfunction and the product of an unrighteous heart (Avalos, Melcher, and Schipper 2007). In Matthew the senses are repeatedly linked to the activity of the heart. It is those who are pure in heart who will see God (Matt 5:3), while those who blaspheme are defiled because what comes out of the mouth (i.e., speech) proceeds from the heart (12:34, 15:18-19).

This biological moral system is contingent upon the Matthean view that sin and impurity is internalized (cf. 5:21-24, 27-28; 15:11). Unethical behavior begins in the heart, and all external manifestations of it (transgressions of commandments, impure speech, etc.) are mediated through the senses. The senses themselves no longer function correctly, as the heart is contaminated, and thus unrighteous persons are unaware of their own infirmity. Once the light of the eyes becomes darkness, individuals become incapable of perceiving anything at all. The same idea is present in TNaph. 2:10: "For if you bid the eye to hear, it cannot; so neither while you are in darkness can you do the works of light" (cf. also LXX Tobit 3:17).

This ethical understanding of sensory function, its relation to perception in the heart, and internalized sin draws upon the intellectual framework of Jewish wisdom literature (Moss 2011). However, if the meaning of Matthean sensory imagery is this straightforward, then why does the evangelist obscure the meaning of the logion in 6:22-23? We are not told how we can find out if the moral lamp in our eye has gone out. As readers we must ask, What is the rhetorical force of leaving the meaning of the logion unresolved and ending with an exclamation? Hans Dieter Betz argues that the purpose of the confusion is pedagogical. The author intends to introduce a sliver of uncertainty into the minds of his audience: "It appears that having heard and understood the logion the thoughtful and conscientious person will be worried: What if my inner light is darkness? How can it be made bright again? The logion is so designed as to provoke this concern, but it does not answer it. It leaves the concerned hearer alone and restless, and this open-ended situation seems to be the parenetical goal of the passage" (1979, 56; cited in Allison 1987, 61–83).

Betz' "conscientious persons" are worried on a number of counts: not only may their eye and indeed whole body be darkness, but if so, the fate of the unrighteous and the darkness of gehenna await them. The force of 6:22-23 is to call into question the salvific status of the Matthean audience; can they truly be sure they are righteous? And if not, how can they tell? The element of confusion and uncertainty over one's own fate plays into the evangelist's larger concern with eschatological judgment that reverberates throughout the Gospel.

From a disability perspective, we can make a number of observations. First, the theories of the body that underpin the interpretation of sensory impairment as associated with ignorance, a loss of understanding, and moral corruption is now outdated. No current medic would subscribe to this theory of vision. Second, even if it were not outdated, the connections in this system are multidirectional. While moral deficiency is connected to blindness (and elsewhere auditory impairment), the character of this moral impairment is not discernible in a physical sense. In other words, a person whose lamp goes out is not (necessarily) physically blind. The rhetorical and exhortatory effects of this passage rest on the assumption that the listener is *not* sensorially impaired. While the association of sin and sensory impairment is unavoidable, the impairment that should concern us is dislocated from any physiological impairment.

Eunuchs for the Kingdom of Heaven (Matt 19:12)

In Matt 19 the evangelist presents the surprising news that Jesus would prefer that his followers live "as eunuchs." Matthew distinguishes between those who were eunuchs from their mother's womb, those made eunuchs by men, those who *live* as eunuchs (presumably celibate lives), and those who make themselves eunuchs for the kingdom of heaven. Matthew's distinction between different kinds of eunuchs mirrors the taxonomy of the Roman jurist Ulpian, who distinguishes between "eunuchs by nature, those who are made eunuchs, and any other kind of eunuchs" (*Digest* 50.16.126). Self-made eunuchs are not a Matthean innovation; they were a feature of the fertility cults of Cybele and Dea Syria.

The reality of the ancient world, however, is that most eunuchs were slaves who were brutalized as a form of punishment, subjugation, or exploitation. While some eunuchs occupied positions of power, they were excluded from traditional structures of succession and were often objects of derision and suspicion. Virgil describes them as strange effeminate foreigners (*Aeneid* 2.693–97), and Lucian calls them "monstrous" (*Eunuch* 6–11). Paradoxically, they were not universally understood to be asexual. Martial portrays them as skilled providers of oral sex (*Epigrams* 3.81; Parsons 2011, 134–35). As a result, we should not dismiss the atypical body of the eunuch and assume that Matthew uses "eunuch" as a mere euphemism or metaphor for celibacy. Eunuchs were not celibate, and there have been some famous examples of early Christians who, reading Matthew literally, castrated themselves (Kuefler 2011).

Clearly, those who "live" as eunuchs and those who make themselves eunuchs are, in some sense, performing disability. They were embracing the marginalizing and socially degrading state that involved abandoning hope of biological procreation. An embodied state that signified social subservience and subjugation is here held up as the desirable state for followers of Jesus. Matthew does not only exhort his audience to celibacy; he exhorts them to become eunuchs.

THE GOSPEL OF MARK

Like Matthew, Mark is a *bios* ("life"), an ancient form of biography. The passion narrative forms the largest section of the Gospel, leading some scholars to argue that the Gospel as a whole is a passion narrative with an extended introduction. Nonetheless, the description of Jesus' ministry focuses on healing stories in particular. After the call of the disciples in chapter 1, Jesus begins by curing Peter's mother-in-law of a fever (Mark 1:29-31). This leads into a succession of healing stories that open the Gospel and shape our understanding of Jesus' mission. The relevancy of the Gospel of Mark to disability stories goes far beyond narratives in which impairments are removed and individuals are reintegrated into the community. The body of Jesus, especially toward the end of his life in the garden of Gethsemane (ch. 14) and crucifixion (ch. 15), presents a counter-narrative about the ways in which ability should be theologized.

HEALING STORIES (MARK 1:21–9:28)

For the author of Mark, bodily wholeness and faith in Jesus are intimately connected. In many ways it is a text that implicitly and explicitly casts persons of disability out of the kingdom of God—implicitly in the sense that everyone who encounters God in Jesus is healed, and explicitly in passages that use the terms "sickness" and "sin" interchangeably. The evangelist relates many instances of healing of blindness, paralysis, and illness resulting from faith. From the healing of the paralytic in chapter 2 to the restoration of Bartimaeus' vision in chapter 10, faith and healing are inextricably connected. In the words of the Markan Jesus, your faith makes you well (Mark 5:34). The message is clear: faithful bodies are healthy, whole bodies.

The prominence of these healing stories and the constant association of faith and wholeness has a marginalizing effect for persons of disability. The Markan Jesus is a cathartic scourge; and as the kingdom of God breaks into the world of Mark's Gospel, disability and illness are systematically removed from it. The blind see, the paralyzed walk, and the sick become healthy. The experiences of the disabled and sick are silenced in a gospel that promotes bodily wholeness as the marker of faithfulness. One cannot help but reach the conclusion that there is no room for disability in the kingdom of God and that salvation and sickness are mutually exclusive.

There are a number of ways that we might wish to interpret this state of affairs positively. We might choose to focus upon the care and attention that Jesus lavishes on the disabled. We might wish to note their privileged positions as the bearers of the greatest amounts of *pistis* ("faithfulness"). We might even offset their faithfulness against the misunderstandings of healthy, bumbling disciples. But we would still have to face the bald fact that the Jesus that traverses ancient Galilee eradicates impairment and that impairment is repeatedly linked to sin and disgrace.

The destructive power of these stories to affect the lives of Christians today should not be underestimated. In an article on epilepsy, Nicole Kelley cites an incident in 2003 in Milwaukee in which an autistic boy named Torrance Cantrell died during a prayer service at Faith Temple Church of the Apostolic Faith. The boy had been repeatedly bound. The church's pastor told the local newspaper that the congregation merely "did what the Book of Matthew said . . . all we did is ask God to deliver him" (2011, 206).

The Opening of the Gospel (Mark 1:29–3:6)

The Gospel of Mark opens with a cluster of healing stories that preempt a cluster of parabolic sayings in chapter 4. Having called the disciples, Jesus heals Peter's mother-in-law (1:29-31), "cleanses" a leper (1:40-45), heals a paralytic who is lowered into a house through slats in the roof (2:1-12), and restores a man's withered hand (3:1-6). Historians have traditionally seen these passages as demonstrations of Jesus' divine power or identity as a "divine man" (*theios anēr*). The evangelist often comments on the magnitude of Jesus' healings such that they are a hallmark of Jesus' missionary activity (1:32-34, 3:10-12, 6:53-56). Additionally, healings are part of the missionary activity of Jesus' disciples (the disciples are chosen to "preach and heal" in 3:15 and fail to exorcize in 9:18).

In the opening chapters of the Gospel, the healing ministry of Jesus is constantly shackled to the idea of faith. Those individuals who show faith (or have friends and relatives who show faith on their behalf) have their sins forgiven and their bodies healed. The demonstration of faith is a necessary precursor to healing in the Gospel. This state of affairs and its accompanying mantra "your sins are forgiven" only reinforce the traditional association of sin and disability. It may well be true that all people are sinful, but in the Gospel of Mark—as in some modern Christian communities—the audience are more frequently asked to reflect upon the sinfulness of the impaired than anyone else.

Given the ubiquity of this theme, it is worth noting that the display of "signs" and wonders is a hallmark of the new age (the longer ending of Mark in 16:17-18 mentions them), but the miraculous is not in and of itself proof of divine sponsorship. We learn that false prophets, too, will show "signs and wonders" (Mark 13:21-22 and Matt 24:24). That the first two evangelists mention the presence of the miraculous among false communities disrupts this idea. Readers should not interpret miraculous cures or able-bodiedness as a sign of holiness or piety.

Sin and Sickness (Mark 2:17)

The synonymy between health and faithfulness is explicitly overlaid in Mark 2:17. In this story Jesus responds to the Pharisees' charge that he should not eat with sinners and tax collectors. Jesus replies by saying, "Those who are well have no need of a physician, but those who are sick; I came not to call the righteous, but sinners." While Jesus' response employs a simile to explain his association with the sinful, the comparison underscores the implicit link between sin and disease. The role of Jesus as physician of souls and the portrayal of sinners as the sick is as striking as it is unsettling. Sinfulness implies failure, and the close association of sickness and sinfulness in this passage implies that sickness likewise connotes failure on the part of those who are sick. In Mark this failure is a lack of faith, for just as Jesus himself says in Mark 9:23, "All things are possible for he who believes."

Possession Stories (Mark 1:23-28; 5:1-20; 7:24-30; 9:14-29, 38-41)

The Gospels contain a number of stories that—using ancient and biblical categories—might be properly described as stories concerned with demonic possession. The author of Mark himself summarizes part of Jesus' missionary activity as "proclaiming the message of the gospel and casting out demons" (1:39), and healing and exorcism are linked in the Gospel (1:32-34).

It is difficult to know whether to think of demonic possession as a disability, an ancient explanation for an impairment, or a wholly other phenomenon (Kelley 2007, 2011). To be sure, demonic possession is the etiology given to certain conditions in the New Testament itself. Modern readers have tended to reset these narratives into modern physiological categories. Some have identified demonic possession as a psychological condition (borderline personality disorders, bipolar disorders, dissociative identity disorders, etc.) but there are other cases, like the Gerasene demoniac of Mark 5, in which supernatural possession has been interpreted as neurological. All of this points to the larger issues of imposing modern diagnostic categories on ancient texts.

In the case of psychoanalytical diagnoses, there have been both varying degrees of success and varying degrees of benefit in these approaches. For those with emotional and neurological disabilities, it has sometimes been helpful to find resources to consult in the text. This approach has been especially successful in dealing with issues surrounding trauma and depression. The association with demonic possession, however, only piles on to the societal prejudices and media caricatures of conditions like autism and borderline personality disorder. There is already the tendency in the broader world to pathologize violence, and layering these uninformed diagnoses with inference of evil can serve to alienate and marginalize persons with disabilities.

It is worth noting at the outset that ancient views of demonic possession did not necessarily view demonic possession as something negative.
"Demons" were not always associated with disruptive behavior or negative
experiences. They were also sources of support, counsel, and inspiration.
The ancient writer Aelius Aristides refers to his *daimon* affectionately. An
accomplished orator, Aelius Aritides traveled the ancient world looking
for a cure for his chronic medical ailment. Even as he went to great lengths
to alleviate his condition, Aristides saw benefits to his condition. He characterizes the relationship between his famous bodily weakness, his personal connection with his daimon, and his oratory as a productive one. He
describes in the *Sacred Tales* how "that famous Pardalas . . . the greatest
expert of the Greeks of our time in the knowledge of rhetoric, dared to
say and affirm to me that I had become ill through some good fortune, so
that by my association with the god, I might make this improvement [in
oration]" (2.259). This twofold approach to the experience of a debilitating
condition in many way maps on to modern studies in which conditions
like depression and bipolar disorder have been linked to creativity and
artistic production.

Legion (Mark 5:1-20)

Even in the New Testament world, demonic possession has its advantages.

In the story of the man known as Legion, we can note how the man's
impairment grants him both superabilities and disables him. The man
appears to be socially alienated and divorced from the community. His living conditions outside the larger community speak to his social marginalization, and the note that no chains could bind him ominously gestures to
the violently restrictive punishments to which he has been subjected. Others have pushed him to the margins and attempted to physically restrain
him. The fact that he is known as "Legion" rather than by his familial
name suggests that in the eyes of those who knew him, his identity had
become coterminous with his condition. He was no longer anything other
than his impairment, and this—in and of itself—was disabling.

At the same time, the man is in possession of superstrength (the chains
were unable to hold him) and, like others possessed by demons, he is one
of the few characters in the Gospel of Mark who actually recognizes Jesus
for who he is. This recognition is unusual. Jesus goes to great lengths to
conceal his identity from others. In fact, only those who are possessed by
demons appear to recognize Jesus for who he is. In New Testament scholarship this is often referred to as the "messianic secret."

The association of specific disabilities with precognitive or supernatural knowledge was common in antiquity. Demons were known for their ability to prophesy the future. In the case of Legion, his special knowledge—however unhappily acquired—gives him the upper hand over other actors in the story. In many ways the exorcism that constitutes the man's "cure" serves to protect Jesus and his identity more than it does the man. The special knowledge afforded to the man on account of his condition narratively acts to disable Jesus by revealing his thus-far-hidden identity. David Mitchell and Sharon Snyder (2013) have referred to "narrative prosthesis" to describe the phenomenon by which a disability appears to facilitate plot development only to vanish in the culmination of the story's plot. In this instance, if demonic possession plays such a role, then its disabling force affects not only the man (who is socially marginalized and mistreated) but also Jesus (whose secret is threatened). The question "Who is disabled by demonic possession in Mark?" is a live one.

The form of the man's healing is notably one of social reintegration. The expulsion of the demons and their reorientation in the swine leads to the acceptance of the man into the community. Ultimately the model presented here is one in which persons with disabilities should be welcomed and accepted into the community rather than rejected and ostracized.

Jairus' Daughter and the Woman with the Flow of Blood (Mark 5:21-43)

The twin stories of Jairus' daughter and the woman with the flow of blood form part of what is typically known as a Markan "sandwich." Jesus is approached and asked to come to the house of Jairus, where his daughter lies dying. As he journeys there, Jesus is approached by a woman with a flow of blood who grasps the hem of his tunic and is healed. The story of the woman's healing is thus sandwiched between the narrative of Jairus' daughter's healing.

Parallels between the two accounts—the girl is twelve years old and the woman has suffered for twelve years—suggest that femininity and womanhood lie at the center of the story. In the history of scholarship, this pericope has attracted the attention of feminist writers interested in the woman's gynecological ailment. These interpretations have centered on the woman's femininity, anonymity, and ritual impurity with great success (D'Angelo 1999).

It is worth noting the way that the woman's gender and the nature of her condition combine to alienate and disable her. While the woman is described as "suffering much [pain]" (*polla pathousa*) as a result of her impairment, it is also socially disabling. She would have been ineligible for marriage, sexually unapproachable, and potentially impure. That the woman had spent the entirety of her financial resources in search of a cure would have added to her socially liminal and imperiled state. Without financial resources or a social network that could support her, the woman was at risk of dying from poverty.

While the healing story follows the traditional Markan scheme of faith and healing, the mechanics of the woman's healing cuts against the dominant Markan narrative that associates disability with sin. I have argued elsewhere that the portrayal of her cure also conforms to the Greco-Roman understanding of the healthy body. In describing her transformation, Mark uses language of hardening and drying up. The Greek term to describe her healing is *exēranthē*, from the root *xērainō*, which literally means "dried up," "scorched," or "hardened." English translations usually render this word as "ceased," presumably to make the event more intelligible for readers, but the Greek implies that the woman's cure is one of bodily hardening and drying. It is noteworthy that where *xērainō* is used elsewhere in the Gospel, it is used to mean scorched or hardened (cf. Mark 3:1, 4:6, 9:18, 11:20-21). The drying up of the woman's blood could have a variety of meanings. It could simply mean that the abnormal bleeding is dried up (D'Angelo 1999, 98). An alternative suggestion cited by Adela Yarbro Collins is that the woman becomes menopausal in anticipation of the genderless eschatological kingdom of God (Collins 2007, 282 n. 149; see also below). Regardless of whether or not we choose to interpret the healing theologically, it is clear not only that the woman's condition has abated but also that her entire body comes to resemble the masculinized healthy body of Greco-Roman medicine (Moss 2010).

Her transition from sickly effeminate leaker to faith-dried healthy follower parallels the faith-based healings of the Gospel of Mark as a whole. The emphasis on her faith as the agent of her healing is typical of Markan miracle stories in general. What is unusual, however, are the *mechanics* of her healing and what these mechanics can tell us about the porosity of Jesus' body. According to Mark 5:30, the woman initiates her own healing by pulling power from an unsuspecting Jesus:

> She had heard the reports about Jesus, and came up behind him in the crowd and *touched his garment*. For she said, "If I touch even his garments, I shall be saved." And immediately *the flow of blood dried up*; and she felt in her body that she was healed of her disease. And Jesus, perceiving in himself *that power*

had gone forth from him, immediately turned about in the crowd, and said,
"Who touched my garments?" (Mark 5:27-30)

According to the narrative, the woman is healed because power
flows out of Jesus through his garments to the woman. The power that
heals the woman does not come from the garments but from Jesus himself. In the words of Mark, the power goes out of him (*ex autou*), not
out of his garments. We cannot argue that Jesus' garments were already
endowed with power by virtue of their proximity to his body because it is
only at the moment that the woman grasps the hem of his garment that
power leaves *the body of Jesus himself*. This is not an act of simple magical
transference from garment to woman; the woman pulls power out of
Jesus himself.

The flow of power is one that is physical and discernible to Jesus himself. He immediately notes the loss of power and demands to know who
touched him. Theological rereadings of this passage have focused on the
apparent loss of power rather than on the body of Jesus itself. But the curious flow of power from Jesus can tell us much about the physiological
composition of the Markan protagonist. In the narrative the flow of power
from Jesus mirrors the flow of blood from the woman. Like the woman,
Jesus is unable to control the flow that emanates from his body. Like the
flow of blood, the flow of power is something embodied and physical; just
as the woman feels the flow of blood dry up, so Jesus feels—physically—
the flow of power leave his body. Both the diseased woman with the flow
of blood and the divine protagonist of Mark are porous, leaky creatures.
Porosity or leakiness was undesirable for ancient Greek and Roman men.
This was predominantly because of the way that corporeal penetrability
affects social status. In the first place, the act of being penetrated—whether
by a disease or by another person—was a marker of inferior social status. It
was morally questionable for a freeborn man to allow himself to be penetrated (Harper 2013). In the second, softer leaky bodies were feminine and
thus inferior and weaker. It is for this reason that the Roman doctor Galen
warned men to abstain from bathing too long in warm water, for fear it
would soften the contours of the body (*On Hygiene* 5.2). This is the situation in which we find Jesus: he is unable to control, regulate, or harden his
porous body. He is not only acutely porous; he is also unable to regulate
and control his own emissions. According to both models, Jesus is sickly.
The nature of his porosity may enable the Markan Jesus to heal others, but
his physiological makeup resembles that of the sick and diseased. Even if
he is the source of healing and the one who creates a legion of able-bodied
followers, the Markan hero is himself physiologically weak. His powers

function along the lines of the pathways of bodily weakness and illness, uncontrollably leaking through his broken skin.

Moreover, in the narrative it is the sickly woman who exerts control over the body of the physician-savior. It is the woman who is able to suck divine power out of the passive, leaky Jesus. This ability is framed using the typical Markan language of faith, but there is no escaping the power that she exerts over his body. This is something of a reversal of fortunes for the physician and patient. Here the disabled woman ably controls the body of the spiritual and physical physician.

Even though the Gospel as a whole promotes health and able-bodiedness as an attribute of the faithful, the Markan protagonist remains porous, leaky, and effeminate. This is a theme that will be picked up again in the Gethsemane agony. The constant affirmation of the power (*dunamis*) of the miracle working Jesus undercuts the traditional association of porosity/sickness and weakness. The porous body—the hallmark of the infirm—is leaky and vulnerable but is nonetheless powerful. In the Gospel of Mark, the one body that truly matters, the body of the Son of God, continues to operate as a sickly diseased body, contaminating others with divine powers but remaining nonetheless porous and, we might say, disabled.

Saying on Autoamputation (Mark 9:42-48)

In chapter 9 of his Gospel, the evangelist Mark offers what is undoubtedly his most concrete statement on the afterlife. In a series of three parallel statements, Mark states that the consequences of sin are dire. Using a rather straightforward formula, Mark's Jesus firmly states and restates that if a body member (here the hand, the foot, or the eye) causes one to sin, then one should cut it off. For it would be better to enter eternal life impaired than to be thrown intact into gehenna, into an unquenchable fire where the worm never sleeps. The nature of the sins alluded to here has drawn a great deal of scholarly attention. The focus of this chapter, however, is on what this passage can tell us about Mark's views of the afterlife and, more specifically, about the continued existence of perceived deformities and disabilities in the kingdom of God.

Traditional scholarship on the nature of the afterlife in Mark 9, based on comparisons with biblical and rabbinic literature, has tended to argue that Mark's references to disability and amputation are primarily metaphorical and rhetorical. Using a two-part argument drawn from rabbinic sources, many scholars have concluded both that Mark thinks that the deformed who enter eternal life will be healed and that the injunction to amputate or blind oneself is not to be taken literally. In response, this commentary will argue two main points: first, that we should not discount the possibility that Mark both envisages the resurrection of deformity and intends his audience to take his injunction literally; second, that even if Mark does not intend his authors to act upon the exhortation, the rhetorical effect of the passage rests upon the assumption that we do understand this passage literally.

With respect to the current question—What does this passage have to say about the preservation of disability in the afterlife?—the situation is more complicated. A number of scholars have pointed to parallels with Second Temple Jewish and rabbinic materials. These texts—most notably *2 Bar.* 50:2 and *Eccl. Rabb.* 1:6—affirm that the dead will rise with the same bodily defects that they possessed in life. As these same scholars have observed, however, the rabbinic texts describe how the disabled will be healed of their infirmities upon entering heaven. To paraphrase Allison, the disabled enter eternal life with their impairments, but they will not remain in that condition once they are there (1998, 140).

At the same time, however, we need to be wary of automatically assuming that Pauline and rabbinic discussions of the afterlife hold the hermeneutical keys to Mark's kingdom. For as even the most cursory reader will note, Mark does not mention eschatological healing at all. While it is possible to infer from other parts of Mark that Mark thinks the eschaton will be marked by healing, he does not give the slightest hint of it here. In fact, the entire rhetoric of the passage hinges on the contrast between deformed eternal life and normal-bodied damnation.

Underlying these scholarly assessments of Mark is the assumption that all ancient constructions of the resurrection and heaven envisioned it as a place of perfection and healing. This idea is strongly supported by passages about the restoration of Israel in Isaiah (29:18; 35:5-7) and the rabbinic examples considered above, yet there were those in the ancient world who were less certain that disability was eradicated in the afterlife. In Greco-Roman mythology, broadly defined, the shade in the underworld preserved all the characteristics of the individual's body in life. Upon learning that he was guilty of patricide and incest, the tragic hero Oedipus famously blinds himself. The act of self-mutilation is a form of punishment that he (mistakenly) thinks will mean that he will no longer serve as a witness to his crimes (Sophocles, *Oedipus rex* 1220-23).

The notion that in the afterlife the anthropomorphized shade preserves the contours of mortal corporeality is found in descriptions of the afterlife in Virgil (*Aeneid* 6.496), in which Deiphobus has neither ears nor a nose. A similar idea is at work in Pindar's myth of the revivification of Pelops, in which Pelops receives a prosthetic shoulder when his bodily shoulder was consumed by Demeter (*Olympian.* 1.26). Such examples are not direct parallels to bodily resurrection, but they hold in common the idea that a person's infirmity persists in one's afterlife, either in one's body or in one's shade. According to these strains of thought, there is "an absolute bodily continuity" between the body as it is now and the individual as he or she will exist after death (Endsjø 2008, 434).

Even if we are not convinced that Mark was familiar with the worldview borne by Homer and Pindar, then we still have to account for the rhetoric of Mark 9:43-48 itself. If Mark holds, with Paul and some rabbinic traditions, that those who are raised are healed, then what does it profit him to omit this concept here? In other words, what is the rhetorical force of eliminating this element of eschatological expectation?

Given that, as we have seen, there are strains of ancient thought in which disability is preserved as a facet of human identity in the afterlife, it is worth reconsidering whether Mark intends us to take his injunction to "cut off" the offending member literally or not. If, as has been argued, the deformed are healed in the hereafter, then why wouldn't Mark encourage his readers to amputate sinful limbs? Self-mutilation could be performed with confidence that the effects are only temporary. Conversely, if Mark is being purely metaphorical, why would it matter whether or not people are healed in heaven? If Mark does not mean to conjure up the notion of actual impairment and physical mutilation, then the rhetorical impact of the pericope is completely undercut.

Not only could Christians read Mark literally, but in many ways the rhetoric of the passage demands that the reader take the injunction literally. In this passage Mark provides an eschatologically oriented commentary on the relative merits of disability and able-bodiedness for the salvation of the individual person. Sin is so corrupting that it would be better to be disabled and enter heaven than to continue to sin as an able-bodied person and be thrown into hell. The argument of the passage is both predictable and unexpected. Mark reproduces a traditional negative evaluation of disability. It is the undesirability of being disabled and the radical suggestion that one should make oneself disabled that makes the saying so powerful. Its efficacy hinges on the assumption that disability is demonstrably inferior to ability. The severity of the audience's situation with respect to sin is amplified by the proposal that they should maim themselves rather than risk damnation. The author harnesses the negativity associated with disability in order to bring home to his audience the imperiled state in which they find themselves. The power of this rhetoric is stymied by the idea that the resurrected dead are healed upon entrance to the kingdom of God.

In this passage Mark employs the negative rhetorical connotations of blindness, lameness, and deformity. It is precisely the undesirability of these conditions that makes the pericope so dramatic and effective. At the same time, however, the passage presents an opportunity for the reinterpretation of Mark's position on disability. The logic of this passage is that sin can be avoided by amputating those limbs or removing those bodily organs that lead one to "stumble." In this passage Mark, like others in antiquity, treats disability not as the consequence of sin but as its preventive. Implicit in this argument is the concept that able-bodiedness can be the *cause* of sin and disability its remedy. The presentation of disability as a prophylaxis for sin rather than as the mark of a sinful person is revolutionary. It muddies the waters of the second evangelist's position on disability. Even as Mark employs the negative rhetorical force of disability, he ultimately revises the standard model of disability in which sin and disability were fundamentally linked. Mark disconnects disability from sin and admits that disabled bodies are accepted in the kingdom of God (Moss and Schipper 2011, 1–2).

Healing of the Boy Possessed by a Spirit (Mark 9:15-29)

The healing of the boy possessed by a spirit (Matt 17:14-21 and Luke 9:37-43) is interesting for a number of reasons. First, the description of the boy's condition is especially vivid. The boy falls down, loses the ability to speak, foams at the mouth, and becomes rigid. It has inspired great commentary by modern readers who have identified the boy as an epileptic (Kelley 2011, 2009). Second, it is not the faith of the boy but his father that is instrumental for the expulsion of the spirit (Mark 9:24). Third, the disciples are unable to drive out the demon from the boy, and Jesus instructs them that there is a specific religious protocol for dealing with the spirit. And, fourth, it is this story that supplies the common rhetoric for the idea that "all things are possible for the one who believes."

The Matthean version of the story augments Mark by supplying a kind of diagnosis. Matthew's version describes the boy only as *seleniazomai* ("moonstruck" or "lunatic"), an interpretation that maintained with popular medicine of the time that the moon could cause periodical disorders of this kind. Matthew's general interpretation of the boy's condition is more therapeutic. All three Synoptic Gospels, however, attribute the cause of the boy's condition to a demon, and the language used in the stories is largely exorcistic.

Bartimaeus (Mark 10:46-52)

As Jesus and the disciples journey to Jericho, they encounter a blind beggar named Bartimaeus, or "son of Timaeus." Traditional interpretations have identified Bartimaeus as an unimportant cipher for faith and healing. But this is the first time we have an impaired character within the narrative who is named. Names have a particular significance to Mark, so we should assume that the beggar's name is also important. Some have taken Timaeus to come from the Aramaic *tamea* ("unclean"). This interpretation would suggest that Mark finds Bartimaeus to be not only blind but also unclean and in need of Jesus' healing. A Greek root is equally plausible; Earle Hilgert (1996), as well as others, has pointed out that Timaeus can also be taken from the Greek word *timaios*, which means "honored." The biases of scholars are clearly on display, but why would Bartimaeus be honored?

A close reading of the passage suggests that Bartimaeus knows more than we think. Not only does he (almost uniquely in the synoptic tradition) recognize that Jesus is the "Son of David," but when he jumps up he also casts aside his cloak. The action of casting aside worldly possession is evocative of the demands of discipleship concatenated earlier in the Gospel (Culpepper 1982, 132; Rowland 2013). The action, says Rowland, lets the audience know that this is a "call to discipleship."

Robert Rowland, a New Testament scholar who experiences vision impairment, has argued that we should consider Bartimaeus in the context of the "blind seer" in antiquity. Drawing upon examples of blind prophets in the ancient world, Rowland argues that blindness was often accompanied by other gifts (foresight, knowledge, philosophy, memory, and vocal abilities). Read in this context, Rowland suggests Bartimaeus' blindness is actually a cue to the reader that Bartimaeus can discern more than other individuals. He is, argues Rowland, a kind of biblical sage who contrasts with the able-bodied disciples, who constantly misunderstand Jesus' identity and message. In the case of Bartimaeus, blindness signifies not sinfulness or doubt but his superior knowledge and understanding of the divine plan.

Rowland concludes his arguments about Bartimaeus with a caution drawn from Martha Rose, concluding that literary topoi like the blind sage can dominate the conversation about lived experiences of blindness (Rose

2006, 77). Impaired persons in the ancient world may have found examples like Bartimaeus (or his classical counterparts) inspiring at the same time they may have been constraining, alienating, and misrepresentative. With this important caveat in mind, however, it is important to note that this story does not in fact present Bartimaeus as a problem to be solved so much as a model disciple (Achtemeier 1978).

Like the Angels in Heaven (Mark 12:24-25)

In chapter 12 the Sadducees, well-known for their opposition to the idea of bodily resurrection, come to Jesus to question him about his opinions on the afterlife. In contrast, Jesus' confident response to the question asserts the fallacy of their belief in sexual relations in the afterlife. He states:

> Is not this the reason you are wrong, that you know neither the scriptures nor the power of God? For when they rise from the dead, they neither marry nor are given in marriage, but are like angels in heaven. (Mark 12:24-25)

Jesus then proceeds to adduce biblical proof for the belief in the resurrection. But the social awkwardness of polyandry in the afterlife is moot, as the dead neither marry nor are given in marriage. Marital relations in heaven do not feature in contemporary Jewish descriptions of eschatological resurrection.

There is no doubt whatsoever about the nature of postresurrection marital life. Whereas just moments before he had used wit to evade the questions of the Pharisees and Herodians over tribute to Caesar (Mark 12:13-17), his response here is straightforward and serious. The focus of his response is to rebuff the claims of the Sadducees that they know Scripture, but in the course of rebuking them, he states quite clearly that the resurrected dead are unmarried, like the angels. Given that Jesus, like all other ancient Jews, thought that sex should be reserved for marriage, it seems that sex is eliminated in the afterlife.

Later interpreters of the story of the healing of the woman with the flow of blood interpreted her healing as a prefiguration of the resurrection of the body (Moss and Baden 2015). They argued that she was *not* restored to fertility but that in her barrenness she becomes a model of the eschatological body. This interpretation is supported by chapter 10 as it eliminates sex, marriage, and procreation in one fell swoop. The question is, then, What counts as healing and salvation in the Gospel of Mark and for us as readers? And, when it comes to the woman with the flow of blood, we have to ask ourselves: Is being healed the same as becoming fertile? Is it possible that the idealized early Christian body is infertile? If eschatological bodies are perfect, it seems that bodily perfection for early Christians—in distinction to other ancient readers—means infertility. The biblical and early Christian interest in infertile bodies as prefigurations of the eschaton can help explain why Matthew instructs his readers to make themselves eunuchs for the kingdom of heaven and why the eunuch of Acts 12 is *not* "healed" (he is already perfect!) and forces us to reassess our own definitions of disability and ability. Infertility here is able-bodiedness (Moss and Baden 2015, chs. 3 and 6). The foundations of ableist assumptions about healing shake when we realize that the resurrection might mean *impairing* rather than healing.

Passion Narrative (Mark 14-15)

Gethsemane Agony (Mark 14:32-42)

The night before his death, after the last supper, Jesus and his disciples go out of the city to the garden of Gethsemane. This incident is known as the Gethsemane agony because it is here that Jesus prays mournfully alone before his death. In Mark's version Jesus is unsteady, passionate, and grieves over his imminent death. He asks his disciples to stay awake with him to keep him company, and he begs God, his father, that "the cup" (i.e., death) might pass from him (Mark 14:36).

In Mark's version Jesus is desperate and in need of comfort. He asks the disciples to stay awake with him because he is grieving. He is described as distressed and agitated and begs God, as his son, using the familial, childlike term "Abba." In Luke Jesus feels no distress at all. He instructs the disciples to pray for themselves and, while he still asks God to remove the cup, the whole scene has an almost businesslike feel to it. What was once a story about the struggle of Jesus has now become something of a test for his disciples. All references to the idea that Jesus suffered emotional anguish, was "disturbed," "agitated," or "distressed," have been removed. In Mark Jesus' distress is apparent even in his comportment: he "falls to the ground" to pray (Mark 14:35). Compare this to Luke's more sturdy and precise "got down on his knees and prayed" (Luke 22:41).

The Jesus of Mark's Gethsemane agony seems to have caused interpretive issues for the author of Luke. The reason for this is Jesus' passionate and emotional response to his predicament. Even his comportment is affected by his distress. To ancient readers this kind of conduct was both effeminate and weak. Ancient readers would have understood Jesus to be more emotional and more distressed than modern readers do. Jesus' conduct is more akin to those suffering trauma and distress and offers a model for catharsis (Kotrosits and Taussig 2013).

Crucifixion (Mark 15:34)

Jesus' desperation only grows more fevered as he dies. On the cross his final words are words of abandonment; he cries out, "My God, my God why have you forsaken me?" (Mark 15:34). The cumulative image is one of a man broken and betrayed, desperately clasping at life, and mournfully accepting death. To paraphrase the words of Bible scholar and Nobel Prize winner Albert Schweitzer, Jesus appears crushed by the wheel of history (1910, 301–11). The very world that he had hoped to influence has trampled him and, at the very end, he is alone and disillusioned. It is a poignant theme full of emotion.

As modern readers, we might be overwhelmed with empathy for Jesus. But if we were to imagine ourselves as ancient audience members, then the death of Jesus appears weak and feminine. Ancient readers—philosophers especially—idealized self-controlled death as the mark of manliness. The Roman stoic philosopher Seneca, for instance, writes that imprisonment and impending death "changed Socrates' soul so little that they did not even change his expression" and that Socrates was an example of "how to die if it is necessary" (Seneca, *Epistle* 104.28, 21). Placed in this context, Jesus' comportment both at Gethsemane and on the cross seems unmanly and feminine. In the binaries that separated male/female, healthy/sick, and strong/weak, Jesus' own body suggests that rather than being a miraculous powerful wonder-worker or a Johannine God-walking-the-earth, he is weak and suffering. He was, in the eyes of ancient readers, disabled.

Christian interpretations of the death of Jesus in Mark have sought to downplay this problem. Since the early church, patristic authors have argued that the apparent weakness of Jesus is highlighted in Mark to show his "human side." Jesus appears weak so that no one could mistakenly think that he's only a god. Bible scholars have pointed out that Jesus' words of despair are citations of psalms that begin despondently but conclude with promises of restoration. Psalm 22, from which the words "My God, my God why have you forsaken me?" are taken, concludes on a much more hopeful note. It is likely that Mark invokes echoes of the whole Psalm in order to imply—to those who catch the allusions—that Jesus' death, though tragic, will in the end turn out for the good.

Whatever the structure of the whole, the passion narrative offers an unlikely frame to the Markan message on healing. If the Gospel begins with the message that Jesus emerges precisely to eradicate bodily differ- ence and that "all things are possible for God," then it concludes with a much cloudier picture of how God responds to and regards disability. The Jesus of the passion narrative is weakened and would have been regarded as weak and feminine. In the garden of Gethsemane he begs that the "cup might pass" from him, and on the cross he cries in anguished despair that he has been forgotten. There is no softening, self-controlled statement to follow this up. Read alongside one another, these two strains of thought create a productive tension:, the God that can and does heal all who approach him in faith does not grant Jesus' request. The source of power is also a site of weakness. And, as we saw in the story of the healing of the woman with the flow of blood, the mechanics of bodily weakness may ever facilitate the problematic healing of others.

The tension between power and weakness and healing and wholeness is itself helpful because it articulates the multifaceted experience of disabil- ity. Traditional readings of the Gospel of Mark have fostered an under- standing of disability as a problem to be fixed by God, but the Gospel also supplies a model of a suffering and weakened savior who faithfully asks for relief and does not receive it. Moreover, the weakened body of Jesus is instrumentally important in the catharsis of others. When we look closely, it appears that Mark's Jesus is not only disabled; he is powerfully disabled.

CONCLUSION

Traditional readings of Matthew and Mark portray them as proponents of the idea that disability is a problem that is fixed by Jesus, provided that the disabled person has the requisite amount of faith. There is plenty of evidence to support this reading. Illness and sensory perception deficits are regularly used as images for sinfulness, and all who encounter Jesus with faith are healed of their condition. At the same time, there are cracks in this story. In contrast to Mark's narrative of bumbling disciples, it is people with disabilities who possess the ability to recognize who Jesus is.

A great deal of the limitations of earlier scholarship on disability in Matthew and Mark is grounded in a failure of imagination that springs from mild ableism. If we put aside our assumptions about the kinds of bodies that are desirable to God, we start to read the Gospels afresh. It is, as we have seen, possible that God instructs us to remove limbs, eye, or genitals. The idea that bodily limitation is preferred and persists in the hereafter is a general point that bears making and remaking.

Perhaps the most exciting area of inquiry, though, is the manner in which disabled experiences can be overlaid onto biblical commands. Our study of proprioception and bodily spatial awareness shows that there are cases in which disabled bodies are better suited to biblical living. A huge area of biblical studies seeks to contextualize these ancient texts in the ancient world. Perhaps in the future this kind of contextualization will cease to assume that day-to-day life in the ancient world was able-bodied.

WORKS CITED

Achtemeier, Paul. 1978. "'And He Followed Him': Miracles and Discipleship in Mark 10:46-52." *Semeia* 11: 115–45.

Allison, Dale C., Jr. 1987. "The Eye Is the Lamp of the Body (Matthew 6:22-23 = Luke 11:34-36)." *New Testament Studies* 33: 61–83.

Avalos, Hector, Sarah Melcher, and Jeremy Schipper, eds. 2007. *This Abled Body: Rethinking Disability and Biblical Studies*. Semeia Studies 55. Atlanta: Society of Biblical Literature.

Baden, Joel S. 2011. "The Nature of Barrenness in the Hebrew Bible." Pages 13–28 in *Disability Studies and Biblical Studies*. Edited by Candida R. Moss and Jeremy Schipper. New York: Palgrave Macmillan.

Betz, Hans Dieter. 1979. "Matthew vi.22f and Ancient Greek Theories of Vision." Pages 43–56 in *Text and Interpretation: Studies in the New Testament Presented to Matthew Black*. Edited by Ernest Best and R. McLachlan Wilson. Cambridge: Cambridge University Press.

Culpepper, R. Alan. 1982. "Mark 10:50: Why Mention the Garment?" *Journal of Biblical Literature* 101, no. 1: 131–32.

Collins, Adela Yarbro. 2007. *Mark: A Commentary*. Hermeneia. Minneapolis, Minn.: Fortress.

Davis, Lennard J. 1995. *Enforcing Normalcy: Disability, Deafness and the Body*. New York: Verso Press.

D'Angelo, Mary Rose. 1999. "Gender and Power in the Gospel of Mark: The Daughter of Jairus and the Woman with the Flow of Blood." Pages 83–109 in *Miracles in Jewish and Christian Antiquity: Imagining Truth*. Edited by John C. Cavadini. Notre Dame Studies in Theology. Notre Dame, Ind.: University of Notre Dame Press.

Endsjø, Dag Oistein. 2003. "Immortal Bodies, before Christ: Bodily Continuity in Ancient Greece and 1 Corinthians." *Journal of the Study of the New Testament* 30: 417–36.

Harper, Kyle. 2013. *From Shame to Sin: The Christian Transformation of Sexual Morality in Late Antiquity*. Revealing Antiquity 20. Cambridge, Mass.: Harvard University Press.

Hilgert, Earle. 1996. "Son of Timaeus: Blindness, Sight, Ascent, Vision in Mark." Pages 185-198 in *Reimagining Christian Origins: A Colloquium*

Honoring Burton L. Mack. Edited by Elizabeth A. Castelli and Hal Taussig. Valley Forge, Pa.: Trinity International.

Kelley, Nicole. 2007. "Deformity and Disability in Greece and Rome." Pages 31–45 in *This Abled Body: Rethinking Disabilities in Biblical Studies*. Edited by Hector Avalos, Sarah Melcher, and Jeremy Schipper. Semeia Studies 55. Atlanta: Society of Biblical Literature.

———. 2011. "'The Punishment of the Devil Was Apparent in the Torment of the Human Body': Epilepsy in Ancient Christianity." Pages 205–22 in *Disability Studies and Biblical Studies*. Edited by Candida R. Moss and Jeremy Schipper. New York: Palgrave Macmillan.

Kotrosits, Maia, and Hal Taussig. 2013. *Re-reading the Gospel of Mark Amidst Loss & Trauma*. New York: Palgrave Macmillan.

Kuefler, Matthew. 2011. *The Manly Eunuch: Masculinity, Gender Ambiguity, and Cheristian Ideoogy in Late Antiquity*. Chicago: University of Chicago Press.

Lawrence, Louise J. 2013. *Sense and Stigma in the Gospels*. Biblical Refigurations. Oxford: Oxford University Press.

Levin, Yigal. 2006. "Jesus, 'Son of God' and 'Son of David': The 'Adoption' of Jesus into the Davidic Line." *Journal for the Study of the New Testament* 28: 415–42.

Mitchell, David, and Sharon Snyder. 2013. "Narrative Prosthesis." Pages 222–35 in *The Disability Studies Reader*. Edited by Lennard J. Davis. New York: Routledge.

Moss, Candida R. 2010. "The Man with the Flow of Power: Porous Bodies in Mark 5:25-34." *Journal of Biblical Literature* 129, no. 3: 507–19.

———. 2011. "Blurred Vision and Ethical Confusion: The Rhetorical Function of Matt 6:22-23." *Catholic Biblical Quarterly* 73, no. 4: 757–76.

Moss, Candida R., and Joel S. Baden. 2015. *Reconceiving Infertility: Biblical Perspectives on Barrenness*. Princeton: Princeton University Press.

Moss, Candida R., and Jeremy Schipper. 2011. "Introduction." Pages 1–12 in *Disability Studies and Biblical Literature*. Edited by Candida Moss and Jeremy Schipper. New York: Palgrave Macmillan.

Parsons, Mikeal C. 2011. *Body and Character in Luke and Acts: The Subversion of Physiognomy in Early Christianity*. Waco, Tex.: Baylor University Press.

Rose, Martha L. 2006. *The Staff of Oedipus: Transforming Disability in Ancient Greece*. Corporealities: Discourses of Disability. Ann Arbor: University of Michigan Press.

Rowland, Robert. 2013. "Bartimaeus: The Blind Paradox." Unpublished paper presented in the Disability and Healthcare Section of the annual meeting of the Society of Biblical Literature, Baltimore, Md.

Schweitzer, Albert. 1910. *The Quest of the Historical Jesus: A Critical Study of Its Progress from Reimarus to Wrede*. London: Black.

.

9

Luke–Acts

David F. Watson

Reading through Luke and Acts with an eye toward disabilities brings out the great extent to which the wellbeing—physical, emotional, and social—of individuals is headlined in these works. Luke cares about bodies—disabled or without disability, poor or rich, sick or healthy. Our existence is not limited to the physical, but our corporeal existence really does matter. It matters to God, and therefore it should matter to us. For Luke it is not the poor in spirit who are blessed (Matt 5:3) but "you who are poor" (Luke 6:20), not those who hunger and thirst for righteousness (Matt 5:6) but "you who are hungry now" (Luke 6:21). Only Luke among the evangelists gives us the parable of the rich man and Lazarus (16:19-31), in which the poor and sick Lazarus is carried away by angels to be with Abraham. Only Luke tells us the story in which Jesus heals ten people with leprosy at once (17:11-19), or the parable of the good Samaritan (10:25-37), the hero of which binds up the wounds and cares for the physical needs of the wounded man. Luke cares about bodies and spends much of his time talking about why we should care for them as well.

Additionally, Luke cares about minds and emotions. Luke's Jesus casts out demons believed to cause insanity or physical harm to the people whom they inhabit (8:27, 9:39). Jesus absolves the pain of feeling oneself sinful (7:36-50) and offers acceptance to people who are shunned (19:1-10). The emotional stress that these conditions cause is compounded by the social isolation that they create. In reading these passages, we do well to remember that disability can occur not just through the body but also through the mind and emotions, and each of these has a social dimension.

Depression, extreme anxiety, and more serious forms of mental illness, as well as cognitive disability, all have the potential to damage one's quality of life, break down healthy relationships, and create isolation.

This leads to an important point: Luke's concern is not simply with the physical, mental, or emotional aspects of life, but the social as well. Indeed, every physical, cognitive, or emotional disability is fraught with social significance. The woman with hemorrhages is not only healed but presumably allowed to return to relationships from which she had been separated because of issues of purity. After healing the ten people with leprosy, Jesus sends them to show themselves to the priests so that they could be restored back into society. He calls a woman "with a spirit that had crippled her for eighteen years" a "daughter of Abraham"—an unusual term, but one that allows her to assume her rightful cultural place (Parsons 2011, 87–89). Luke shows a clear awareness that to deviate from physical, cognitive, or emotional norms is to stand at a considerable social disadvantage.

The following pages will approach Luke–Acts from a social-scientific and historical perspective. We will work through an inventory of and commentary upon passages in Luke–Acts that depict people with disabilities. We will attempt to pull back the curtain on the world of Luke–Acts in terms of some of its important cultural assumptions. In so doing we will need to look at the ways in which common ideas about the body, appearance, and gender come to bear on Luke's presentation. Luke does not have a modern concept of disability, nor should we expect him to. Within the Greco-Roman context, what we think of as "disability" today would probably have been thought of in terms of "defect" or "inability." The physiognomic assumptions of the day meant that persons with disabilities could be perceived as deficient in character. Likewise, people throughout the Greco-Roman world, including within Judaism, often assigned negative religious significance to the conditions of people with disabilities. For example, a disability might be seen as a divine punishment, or a child born with some type of visible physical deviation from a "normal" infant might be perceived as a divine portent.

Additionally, it will be important to bring the social-scientific and historical perspective into dialogue with concepts derived from the modern social and cultural models of disability. As Amos Yong writes, "Whatever else disability is, it is also the experience of discrimination, marginalization, and exclusion from the social, cultural, political, and economic domains of human life" (2007, 99). Proponents of the social model of disability suggest a distinction between impairment and disability. An impairment is a physical, mental, or emotional nonnormative characteristic that one can diagnose medically. A disability, however, is the social disadvantage that a person with an impairment encounters as a result of his or her impairment (see Moss and Schipper 2011, 3–4). According to the cultural model, disability is "a product of the ways that cultures use physical and cognitive differences to narrate, organize, and interpret their world. Whereas in the social model, disability refers to a type of social discrimination, in the cultural model descriptions of disability become one way by which we create or shape culture" (4). Clearly, the social and cultural models share a great deal in common, particularly that disability is a category brought about by commonplace attitudes, actions, and practices.

As Hans Reinders points out, however, the understanding of disability as a social construction has come under some critique because "not only social conditions but also physical conditions may be responsible for the fact that people suffer from their disability, none of which the social model has any interest in pursuing" (2008, 63). This critique would apply to the cultural model as well. There can be disadvantages to a physical or mental impairment other than those that are socially and culturally determined. To put the matter more concretely, even if one were to eliminate all the social stigma around leprosy in Luke's world, and even if "leprosy" was not used as a category of creating and organizing the culture itself within the world of Luke's narrative, the person who experienced the symptoms we associate with leprosy would still suffer from his or her condition. It would hurt. It might lead to infections. It might shorten one's life. The social and cultural aspects of this condition do not exhaust its effects upon a person's life.

Within Luke–Acts, which makes up about one-fourth of the New Testament, the range of impairments is indeed broad and varied. The forms of isolation, exclusion, stigma, and taboo related to these impairments are proportionally broad. With these issues in mind, I will offer an analysis of relevant passages in canonical order, treating some very brief passages and passing references at the end. I will focus primarily on exegetical concerns, with special attention to the ways in which impairments create social dislocation. I will then offer some concluding comments on Luke, disability, and the social world.

PEOPLE WITH DISABILITIES IN LUKE–ACTS

LUKE 1:5-25: ELIZABETH'S DISABILITY

In the world in which the story of Elizabeth takes place, the inability to conceive carried with it serious social consequences (Schaberg 1998, 371).

According to Rebecca Raphael, infertility is "the defining female disability in the Hebrew Bible (and in other ancient Near Eastern literature)" (2008, 57–58). Elizabeth herself refers to her inability to conceive as "my reproach (ὄνειδος, *oneidos*) among people" (Luke 1:25), echoing in Greek the words of Rachel, freed from such reproach after she has given birth to Joseph (LXX Gen 30:23). Luke describes God's granting of a son to Elizabeth as an act of "mercy" (ἔλεος, *eleos*; 1:58). In addition to the verbal allusion to Rachel, the story calls to mind Old Testament accounts of Sarah and Hannah. After Abraham and Hagar conceive a child together, we read that Hagar looked contemptuously upon Sarah (Gen 16:5). Of Hannah we read, "Her rival used to provoke her severely, to irritate her, because the Lord had closed her womb" (1 Sam 1:6). With these stories as a backdrop, we are to see that Elizabeth's infertility is a source of disgrace and isolation.

This narrative points forward to God's plan to redeem Israel and bring salvation to the gentiles. Elizabeth becomes an agent of God's saving work. From the perspective of the story, the conception of John is a sign of God's favor toward Elizabeth and a removal of her reproach among her people. For those who might have thought of Elizabeth's "barrenness" as a sign of divine disfavor, Luke shows that quite the opposite is true. Elizabeth is the recipient of divine favor in God's good time, as were Sarah, Rachel, and Hannah. One cannot assume, then, the absence of divine favor based upon infertility.

Yet we should note that Elizabeth's reproach is taken away only *after* she becomes pregnant. Her social dislocation is healed not by, say, a divine message that she should not be the object of reproach because she cannot bear children but by her pregnancy. Of course, the pregnancy is necessary to advance the story and narrate the miraculous conception and birth of John. It also ties the story into the broader salvation history of Israel. Yet it is worth noting that the system of values that allows for the disgrace of women who do not bear children remains in place. To the extent that Luke challenges this system of values in this story, the challenge is slight.

Later in Luke, however, there is an interesting exchange between Jesus and a woman listening to his teaching. According to Luke 11:27, she raises her voice and says to Jesus, "Blessed is the womb that bore you and the breasts that nursed you!" Jesus' response is, "Blessed rather (μενοῦν, *menoun*) are those who hear the word of God and obey it!" (11:28). The Greek word *menoun* is used to emphasize or correct (Culy, Parsons, and Stigall 2010, 391). If the bearing of children was considered a blessing, the bearing of Jesus would be all the more so. Yet here Jesus corrects the attribution of blessing: it is not through childbirth, his or some other, that blessing is conferred, but through the hearing and obeying of the word of God. In this case Luke expresses a more countercultural view of the significance of childbearing than in the story of Elizabeth.

LUKE 4:31-37: A MAN WITH THE SPIRIT OF AN UNCLEAN DEMON

Modern Western academics have most often dismissed or avoided the matters of possession and exorcism as products of an ancient worldview unacceptable for serious consideration in the modern context. The influence of Pentecostal and charismatic traditions increasing in the global south and a greater number of scholars of these traditions contributing to academic conversations worldwide has mitigated this tendency somewhat.[1] Regardless of the way in which we understand the New Testament stories of possession, however, it is important to identify the dangers involved in attributing disabling conditions to demonic forces (Kelley 2011). In particular, the stigma of mental illness can be compounded by the stigma of demonic influence. Failure to treat appropriately a mental or emotional disability could result from attributing it inaccurately to demonic influence. A person experiencing mental illness could be traumatized by practices of exorcism. The list could go on. Certainly in Luke's worldview, however, demonic possession was quite real, as were its consequences, and exorcism was the effective remedy.

In 4:31-37 Jesus encounters a man with the "spirit of an unclean demon" (v. 33). The man is described as being "in the synagogue," so perhaps he was not manifesting unusual behavior before Jesus' arrival. Nevertheless, the possessed man regards Jesus with fear and hostility, and he seems to know preternaturally of Jesus' identity. Jesus commands the demon, "Be silent, and come out of him!" (v. 35). The Greek word φιμώθητι (*phimōthēti*, lit. "be muzzled") is part of a common exorcistic formula (Luz 1983, 81). The demon does leave the man, but not before hurling him upon the ground in the midst of the onlookers. We do not gain from this story very much knowledge of the possessed man's behavior

---

[1] "Pentecostals in general share a New Testament belief in the possibility of demonic influence in human behaviour. Some will call this 'demon possession,' 'oppression,' or 'demonisation,' but the net result is that the persons suffering from this form of affliction need 'deliverance' or 'exorcism.' This has always been a prominent part of Pentecostal and Charismatic practice (esp. in the Majority World), often conducted in the inner rooms and private counselling sessions of churches and exhibiting a wide variety of procedures" (Anderson 2006, 117; see also Park 2011, 85–103).

except for the fact that he shouts, speaks from the perspective of a persona not his own, and does not have control of his own body. Today, in much of the world, a person exhibiting these characteristics would be diagnosed with some form of mental illness. The stigma of mental illness in our own context can be considerable, but the stigma of being possessed by "the spirit of an unclean demon" in Luke's day must have been even more severe. Quite apart from the fear that demon possession would inspire and the designation of the demon as "unclean," no one who appears to be out of control of his or her mind and body could function effectively in normal social relationships.

LUKE 5:12-16: A MAN WITH LEPROSY RESTORED TO COMMUNITY

In the world of first-century Judaism, which is the background for Luke's narrative through Acts 7, bodily boundaries are of considerable importance regarding issues of purity and pollution. Certainly it was not the case that most Israelite people walked around consistently in a state of ritual purity. Purity related primarily to a bodily state acceptable to temple-related religious activities. Some Jewish people, such as Pharisees, seem to have viewed things differently than most other Jews, bringing matters of purity much more squarely into everyday life rather than understanding it primarily in terms of cultic matters. Broadly speaking, however, the potential for people to pollute by way of transgression of bodily boundaries was a serious matter.

One form of the violation of bodily boundaries occurs in the variety of skin diseases grouped under the broad heading of leprosy. In the modern context, when we speak of leprosy we most often mean Hansen's disease, a bacterial infection that causes pronounced lesions and bumps on the skin. As Joseph Zias notes, however, to identify biblical leprosy with Hansen's disease is a mistake:

> For decades, medical historians have realized that Levitical leprosy (chapters 13–14) is a generic term covering a wide range of skin diseases (e.g., psoriasis) that were regarded as being cultically unclean. Due to complicated semantic issues and errors in translation of the Old Testament into other languages, the lay public continues today to view true leprosy or Hansen's disease with horror. The biblical command that they should reside outside the camp of Israel (Leviticus 13:46) is still taken literally around the world, despite the fact that the Bible is not referring to modern leprosy. The 12 million estimated sufferers of the disease (World Health Organization) are still shunned by many people. (1991, 149)

The point from the biblical perspective is not the medical diagnosis but the symptoms. Skin diseases designated as "leprous" allow for one person to pollute another. Leviticus 13 discusses many criteria by which a person with a skin disease may be designated as unclean. There were indeed consequences for such a designation:

> The person who has the leprous disease shall wear torn clothes and let the hair of his head be disheveled; and he shall cover his upper lip and cry out, "Unclean, unclean." He shall remain unclean as long as he has the disease; he is unclean. He shall live alone; his dwelling shall be outside the camp. (Lev 13:45-46)

Until such a person underwent rituals for purification described in Lev 14 and was certified as clean by a priest, he or she would be ostracized. We see this again in Num 5:2-4, in which God instructs Moses, "'Command the Israelites to put out of the camp everyone who is leprous, or has a discharge, and everyone who is unclean through contact with a corpse; you shall put out both male and female, putting them outside the camp; they must not defile their camp, where I dwell among them.' The Israelites did so, putting them outside the camp; as the Lord had spoken to Moses, so the Israelites did."

The extent to which these regulations were imposed in different times and places is unclear. Within Luke's narrative, however, it does appear that lepers are ostracized, and Jesus' healing of them represents the potential for their return to society and normal relationships. After Jesus heals the leper of Luke 5:12-16, he instructs him to show himself to the priest and, "as Moses commanded, make an offering for your cleansing, for a testimony to them" (5:14). This is as much a social healing as it is physical. By healing the medical condition, Jesus opened the way for this man's return to normal relationships.

It is noteworthy that in healing this leper Jesus touches him. Jesus does not need to touch in order to heal. In the healing of the centurion's servant recounted in 7:1-10, Jesus is not even in the house where the servant lies. Likewise, in the healing of the ten lepers in 17:11-19, there is no indication that Jesus touches them. Yet here, in the healing of this leper, the text is clear: "Jesus stretched out his hand [and] touched him" (5:13). As in many other cases, Jesus cures the disease, but here he does so in such a way as to reject the social boundary created by leprosy. Without Jesus' touching the leper, one could read his healing as an accommodation to or even perpetuation of the system of exclusion. Instead, Luke portrays Jesus as rejecting the system of exclusion. Contrast this with the story of Naaman the Syrian in 2 Kgs 5:1-19 (mentioned in Luke 4:27). Elijah does not touch Naaman.

Indeed, he does not even come out of his house but instead sends a messenger telling Naaman to bathe in the Jordan seven times.

Yet what of Jesus' instruction to the man to "show yourself to the priest, and, as Moses commanded, make an offering for your cleansing, for a testimony to them" (Luke 5:14)? Perhaps this is also an accommodation to prevailing norms of exclusion, but there are two items that we should consider before rendering judgment. First, regardless of Jesus' own rejection of the norms excluding this man, the wider culture does not share Jesus' perspective on this matter. Without going through the ritual for purification, the man will not be restored to society. Second, Jesus sends the man to the priest "as a testimony to them" (5:14). Perhaps the meaning of this qualifying statement is that Jesus' act of healing will witness not only to his power but also to his refusal to exclude the leper on the basis of purity laws.

LUKE 5:17-26: A PARALYZED MAN WITH FAITHFUL FRIENDS

Commonly in Luke–Acts, though particularly in Luke, we encounter characters with impaired limbs or impaired mobility. The first of these to appear in the narrative is the paralytic of Luke 5:17-26. Jesus is healing in a house, and some men bring a paralyzed man on a bed. They cannot get to Jesus because of the great crowd around him, so they climb on top of the roof and lower the paralytic through a hole they make. Jesus is impressed with their faith and says to the paralytic, "Friend, your sins are forgiven you" (5:20). When the scribes and Pharisees who see this raise questions and accuse Jesus of blasphemy, Jesus asks them, "Which is easier, to say, 'Your sins are forgiven you,' or to say, 'Stand up and walk'?" Jesus continues, "'But so that you may know that the Son of Man has authority on earth to forgive sins'—he said to the one who was paralyzed—'I say to you, stand up and take your bed and go to your home'" (5:23-24). The paralyzed man does exactly that.

Immediately, the question arises: Do Jesus' words indicate a connection between impairment and sin? In other words, does Jesus heal the paralysis by forgiving the sin, an act that would indicate that the paralysis is a punishment for sin? Or is it the case that Jesus is demonstrating his authority to forgive sins by a more tangible demonstration of his authority to heal the sick? The sequence of events, taken over from Mark 2:1-12, is

a. demonstration of faith by the friends of the paralyzed man, and possibly by the paralyzed man himself (Luke 5:18-20)
b. pronouncement of the forgiveness of sins (5:20)

a¹. demonstration of faithlessness on the part of the scribes and Pharisees (5:21)

b². instructions to the paralyzed man to take up his bed and go home (5:24).

It is possible to read this story in such a way that Jesus' forgiveness of sins effects the healing. In this case one could draw a connection between the man's paralysis and unforgiven sin. This reading, however, is problematic. If there is a direct connection implied between sin and sickness, one wonders why the paralytic did not immediately get up after Jesus pronounced the forgiveness of his sins. John Nolland (1989, 236) argues, "The challenge of Jesus' question is: 'You are scandalized at this act of mine which is not subject to public verification. What will you make of this other which is plain for all the world to see?'" One could, in fact, read this passage to suggest that Jesus sees in this man more than the man's physical impairment. Rather, Jesus attends to his state of righteousness before doing anything else, and then he tends to the man's physical and social well-being. The phrase "so that you may know that the Son of Man has authority on earth to forgive sins" (5:24) suggests that the healing demonstrates Jesus' authority to forgive sins. It does not, however, necessarily mean that the healing *results from* the forgiveness of the sin. Jesus possesses the authority of God, and therefore he has the authority to forgive sins. The visible expression of Jesus' divine authority lends credence to the invisible one.

Luke 6:6-11: A Man Who Is Unable to Use His Hand and a Sabbath Controversy

Three healing stories in Luke highlight Jesus' interpretation of the Torah in ways that relate to human well-being (6:6-11, 13:10-17, 14:1-6). In the first of these, Jesus encounters a man who has an impaired hand. Unlike the parallel stories in Matthew (12:9-14) and Mark (3:1-6), Luke's story specifies that the impairment occurred in the man's right hand, which was associated with work, prowess, and honor. In other words, this man's condition seriously limits the extent to which he would be able to engage in certain activities that were expected of men in his day, such as wage-earning labor. An ancient audience would immediately perceive that this man's impairment has not only a physical dimension but economic and social dimensions as well. The scribes and Pharisees watch to see if Jesus will heal on the Sabbath, planning to make an accusation against him if he does so. Jesus, in fact, does heal the man, asking the scribes and Pharisees if it is lawful to "do good or to do harm on the Sabbath, to save life or destroy it" (6:9). The implication of Jesus' question is that there are exceptions to strict Sabbath observance. Therefore, why not make an exception for this man in need?

LUKE 8:26-39: A DEMON-POSSESSED MAN, ISOLATED AND LIVING AMONG THE TOMBS

The story of the Gerasene demoniac (Luke 8:26-39) underscores the matter of social dislocation. This man is possessed not by one demon but by many (v. 30). His life is one of extreme isolation. He has worn no clothes for a long time and lives among the tombs (v. 27). Gerasa was a gentile area, and Jewish purity concerns would not come to bear on the man's location in the tombs. Nevertheless, a graveyard clearly would not be a place where people would meet for normal social interactions. Further, the people who were likely his peers and kin group before now keep him under guard and bind him with chains and shackles, "But he would break the bonds and be driven by the demon into the wilds" (v. 29). This man is utterly alone. His lack of clothing, his habitations, his behavior, and the stigma of the demonic prevent his engaging in any positive relationships with other people. In a culture in which people were much more interdependent than in our own, he has no peers or kin group with which to interact. By casting out the demons, Jesus allows the restoration of this man's most important relationships. In fact, Jesus even tells him, "Return to your home, and declare how much God has done for you" (v. 39).

Without attributing mental illness to demonic possession, we can see certain parallels between the situation of this man and many people with mental illness today. Mental illness can manifest itself in an inability to relate to others in positive or meaningful ways. Its symptoms can create fear of the person who suffers from mental illness. It can result in extreme social isolation, manifested through homelessness or institutionalization. Jesus, first of all, shows no fear of the possessed man. There is likely no other reason for Jesus to enter a gentile graveyard than to approach this man. Jesus refuses to participate in the isolation of this individual, and in so doing begins the process of restoring this man to meaningful relationships. Likewise, were we to refuse to accept many of the stigmas and negative stereotypes around people with mental illness, we too could more often make strides in restoring broken relationships.

LUKE 8:43-48: A WOMAN WITH A FLOW OF BLOOD AND THE REJECTION OF POLLUTION

In this passage we encounter a woman who suffers from abnormal menstrual flow. Literally, the text describes her as "being in a flow of blood" (οὖσα ἐν ῥύσει αἵματος, *ousa en hrusei haimatos*; 8:43). In addition to health problems that she may have experienced because of this condition, there are other quite serious social consequences for such a person. According to Lev 15:19-24, when a woman has a regular menstrual discharge: (1) she is considered impure for seven days, (2) anyone who touches her is considered unclean until the evening, (3) everything upon which she lies or sits is considered unclean, (4) anyone who touches her bed or anything upon which she sits will be unclean until evening and must wash his or her clothes and bathe, and (5) a man who has intercourse with her is considered unclean for seven days, and every bed on which he lies is considered unclean. Irregular menstrual discharge, which Leviticus defines as "a discharge of blood for many days, not at the time of her impurity" or "a discharge beyond the time of her impurity" (Lev 15:25) has additional consequences. Essentially, the stipulations of verses 19-24 occur until seven days after the end of the discharge, after which the priest will perform on her behalf the sacrifice of two turtledoves or pigeons, one as a sin offering and one as a burnt offering: "The priest shall make atonement on her behalf before the Lord for her unclean discharge" (Lev 15:30).

With this in the background, the social isolation of this woman must have been acute. Perhaps the reason that she tries to touch Jesus without his knowing is that her presence among such a large crowd would cause offense were her condition to be made known. Alternatively, perhaps she believes in particular that a holy man such as Jesus would be offended by the presence of someone who is considered unclean. Regardless, the narrative shows that Jesus rejects the idea that people may defile through pollution. As we have already seen, he touches the leper of 4:12-16. In this story Jesus looks upon the woman who touched his cloak with approval, saying, "Daughter, your faith has made you well; go in peace" (Luke 8:48). Jesus not only cures the illness (however inadvertently) but by his approval of her actions also challenges the purity system that results in her exclusion. He rejects the social/religious structures that caused her social dislocation.

Candida Moss has put forward a very interesting argument regarding the Markan parallel to this story (Mark 5:25-34). She focuses on the involuntary nature of the healing power that goes out from Jesus. Porosity, she writes, is an ancient medical category particularly associated with women.

"Oversaturation and softness are equated with weakness and femininity" (2010, 513). While no one would wish to display these characteristics too abundantly, men would particularly want to avoid them: "A soft, thin, feminine body is one that is vulnerable to external attack and forces" (514). Ancient people would see the woman in this story as unduly porous. Her body lacks the appropriate boundaries, which is why she has been leaking blood for twelve years. When the power flows out from Jesus through his robe, the woman "dries up." It is curious, however, that the power flows out from Jesus in the same involuntary manner as the blood flows from the woman. Jesus, then, displays a characteristic that was identified more with women than men. Yet Moss argues that his porosity would also have subtly conveyed that Jesus was divine. As she explains, "The epiphany motif, the idea that the gods travel the earth in disguise as human beings before revealing themselves in displays of greatness, was a well-established convention of Greek mythology. . . . The principle of divine light flooding through the confines of the fragile form provides another example of the inability to regulate the boundaries of the body viewed positively as a sign of power" (518).

Luke 9:37-43: A Demon-Possessed Boy

The Gospel of Luke's final exorcism story occurs in 9:37-43. In this story a man begs Jesus to look at his son. The son exhibits what look like symptoms of epilepsy. As the father describes his condition, "Suddenly a spirit seizes him, and all at once he shrieks. It convulses him until he foams at the mouth; it mauls him and will scarcely leave him" (9:38-39). Later, as Jesus approaches, the demon throws the son to the ground in convulsions (v. 42). Adela Yarbro Collins, drawing heavily on the work of Max Krenkel, argues that epilepsy, sometimes called the "divine illness," was, in almost all cases in the Greco-Roman context, attributed to demonic spirits. It carried with it considerable shame and stigma and was also called "the disease that is spit out" because when one saw a person exhibiting symptoms of epilepsy, one would spit on the ground as a charm against it (2011, 173). The suffering of the son in this story has to do with much more than the physical symptoms of his condition. It also has to do with the special stigma attached to epileptics. Because of the group-oriented nature of ancient Mediterranean cultures, the stigma would affect not only the son but his family as well. Once Jesus rebukes the unclean spirit and heals the boy, the family could return to normal patterns of social relationships.

LUKE 13:10-17: A WOMAN WHO CANNOT STAND UP STRAIGHT AND A SECOND SABBATH CONTROVERSY

In this passage Jesus heals a woman who has suffered for eighteen years from an impairment that has rendered her unable to stand up straight. Mary Ann McColl and Richard S. Ascough note the social consequences of this condition: "From a practical standpoint, it prevents her from having social intercourse with the community, since she cannot meet them face-to-face. It further prevents her from fully partaking of the usual social roles for women, including marital, parental and household roles. It should be noted however that the extent of the disability is not so great as to keep her from moving or functioning independently" (2009, 6).

The synagogue leader becomes indignant and says to the crowd, "There are six days on which work ought to be done; come on those days and be cured, and not on the Sabbath day" (13:14). This time Jesus responds by calling his opponents "hypocrites" (v. 15). He points out that each of them would, on the Sabbath, make an exception to untie an ox or donkey from a manger and lead it away in order for it to have water. How much more important, then, is it that this "daughter of Abraham, whom Satan bound for eighteen long years" (v. 16), be set free from her impairment immediately? An ox or a donkey cannot compare in importance to a daughter of Abraham. The reference to Satan, moreover, does not indicate that she has done something wrong to endure this condition. Rather, as McColl and Ascough put it, "She was a victim of his evil power as were all ill persons. Rather than impugning the woman's virtue, it appears that the mention of Satan in this story is meant to add a cosmic dimension, portraying the disability as spiritual as well as physical bondage. Thus the healing of illness is interpreted as the defeat of Satan and the triumph of Jesus and of God" (2009, 6).

LUKE 14:1-6: A MAN WITH DROPSY AND A THIRD SABBATH CONTROVERSY

The encounter between Jesus and a man with dropsy in Luke 14:1-6 provides another example of Jesus' healing with a sense of urgency: "Dropsy is a symptom, not a disease. It refers to massive retention of fluids in the body because of what are, mostly, quite serious and even life-threatening health problems" (Nolland 1993 746). Dropsy, or edema, at times results from a heart condition (748). Chad Hartsock explains dropsy as "a condition marked by the body's inability to process fluids, thus the victim continues to drink more and more until he or she eventually dies from drinking too much. The victim drinks because he or she is thirsty, but the body retains the fluid rather than processes it; thus the victim remains thirsty and continues to drink until something bad happens, like the bursting of organs" (2013, 342). According to Hartsock, because of the insatiable thirst of the person suffering from dropsy, this condition became a metaphor for greed and wealth (see also Braun 1995, 30–38). Adding credence to his argument is the fact that this passage immediately precedes a short discourse on humility (14:7-11), which is followed by the parable of the great dinner (14:15-24). At the end of this parable, the people who are invited are "the poor, the crippled, the blind, and the lame" (v. 21). Luke, who is often critical of excessive wealth, shows that the people who are often lacking in financial resources will be the favored recipients at the divine banquet. If this is the case, the dropsy, clearly a disabling condition, is used like the inability to see or hear as a metaphor for spiritual shortcomings. Indeed, Luke seems to have no compunctions about identifying physical impairments with spiritual deficiencies.

The effect of the metaphor of dropsy is mitigated by the inclusion of people with disabilities in the parable of the great dinner. Here people with disabilities are the favored guests of the host of the banquet, clearly a metaphorical representation of God. Additionally, we should bear in mind that in the story of the healing of the man with dropsy, Jesus again emphasizes compassion and physical and social restoration over strict Sabbath observance. In so doing he refers to the kinds of exceptions to Sabbath regulations that his opponents would affirm: "If one of you has a child or an ox that has fallen into a well, will you not immediately pull it out on a Sabbath day?" (14:5). The reference to falling into a well may also point to the seriousness of the man's condition. The causes of edema may be imminently life threatening. What is most important is to extend physical and social restoration to this man. Other concerns are subordinate to this one.

In none of these stories is it the case that Jesus' opponents care about the law while he sees fit to neglect it. Rather, both Jesus and his opponents care about the law, but they have different ways of interpreting and applying it. Scribal tradition would have it that a non-life-threatening condition would not supersede Sabbath regulations (Green 1997, 255). It is likely that, of the three conditions present in these passages, only dropsy could be perceived as immediately life threatening. Jesus seems to operate from the principle that conditions that cause people pain or loss of honor should also qualify for exemption from Sabbath rules. In the one case, we have a man who may have lost his ability to earn wages and who is forced to do things with what was considered the less honorable hand. In the other, we have a woman whose condition not only must have been very painful but also seems to have signified for Luke some kind of satanic oppression. These are very serious matters, even if not life threatening. Jesus is not simply curing the physical impairments of these two people but challenging ways of interpreting Sabbath law that would perpetuate these conditions longer than necessary.

Luke 16:19-31: Lazarus, Covered with Sores

A different set of concerns is present in the parable of the rich man and Lazarus (Luke 16:19-31). Lazarus is covered with sores (v. 20), but this does not necessarily imply that he is unclean. Leviticus 13:18-28 discusses the conditions under which a boil should be considered "leprous." For example, if the boil heals, and in its place there appears a white swelling of a reddish-white spot, then the priest should judge it leprous. There is nothing to indicate that Lazarus' sores are of this type. They may, however, call to mind a common Old Testament symbol of divine judgment. The word here translated "covered with sores" (16:20) is the passive participle εἱλκωμένος (*heilkōmenos*), which is related to the word ἕλκος (*helkos*). In the Septuagint *helkos* refers mainly to "boils," such as those that affected the people and livestock of Egypt during the first plague (see Exod 9:9-11). These "boils of Egypt" are also listed among the curses that God will send upon the Hebrews if they do not obey God's commandments (Deut 28:27, 35). The healing of a *helkos*, which saves Hezekiah's life, is a sign of divine favor in 2 Kgs 20:7. In the New Testament, Revelation picks up on this motif, describing the first of seven bowls of the wrath of God poured out upon the earth as consisting of "a foul and painful sore" that "came on those who had the mark of the beast and who worshiped his image" (16:2). These sores cause their bearers to curse God in their misery, but they do not lead them to repentance (16:11).

If divine judgment and divinely caused affliction are somehow in mind here, Luke overturns this expectation in what follows. Both Lazarus and the rich man at whose gate he lies die, and while Lazarus is taken away by angels to be with Abraham (v. 22), the rich man is consigned to Hades (v. 23). Lazarus, who suffered in life, is the recipient of divine favor. The rich man, who lived in opulence, receives divine condemnation. Perhaps Luke, then, is playing upon the Old Testament motif of affliction with boils intentionally to overturn it. The illness that Lazarus experiences is clearly not the result of divine judgment. Like Job, who also is covered with sores (Job 2:7), Lazarus has done nothing to deserve these.

If Luke is overturning the connection between affliction with boils and divine judgment, however, then what is the reason for Lazarus' impairment? The sores with which Lazarus is afflicted are signs of his poverty (Sussman 1992, 11). Bernard Brandon Scott argues that there is a direct and parallel contrast between Lazarus, on the one hand, covered with sores and desiring to be fed with the scraps from the rich man's table, and the rich man, who is clothed in purple and feasts sumptuously every day (1989, 149–50). Perhaps his impairment is such that Lazarus cannot work. He seems to have no family to care for him, since he longs to sate his hunger with what falls from the rich man's table. It seems he has been reduced to begging, or perhaps his presence at the rich man's gate indicates his desire to become the rich man's client (Scott 1989, 151). Therefore, the symptoms normally associated with divine punishment are reinterpreted as a symptom of social sinfulness. It is not Lazarus who is sinful, but those who will not help him in his impairment and poverty.

LUKE 17:11-19: TEN LEPERS AND A GENTILE WHO "GETS IT"

Jesus heals ten lepers as he travels "through the region between Samaria and Galilee" (17:11).[2] Because they are outsiders to village life, Jesus encounters them at its boundary. The lepers approach him, but they stand at a distance in deference to their assigned social space. Jesus simply commands them to show themselves to the priests. They obey and are healed as they do so. Although the one leper who returns to Jesus and does not go to the priest is not an Israelite, he would be required to appear before a priest, though in this case a Samaritan one (Fitzmyer 1985, 1151). His return to Jesus, therefore, is not because he lacks the same obligation as the Israelites. Rather, it is one of many examples of Luke's presaging of the gentile mission. Rather than keeping his distance, this leper now falls at Jesus' feet, thanking Jesus and praising God. Jesus commends his faithfulness and recognition of the source of his healing. This leper—the gentile—is the one who "gets it." The command that the lepers show themselves to the priest is a concession to common religious values, but the leper who falls at Jesus' feet shows that the priest's certification of cleanliness is not necessary.

Coupled with the story of the leper's healing in 5:12-16, this story suggests that lepers have *always* been acceptable before God. Luke simply rejects this aspect of the purity system (along with most others, though; see

---

[2] Exactly what region this might be is unclear. Perhaps Luke does not have a strong working knowledge of Palestinian geography. The point seems to be that Israelites and Samaritans need to be grouped together for the sake of the story that follows.

Acts 15:19-21). Jesus seems to have no trouble with lepers who have not been certified as clean in keeping with priestly regulations, even touching one of them in order to heal him. Jesus' healing of the impairment may be understood as an act of mercy to remove the painful physical symptoms of the skin disease. It is indeed a sign of his messianic office (see 7:22). Further, it creates a state of affairs whereby the lepers may be restored to social relationships: to participate fully in society again, the lepers must be certified as clean by the priests. Yet even as Jesus acquiesces to the religious requirements necessary for the social restoration of these lepers, he subtly undermines these requirements by his behavior toward the lepers, both before and after their healings.

LUKE 18:35-43: A PERCEPTIVE BLIND MAN

People who are unable to see, hear, or speak are commonly represented in Luke, and occasionally in Acts. Of these, blindness is the most frequently mentioned (explicit references occur in Luke 4:18; 6:39; 7:21; 7:22; 11:34; 14:13, 21; 18:35-43; Acts 9:8 [and 22:11]; 13:11). Deafness occurs far less often (Luke 7:22, 28:27). The inability to speak also receives mention in two places (Luke 1:20-22, 11:14). Within these works, the healings of blind and deaf people are representative of the inbreaking of God's kingdom. Jesus lists "recovery of sight to the blind" among the reasons for his being sent by the Lord (4:18). As noted above, when John's disciples ask Jesus whether or not he is "the one who is to come," he answers them by referring to a number of miraculous events, including the healing of blind and deaf people (7:22).

The conditions of blindness, deafness, and the inability to speak are cast in a particularly negative light. It is not simply the case that these impairments have a negative effect upon an individual by making life generally more difficult. Rather, they can at times metaphorically represent spiritual conditions or display divine punishment. Such is the case in Luke 6:39 when Jesus asks, "Can a blind person guide a blind person? Will not both fall into a pit?" Luke 11:34 states, "Your eye is the lamp of your body. If your eye is healthy, your whole body is full of light; but if it is not healthy, your body is full of darkness." As Mikeal Parsons points out, there is a close connection in Greek physiognomic literature between the eyes and moral character: "Persons with 'good eyes' were morally sound" (2011, 77). This is not to be construed in an over literal way, such as to say that strong eyesight meant strong character, but rather that various characteristics of the eyes could stand for various moral attributes. They were not only indicators but also symbols of one's moral state. The persecutor Saul is struck blind for three days (Acts 9:8). When Ananias lays hands upon him and says that Jesus "has sent me so that you may regain your sight and be filled with the Holy Spirit" (9:17), Saul's sight is restored. Immediately thereafter he is baptized. In an ironic turn of events, Paul later curses and strikes blind a magician named Bar-Jesus who is hindering the evangelistic work of Paul and Barnabas (Acts 13:11). Still later in Acts, spiritual imperception is explicitly linked with blindness as Paul recounts his encounter with Jesus on the road to Damascus. Jesus states, "I will rescue you from your people and from the gentiles—to whom I am sending you to open their eyes so that they may turn from darkness to light, and from the power of Satan to God, so that they may receive forgiveness of sins and a place among those who are sanctified by faith in me" (Acts 26:17-18). As Acts draws to a close, Paul references Isa 6:9-10 when speaking to local leaders:

> Go to this people and say, "You will indeed listen, but never understand, and you will indeed look, but never perceive. For this people's heart has grown dull, and their ears are hard of hearing, and they have shut their eyes; so that they might not look with their eyes and listen with their ears, and understand with their heart and turn—and I would heal them." (28:26-27)

Zechariah's inability to speak is punishment inflicted by Gabriel for Zechariah's disbelief that Gabriel's words were true. In the other instance of the inability to speak in Luke–Acts (Acts 11:14), this condition is attributed to demonic possession. Once the demon is gone, the person who was possessed can once again speak.

Blindness is among the conditions of Lev 21:16-24 that prevent priests from offering sacrifices to God. These "blemishes," designated by the Hebrew term מוּם (*mûm*), appear to be deviations from the ideal of a physically whole (male) body, though the criteria to establish what constitutes a "blemish" is unclear. Saul Olyan writes that most of these "blemishes" are "visible to the eye, long lasting or permanent in nature, and characterized by physical dysfunction, and more than a few share asymmetry as a quality" (2008, 30). These blemishes change the status of the priest. The blemished priest cannot fulfill the most significant function of the priesthood. His status is not entirely degraded, but it is diminished. Raphael explains the matter thus: "Leviticus associates holiness with physical beauty. The implied aesthetic criterion also helps explain the omission of invisible disabilities, for a deaf priest presents the same unruptured surface that a hearing one can. If ugliness makes a priest less holy (although still holy), then beauty makes him more holy" (2008, 36). Similar logic extends to the animals that may be offered to God in sacrifice: "To be acceptable in your behalf it shall be a male without blemish, of the cattle or the sheep or the goats. You shall not offer anything that has a blemish, for it will not be acceptable in your behalf" (Lev 22:19-20). We should note that the priest may still work in the temple and may still "eat the food of his God, of the most holy as well as of the holy" (Lev 21:22). It is sacrifice that is forbidden. In 2 Samuel, however, the exclusion of disabled people is more extreme: the "lame" and the blind are said to be among the people whom "David hates": "Therefore it is said, 'The blind and the lame shall not come into the house'" (5:8). As Olyan states, "Persons with 'defects' are frequently stigmatized by biblical authors, who also assign them marginal social positions" (2008, 26).

By contrast, one passage that mitigates the overall portrayal of blindness, deafness, and muteness in Luke–Acts is Luke 18:35-43. The blind man in this story demonstrates a level of perception that many others do not. He can see that Jesus is the "Son of David," a messianic title tied to Jesus' ancestry. Even when others try to silence him, he persists in calling out to Jesus using this title. Jesus sees his perception and perseverance as examples of faith. As Joseph Fitzmyer notes, "Coming immediately after the announcement of the passion, which the Twelve did not comprehend (18:31-34), this episode depicts a physically blind person coming to physical sight, but also recognizing in Jesus what others did not want him to recognize. . . . The blind man is presented as a foil to the uncomprehending Twelve" (1985, 1214). Significantly, the blind man's spiritual discernment precedes his physical healing. Jesus restores the blind man's physical sight, but this man's spiritual sight was already in good working order.

LUKE 19:1-10: ZACCHAEUS' SOCIAL HEALING

The story of Zacchaeus (19:1-10) has not always been interpreted as a story about a person with a disability. Normally, interpreters have simply thought of Zacchaeus as relatively short. As Parsons has argued, however, being of small physique could open one up to ridicule and invective in the Greco-Roman world (2011, 100–101). From a physiognomic perspective, Zacchaeus' stature would have cast doubt upon his character. The issue may have been more serious than this, however. Parsons also states, "Both lexical and contextual evidence suggest that at least some in Luke's audience would have viewed Zacchaeus' shortness as so extreme as to be pathological" (102). Not only would Zacchaeus have been of suspect character, then, but he also would have fallen into the Greco-Roman category of the "monstrous." Those unfortunate souls who were deemed such were regarded as objects of entertainment, and particularly humorous entertainment. Life for such people must have been quite difficult. The social discrimination that takes one from impairment to disability would have been especially pronounced. It may be that we are to understand Zacchaeus as both religiously ostracized and socially alienated (104). All of this would be in addition to his negative reputation as a tax collector.

Of all the people to whom Jesus can speak, he chooses to speak to Zacchaeus. Moreover, he asks to go to Zacchaeus' home and to stay with him, which would naturally involve accepting Zacchaeus' hospitality and sharing table with him. Jesus' behavior stands over against the ostracism of Zacchaeus. Staying with Zacchaeus and sharing table with him meant identifying with him socially, sharing in his reputation and his social ranking. Likewise, Zacchaeus' social standing will go up because he is sharing table with Jesus. The fellowship between the two is a rejection of the social norms that would prevent a person regarded as a holy man by many from close association with one widely regarded as a "sinner."

The story shows that Jesus is redefining the norms of proper social interaction. Yet as Parsons has pointed out, it is also a critique of prevailing physiognomic assumptions, an argument he also makes with regard to the woman who is unable to stand up straight in Luke 13:10-17 (2011, 105–7). Just as Jesus calls this woman a "daughter of Abraham" (13:16), he calls Zacchaeus a "son of Abraham" (19:9). These people might be assumed to be of low moral character, but Jesus rejects this notion. In the case of Zacchaeus, it appears that he has defrauded people in the past (19:8). He repents of this behavior, however, vowing even to pay back four times as much as he has taken from others fraudulently. Zacchaeus may have sinned in the past, but his future looks very different.

Of interest is that, assuming Zacchaeus' stature is pathological, Jesus does not attempt to heal him. Rather, this is one of the few places in which Jesus foregoes physical healing but engages instead only in social healing. In this case the absence of physical healing foregrounds the social: this is a story about relationships, character, and repentance, and it talks about each of them in unexpected ways.

Luke 23:33: The Crucifixion

Like the other evangelists, Luke provides few details about the crucifixion itself. One may surmise that the details of crucifixion were known all too well among the early followers of Jesus. Despite the sparse accounts of Jesus' crucifixion, however, we may infer a great deal about its social significance. Several times in the preceding pages we noted issues related to prowess, honor, and masculinity. The loss of these could have serious social consequences, particularly for males. When Jesus heals people such as the man who was unable to use his right hand, he allows this man to engage in the kind of behavior generally expected of him. He can engage others socially in ways that he could not before. In the crucifixion, however, Jesus experiences physical disempowerment and social isolation. Martin Albl puts the matter thus: "In the ancient world, a crucified person was the ultimate example of 'disability.' On the one hand, a crucified person was the ultimate symbol of 'functional limitations'—a person stripped of all ability to do anything for him or herself. With regard to the second aspect of disability, a crucified person bore the ultimate in social stigmatization" (2007, 149). Jesus experiences unmitigated social isolation. This was the point of crucifixion—not simply to inflict physical pain, though it certainly did that, but to humiliate, emasculate, and disempower the victim. No one wanted to be associated with someone who was crucified.[3] Jesus' followers are nowhere to be found when the events leading to his death begin to unfold. While crowds attend his crucifixion, "all his acquaintances" (οἱ γνωστοὶ αὐτῷ, *hoi gnōstoi autō*) watch from a distance (Luke 23:49).

There is, then, a very immediate identification of Jesus with those who suffer and experience social dislocation. The crucifixion is a physical manifestation of Christ's identification with those people who are on the margins of society. Jesus, after all, retains the marks of the crucifixion even after he is raised (24:39): "Like Job, the Lukan Jesus insists that we must not look away from suffering, even in light of the resurrection" (Gaventa 2008, 322). In fact, one might argue that the resurrection intensifies Jesus' identification with the suffering. When Jesus is raised, he and all those who suffer, all those who are "on the outs," are vindicated as the objects of God's special concern. With God's favor to the crucified one, God revalues the crucifixion and thereby turns the standard ways of reckoning honor, shame, human value, strength, weakness, and power upside down. Those who face the greatest challenges in life—it is they whom God honors most fully, and those who wish to honor God must assume a new system of values. God's

---

[3] Indeed, quite apart from issues of disability, many early Christians may have experienced social dislocation by virtue of their association with Jesus. Early on, Jesus' followers stood over against many of the values of the wider Mediterranean culture in which they lived. See Watson 2010a (especially in the conclusion, "Why *This* Story, Told in *This* Way?") and Watson 2010b. While these works are focused on the Gospel of Mark, many of the arguments therein also apply to the Gospel of Luke.

favor to Jesus after the crucifixion means that Jesus' followers must stand in solidarity with those who suffer physical pain, stigmatization, and isolation.

ACTS 3:1-10: PETER AND A MAN UNABLE TO WALK SINCE BIRTH

In Acts 3:1-10 we read of Peter's healing of a man who has been unable to walk since birth. The disabled man wishes to receive alms; Peter instead commands him to stand up and walk, and he does so (v. 6). The man's reaction is exuberant: "Jumping up, he stood and began to walk, and he entered the temple with them, walking and leaping and praising God" (v. 8). Such a reaction is reminiscent of Isa 35, an oracle of God's salvation. Particularly relevant is verse 6, which refers to the "lame" leaping like a deer. Parsons sees this behavior in contrast to common physiognomic conventions: "The lame man, once healed of his former 'inadequacies,' does not immediately adopt a slow, dignified gait, the sort of deportment that would show him to be a man of courage and vigorous character—in other words, a 'manly man.' Rather, by depicting the formerly lame man as leaping and praising God, Luke shows that he is an enthusiastic and grateful member of the eschatological community of God" (2011, 121). By telling the story in this way, Luke privileges proper gratitude for the benevolent work of God over commonplace standards of masculinity.

ACTS 8:26-40: CREATING SPACE FOR THE EUNUCH

The Ethiopian eunuch of Acts 8 presents a complex set of issues within the world of first-century Judaism. In that context a eunuch represented a less-than-complete male, diminished in holiness. Leviticus 21:20 forbids priests with crushed testicles from offering sacrifice. Because of this perceived deviation from wholeness, such a priest lacks the requisite level of holiness. Deuteronomy 23:1 takes this notion much further, forbidding eunuchs from admission to the "assembly of the LORD." This probably means that they are forbidden to enter "the sanctuary sphere for worship" (Olyan 2008, 11). They lack the holiness, from this perspective, to gather among the assembly of YHWH's worshippers. In this sense they are perennial religious outsiders, which in the ancient world creates perennial social dislocation.

Further, within the broader ancient Israelite context, fatherhood is held up as an ideal. To have a loyal wife who bears children and maintains a well-ordered household is a core component of masculinity (see, e.g., Ps 127:5; Prov 31:10-11; Sir 3:1-16, 22:3-6, 26:1-12, 30:1-13). Those who could not do so were therefore all the more outsiders, caught in an ambiguous space outside reified gender roles, and particularly set apart from ideals related to masculinity. It was common to find eunuchs in positions of political prominence, as we see in this narrative, in which the eunuch belongs to the court of the Ethiopian queen. Nevertheless, "Their peculiar impairment usually rendered them among the most scorned and stigmatized members of society. In a patriarchal culture where honor was tied to male domination, the effeminate, impotent eunuch was viewed with shame and as a threatening social deviant" (Spencer 2000, 434).

Yet Isaiah holds out eschatological hope for the eunuch: "Do not let the eunuch say, 'I am just a dry tree.' For thus says the LORD, 'To the eunuchs who keep my sabbaths, who choose the things that please me and hold fast my covenant, I will give, in my house and within my walls, a monument and a name better than sons and daughters; I will give them an everlasting name that shall not be cut off' " (Isa 56:3-5). In God's eschatological future, the criteria for inclusion among the most honored of God's people changes: "Thus says the LORD: 'Maintain justice and do what is right, for soon my salvation will come and my deliverance be revealed. Happy is the mortal who does this, the one who holds it fast, who keeps the sabbath, not profaning it, and refrains from doing any evil' " (Isa 56:1-2). The baptism of the Ethiopian eunuch in Acts 8 represents the fulfillment of Isaiah's prophecy. The eunuch is, in fact, reading from Isaiah (53:7-8) when Philip encounters him. He is likely a diaspora Jew: he is reading from the Jewish Scriptures and traveling in Israel to worship (though one wonders what form this could take). Despite his heritage, however, the eunuch is an outsider. Philip provides him with the opportunity to become an insider, and he seizes it (Acts 8:36). After his baptism he is fully a part of God's covenant people. Baptism, rather than physical characteristics, now determines acceptability before God and the receipt of divine favor.

It is noteworthy that Philip does not physically heal the eunuch. We know that he has the power to do so (see, e.g., Acts 8:7). This is one of the few places in Luke–Acts where a person with an impairing condition is welcomed into a new social reality without the elimination of the impairment that caused the stigmatization. Perhaps the reason for this is to maintain continuity with the prophecy of Isa 56. If the eunuch is no longer a eunuch, he cannot receive the monument and everlasting name that God promises.

ACTS 14:8-20: A MAN WHO IS UNABLE TO WALK

Acts depicts the healing of another man unable to walk in 14:8-20. The severity of the man's condition is emphasized by repetition. We are told that he could not use his feet, that he had never walked, and that he had been "crippled from birth" (14:8). In this case the healing, which takes place in Lystra, a primarily gentile context, is taken by the onlookers to demonstrate that Barnabas and Paul are the gods Zeus and Hermes in human form. Such powerful benevolence would require a divine visitation. Indeed, the people of Lystra have witnessed the power of a deity, though not the deity they thought. The apostles thereby seize upon the opportunity to testify on behalf of the God of Israel. In verse 19, however, the Jews of the city are said to stone Paul until they believed he was dead. In verse 20 we read that "when the disciples surrounded him, he got up and went into the city," which seems to indicate the miraculous healing of his wounds. The man who is unable to walk at the beginning of this story is not the story's real focus. Rather, the real focus of the story is the testimony of Paul and Barnabas, to which the miraculous healing gives occasion. In light of the larger narrative of Luke–Acts, however, this story continues the themes of God's benevolent care for those who are marginalized, first through Jesus, and then through the work of the apostles.

PAINTING IN BROAD STROKES: GENERAL STATEMENTS AND PASSING REFERENCES

In some places Luke tells us very little about the ailments and impairments from which people suffer. The account in which we learn of these impairments may be quite brief, or they may be only passing references (see, e.g., Luke 4:38-39, 7:2, 8:2, 10:30; Acts 9:32-35, 28:8-9). In Luke 4:40-41, 7:21, and 9:11, we read of Jesus performing mass healings, and the first two of these specifically mention exorcisms. In Luke 9:1 and 6, Jesus empowers the Twelve to cast out demons, and we read that they cured diseases everywhere they went. Similarly, in 10:9 Jesus appoints seventy more people to cure the sick. These large-scale healings continue in Acts. For example, 5:16 mentions many who were sick or possessed being cured by the apostles, and in 8:6-7 Philip is said to have healed many people who were "paralyzed or lame." In 10:38 Peter hearkens back to the story of Jesus healing all who were "oppressed by the devil." In 19:11 we read that people who touched handkerchiefs or aprons that Paul had touched were cured of sickness and demonic possession.

Many of these people would have suffered from social stigmatization. Luke teaches, however, that in Jesus' program these are the very people to whom his followers should extend hospitality. We read in Luke 14:12-14, "When you give a luncheon or a dinner, do not invite your friends or your brothers or your relatives or rich neighbors, in case they may invite you in return, and you would be repaid. But when you give a banquet, invite the poor, the crippled, the lame, and the blind. And you will be blessed, because they cannot repay you, for you will be repaid at the resurrection of the righteous" (see also 14:21). One way to read this passage is to understand people with disabilities as needing charity, and indeed Luke does seem to see them in this way. They are those who are unable to repay the one who throws the banquet. On the other hand, Luke is also challenging social conventions around those who would qualify as desirable company. Normally one's companions at a banquet would be social equals. Then, as is often the case now, people would commonly wish to associate with others who represented the social ideals that they themselves valued. In the Greco-Roman world, these social ideals would relate to honor expressed through wealth, influence, reputation, prowess, and favorable physiognomic characteristics. Here Jesus teaches that this conventional perspective of "desirable" companions is wrongly directed and out of keeping with the values of God's kingdom.

In these passages the ailments and impairing conditions of which people suffer are not the focus of the story. Rather, they are narrative elements by which Luke can "paint in broad strokes." They show the widespread work of Jesus and the apostles, who usher in the kingdom of God by the power of the Holy Spirit. As Jesus says in Luke 13:31 when some Pharisees tell him that Herod wishes to kill him, "I am casting out demons and performing cures today and tomorrow, and on the third day I finish my work." Many illnesses and disabling conditions could prevent people from experiencing the fullness of life, at times from employment or participation in social structures and meaningful relationships. The work of Jesus and the apostles reverses this. God is at work so that human beings may flourish as humans. Of course, some of the conditions in the New Testament—leprosy, fevers, and dropsy, for example—could range from physically uncomfortable to miserably painful. The healings of which we read are also a way of alleviating physical pain. Yet in the group-oriented culture of the ancient Mediterranean world, conditions that could impair one's ability to fulfill one's role within the household and engage with family and friends would be particularly devastating. Therefore, the "broad stroke" accounts of healings and exorcisms speak not only to the alleviation of ailments and impairments but also to the restoration of meaningful relationships.

CONCLUSION: LUKE–ACTS, DISABILITY, AND THE SOCIAL WORLD

When it comes to people with disabilities, Luke–Acts provides some wonderful insights and resources along with some serious challenges and liabilities. Again and again, Luke–Acts stands with the people who are vulnerable, marginalized, and isolated. The social and cultural models of disability tell us that our culture often pushes people with disabilities into these categories. In this sense Luke is very much our ally. Yet at times, Luke–Acts expresses values and solves problems in ways that we may find unsettling. This is an ancient work, and while we find many concepts in Luke–Acts that challenge the status quo in Luke's day and our own, the worldview assumed by the text is still that of the ancient Mediterranean, Greco-Roman context. The concept of "disability" as we know it today simply did not exist in the world of Luke–Acts. This work has no developed agenda regarding people with disabilities, and the author does not directly address certain social practices that readers today might find uncomfortable, offensive, or unacceptable. Recall, for example, the case of Elizabeth. In Luke's story the remedy to her social dislocation is not a prophetic challenge to people who discriminate against women who cannot bear children. Rather, the remedy is that she gives birth to a son.

The Healings in Luke–Acts

We must also consider the implications of the many healings in Luke–Acts. When people are healed, this does resolve the immediate problem: the physical suffering the person with a disability may experience will go away, and the conditions resulting in his or her social isolation will be resolved. In other words, from the perspective of Luke–Acts, a disability is a problem to be resolved, and Jesus and the apostles resolve such problems quite frequently. As noted above, however, the social structures that magnify the difficulty of the impairments are often left unchallenged, or are challenged very slightly. Or, to put the matter differently, within this first-century work, the challenge to social structures is subordinate to the immediate resolution of physical, mental, and emotional conditions that cause pain and social isolation. From the perspective of the text, healing is a gift of God. Many people today who have experienced relief from disabling conditions will be inclined to agree.

Some scholars suggest another positive angle on the healings in the Gospels and Acts. As McColl and Ascough point out:

> From the perspective of those who work alongside people with disabilities and provide care or service, the healing miracles in the gospels consistently evoke themes of inclusiveness, advocacy and courage. In each story (with the exception of the paralytic lowered through the roof), the disabled person appears alone, with no one to help him or her. By healing, Jesus restores these individuals not only to health, but to full humanity, standing in religious terms, and a place in the community. (2009, 8)

While our categories of disability, stigma, socialization, and culture are not a part of Luke's worldview, he does know that certain physical, mental, and emotional conditions cause the social bonds between people to break down and require restoration. Insofar as he sees God's redemptive work in overturning various types of stigmatization, Luke challenges these in many of his healing stories. Jesus touches a leper. He interprets Sabbath law in such a way as to emphasize the relief of suffering over strict observance. He shows no resentment over being touched by a woman with a flow of blood. The healing stories provide circumstances under which Jesus can demonstrate his own system of values, while at the same time relieving the physical and social suffering of the people whom he heals.

Yet some interpreters of Luke–Acts find the emphasis on healing in this work unhelpful, even harmful (McColl and Ascough 2009, 1–11). In many cases the concern over the healings in Luke–Acts arises because of the ways in which the Gospel narrative could translate into contemporary practice. The practice of healing is at the core of some contemporary Christian traditions, particularly those associated with Pentecostalism and the wider charismatic movement. Yet as Pentecostal theologian Amos Yong writes, "The experience of disability scholars such as Nancy Eiesland suggests that the Pentecostal Movement's emphasis on healing is counterproductive and even offensive to those scholars of disability who themselves have disabilities but understand these not as problems to be resolved (or healed or cured) but as part and parcel of their identity as human beings" (2009, 169). Likewise, Deborah Creamer identifies her disability as "an essential part of who I am" (1995, 80). In other words, there are complex issues related to disability and identity that problematize the matter of the curing of impairments. Some people with disabilities can and do choose treatments that will cure their impairments. Some see their impairment as a core part of their being and therefore not something that they could eliminate without changing who they are. The connection between disability and identity is one that warrants considerably more analysis than it has yet received.

LUKE'S COMMUNITY ETHOS

Luke's Gospel is creating a community ethos. It is not specifically concerned with people with disabilities, but it does include such people. It is an ethos that makes sense within the Greco-Roman world. This world was infused with the values of honor and shame, and it was strongly group oriented. It was intensely religious. It was a world in which health care and religion were closely related. The matrix of concepts related to family, honor, shame, religion, and health meant that to be deprived of one of these would come to bear on all the others. The loss of honor could mean rejection by the family; rejection by the family certainly meant the loss of honor. Misfortune could be attributed to fate, spirits, the gods, or God, and it too could bring dishonor upon an individual and a family.

A person with nontypical physical and mental characteristics was especially vulnerable to the loss of honor and the breakdown of familial relationships. It is not an overstatement to say that in the Greco-Roman world people were often amused by those they considered "deformed." As L. L. Welborn points out, humor in this context was often "grounded in contemplation of the ugly and defective" (2005, 33). Far from being people whom one should include in one's community, regard as friends, and care for when in need, people with disabilities were often objects of scorn, shame, and absurd comedy. Moreover, this tendency, though not as overt as in the ancient world, still lurks in our own context.

From this vantage point, Luke–Acts is quite countercultural. The community ethos that we see developing in Luke's Gospel is not one that we could say is a fully formed ethic of disability. Rather, it challenges practices regarding disabilities in its own day, and it holds within it the seeds of life-giving attitudes and practices as they relate to people with disabilities in our day. Luke–Acts provides a scriptural basis for the care of people who are marginalized. If we consider the story of Zacchaeus or the parable of the rich man and Lazarus, we see in Luke an unconventional regard for those who experienced social isolation. At times Luke seems to reinforce actions and attitudes that are less consistent with this ethic and that may seem objectionable to us. In order to draw out what is most helpful, most life giving in Luke–Acts, we must read this narrative in dialogue with the broader canon of Scripture, and our broader theological and ethical frameworks. At the core of the Christian faith is the love of God expressed through the saving work of Jesus Christ and the ongoing presence of the Holy Spirit. Luke–Acts represents a significant landmark on a trajectory of the development of Christian doctrine and practice. It informs Christian ethical systems but is not wholly determinative of them. While we will wrestle with particular passages in Luke–Acts, we can learn from them that God cares for people who have been pushed to the margins of society. If we are wise, our lives will reflect this same care and concern.

WORKS CITED

Albl, Martin. 2007. "For Whenever I Am Weak, Then I Am Strong: Disability in Paul's Epistles." Pages 145–58 in *This Abled Body: Rethinking Disabilities in Biblical Studies*. Edited by Hector Avalos, Sarah J. Melcher, and Jeremy Schipper. Semeia Studies 55. Atlanta: Society of Biblical Literature.

Anderson, Allan H. 2006. "Exorcism and Conversion to African Pentecostalism." *Exchange* 35, no. 1: 116–33.

Braun, Willi. 1995. *Feasting and Social Rhetoric in Luke 14*. Society for New Testament Studies Monograph Series 85. Cambridge: Cambridge University Press.

Collins, Adela Yarbro. 2011. "Paul's Disability: The Thorn in His Flesh." Pages 165–83 in *Disability Studies and Biblical Literature*. Edited by Candida R. Moss and Jeremy Schipper. New York: Palgrave Macmillan.

Creamer, Deborah. 1995. "Finding God in Our Bodies: Theology from the Perspective of People with Disabilities." *Journal of Religion in Disability & Rehabilitation* 2, no. 2: 67–87.

Culy, Martin M., Mikeal C. Parsons, and Joshua J. Stigall. 2010. *Luke: A Handbook on the Greek Text*. Baylor Handbook on the Greek New Testament. Waco, Tex.: Baylor University Press.

Fitzmyer, Joseph A. 1985. *The Gospel According to Luke X–XXIV*. Anchor Bible 28A. Garden City, N.Y.: Doubleday.

Gaventa, Beverly Roberts. 2008. Review of *Body and Character In Luke and Acts: The Subversion of Physiognomy in Early Christianity* by Mikeal Parsons. *Perspectives in Religious Studies* 35, no. 3: 319–22.

Green, Joel B. 1997. *The Gospel of Luke*. New International Commentary on the New Testament. Grand Rapids: Eerdmans.

Hartsock, Chad. 2013. "The Healing of the Man with Dropsy (Luke 14:1-6) and the Lukan Landscape." *Biblical Interpretation* 21, no. 3: 341–54.

Kelley, Nicole. 2011. "'The Punishment of the Devil Was Apparent in the Torment of the Human Body': Epilepsy in Ancient Christianity." Pages 205–21 in *Disability Studies and Biblical Literature*. Edited by Candida R. Moss and Jeremy Schipper. New York: Palgrave Macmillan.

Luz, Ulrich. 1983. "The Secrecy Motif and the Marcan Christology." Pages 75–96 in *The Messianic Secret*. Edited by Christopher Tuckett. Philadelphia: Fortress.

McColl, Mary Ann, and Richard S. Ascough. 2009. "Jesus and People with Disabilities: Old Stories, New Approaches." *Journal of Pastoral Care and Counseling* 63: 3–4.

Moss, Candida R. 2010. "The Man with the Flow of Power: Porous Bodies in Mark 5:25-34." *Journal of Biblical Literature* 129, no. 3: 507–19.

Moss, Candida R., and Jeremy Schipper, eds. 2011. *Disability Studies and Biblical Literature*. New York: Palgrave Macmillan.

Nolland, John. 1989. *Luke 1–9:20*. Word Biblical Commentary 35A. Dallas: Word.

————. 1993. *Luke 9:21–18:34*. Word Biblical Commentary 35B. Dallas: Word.

Olyan, Saul M. 2008. *Disability in the Hebrew Bible: Interpreting Mental and Physical Differences*. Cambridge: Cambridge University Press.

Park, Nam Shin. 2011. "Hermeneutics and Spiritual Warfare." *Didaskalia* 22: 85–103.

Parsons, Mikeal C. 2011. *Body and Character in Luke–Acts: The Subversion of Physiognomy in Early Christianity*. Waco, Tex.: Baylor University Press.

Raphael, Rebecca. 2008. *Biblical Corpora: Representations of Disability in Hebrew Biblical Literature*. New York: T&T Clark.

Reinders, Hans. 2008. *Receiving the Gift of Friendship: Profound Disability, Theological Anthropology, and Ethics*. Grand Rapids: Eerdmans.

Schaberg, Jane. 1998. "Luke." Pages 363–80 in *Women's Bible Commentary*. Edited by Carol A. Newsom and Sharon H. Ringe. Expanded ed. Louisville, Ky.: Westminster John Knox.

Scott, Bernard Brandon. 1989. *Hear Then the Parable: A Commentary on the Parables of Jesus*. Minneapolis: Fortress.

Spencer, F. Scott. 2000. "Eunuch." Pages 434–35 in *Eerdmans Dictionary of the Bible*. Edited by David Noel Freedman, Allen C. Myers, and Astrid B. Beck. Grand Rapids: Eerdmans.

Sussman, Max. 1992. "Sickness and Disease." Pages 6–15 in vol. 6 of *The Anchor Bible Dictionary*. Edited by David Noel Freedman. Garden City, N.Y.: Doubleday.

Watson, David F. 2010a. *Honor among Christians: The Cultural Key to the Messianic Secret*. Minneapolis: Fortress.

————. 2010b. "The Life of Aesop and the Gospel of Mark: Two Ancient Approaches to Elite Values." *Journal of Biblical Literature* 129, no. 5: 697–714.

Welborn, L. L. 2005. *Paul, the Fool of Christ: A Study of 1 Corinthians 1–4 in the Comic-Philosophic Tradition*. New York: T&T Clark.

Yong, Amos. 2007. *Theology and Down Syndrome: Reimagining Disability in Late Modernity*. Waco, Tex.: Baylor University Press.

————. 2009. "Many Tongues, Many Senses: Pentecost, the Body Politic, and the Redemption of Disability." *Pneuma* 31: 167–88.

Zias, Joseph. 1991. "Death and Disease in Ancient Israel." *Biblical Archaeologist* 54, no. 3: 146–59.

10

John, First–Third John, and Revelation

Jaime Clark-Soles

The Johannine Literature consists of the Gospel of John, 1–3 John, and Revelation.[1] Different genres of literature are represented by each. The Gospel is a literary narrative that intentionally aims, through story, to persuade the reader of its thesis statement: "These are written so that you may come to believe that Jesus is the Messiah, the Son of God, and that through believing you may have life in his name" (John 20:31). First–Third John are epistolary and hortatory. Revelation is an apocalypse, replete with visionary experiences; fantastic imagery; highly symbolic, allegorical language; an interest in numerology; and an urgent sense of the eschaton. Apocalyptic literature is written for and tends to appeal to those who find themselves oppressed politically and socially and on the verge of losing faith and hope. The author encourages the readers by insisting that, despite all appearances, God's justice will finally inhere in the world and the great reversal will occur: the lowly will be exalted and the haughty will be brought low. The author exhorts the readers to remain faithful through the struggle, even unto death.

Though all this literature is considered "Johannine," only Revelation names its author as John but does not say which John (a name as common then as it is now). Unlike 2 and 3 John, the author of 1 John remains entirely unnamed but claims to be an eyewitness to the earthly Jesus (1 John 1:1-4). Due to apparent knowledge of and dependence upon

---

[1] I must thank Rev. Helen Betenbaugh and Dr. Sang Soo Hyun for engaging this chapter seriously and offering important critiques and suggestions.

the traditions evinced by the Fourth Gospel, some assume that the same author penned both texts. Based upon differences in theology and style, however, others attribute 1 John to a different author, perhaps the "elder" referred to in 2 John 1 and 3 John 1. The composition history of the Fourth Gospel itself is quite complex and probably reflects various stages of the Johannine community and more than one authorial or editorial hand. As a result, theories concerning the authorship and dating of the Gospel and each epistle abound.

Also unlike 2 and 3 John, 1 John is more a hortatory address or essay than an epistle. It lacks the conventional features of a letter, including the names of the sender and recipient, opening and closing greetings, or a thanksgiving. Second John is written to "the elect lady and her children" and 3 John to Gaius. First John does not designate its audience, but its rhetoric, allusions, and assumptions indicate that the audience is part of the "Johannine community." In each case, the author is concerned with both the theology and ethics of the community.

In disability studies it is customary to distinguish between impairment (a physiological, medical phenomenon) and disability (a social phenomenon). A society disables people with impairments when it refuses to take steps to ensure that all members of society have equal access to the benefits of that society (including education, transportation, employment, architecture that can be navigated, political power, etc.—all entitlements that people with normate bodies usually take for granted). Another crucial matter of definition relates to the language of "cure" and "healing." In this essay "cure" refers to the elimination of impairment and is experienced at the individual level. "Healing" refers to a person who has experienced integration and reconciliation to self, God, and the community. "Healing" may or may not involve a "cure." Just as impairment is experienced on an individual basis, so is a "cure." Just as a disability is a communally imposed limitation, so also "healing" is a communally based liberation.

The differences in genre (and therefore purpose) of the material necessitate an eclectic methodology. Drawing upon insights from different models and methods to illuminate or interrogate different aspects of the texts, we will explore them with a view to answering this question: From a disability perspective, what are the promises and pitfalls of these texts with respect to ancient audiences and later interpreters? That is, in what ways does the text have liberative potential and in what ways does it present obstacles for those seeking abundant life (John 10:10)?

FOURTH GOSPEL

The Fourth Gospel is a narrative. Its rhetoric depends, therefore, upon literary techniques including plot, characters, setting, and point of view (omniscient narration, in this case). To interpret the Fourth Gospel from a disability perspective, one must attend not only to obvious texts, such as the healing/cure narratives and passion and resurrection stories, but also to the Gospel's emphasis on creation, incarnation, and the peace of Christ. Comparatively speaking, few healing/cure stories appear: one at Cana (4:46-54), one at Bethesda (5:1-15), and one at Siloam (ch. 9). Only those in chapters 5 and 9 involve a disability.

THE PROLOGUE: JOHN 1:1-18

Diversity in Creation: And God Said, "It Is Good"

Using the same opening phrase as Genesis, "In the beginning" (Ἐν ἀρχῇ, *en archē*), the Gospel commences its narrative about the incarnation, the Word (λόγος, *logos*) made flesh. Christians typically equate the Word with Jesus of Nazareth. Striking is the author's insistence that "Everything came into being through him and without him not even one thing (οὐδὲ ἕν, *oude hen*) came into being" (1:3; my trans.), since it implies that the diversity of creation is by God's design. Is this diversity to be celebrated or overcome? Immediately, then, we are drawn into some of the most difficult questions debated in disability studies.

Are disabilities the mark of the demonic, the divine, both, or neither? The ancients commonly ascribed physical or mental disabilities to demonic forces. In the Gospel of John, Jesus' opponents, who seek to disable him throughout the narrative, routinely accuse him of having a demon (ἔχει δαιμόνιον, *echei daimonion*), which is equated with being mentally insane (μαίνεται, *mainetai*) (7:20, 8:48-52, 10:20-21). Diane Devries, a disabilities activist, was born with arm stumps and no lower limbs. Her grandmother ascribed her deformities to a tryst between her mother and the devil. The delivering physician considered her impairments a tragedy, which is common for those operating from a medical model of disability: "The medicalization of disability casts human variation as deviance from the norm, as pathological condition, as deficit, and significantly, as an individual burden and personal tragedy" (Linton 1998, 11). For Devries, "It seems no more necessary to ask why she was born with her body, than it does to pose the same question of her able-bodied younger sister. In refusing to define her own birth as a tragedy, Devries rejects dominant conceptions and reconceives it as the natural beginning of an ordinary life" (Eiesland 1994, 34).

Verse 3 implies that "good bodies" come in a variety of forms. Rather than "fixing" bodies that deviate from the "norm," the concern should be to fix society to make it inclusive of all bodies. Rather than eradicating difference, society should accommodate, even celebrate it. To denigrate differently abled bodies is to denigrate creation and, by extension, its creator.

Some would find the notion that disability is a part of God's creative design to be oppressive rather than liberating. Part of the problem with the conversation is that, for the sake of sustaining a dialogue and debate, a vast variety of experiences are placed under the label "disability." The experience of a congenital impairment is almost always quite different from one that develops later in life. In the latter case, people often experience a deep sense of loss and grief that does not characterize the experience of the former. The difference between intellectual disabilities and physical disabilities causes immense tensions and problems in the disability community. In their own struggle for justice, some people with physical disabilities fight very hard to distinguish themselves from those with intellectual disabilities in the eyes of temporarily able-bodied (TAB) people. People who are blind or are in wheelchairs often have the experience of people speaking to them more loudly or slowly or simply, as if they were cognitively impaired. Next, a chronic impairment is vastly different from an illness. While some impairments cause inconvenience, others cause unmitigated, debilitating pain. Some impairments are obvious to the onlooker, while others are hidden such that the person with a disability (PWD) can "pass" as "normal." This immense variety and complexity makes any analysis of the scriptural texts from "a" disability perspective a bit unwieldy and susceptible to critique and demands for further nuance than a brief chapter can provide, but the matter is important enough to risk making some suggestions anyway.

There is a vigorous debate in the disability literature about whether those with impairments should seek a cure if possible or whether to do so is to acquiesce to, rather than resist, the oppressive, narrow values of normate society. For instance, many in the Deaf community do not find deafness to be a disability. Just as Spanish and German are languages, so is American Sign Language. If others are ignorant of a language, they should not look down on those who know it. Many in the Deaf community criticize the insertion of cochlear implants as a means to join the "normate" community. Christopher Reeve serves as a lightning rod; many in the disability community have a negative view of him insofar as he sought a cure until his death rather than embracing his differently abled body. He is contrasted to a person like Nancy Mairs, who has multiple sclerosis. Mairs declares, "I'd take a cure; I just don't need one" (Wynn 2007, 66).

When my daughter was in fifth grade, the science teacher was covering genetics. As she explained that males have an XY chromosome and females an XX, my daughter raised her hand to ask about hermaphrodites. The teacher responded, "They are a genetic mistake." How does this cohere with John 1:3? Theologian Amos Yong has a brother with Down syndrome, which can be described in terms of physical or cognitive features, or genetically: a trisomic mutation of the twenty-first chromosome. As Yong indicates, "Mark has all of these 'normal' features for a person with trisomy 21" (2011, 3). Is he a "genetic mistake" who needs to be rehabilitated to resemble more closely the normate ideal, or is he part of God's intentional creation just as he is, gifted to testify to the gospel and serve as one member of the body of Christ? Furthermore, what would it mean to cure Mark of his cognitive or physical disabilities; would that not erase Mark himself? Does erasure of difference honor God as the potter who makes the clay and who shapes the pot?

Verses 1-5 insist that God is in the business of *life* (ζωή, *zōē*, and its cognates occur frequently, fifty-six times). At all times when reading the Johannine texts through the lens of disability, Christians are to ask: What gives life and what hinders life? Once they discern the answer, they are to work the works of God and thereby serve life.

Children of God

John 1:11-13 adumbrates the plot of the Gospel. Jesus will be rejected by some and accepted by others. All who receive him become children of God, born "not of blood or of the will of the flesh or of the will of a husband, but of God" (v. 13; my trans.). People with disabilities sometimes find themselves cast as children of a lesser God. Do people with disabilities have to be cured or healed to be considered fully children of God? Are people with disabilities farther from the grace of God: "There but for the grace of God, go I"? This is an expression that many PWDs have heard, and it is deeply problematic in its implications. It implies that the PWD is outside the grace of God; it implies that the reason one is TAB is because one is especially favored or blessed by God. It entirely misses the meaning of grace and blessing, not to mention the cross. It makes God appear capricious or malevolent. And the list goes on.

Too often readers move from the occasional miracle story that connects faith and cure to a generalized notion that cure depends upon faith or forgiveness of sin. This is not a defensible move, as one discovers upon further study. In chapters 5 and 9, Jesus takes the initiative to cure the two men; one becomes a follower, the other does not. In the only other story of a cure in John, faith comes as a *result* of the cure; this continually frustrates Jesus, who expresses impatience with "signs faith": "Unless you see signs and wonders you will not believe" (4:48). A mature faith requires no magic tricks. When someone advises a disabled person simply to pray harder or have more faith in order to be cured, the adviser operates against the grain of the Fourth Gospel and burdens the disabled person with blame and judgment. Where the health and wealth "gospel" reigns, Christ does not.

Incarnation

John 1:14 is central for the consideration of the intersection of disability studies and the Bible, the intersection of bodies and theology: "And the Word became flesh (σάρξ, *sarx*) and tabernacled (σκηνόω, *skēnoō*) among us, and we have seen his glory, the glory as of a father's only son, full of grace and truth" (my trans.). Many implications derive from this statement.

First, the embodiment of the divine undergirds the whole Gospel. Plato emphasized the distance between the material order (the phenomenal world) and the higher realm (the noumenal world), which is summarized by his memorable phrase *soma sēma* ("the body is a tomb"). In contrast, John finds the body to be a locus and instrument of the divine (hence the use of the word σκηνόω [*skēnoō*, "tabernacle"]) and the reference to Jesus' body as a temple [ναός, *naos*] in 2:21). In fact, the whole created order reflects and symbolizes God's nature and activity (1:3). Bread is no longer just bread (6:35); water is no longer just water (4:14); flesh is no longer just flesh (6:51).[2]

---

[2] "If the Word of God became flesh and dwelt among us—i.e., if the Word of God came out of the birth canal of a woman's body, grew, ate, went to the bathroom, bathed, struggled against demons, sweated, wept, exulted, was transfigured, was physically violated, and rotted away in a tomb just before being gloriously resurrected—then the Bible must have flesh on it. If a valley of dry bones can live again, then bones and blood and bread and flesh and bodies should never be left behind when we are trying to understand the grime and glory of Scripture. Any interpretation that denounces the material, created order, including our own bodies, should be suspect. From birth to death our bodies swell and shrink; they are wet with milk and sweat and urine and vomit and sex and blood and water, and wounds that fester and stink and are healed and saved and redeemed and die and are resurrected. If you can't glory in or at least talk about these basic realities in church while reading Scripture, then how can Scripture truly intersect with or impact life? We might as well just go read a Jane Austen novel—though I doubt we'll ever be transformed or made whole or saved by it" (Clark-Soles 2010, 32).

Second, this Gospel is particularly intimate both physically and emotionally. Bodies touch. Jesus is in God's bosom (κόλπος, *kolpos*; 1:18) just as the Beloved Disciple reclines upon Jesus' bosom (ἐν τῷ κόλπῳ, *en tō kolpō*; 13:23). Jesus rubs mud on the eyes of the man in chapter 9. Mary, the sister of Martha, wipes Jesus' feet with her hair (11:2). Jesus washes the disciples' feet and wipes them (13:5). Joseph and Nicodemus wrap and bury Jesus' dead body (19:39-42). Mary Magdalene holds on to Jesus (20:17). Thomas is invited to touch Jesus' wounded hands and side (20:27). Those who perpetrate violence against another's body in the Gospel always do so with an object such that the bodies do not, in fact, touch (Peter chops off the ear with a sword (18:10); Pilate's lackeys flog Jesus with a whip (19:1); the soldier's jam the crown of thorns onto Jesus' head and spear Jesus' side (19:2, 38)). They use objects to objectify the body of the other.

Third, the Gospel is highly sensual: seeing, hearing, smelling (11:39), touching, and tasting (2:9) all figure into the narrative.

Fourth, bodies do not need to be "overcome." They are sites of vulnerability, connection, shame and glory. Jesus' body experiences a range of states and experiences—God is in them all (note that this Gospel never finds Jesus feeling forsaken by God as he does in Mark 15:34 and Matt 27:46). He does not try to escape his ordeal and does not feel abandoned. He knows that it is not God but society that attempts to disable him. Notably, when he appears in his resurrection, his body is not repaired but continues to bear the wounds in his hands and side.

Is it any wonder that the Gospel that focuses most overtly on incarnation is also the Gospel that uses the language of love (φιλέω, *phileō*; ἀγαπάω, *agapaō*) more than any other Gospel? Furthermore, when one considers those relationships that are usually deemed most intimate, they all appear in John (mother, father, child, sibling, friend, spouse, partner).

JOHN 5:1-18: WILLING TO BE HEALED?

Along with chapter 9, 5:1-18 is a *crux interpretum* for those interested in disability and the Bible. The Fourth Evangelist typically relies upon intercharacterization; that is, characters can only be fully understood by comparing them with other characters in the narrative.

The man provides a negative example for readers in at least two ways. First, he represents failed discipleship. He encounters Jesus, but by the end of the narrative he not only does not follow Jesus, but he also works against Jesus by implicating him to the religious authorities. Second, he appears to represent those who suffer impairment as a result of their own sinful behavior.

An Interpretation

This cure story immediately follows the one in chapter 4 where the father, a "royal official" (βασιλικός, *basilikos*) exemplifies a faithful response to Jesus' curing of his son's illness. In chapter 5 we find the man who was ill for thirty-eight years in Jerusalem at the "hospital" called Bethesda. Since it served as a hospital of sorts, it is not surprising that "a multitude of invalids" (πλῆθος τῶν ἀσθενούντων, *plēthos tōn asthenountōn*) were there. The word translated as "invalid" here comes from the verb ἀσθενέω (*astheneō*), meaning to be sick or weak. It is a generic term covering a variety of impairments. In this case the author further modifies *astheneō* with the tripartite phrase blind (τυφλῶν, *tuphlōn*; 5:3; 9:1-2, 13, 17-20 24-25, 32, 39-41; 10:21; 11:37), lame (χωλῶν, *chōlōn*; only occurrence), and paralyzed (ξηρῶν, *xērōn*; only occurrence). The word *astheneō* occurs eight times in the Fourth Gospel (4:46; 5:3, 7; 6:2; 11:1-3, 6). Of course, the heteronyms *in*valid and in*valid* should not be lost on the modern reader concerned about disability issues.

At verse 6 Jesus asks the unnamed man if he wills or wishes (θέλω, *thelō*) to be healthy (ὑγιής, *hygiēs*; 5:6, 9, 11, 14-15; 7:23). On the face of it, it is a stupid or insensitive question: Who does *not* wish to be healthy? Notice, however, that the man does not actually answer the question; he says neither yes nor no. Many readers of this Gospel understand this to be the question of all questions—unless one has the will (1:43; 3:8; 5:6, 21, 35, 40; 6:11, 21, 67; 7:1, 17, 44; 8:44; 9:27; 12:21; 15:7; 16:19; 17:24; 21:18, 22-23) to be well, the likelihood of wellness remains slim. What one wills or wishes matters. In fact, it would appear that some people find their equilibrium precisely in misery. Sometimes our sense of identity is based upon our impairment. If one does not actually wish or will to become healthy, it might be difficult for anyone, including Jesus, to help one to do so. Does the man in chapter 5 wish to be made well? The evidence is not in his favor. First, he produces an impressive litany of excuses: (1) I have no one to help me when the time is right, and (2) when I do try, I get trumped by someone more able. Second, he clearly has not made any connections or built any community in thirty-eight years. Third, he never declares that he wants to be made well (though he readily follows Jesus' orders). Finally, though Jesus grants him healing, he shows no sign of gratitude, transformation, or understanding. One may imagine that he ended up right back by the pool, drowning in his self-chosen illness, totally unlike the blind man in chapter 9. He takes no risks for the gospel but protects his own interests at the expense of Jesus.

Are there benefits to remaining ill? Might it alleviate responsibility? What is the cost of becoming well? Perhaps it would involve radical change and the adoption of a new persona to some degree. If one is in a family or a web of relationships, it might mean potential rupture of those relationships as one steps out into health and refuses to play or matures past an assigned role in the family drama.

Though the man never overtly agrees to the cure, Jesus assumes center stage in the drama and effects it. He commands the man to stand up and walk (which obviously further defines the author's meaning of healthy [ὑγιης, *hygiēs*; 5:9]). The fact that the whole event occurred on a Sabbath (a recurring theme in John: 5:9-10, 16, 18; 7:22-23; 9:14, 16; 19:31; 20:1, 19) antagonizes the religious authorities (gatekeepers of said Sabbath), who accost the man who had been therapeutized (θεραπεύω, *therapeuō*). Just as the man took no responsibility for his illness, he takes no responsibility for his healing. He immediately blames the incident on the man (ἄνθρωπος, *anthrōpos*) who directed him, a man whom he does not know. These are apparently damning facts. First, those who do not grasp Jesus' full identity refer to him merely as an *anthrōpos*, culminating in Pilate's famous dictum: "Behold, the *anthrōpos*" (19:5). Second, the verb "to know" (γινώσκω, *ginōskō*) serves to mark insiders and outsiders in the Fourth Gospel. Insiders know; outsiders do not. The fact that the man confesses that he does not know Jesus implies that he does not become a disciple of Jesus and, in fact, serves as a failed example of discipleship.

Once again, Jesus takes it upon himself to approach the man in verse 14. He finds the man in the temple, of all places, and declares, "Behold you have become healthy (ὑγιής, *hygiēs*). No longer keep sinning, in order that nothing worse happens to you" (my trans.). The command occurs in the second-person present imperative. The present implies ongoing, habitual action. As controversial and problematic as Jesus' command might be here for modern readers, there is no question that Jesus assumes this man to be an ongoing sinner of some sort. Note that the man's reaction to his cure is not one of gratitude or discipleship; rather, he tattles to the antagonistic religious authorities with whom Jesus has already clashed in the temple (2:13-20). As a direct causal result of the man's actions (διὰ τοῦτο, *dia touto*), the religious authorities persecuted Jesus for curing on the Sabbath. At this point the narrative morphs into a Sabbath controversy story focused upon Jesus' identity and authority vis-à-vis God.

In 1:11 we were informed that Jesus came unto his own and his own did not receive him. This seems to be the case with this Jewish man and the religious authorities in chapter 5, especially when juxtaposed with the

Samaritan (non-Jewish) woman in 4:1-42, who engages Jesus deeply and becomes the first evangelist in the Gospel, or the royal official (gentile) in 4:46-54 who rounds out the Cana-to-Cana cycle with his own belief and that of his whole household.

Is there any way that chapter 5 might be useful or suggestive for those who seek justice for people with disabilities?

Questions Raised

From a disability perspective, this text evinces problems. First, both the person and the disability are *erased* in a number of ways. He has no name, and no specific details are given about his impairment or how he became impaired. In a sense, he does not figure as a person but as a pawn in a nor-mate narrative about Jesus revealing his own identity, power, authority, and ability as God's agent. He is useful to the "normate" interpreter only insofar as he has a disability. The encounter functions primarily as an epi-sode in Jesus' escalating controversy with the religious authorities. In fact, the text launches into a christological monologue from 5:19 to 47. The man himself is a cipher. As Kathy Black notes,

> We tend to use them [the people in the biblical stories who are disabled or differently abled] as objects to make some other point. The problem with this is that persons with disabilities today likewise find themselves treated as objects. Health care, education, employment, social services—all the basic institutions of our society often view persons with disabilities as objects to be dealt with, rather than as subjects that have something to contribute. (1996, 13)

This is an example of what David Mitchell and Sharon Snyder have termed "narrative prosthesis." They explain, "Our thesis centers not sim-ply upon the fact that people with disabilities have been the object of rep-resentational treatments but rather that their function in literary discourse is primarily twofold: disability pervades literary narrative, first, as a stock feature of characterization and, second, as an opportunistic metaphor-ical device" (2013, 274). Such narratives expose and explain differences as deviances before providing some sort of remedy that often eliminates difference or reinterprets it in a manner that is acceptable for the social context: "Narratives turn signs of cultural deviance into textually marked bodies" (279).

This leads to a second issue: For whose sake was the man "cured" in this story? Jesus asks if the man "wills" the cure; the man never says that he wills the cure, but Jesus cures him anyway. Is this an opportunistic move on Jesus' part? A normate hermeneutic assumes that "cure" is the goal of all who have impairments of various sorts so that the disabled person's body will resemble more closely the normate body that the society deems as ideal. But some people with impairments are not, in fact, obsessed with achieving a normate body. Rather, they maintain that creation radiates diversity—that bodies come in all different shapes, sizes, colors, forms, and configurations—and that there is no reason to value one more than the other. What if, instead of focusing upon "curing" differently abled bodies to bring them in line with a cultural ideal, a society began to honor the true diversity of embodied existence and valued that diversity, resulting in creating societies whose architecture (literal and metaphorical) accommodated—no, celebrated—that wide variety as testifying to the full image of God, rather than valuing only one type of body (so-called "able")? In a society driven by the medical model, which sees impairment as a problem to be eradicated, judgment looms large upon those who do not cooperate in the effort to "overcome" their difference. This is one of the places where vigorous debate ensues in the disability community about issues of "passing" and the place of "Otherness."

Third, both ancient and modern interpreters reflect what Warren Carter cites as a "physiognomic consciousness" that "posits a correlation between physical appearance and moral character and shifts attention to matters of character. Thus it focuses on physical ugliness and somatic deformity in that they represent evil, vice, stupidity and low status" (2011a, 130). Jesus makes this move, according to Carter, when he insists that the man's illness is connected to poor moral character. Some illnesses are. Carter's review of commentaries on this passage demonstrates that this is a common approach. Such interpretive moves are made by the likes of B. F. Westcott, who opines that

> the paralyzed man *acquiesces* in his condition by failing to get into the "stirred up" waters in time to be healed. Marked by apathy, he lacks willingness to "make any vigorous effort to gain relief." Raymond Brown describes him as marked by "obtuseness," an "unimaginative approach to the curative waters," "a chronic inability to seize opportunity," "real dullness," and "persistent naiveté." C. H. Dodd thinks that the man "refused to make use of [Torah's] means of grace;" he "has not the will" to live, and offers a "feeble excuse" for not getting into the water. (Carter 2011a, 131; emphasis added)

One of the chief problems with this physiognomic approach is, again, erasure of actual physical disability. That is to say, the focus becomes centered on the man's (supposed) character or (speculative) psychological motivations; the fact of the man's actual physical disability and the social, spiritual, political, and economic realities or consequences of that fact are rendered invisible. This is a problematic hermeneutical approach that erases the importance of those realities for contemporary individuals, communities, and societies. But the problem is generated by the Johannine text itself.

Fourth, linking sin with impairment can be a dangerous, destructive habit. A connection may be possible in particular cases, but such is not inevitable. Similarly, tying salvation and forgiveness of sins to a "cure" is also problematic. It can imply that disabled persons who remain "uncured" remain unsaved or unforgiven or lacking in faith or, in fact, unhealed. This can victimize the victim, falsely identify disabled persons as "victims," and make TAB people feel superior in body and soul. Remember, "healing" and "cure" are not synonymous.

Chapter 5 as a Negative Example: Individual Sin—Wynn

Kerry Wynn admits that there is no denying Jesus' bald connection between sin and disability in the case of the man in chapter 5. Wynn commences his essay thus: "The two most common assumptions in popular theology that marginalize people with disabilities are (1) disability is caused by sin, and (2) if one has enough faith, one will be healed" (2007, 61). In his comparative analysis between the man in chapter 5 and the man born blind in chapter 9, he argues that the relationship between sin and disability in each narrative has to do with the person's *reaction* to his disability. In the case of the man in chapter 5, he writes,

> The man who had been disabled for thirty-eight years is located in the institutional healthcare system of the normate society. It is no accident that "Bethesda" is a popular name for hospitals. This is not to say that curative pools and modern medicine do not have a vital role to play in the reality of disability in the first and the twenty-first centuries. The problem is that after thirty-eight years he is still looking for a miracle cure and life has passed him by. He has bought into the role of the helpless dependent and the normate society has affirmed him in this role. That a normate society still affirms that role today can be seen in modern interpretations of this passage. (65)

The man has acquiesced to the shallow, myopic values of the dominant culture (represented by the religious authorities) rather than adopting Jesus' alternative way, truth, and life that incarnationally affirms the value and legitimacy of a wide variety of embodied existences.

As with numerous other stories in John, commentators reflexively associate this story with baptismal themes. The man never makes the healing waters before Jesus arrives and never enters the baptismal waters after: "He has failed to heed Jesus' admonition not to sin any more by remaining subject to normate society and thus 'something worse' has happened to him" (Wynn 2007, 70).

Chapter 5 as Negative Example: Systemic, Structural Sin—Carter

Warren Carter views the man more sympathetically than Wynn as he addresses this passage through a postcolonial lens, arguing that the man is disabled by the Roman Empire and his own society, a territory occupied intensively by Rome. As feminists and womanists know deeply, the politics of a society get mapped onto real bodies, particularly bodies considered deviant from the "normate" body of a given society: "These bodies [disabled bodies in John's Gospel] reveal the lie of imperial claims to be a force for wholeness and healing even while they compete with and imitate this imperial vision. John constructs an alternative world that participates in, imitates, and contests Roman power" (2011a, 129–30). Carter creatively analogizes from Frantz Fanon's *The Wretched of the Earth*, whose work is set in the context of French rule in Algeria, and Salmon Rushdie's novel *Midnight's Children*, whose context is British imperial rule over India and its consequences. Imperial powers, both ancient and modern, posture as providers of health and peace, whose leaders are often referred to as saviors. In truth, imperial powers disable people in multifarious ways from very basic needs such as access to nutritious food, clean water, medicine, sanitary living conditions, education, employment, and social mobility. Empires send their own people to war, where they sustain disabilities and invade other groups, inflicting further disabilities. Carter interrogates the narrative in chapter 5 to discern how the man's disabilities relate to empire:

> In Fanon and Rushdie's psychosomatic framing, blindness and paralysis ambiguously exhibit the overwhelming power of imperializing agents along with the reticence of the subjugated. Does the inability of the paralyzed man to move in John 5 attest overwhelming paralyzing imperial power and/or does it attest the subjugated's refusal to be moved? Does the inability of the blind man in John 9 to see attest overwhelming "shock-and-awe," blinding, imperial power (military power and every imperial structure) and/or does it attest a means whereby the subjugated refuses to acknowledge power? (136)

While most commentators worry about the link between individual sin and disability, Carter asks the important larger question of the role of social systems in disabling people: "Who sinned? At least in part, the empire and every and any politico-economic-cultural societal system that deprives people of adequate food resources and creates unjust living conditions that damage and disable people. Imperializing power and practices—whether ancient or modern, governments or multinationals—should come with a warning: they can be bad for people's health" (2011a, 145).

The man in chapter 5 raises questions for those in (post)modern societies. Is this man truly a whining victim, or are commentators blaming the victim? If he is repulsive to behold, is it because of his own weak character, or is it a result of what the system has done to him? Of course, all colonizing agents know that the best way to keep a people subjugated is to have them internalize messages of nonagency and weakness and worthlessness, and simultaneously to have the subalterns mimic the values of the colonizers such that to "make it" means to associate with and be what those in power most respect: strong, able-bodied people.

Where Caesar fails, Jesus can deliver. He can heal and save (and, perhaps incidentally, he also cures). He can provide true peace based on justice, and he can bring abundant, eternal life. In Jesus, not Caesar, one may find healing. The man in chapter 5 may be cured, but he is not healed. He chooses to side with the empire and its values and is not, in fact, depicted as restored to himself, to God, or to his own (Jewish) community. Whether or not one declares him a victim, he has sided with the values of the empire/normate society.

JOHN 9: SIGHT AND INSIGHT

Like the Samaritan woman in chapter 4, the man born blind bedazzles the reader as a paradigmatic disciple to be imitated. John's Gospel features several dramatic aspects such that its lengthy narratives can often be effectively divided into scenes.

Scene 1: The Cure (vv. 1-7)

"As he walked along, he saw a man blind from birth" (v. 1). Unlike the man in chapter 5, this man is designated as having a congenital impairment. Immediately, Jesus' disciples reflect the problematic physiognomic tendency to attach disability to moral character. They assume that the blindness is a punishment for sin, either the man's or his parents. Jesus promptly extinguishes their logic and separates sin and disability. While many modern readers applaud Jesus for that, their relief is short-lived when they consider Jesus' next words, which the NRSV translates thus: "Neither this man nor his parents sinned; he was born blind so that God's works might be revealed in him. We must work the works of him who sent me while it is day; night is coming when no one can work" (vv. 3-4). Did God cause the man to be born with an impairment for the sole purpose of using him as a prop in a divine magic show? Does the God who sent Jesus into the world that he loved so much, in order to give people abundant life, cause congenital blindness so that he might show off by curing the problem God caused? If so, why does God choose to cure some congenital impairments and not others? There is certainly never an indication in this story that faith is a prerequisite for a cure. In fact, there is no indication that the man was seeking a cure.

Two comments about the ancient Greek text are in order here. First, the ancient manuscripts with which translators work are composed in *scripta continua*, continuous script. There are no spaces between words, no punctuation marks, no distinctions between capital and lowercase letters, and certainly no chapter or verse numbers. All those features are judgments made by modern translators of different English versions. Second, the phrase which the NRSV translates as "he was born blind" does not actually appear in the Greek text at all. It makes more sense, given the rest of the Gospel, to translate the passage this way: "Jesus answered, 'Neither this man nor his parents sinned; [he was born blind]. In order that God's works might be revealed in him, we must work the works of him who sent me while it is day; night is coming when no one can work.'" Reading the text this way, we see Jesus moving away from an obsession with determining whose fault the man's impairment was, whether the man's, the parents', or God's. It is simply a fact: the man was born blind. The reality is, he continues to be blind at that moment. While the disciples busy themselves with an academic exercise in theological hair-splitting, here sits a person (a person, not a "case") with an impairment. Even if they were able to determine whose fault it is, it does not change the fact that the man cannot see. Jesus turns them away from speculating about the past, focuses their gaze on the person in front of them, and asks them to consider whether or not they are going to work for and with God or, as we see later in the story in the case of the Pharisees, whether they are going to work for themselves and against God. Jesus definitively declares and demonstrates that, for his part, he sides with God. We have already heard about light (1; 8) and works (4:34; 5:34 describes the man in ch. 9; 5:36 describes Jesus' works).

Once again (cf. 1:1), the author alludes to the creation accounts of Genesis by showing Jesus' creative act, using the earth for the sake of the earth creature. As in chapter 5, the man does not ask for a cure; Jesus acts upon him. Does this make the blind man a pawn without agency? The man does, as in chapter 5, obey Jesus' command and, as a result, receives sight. The reference to washing in the pool of Siloam raises baptismal echoes for many. Whereas the man in chapter 5 never enters the waters, this man does.

Scene 2: What Do the Neighbors Think? (vv. 8-12)

The rest of the story narrates various reactions to the healing: the man's, the neighbors', the parents', and the religious authorities'. So completely have the neighbors identified the man with his impairment that they are bemused, trying to decide whether or not it is the same man. The man refuses their binary categories and claims an integrated identity with his response: "I am" (Ἐγώ εἰμι, *egō eimi*; note that the word "the man" does not appear in the text but has been inserted by the translators). That is, he is both the very man who used to sit and beg and he is something more than that, all at once. Moving into one's future story with God, for John, does not mean denying one's former life (see chs. 4 and 21). Like most normate gazers, the neighbors identify him with his disability; he does not. He is the same person blind or sighted. The "I-Am" (*egō eimi*) statements constitute one of the most famous and celebrated features of the Gospel's conveyance of its christological claims. Use of the *egō eimi* on his part associates him with Jesus and is a bold expression of identity. The fact that he had to keep saying it (ἔλεγεν, *elegen*) implies an ongoing interaction and interrogation.

The neighbors repeatedly (ἔλεγον, *elegon*) demand an explanation. Healing usually has social ramifications. When one person receives healing, others want to know whether it will disturb their own equilibrium. We will see the same fear and lack of support from the parents and the religious leaders. The man recounts the experience using Jesus' name (which implies some knowledge of Jesus) and the same words as the narrator used: the man is a reliable character.

Verse 13 again raises the question of the man's agency. Why would the neighbors "bring" the man to the Pharisees when he can see? If the language is merely figurative, by what authority do they act upon the man? The neighbors continue to treat the man as "lesser than" (implied already by their naming him a beggar) and assume that they have the right to drag him to the authorities. Those who are in wheelchairs may recognize the experience where someone may approach them and take the handles of the wheelchair and move them "out of the way" without even asking permission. No one would walk up to a TAB person and grab their shoulders without permission and move them.

Scene 3: Pharisees (vv. 13-17)

The reader now learns that, as in chapter 5, Jesus performed the cure/miracle on the Sabbath. On the surface the conversation appears to be about the miracle cure, as verse 14 repeats that he "opened his eyes" and verse 15 has the Pharisees continually ask him "how he had received his sight." The verb is in the imperfect tense (ἠρώτων, *ērōtōn*), stressing the ongoing ordeal to which the man is being subjected. He stands firmly confident and unabashed as he epitomizes his experience, giving his testimony and becoming an evangelist. Like the neighbors, instead of celebrating with the man and giving glory to God, the Pharisees bicker among themselves, but this time about the identity of Jesus rather than the man born blind, so that the story transitions to the question of whether Jesus is a sinner, not whether the man is a sinner. The man is now called to testify. Whereas he first identified Jesus merely as a person (ἄνθρωπος, *anthrōpos*), he now reveals a deeper understanding of who Jesus is: a prophet.[3] To call Jesus a prophet is to ascribe him religious authority; recall that Moses, Elijah, and Elisha all performed healing miracles.

Scene 4: The Parent Trap (vv. 18-23)

The religious leaders next interrogate the man's parents in order to build a case against Jesus. To say that the parents fail to support their son in any way as he attempts to negotiate the power structures of his society is an understatement. They cower, fearing the cost of defending their son, while the formerly disabled man speaks truth to power. No matter—he is probably used to standing *alone* and *against*. But who is more disabled here, the man or his parents?

Scene 5: Pharisees, Round Two (vv. 24-34)

This passage drips with irony based on the verb "to know" (γινώσκω, *ginōskō*). They declare to know that Jesus is a sinner and they want to bully the man into siding with them and against Jesus. The man pleads ignorance concerning their academic debate but insists on what he does know—Jesus did, in fact, open his eyes (literally and metaphorically). They continue to badger him, but he knows that they are impervious to the gospel so he has a bit of fun at their expense. He acts up.

---

[3] Old Testament prophets, such as Elisha, Elijah, and Moses, often performed miracles. The same pattern of burgeoning comprehension regarding Jesus' identity appears in 4:1-42.

As usual, acting up to the powers that be brings swift castigation, threat, and rejection. They attempt to dissociate Jesus from Moses in order to make the man choose Moses. They base this on their so-called knowledge. The irony remains thick about who knows what. They declare that they do not know where Jesus is from and base their rejection of him upon that fact. The experienced reader of John knows that the question of where Jesus is from (above), by whom he has been sent (God),[4] and where he is going (to God) is paramount and that the leaders condemn themselves by accidentally speaking the truth because, in fact, they do not know where Jesus is from and they do not care to learn the truth about him. Both what they know and what they do not know indict them. The man commandeers the floor and presents a logical theological argument. They try to subordinate the man with the statement: "*We* . . . but *you* . . ." He dismisses their move and in verses 31-33 declares, "*We*[5] know that God does not listen to sinners, but he does listen to one who worships him and obeys his will [which the leaders are patently failing to do]. . . . If this man were not *from God*, he could do nothing [let alone miraculously provide sight]." They immediately dissociate themselves once again, using categories of "you" and "us." The plot of the entire narrative (beginning with 1:11) involves the quest of the religious leaders to disable Jesus because of his refusal to accept the unjust, death-dealing, violent terms of normate society. When this formerly blind man chooses to side with Jesus, they move to ad hominem attack that focuses on the man's sin, just as the disciples had done at the beginning. The verb used in verse 34, ἐκβάλλω (*ekballō*), is quite violent; it is the word used for driving out demons. Demonizing those who refuse to cooperate with hegemonic systems is common, of course (recall that Jesus is accused of having a demon in the very next chapter), and is a general claim even today about PWDs.

Scene 6: Fade to Black (vv. 35-41)

In the final scene, Jesus once again initiates the action between the man and himself and the man's insight about Jesus' revelation as the Son of

[4] The author plays on this theme by telling the reader that Jesus sends (9:7) the man to the pool of Siloam (which means "Sent") to wash (which amounts to doing the works of God).

[5] "The most stringent power we have over another is not physical coercion but the ability to have the other accept our definition of them" (Hauerwas 2004, 40). "Bodies show up in stories as dynamic entities that resist or refuse the cultural scripts assigned to them" (Mitchell and Snyder 2007, 276).

Man is revealed: "You have seen (ὁράω, *horaō*) him" (v. 37). Note the use of the perfect tense here, whose force is to highlight that the completed action has ongoing effect in the present. So complete is the man's understanding and commitment that he now calls Jesus not "person" or even "prophet," but "Lord" (Κύριε, *Kyrie*) and declares his belief. Given that the author clearly states that the purpose of the Gospel is to engender belief (20:31), the man perfectly exemplifies the call to discipleship. His willingness to engage Jesus and ask questions about his identity (reminiscent of the Samaritan woman earlier) leads him, finally, to worship (προσκυνέω, *proskuneō*) Jesus (v. 38).

Jesus then speaks for the benefit of the Pharisees when he says, "I came into this world for judgment so that those who do not see may see, and those who do see may become blind" (v. 39); the reader is reminded of Jesus' earlier statements about seeing, light, and darkness: "Very truly, I tell you, no one can see the kingdom of God without being born from above" (3:3). Clearly the man born blind sees the kingdom of God. Further, Jesus says, "And this is the judgment, that the light has come into the world, and people loved darkness rather than light because their deeds were evil. For all who do evil hate the light and do not come to the light, so that their deeds may not be exposed. But those who do what is true come to the light, so that it may be clearly seen that their deeds have been done in God" (3:19-21). Jesus, the light, has come into the world and is shining in the faces of the religious leaders. They hate the light and want to do the evil deed of disabling Jesus through death. The man born blind sees the light and does the work of God by believing in Jesus. The Pharisees intuit that Jesus refers to them, and they find it incredible that they, given all their knowledge, status, and power, should be considered blind (which is a code word for "ignorant" here: as the saying goes, "There are none so blind as those who will not see"). Jesus disrupts the analogy by indicating that those born blind (as was the man they have just accused of being a sinner) are not sinners. Those who stand judged are the temporarily able-bodied, physically sighted who claim too much for themselves with respect to insight and commit the sin of willful ignorance, not to mention abuse of power (cf. 15:22) and the demeaning of those without physical sight.

Promises

John 9 houses liberative potential for persons with disabilities. First, Jesus corrects the assumption that impairment is caused by sin. Second, he calls his disciples to work on behalf of those pushed to the margins socially, religiously, and economically by impairment. Third, this nameless man born blind gets the spotlight as one of the exemplars of the narrative; all readers should aspire to imitate him. He achieves this role not by showing that if one has great faith, one can be cured of a physical impairment. He is not a hero because he was cured (after all, the man in chapter 5 was also cured) or because he "overcame" his disability through pluck and determination. He was not even seeking a cure, as far as we know. He is a paragon because when he has a transformative encounter with Jesus, he responds by giving glory to God, becoming a disciple of Jesus, and evangelizing those around him. He himself, then, shows the fulfillment of Jesus' promise that his disciples would do greater works than Jesus himself did. Fourth, the man claims his voice and insists on the truth as he knows it, even though those with more education, power, and status try to induce doubt and "keep him in his place." The text supports acting up on behalf of justice.

The text overtly challenges any TAB reader who views persons with disabilities physiognomically, assuming to know something about the person's character or life by a mere gaze.[6] Furthermore, able-bodied people who paternalistically think that they know what is best for those with disabilities should feel addressed by the text. The voices of those actually experiencing the disability should be heard and heeded. That is, the voices of the "invalids" are *valid* beyond all telling of it. At first the narrative displays able-bodied people who objectify the man. The more the man himself speaks, the more the categories of center and margins are redefined. In Colleen Grant's view, "The typical sin/sickness metaphor is reversed so that blindness is no longer a symbol for humanity's sinfulness, but instead representative of a state of innocence and openness to revelation" (1998, 85).

As noted in our treatment of chapter 5, Carter indicts imperial systems for the ways that persons are disabled. The fact that the man was born blind may have to do with economic and social realities such as lack of access to food, nutrition, and medicine. His disability may have made him a mendicant, as his career options would have been limited. When Jesus cures the impairment caused by poverty, he "repairs imperial damage" by raising his social class (2011a, 144).

Wynn finds a vigorous, heroic figure in the man born blind, especially in contrast to the man in chapter 5. He has a rather optimistic view of the

---

[6] Grant suggests that the punch might be that we able-bodied folks in our hubris and pride about our able-bodiedness compared to the poor disabled in need of healing may not realize we are more in need of healing because our sin of stereotyping and excluding remains (1998, 85). Referring to the diagnostic gaze of Ezra/Nehemiah, Wynn writes, "The 'gaze' in Ezra–Nehemiah creates a narrative based on the presuppositions of the observer which shapes the image of the object observed" (145 in this volume).

man's begging activity, claiming that it was a legitimate job that made him a part of the religious system of his day (since giving to a beggar was a good deed). "It is more blessed to give than to receive," as the saying goes. The man is living a meaningful life and seems to have dealt with his impairment in such a way that he did not feel a severe lack: "He has rejected the normate stereotype of one disabled as 'victim' but has not substituted a need to 'overcome' his disability or 'pass' as 'normal.' He is comfortable in his identity as 'other' than the normate social stereotypes. . . . It is in his ability to reject the normate perspective and to embrace Jesus in their mutual 'otherness,' not in the act of healing, that 'God's work might be revealed in him' (9:3)" (2007, 68).

Pitfalls

While the text clearly stands as one of the most liberative in the Bible with respect to disability, a few concerns should be noted. First is the use of blindness as a metaphor for sin and ignorance. On the positive side, the person who is literally blind in the story is good, and those who are only metaphorically blind are bad. On the negative side, the association between sin and ignorance, if only metaphorical, remains unhelpful to actual blind persons trying to function in normate society (cf. 12:40 esp.). In his treatment of John 9 in *In the Beginning There Was Darkness: A Blind Person's Conversation with the Bible*, John M. Hull explains that the Gospel of John is problematic:

> Although blindness is symbolic of sin and unbelief in the three earlier Gospels, it is in the Fourth Gospel that this connection reaches its climax. John's Gospel was the first book in Braille that I read after I had become blind in my adult life. As I read it, rather laboriously, I was delighted to have access once again to so many familiar and greatly loved passages. However, the symbolism made me feel uneasy and I soon came to realize that this book was not written for people like me, but for sighted people. No other book of the Bible is so dominated by the contrast between light and darkness, and blindness is the symbol of darkness.[7] (2002, 49-50)

Second, readers should be careful about the tendency to erase disability by interpreting the narrative metaphorically, as the text pushes the reader to do. It lulls the reader away from "the real world" and interrogating hegemonic systems that disable real people. It also reduces persons

---

[7] African American interpreters routinely draw attention to the association of darkness with negative characteristics.

with disabilities to a mere "moral lesson" of one sort or another for able-bodied persons.

JOHN 11: I AM THE RESURRECTION AND THE LIFE

The language of illness or weakness occurs five times in the first six verses of chapter 11:

> v. 1: Now a certain man was ill (Ἦν ἀσθενῶν, ēn asthenōn).
> v. 2: Her brother was ill (ἠσθένει, ēsthenei).
> v. 3: Lord, he whom you love is ill (ἀσθενεῖ, asthenei).
> v. 4: This illness (ἀσθένεια, astheneia) does not lead to death.
> v. 6: having heard that Lazarus was ill (ἀσθενεῖ, asthenei).

The use of the imperfect tense in verse 1 might imply a chronic illness or disability. Jesus heads back to Bethany near Jerusalem, the center of opposition to him. Thomas (the Eeyore of the Gospel), expecting the worst violence to be perpetrated against them, resignedly declares, "Let us also go, that we may die with him" (v. 16).

What follows is a story less about Lazarus and more about Mary and Martha, the siblings of the utterly disabled man. They are grief-stricken. Like the disciples in chapter 9, they focus on the past rather than the present: "If only the past had been different, this tragedy would not have materialized" (v. 21; my paraphrase); they both indicate that "if only" Jesus had been there, Lazarus would not have died. They subtly, if bitterly, accuse Jesus for allowing tragedy. As in chapter 9, Jesus tries to draw their attention to the only time that they have any control over—the present: "Your brother will rise again" (v. 23). At this point Martha is in danger of whiplash as she jerks her gaze from the useless past to the distant future: "I know that he will rise again in the resurrection on the last day" (v. 24). But Jesus wants her to turn her face and train her eyes on the very full, abundant present that is available here and now in his presence, so he declares, "I am the resurrection (ἀνάστασις, anastasis) and the life (ζωή, zōē). Those who believe in me, even though they die, will live, and everyone who lives and believes in me will never die. Do you believe this?" (vv. 25-26). Martha then makes a full confession of Jesus by nearly quoting the author's thesis statement from 20:31: "Yes, Lord, I believe that you are the Messiah, the Son of God, the one coming into the world" (v. 27). "The one coming into the world" (ὁ εἰς τὸν κόσμον ἐρχόμενος, ho eis ton kosmon erchomenos) is a christological title in John and is tied directly to the incarnation (cf. 1:9). The point is not to escape the world but to transform it such that it promotes the flourishing of all creation, the creation that God carefully orchestrated. God is always at work in the world, in embodied lives. For John, verses 25-27 constitute the primary point to be made in 11:1-44. The story serves to reveal Jesus' identity and invite the reader into relationship with the Johannine Jesus and community. The healing story that follows simply fleshes out this main point.

Jesus weeps. This matters. Those who see it and understand his deep love for his friend ask the poignant perennial question that arises for persons with disabilities and those who love them: "Could not he who opened the eyes of the blind man have kept this man from dying?" (v. 37). The reader already knows that the simple answer to that is yes, based on the healing story in chapter 4. But this is not that story. Jesus comes to the tomb (μνημεῖον, *mnēmeion*) in verse 38. The word first appears at 5:28 where Jesus says, "Do not be astonished at this; for the hour is coming when all who are in their graves (μνημεῖον, *mnēmeion*) will hear his voice." The next time we see the word, Jesus is calling out to Lazarus in a loud voice to "come out." The next occurrence after that is Jesus' own tomb, where another stone (λίθος, *lithos*) appears, and is taken away, as in verse 39 (cf. 20:1). Clearly, the author ties our suffering to that of Jesus, infusing it with meaning and hope.

Verse 44 tells us that the "dead man (ὁ τεθνηκὼς, *ho tethnēkōs*) came out." Notice that the verb is in the perfect tense, the tense used to indicate an action in the past that has continuing effect in the present. This is a crucial point, especially from the social model of disability. Jesus has raised him up, but the man is still described as dead. He is also still bound. Notice what Jesus does. He does not zap away the bindings; rather, he calls the community to unbind the man who had been held captive by the rancid stench of death. Communities disable and enable. Throughout the chapter the whole community has gathered around to fret and mourn dramatically for a few days; but does the community have the will to enable Lazarus, and not just in those first dramatic moments, but for the rest of his life? The miraculous healing symbolically makes the christological point that Jesus, like God, is in the glorious business of life. But the physical cure itself is evanescent since Lazarus will die again at some point. The story is about Jesus, but the story is, more important, about what kind of communities we create: Are they disabling or enabling? Jesus cured the impairment, but the community has the power to remove the disability/bindings.

It is worth noting that scholars do not at all agree about how to interpret the statements referring to Jesus' emotional state in verses 33, 35, and 38. Most people simply associate Jesus' emotions with grief over loss. But the verbs express anger and frustration, and it is not unreasonable to assume that Jesus is upset because, while flamboyant theatrics and concern arise once the disabled Lazarus is dead, one wonders whether the level of energy and concern were there before he died, and will it be there once he is among them again?

This is a story about God's glory insofar as it displays God's character as one coming into the world to make a way out of no way. Notice that Jesus never promises that believers will not suffer or die (in fact, quite the opposite; cf. the Farewell Discourse in chs. 14–17). Jesus relativizes suffering and death; it is no longer ultimate. Eternal life, which is a certain quality of life marked by abundance, joy, peace, and love, is available now and will continue forever. Death does not and cannot interfere with any of that ultimately, because Jesus has cast out that power through his exaltation on the cross whereby he accomplished his promise declared at 12:32: "And I, when I am lifted up from the earth, will draw all people to myself." *All* people, not just some. On the other hand, there are people walking around us all the time who might as well be dead—they have not seized the abundant life readily available to them. This is what John is saying: there is living and then there is *living*. Or, using Irenaeus' terms, there is *existing* and there is *flourishing* (*Haer.* 4.34.5–7).

As in chapters 5 and 9, the healing of Lazarus does not cause the authorities to celebrate or give glory to God; rather "the chief priests planned to put Lazarus to death as well, since it was on account of him that many of the Jews were deserting and were believing in Jesus" (12:10-11). Certain social, political, economic, and religious systems benefit from keeping some people disabled or dead. The raising of Lazarus serves to foreshadow Jesus' own death and resurrection. Jesus dies only once, of course. Lazarus will eventually die again, but that will not be ultimately devastating. John assures us that once one grasps the ultimate eternal power of the resurrection and the life available through Jesus and the fact that both start here and now, the grave can offer no real threat. Only three chapters later Jesus will reiterate the point by announcing: "I am the way; that is, the truth and the life" (14:6; my trans.).

Promises and Pitfalls

From a disability perspective, the story has liberative potential. It calls readers to stop playing the "if only" game, to embrace abundant life in the present, and to enjoy the peace that Christ brings even in the face of suffering and death. It challenges society to understand that both disability and liberation are a communal project, not an individual's problem that the person should figure out how to solve. Many would like to take the approach of Pontius Pilate, whereby they wash their hands of the whole matter. Alas, Pontius Pilate is not a strong role model.

But the text may leave us unsatisfied in other ways. First, Lazarus never gets to speak anywhere in the Gospel. He has no agency but appears only as an object to be discussed and acted upon. It is another example of narrative prosthesis in which Lazarus is more of a device to convey the Gospel's Christology than a character in his own right. Second, the theodicy question (the defense of God's love and justice in light of evil, suffering, and death) will still burn in the hearts of many: "Could not he who opened the eyes of the blind man have kept this man from dying?" (11:37). And further, why are some cured and others not? Third, the notion that Jesus intentionally allowed Lazarus to die in order to allow God to perform a publicity stunt to get more adherents (as the text seems to indicate in vv. 4, 15, and 40-42) remains problematic at best.

THE PASSION

In the passion we see the full unleashing of the power of both the religious establishment and imperial authorities brought to bear upon Jesus' body. The high priest's police hit Jesus in the face (18:22). After Pilate has Jesus whipped, the soldiers mock and abuse him. Pilate has Jesus (and two other deviants) crucified. Their brutal, exterminatory lust still unsatiated, the soldiers not only break the legs of the other two but also spear Jesus in the side, whence blood and water issue forth.

Rome dominates the native government, and both map their power onto Jesus' body. Rome symbolically whips Israel; the religious leaders oppress those less powerful and collude in Jesus' death through scapegoating and stigmatizing.[8] Recall Caiaphas' (ironic) words: "You do not understand that it is better for you to have one man die for the people than to have the whole nation destroyed" (11:50). Some people with disabilities will relate to society's habit of stigmatizing and scapegoating.

Promises

The Passion has liberative potential because it is tied to the incarnation. Jesus himself truly experienced disdain, shame, humiliation, and even

---

[8] "The convention of metaphoricalizing disability invisibilizes the somatic impact of collisions between colonizers and colonized. Such encounters literally disable bodies as both sides pursue and contest the imperial agenda of subjugating people and seizing resources and land" (Carter 2011a, 137).

physical violence. In this way he has intimately assumed the experience of many people with disabilities.

By his own estimation, his suffering has a redemptive quality to it as seen by his analogy between his crucifixion and Moses' lifting upon the serpent in the wilderness (3:14) for the healing of his people. Others throughout Christian history have understood their own suffering to have a redemptive quality (cf. 12:24). How do we honor suffering without glorifying and sensationalizing it? Suffering does not guarantee wisdom, but no great wisdom comes without suffering. Only the sufferer has the right to discern whether her own suffering is of the redemptive sort; no one should ever attempt to coerce or even suggest to one suffering that this must be so in her case.

At the very least, the disabled body of Jesus on the cross serves as an indictment of the ways societies disable some of their members. It may demand soul-searching, renew our commitment to justice, and bring healing and freedom for those on both ends of the whip.

RESURRECTION AND ETERNAL LIFE

The Gospel of John narrates four different resurrection appearances. First, Jesus appears to Mary Magdalene in the garden. Like other passages in John that point to God's creative power, this scene in the garden undoes the fall in Eden. Creation is reconciled and restored to wholeness. Jesus then appears to his disciples. In keeping with the Gospel's insistence on the incarnation and the goodness of somatic existence, Jesus appears in bodily form. But this body is both like and unlike his preresurrection body. On the one hand, it penetrates locked doors; on the other, it retains the marks (which Paul refers to as stigmata in Gal 6:17) of his disabling experience. The disciple Thomas was not present at this appearance and, famously, declares, "Unless I see the mark of the nails in his hands, and put my finger in the mark of the nails and my hand in his side, I will not believe" (John 20:25). Jesus appears a third time and invites Thomas to touch his wounds. It is the sight of Jesus' marks of disability that cause Thomas to ejaculate confessionally, "My Lord and my God!" (20:28).

The fourth appearance occurs on the shore of Galilee where Jesus materializes in recognizable bodily form. He reconciles with Peter, releases him from the debilitating effects of his guilt and shame, and commissions him to ministry, with a warning: "Very truly, I tell you, when you were younger, you used to fasten your own belt and to go wherever you wished. But when you grow old, you will stretch out your hands, and someone else will fasten a belt around you and take you where you do not wish to go"

(21:18). Clearly this is a reference to Peter's impending martyrdom. It may also be suggestive for those who have developed a disability in adulthood or even old age. Moving from able-bodiedness to disability may involve some loss of autonomy, but it need not entail a loss of meaning or mission.[9] It may, however, require assistance.

Promises

For Christians, resurrection and eternal life are somatic experiences. Images of feasting (chs. 6, 13, 21) point to a messianic feast where none will be disabled through hunger. Jesus' own body bears the marks of his specific lived experience, but his body transcends all finite limits. Wynn asks, "If disability is to be affirmed as a meaningful and valid life experience, what are we to say about disability in the resurrection?" (2007, 75). He proceeds to note of the man in chapter 9 that even though the man moves into a normate body, the important point is that he retains the lessons from his disabled experience. Regardless of what the resurrected body entails, those lessons will be retained.

Like Paul, John presents both the disabled ("crucified in weakness"; 2 Cor 13:4) Christ and "the glorified, powerful Christ—the Christ beyond all disabilities and limitations. . . . It is the paradoxical connection between the two that is the center of Paul's message" (Albl 2007, 147). Paul used his disability to manifest God's power and anticipated a day when his limitations would be overcome. He called others to use their circumstances the same way and to stand firm in the hope of finally overcoming all limitations.

In John, Jesus repeatedly refers to his cross as his exaltation (ὑψόω, *hypsoō*). What the ignorant world takes to be his moment of deepest shame, the expert reader understands to be his moment of victory: "And I, when I am lifted up, will draw all people to myself" (12:32). That moment is not separable from the resurrection for John. Disability does not have the last word either for Jesus or for us. By sharing in Jesus' disability (Jesus warns the disciples that the world will hate them as it hated him and informs Peter that he will be martyred), Christians can "overcome all disability" by sharing Christ's resurrection and glorification.

Pitfalls

Mitchell and Snyder raise important concerns about what they term "the limits of redemption narratives" (2007, 178). Miraculous healings and

---

[9] Read Philip Simmons, *Learning to Fall: The Blessings of an Imperfect Life*, 2003.

resurrections are problematic insofar as they rely on the eradication of disability as a resolution to human-made exclusion. The social constructions that propagate the exclusion and oppression of people with disabilities remain intact. Take note of Zacchaeus. He was a little person (μικρὸς, *mikros*; Luke 19:3). He was "healed" by Jesus insofar as he was restored to the community with a sense of honor and validation, without Jesus "curing" him by adding inches to his physical height.

With this in mind, it would be more impressive and hope inducing in some ways if, instead of curing the disabled body to fit normate society, normate society were healed so that the society would accommodate all types of bodies. As noted, "The acceptance of disabled people can no longer be predicated on the perverse interests that underwrite fantasies of erasure, cure, or elimination of bodily difference. Such longings for human similitude ultimately avoid rather than engage the necessity of providing provisions for our meaningful inclusion in social life" (Mitchell and Snyder 2007, 183).

Summary/Conclusion

With respect to persons with disabilities, the Gospel of John has both liberative and problematic potential. The emphasis on diversity in creation, the incarnation, a blind man as a hero, the role of the community in healing, and the ability to seize life, joy, and peace in the present even in the midst of difficulty are a welcome balm. The texts also sound warnings. Empires and societies tend to disable some people. TABs assume a normate view that disables people with certain impairments. This happens in the way that they narrate stories and the way that they interpret stories. In the process, people with disabilities are often presented as a morality lesson and remain objects rather than agents in the plot. Erasure occurs. Finally, by insisting upon material creation as the locus of God's attention and activity, the Fourth Evangelist emboldens the reader to interpret in ways that promote the flourishing of all, even when that entails resisting some of the Evangelist's own moves.

THE JOHANNINE EPISTLES

Reading the Johannine Epistles from a disability perspective invites attention to (1) the role of the senses, (2) ethics and incarnation as expressed in embodied love, (3) hospitality, (4) the role of prayer, and (5) the "prosperity" gospel.

First John

The Senses

Like the Gospel, 1 John begins at the beginning (ἀγχῆ, *archē*). The prologue anticipates a major theme of the Epistle—namely, the incarnation, the embodiedness of the Messiah, such that he could be perceived by the senses: he was seen, heard, and touched. In addition, the transmission of the gospel involves the embodiedness of one's brothers and sisters (3:16-18) and abiding with another in love; as the text demonstrates, this ideal can be elusive. The author claims epistemological authority based on sensory experiences. Their testimony is to be trusted because they were able to see and hear. Hearing (ἀκούω, *akouō*) language occurs fourteen times in the Epistles and fifty-nine times in John. Seeing language (ὁράω, *horaō*; βλέπω, *blepō*; and θεωρέω, *theōreō*) appears often as well: 121 times in John and 12 times in the Epistles. What might this mean for people who are blind or deaf? Can they know God as well and authoritatively transmit the tradition? Hector Avalos' work on sensory criticism aims, in part, to "examine how the valuation of the senses is intimately related to the differential valuation of persons that lies at the core of defining disabilities" (2007, 47). In antiquity a blind person was not necessarily disabled in terms of valuation of knowledge, as the trope of the blind prophet proves (both in biblical and pagan literature). Prophets hear the word of the Lord. Job, on the other hand, depends upon vision. Avalos argues, "Sensory criticism can render us more sensitive to how the gathering and processing of information has been a continuing theme in the differential treatment of human beings that underlies all notions of disability, whether in the medical or social models" (59).

In 1 John sighted people have no advantage over unsighted people in apprehending God: God is not visible to the human eye at this point in history but only through acts of love (4:20); until the eschaton (and the full unveiling of God's face), the only way to surely connect to God is to practice loving with the expectation that practice will make perfect, eventually.

Love Embodied in Action—Ethics and Incarnation

The author enjoins the audience to "walk" (περιπατέω, *peripateō*) in the light, the truth, and the commandments (1 John 1:6-7; 2:6, 11; 2 John 1:4, 6; 3 John 1:3-4). The language of "walking" as a metaphor for ethical behavior is common in the Hebrew Bible and stems from the verb הלך (*hālak*, "to walk"). Hence, even today the collection of rabbinical ethical teachings is called the halakah. The language is, of course, metaphorical here.

The leitmotif of 1 John is love. To behave ethically in the Epistles is to love as Jesus has loved—to the extent of laying down his life. This love commandment dominates as it has "from the beginning." The latter is a favorite phrase of the author and is multivalent. Surely it means at least: from the beginning of everything, since it defines God's character (4:16); from the beginning of creation; from the beginning of humanity's story (Cain and Abel are representative of the fruits of love and hate); from the beginning of Jesus' particular work in the incarnation (cf. the Gospel of John); and from the beginning of the Johannine community in Palestine to the later stages in Ephesus. Love is foundational.

Love and incarnation are inseparable. Those who have left the community are antichrists and liars and do not love God. What makes these apostates antichrists? Their Christology does. They not only deny the Father and the Son and that Jesus is the Messiah (2:22) but also deny the flesh of Jesus. For the author it appears to be a short step from denying the importance of Christ's fleshly embodiedness to denying the importance of a neighbor's bodily needs. When one does this, one walks in the footsteps of Cain, who is associated with the evil one and traffics in fratricide (3:12-15). The author makes the ethical demand clear: "We know love by this, that he laid down his life for us—and we ought to lay down our lives for one another. How does God's love abide in anyone who has the world's goods and sees a brother or sister in need and yet refuses help? Little children, let us love, not in word or speech, but in truth and action" (3:16-18).

The emphasis on care and justice for those in need draws attention to disability concerns. Who is poor and why? Certainly disability is more prominent where poverty prevails. Faith and love belong together and coalesce in a concern for justice. Beutler declares,

> Christians living in affluence must share their material goods with their brothers and sisters beyond the boundaries of their Christian communities on a worldwide scale and challenge unjust social structures. . . . For the nations of the northern hemisphere, this responsibility means sharing their wealth with the nations of the south. But this commandment also applies to the developing nations that are characterized by vast inequality in material wealth. A rich ruling class often exploits the masses of the poor. (2004, 556, 558)

For this author, having the right Christology is not merely an academic exercise but is essential for acting justly, which is to say, loving in the way that God loves (ἀγάπη, agapē, language occurs forty-eight times in 1 John). The denial of Jesus' fleshly existence along with the overwhelming use of "knowing" language (γινώσκω, *ginōskō*, twenty-five times; οἶδα, *oida*, fifteen times) immediately raises the specter of docetic or gnostic Christology. It is no accident that the noun "knowledge" never appears in 1 John; the emphasis is on action. Knowing is doing, and knowing rightly is tied to acting rightly. Those who disembody Jesus easily disembody their neighbor. Certain ways of "knowing" cause arrogance and disdain for others in the community. Readers should be reminded of the Pharisees in John 9 and their treatment of the blind man and ask whether they, like those Pharisees, operate from a normate standard that oppresses persons with disabilities.

Furthermore, 1 John's focus on the incarnation implies that Christians ought to be concerned with ecological matters. The prologue to John proclaims, "The Word became flesh (σάρξ, *sarx*) and tabernacled among us" (1:14). Though Jesus is the unique Son of God, he is related to us insofar as we have become children of God through his blood. As the Son, he has authority over all flesh (πᾶς σάρξ, *pas sarx*; John 17:2). Since the prologue narrates the Word's participation in the creation of everything (John 1:3), "all flesh" presumably includes the whole created order, not just human beings (cf. Rom 8). First John eschews docetist theologies that denigrate the material order. Do we? Should human beings relate to the earth in a hierarchical, dominating fashion by which the earth exists merely as an object to be used in the gratification of human greed and gluttony as described in 1 John 2:16?

Ecofeminists argue that denigration of creation is usually connected to denigration of female bodies. The power dynamic of patriarchy involves a system of hierarchy where the male rules as lord (Latin *dominus*, tied to the word "dominate") and the female (and children) are subjects (objects, really) to be used as the male sees fit. Genesis 1:28 is often brought to bear on such a discussion: "God blessed them, and God said to them, 'Be fruitful and multiply, and fill the earth and lord over (κατακυριεύσατε, *katakurieusate*) it; and rule over (ἄρχετε, *archete*) the fish of the sea and over the birds of the air and over every living thing that moves upon the earth'" (my trans. of the LXX) followed by Gen 3:16: "To the woman he said, 'I will greatly increase your pangs in childbearing; in pain you shall bring forth children, yet your desire shall be for your husband, and he shall lord over (κυριεύσει, *kurieusei*) you'" (my trans. of the LXX). Rape, of the earth or of people, is inherent in such a system. As discussed above in relation to the man who was paralyzed (John 5), postcolonialism extends the conversation to other bodies, colonized bodies, including disabled bodies.

As discussed in the treatment of the passion narrative in John, Jesus' body was disabled by the religious and political structures of his society.

He was physically violated, beaten, stabbed, and crucified. First John 5:6-7 may refer to John 19:34, where Jesus is stabbed in his side with the spear and water and blood come out. Even apart from that possible allusion, the language fits well in 1 John where the "begetting" language implies birth language, which involves both blood and water (cf. the woman in labor in John 16:21 and the womb [κοιλία, *koilia*] and water language in John 7:38 and 3:4). Furthermore, the blood of Jesus has already been mentioned in chapter 1 in relation to his salvific death. By insisting upon this earthy, earthly, wet, and bloody reality that Jesus experienced, the author may be emphasizing his actual death, thus countering once again a docetic Christology that insists that Jesus only "seemed" human.

The Power of Prayer

First John 5:14-15 raises the important issue of the place of prayer with respect to disability: "And this is the boldness we have in him, that if we ask anything according to his will, he hears us. And if we know that he hears us in whatever we ask, we know that we have obtained the requests made of him." For some people with disabilities or those who love them, these verses may feel like a mockery as they lift continual prayers for healing but healing does not come. Or they are accosted and victimized by other Christians who assure them that if they just pray harder, or have more faith, they will be healed. That is too vast a subject to treat here, but the text does insist that prayer is an essential aspect of Christian faith. The author proceeds to draw particular attention to intercessory prayer. He indicates that all injustice (ἀδικία, *adikia*) is sin. When Christians do not "do justice," do not love a brother or sister, they are not acting in accordance with God's will or loving the way God loves. They need to recognize that they are out of step with God and the community and are thereby affecting the whole group negatively. They need to recognize their sin, rely on Christ's advocacy (2:2), and move back into harmonious relationship with God and neighbor. The result will be, as usual, life.

Perhaps those with disabilities are called by this text both to point out ableist injustice and to pray for those who are in its grip, either by ignorance or malevolence. In "Disabling the Lie: Prayers of Truth and Transformation," Helen Betenbaugh and Marjorie Procter-Smith write,

> Prayer is encounter and discourse with the Holy One, and as such it demands honesty and authenticity. How then are persons with disabilities to pray? In what ways does their embodied knowledge of difference, suffering, exclusion, and rejection shape their prayers before God in the midst of the community?

How have the conventions of traditional Christian public prayer enabled or inhibited the full participation of persons with disabilities in public worship? (1998, 281)

Eschewing Idolatry

The author concludes his message to his flock on an urgent hortatory note, one that is particularly relevant for our own study: "Little children, keep yourselves from idols" (5:21). What constitute idols in our contemporary context? Do wealth, status, power, ego, vanity, and nationalism qualify? What is more idolatrous than ableism?

Just as racism is a set of cultural attitudes and sociopolitical structures that privilege the dominant race over ethnic minorities, and just as sexism is a similar set of cultural presuppositions and sociopolitical structures that perpetuate male domination over women, so ableism names the discriminatory attitudes, negative stereotypes, and sociopolitical and economic structures and institutions that together function to exclude people with disabilities from full participation in society. Ableism thus identifies the normate bigotry, evaluative chauvinism, and structural injustice that people with disabilities have to endure at the hands of the dominant (read: nondisabled) culture (Yong 2011, 11).

SECOND JOHN

Second John contains many of the same themes and uses similar language as 1 John. The ethical life is metaphorized with walking language (vv. 4, 6). The incarnation is emphasized through the author's concern about the many antichrists, former members of the community who "do not confess that Jesus Christ has come in the flesh" (v. 7; cf. 1 John 2:18, 22; 4:3). While disability per se does not overtly appear, the author's command to deny physical hospitality to those who hold differing views might deserve further attention. Their holding a different view is equated with evil deeds, and the author has a sense of "contagion" whereby welcoming someone with different views is not only to condone evil but to participate in it. Upon what basis should hospitality be extended or denied to the "other"? Most certainly, many people with disabilities have experienced inhospitality and the fear of "contagion." What is the relationship between hospitality and justice?

THIRD JOHN

As in 1 and 2 John, the language of "walking" appears. As in all the Epistles (and the Gospel of John), concern for truth predominates (vv. 1, 3, 4,

8, and 12). Like 2 John, the author raises the issue of hospitality in two ways. First, the elder sends Demetrius with a letter to Gaius, instructing him to prepare to offer hospitality to the missionaries that the elder will send. Second, the elder derogates Diotrephes, because Diotrephes not only refuses hospitality to the elder's people but also punishes anyone else who welcomes them. The same questions posed above apply to this situation.

What 3 John adds to the topic of disability and the Bible is a consideration of the relationship between one's physical health and one's spiritual health. Heather Landrus' essay canvasses interpretations of 3 John 2 over time. At issue is whether verse 2a finds Gaius in poor physical health. Lord Bishop Sumner takes him to be in poor physical health but vigorous spiritual health (Landrus, 2002, 78). Much of the interpretive history deemphasizes the importance of physical (or financial) health and draws attention to spiritual health as far more crucial. According to Landrus, having made a sharp distinction between the prosperity of the body and the prosperity of the soul, some quickly move to asceticism (Tertullian and Augustine), while others like the Benedictine Bede see prosperity as a communal category such that prosperity was a way to gift others in need. More recently, one finds figures such as Carol Judd Montgomery, Oral Roberts, and Kenneth Hagin. All experienced poor physical health, all considered this biblical verse important for their own theology, and all saw attending to the physical health of people important. In fact, Montgomery opened places of rest and healing. Hospital and hospitality are etymologically related terms, not accidentally. Oral Roberts' physical illness was combined with poverty, as was the case with Kenneth Hagin.

The interpretation of verse 2 raises questions about the relationship between faith and physical well-being as well as faith and financial well-being. Those committed to the "prosperity gospel" (also known as "the health and wealth gospel") suggest that faithful believers should expect physical and financial deliverance. Others link holiness with poverty. Are Christians free to or even obligated to succeed financially? Does wealth necessarily cause spiritual injury? Is poverty a sign of a lack of faith or a sign of blessedness? Disability studies has taught us to ask these questions about physical health as well. Should those who are physically or mentally disabled seek physical healing to conform to "normal" bodies, or can physical suffering lead to holiness (cf. 2 Cor 12)? These thorny questions beg to be addressed in community.

APOCALYPSE OF JOHN

The Importance of Genre

The Apocalypse falls into three different genres, all of which are pertinent to reading through the lens of disability. First, John considers himself a prophet and his book to be prophecy (1:3). Prophets share their message from God with God's people; the message routinely entails a call away from idolatry and the adoption of the world's values, attention to the well-being of the particularly vulnerable or marginalized, and promises of reward or punishment depending upon whether the group acts in accordance with God's sense of justice. God's people were called to repent of their sin, whether individual, communal, institutional, or national. The prophets always judged Israel by their care for those on the margins: the widow, the orphan, and the stranger in the land. This could easily include persons with disabilities. God always sides with the marginalized and takes the wealthy or privileged to task for creating religious, economic, and political systems that benefit the few at the expense of the many.

Second, the unveiling of the vision is conveyed through letters directed to the angels of seven churches in Asia Minor. John shares the vision with an eye to embodied praxis. He patently wants them to do certain things and avoid others. Some of them may complain that they should not be held responsible for faithful action because they are so powerless, but John would dismiss the complaint immediately (3:8). The importance of embodied agency for those facing difficulty or exclusion may also be empowering for people living with disabilities. Each of the seven letters follows a pattern. First, the particular church is tied to symbolism that was first presented in the vision of Christ in 1:9-20. Second, the church is praised for what it is doing well. Third, it is rebuked for what it is doing wrong. Fourth, it is given a challenge relevant to its particular situation. Finally, it is promised reward or punishment based upon whether or not it conquers (νικάω, *nikaō*). The fact that Revelation was written to seven real, specific human communities (as opposed to a random, disembodied vision) undergoing suffering and trials of various sorts by a specific person who finds himself in exile, along with John's coalescing of the language of embodied agency and conquering, may be liberative for disabled persons. The conquering is not tied to becoming or remaining able-bodied but rather is related to patient endurance (ὑπομονή, *hypomonē*; used seven times in Rev, accounting for one-quarter of all New Testament uses) and faithfulness, even if that leads to death. On the other hand, the language may oppress insofar as PWDs are expected to become exemplary paragons of "overcoming" adversity, and if they choose *not* to adopt this role, they may find themselves maligned or unworthy of attention.

Third, the Apocalypse is an apocalypse (1:1). While there are many extracanonical examples of the genre (*1 En.*; *4 Ezra*; *2 Bar.*), this is the only one included in the Christian canon. Apocalyptic is literature of protest and, most importantly, hope. It emerges from communities that perceive themselves to be under severe stress and perhaps even physical danger. It is written for and by people on the margins who do not have access to political power, and it asks hard questions: Is there any justice for the powerless and oppressed? Does God have the goodwill (benevolence) to act or the power (omnipotence)? Negatively put, is God malevolent or impotent? Apocalyptic, then, takes up the question of God's love, justice, and power. Revelation insists that God is just and powerful and, imminently, will set everything aright. The innocent who suffer will be vindicated, and the supercilious wicked will be harshly punished. Apocalyptic is literature of hope that sustains the downtrodden and exhorts them to remain faithful even under the worst of circumstances. Such literature inherently has the potential to inspire people with disabilities who presently see no light at the end of the proverbial tunnel.

Typically the members of such communities do not have political power and cannot leverage the social or economic systems of their host culture. In this case the host culture is the Roman Empire. John has been exiled to Patmos; the fact that he was not summarily executed implies that he might have enjoyed some level of social status. John sees Rome as irrevocably satanic. It cannot be overthrown by grassroots organizing and democratic vote. The only hope for its overthrow and the restoration of a just system lies in a dramatic, decisive, imminent act of God. John graphically and resolutely names the rottenness of the political, social, economic system that is Rome (see esp. ch. 18) and demands that Christians avoid participating in the system. He calls them to patient endurance (ὑπομονή, *hypomonē*) and faithfulness, even unto death. Apocalyptic, like Christian hope itself, depends upon irony. Reality is far different than it appears. On the surface it may appear that God has abdicated or lost interest in God's will being done on earth as it is in heaven. The wicked prosper and the innocent suffer. But in reality God sees it all and judges it all and will, in fact, set things right sooner rather than later. Justice will prevail. Certainly, many PWDs, like other groups before them who have wondered "How long, O God?" can relate to this scenario. The liberative potential of apocalyptic is strong because it teaches all of us, including PWDs, to name evil structures for what they are, resist their evil, and rest assured that they oppose God's own vision (that is, that the suffering stems from a problem with "the system," not the PWD) and that they stand under God's just judgment. The potential pitfall lies in encouraging passivity when it is unnecessary. That is to say, while in Rome it was impossible for Christians to "act up" politically in a way that would effect real systemic change in the government, in modern America it is possible (hence the Americans with Disabilities Act). All such avenues should be pursued actively. As with the strategies of Martin Luther King Jr.'s groups, Revelation's model of nonviolent resistance to the power structures of its society coheres well with the efforts of organizations such as ADAPT, whose mission statement reads, "ADAPT is a national grass-roots community that organizes disability rights activists to engage in nonviolent direct action, including civil disobedience, to assure the civil and human rights of people with disabilities to live in freedom."[10]

SENSORY OVERLOAD

Immediately one is struck by the sensory language that infuses this text (1:1, 2, 3). Revelation is a particularly noisy book. One hears loud voices (6:1), singing (5:9), and instruments (harp, trumpet). Hearing (ἀκούω, akouō) language occurs seventeen times. Voice or sound (φωνή, phōnē), fifty-five times.

Often hearing is accompanied by seeing. "Eyes" (ὀφθαλμός, ophthalmos) occurs ten times. At 5:6, John, drawing upon Zech 4:10, presents the lamb as having seven eyes: "Eyes represent divine omnipresence and omniscience" (Meeks 1997, 2316). Verbs of seeing loom large in the text.

As noted by Greg Carey (2009), John employs rhetography, "the rhetoric of the senses." Carey attends to language of seeing, touching, tasting, hearing, and smelling in Revelation. How might a person with one sensory impairment or another experience the book of Revelation? On the one hand, one might argue that in a book that reiterates the statement "Let anyone who has an ear listen to what the Spirit is saying to the churches" (2:11) or that equates blindness with wretchedness (3:17), the effect is detrimental to PWDs and implies that they may not be able to know God as well as TABs, who can perceive God in multiple ways. On the other hand, the fact that all the senses are highlighted and employed implies that God can be known in a variety of ways, such that a person with a particular impairment is not epistemologically disadvantaged: "The entire

[10] ADAPT's mission statement can be found at http://www.adapt.org.

discussions about the value of hearing and seeing ... may be considered part of a larger struggle with epistemological questions that continue today—namely, what are the best instruments available to human beings to perceive the world and the divine?" (Avalos 2007, 58).

Power and/in Weakness

Theologian Marva Dawn contends with multiple disabilities. In her book *Joy in Our Weakness: A Gift of Hope from the Book of Revelation*, she explores a theology of weakness. How does such a theology cohere with Revelation's emphasis on overcoming? Seventeen times, from start (2:7) to finish, the verb "to conquer" (νικάω, *nikaō*) appears, culminating with 21:7: "Those who conquer will inherit these things, and I will be their God and they will be my children." Dawn writes,

> Because I am weak and not weak enough, this book is written from two sides. As one who is handicapped, I plead for all of us to learn better to care for and listen to each other, and especially those who struggle with particular physical, emotional, and mental challenges. On the other hand, my calls to repentance are written by one who needs this prodding.... [A] theology of weakness also realizes that those who accept their weakness and acknowledge their dependence can teach us best about the grace that invades all our lives. Therefore, this theology challenges our churches to encourage the gifts and teaching potential of those who suffer and to become more truly a Christian community that cares deeply about each person. (2002, xi)

The mutuality and interdependence that inhere in such a model serve as a radical antidote to the hierarchical binary categories with which modern American society (and, for that matter, the imperial framework of Revelation) operates (rich/poor, educated/uneducated, documented/undocumented, TAB/PWD, white/black, young/old, etc.). Even the notion that "it is more blessed to give than to receive" propagates such top-down categories. Those in power get the hubris-building experience of handing something down to those in need. Those in need are taught to fantasize about being in power. But a theology of weakness understands that all have need and all have something to give. We would do well to learn not only how to be better givers but, perhaps more important, to become better at receiving.

A Call to Patient Endurance

The conquering that John has in mind is ironic: it involves no violence and no show of force. Rather, in the face of uncertainty, persecution, and suffering, John emphasizes patient endurance (ὑπομονή, *hypomonē*;

1:9; 2:2-3, 19; 3:10; 13:10; 14:12) as the primary strategy of victory. Dawn wisely notes that people with disabilities often develop patient endurance and discipline due to their lived reality: "The value of our weakness is that it teaches us to wait for God's timing" (2006, 16). Closely tied to this patient endurance is faithfulness in spite of powerlessness, as evidenced by the church at Philadelphia: "I know that you have but little power, and yet you have kept my word and have not denied my name" (Rev 3:8). And yet. Everything depends upon that "and yet" (καὶ, *kai*). Suffering with patient endurance has evangelistic potential. Indeed, Revelation is the first instance of the word "martyr" in the sense of one who dies for the faith. The word is a transliteration of the Greek word meaning "witness."

Of course, John is not the only New Testament witness to highlight a theology of weakness. Recall Paul's words from 2 Cor 12:10: "Therefore I am content with weaknesses, insults, hardships, persecutions, and calamities for the sake of Christ; for whenever I am weak, then I am strong." One would think that a tradition based upon a crucified Messiah who is depicted as a slain lamb would (1) not value power unduly and (2) readily intuit the potential power of the "weak" among us. But the values of empire remain seductive.

There is a potential danger that the call to patient endurance might be confused with living in a passive manner and settling for oppression. Or it might manifest itself in not taking care of oneself by getting what medical help one can. Other critiques arise from feminist and postcolonial interpreters who note that Revelation itself, despite its elevation of weakness, buys into the empire's power structures when it depicts God as uber-masculine (and violent; Moore 2009) and denigrates women, the "weaker sex" in the minds of the ancients. Revelation is notorious for its problematic portrayal of females (see, e.g., the work of Tina Pippin 2012). Concomitantly, I would argue that God is, therefore, also depicted as uber able-bodied. Whatever power Caesar is said to yield, God wields more with eternal, not temporary, effects. This would appear to have negative ramifications for those who are physically weak. But is the focus on the mighty tempered by the image of the Slain Lamb and the blood of the martyrs? As Carter notes, while the envisioned fantasy thrives on violent imagery, at no point are actual Christians enjoined to actual physical violence. Rather, they are to endure. If anything, there is a danger that Revelation trains readers to become too passive and not to consider it their duty to actively oppose oppressive structures and regimes (Carter 2011b).

DIVERSITY AND INCLUSIVITY

At 4:11 John echoes John 1:3 in declaring that everything has been created by God. Recall Amos Yong's contention that perhaps those with Down syndrome were created that way and do not need a medical cure. The passage in 3:15-22 raises issues, however. In addition to the association between blindness and wretchedness, Jesus tells the church at Laodicea, "I reprove and discipline those whom I love" (v. 19). Are disabilities a sign of God's special love or are they a sign of wretchedness? Furthermore, given Revelation's constant reference to names being inscribed in the book of life before the foundation of the world (3:5, 13:8, 17:8, 20:15, 21:27), were they predestined to have their particular disability? If so, how does this cohere with notions of illness and impairment as a sign of the demonic?

Revelation harbors within itself an irony: on the one hand, the author demands complete adherence to his construal of Christianity such that anyone who disagrees is labeled a Jezebel or Balaam; on the other hand, the same author envisions "every creature in heaven and on earth and under the earth and in the sea, and all that is in them, singing, 'To the one seated on the throne and to the Lamb be blessing and honor and glory and might forever and ever!'" (Rev 5:13). Every creature. Does this sectarian book contain within it the seeds of radical inclusivity?

OVERCOMING FEAR

Often, suffering is exacerbated by fear or ameliorated by confident faith. John faces this fact directly in his letter to the church at Smyrna: "Do not fear what you are about to suffer. Beware, the devil is about to throw some of you into prison so that you may be tested, and for ten days you will have affliction. Be faithful until death, and I will give you the crown of life" (2:10). John is not Pollyanna and does not infantilize his people. I am reminded of a word from Tobias Wolff. He is referring to short stories, but it applies to Scripture as well:

> As it happens, many of the stories in this book confront difficult material: violence, sickness, alcoholism, sexual exploitation, marital breakup. Well, so do we. I have never been able to understand the complaint that a story is "depressing" because of its subject matter. What depresses me are stories that don't seem to know these things go on, or hide them in resolute chipperness; "witty" stories, in which every problem is an occasion for a joke, "upbeat" stories that flog you with transcendence. Please. We're grown-ups now, we get to stay in the kitchen when the other grown-ups talk.
>
> Far from being depressed, my own reaction to stories like these is exhilaration, both at the honesty and the art. The art gives shape to what the

honesty discovers, allows us to face what in truth we were already afraid of anyway. It lets us know we're not alone. (1994, xiv–xv)

Like John, Wolff understands that almost anything is bearable as long as it is not borne alone. The real problem for many PWDs is the excruciating experience of being alone and Other.

Fear increases both physical pain and psychosomatic agony. Most of the things we spend time dreading turn out to be harder because of our panic. At first when I shattered my foot, alarm about the probability of amputation prevented me from thinking of ways to cope with the daily difficulties. Only after ten days of traveling and teaching did I begin to trust that other people and ingenuity would help me get around all right and that Christ could use me for his work anyway. When I panic about the unknowns of the future, I need to remember those lessons in trust (Dawn 2002, 59).

SALVATION (AND DAMNATION) IS COMMUNAL

Like the Fourth Gospel, Revelation is incarnational and relational. Jesus, the Word made flesh, declares at 2:9, "I know (οἶδα, *oida*) your affliction (θλῖψιν, *thlipsin*; cf. 1:9, 2:10, 2:22, 7:14) and your poverty." The use of the perfect tense, whose force denotes action completed in the past with ongoing effect in the present, speaks a word to those currently struggling. Jesus knew it then; he knows it still. All the letters are addressed to churches, not individuals. As the vision of God's justice being brought to bear upon earth unfolds, it is clear that God's salvation is worked out communally. God does not simply judge individual emperors but Rome as a nation, an empire, a social, political entity that causes the oppression of whole groups of people. From Genesis to Revelation, we are saved together or we are damned together. As Martin Luther King Jr. proclaimed, "Justice is indivisible, and injustice anywhere is a threat to justice everywhere."[11] The Johannine material urges TABs to see the experience of PWDs as part of their own experience. Disability and healing are communal experiences, by definition.

IMPERIAL IMPLICATIONS

The language of war, power, violence, and conquering permeates Revelation. Postcolonial scholars routinely note that the oppressed mimic the

---

[11] In a speech delivered at an antiwar rally the University of Minnesota, April 27, 1967. At the twenty-minute mark in the following video of King's speech: http://www .mnvideovault.org/index.php?id=17397&select_index=3&popup=yes#3.

oppressor. John envisions God's justice ousting Caesar at some point, but ironically God adopts the very techniques employed by Caesar himself. The dynamics remain the same; the only difference is who gets to stick it to whom. Instead of Caesar's misogynistic, sexually perverted, murderous rage, we find John exulting in Jesus murdering Jezebel's children (2:22-23) and "the whore [Rome], being stripped naked, gang raped (by the kings, merchants, and sailors), cannibalized, and burned forever (17:16)" (Pippin 2012, 630). This is a crucial issue for our analysis. Part of the disabling dynamic has to do with the constant fixation on binary categories: able-bodied/disabled, sick/healthy, ruler/ruled, powerful/impotent, conqueror/conquered. The modern world gave us the categories of either/or; post-modernism has given us the life-saving gift of both/and. Unfortunately, just as John contests Rome's behavior, he himself adopts it, valuing some bodies far more than others (note that the "144,000" are all males who have not "defiled" themselves with women [14:1-5]). We can, with John, protest the ways that empires oppress many of their members, but we must simultaneously critique John wherever he propagates the same destructive ideology.

In the end, Jesus' way of nonviolent resistance defeats Rome's arrogant, oppressive violence against bodies of all kinds. Carter explicates the significance of the phrase "slain but standing" in 5:6 to describe Christ, showing the violent nature of his death while maintaining his resistance to powers that be. He states, "It reveals that the world to which some or many of the Jesus-believers in the seven cities were happily accommodated violently rejected Jesus, the agent of God's purposes. But it also reveals that God sided with Jesus, not Rome, in raising Jesus from the dead. Roman power and violence are not ultimate; they do not have the last word. God's life-giving actions prevail" (2011b, 57). This is good news not only for PWDs but for everyone.

THE HOPE OF HEAVEN (REV 21:1-5)

The hope of heaven articulated at the close of the Christian canon has sustained sufferers of all kinds for centuries. Revelation is nothing if not a manifesto of hope. Writing to seven churches in Asia Minor who, by all appearances, had little reason to believe that God had the interest, the will, or the power to rectify rampant injustice and chaos, John conveys the contents of his singular "revelation of Jesus Christ" (1:1).

This vision of ultimate restoration does not countenance escapist fantasies or flight from earthly reality and its attendant problems; quite the opposite. In fact, it insists that God's home, as usual, is among mortals. Death (and its comrades Sin and Suffering) does not hold ultimate sway, for the Son of Man declares, "I was dead, and see, I am alive forever and ever; and I have the keys of Death and of Hades" (1:18). Thus, Revelation provides hope for all people, including PWDs. Dwight Peterson, himself a PWD, finds in Revelation a twofold call: "First, we ought to *wait in hope*; second, we ought to *act in hope*" (2005, 166; emphasis in original). He defines acting in hope as visiting those who are sick, accompanying them to appointments, and working on policy initiatives: "This is no laundry list, of course. Instead, practicing the presence of Christ calls for thoughtful and collaborative creativity" (168).

One should be careful not to assume, however, that all people with disabilities imagine themselves as having normate bodies at this time of restoration. Instead, some people who have lived their entire lives in a wheelchair imagine heaven as a place with no stairs and fully accessible. This may be especially interesting to consider in Revelation because standing and mobility play a large role (ascending to the throne, one foot in the river, one on land, etc.). For them, the hope is not to become someone or something else but to become one's self fully without obstacles, to inhabit a world where impairments are not necessarily disabling.

As in the Fourth Gospel where Jesus' stigmata remain, so in Revelation we have the image of the Slain Lamb. Helen Betenbaugh[12] wonders about the "stigmata" on the bodies of those who sustained them by doing good works. Might there be a positive link between them and the Lamb, especially in chapter 5 since the Lamb was outcast, disabled, wounded, and is suddenly at the center as the major actor? Might this function in the same way as the vision of the eschatological banquet where "the right people" are too busy to attend, and so the PWDs, the outcasts, and the poor become the feted guests? Certainly the theme of the great reversal, wherein the last shall be first, predominates all apocalyptic literature.

Promises and Pitfalls

Most religions attempt to account for suffering. Typically, pain may be viewed as punishment, as an opportunity for transcendence or "overcoming," or as redemptive and salvific (Conwill 1986). One might argue that the latter two are represented in Revelation (and all apocalyptic literature) as John relativizes the suffering of his audience by pointing them to the

---

[12] Personal correspondence, October 1, 2013.

rewards that accrue for endurance. Certainly Jesus' death is considered redemptive, and perhaps those of the prognosticated martyrs as well. This fact might help those with disabilities discern or create meaning out of their experiences of pain and suffering. Clearly this is the approach taken by Marva Dawn. She would fully resonate with Betenbaugh's notion of "an Easter faith in a Good Friday body" (2000, 208).

But a warning is in order. In his article "Why Do the Innocent Suffer?," Thomas Tracy cautions against the facile explanation of suffering as a tool for character formation. The question of proportion immediately arises. If one posits that suffering is useful for character formation, one has to ask, "How much suffering?" Too much suffering destroys. Also, logically speaking, if we believe this, we might argue that it is incumbent upon us to *cause* suffering for others for their own moral formation. This is logically absurd reasoning, but it is implicit when people try a "one-size-fits-all" approach to accounting for the experience of suffering and God's place in it. As Tracy so eloquently states, if one is not careful, one subscribes to a notion of "a vast pedagogy of pain" where life is a "cosmic nursery school" (1998, 49–50). This notion that God never gives a greater burden than one can bear has been deployed with devastating results. Anyone paying attention in the least can discern that such is not the case in a general way, else one would not find people in a catatonic state, suffering a nervous breakdown or severe depression, ulcers, high blood pressure, or, in the case of my son's seventh-grade peer, hanging oneself to death.

CONCLUSION

The word "healing" (θεραπεία, *therapeia*) occurs only once in Revelation, in the final chapter: "Then the angel showed me the river of the water of life, bright as crystal, flowing from the throne of God and of the Lamb through the middle of the street of the city. On either side of the river is the tree of life with its twelve kinds of fruit, producing its fruit each month; and the leaves of the tree are for the healing [not *curing*!] of the nations" (22:1-2). This is a stunning image of universal luxurious abundance for the flourishing of all creation. May those presently deprived draw hope from it; may those disproportionately privileged feel convicted by it; may it be on earth as it is in heaven; and may the new Jerusalem arrive sooner rather than later.

WORKS CITED

Albl, Martin. 2007. "For Whenever I Am Weak, Then I Am Strong." Pages 145–59 in *This Abled Body: Rethinking Disabilities in Biblical Studies*. Edited by Hector Avalos, Sarah J. Melcher, and Jeremy Schipper. Semeia Studies 55. Atlanta: Society of Biblical Literature.

Avalos, Hector. 2007. "Introducing Sensory Criticism in Biblical Studies: Audiocentricity and Visiocentricity." Pages 47–59 in *This Abled Body: Rethinking Disabilities in Biblical Studies*. Edited by Hector Avalos, Sarah J. Melcher, and Jeremy Schipper. Semeia Studies 55. Atlanta: Society of Biblical Literature.

Betenbaugh, Helen R. 2000. "Disability: A Lived Theology." *Theology Today* 57: 203–10.

Betenbaugh, Helen, and Marjorie Procter-Smith. 1998. "Disabling the Lie: Prayers of Truth and Transformation." Pages 281–303 in *Human Disability and the Service of God: Reassessing Religious Practice*. Edited by Nancy L. Eiesland and Don E. Saliers. Nashville: Abingdon.

Beutler, Johannes. 2004. "1, 2, and 3 John." Pages 553–58 in *Global Bible Commentary*. Edited by Daniel Patte. Nashville: Abingdon.

Black, Kathy. 1996. *A Healing Homiletic: Preaching and Disability*. Nashville: Abingdon.

Carey, Greg. 2009. "A Man's Choice: Wealth Imagery and the Two Cities of the Book of Revelation." Pages 147–58 in *A Feminist Companion to the Apocalypse of John*. Edited by A. Levine and M. M. Robbins. New York: T&T Clark.

Carter, Warren. 2011a. "'The Blind, Lame and Paralyzed' (John 5:3): John's Gospel, Disability Studies, and Postcolonial Perspectives." Pages 129–50 in *Disability Studies and Biblical Literature*. Edited by Candida R. Moss and Jeremy Schipper. New York: Palgrave Macmillan.

———. 2011b. *What Does Revelation Reveal? Unlocking the Mystery*. Nashville: Abingdon.

Clark-Soles, Jaime. 2010. *Engaging the Word: The New Testament and the Christian Believer*. Louisville, Ky.: Westminster John Knox.

Conwill, William L. 1986. "Chronic Pain Conceptualization and Religious Interpretation." *Journal of Religion and Health* 25: 46–50.

Dawn, Marva. 2002. *Joy in Our Weakness: A Gift of Hope from the Book of Revelation*. Rev. ed. Grand Rapids: Eerdmans.

Eiesland, Nancy L. 1994. *The Disabled God: Towards a Liberatory Theology of Disability*. Nashville: Abingdon.

Grant, Colleen C. 1998. "Reinterpreting the Healing Narratives." Pages 72–87 in *Human Disability and the Service of God: Reassessing Religious Practice*. Edited by Nancy L. Eiesland and Don E. Saliers. Nashville: Abingdon.

Hauerwas, Stanley. 2004. "Community and Diversity: The Tyranny of Normality." Pages 37–43 in *Critical Reflections on Stanley Hauerwas' Theology of Disability: Disabling Society, Enabling Theology*. Edited by John Swinton. Binghamton, N.Y.: Haworth Pastoral.

Hull, John M. 2001. *In the Beginning There Was Darkness: A Blind Person's Conversations with the Bible*. Harrisburg, Pa.: Trinity International.

Landrus, Heather L. 2002. "Hearing 3 John 2 in the Voices of History." *Journal of Pentecostal Theology* 11: 70–88.

Linton, Simi. 1998. *Claiming Disability: Knowledge and Identity*. New York: New York University Press.

Meeks, Wayne, ed. 1997. *The HarperCollins Study Bible*. San Francisco: HarperCollins.

Mitchell, David, and Sharon Snyder. 2007. "'Jesus Thrown Everything Off Balance': Disability and Redemption in Biblical Literature." Pages 173–83 in *This Abled Body: Rethinking Disabilities in Biblical Studies*. Edited by Hector Avalos, Sarah J. Melcher, and Jeremy Schipper. Semeia Studies 55. Atlanta: Society of Biblical Literature.

———. 2013. "Narrative Prosthesis." Pages 222–35 in *The Disability Studies Reader*. Edited by Lennard J. Davis. New York: Routledge.

Moore, Stephen. 2009. "Hypermasculinity and Divinity." Pages 180–204 in *A Feminist Companion to the Apocalypse of John*. Edited by A. Levine and M. M. Robbins. New York: T&T Clark.

Peterson, Dwight N. 2005. "Barriers, Boundaries, Limits: Revelation 21:1-4." *Ex Auditu* 21: 165–69.

Pippin, Tina. 2012. "Revelation/Apocalypse of John." Pages 627–32 in *Women's Bible Commentary*. Edited by Carol A. Newsom, Sharon H. Ringe, and Jacqueline E. Lapsley. Louisville, Ky.: Westminster John Knox.

Simmons, Philip. 2003. *Learning to Fall: The Blessings of an Imperfect Life*. New York: Bantam.

Tracy, Thomas F. 1998. "Why Do the Innocent Suffer?" Pages 40–55 in *Why Are We Here? Everyday Questions and the Christian Life*. Edited by R. F. Thiemann and W. C. Placher. Harrisburg, Pa.: Trinity International.

Wolff, Tobias, ed. 1994. *The Vintage Book of American Short Stories*. New York: Random House.

Wynn, Kerry H. 2007. "Johannine Healings and Otherness of Disability." *Perspectives in Religious Studies* 34: 61–75.

Yong, Amos. 2011. *The Bible, Disability, and the Church: A New Vision of the People of God*. Grand Rapids: Eerdmans.

11

Paul

Arthur J. Dewey and Anna C. Miller

The Pauline corpus in the New Testament comprises thirteen letters attributed to the apostle Paul. However, through a comparative analysis of the letters, the majority of contemporary New Testament scholars consider seven letters (1 Thess, Gal, 1 and 2 Cor, Phlm, Phil, and Rom) were authored by Paul in the mid-first century (48–55 CE). A follower of Paul may well have written Colossians and Ephesians in the last quarter of the first century, while Titus and 1 and 2 Timothy were written sometime before the mid-second century. Second Thessalonians may be the latest written, a second-century reworking of 1 Thessalonians dealing with the delay of the end of the world. In treating the overarching question of the Pauline corpus and disability, we therefore shall divide our treatment into two sections: the authentic Pauline letters and the later letters written in his name. We shall note how the remarkable insights included in Paul's letters were, to a great extent, frustrated, deflected, and even erased by the later letters.

Beyond the determination of the authentic letters of Paul, we need to be aware of the significant critical factors in reading this material. In raising the question of disability with regard to the Pauline corpus, we must recognize the limits and possibilities of this investigation. It should be noted right from the start that the concept of disability is a modern construction. While persons with a variety of physical or mental impairments were set within disabling social situations and institutions in the first and second centuries, the classification of people according to "disabled" or "nondisabled" categories did not exist in antiquity (Kelley 2007, 33). Such a classification system owes much to the requirements of modern Western governments both to control citizens and to respond to the needs, the "political problem," of citizens with certain impairments (Hedlund 2009, 6). Nevertheless, those who have considered disability in antiquity have recognized that there is a wide, albeit often vague, range of terms for various physical and mental impairments in the Greco-Roman world. At the same time, scholars like Jeremy Schipper have shown that representations of "disabled" bodies are used in antiquity, as today, to "help to develop and work out social and cultural ideologies or worldviews" (2006, 20). In our work with Paul, we aim to respect the differences in terminology and construction between modern and ancient understandings of disability, even as we interrogate the way that Paul's deployment of impairment impacts his theological formulations. Finally, we will explore insights that arise from putting Pauline texts into conversation with a modern disability perspective.

In our own investigation of the Pauline corpus, we shall keep in mind three modern models of disability. The medical model focuses on disability as personal illness, injury, or other health issue that prevents active engagement in life. This model assumes these issues will "be improved through medical intervention in the form of treatment methods, medicine, and therapy or rehabilitation measures" (Hedlund 2009, 9). The medical model has definite limitations, since it focuses heavily on the individual and usually reflects the modern therapeutic situation. By contrast, the social model focuses on disability as a result of poor adaptation and organization on the part of the wider society. In effect, society disables when it excludes or makes it impossible for persons with disability to participate (Hedlund 2009, 10). Yet another model of disability, what Jeremy Schipper and David Mitchell call the "cultural model," has become an important part of the conversation in disability studies. Schipper explains regarding the cultural model:

> As with the social model, disability remains a social construction, but the cultural model views it as part of the construction of the very nature of society itself rather than only the result of social discrimination. In other words, according to the cultural model, disability is not only a result of social organization, but integral to social organization itself. . . . In this sense, representations of disability are not value-free or transparent, but help to develop and work out social and cultural ideologies or worldviews. (2006, 20)

These last two models will most heavily affect our analysis of Pauline literature, but we will draw insights from all three in the course of our discussion.

These models of disability come into historical focus when we consider the economic and political assumptions of the ancient world. If the Greco-Roman world lacked a distinct classification of "disabled," Rose has suggested that, culturally, an individual's physical or mental (dis)ability in antiquity cohered with how well they met the demands of family, and especially civic, life (2003, 3). In the first-century world, these demands were often refracted through an agonistic perspective that played out in competition, mastering stances, and posturing. It was a world where the question of gaining an advantage was ever present. In this competitive social field, the contrast of "weakness" and "strength" was essential to discussions of civic service and participation.

One might expect anyone experiencing a significant physical or mental impairment in the ancient world to be disqualified for this competitive social environment. However, Rose points out that physical impairments did not automatically exclude someone from such civic participation. Indeed, ancient authors used the examples of Demosthenes (Cicero, *De or.* 1.61.260–261; Plutarch, *Dem.* 11.1) and Thersites (Libanius, *Progymnasmata, Encomium* 4) to show the opposite, that a verbal or physical impairment could be overcome so that an individual could be an adequate or even an extraordinary citizen. Rose argues that the ultimate "impairment" for acting out full citizenship was being a woman—and, we would add, being a slave (2003, 62–63). As we shall show, women and slaves were constructed as essentially impaired in intellect and morality, ever lacking in the critical abilities required by full citizens. To this short list of what Charles Hedrick calls the "utter anti-citizens" of the ancient world (1994, 302), we might add those punished through crucifixion. Crucifixion was no mere physical fate; it entailed social liquidation. Crucifixion rendered victims socially impure. But death—the ultimate disablement—was not enough. Memory of the crucified was damned to oblivion. The social ritual of crucifixion attempted to remove all human traces. Paul's letters are unusual—indeed, extraordinary—documents in that they not only call for solidarity with the crucified but also record the claim of the very earliest Christians that, in the Anointed One, "there is no longer slave or freeborn, no longer 'male and female'" (Gal 3:28).[1] For those most thoroughly disabled by ancient social constructions, this

---

[1] N.b.: all quotations of the authentic Paul come from the Scholars Version Translation found in the *Authentic Letters of Paul* (2010). Otherwise, the translations are from the NRSV.

formula holds out the promise of equality and full citizenship in the community gathered around the crucified Anointed One.

Examining the question of disability in the Pauline letters provides critical insights into Paul's rhetorical and theological project. As we shall see, Paul's theological construction depends heavily not only on contrasts between weakness and strength, "disabled" flesh and "enabling" spirit, but also on his focus to know nothing "while I was with you except Jesus, God's Anointed, crucified" (1 Cor 2:2). With this choice Paul centers his theology on a figure that we may explain as disabled, not only in terms of suffering flesh but also in terms of a punishment aimed to socially annihilate, to permanently "disable" the victim. As we shall see below, Paul engages one of the fundamental, countercultural insights of early Christian theology: that the God of Israel has accepted this disabled figure. To say that God has accepted Jesus is equivalent to declaring that God values the person who is totally marginalized. In accepting this liquidated victim, God overturns given social values by making him his "son" (a divine title usually bestowed on emperors and other civic heroes). In urging his listeners to join in the suffering of the Anointed, Paul opens up the possibility for their own transformation. They even act like God in accepting the crucified one against the values of the world. By joining in solidarity with this crucified one, they enter a community where their humanity in all its frailty has both a value and a creative role to play in cosmic transformation (Rom 8).

This theological focus deeply influences Paul's construction of his own authoritative role and the way he envisions the community of Jesus' followers. Paul repeatedly bases his claims to leadership in his suffering with and for the Anointed. Moreover, he calls for the Anointed's followers to be a community of sufferers who, with Jesus, "experience the same abuse as he did in the hope that we may share his exaltation" (Rom 8:17). This last statement highlights the rhetorical power in Paul's letters created by the contrast of the suffering, crucified Son of God and the resurrected, exalted one to whom "every knee should bend, above the earth, on earth and under the earth" (Phil 2:10). For his readers, Paul urges them to become a community of sufferers that gives the greatest honor to its weakest members. He promises that this experience will mean their own stunning transformation of resurrection in which they will inhabit imperishable (perfectly abled?) spiritual bodies.

From a modern disability perspective, Paul's call to solidarity with the crucified, entwined with this vision of triumphal resurrection, offers great potential for liberation— but also great risk of limiting, or even reversing, such liberation. Too often, subsequent Pauline interpretation—including those New Testament letters written in Paul's name— works toward this reversal of the liberative strain in Paul's letters. Later interpreters tend to silence those who would speak from their genuine experience of loss and impairment. The task of the Pauline interpreter, then, is to see the tension in Paul's language, to see the utopian liberating possibilities, while at the same time noting the ways in which Paul's choices of language and metaphor often subvert these possibilities by reinforcing standard power hierarchies that are deeply implicated in constructions of "ability" and "disability" in antiquity.

The lens of disability studies thus enhances our reading of Paul and facilitates significant questions regarding the power and impact of these texts. This very process of questioning and critiquing may give us entrance into a surprising renewal with the tradition. Indeed, as we shall see, Paul stresses not only the worth of his experience but also that of his listeners. In bringing the question of disability to the letters, readers, especially readers with disabilities, can thus actively enter into conversation with their ancestors in faith. By valuing their experience, readers can see the possibilities and limits of their conversation over time and space. In effect, the conversation is not a one-way street. Modern readers, in fact, bring an urgent inquiry to these ancient texts. Readers with disabilities, empowered by their experience, can detect what is at best problematic and ambiguous in the Pauline materials. The consequences of such a conversation speak volumes for the task of theology. Each reader has the responsibility to enter into an interpretive dialogue with Paul and his "schools." The Pauline letters cannot be accepted simply as theological givens, never to be questioned. The task of theological reflection comes alive through an open-ended conversation that is not silenced by previous formulations, not unlike the interpretive efforts of Schüssler Fiorenza (1988, 791). In effect, new and unexpected theological avenues are opened up by this critical negotiation with the tradition. The Pauline letters therefore become not the final punctuation but a starting point of an involved and unending conversation.

THE AUTHENTIC PAUL

THE PAULINE BREAKTHROUGH

It is crucial to begin an analysis of Paul with the fundamental insight underpinning all his letters and mission. By understanding Paul's initial experience, we may begin to see the bearing this insight has on the matter of disability.

Our primary information comes from Gal 1:13-17. Here Paul describes his former behavior as a practicing Jew, claiming he went beyond most of his contemporaries in the observance of Jewish traditions. In this claim Paul expresses the competitive expectation of his world and his own "advantage" within Judaism. As a Pharisee, Paul would have been concerned particularly with purity matters and the integrity of the God of Israel. His harassment of Jesus communities may have come as a reaction to what those communities were doing (Mack 2004, 371; Koester 1998, 345)—celebrating the death of Jesus as a hero's death (1 Cor 11:23) and, in their meal commemorations, invoking the God of Israel. Such a reimagining of the death of Jesus was a significant move by the early (probably Syrian) community. Crucifixion, seen in all its first-century horror, represented the ultimate liquidation of a person. The victim was shamed publicly and any memory was to be erased. Those who raised a sandal against the empire were condemned to such a "disappearance." Thus, to associate the God of Israel with a criminal who had been so shamefully executed would have touched on blasphemy. Paul's concern for the integrity of God may well have ignited his harassment of those communities (Matthews 2004, 362–63).

Paul spoke of his breakthrough insight as a prophetic experience. He employed traditional language to describe what he considered a prophetic call ("when the One who designated me before I was born and commissioned me to be an envoy"; Gal 1:15). He did not see himself as what we today would call a "convert." He never stopped being a Jew (cf. Rom 9:3; Eisenbaum 2009). He continues in the line of Jewish prophets in their call to the nations. With God's acceptance of the physically and socially disabled Jesus, Paul saw the God of Israel in an entirely new light. God had taken an outrageous step in accepting that shamed criminal. God had accepted the impure without condition. Because God has accepted this nobody, the usual conditions of human existence have been forever changed.

Beyond Paul's brief description in Galatians, we do not have any more information about his initial experience. We cannot use the material in Acts 9:1-9, since it reflects a second-century (Pervo 2006; Smith and Tyson 2013) commonplace of someone opposing a god (cf. *Bacchae*). Nor does the heavenly vision in 2 Cor 12:1-10 provide any help. At best it is a Pauline parody of an apocalyptic vision. However, there may be an indirect possibility in 1 Cor 14:23-25, where Paul describes an outsider's experience whose deepest dreams are revealed in communal action. In the first century, only God was thought to know the human heart's deepest wishes (Malina 2001, 71ff.). The outsider, discovering that his deepest secrets are sounded in the midst of the community's conversation, concludes, "God really is present among you" (1 Cor 14:23-25). Could Paul's experience have been that "God was really present" among those he zealously sought to destroy? In effect, Paul's insight would not have been a solitary experience but one embedded in his encounter with the Syrian community. He saw that the modus vivendi for living had been drastically altered. The competitive search for an advantage falls before a vision of a God who accepts one with no advantage. From this insight all Paul's subsequent actions and missionary fervor follow.

It is crucial that we notice that Paul's breakthrough was not a simple endorsement of vicarious suffering. Paul's insight was based on the earlier attempt by (probably Syrian) Jesus followers to turn the disaster of Jesus' crucifixion into a meaningful death. In setting the fate of Jesus within the narrative of martyrdom (such as is found in 4 Macc 16:16-23, 17:8-22), the Syrian Jewish followers of Jesus refuted a meaningless end for that artisan of wisdom. By contrast, Paul does not focus on the heroism of Jesus but on the election of God ("in order to show God's reliability"; Rom 3:25). His insight into what God has done by accepting the one who has been disabled beyond death recasts the direction of meaning. The subsequent history of interpretation tends to reverse this focus and, instead, fixates on Jesus' heroic death. This focus obscures the reality of crucifixion with its horrendous physical and social cost. For people with disabilities, such a narrative frame not only sets up expectations but even encourages the disabled to overlook their own experience. What if someone has no choice in being disabled? Does one then accept what Jesus has done "for them" at the very cost of denying their situation? Does one have to live vicariously through Jesus' sacrifice? Paul lends some advice on this point. He never gives up on his experience, nor does he urge his listeners to give up on their experience (e.g., Gal 3:2-4; Rom 4:16, 24). For those reading Paul today, it would be vital to continue this advice. Begin with experience, not with what is theologically prescribed. Second, Paul's insight is not that Jesus is heroic but that God has accepted the godless one, the one who has no advantage (Gal 3:1b; 1 Cor 1:21-22). Third, when Paul does speak of Jesus, he talks of his "trust" or "confidence in God." He maintains that his listeners can also manifest such trust in a reliable God, as he points to their trusting experience (e.g., Gal 3:2). Does that insight have anything to say to a disabled person? Does God's mystery directly touch people where they are at, particularly beyond physical and social advantages? And from this experience can they speak? Only they have the final word on this.

FIRST THESSALONIANS

In his earliest surviving letter, Paul notes that the Thessalonians had first received him just after he was "assaulted and insulted in Philippi" (1 Thess 2:2). Paul did not conceal that his original encounter with them was not a triumphal entrance. Nevertheless, at that time he offered to share with them not only the radical message of the Anointed but also his very life (2:8). As we shall see, such human vulnerability continues to mark the entire Pauline mission. It is not an obstacle but the very means of communicating what is most important.

In this letter Paul praises the Thessalonians themselves for their willingness to accept the vulnerability of persecution as they pursue the gospel. In 1 Thess 1:6, Paul suggests that the Thessalonians became imitators of Paul, his fellow missionaries, and the Anointed himself by receiving the word with joy in the midst of trials. While we cannot specify the nature of the Thessalonians' trials, this formulation unites this community with Jesus and with Paul because they all suffer "persecution at the hands of surrounding communities" (Castelli 1991, 93). As Castelli notes of the Thessalonians in 1:6 (and in the similar formulation at 2:14-15),

> Their suffering, for which they are praised by Paul in both the passages, ties their experience to that of everyone else in the mimetic system: Paul, the Lord, and the other persecuted communities . . . Their sufferings become a way of establishing identity within the group and in the face of outsiders. (94)

In this way 1 Thessalonians defines the very identity, the worthiness, of Jesus' followers by a willingness to come together as a community of sufferers imitating both Jesus and Paul.

It is in 1 Thess 4:13-18 that we see one critical reason for Paul's letter. Evidently, some members of the community have died, and the living members of the community wondered whether the deceased would be forgotten at the arrival of the Anointed One. Paul uses two oracular utterances to undermine these fears, stating that at the Lord's arrival those who have already died will "ascend first," to be followed to the clouds by those still living. In this passage Paul speaks to the fears of those for whom death was the ultimate disability, preventing the ones who had died from enjoying the arrival of the Anointed. Apparently the apocalyptic scenario they entertained could not account for these beloved dead. It is crucial to see that Paul reiterates here the lack of advantage for one community member over another.

In assessing Paul's use of these oracular utterances to reconfigure the Thessalonians' sense of the future, we should be cautious about uncritically taking over this scenario for the modern world. We should note that Paul's vision of the end time significantly changes in the course of his letters. By the time we reach Rom 8, the final scene is quite different. The entire cosmos is laboring to bring forth the children of God (Rom 8:18-23). In effect, we can say that Paul does not subscribe to some wooden and pre-scribed scenario. Sadly, there are some modern Bible readers, reacting to the terrors and upheavals of this uncertain world, who conjure up apoc-alyptic scenarios from a number of New Testament scenes (such as Mark 13; 1 Thess 4; Rev; 2 Thess) to weave a tapestry of shock and awe. Do the creators of such scenarios forget Paul's point that no one has need of an advantage before God and focus instead on a way of gaining some leverage over others in a collapsing society? What underlying image of God comes through such scenarios? Has the model of the dominating overlord once again won the day?

It is interesting that, as Paul continues to explore what is to come in 1 Thess 5, he stresses the present possibilities for community life and action. He calls the Thessalonians "day-people" who protect themselves with the "armor of God" and, with unselfish love for one another, wear the "helmet of liberating hope" (v. 8). It is significant that humans wear both the armor and helmet, for these items are elsewhere proclaimed as posses-sions of God (Isa 29:17; Wis 5:18; Job 2:9 LXX). In this vision Paul locates the presence of the divine precisely in the life the community shared with one another. In their limitations, in their fragmented condition, they were encouraged to live in the divine presence.

In 1 Thessalonians Paul's construction of community underlines soli-darity with the suffering, crucified Anointed. This construction also makes a significant authority claim that Paul in his own suffering is worthy of imitation alongside the Anointed. By locating the divine in a community's endurance and compassion when faced by social, and even physical, perse-cution, 1 Thessalonians may empower modern communities—including communities of the disabled—who have likewise experienced suffering and persecution from the society around them. However, by giving such a high theological value to suffering, we may also question whether 1 Thes-salonians encourages a passive acceptance of suffering and pain that might contribute to, rather than combat, the disabling effects of society on those struggling with impairments or marginalization.

Galatians

More than an exasperated response by Paul to the prospective actions of the Galatian community, this letter delivers a well-crafted argument meant to shape the Galatians' choices about their new life and practices in the Anointed. Paul reminds them that their experience of trust in the God who raised Jesus entails a life lived in compassion rather than competition. It has been argued that this letter is an articulated personal defense by Paul (Betz 1979). However, it seems Paul's main intent was making not a personal defense but a case for the best way for the Galatians to create community. It is this question that modern readers can continue to raise and explore, taking into consideration Paul's advice.

Originally, Paul was well received by this community. He had found out, however, that other Jesus missionaries arrived after his departure and sought to persuade the community to reconsider their involvement in the Jesus movement. The recent missionaries did not seem to dismiss Paul's original message to the Galatians. They attempted to build upon what Paul had done in order to introduce the community to what many would have considered a fuller and richer religious life. At the nub of the dispute is the notion of "traditional religious practices." The missionaries apparently interpreted Paul's message within the wider frame of the Hellenistic Jewish tradition. They claimed that Jesus' confidence in God was a testament to the faith of Judaism and that the Galatians could magnify their experience of God by accessing the fullness of the Jewish tradition. Certainly, this would entail the matter of circumcision and the keeping of religious festivals and requirements. All of this would be the fulfillment of the covenant to Abraham among the nations.

Paul takes exception to this approach. He contends that there is no reason for those of the nations to become Jews (Gal 2:14-16). Rather, their trust in the God of Jesus has brought them already to a genuine relation with God. They do not need the assurance of identifying religious practices. Paul reminds them that doing so actually entails a forgetting of their own experience. He asks them rhetorically how they really experienced the presence and power of God (3:2, 4-5).

Just as Paul remained faithful to his breakthrough experience of the God of Israel, he counsels his listeners to be attentive to their experience. He reminds them that this experience comes through the announcement of what God had done to Jesus, "graphically portrayed on a cross" (Gal 3:1b). This allows him to quote what may well have been a familiar melody in their community: "You are no longer Jew or Greek, no longer slave or freeborn, no longer 'male and female'" (Gal 3:28a). To which he adds: "You all have the same status in the service of God's Anointed, Jesus" (v. 28b). In recognizing that God accepted one who "was cursed" (3:13), the Galatians no longer needed to seek for any competitive edge before the divine or with others. They already had gone beyond the usual cultural delimitations and could live "a life of freedom" (5:13). Their adoption as "God's children" (4:5) was no second-class citizenship; rather, this meant that they shared the status of God's Anointed. And the very presence and power of God was to be manifested by their compassionate life together, of which there is no prescribed formula (5:22-23). Paul concludes that they are living in a new situation, a transformed world (5:15).

Paul asks the Galatians to recognize the depths of their experience of trust. One could have confidence in a God who is trustworthy, who surprises all by accepting someone who has no advantage. There are no conditions for those who enter this trusting relationship. Life becomes a creative response to the mystery of this powerful presence in their midst. There is no need to score points or to win at another's expense. To think otherwise, to play the usual cultural game of one-upmanship, was to deny one's experience of trust and to revert to the competitive demands of the first-century world.

We should pause here to consider a dichotomy in Paul's rhetorical argument. He presents two options (e.g., in Gal 3:2, 4-5). While Paul does stress the experience of the Galatians, does he consider that the experience of the Galatians might have gone beyond what he understood? Here is where some of the assumptions of ancient rhetoric must be noted. Such rhetoric comes out of a competitive culture, where opposition is the natural cast of imagination. Paul's own participation in this rhetorical process of contest reveals some elements of the Galatians' practices and beliefs while obscuring others.

We have already mentioned above that Paul had his limits as a first-century person. Ironically, the person who would counsel others not to be competitive is using competitive means. Modern Bible readers should be aware of these limits. Paul was not delivering unalterable prescriptions for behavior but seeking to persuade his readers to a certain vision of community and practice. The attentive reader needs to recognize the power for decision and action on the part of the Galatians.

In Galatians Paul's rhetorical style is characterized by binary oppositions—most notably the opposition between πνεῦμα and σάρξ, often translated as "spirit" and "flesh." The term σάρξ is particularly difficult since its meaning can range from the "physical body" to "the realm of human activity apart from the divine." Likewise, πνεῦμα can range from "breath" to "the realm in which people enjoy God's power and presence" (Brandenburger 1969).

These distinctions become crucial when readers consider Gal 4:13-14. Here Paul reminds his listeners that they neither "disdained nor scorned him" due to his earlier "weakness of the flesh" (ἀσθένειαν τῆς σαρκός). The nature of Paul's "weakness" is not evident in this text (Lambrecht 1999, 205). Amos Yong has wisely suggested that Paul's infirmity may well situate him as a person of disability (2011, 86). However, despite much hypothesizing, the identification of Paul's exact disability has defied researchers (Lambrecht 1999, 205). Nevertheless, it is clear that Paul rhetorically deploys this weakness toward the realization of his ideal community. Paul praises the Galatians for not excluding the disabled Paul but receiving him with compassion and care. It is significant that Paul sets "flesh vs. spirit" off quite decidedly in exhorting his listeners to live a life of freedom in the πνεῦμα instead of a life according to the σάρξ.

Here (Gal 5:16-26) we see two contrasting life-worlds, one of compassion and self- giving versus one of self-serving and alienation. It is crucial to see that Paul uses the two contrasting life-worlds to describe the kinds of community on the Galatians' horizon. Living according to the σάρξ entails fragmentation and mutual destruction, while living according to the πνεῦμα begets a world of confidence and trust. We see that Paul is talking here about practices that either build or break community. Here σάρξ is an atmosphere in which the behavior is self-serving and self-defeating. It fails to build community. On the other hand, life according to the πνεῦμα is a life characterized by the building of community, of generating solidarity.

We have stressed that Paul is asking his audience to remember their experience. In this letter we can see that there is a certain angle to this experience. Paul would advise them that it is their experience that includes the disabled through acts of compassion and self-giving. As they accepted the weakened Paul, they accepted the crucified Anointed. This becomes the way in which community is created. This is living according to the "breath" of God.

This letter from Paul thus offers significant points to continue in our conversation over disability. How often are the disabled tempted to see themselves through the expectations of the able-bodied person? How often does the able-bodied person consider the disabled as deficient or needing a variety of supplements to be seen as "whole"? Paul would advise us to look first to our experience and to find that the presence of God already is there, precisely where there is a disabling condition. One can live in confidence in the very midst of disability. In fact, by taking seriously their experience, the people with disabilities enter into the theological conversation. Their contribution promises a more inclusive discussion about genuine human community.

THE CORINTHIAN CORRESPONDENCE

The Corinthian correspondence represents remnants of the longest sustained conversation with a community in the New Testament. To see this, readers need to note that 1 Corinthians was not Paul's first letter to the community at Corinth. First Corinthians 5:9 indicated that an earlier, lost letter was delivered. So 1 Corinthians is actually a second letter to the community. First Corinthians shows a conversation between Paul and the community already underway. However, the canonical 2 Corinthians itself has been a matter of dispute. The literary unity of 2 Corinthians has been much debated. It appears that one section is a later interpolation (2 Cor 6:14–7:1) and that the remaining material can be divided into a number of parts ([a] 2:14–6:13; 7:2-4; [b] 10–13; [c] 1:1–2:13; 7:5-16; [d] 8; [e] 9). In effect, we may well have six letters of Paul to the community at Corinth.

When read diachronically, the Corinthian correspondence presents a number of moments in Paul's relation to the Corinthian community. We begin with Paul attempting to persuade the community in light of what seem to have been significant divergences of understanding about what solidarity with God's Anointed entailed. Evidently the Corinthians had interpreted the message Paul shared in a number of ways, some of which Paul found not supportive of the common life they shared. Yet it seems that 2 Corinthians records the most difficult time in Paul's relationship with the community, precipitated by the Corinthians' encounter with other Jesus missionaries (2 Cor 2:14–6:13). Paul attempted to remind the community that it was their shared experience of God's presence and power—not the missionaries' elitist program—that was the basis for their life together (2 Cor 3:2-3, 18). The Corinthians failed to catch this point, and it became clear that when Paul visited them, he was not only insulted but found to be "unimpressive" (2 Cor 10:10). Paul, at a complete loss, delivered what amounted to a "fool's speech" (2 Cor 10–13) in which he attempted to get the Corinthians to look at their competitive assumptions through a variety of comic masks. This letter appears to have helped to restore relations (2 Cor 1:1–2:13; 7:5-16). There then follow two separate letters regarding the collection for God's people in Jerusalem.

First Corinthians

First Corinthians is a perennial favorite for scholars and congregations alike, in part because this letter provides some of Paul's most sustained arguments regarding community and theology. At the same time, 1 Corinthians also contains some of our most fascinating glimpses of a particular early group of Jesus' followers negotiating practice and belief in the decades after his death. These attributes make this letter a remarkable resource for the disability conversation, demonstrating extremes when it comes to the potential pitfalls of Pauline theology and social construction for this conversation.

Paul devotes much of the early chapters of 1 Corinthians to a comparison of divine and worldly wisdom that directly relates to his construction of the ideal community. In these first chapters, Paul creates a strong opposition between the wisdom of God and the wisdom of the world (1:20-21). This division of wisdom effectively divides human beings into two groups as well. Paul places himself among those who speak and possess divine wisdom. By contrast, Paul aligns the Corinthians with the inferior wisdom of the world.

For Paul, God's wisdom manifests most powerfully in the figure of the crucified Anointed, a figure who appears as "an offense to Jews, nonsense to the nations" (1:23). Paul argues repeatedly that God chooses what is foolish or worthless in the eyes of the world in order to bring salvation to those who believe, to make manifest divine wisdom that subverts the normate world. Amos Yong raises a most challenging question:

> Might thinking about the cross in terms of intellectual disability in particular, with its broad spectrum of physical and mental impairments, serve as an even more subversive symbol of the divine undermining of the world's claims to wisdom and power? (2011, 101)

Here, Paul deepens this reimagining by stating that the Corinthians' own call demonstrates this divine choice. Before they heard the gospel, Paul claims that not many of the Corinthians were wise, powerful, or well born according to human standards (1:26). However, "God has chosen people who have no status in the world, and even those who are held in contempt, in order to bring to nothing those who are thought to be really something" (1:28). Paul argues that his own proclamation to the Corinthians embodied wisdom that is disabled, since it does not contain persuasive words of the competing culture but "was accompanied by visible evidence of God's power and presence" (2:4). In fact, Paul illustrates his own separation from the dominant system with the very trepidation and weakness in his initial proclamation (2:3).

In stark contrast to the paradoxical divine wisdom, Paul establishes the inferiority of worldly wisdom by linking it with the human (2:5) and the fleshly (3:1-4), and, by extension, with immaturity (2:6, 3:1-4). Paul also ties this wisdom to the human hierarchy of power, to the rulers of this age (ἀρχόντων τοῦ αἰῶνος τούτου) who are "doomed to perish" (2:6). As in Galatians, the human and fleshly manifest with behaviors like jealousy and quarreling, behaviors that Paul puts in opposition to community harmony and understanding. In their own debates, their "quarreling" regarding leadership, Paul suggests that the Corinthians demonstrate an immaturity that marks them as "people occupied with worldly concerns, as mere toddlers in the Anointed new way of life" (3:1).

These initial chapters of 1 Corinthians lay out a powerful vision of community based in solidarity with the crucified, disabled Anointed One. Paul himself argues that this vision is "countercultural," a rejection of the prevalent values of competition and self-aggrandizement that characterize the wisdom of the world. The solidarity Paul advocates occurs in part through finding worth in those things understood as despicable or foolish in this worldly perspective. Paul asks the Corinthians to make the choice that God has made—the choice for finding divine wisdom through the crucified and in their own lowly, weak position. This model has significant implications for disability studies. To better understand the range of these implications, it is helpful to put 1 Cor 1–4 into conversation with another passage in which Paul visualizes the ideal community united in the "body of the Anointed": 1 Cor 12.

In 1 Cor 12, Paul draws on the metaphor of the human body to speak of the community formed when believers are baptized "by the same power of God" (v. 13). Paul's use of this metaphor exploits interdependence between the different members of the body in order to call for an honoring of diversity and mutual interdependence within the community of Jesus' followers (Dewey 2010, 132–37). To understand the radical nature of Paul's construction in this passage, one must remember that the political metaphor of the body was a commonplace in Roman society. Indeed, the body as political metaphor often served to instantiate the hierarchical, patriarchal, and political dominance of the imperial system (Aesop, *Fab.* 130; Livy, *History of Rome* 2.32.9–12; Dionysius of Harlicarnassus, *Ant. Rom.* 6.86.1–3).

In his own use of the body metaphor, Paul first insists that the body is composed of diverse elements. In the case of the Corinthians, this means each "member" manifests the spirit in a variety of different gifts serving the one body (12:4-13). However, Paul emphasizes not only diversity in 1 Cor 12 but also the critical role played by those parts of the body that "seem to be weaker," "less respectable," or "less honorable" (vv. :22-24; see Yong 2011, 90ff.). Paul literally "gives voice" to these weaker members of the body in a comic diatribe starting in 1 Cor 12:15. In this comic moment, it is not the head that goes first as the body part usually assigned leadership by ancient writers.

Instead, the foot begins the snobbish comedy (if the foot would say, "Because I am not a hand, I am not part of the body," that would not make it any less a part of the body; 12:15). Paul uses this comic voice as part of his larger argument that all parts of the body are indispensable to the body's function and integrity. In these verses he also claims that God has arranged the body "giving the inferior part greater value," that there may be no dissension within the body, but the members may have the same care for one another (12:24-25). In this relationship of interdependence, the suffering of one member means the suffering of all, even as honor for one is honor for the entire body (v. 26). In the concluding verses of the chapter, Paul leaves no room for doubt as to the application of his metaphor, stating directly to the Corinthians, "Now you are the body of the Anointed and individually members of it" (v. 27).

What implications does Paul's vision of community in 1 Cor 1–4 and again in 1 Cor 12 have for a conversation over disability? One may read in these passages an insistence that the accepted categories of the "world" be reevaluated. These verses ask the reader to look again at just those people in everyday life who are routinely judged, and rejected, as weak, low, and lacking in respect or honor. And yet Paul does more. He insists that divine favor resides with just these members of society that are rejected by the world. God chooses the crucified and the weak as the site to manifest true wisdom and genuine salvation. Moreover, Paul predicates community in 1 Cor 1–4 and 12 with making solidarity with these rejected ones— including, but not limited to, the crucified, disabled Anointed One. As God shows greater honor to the "less respectable," "less honorable" members of our bodies, Paul suggests that communities may be judged by the care shown to all members and by the willingness to share in the honors and suffering of all.

From a disability perspective, these passages might facilitate the interrogation of a normate worldview that too often rejects or disregards those labeled as "weak" or "disabled." Indeed, Paul's contention that divine favor and wisdom rests with just such ones could be used to critique the medical model of disability in which impairment appears as a problem to be solved. Paul's formulations suggest instead that the perspective and experience of the disabled be viewed as valuable, even uniquely valuable, in the life of the community and in the economy of salvation. Moreover, Paul's discussion of the "body" of the Anointed in 1 Cor 12 makes an important connection with claims from the social model of disability that it is society itself that "disables" the participation of the full range of its citizens. First Cor 12 argues that the social body only functions successfully when it welcomes the contributions, the gifts, of all its members. However, Paul also suggests that the success of the community is determined by its ability to act like God in making possible the contributions of all—by giving greatest honor to the weakest and by providing consistent care to all.

Paul's theological formulations regarding divine wisdom and the body of the Anointed in 1 Cor 1–4 and 1 Cor 12 may indeed have radical potential for unsettling standard constructions and hierarchies regarding the disabled in antiquity and today. However, this potential stands in profound tension with those parts of this letter that strongly reinforce the standard sociopolitical hierarchy of antiquity, a hierarchy dominated by the able-bodied free male citizen.

Indeed, these very chapters of 1 Cor 1–4 and 12 demonstrate Paul's rhetorical efforts to develop a hierarchy that serves his own authority claims. First Corinthians 12 itself ends with Paul's assertion of a hierarchy of roles within the *ekklēsia* that is topped by the title Paul gives himself— the title of envoy (see Wire 1991, 136–38; Miller 2015, 157–58). Meanwhile, the terms in which Paul represents the debate of the Corinthians—that some claim to "follow Paul" and some Apollos—show that some of the Corinthians are questioning Paul's own leadership (3:4). If Paul rhetorically constructs himself as a servant leader who has become like "the scum of the earth" (4:13), he also uses the opposition between divine and human wisdom to appropriate an authority that he denies to the Corinthian *ekklēsia*. Paul asserts the immaturity of the Corinthians by associating them with the wrong kind of wisdom, the human wisdom that signals their fleshly nature and separation from the divine. By contrast, Paul claims for himself divine wisdom that allows him to deliver his proclamation with a demonstration of "God's presence and power" (2:4). Indeed, Paul appeals to this divine authority in arguing that he is impervious to the Corinthians' judgment (2:14, 4:3-4). Paul may seem to critique a competitive search for advantage among the Corinthians. However, his own goal regarding his place in this community does not appear to be establishing his place among equals—or even his equal place among his fellow envoys. Instead, as Elizabeth Schüssler Fiorenza points out, Paul frames his authority as the community's "sole founder and father" (1999, 119). Paul claims this role of father at the end of 1 Cor 4, and he asks rhetorically regarding his future visit to the Corinthians, "So what do you prefer? Shall I come to visit you with a stick or with affection and gentleness?" (4:21; see Fee 1987, 193; Conzelmann 1975, 93).

We may ask, How does Paul's metaphorical claim to be father of the community with the right to exercise physical punishment against his "children" reverse, or at least undermine, his own attempts elsewhere to unseat traditional hierarchies in the ancient world? Scholars like Antoinette Wire have pointed out this difficulty in 1 Corinthians—the tension in Paul's rhetoric between the patriarchal hierarchy of the ancient world, the model for the empire, and the solidarity Paul advocates with the crucified, disabled Anointed One. However, Wire has also illuminated evidence for other theological constructions within the Corinthian community. Namely, she argues the Corinthians believed that the Anointed's action in the world represents not a call for them to maintain their original humble position, but "God's choice to lift them up into wisdom, power, and honor through the practice of God's gifts in assemblies that reject the privileges of gender, caste, and nation (1 Cor 4:7, 10; Gal 3:28)" (2000, 127). The gendered hierarchy that Paul upholds not only in 1 Cor 4 but also in other key passages of the letter provides a serious challenge to such a theological formulation—and to Paul's own call to make common cause with the weak and despised of the world. The scope of this commentary precludes a full exploration of these passages, but in her monograph, Miller (2015) argues that Paul's construction of gendered hierarchy in 1 Cor 11:2-16 and 14:33-36 works to question women's intellectual ability and their connection to the divine, thus serving the "disablement" of their vocal agency as full "citizens." As we will show, gendered hierarchy in 1 Cor 4 and 11:2-16 has a strong connection with the gendered vision of resurrection in 1 Cor 15.

First Corinthians 15 stands as a particularly important chapter when read from a disability perspective. In this chapter Paul addresses the skepticism of those in the community over the matter of the body's resurrection. Since the community already shared in the life of God, they might ask, Why was there any need to consider the future of the mortal shell? Paul seeks to persuade his listeners that their relationship with God's Anointed was still unfolding in a process of resurrection. More specifically, Paul frames the Anointed's ongoing role in this "process" of resurrection as a matter of imperial rule and conquest. In order to explain the nature of this resurrection, Paul includes here a contrast of earthly bodies to the spiritual bodies inhabited by the resurrected. Both these conversations offer critical insights into the way that Paul uses "perfect" resurrected bodies to explain the nature of salvation for believers. Moreover, both conversations also demonstrate that Paul genders the perfection of resurrected bodies, and thus the divine itself, as male. Paul's portrayal of the risen one as the imperial Son of God, and his gendering of the perfect resurrected body creates a deeply hierarchical system that replicates in many respects the hierarchies of the wider Roman Empire. In this vision of resurrection, we may ask what has become of the weak, disabled body of the suffering Anointed One and the honor accorded to it. Indeed, what does this understanding of resurrection mean for those who might find empowerment and voice in the divine power Paul accords weak and scorned bodies in the preresurrection state?

Richard Horsley identifies 1 Cor 15:20-24 as the "center and substance" of Paul's larger meditation on resurrection in 1 Cor 15 (2000, 99). In this pericope Paul describes a process of resurrection inaugurated by the Anointed's death and resurrection. Here he makes a connection between Adam and the Anointed One. Death comes to humanity through Adam, but resurrection and life come through the Anointed as "the first fruit of those who have died" (vv. 21-22). Here Paul asserts a necessary order to resurrection. The Anointed must be raised first so that those who believe in him may be resurrected "at his coming" (ἐν τῇ παρουςίᾳ αὐτοῦ; v. 23). However, Paul locates the completion (the τέλος) of this process in the Anointed's destruction of "every ruler and every authority and power" (v. :24). Only at this point can the Son's reign comes to an end as he hands over the kingdom to God, the Father, and is himself subjected, "so that God may be the one who rules everything everywhere" (15:28).

In Paul's rendering, both life and death originate in the male body: death in the body of Adam on the one hand, and life in the Anointed on the other. For Paul, resurrection springs from the anointed, risen, imperial "Son" of God, whose role is not only life giver to believers but also dealer of destruction to his enemies. With this depiction Paul reinscribes the positive valence of imperial "images and relations" (Horsley 2000, 93). The Anointed himself takes on the guise of the all-powerful, violently conquering emperor. However, Kittredge points out that Paul has also located the Anointed as the necessary, mediating term in a hierarchy that extends from human beings to God. Kittredge argues that this construction is not an isolated "exegetical afterthought" but a reinforcement of those hierarchies found in 1 Cor 4, and especially in 11:2-16, in which the Anointed acts as the critical intermediary between the Father and all creation. She concludes, "In the symbolic universe of the letter, God's subjection of the Anointed is the ultimate symbolic legitimization of the father's position between the children and the Anointed One and the husband's position between his wife and God" (2000, 107).

Within 1 Cor 15 the process of resurrection remains mysterious. Yet while the process itself is mysterious, we can also see that in his vision of the transformative process of resurrection, Paul employed two assumptions from the ancient world: first, that seeds sown in the ground died and that growth represented a miraculous effect of the divine; and second, that bodies in the heaven were not material but actually immaterial and living minds (Dewey 2010, 140–41). However, Paul illustrates the transformative power of this resurrection through a comparison of the body before and after resurrection. Amos Yong has pointed out the potential from a disability perspective in Paul's claim of 1 Cor 15:42-44 that there is some continuity between the present and resurrected body (2011, 123–24). But this sense of continuity—and thus much of this potential—is undermined by Paul's thorough comparison in 1 Cor 15:35-54 of the "earthly" (ἐπίγεια) body with the "heavenly" (ἐπουράνια) resurrected body. Paul describes this earthly body, sown in preparation for resurrection, as physical, weak, dishonorable, and perishable. By contrast, the risen body is defined by its spiritual and imperishable nature, along with its honor, glory, and power. Paul again draws on Adam and the Anointed as models to illustrate the difference. In this case Adam as "a man of dust" represents the earthly, physical body. In our own physical bodies, we have born the "likeness of the earthly man" (τὴν εἰκόνα τοῦ χοϊκοῦ; v. 49). By contrast, Paul contends that our spiritual bodies will bear the image of the second man, the man of heaven (τὴν εἰκόνα τοῦ ἐπουρανίου; v. 49).

In Paul's description of resurrection, the perfect risen body replaces—and in effect erases—the inferior physical body. With the lens of disability studies, it may be argued that Paul constructs resurrection as a "cure" for the impairment that characterizes the physical human body. Part of this cure appears to be taking on the image of the Anointed, portrayed most strikingly in 1 Cor 15 as the heavenly male emperor exercising power through force and subjugation. This risen Anointed One becomes the means for the cure of resurrection, even as he is the model of divine bodily perfection to which our own resurrected bodies aspire.

With regard to disability, Paul's rhetoric in 1 Cor 15 has several implications. Paul's depiction of all earthly, physical bodies as essentially impaired renders disability itself as a generic element of the human experience. Lost is the rich diversity of voice and experience that is connected with a range of physical and mental differences among those commonly labeled "disabled." Indeed, when the transformation of weak and disabled bodies to perfect powerful bodies is portrayed as the ultimate goal, the telos of salvation, one may question how the state of being disabled may be honored or appreciated. Does this construction in fact give greater force to the medical model, in which impairment exists to be repaired?

Paul's portrayal of resurrection and the risen Anointed One also rein-forces hierarchy that deeply affects representation of bodies as abled or disabled. In 1 Cor 15, Paul reproduces the imperial hierarchy with the resurrected Anointed One at its apex in the guise of the ultravirile war-rior emperor. It is this gendered persona, this male body, that becomes the model for the perfect resurrected bodies that Paul promises believers will inhabit at the Anointed's coming. This formulation naturalizes the dominant sociopolitical hierarchy of the ancient world in which the male body of the free citizen was held up as the ideal, defining what it meant to be a realized human being. We can see this in the imperial art, where the deified Augustus sits on what was once Zeus' throne, the perfect man now elevated to the heavenly realm (*Gemma Augustea*).

Against this ideal, all other bodies were commonly portrayed as lim-ited or disabled. This "disabling" of the nonmale citizen body becomes especially severe in the case of women and slaves, whose physical, mental, and moral abilities were routinely identified as different and, of course, inferior to those of male citizens. This construction of disability under-wrote the reasoning that those inferior to the male citizen were naturally subjected to him. As Kittredge (2000) explains, the hierarchy that Paul describes in 1 Cor 15 is isolated neither from the wider culture nor from the gendered hierarchy seen elsewhere in 1 Cor 4 and 11 that distances women from the divine, and legitimates the "rule" of the stern father who comes "with a rod" (4:21).

With 1 Cor 15, we must ask what has become of the honored disabled body of earlier chapters in this letter. Does the telos of salvation, the perfect risen body, entirely erase what has come before in the crucified, disabled body? Does the importance of that earlier body only lie with its function as a foil for the manifest superiority of the resurrected state? We might also question, postresurrection, what has become of the divine truth and solidarity that Paul associated with those things considered weak, low, and despised "in the world." Along with Amos Yong, we can ask, "Why didn't Paul more radically rethink his notion of the resurrected body based on his theology of weakenss?" (2011, 124).

At a distance of many centuries from Paul's intense eschatological expectation, we suggest it is critical to seek ways of retaining the hope of transformation Paul envisions with resurrection while also holding up the ways in which God's truth manifests in our weakness and falli-bility. How might we act out God's will when, according to the domi-nant vision of 1 Cor 12, we form communities that enable the full range of human beings to participate as valued equals? The enemies to such "beloved" communities are those very sociopolitical structures that hinder or make impossible such equal participation for the greatest possible range of humanity. In our own role as critical interpreters, we may consider whether Paul's portrayal of resurrection in tones of imperial purple ultimately serves to reinforce these structures that disable. In turn, such questioning may allow us to create fruitful dialogue that enables modern voices—including voices of people with disabilities—to join a debate both with Paul's perspective and with other early Christian voices like those Paul himself addresses in 1 Corinthians. We argue that it is in this debate that modern readers may find powerful and healing alternative ways to envision the "risen" Anointed One and our own ultimate salvation.

Second Corinthians

The competitive atmosphere of the Corinthian correspondence heated up with the fragments of 2 Corinthians. Other Jesus missionaries arrived, carrying letters of recommendation from other communities and demonstrating their worth by a compelling performance of scriptural interpretation. They criticized Paul for his lack of credentials and competence. In 2 Cor 2:14–6:13, 7:2-4, Paul actually plays their game by delivering a speech that tried to turn his opponents' claims on their heads. Paul argues that his competence was not the issue, nor was there any need for scriptural expertise since the community themselves were his best credential, and that the life they already enjoyed was the heart of their genuine transformation (3:2-3, 18). It was from their own lived experience that they could creatively engage the world.

As Paul continues his defense, rereading Gen 1:3, he claims that the power and presence of God is manifested precisely in his limited humanity (4:5-6). Creation was not a past matter for Paul; it was happening now, particularly as his words reflected on the Corinthian community. The mutual transformation noted in 2 Cor 3:18 continued here. Paul's letter, as well as his person, was a mask through which the splendor of God enlightens hearts. This mutual enlightening process comes about in very human terms. Paul saw himself like the grotesque pottery of the first century, proving that whatever energy was manifested, it came from the divine (4:7-12). This passage is crucial for understanding the radical humanity of Paul. He is saying that it is precisely through his human limitations that the divine communicates with the community. Even as he moves toward death, the life of God continues to abound. In effect, our limited, mortal human condition bears and transmits the revelatory liberation of God. It is not the perfect, ideal winner who communicates God's image; rather, "ordinary earthenware," with all its limitations, transmits the divine. This means for us that being disabled is not a condition to be wished away but instead can be seen as a revelation of our true relation to the living God.

Paul continues to explore this radically new condition in 2 Cor 5:16-21. Paul declares that the condition for anyone connected to God's Anointed is tantamount to "a new world order" (v. 17). Now this new order is not a return to the old status quo. Often this passage's interpretation turns on the notion of reconciliation to suggest that there is a return to one's old relationship with God. This misses the underlying metaphor of regime change and the use of coinage to express this transformation. In the ancient world, a new regime entailed a new minting, or at least a reminting of old coins (Dewey, Hoover, and McGaughy 2010, 128–29, notes on 5:17, 18, 21). These coins did not signal a return to old ways but the inauguration of a new era. Paul thus calls the Corinthians to see that their life is part of a radically new situation. They, just as he, function as agents of change in this new regime.

Evidently, despite the rhetorical success of this fragment, the Corinthians failed to see Paul's fundamental point: that the competitive world of gaining an advantage was no longer the way to live in solidarity with the Anointed. The Corinthians judged Paul's advice to be worthy of acceptance on the strength of his rhetorical performance!

Ironically, he had won the battle but lost the war. Moreover, the competitive propensity of Paul, indicated in Gal 1:13-14, comes out in this material. Then, when he visited them, they found his real-life presence to be a pale comparison to the persona delivered through his letter's interpreter. He left Corinth insulted by those who thought his presence unimpressive and pathetic (2 Cor 10:10). The community still played in terms of competitive advantage.

Paul wrote his next letter (2 Cor 10–13) aware that he could well lose any further connection with the community he founded. He tries one last time to persuade them to reconsider not simply him but also the way in which they imagine how reality works. He tries a rather different approach: comedy. In what is a parody of the ancient "fool's speech," Paul puts on a variety of comic masks to "boast" as people would want him to boast. But he does not boast in the usual way. Instead, he proceeds to deliver a series of comic bombasts that dissolve the usual ways of documenting success in the ancient world. Even a heavenly ascent and a divine oracle that should substantiate his superiority become comic fodder (12:2-6). Here Paul is delivering a parody of a heavenly vision. He should be confident in his experience and knowledge. Yet his language is a mass of contradictions. He should know what was going on, but he speaks as if "someone else" had the experience. In fact, he cannot even utter what it was that was seen! Hardly a success story. In addition, Paul speaks of a chronic disability. Much ink has been spilled over determining what the disability might have been. There has been no resolution. Such a search is rather beside the point. Here we have an oracular account (12:7-9a). As such, it should be a success story. Instead, it abounds in frustration. But this leads Paul to a major insight that is actually consistent with his insight into God's acceptance of Jesus: "So, for the sake of God's Anointed, I accept limitations, insults, calamities, persecutions, difficulties. For when I accept my limitations, then I am empowered" (v. 10).

Paul reiterates what we have already seen in 2 Cor 4:7-12. It is precisely in the acceptance of limits, of negativities, of disabilities that the revelatory action of the divine is perceived. Such material has bearing upon our discussion of disability. The attempt to escape from one's situation, or to paint over it with a theological gloss, is precisely what Paul does not do. The physical reality of his situation is the starting point for meaningful life. What would have been considered both a physical and social impediment, rendering Paul incapable of divine access, turns out to be the avenue of genuine mystery.

The third fragment of 2 Corinthians celebrates Paul's reconciliation with the community. In fact, part of the opening of this fragment (1:4-7) has been used over the centuries to begin discussions over the interrelationship between those who suffer and those who support. Caution needs to be used when applying this passage. The words were delivered after a very difficult social situation. These words highlight the breakthrough experienced by Paul and the Corinthians in their deteriorating relationship. To read and apply these words without context or any sense of that tenuous historical experience renders them hollow and can prove counterproductive. Too often these sentences are quoted and applied without paying attention to the reality of the present situation. They cannot be used to gloss over an unreconciled condition. Paul, on the other hand, can look back at what was a difficult situation and say to the Corinthians that the painful estrangement they all experienced had turned into a moment of transformation. In Paul's estimation they had gone beyond a self-serving attitude to a basic openness to what God was doing (7:10). The fundamental relationship between the Corinthians and Paul was ultimately recovered and celebrated (7:12).

Finally, the two remaining fragments (chs. 8 and 9) present Paul's appeal specifically to the Corinthians and to all the province of Achaia. It is important to see what Paul was trying to achieve by this collection for the community in Jerusalem. Paul did not consider this to be an assessment by one community on another. It was not a tax to be collected. Rather, for Paul this collection expressed a fundamental equality among Jesus followers. The collection, for Paul, indicated the equality of the nations with Jews before the God of Israel. Moreover, the contributions further expressed the interdependent way life together was to be lived (8:14-15). The basic equality among followers of the Anointed comes from a fundamental poverty. In recognizing that God has accepted the one who had nothing, then what one had could be seen as a surplus to be used in a similar fashion. Further, Paul saw that this new situation could well lead to a constant interdependence and mutual sharing within the community of the Anointed. Such an economic model contrasts sharply the extractive economy of the empire. Paul spells this out further in 2 Cor 9:10-15, where he turns the benefits model underpinning the economic reality of the empire into a shared generosity of the nations, which leads to a surprisingly widespread thanksgiving to God. This sharing of abundance would be seen as an acknowledgment of the effectiveness of the world-transforming message of what God has done to Jesus. For Paul, surplus could come from unexpected places—from those who seemingly had little or nothing. It would be used not to maintain dominance but to provide for those in need. Interdependence and mutual assistance would be the fundamental characteristics of this economic enterprise. The usual social positions and postures, maintaining social disability, were overcome by this interdependent strategy.

THE LETTER TO PHILEMON

Any analysis of Paul's letter to Philemon must acknowledge that its dominant interpretation over the last millennia and a half has rendered this a deeply disabling text for slaves from antiquity into the early modern period. From the time of John Chrysostom forward, exegetes have argued that Philemon demonstrates Paul's support of slavery and the harmonious coexistence of Christian ethics with slaveholding.

Demetrius Williams notes that the use to which supporters of slavery put this letter in our own American history has meant its continuing exclusion from the "canon" of Scripture that black churches include in their liturgy and study (2012, 37). Our interpretation of this letter suggests that Paul's appeal to Philemon in this letter offers the possibility of departure from a construction of slaves as essentially other, as "disabled" in antiquity. However, this very appeal to Philemon's authority of decision also reinscribes the structure of domination that underwrote slavery as an institution.

From an early date, the dominant reconstruction of the letter's circumstance explained the primary addressee in the letter, Philemon, to be the owner of the runaway slave Onesimus. In this remarkable rhetorical gem, Paul attempts to do much in just twenty-five verses. While addressing the entire household of Philemon, Paul focuses his attention directly on Philemon in order to make an intercession for Onesimus, present with Paul in his imprisonment. Paul proceeds carefully in this intercession. He states that he has the power in the Anointed to command but chooses to appeal to Philemon on the basis of their shared relationship, the love they have developed in solidarity with God's Anointed. Paul explains that he sends Onesimus back to Philemon despite the fact that Onesimus has become his dear child during his time in prison (Phlm 1:10). He adds that Onesimus was formerly "useless" to Philemon, but has now become "useful" to both Paul and to Philemon (v. 10). Paul urges Philemon to take Onesimus back "no longer as a slave but more than a slave, a beloved brother" (οὐκέτι ὡς δοῦλον ἀλλ᾽ ὑπὲρ δοῦλον, ἀδελφὸν ἀγαπητόν; v. 16).

This letter poses a challenge to interpreters in the many questions it leaves unanswered. How did Onesimus come to be with Paul in the first place? Was he indeed a runaway slave, or did Philemon originally send him to Paul? What prompts Paul to send Onesimus back to Philemon? And most urgently, What does Paul envision as Philemon's ideal action? Does his carefully phrased request that Philemon treat Onesimus as a brother, and his optimistic statement that Philemon will do "even more than I say" (v. 21), indicate Paul's oblique appeal for Onesimus to be legally freed? Or does Paul send Onesimus back into long-term slavery with an appeal that Philemon alter the nature of their master/slave relationship so that it is defined by their mutual solidarity in the Anointed? These last questions have been at the heart of the long debate over this letter's import for Christian believers. Historically, the dominant interpretation has been this last possibility—namely, that Paul sends Onesimus back to take up his role as Philemon's slave (D. Williams 2012). Even as many modern interpreters now argue for a "manumission" reading of the letter (R. Martin 1974, 166; Winter 1993, 301–6), this earlier legacy continues to color this letter's reception.

In a commentary on disability, it is critical to make several notes about slavery that have a bearing on the reading of this letter. Paul, Philemon, and Onesimus all lived in one of history's great slave societies. In the

Roman Empire, slaves and slavery were present in all aspects of life, even as vast numbers of new slaves were entering the empire through conquest in the first century. The subjugation of slaves, like that of women, was justified in Greco-Roman literature with assertions that slaves were essentially different than the free male citizen. Aristotle, for instance, argues that slaves were naturally ruled since they did not possess the part of the soul that allowed them to deliberate rationally, or to "foresee with their mind" (*Pol.* 1252a32, 1260a12–15). Aristotle was in good company with this observation, and with his contention that such impairment affected not only the slave's intellectual capacity but also his or her moral character. In the ancient world, slaves were regularly described as "naturally" lazy, dishonest, and criminal in various respects (Noel 2012, 61). This condemnation of slaves as morally compromised was not matched in antiquity, as it was in American history, by a condemnation of slavery itself as an immoral institution.

This ancient understanding of slaves and slavery is a critical context for our reading of Philemon. In a culture that asserted the inherent difference and inferiority of slaves, Paul's call for brotherhood between (former?) slave and master might be interpreted as a revolutionary expression of solidarity with the Anointed. Paul appeals to Philemon not in a private letter but in a letter addressed to the *ekklēsia* as a whole. By addressing this letter to the community, Paul makes this a public matter to be discussed, and a matter in which Philemon's decision could be strengthened in the eyes of this community by Paul's own authoritative voice. In the context of this letter, Paul not only urges brotherhood "both as a man and as one who belong to our lord" (v. 16) but also asks Philemon to welcome Onesimus just as he would receive Paul himself. Some interpreters read Philemon as realizing the liberative potential in the baptismal formula of Gal 3:28, which states, "There is no longer slave or free" in the Anointed (Lewis 1991, 232–46).

What we detect in Philemon could well be one of the first instances where the utopian dreams of Gal 3:28 gain concretization. In this letter Paul shows his affection for both Onesimus and Philemon and persuasively urges that this love be the model for a new relationship between these two believers.

If we accept this positive reading of Philemon, we are still left with challenging questions regarding Paul and his interaction with the "disability" of slavery in the ancient world. If Paul does proceed with revolutionary intent in this letter, supported by the paradigm-changing implications of Gal 3:28, why does he stop short of asking openly for Onesimus' manumission? Or more radically still, why does Paul not condemn slavery here, or elsewhere in the controversial 1 Cor 7:21? It may well be that Paul's apocalyptic perspective that "the world in its present form is passing away" (1 Cor 7:31) obscures the need to confront embedded social structures. Yet we may ask why Paul does seem comfortable challenging certain social structures—namely, the difference between Jew and gentile—but is unable to challenge other social structures.

Sheila Briggs has argued persuasively that any critique Paul might offer regarding the social system of slavery—and the lived experience of slaves—was complicated by the theological metaphor of slavery that permeates his writing. Paul describes the Anointed One as a slave (Phil 2:7) and his own apostolic role with the language of slavery (1 Cor 9:19), even as he calls on Jesus' followers to remember they "were bought for a price" (1 Cor 6:20). Such a metaphor might have a leveling effect within early Christian communities when all are called to be slaves of the Anointed. However, Briggs notes, conversely, "When salvation itself is seen as a process of domination, then the critique of social arrangements, resulting from processes of domination, is made, to say the least, more difficult" (2000, 118).

In the case of Philemon, Paul's call for Onesimus to be welcomed as a beloved brother departs from an ancient script in which slaves were commonly portrayed as inherently inferior to free citizens in their moral and intellectual capabilities. However, Paul's appeal to Philemon may be argued ultimately not to unsettle but to reinforce the hierarchy between slave and master. The very nature of this appeal acknowledges Philemon's power of decision, thus reinforcing the authority of the slaveholder. Meanwhile, Onesimus remains, at least in the moment of the letter, lacking in the voice or agency associated with the free person (unless Onesimus actually performed the letter before Philemon's household). Even as Paul seems to call for a new and loving relationship between Onesimus and Philemon, he remains apparently complicit in the power hierarchy that degrades any such relationship (Glancy 2002; Osiek 2003).

THE FRAGMENTS OF PHILIPPIANS

Philippians offers rich content for a discussion of disability—not least in the famous "Christ hymn" of Phil 2 in which Jesus makes common cause with the marginalized by taking the form of the slave. While this commentary is not the place to address the complicated textual arguments regarding Philippians' composition, we will address this text as a series of letter fragments from Paul to the Philippian community that were gathered into a single document in the second century. The fragments identified as the first (4:10-20) and third (3:2-11, 20-21) find resonance in other Pauline material (such as in 1 Cor and Rom) with their assertion that life in solidarity with the Anointed means a truly interdependent tissue of trust and a future of transformation and hope beyond an individual scenario. Because we examine those Pauline claims more thoroughly in the letters of Romans and 1 Corinthians, here we will concentrate most fully on the surprising content of the Christ hymn of Phil 2.

Before moving onto the matter of the hymn in Phil 2, we should not overlook a theme that ties the first and second fragments together. Despite the fact that Paul describes himself as being able "to manage in whatever circumstances" he finds himself (exhibiting the self-sufficiency of the Stoic sage), his "thank you" letter (4:10-20) makes it quite clear that he sees his particular relationship with the Philippians as the ideal expression of mutual life and interdependence. Paul, in effect, transcends the ancient model of self-sufficiency by recognizing how the Philippians became his partners when he "was having a hard time" (4:14). Their continued financial support for him was not done to affirm anyone's superiority; rather, it reinforced what Paul understood to be the benefit cycle initiated by the God of Israel and sustained through their generosity. Likewise, in the second fragment, the Philippians' concern for the welfare of Epaphroditus (2:25-30) is a further example of this interdependence. Sent by the community, Epaphroditus risked his health to assist Paul. Mutual giving and interdependence mark the relationship between the Philippians and Paul. Such a sense of life together flies in the face of the modern delusion of self-sufficiency. How often do the able-bodied misunderstand the interconnectedness of life, especially in those moments of weakness and limits where the value and contribution of each person can come to life?

In the second fragment (1:1–3:1a; 4:4-9, 21-23), Paul directly deals with his imprisonment (probably at Ephesus). Paul sees his predicament as an opportunity to spread the world-transforming message of God's Anointed (1:12-14). Indeed, he can even look equally upon the prospect of his death or survival as a further means of increasing the life of trust (1:20-26). He urges them to maintain the attitude of love, of keeping others' interests in mind rather than their own (2:4). He then reminds them of a hymn about the Anointed, which may well have been familiar in their gatherings (2:6-11).

In the hymn of 2:6-11, Jesus "is raised higher than anyone and awarded a title above all others" (v. 9) precisely because of his resolution to "belong to humankind" (v. 7) and to trust "all the way to death, even by crucifixion"

(v. 8). Jesus' choice in this hymn to take on not only a human form but the form of a slave stands in dramatic tension with the standard constructions of power and authority in the empire. Katherine Shaner (forthcoming) has pointed out that this tension is especially profound in verse 6 where the word ἀπαγμὸν appears, a word most literally translated as "rape" or "robbery." The "rhetoric" of imperial imagery commonly portrays the divine emperor as a warrior in the midst of conquering, of raping and robbing, a woman who represents subject peoples. Given Shaner's suggestion that this hymn can be contextualized by such imagery, a dynamic translation of verse 6 could yield, "Jesus did not equate being like God with rape and robbery." In this reading, Jesus' rejection of divinity in the violent exercise of imperial power explains his choice to stand at the very bottom of the imperial hierarchy—to make common cause with the physically and sexually brutalized slave woman. In effect, Jesus has refused to live above those who are plundered and raped.

Yet this hymn features a final transformation—one we have examined in 1 Corinthians. At the end of the hymn in Philippians, the Anointed is "raised higher than anyone and awarded the title that is above all others . . . so that on hearing the name 'Jesus' every knee should bend" (Phil 2:9-10).

While the earlier half of the hymn seems to condemn imperial domination, the latter part still uses the mythic structure of divine elevation and dominance to portray Jesus as a heavenly imperial figure. Modern readers have become cautious in simply accepting the social structure implicit in such language. The exultation of Jesus as "lord" can easily morph into a triumphal figure, hardly distinguishable from the imperial cast. The modern reader has interpretive choices to make here. Has Paul returned to the paradigm of domination, or does he keep the one who went trustingly to death in mind? Certainly by the fourth and fifth centuries, the answer was clear: Jesus now wore the victorious imperial purple. The tortured one was left behind.

Joseph Marchal has illuminated the dangers this hymn, and its reverberations elsewhere in the letter, hold for the marginalized reader. Marchal notes that the placement of the hymn serves as a call for obedience and humbleness on the part of the Philippians. Indeed, much of the letter can be read as counseling an "ethics conditioned by obedience, humility, and sacrifice" (2007, 253). For a reader with disabilities, whose impairment might have led to an experience of marginalization, such an ethics has the possibility of valorizing, and thus reinforcing, marginalization. Moreover, the hymn highlights the Anointed's choice in taking on the "disability" of slavery and crucifixion. Marchal explains that this "choice" of voluntary obedience in the hymn ultimately "idealizes and obscures the compulsive dynamics of slavery" (253). We suggest a similar formulation regarding disability. The Anointed's freedom to choose a disabled state in the hymn obscures the lived experience of disability that is often defined by its very lack of choice.

The final fragment begins on a discordant note, warning the listeners to "watch out for those curs" (3:2) (apparently a reference to leaders conceived of as competitors). However, Paul moves quickly beyond the competitive claims of opponents to explore briefly what confidence in God's world-transforming message entails (3:8-11, 20-21). Paul asserts that a life lived in trust and confidence leads somewhere. It is no dead end; rather, it is already on the road to transformation. One can see connections to 1 Cor 15:35ff. and anticipation of Rom 8:18ff. Paul presents this life as a truly interdependent tissue of trust and envisions a future of transformation and hope beyond an individual scenario. Such a sense of transformation can be seen when Paul declares that he would know the "unconditional trust of the Anointed and the power of his resurrection" (Phil 3:10) by joining in his sufferings to attain the goal of "resurrection from among the dead" (3:11). Such a declaration reiterates the solidarity Paul sees in what God has done for the godless Jesus. Paul can experience his own mortality, live out his life with whatever sufferings, just as Jesus did. Like Jesus, he can approach his experience in confidence that the trustworthy God delivers unending life. In the key of disability studies, Paul here frames his own disabling experience as an expression of solidarity with the Anointed One. His own suffering becomes a further chapter in God's unfolding and surprising story. As we have said elsewhere, such a model may offer promise of empowerment for those experiencing disability. However, this formulation likewise requires us to deal with the very questions and conundrums we discussed with regard to the hymn of Philippians. Paul's presentation of his own suffering and that of the Anointed One evokes questions of choice and valorization of suffering that must be included in any discussion of Paul's theology and disability.

ROMANS

Paul addresses this letter to people he did not yet know but hoped to meet and to rely on for future assistance. Paul takes pains in Romans to envision life in solidarity with God's Anointed for a community composed of both Jews and "the nations." One cannot read Romans without recognizing, even from the outset (1:1-7), that Paul understands the Jesus movement to be an alternate regime, already underway. Unless the modern reader sees that the one titled "Son of God" completely overturns the standard paradigm of divine favor (i.e., Paul's fundamental insight of God accepting the godless one), then the very structure of this enthronement scene (1:3-4) reinforces the dominance Paul would subvert.

After a remarkable salutation (1:1-7) performed in ambassadorial tones, there comes the usual thanksgiving (1:8-15). Thereupon follows the first major section (1:16–4:25) of the body of the letter (1:16–11:36). Romans 1:16-17 sets the perspective of the world-transforming news to Jews and Greeks: living out of trust is the way to exist.

Within that frame Paul inserts what was essentially a standard synagogal critique of "the nations" (1:18-32; see Georgi 1986, 83–163; Käsemann 1980) where the relationship of the nations to the God of Israel was characterized as "disordered." The "nations'" failure to recognize and thank the One God meant their existence and practices were essentially compromised. In this construction of the cosmos, the divine provides the life and benefits of life for which humanity must give thanks. This is not a factual assessment but an ideological brief against non-Jews. There is a tendency for modern readers to obsess over the sexual disorders of "the nations," over the abandonment of "natural sexual relations" (1:26-28), and to glide by "injustice, greed, arrogance, jealousy, slander and pitilessness" (1:29-31).

Paul's condemnation of certain kinds of sexual acts and "dishonorable passions" is best contextualized as part of a larger ancient Jewish critique of "the nations'" idolatry. Nevertheless, we must also acknowledge that these verses continue to be mobilized in modern conversations so as to "disable" certain identities and sexual practices. Dale Martin notes the frequent association of these verses with the "fall" of Adam and Eve in Genesis. This association, unsupported by the text of Rom 1:18-32 itself, contributes to a logic that aligns not only homosexual acts but also homosexual desire and identity with "fallen human nature" (Martin 2006, 52–53). Such a reading does violence to the text in its failure to address adequately the historical context of these verses, even as it introduces a modern understanding of sexual identity not available in Paul's own time. These verses can only be responsibly analyzed with awareness of the significant differences in worldview that separate Paul and the modern reader when it comes to the subject matter of this passage. Paul's assumption of a functional understanding of procreation, based on the prevalent Stoic metaphysics, is quite different from a modern relational understanding of sexuality. Moreover, as Martin points out, the contemporary reader comes to this text with a very different understanding of the relationship between Jews, gentiles, and idolatry than Paul and his readers. Moreover, at a distance of two thousand years from Paul, we are part of a radically different, and still evolving, conversation over sexual identity and justice issues.

In chapter 2 Paul turns away from this synagogal critique to the very assumptions Jews made about the non-Jew and about themselves (vv. 3, 17). In fact, Paul set up the listening Jew (as well as the sympathetic non-Jew who shared the Jewish mindset) to judge "the nations" as failing to honor God. In Rom 2:2 Paul cites what right-thinking Jews would say: "God judges rightly those who do such evil deeds." He then immediately turned the tables on those Jewish Jesus followers who made such a judgment through a series of rhetorical questions (vv. 3-4) and observations of self-contradiction (vv. 5-11). The result is to see that the ones who felt so content in their integrity were no better than the ones they criticized. Paul wanted his listeners to see that neither Jew nor Greek had any advantage before the God of Israel. Nor did they need one. For Paul, authentic life comes from living "inwardly," as a "matter of the heart," "transformed by God, not conformed to tradition" (2:29). But who lives this life? Those who trust, as Jesus did, in an ultimately reliable God (3:22-26). Romans 3:25 indicates that Paul, knowing an earlier hero tradition (S. Williams 1975), places the emphasis on the election of God, not on the sacrificial heroism of Jesus. His insight focuses upon what God has done by accepting the one who has been disabled beyond death.

It is crucial to place the entire first section of the body of the letter within this perspective of trust. Otherwise this material becomes a fruitless *j'accuse* for anyone with an ax to grind. To read this section as a litmus test for religious behavior is to miss Paul's fundamental point: Is a trusting relationship the basis for your life? Using this material to judge others (thereby maintaining a dominating advantage) destroys the possibility of examining and appreciating the life of trust.

Through this prism of trust, Paul recast the story of the Jews. He saw in the primordial figure of Judaism—Abraham—the primary example of one who has confidence in the reliability of God (4:1-25). Indeed, even the impotent Abraham and the childless Sarah (v. 19) grew in their confidence in God (v. 20). Abraham anticipated Jesus, who was raised from among the dead (v. 24).

Paul could further rewrite the story of Adam, turning that mythic "costly blunder" into an antitype of the one whose death assured liberation and life (5:9, 15, 18-21). In his discussion of Adam, Paul brings in the "corrupting seduction of power" (5:12): *hamartia*, usually translated as "sin." Unfortunately, the English term "sin" is limited in its linguistic scope today, inhabiting a religious ghetto. On the other hand, the Greek *hamartia* was fraught with nuance. This word was invoked in situations beyond a person's control. It spoke to the deeper and darker parts of human experience. Thus the term *hamartia* carries with it the sense of being overwhelmed, the sense one is entangled in something larger than oneself. When we begin to see the mythic range of *hamartia*, we can then explore a variety of questions about those forces that dominate and overwhelm our life. We can begin to name a situation for its true effect upon us. In giving us the contrast between "one man's rebellious mindlessness" and "one man's trusting mindfulness" (5:19), Paul offered a hopeful way to negotiate the exigencies of life.

It is in Rom 7:6-25 that Paul offers a graphic examination of life's self-contradiction. The "ego" in this material is not Paul. Rather, Paul uses the form of a teaching diatribe to guide his listeners in recognizing the forces that govern their existence. He thus personifies the individual as one who successfully internalizes the cultural expectations promised by the law (whether it was Jewish or Roman). In the ancient world, the law reflected and reinforced society's expectations. The ancients assumed that embodying the law would guarantee freedom. Paul argues conversely that those who seek to internalize social expectations become aware of an internal rebellion. Self-contradiction is the fate of social success. The seeker of success becomes embedded in the coils of *hamartia*, the seductive corruption of power. The overwhelmed "ego" cries out, "What a sorry creature am I! Who will rescue me from this earthly self which is captive to death?" (v. 24). Paul anticipates the modern critique of society by exposing its disabling and contradictory effect. The deepest desires of the individual prove to be radically frustrated. Here is a devastating evaluation of those individuals who internalized the competitive expectations of the ancient world. The judging of others turns inward. The solitary "ego" feels the gap between desire and attainment. The disabling nature of the social world of the first century becomes clear. The prized vision of attaining success at the top of the social pyramid comes tumbling down in a crash of self-contradiction. Advantage over others provides no ultimate hope, for the "ego" realizes it is fundamentally incapable of effecting what it wants. It is crippled by contradiction.

The way out of the "ego's" death spiral is discovered in the solidarity (ch. 8) with the "beloved community." We can see the change in pronouns from chapter 7 to chapter 8, from "ego" to "you" (pl.) as an indication of the reframing of human existence by Paul. Recognizing that God has accepted Jesus as the Anointed brings about a different way of living. Paul uses liturgical language to reinforce the communal experience of trust (8:14-17). He declares that they have received genuine adoption into the life of God. They exist in solidarity with the Anointed as God's children and with a future as God's heirs.

Indeed, Paul explored the implications of that shared life. All creation "anticipates the disclosure of who God's children really are" (8:19). Creation and all those who "have savored the first taste of God's power" (8:23) are caught up in the hope of cosmic transformation. And in the midst of this labor, God's power is ever present in our frailty and disability, even in the obscurity of the human heart (8:26-28).

This presence of God survives all forces arrayed against it; no dominating power or element can keep away the reliable love of God. In fact, Rom 8:38-39 lists all the lines of domination and exclusion. *Significantly, God is not in any of them. In fact, God's love is inclusive and non-domineering.* Such an image of God is largely lost in Christian history. For Paul, God's acceptance of the godless Jesus shows there is no power that can prevent this fundamental connection, this lasting tissue of trust. This God does not harness the usual forces of domination and alienation. Rather, God's "power" takes on a countercultural cast as it is revealed as unending, accepting, and faithful love.

It is in light of this persistent confidence that Paul brought up his relationship with his fellow Jews and their refusal to accept the world-transforming message about the Anointed One (Rom 9–11). How did Paul make sense of the fact that his new life and vision seemed to alienate him from his kinfolk? How did he attempt to make sense of their rejection or inattention to what to him was the crucial message for the world? First, Paul did not give up on either his experience or his people. This stance is consistent with how Paul reminded others to recognize and affirm their experience. Here Paul attempts to reimagine what their rejection of the message entailed. He turns a negative situation into a surprising opportunity by accessing the traditional notion of the remnant. Jews had used the notion of the remnant to speak of the survival of at least some of the people during a time of devastation. God's fidelity to the people was maintained through that interpretation. Paul, however, does not use the idea of the remnant to interpret his people's fate but the presence of "the nations" in the growing Jesus community. For example, Paul inverts the meaning of Hos 2:1 (9:25-26; Hos 2:1), originally intended to point out the survival of the people of Israel. Those without an identity are now "God's people," "beloved," and "children of the living God." Paul saw in this new situation the proof that no one can bring about this new situation on one's own. No advantage can bring this about. On the other hand, "the nations" cannot use their new situation to their advantage, for that would be another example of misunderstanding God's relationship with the world (11:21). But what, then, of Israel? Was there no hope for his people? Paul did not have a definitive answer. Instead, he declared at the end of his wisdom speculation that ultimately Israel "would receive God's mercy" (11:31). Paul concludes by acknowledging the inscrutable wisdom of God (11:33-36). Paul's lack of a resolution speaks volumes today. How often do we foreclose possibilities because of our preconditioned understanding? How do we interpret those moments in our life when the unexpected, the undesired occurs? How often are we tempted to abandon important relationships due to increasing strain and difficulty? Can we learn to be faithful to the depths of our experience? Can we begin to reframe our disablements in new ways? Can we enter this examination with the confidence that ultimately God will come through?

Such a meditation on the reliability of God stands in stark contrast to a society that is "ever in control" and sets expectations for those they define as disabled. In essence, these stances are actually indications of a fundamental lack of trust. Because we cannot assure ourselves of our total safety and perfect health, we take measures that go in that direction. Yet life mysteriously intervenes. Disabilities, complexities, and unforeseen developments throw us for a loop. Too shocked by what life gives us, we cannot imagine a way forward. Here is where Paul provides some advice: look at the depths of your experience and trust that somehow God's presence and power abides in those shadows. God awaits what you will say—a word from you never spoken until you respond to heartache. It is out of our struggles that we build a community of genuine life together.

In the final exhortation in Romans (12:1–15:32), Paul asks his listeners to acknowledge genuine worship as the lived response to God's mercy. This response is not limited to religious confines. Rather, it defines life together in solidarity with the Anointed. This means a critical assessment of the powers that would dominate us (12:2). The new basis for behavior is fundamental: God's unending connection with the lost (14:7-9) allows everyone to live creatively for one another. Life is no longer lived according to prescription and decree. Rather, life becomes a time for surprising one another in compassionate ways yet to be imagined.

The final chapter of Romans may well have existed originally as a letter of recommendation for Phoebe, a leader of the community at Cenchreae, who could have performed the letter to the Romans. Over a third of the people mentioned are women, and Junia (16:7) is described as being a person of "distinction among the Anointed's envoys (apostles)." This brief correspondence points to the significant and abiding leadership (even apostleship) of women among the early Jesus communities and begins to fill out the political implications found in Gal 3:28.

THE SECONDARY PAULINE CORRESPONDENCE

COLOSSIANS

Most New Testament scholars believe Colossians was written after Paul's death, perhaps in the last quarter of the first century. Questions of language, style, theology, and social situation convince many that this letter was written in Asia Minor for a community continuing the Pauline legacy. Since an earthquake in 60–61 CE destroyed the city of Colossae, this document was probably written sometime later for another congregation in Asia Minor. In fact, Colossians (and Ephesians) may well represent another side of life of those communities within Asia Minor addressed by the Apocalypse. Revelation's author draws on the seismic fall of Jerusalem and a profound antipathy to Roman domination to provide a bracing vision and radical critique of the empire. Meanwhile, Colossians (and Ephesians) rejects an apocalyptic worldview, adopting instead a vision of vertical, if not static, transcendence. If the Apocalypse encourages a radical rejection of the imperial world, Colossians (and Ephesians) urges followers to "think about what is above, not on the earth, for you have died and your life is hidden with the Anointed in God" (3:2). These letters suggest that peaceable coexistence with the imperial context is possible and that Jesus' followers may live a life consistent with Roman virtue and behavior.

Colossians' use of the "body of the assembly/church" (1:18) metaphor marks a significant contrast with 1 Cor 12, where Paul uses the Anointed's body to illustrate the interdependence of all the body's parts. In Colossians (1:15-20) the body metaphor elucidates the preeminence of the Anointed within a vertical cosmos. Nothing of the democratic horizontal movement of 1 Cor 12 survives. Rather, Colossians reminds its readers that they were once "alienated and hostile in mind" (1:21) but are now reconciled and urged to continue to persevere in a hope that has been hierarchically cast.

With that urging, the author, writing as Paul, describes joy "in his sufferings" for the community that would "complete what was lacking in the sufferings of the Anointed" for the sake of "his body, the *ekklēsia*" (1:24). This line reflects the authentic Pauline material, where his suffering serves the communities' experience of the Anointed's power (see 2 Cor 4 and Phil

3:10-11 above). But this passage deepens the matter. The recognition of suffering opens up a hidden dimension, the "mystery that has been hidden from the world powers and past generations" (1:26). Colossians attempts to keep its audience's eyes upon an invisible, heavenly realm in which they are "complete/whole" (*teleios*) in the Anointed.

Such a passage is filled with both possibilities and pitfalls in a discussion over disability. On the positive side, one can read this advice as urging people to see beyond visible limitations. By contrast, this passage may also reinforce a sort of disjointedness between the actual disabled condition and the ideal. Furthermore, the letter's support for the values of late first-century Roman domination may limit its worth for a modern assessment of disability. How, for example, is the notion of "perfect or complete" to be understood? Is this done at the expense of overlooking the actual condition of the person?

In Col 2:18-23, the authentic Pauline understanding seems to be continued where the congregation is advised not to let others "disqualify" (καταβραβεύω) them. The term comes from the Greek word βραβεῖον for "award" or "prize." Colossians urges its audience not to let others "deprive" them ("of their prize") because they did not excel in various ascetic practices. Such advice picks up Paul's concern about not needing to have an advantage over others. In this passage the writer evidently opposes those calling for distinctive religious practices. However, after asserting that the congregation should live a life of compassion and patience toward one another (again reiterating what was advised in the authentic letters of Paul), the writer then enjoins wives to be "submissive" to their husbands (3:18) and slaves to their masters (3:22). It is important to see that the writer has reverted to the dominant values of Roman life, a contrast to the much more equal relationship between husband and wife advocated by Paul in 1 Cor 7:3-4.

As the Pauline tradition moved forward in time, his followers made a variety of adjustments. Paul described the dramatic intrusion of an apocalyptic future into the present with surprising possibilities. Colossians transforms this into a vertical cosmic vision where the earthy realm disappears into the hidden heavenly realms. The focus is no longer a forward vector but an upward gaze—not unlike that of their contemporaries in the empire. The social values of the Roman world have now become the modus operandi of that Jesus community.

Ephesians

The so-called letter to the Ephesians is actually a treatise or homily. Scholars are uncertain about the audience for this homily. The place name

"Ephesus" is in fact a second-century insertion. Many scholars argue that Ephesians was the companion letter of Colossians directed to Laodicea (Col 4:16). It would seem that this homily circulated in the 80s and 90s CE in western Asia Minor. As with Colossians, it places the community addressed within the vertical stasis of a cosmic reality. The social situation has moved beyond individual congregations to a more abstract notion of *ekklēsia*. Here the notion of "church" as an overarching concept comes into play. In fact, the "church" is seen as intrinsic to the cosmic Anointed One, who is now head of the body—that is, the "church" (Eph 1:22). Moreover, the author considered that this situation is where Jew and gentile can meet in reconciliation. Through Jesus' death a "new human" comes into being, transcending the limits of the past (2:15). Ephesians calls its readers to a reconciling unity so that each and every person can grow into "the one who is the head" (4:15). Having established this basic insight, the author then exhorts his listeners to live in this new life. This leads directly into a series of ethical instructions that imagine proper church order as the household of God. This household metaphor facilitates commonplace Roman social values. Instead of the interdependence of husband and wife (1 Cor 7), wives are advised to submit to their husbands. Moreover, the image of the Anointed as the head of the subordinate church is brought to bear on the relationship between husband and wife (5:21-23). The patriarchal hierarchy of Roman social values continues in regard to children (6:1-4) and slaves (6:7-9). The emancipatory song of Gal 3:28 has been forgotten. This treatise speaks to Jesus followers over the long term, individuals who endure the imperial reality of their lives and keep their eyes focused upon the eternal and invisible realm.

Precisely because of this bifurcated vision (heavenly versus earthly), there is a danger to downplay the historical reality of life. The static quality of the mythic vision concentrates the believer's attention without offering any of the transformative imagination found in the authentic letters of Paul. The audience was asked to maintain, to hold on. The one note of transformation (the emergence of the "new human" [Eph 2:15]) is relegated to the space of the "church." Even the cosmic vision is quite unlike the transformative vision found in Romans (8:19-23), where all are caught up in a radical re-creation.

Ephesians does not envision any social transformation; instead, it reiterates the social norms of the Roman world. Such an affirmation may sound attractive to those who espouse "family values" today. However, those Roman values reinforce the supremacy of the able-bodied free male and allowed generations to overlook the needs and concerns of those who deviated from the established pattern of a patriarchal culture and power scheme. The first-century culture surviving on exclusion and competitive advantage returns with a vengeance. One needs to be quite cautious in applying this material to the modern situation. Only a nuanced and critical appreciation of the original context can give the contemporary reader a way to negotiate a meaningful outcome.

SECOND THESSALONIANS

This letter raises questions about the place of apocalyptic literature in discussions over disability, especially for those who experience profound loss and suffering in that disability.[2] Second Thessalonians appears to address a situation from the time during or soon after the Jewish War. Many apocalyptic visions and writings emerged from that seismic event. This letter's apocalyptic language would be a fitting response to such shattering times. For many, the Jewish War produced extraordinary social vertigo and loss. Apocalyptic scenarios allow those experiencing such trauma to gain an imaginative space in which they can move beyond their pain and loss to visions of justice and positive change. However, this literature often lacks nuance; rather, the stark situation is met with a grim scenario. The logic of violence within apocalyptic language does not always leave room for complexity or compassion.

Second Thessalonians advises a community shaken by some communication (a prophetic oracle or a letter purportedly by Paul) declaring the arrival of the Lord's Day (2:2). Couched in apocalyptic speech, the letter urges the community to hold on—particularly to the "traditions" (2:15, 3:6). Indeed, the language of retribution (1:6, 9) comes right out of such apocalyptic rhetoric. Second Thessalonians counsels its audience to stay away from those who do not keep the traditions that Paul has given them.

To read this letter today without context or awareness of the limits of apocalyptic language impoverishes any responsible interpretation. Such apocalyptic language contradicts other biblical messages, such as that in the Gospels where Jesus speaks of a God who does not discriminate, providing benefits to good and bad without an eye to punishment (Matt 5:45). We should be aware that people reach for apocalyptic rhetoric when they

---

[2] Despite attempts to consider 2 Thess as a genuine Pauline letter, modern scholarship considers this letter to be pseudepigraphic and occasioned by a situation sometime after Paul's death. While there are some verbal agreements between 1 and 2 Thess, the changed tone—much more impersonal—and the unusual stress on authenticity (2 Thess 3:17) argue for another hand. It may well be that 1 Thess served as a model for 2 Thess.

feel that they "have come to the end." Their sense of loss carries with it a cry for justice (usually embedded in a scenario of vengeance on a divine scale). Such language should alert us to the presence of pain, loss, and the desire for things to be set right. At heart are questions familiar to many experiencing disability: How can God permit this? When the innocent suffer, where is God? The pastoral response, however, cannot be a simplistic reduplication of an apocalyptic scenario. The history of Christianity is riddled with such reactions. Does this language allow for those who are suffering to deepen their vision? Or does it perpetuate a violent reaction? Perhaps it is time not to react but to be patient and to listen for more than what is usually offered for consolation in order to go in unexpected and creative directions.

THE PASTORAL LETTERS: 1 AND 2 TIMOTHY, TITUS

The Pastoral Letters, 1 and 2 Timothy and Titus, differ significantly from the authentic letters of Paul.[3] When scholars compare these letters with what is considered authentic, differences in the language, historical situation, and theology are quite evident. The letters are no longer addressed to communities but to a leading individual. These letters focus on questions of order and authority, concerns particularly characteristic of the second century. Indeed, the Pastorals present just one of several ways in which the Pauline legacy was being shaped and transmitted in the second century (see MacDonald 1983). Here, Paul's authority is invoked to support a developing institutional framework that in many ways replicates the patriarchal/imperial hierarchies of antiquity.

Each of these letters advises Timothy and Titus on governing well. Despite the Christian frame, the advice provided coheres with the Roman value system. In this system the domination of the able-bodied free male over his "natural" subordinates serves to illustrate his right to ultimate social and political power. In this vein, 1 Timothy requires the one holding the highest church office, the office of bishop (lit. "overseer"), to "manage his household well"—in part by keeping his children submissive (3:4). Likewise, the Pastorals present the submission of both women and slaves as a necessity for correct order. As in 1 Cor 11:8-9, 1 Tim 3:13 appeals to Eve's secondary creation "for man" in Gen 2 as justification for women's natural subordination—while adding that Eve was the first deceived. For

[3] The Pastorals do not appear in any of the earlier collections of the Pauline material. Their first known use comes with Irenaeus (180 CE) and the earliest extant fragment (of Titus) is from the third century.

women, this subordination means their very voice is disabled, as they are required to learn in silence. These letters thus strongly reinforce a construction of ability/disability we have examined elsewhere. In this construction the free male constitutes the ideally "abled" and thus politically powerful figure. The abilities of all others are determined by their lesser place and role within this hierarchy, whether for women it is being "saved through childbearing" (2:15) or for slaves, serving God through faithful submission to the believing master (6:1-2). With this model the Pastorals retain little sense of the solidarity with the crucified one (Schüssler Fiorenza 1994) or of a transformational sense of communal empowerment. Instead, the power structure of the *ekklēsia* is linked to the power pyramid of the ideal Roman household. However, even within the patriarchal perspective of the Pastorals, some women have a status not found in some present-day churches. First Timothy 3:11 would suggest that there were female deacons, equal to their male counterparts. Further, the role of widows (5:9-16) provides another example of female leadership and contribution to the community. Nevertheless, apart from these pragmatic notes, the role of women within the Pastorals represents a decline from what can be found in the authentic letters of Paul.

Modern readers must not overlook the social, political, and theological frame of these values. A simplistic reading of the Pastorals actually continues the domination scheme of the Roman Empire. Such a reading does not see that the advice given by Paul in Rom 12:2 ("Do not accept the life of this age as your model, but let yourselves be remodeled by the recovery of your true mind") greatly contradicts simply carrying forward the values of the ancient social world.

CONCLUDING REMARKS

The ancient Scriptures emerge from real human situations and are written by authors limited in time and space. To overlook their perspective and to assume it is already ours is to fail to see that there may well be a significant difference between them and us. It is patently unfair both to those who created these texts and to the present interpreters to bypass this task. On the other hand, when Bible readers understand that these letters came from real people undergoing real challenges, they gain a remarkable perspective into where these texts can lead. Such a consideration has a direct bearing on our conversation on disability. It is not enough to secure verses that will aid in our discussion; proof-texting is quite limited and ultimately bankrupt. For such a method does not get into either side of the conversation.

We cannot use Scripture simply to justify one position or another. Such an approach often can perpetuate the structures of domination that people with disabilities feel and fight everyday. Instead, an imaginative exploration of scriptural texts can open sensitive readers up to possibilities and limitations of our ancestors in faith. They did not have all the answers, and they did not provide us with a volume of ready-made solutions. On the contrary, a historical reading of the Pauline corpus provides us with the chance to recognize how meaning was achieved and at what expense. Paul, for example, was a first-century messianic Jew who discovered that the God of Israel was more than he had ever imagined. He found hope where no hope should exist. His insight was that God had accepted the godless Jesus. From this everything followed for him. He could go into the world, seeking the godless nations, telling them that they had no need to achieve a competitive advantage over others in order to be accepted. The simple act of trust, in whatever condition they found themselves, was enough. Indeed, genuine life grew out of this tissue of trust.

We have also seen that Paul was very much a person of his time and place. We cannot overlook his own competitive propensity, particularly when he argues against that cultural habit. Moreover, his attempts to speak of the "other side" of death, of the utopian possibility discovered in the crucified one, were conflicted by the language and images he used. In his own claims to authority, and in the apocalyptic images of victory and success he chooses, Paul's rhetoric often reinforces, rather than undermines, the sociopolitical hierarchies of his time. If we are to exploit the liberative potential of these letters, we must be ready to identify and critique those elements that contribute to a logic of domination and injustice. Paul's own theology of the disabled Anointed One can aid such a critique. However, Paul's letters also can provide evidence for the voices of other early Jesus followers with whom Paul was in dialogue. In those voices and in that dialogue we may find other liberative possibilities that will contribute to our critical reading of these letters (Wire 1990; Schüssler Fiorenza 1999; Miller 2015).

Without such a critical reading, the logic of domination present in different parts of the letters can easily come to the fore. This certainly happens in much of the secondary Pauline letters; much more so does this haunt subsequent Christian tradition. With the lens of disability studies, we may ask particularly important questions of these letters, questions that cut to the heart of Paul's theology and exercise of power. Such questions that we have asked throughout this commentary involve the encounter between Pauline text and the reader with disabilities. We have pointed out many ways in which such a reader might critique or struggle with Paul's arguments and vision. However, we have also suggested that Paul's own formulations suggest that the experience of the reader with disabilities is crucial for the act of interpretation. Taking Paul's own advice to value one's experience, the reader with disabilities can do nothing less. The reader with disabilities no longer submits to those who would claim advantage or who would exclude the experience of the disabled from the conversation. On the contrary, if the God of Israel has accepted Jesus in his ultimate disability, then the reader with disabilities can see that her or his life experience is valuable as it stands and can even be used to enable Paul to express his vision more fully. Indeed, Paul has seen that the death of Jesus becomes the way in which God communicates unending trust and love. To join in solidarity with this godless one does not mean that one has to add more suffering or pain. Rather, it means that we can see in our human condition, in our impairments, in our countless limits, the very way in which the divine communicates with us. Our impairments thus can be revelatory and constitutive of a community that is finally discovering what it means to be human. Nothing less than an inclusive community of fellow sufferers will bring this dream to fruition.

WORKS CITED

Betz, Hans Dieter. 1979. *Galatians: A Commentary on Paul's Letters to the Churches in Galatia*. Hermeneia. Philadelphia: Fortress.

Brandenburger, Ego. 1969. *Fleisch und Geist. Paulus und die dualistische Weisheit*. Wissenschaftliche Monographie zum Alten und Neuen Testament. Neukirchen-Vluyn: Neukirchener.

Briggs, Sheila. 2000. "Paul on Bondage and Freedom in Imperial Society." Pages 110–23 in *Paul and Politics: Ekklesia, Israel, Imperium, Interpretation: Essays in Honor of Krister Stendahl*. Edited by Richard A. Horsley. Harrisburg, Pa.: Trinity International.

Castelli, Elizabeth A. 1991. *Imitating Paul: A Discourse of Power*. 1st ed. Literary Currents in Biblical Interpretation. Louisville, Ky.: Westminster John Knox.

Conzelmann, Hans. 1975. *1 Corinthians: A Commentary on the First Epistle to the Corinthians*. Hermeneia. Philadelphia: Fortress.

Dewey, Arthur J. 2010. "Paul and the Remapping of the Body." *Classical Bulletin* 86, nos. 1 & 2: 130–55.

Dewey, Arthur J., Roy Hoover, and Lane McGaughy, eds. and trans. 2010. *The Authentic Letters of Paul*. Salem, Ore.: Polebridge.

Eisenbaum, Pamela. 2009. *Paul Was Not a Christian*. New York: HarperOne.

Fee, Gordon D. 1987. *The First Epistle to the Corinthians*. New International Commentary on the New Testament. Grand Rapids: Eerdmans.

Georgi, Dieter. 1986. *The Opponents of Paul in Second Corinthians*. Philadelphia: Fortress.

Glancy, Jennifer. 2002. *Slavery in Early Christianity*. Oxford: Oxford University Press.

Hedlund, Marianne. 2009. "Understandings of the Disability Concept: A Complex and Diverse Concept." Pages 5–18 in *Disabilities: Insights from across Fields and around the World*. Edited by Catherine Marshall, Elizabeth Kendall, Martha E. Banks, and Reva Mariah S. Grover. Westport, Conn.: Praeger.

Hedrick, Charles. 1994. "The Zero Degree of Society: Aristotle and the Athenian Citizen." Pages 289–318 in *Athenian Political Thought and the Reconstruction of American Democracy*. Edited by J. Peter Euben, John R. Wallach, and Josiah Ober. Ithaca, N.Y.: Cornell University Press.

Horsley, Richard A. 2000. "Rhetoric and Empire and 1 Corinthians." Pages 72–102 in *Paul and Politics: Ekklesia, Israel, Imperium, Interpretation: Essays in Honor of Krister Stendahl*. Edited by Richard A. Horsley. Harrisburg, Pa.: Trinity International.

Käsemann, Ernst. 1980. *Commentary on Romans*. Grand Rapids: Eeerdmans.

Kelley, Nicole. 2007. "Deformity and Disability in Greece and Rome." Pages 31–45 in *This Abled Body: Rethinking Disabilities in Biblical Studies*. Edited by Hector Avalos, Sarah J. Melcher, and Jeremy Schipper. Semeia Studies 55. Atlanta: Society of Biblical Literature.

Kittredge, Cynthia Briggs. 2000. "Corinthian Women Prophets and Paul's Arguments in 1 Corinthians." Pages 103–9 in *Paul and Politics: Ekklesia, Israel, Imperium, Interpretation: Essays in Honor of Krister Stendahl*. Edited by Richard A. Horsley. Harrisburg, Pa.: Trinity International.

Koester, Helmut. 1998. "The Memory of Jesus' Death and the Worship of the Risen Lord." *Harvard Theological Review* 91: 335–50.

Lambrecht, Jan. 1999. *Second Corinthians*. Sacra Pagina Series. Collegeville, Minn.: Liturgical.

Lewis, Lloyd A. 1991. "An African American Appraisal of the Philemon-Paul-Onesimus Triangle." Pages 232–46 in *Stony the Road We Trod: African American Biblical Interpretation*. Edited by Cain Hope Felder. Minneapolis: Augsburg Fortress.

MacDonald, Dennis Ronald. 1983. *The Legend and the Apostle: The Battle for Paul in Story and Canon*. Louisville, Ky.: Westminster John Knox.

Mack, Burton L. 2004. "Why Christos? The Social Reasons." In *Redescribing Christian Origins*. Edited by Ron Cameron and Merrill P. Miller. Atlanta: Society of Biblical Literature.

Malina, Bruce. 2001. *New Testament World: Insights from Cultural Anthroplogy*. Louisville, Ky.: Westminster John Knox.

Marchal, Joseph. 2007. "Expecting a Hymn, Encountering an Argument: Introducing the Rhetoric of Philippians and Pauline Interpretation." *Interpretation* 61: 245–55.

Martin, Dale B. 2006. *Sex and the Single Savior: Gender and Sexuality in Biblical Interpretation*. Louisville, Ky.: Westminster John Knox.

Martin, Ralph P. 1974. *Colossians and Philemon*. New Century Bible Commentary. London: Oliphants.

Matthews, Christopher. 2004. "From Messiahs to Christ: The Pre-Pauline Cult in Scholarship." Pages 349–63 in *Redescribing Christian Origins*. Edited by Ron Cameron and Merrill P. Miller. Atlanta: Society of Biblical Literature.

Miller, Anna C. 2015. *Corinthian Democracy: Democratic Discourse in 1 Corinthians*. Eugene, Ore.: Pickwick.

Noel, James A. 2012. "Nat Is Back: The Return of the Re/Oppressed in Philemon." Pages 59–90 in *Onesimus Our Brother: Reading Religion, Race and Slavery in Philemon*. Edited by Matthew V. Johnson, James A. Noel, and Demetrius K. Williams. Paul in Critical Contexts. Minneapolis: Fortress.

Osiek, Cynthia. 2003. "Female Slaves, Porneia, and the Limits of Obediance." Pages 255–76 in *Early Christian Families in Context: An Interdisciplinary Dialogue*. Edited by Cynthia Osiek and David L. Balch. Grand Rapids: Eerdmans.

Pervo, Richard. 2006. *The Dating of Acts*. Salem, Ore.: Polebridge.

Rose, Martha L. 2003. *The Staff of Oedipus: Transforming Disability in Ancient Greece*. Ann Arbor: University of Michigan Press.

Schipper, Jeremy. 2006. *Disability Studies and the Hebrew Bible: Figuring Mephibosheth in the David Story*. New York: T&T Clark.

Schüssler Fiorenza, Elisabeth. 1988. "The Ethics of Interpretation: Decentering Biblical Scholarship." *Journal of Biblical Literature* 107: 3–17.

———— 1994. *In Memory of Her: A Feminist Theological Reconstruction of Christian Origins*. New York: Crossroad.

————. 1999. *Rhetoric and Ethic: The Politics of Biblical Studies*. Minneapolis: Fortress.

Shaner, Katherine A. Forthcoming. "Seeing Rape and Robbery: *harpagmos* and the Philippians Christ Hymn." *Biblical Interpretation*.

Smith, Dennis, and Joseph Tyson, eds. 2013. *Acts and Christian Beginnings*. Salem, Ore.: Polebridge.

Williams, Demetrius K. 2012. "'No Longer a Slave': Reading the Interpretation History of Paul's Epistle to Philemon." Pages 11–46 in *Onesimus Our Brother: Reading Religion, Race and Slavery in Philemon*. Edited by

Matthew V. Johnson, James A. Noel, and Demetrius K. Williams. Paul in Critical Contexts. Minneapolis: Fortress.

Williams, Sam K. 1975. *Jesus' Death as Saving Event. The Background and Origin of a Concept*. Missoula, Mont.: Scholars.

Winter, Sarah C. 1993. "Philemon." Pages 301–12 in *A Feminist Commentary*. Edited by Elisabeth Schüssler Fiorenza. Vol. 2 of *Searching the Scriptures*. New York: Crossroad.

Wire, Antoinette Clark. 1990. *The Corinthian Women Prophets: A Reconstruction through Paul's Rhetoric*. Minneapolis: Fortress.

———. 2000. "The Politics of the Assembly in Corinth." 124–29 in *Paul and Politics: Ekklesia, Israel, Imperium, Interpretation: Essays in Honor of Krister Stendahl*. Edited by Richard A. Horsley. Harrisburg, Pa.: Trinity International.

Yong, Amos. 2011. *The Bible, Disability, and the Church: A New Vision of the People of God*. Grand Rapids: Eerdmans.

12

Hebrews and the Catholic Letters

Martin C. Albl

INTRODUCTION: APPROACHING DISABILITY IN HEBREWS AND THE GENERAL LETTERS

This introductory section has two tasks: (1) to clarify the understanding of disability used in this contribution and (2) to specify the general hermeneutical approach taken.

THINKING ABOUT DISABILITY: THREE MODELS

Recent scholarship on disabilities recognizes that that the term "disability" is difficult to define with precision. Leading disabilities scholar Lennard Davis writes simply, "Disability is itself an unstable category" (2013, 269). Deborah Creamer comments that "disability may be best seen less as a precise category (where one either is or is not disabled) and more as a broad descriptive term for a cluster of somewhat related experiences or situations" (2009, 22).

Rather than offering a strict definition, then, I follow Creamer in working with three "models" of disability: the medical (functional-limitation) model, the social (minority-group) model, and what Creamer herself calls a "limits model" (2009, 22–33). With Creamer, I find that the three models mutually balance and correct one another, thus allowing for a more nuanced approach to the complex reality of disability. Following is a brief summary of Creamer's models.

Medical (Functional-Limitation) Model

The medical, or functional-limitation, model focuses attention "on what one can or cannot physically or functionally do" (Creamer 2009, 22). This model sees a disability "as primarily a medical or biological condition": a disabled person is one whose "functional ability deviates from that of the normal human body" (23).

The limitations of this model have often been discussed in disabilities literature. This model tends to focus on the limitations of people with disabilities and their dependence on the "able-bodied" (Creamer 2009, 23). It also operates with what Creamer calls the principle of "normalization": the attempt to "modify, repair, or relocate individuals with disabilities until they are congruent with societal expectations of normalcy and acceptability" (23). Amos Yong identifies the harmful effects of this "normate bias": the assumption whereby "non-disabled people take their experiences of the world as normal, thereby marginalizing and excluding the experiences of people with disabilities as not normal" (2011, 10–11).

A further drawback of the medical model is that it prevents an analysis of the role society itself plays in disabling people; it ignores the "architectural or attitudinal barriers in society" and thus provides no motivation for "a community to change its exclusive practices towards those with disabilities" (Creamer 2009, 24).

Despite these legitimate criticisms, the medical model retains its value. The reality of functional limitation remains essential for any thinking about disabilities. Beyond the socially constructed handicaps placed on people with disabilities, there remains an objective reality to functional limitations. Many people with disabilities do in fact experience their disability (whether it be chronic pain or other limiting conditions) as a limitation of a natural function of the body and thus as a hindrance to their well-being.

Social (Minority-Group) Model

The social, or minority-group, model is in many ways the polar opposite of the medical model. This model distinguishes sharply between an impairment, understood as a physical limitation, and a disability, understood as the social limitations imposed on people with impairments (Shakespeare 2013, 216). These social limitations can take the form of social policies (e.g., failure to make accommodations for people with impairments) or the fostering of stereotypes about people with disabilities (e.g., regarding them as dependent, morally or intellectually inferior to the able-bodied, or, alternatively, unrealistically saintly or heroic [Creamer 2009, 26]). The common denominator in the stereotypes is the categorization of people with impairments as "other than normal." According to this paradigm, then, people with disabilities are an oppressed group, excluded from full participation in society (Shakespeare 2013, 216; Creamer 2009, 25).

This stereotyping tendency of mainstream society is sometimes defined as "ableism." According to Yong, "Ableism names the discriminatory attitudes, negative stereotypes, and sociopolitical and economic structures and institutions that together function to exclude people with disabilities from full participation in society" (2011, 11).

The great advantages of the minority model are its ability to analyze the role of a mainstream society in discriminating against people with disabilities and to mobilize a minority group to work to effect practical changes to improve its condition (Shakespeare 2013, 216). Its limitation, as Creamer notes, is its implication that people should accept or even embrace their impairments, since the disabling nature of the impairment is attributed solely to mainstream society (2009, 27). This implication, however, does not do justice to those who experience their impairment in an ambiguous or even negative way (e.g., those who are suddenly impaired by an accident or illness and thus are frustrated by their new limitations, or those who suffer from chronic pain).

The minority model also tends to overlook both the wide variety of disabilities and the marked differences between people with disabilities by lumping widely disparate groups together under the one overbroad label of "disabled": "a legally blind person may in some ways be more similar to a person who wears glasses than to a person who uses a wheelchair" (Creamer 2009, 31–32).

Both the medical model and the social model, furthermore, tend to be reductionist in that both define the person in terms of disability. Both models thus miss the complexity of the lived experience of disability since no person can be defined simply by his or her disability alone (Creamer 2009, 28).

Limits Model

Creamer offers a "limits" model as a complement to the medical and social models (2009, 31). Under the limits model, disability is not defined as an either/or condition. Rather, the category is seen as fluid: a particular person might be more or less "disabled" depending on particular conditions. The limits model thus does not categorize people into sharply defined "disabled" and "nondisabled" groupings.

Against the medical model's view of disabilities or limitations as aberrations to be overcome, the limits model strives to understand disabilities as an expected and natural aspect of the human condition. Creamer writes, "Good health is never a permanent state, so the 'exception' (disability) is perhaps actually more 'normal' than the norm (able-bodiedness)" (2009, 32). Experiencing limitations is part of what it means to be human.

Lennard Davis' reflections on "dismodernism" coincide significantly with Creamer's suggestions. For Davis, the standard in thinking about disability should not be that of a fictitious, socially constructed "normal person." Rather, every person should be seen as an "incomplete subject whose realization is not autonomy and independence but dependency and interdependence . . . What is universal in life, if there are universals, is the experience of the limitations of the body" (2013, 273).

Approaching the Text from a Disabilities Perspective

In this contribution each biblical text is read with a special attention to issues relevant to disabilities studies. I shall use Creamer's three models to illuminate issues such as the following: (1) Does the text refer to people with disabilities? (2) What attitudes or practices toward the disabled are evident? and (3) What assumptions regarding the cause of disabilities can be discerned in the text?

I shall also employ a method of correlation: identifying a theological theme in Scripture and correlating it with related themes or examples from the disability studies literature. This method serves to highlight what I find to be a remarkable congruity between the values of Scripture and the values expressed by many authors writing on disability issues.

THE LETTER OF JAMES

Identifying People with Disabilities: The "Sick" in the Medical Model Perspective

The clearest reference to people with impairments occurs in Jas 5:14: "Are any among you sick? They should call for the elders of the church and have them pray over them, anointing them with oil in the name of the Lord." The term translated here as "sick" is the verb ἀσθενέω (astheneō). As James provides no further description of this group, we must turn to linguistic evidence outside James in order to gain a clearer sense of this group's possible identity.

Astheneō with its cognates (noun: ἀσθένεια, *astheneia*; adj.: ἀσθενής, *asthenēs*) refers to any kind of human limitation or weakness. In a standard

New Testament lexicon, the first definition for *astheneō* is "to suffer a debilitating illness; be sick" (Danker 2000, s.v.). It is used frequently in the New Testament in general references to the healing of those with disabilities, both by Jesus (Matt 8:17, 10:8, 25:36-44; Mark 6:5; Luke 4:40, 5:15, 8:2, 10:9; John 6:2) and by the apostles (Acts 5:15-16, 19:12, 28:9). Thus Acts 5:15 reads, "They even carried out the sick (*asthenēs*) into the streets, and laid them on cots and mats."

In addition to these general references, we find *asthenēs* and its cognates applied to more specific disabilities: a man described as "lame" (χωλός, *cholos*) from birth (Acts 3:2) is also labeled *asthenēs* (Acts 4:9), as is a woman who "was bent over and was quite unable to stand up straight" (Luke 13:11). We also find it used as a collective term for "the blind, lame, and paralyzed" (τυφλός, *typhlos*; χωλός, *cholos*; ξηρός, *xēros*; John 5:3).

Thus *asthenē* and its cognates "are the most common NT expressions for sickness" (Stählin 1964, 492). In the wider cultural context of New Testament times, Nicole Kelley lists *astheneia* as one of the generic terms for disability used in the ancient Greco-Roman world (2007, 33). Thus, while the term can carry a more generalized meaning referring to any weakness, most commentators (e.g., Johnson 1995, 330; Allison 2013, 754) rightly see in Jas 5:14 a reference to a physical impairment.

THE POOR IN JAMES: THE DISABLED IN THE SOCIAL AND MEDICAL MODEL PERSPECTIVE

From the perspective of the minority model, people with disabilities are an oppressed group, excluded from full participation in society (Shakespeare 2013, 198). In this sense the term can be used quite broadly: "Under this model, individuals are considered disabled insofar as they experience prejudice and exclusion" (Creamer 2009, 25), or more simply, "To be disabled means to be discriminated against" (Barton 1996, 13, quoted in Creamer 2009, 25).

In James the group that fits this description is simply labeled "the poor." The concern for the poor and weak, understood as the economically and socially marginalized, is central to James (see, e.g., Maynard-Reid 1987). This concern, coupled with a correspondingly critical attitude toward a group simply labeled as "the rich," emerges explicitly in Jas 1:9-11, 2:1-12, and 5:1-6.

In James the poor include widows and orphans (1:27), those who are ill fed and ill clothed (2:2, 15), and agricultural wage earners (i.e., tenant farmers who do not own their own land (5:4). The poor are clearly marginalized and oppressed: they are exploited in law courts by the rich (2:6; Davids 1982, 112–13) and deprived of their just wages (5:4). They lack the power of self-determination: they either depend on others to meet their daily needs (widows and orphans, those who lack daily clothing and food) or they are at the mercy of landowners who may or may not pay them a just wage. They are thus vulnerable to exploitation.

James uses two terms for the poor: ταπεινός (*tapeinos*; 1:9, 4:6; cf. cognate uses in 1:10 and 4:10) and πτωχός (*ptōchos*; 2:2-6). *Ptōchos* refers primarily to economic poverty. Luke, for example, uses this word to describe Lazarus, the man who lay at the rich man's gate, "covered with sores, who longed to satisfy his hunger with what fell from the rich man's table; even the dogs would come and lick his sores" (16:20-21).

The word *tapeinos* also refers to economic status; in the Greek translation of the Old Testament (the LXX), it translates a variety of Hebrew terms referring to people in lowly conditions: the poor, the oppressed, and the crushed (e.g., Amos 8:6; Ps 10:18 [LXX: 9:39]; Ps 34:10 [LXX 33:19]). It also connotes a humble social status. In the Hellenistic world, *tapeinos* refers to anything insignificant, poor, or lowly (e.g., Demosthenes, *Eub.* 57.45 refers to a nurse as a "lowly" occupation), including people born into a low social position. We can correlate this lower social status with the low status that people with disabilities have traditionally held in society (cf. the classic study of Goffman 1963).

If "the poor" in James clearly can be understood as disabled from a social model perspective, we also have reason to suspect that people with functional impairments were included in their ranks as well.

The word ταπεινός (*tapeinos*) and its cognates, in fact, are directly associated with impairments in the Bible. For example, LXX Ps 38:8-9: "For my soul is filled with mockings; and there is no health in my flesh. I have been afflicted and brought down (ταπεινόω, *tapeinoō*) exceedingly."

At a level of factual observation, disability has always been associated with poverty. According to a 2010 U.S. Census report, 28.6 percent of people aged fifteen to sixty-four with severe disabilities and 17.9 percent of adults with nonsevere disabilities were under the poverty line, compared with 14.3 percent of the nondisabled population (Brault 2012, slide 17). A 2013 UNICEF report notes multiple links between poverty and disability, including a higher incidence of cognitive disabilities among children in poorer households (71). Disability in the family was linked with a higher risk of becoming or remaining poor (81), and malnutrition was identified as both a cause and a consequence of disabilities (24–25). These findings suggest that in James, those lacking sufficient food (2:15) and orphans (1:27) would be particularly at risk for being impaired.

In the ancient world, the correlation between disability and poverty was even stronger. Since only those with substantial resources could afford to consult a physician, even a minor trauma such as a broken leg or dislocated shoulder was likely to result in permanent disability (Garland 1995, 21). One subgroup of "the poor," slaves, were particularly vulnerable to the cruel whims of their masters. The emperor Commodus, for example, "nicknamed certain individuals one-footed or one-eyed after breaking one of their legs or plucking out one of their eyes" (*Lampridius Commod.* 9.6; cited in Garland 1995, 51).

Gospel traditions frequently make the connection between poverty and disabilities. Thus Luke records Jesus' teaching: "But when you give a banquet, invite the poor, the crippled, the lame, and the blind. And you will be blessed, because they cannot repay you, for you will be repaid at the resurrection of the righteous" (Luke 14:13-14). Other traditions portray the disabled as engaged in begging (e.g., the blind man Bartimaeus [Mark 10:46] and a man lame from birth [Acts 3:2]). A woman suffering from a hemorrhage "had spent all that she had; and she was no better" (Mark 5:26).

The Rich in James: The Social Model Perspective

James uses the term πλούσιος (*plousios*) to refer to the rich (1:10, 2:6, 5:1). Among the rich are traveling businessmen (4:13) and landowners wealthy enough to hire workers (5:4). The rich oppress the poor: they drag them into court (2:6; likely a reference to debtors who are unable to repay their loans) and defraud the workers of their fields of their wages (5:4). Their oppression goes as far as murder: "You have condemned and murdered the righteous one, who does not resist you" (5:6).

The wealth of "the rich" is conspicuous: they wear gold rings and fine clothing (2:2-3); they store up gold and silver (5:2-3); they live lives of pleasure and self-indulgence (5:5). They expect to receive preferential treatment and public recognition of their high social status (2:2-3).

From the social model perspective, "the rich" correspond with a mainstream culture that often discriminates against people with disabilities. The rich, with their callous disregard for the basic rights of the poor in general (2:6; 5:4, 6) certainly would have no regard for the special needs and rights of those with disabilities.

RICH AND POOR IN RELATIONSHIP TO GOD: DISABILITIES FROM THE LIMITS PERSPECTIVE

For James the terms "poor" and "rich" designate not only social groups but also two distinct worldviews with respect to God. The rich rely on their own social power and prestige to deal with all of life's challenges. They act with an attitude of smug self-sufficiency, confidently making their future plans: "Today or tomorrow we will go to such and such a town and spend a year there, doing business and making money" (4:13). James sharply criticizes their attitude, reminding them, "Yet you do not even know what tomorrow will bring. What is your life? For you are a mist that appears for a little while and then vanishes. Instead you ought to say, 'If the Lord wishes, we will live and do this or that.' As it is, you boast in your arrogance; all such boasting is evil" (Jas 4:14-16). These self-confident rich "will disappear like a flower in the field" (1:10), "in the midst of a busy life, they will wither away" (1:11).

The limits model helps us to see that the rich fail to acknowledge their own limits. They are under the illusion that they control their own lives and fail to recognize the fragility of human life. This can be understood as sinful arrogance in Creamer's terms. She writes that sin "might now be redefined as an inappropriate attitude toward limits as we both exaggerate and also reject our own limits and the limits of others" (2009, 33). James would agree, delivering this judgment on the arrogant self-confidence of the rich: "All such boasting is evil" (4:16).

The poor, in contrast, are humble (*tapeinos*; e.g., 1:9), recognizing their dependence on God by calling out to him in their oppression: "The cries of the harvesters [those deprived of their just wages] have reached the ears of the Lord of hosts" (5:4). The poor's dependence on God is a recognition of their own limits. Their reliance on God is also expressed through their faith—a faith that James characterizes as "rich": "Has not God chosen the poor in the world to be rich in faith?" (2:5).

The humble poor, then, including those with disabilities, have a special relationship with God: they will inherit "the kingdom that he has promised to those who love him" (Jas 2:5). For "God opposes the proud, but gives grace to the humble" (Jas 4:6).

Stanley Hauerwas recognizes that one factor in why "normal" people are often uncomfortable in the presence of people with cognitive disabilities is precisely because this group is a reminder of the limitations that we all share as humans. Unfortunately, Hauerwas uses the term "retarded" in the following excerpt:

Perhaps that is why the retarded scare us so much—namely, they remind us that for all our pretension we are as helpless as they are when all is said and done. Like them, we depend on others for our lives and for simple things that make life livable. We prefer to keep our dependence hidden, however, as we are under the illusion that, unlike the retarded, we are in control of our existence. Thus we label those who are so clearly dependent as "retarded" in order to mark them off from us. To Christians, such a distinction must be particularly anathema, for the very content of revelation is to teach us precisely that we are indeed a dependent people. (1986, 184)

John Swinton writes that Hauerwas emphasizes here the fundamental Christian belief that as created creatures, all people are dependent: "Our encounters with people who have profound intellectual disabilities remind us of a fundamental theological truth that modernity has hidden from us: It is dependency and not autonomy that is one of the ontological characteristics of our lives" (2012, 519).

Jean Vanier is the founder of L'Arche, an organization that fosters communities where people with disabilities live together with the able-bodied. In his writings Vanier regularly refers to people with disabilities as "the poor," not simply in economic terms but also in terms of their lack of power in the world—influence, prestige, abilities, connection and community with others. Vanier insists that when the nondisabled encounter "the poor" in community, they receive as great a benefit as those they are assisting:

> People who are poor seem to break down the barriers of powerfulness, of wealth, of ability, and of pride; they pierce the armor the human heart builds to protect itself; they reveal Jesus Christ. They reveal to those who have come to "help" them their own poverty and vulnerability. These people also show their "helpers" their capacity for love, the forces of love in their heart. A poor person has a mysterious power: in his weakness he is able to open hardened hearts and reveal the sources of living water within them. (1989, 97)

THE VALUES OF "THE WORLD" AND THE VALUES OF THE KINGDOM

The contrast between the humble perspective of the poor and the arrogant perspective of the rich correlates closely with the dichotomy that James points out between the wisdom "from above" and a wisdom that is "earthly, unspiritual, devilish" (3:15). In this passage "wisdom" refers to any philosophy, worldview, or value system that governs one's life choices.

This "earthly wisdom" is associated with the values of "the world" (κόσμος, *kosmos*): a term that has thoroughly negative connotations for James. The values of "the world" are opposite to the values of God: "Do you not know that friendship with the world is enmity with God?" (4:4). James thus exhorts his readers to keep themselves "unstained by the world" (1:27).

In 3:13-18 James details the differences between the two "wisdoms." The wisdom of the world is characterized by "bitter envy and selfish ambition"; those who follow this "wisdom" are "boastful and false to the truth" (Jas 3:14). The wisdom of the world, then, is essentially competitive. The Greek word translated as "envy" here is ζῆλος (*zēlos*)—a term that the ancient Stoic philosophers defined as "a pain at someone else having things which one desires oneself" (Diogenes Laertius, *Lives* 7.111). In contrast the wisdom that comes "from above" is "first pure, then peaceable, gentle, willing to yield, full of mercy and good fruits, without a trace of partiality or hypocrisy" (Jas 3:17).

James' division here closely parallels the division reflected in 1 Cor 1. Here Paul also contrasts the "wisdom of the world" with the "wisdom of God" (1:20-21). The wisdom of the world centers on power and prestige (noble birth; 1:26). God's wisdom, in contrast, is centered on Christ crucified (1:23), a wisdom that chooses "what is weak (*asthenēs*) in the world" and "what is low and despised in the world" (1:27-28).

In James the values of "the world" correspond with the values of "the rich," and include a promotion of "ableism" and the "normate bias." What counts in "the world" is physical and intellectual strength, power, wealth, and prestige. These values are considered "normal"—the norm to which all people should strive. Those who are "weak" or disabled are despised or simply ignored.

The "wisdom" followed by the poor and disabled in James, in contrast, is a "wisdom" that finds value in weakness. It is a wisdom that knows that life is fragile and that human accomplishments come not through one's own strength alone (contrast the attitude of the rich in Jas 4:13-16). It is the wisdom of the lowly who will in the end be exalted by God (1:9, 2:5). James exhorts his readers, "Humble yourselves before the Lord, and he will exalt you" (4:10).

The values of the poor, then, are the values of the kingdom of God, which the poor will inherit (2:5). James has learned these values from Jesus, especially in Jesus' teaching found in Matt 5–7 and Luke 6:20-49: "Blessed are you who are poor, for yours is the kingdom of God" (Luke 6:20). Although James never directly cites Jesus' teaching, he has clearly taken the wisdom of Jesus as the foundation of his own instruction (Davids 1982, 47–48; Kloppenborg 2009).

TESTING, DISABILITY, AND ENDURANCE

After the initial greetings, James announces a central theme of his letter: the close connection between testing and trial, genuine faith, and wholeness: "My brothers and sisters, whenever you face trials of any kind, consider it nothing but joy, because you know that the testing of your faith produces endurance; and let endurance have its full effect, so that you may be mature and complete, lacking in nothing" (Jas 1:2-4). William Wuellner identifies this passage as the exordium of the letter: the introductory "thesis statement" (1978, 37). The following sections seek to "unpack" James' thesis from a disabilities perspective.

Disability as a Peirasmos (Trial/Temptation)

The concept of "trial" or "testing" (πειρασμός, *peirasmos*), together with its cognate verb πείραζω (*peirazō*), is key for James. The basic meaning of *peirasmos* is any sort of test or trial. There are two basic types of *peirasmoi*: (1) any type of suffering or persecution caused by an *external* force and (2) a person's own *internal* temptation to do wrong (Danker 2000, s.v.). One sees this dual meaning in James: *peirasmos* is typically translated as "trial" in Jas 1:2 ("whenever you face trials of any kind") but as "temptation" in Jas 1:12 ("Blessed is anyone who endures temptation").

Though James does not explicitly link *peirasmos/peirazō* with disability, the link is a natural one. Disability is frequently experienced as a trial or test of a person, or of the person's family. At the same time, a disability may lead one to an inner temptation to question the goodness of God and the fairness or even the value of living life with disabilities, to self-blame, or to feelings of inadequacy or despair.

Ancient Christian authors regularly identify disabilities as a *peirasmos*. John Cassian (*Conf.* 1.23) and Clement of Alexandria (*Strom.* 2.20), for example, use this word to describe the suffering of Job. Externally, Job was tested by the loss of family and fortune and by his affliction with a loathsome skin disease. Internally, Job was faced with the temptation to question God's goodness and (in the form of the accusations of his friends) to question whether his own sin had brought the suffering and illness upon him.

A passage in Hebrews links πειράζω (*peirazō*) with ἀσθενής (*asthenēs*)—the word commonly used for a variety of disabilities (see Jas 5:14). Hebrews says of Jesus, "For we do not have a high priest who is unable to sympathize with our weaknesses (ἀσθένειαι, *astheneiai*), but we have one who in every respect has been tested (πειράζω, *peirazō*) as we are, yet without sin"

(Heb 4:15). Disability, then, can certainly be understood as a kind of trial/temptation.

The Virtue of Endurance and Disabilities

James insists that a testing should be accepted with joy, since "the testing of your faith produces endurance" (ὑπομονή, *hypomonē*; 1:3). The ancient Greek philosophical tradition saw *hypomonē* not as a passive endurance of trials but as an active act of courage in facing them (e.g., Aristotle, *Eth. nic.* 3.7) and the active capacity to hold out or bear up in the face of difficulty. In the gospel accounts, Jesus singles out the virtue of *hypomonē* as necessary for enduring the trials of the end times: "But the one who endures (*hypomonē*) to the end will be saved" (Mark 13:13 par.).

Within disabilities studies we find several parallels to James' exhortation to accept disabilities with joy, since they are an opportunity to develop the virtue of endurance. Creamer writes that thinking of a disability as a natural human limitation "offers us the ability to think of the presence of limits as a natural and good aspect of being human that at the same time is inherently difficult and challenging" (2009, 32).

For those who live with disabilities, the virtue of endurance is essential. Nancy Mairs, an author who writes eloquently of life with multiple sclerosis, reflects, "Perhaps because I have embraced a faith with crucifixion at its heart, I do not consider suffering an aberration or an outrage to be eliminated at any cost, even the cost of my life. It strikes me as intrinsic to the human condition. I don't like it. I'm not asked to like it. I must simply endure in order to learn from it" (1998, 481).

This virtue of endurance, however, can be unduly romanticized. Writers on disability rightly critique an "ableist" bias that labels those struggling with disabilities as "saintly" or "heroic" (Creamer 2009, 25–26). Such an attitude presupposes a sharp division between "normal" people and people with disabilities. In her work, Nancy Eiesland strives to correct this stereotype by showing how the daily lives of those living with disabilities can be quite "ordinary," in spite of the unique challenges they face (1994, 31–48).

WHOLENESS IN JAMES

Becoming Whole through Facing Disabilities

James continues his teaching on endurance: "And let endurance have its full effect, so that you may be mature and complete, lacking in nothing"

(1:4). The word translated as "mature" here, the adjective τέλειος (*teleios*), is also often translated as "perfect." This word and its cognate noun and verbal forms are used often in James: *teleios* in 1:2-4 (two times), 1:17, 1:25, 3:2; the verb τελειόω (*teleioō*) in 2:22; the verb τελέω (*teleō*) in 2:8; ἀποτελέω (*apoteleō*) in 1:15; and the noun τέλος (*telos*) in 5:11.

The essential meaning of *teleios* refers to something that is complete or whole. Aristotle teaches, "Things which have attained their end (*telos*), if their end is good, are called perfect (*teleios*)" (*Metaph.* 1021b). In the New Testament, Hebrews applies this meaning to those who are mature (*teleios*) in their faith as opposed to those who are still children in their faith (5:11-14). The Stoics used the term to designate an ethical completeness: "Every honorable and good man is complete (*teleios*) because he lacks none of the virtues" (Stobaeus, *Anth.* 2.7.11).

James develops the ethical sense of the word. The testing of one's faith allows one to develop the virtue of endurance (*hypomonē*); this virtue in turn allows one to become "perfect" or, perhaps better stated, a whole and complete person (Jas 1:2-4).

People with disabilities often reflect on how experiencing the limitations forced on them by their disability opens up other areas of growth in their lives, paradoxically allowing them to become more whole. A woman permanently disabled by polio writes,

> But now, far away from the hospital experience, I can evaluate what I have learned. For it wasn't only suffering: it was also learning through suffering. I know my awareness of people has deepened and increased, that those who are close to me can count on me to turn all my mind and heart and attention to their problems. I could not have learned *that* dashing all over a tennis court. (Goffman 1963, 11)

Joni Eareckson Tada, an artist paralyzed from the neck down in a diving accident, was forced to use her teeth to grasp her tools:

> All I could see were the obstacles. My teeth grasped the pencils and paintbrushes. My eyes were only inches from the canvas. My weak neck muscles tired easily. My hands were unable to hold an eraser. . . . But my limits had a purpose. I was forced to plan my compositions more carefully. And because I couldn't erase, I had to sit and think more—probably the most important discipline of any artist. Now I delight in my weakness and hardships, because my paintings are far more beautiful. Praise God for limitations! (1993, 5)

Wholeness: Avoiding Double-Mindedness

James admonishes his readers to pray in faith, not doubting, since doubt reveals that the person is "double-minded and unstable in every way"

(1:6-7). In chapter 4 James gives a fuller sense of his meaning for "double-mindedness" in connection with a discussion on the inner conflicts within a person, the "cravings that are at war within you" (v. 1). These internal cravings for selfish pleasures in turn lead to outward expressions of jealousy and conflict (vv. 2-3).

Ultimately, James sees in both internal and external conflicts a deeper conflict between the values of God and the values of the "world" (4:4: "Whoever wishes to be a friend of the world becomes an enemy of God"). This is in fact the source of "double-mindedness": a person doubts and hesitates because he is torn between following the values of God and the values of the world. So James can admonish his readers, "Draw near to God, and he will draw near to you. Cleanse your hands, you sinners, and purify your hearts, you double-minded" (4:8).

Wholeness and Integrity of the Body

In modern Western cultures, the word "perfect" usually connotes characteristics of strength, beauty, and intelligence in all areas of life. The "perfect" or "ideal" employee or spouse is physically strong, attractive, intelligent, socially adept, and capable. Measured against this ideal, then, the person with disabilities is judged as inadequate and incomplete.

Susan Wendell writes of one consequence when people with disabilities internalize this societal norm. When she was disabled by an illness, she experienced a "profound alienation from my body. After a year spent mostly in bed, I could barely identify my body as my own. I felt that 'it' was torturing 'me,' trapping me in exhaustion, pain, and inability to do many of the simplest things I did when I was healthy" (2006, 248).

One source of this alienation, in Wendell's view, is the discrepancy between a person's actual body and the idealized human body constructed by "normate" expectations (the values of "the world," in James' terms). This ideal includes not only acceptable appearance but also "ideals of strength and energy and proper control of the body" (Wendell 2006, 248). Society promotes the illusion that a "strong" person is in complete control of his or her body, just as "the rich" in James falsely assume that they control their own destiny (4:13-16). This ideal prevents both the able-bodied and disabled person "from identifying with and loving her/his real body" (248). Here is an example of James' "double-minded" person: one who is internally conflicted by the pursuit of the (unattainable) norms of "the world."

In contrast, Eiesland describes a woman with disabilities who has been able to attain a sense of wholeness and integration—the *teleios* of

James. Eiesland describes Diane DeVries, a woman born without lower limbs and with above-elbow stumps as her upper appendages. In a normate view, DeVries' body would be considered incomplete and thus inadequate. Eiesland relates how DeVries, in contrast, understands her body as whole and integrated.

DeVries is accepting of her body: "Because that's the only thing that's wrong with me, is just that I don't have no arms and legs." She notes further that she has always been "really in tune with my body." Eiesland comments, "Despite others' perceptions of her physical imperfections, DeVries evaluated her body positively as compact and streamlined. Her awareness of the differences between her and others did not lead her to conclude that her body was incomplete. Although her body was different, it was, nonetheless, intact and healthy" (1994, 34).

DeVries also resists seeing her disabled condition as "abnormal." She seeks no special explanation for why she was born this way: "Dad believed and I do, too, that it was just something that happened." As Eiesland comments, "In refusing to define her own birth as a tragedy, DeVries rejects dominant conceptions and reconceives it as the natural beginning of an ordinary life" (1994, 34).

Eiesland further notes how DeVries is able to understand aids to her mobility as a "natural" extension of her body: "She describes the battery for her electric wheelchair as 'my legs' and the mobility she gains from her wheelchair as 'walking'" (1994, 37–38). Eiesland comments, "Her body doesn't stop with the bones and flesh. She incorporates devices that promote her self-definition as a healthy, mobile, and intact woman" (38). In a similar fashion, Mairs, speaking of her leg brace and cane, reflects, "I've incorporated them, I suppose: made them, in their necessity, insensate but fundamental parts of my body" (1998, 89).

Integrity and Wholeness: Harmony of Words and Action

Another important aspect of James' overriding concern with "wholeness" is his insistence that those in the community must maintain a harmony between words and actions. In his famous critique of the inadequacy of a "faith" that consists in merely verbal expression, James challenges his readers, "What good is it, my brothers and sisters, if you say you have faith but do not have works? Can faith save you? If a brother or sister is naked and lacks daily food, and one of you says to them, 'Go in peace; keep warm and eat your fill,' and yet you do not supply their bodily needs, what is the good of that?" (2:14-16).

For James, then, religion is not merely a matter of verbal statements; it must also involve actions that show concern for "the poor": "Religion that is pure and undefiled before God, the Father, is this: to care for orphans and widows in their distress" (1:27). In another context, in speaking of the "word" of the Lord that is "implanted" within a person (1:21) and expressed in the scriptural law (1:23-25), James insists, "But be doers of the word, and not merely hearers who deceive themselves" (1:22). For the whole person (as opposed to the double-minded person), integrity between actions and verbal statements of faith is a must.

James' attitude correlates well with the pragmatic bent of disabilities studies. In particular, those writers employing the social model of disability have sought to apply their studies in practical ways in order to bring about changes in social laws and policies. In the United States, the development of the social model is historically linked with the independent living movement in Berkeley of the late 1960s and early 1970s (Creamer 2009, 26). The applied research using the social model was a key element leading to the passing of such laws as the British 1995 Disability Discrimination Act and the 1990 Americans with Disabilities Act. As Tom Shakespeare notes, "The social model has been effective *instrumentally* in the liberation of disabled people" (2013, 215; emphasis in original). Michael Oliver simply asserts that the social model is a "practical tool, not a theory, an idea or a concept" (quoted in Shakespeare 2013, 215).

LACK OF WHOLENESS: DISCRIMINATION AGAINST THE POOR AND THE DISABLED WITHIN THE CHURCH

James condemns internal division (double-mindedness: 1:7, 4:8) just as he condemns external divisions within the church (e.g., 4:1, 11-12). He strongly criticizes those who discriminate against the poor and show favoritism toward the rich within the church community:

> For if a person with gold rings and in fine clothes comes into your assembly, and if a poor person in dirty clothes also comes in, and if you take notice of the one wearing the fine clothes and say, "Have a seat here, please," while to the one who is poor you say, "Stand there," or, "Sit at my feet," have you not made distinctions among yourselves, and become judges with evil thoughts? (Jas 2:2-4)

Peter Davids describes the gathering as a "judicial assembly of the church" or a "church court" (1982, 109), while Dan McCartney argues that it refers to the gathering of the church for worship (2009, 138–39). In either case, however, James portrays a meeting of the church community. James criticizes church members for the sin of favoritism: they pay special attention to the wealthy, placing them in seats of honor, while dishonoring the poor (see Jas 2:6) by shunting them off to the side or assigning them seats with less status. People with disabilities have often experienced this marginalization within church communities.

In 1986 the American Lutheran Church at its general convention announced that people with "significant" physical or mental disabilities would be excluded from serving as ordained ministers. The rationale was that pastors should be sufficiently ambulatory and able-bodied to carry out parish duties and to respond to emergency situations (Lischer and Lischer 1985; Eiesland 1994, 75–86). For Eiesland, this is a clear example of James' double-mindedness: while the church had expressed verbal approval of welcoming those with disabilities, it did not follow through with this principle in its actions (86).

Examples of churches dishonoring those with disabilities by not facilitating their full access could be multiplied. Diane DeVries' (the woman born without lower limbs and with above-elbow stumps) request to join the church choir was denied; a pastor told her that "it just wouldn't look right" (Eiesland 1994, 36). Those in wheelchairs have not been allowed to process to the front of the church to receive palms on Palm Sunday (Lees 2007, 161). The family of Jessica, a child with profound disabilities, routinely encounters physical (e.g., non-wheelchair-accessible rooms) and social (e.g., the silent stares of uncomfortable parishioners) barriers when taking her to worship services (Beates 2012, 18).

Vision of a Unified, Inclusive Church

For James such favoritism toward the rich and powerful and such lack of respect for the poor is not simply objectionable; it is incompatible with being a Christian: "My brothers and sisters, do you with your acts of favoritism really believe in our glorious Lord Jesus Christ?" (2:1). No group should be shown favoritism based on their greater wealth and social prestige; all such distinctions are evil (2:4).

Full participation in the life of the church community has long been one of the goals of the disability rights proponents. As Yong writes, "I envision a fully inclusive church—at the congregational, parish, community, and missiological levels—to be one in which people with disabilities are honored and in which they are fully ministers alongside non-disabled people" (2011, 146). Writers on disability note the relevance of Paul's image of the church as the body of Christ, in which all members have need of one another (Beates 2012, 16; 63–64). Yong finds special significance in 1 Cor

12:22 ("the members of the body that seem to be weaker are indispensable"). He thus challenges churches to invite people with disabilities into their congregations not as objects of charity but as proactive agents capable of offering their own unique contributions (2011, 90–96).

Just as Paul calls on the body to accept all gifts equally, so James insists that all should be welcomed equally; no distinctions based on social prestige should be made. James provides a glimpse of this inclusive community toward the end of the letter. Those who are "sick" (disabled) should call for the elders of the church, who will pray over them and anoint them with oil (Jas 5:14). This gathering together of the community in prayer and concern for the needs of others is a concrete sign of a community that does not shunt aside those with disabilities but rather includes them as an integral part of the one body of believers.

Following closely on his description of the anointing ritual, James advises, "Confess your sins to one another, and pray for one another, so that you may be healed" (5:16). This shows that the activity of praying for the "sick" is not an anomalous activity done for the disabled with a paternalistic or condescending attitude: rather, the expectation is that all church members, "abled" and disabled, pray without distinction—for one another.

Vanier's L'Arche communities can serve as a model for inclusive, unified church communities. As noted above, Vanier's paradigm is not one of the able-bodied helping to meet the special needs of the disabled. Rather, the paradigm is nearly the opposite: the able-bodied learn from those with disabilities:

> When I speak of the inclusion of those who are marginalized, I am affirming that they have a gift to give to all, to each of us. . . . The excluded, I believe, live certain values that we all need to discover and to live ourselves before we can become truly human. It is not just a question of performing good deeds for those who are excluded but of being open and vulnerable to them in order to receive the life that they can offer; it is to become their friends. If we start to include the disadvantaged in our lives and enter into heartfelt relationships with them, they will change things in us. They will call us to be people of mutual trust, to take time to listen and be with each other. They will call us out from our individualism and need for power into belonging to each other and being open to others. They will break down the prejudices and protective walls that gave rise to exclusion in the first place. (1999, 183–84)

The Cause of Disability in James

Many disability studies writers have discussed the harmful effects of uncritical Christian theologies that understand disabilities as a punishment for personal sins, associate disability with impurity, or understand disability as a test sent by God (e.g., Eiesland 1994, 71–72; Creamer 2009, 35–36, 42–43).

How does James understand the cause of disabilities? If disability can be understood as a "trial" or "test" (*peirasmos*) then James is unequivocal; God is not the cause of disability, nor does he send it to people as a test: "No one, when tempted, should say, 'I am being tempted (*peirazō*) by God'; for God cannot be tempted by evil and he himself tempts (*peirazō*) no one" (1:13). God can only be the source of good gifts: "Every generous act of giving, with every perfect gift, is from above, coming down from the Father of lights" (1:17).

James also rejects the related view that disability is God's punishment for sin. After advising the disabled to call upon the elders for prayer and anointing, James adds, "The prayer of faith will save the sick, and the Lord will raise them up" (5:15a). James then says carefully, "and *if* (κἀν, *kan*) the sick person has committed sins, it will be forgiven that person" (5:15b).[1] Clearly, James assumes no necessary connection between disability and sin. At the same time, James does assume that they are related in some way, since he just as clearly connects confession of sins and physical healing: "Therefore confess your sins to one another, and pray for one another, so that you may be healed" (v. 16). Here one may note James' integrated, holistic view of the human: physical healing cannot be separated from spiritual healing.

DISABILITY IN THE LETTER TO THE HEBREWS

THE HUMANITY AND DIVINITY OF JESUS FROM A DISABILITIES PERSPECTIVE

Hebrews strongly emphasizes the divinity of Jesus. This letter features one of the few New Testament texts that explicitly refers to Jesus as God. Applying Ps 45:6 to Christ, the author writes: "But of the Son he says, 'Your throne, O God, is forever and ever, and the righteous scepter is the scepter of your kingdom'" (1:8). Oscar Cullmann remarks, "Outside the Johannine corpus only Hebrews unequivocally applies the title 'God' to Jesus" (1963, 310).

At the beginning of the work (Heb 1:2), the author identifies Christ as God's preexistent Son through whom God created the universe (cf. Prov 8:27; Sir 24:1-7; John 1:1-3; Col 1:16). The Son is called the reflection

---

[1] I provide a more literal translation than does the NRSV in order to bring out the conditional force of the Greek κἀν (*kan*).

(ἀπαύγασμα, *apaugasma*; better translated as "radiance": see Witherington) of God's glory and the exact imprint (χαρακτήρ, *charaktēr*) of God's very being (Heb 1:3) (2007, 103). The precise meaning of these terms is debated, but Harold Attridge is surely correct to say that these verses function to "express once again the conviction that the Son is the fully adequate representation of the divine" (1989, 44).

Paradoxically, Hebrews also emphasizes strongly the true humanity of Jesus, including Jesus' weakness. Hebrews unabashedly affirms Jesus' humanity and limitations. Jesus became "like his brothers and sisters in every respect" (2:17). Hebrews repeatedly states thatl Jesus suffered (2:10, 2:18, 5:8), indeed that "he learned obedience through what he suffered" (5:8). Jesus "himself was tested (*peirazō*) by what he suffered" (2:18); in fact he was tested in every way in which other humans have been tested (4:15). Although Hebrews provides no narratives about Jesus' earthly life, a brief reference to his life again emphasizes Jesus' weakness and vulnerability: "Jesus offered up prayers and supplications, with loud cries and tears, to the one who was able to save him from death" (5:6).

Thus, the Christology of Hebrews expresses in a remarkably direct way the paradoxical belief that Jesus was truly divine and truly human: he is divine in the fullest sense, the "exact imprint of God's very being" (1:3), yet at the same time, he truly shared every human weakness and limitation.

THE DISABLED JESUS IN HEBREWS

The Jesus of Hebrews is closely connected with disabilities. First, Jesus is said to be like other humans "in every respect" (2:17), and this of course includes the full range of human limitations and disabilities. Hebrews also affirms that Jesus was tested (2:18, 4:15); we saw above that testing (*peirazō*) is associated with physical disabilities in the Bible and Christian biblical interpretation. Hebrews further affirms, "For we do not have a high priest who is unable to sympathize with our weaknesses" (4:15); the word for weakness (*asthenēs*) is one of the words that regularly refers to physical disabilities in the ancient Greek-speaking world. While Hebrews does not state that Jesus was disabled according to the medical model definition, it does insist that he experienced the full range of human limitations and thus was disabled in some sense according to the limits model.

From the social model perspective of disability as oppression, marginalization, and exclusion, Yong can say that Jesus, as portrayed in Hebrews, "entered into the experience of disability fully in his suffering, persecution, and execution at the hands of others. Thus, he is able to identify with people who have disabilities as one who has shared in their ostracism 'in every respect'" (2011, 126). Yong writes further, "My claim is that even if Jesus was neither impaired nor disabled, he penetrated the depths of the human experience of weakness, exclusion, and marginality" (128).

The Christian doctrine of the incarnation (God's eternal Son surrendering his own divine power in order to share in human weakness)—so clearly emphasized in Hebrews' insistence of the full divinity and full humanity of Jesus—can be understood as the Son accepting a disabled condition. Amanda Shao Tan writes, "In the willing forfeiture of everything that he could have and everything that was his [in his eternal life with the Father], and in the suffering that came as a result of his voluntary deprivation, Jesus became disabled" (1998, 12). Tada agrees that in accepting human limitations Christ "*chose* to be handicapped" (1989, 192; emphasis in original).

CRUCIFIXION AND STIGMA

Yong writes that Jesus shared fully in the social marginalization and ostracism of people with disabilities (2011, 128). This marginalization is nowhere more apparent than in his death by crucifixion. Hebrews, too, is fully aware of this stigma, relating how Jesus "who for the sake of the joy that was set before him endured the cross, disregarding its shame" (12:2). Here Hebrews pictures Jesus as fully aware of the horror and degradation of crucifixion but still accepting it in order to fulfill God's plan of salvation.

The word translated as "shame" here is the Greek αἰσχύνη (*aischynē*). The word has a range of meaning, including a subjective sense of shame, but here it clearly refers to a social concept—the stigma placed by society on individuals who violate society's norms. One often sees this social sense of the word in the New Testament: in Jesus' parable, a man who had to give up his seat of honor at a banquet moves "with shame" to a lower seat (Luke 14:9). The Wisdom of Sirach asserts that it is a "great disgrace" (*aischynē*) when a wife supports her husband financially (25:22).

In addition to the inhuman physical cruelty of crucifixion, the crucified person also suffered the ultimate social stigma and degradation. In Roman society, the penalty was for the most part reserved for foreigners and slaves (O'Collins 1992, 1207–8). The Roman historians Tacitus and Livy, in fact, simply refer to it as the "slaves' punishment" (*servile supplicium*; see Hengel 1997, 51). Roman citizens, especially members of the upper class, were generally spared crucifixion, no matter the gravity of their crime, because of its great stigma. Thus Cicero writes that the very thought of crucifixion was beneath the dignity of a Roman citizen:

> But the executioner, the veiling of the head, and the very word "cross" should be far removed not only from the person of a Roman citizen, but from his thoughts, his eyes and his ears. For it is not only the actual occurrence of these things but the very mention of them, that is unworthy of a Roman citizen and a free man. (*Rab. Perd.* 16)

Those who were crucified were the powerless of society. Martin Hengel comments that they were "primarily people who had been outlawed from society or slaves who on the whole had no rights" (1997, 88).

As employed by the Romans, the punishment was designed to produce both the greatest physical torture and the maximum humiliation. Crucifixions were public in order to serve as a deterrent to others. Quintilian (ca. 35–95 CE) writes, "When we crucify the guilty, the most crowded roads are chosen, where the people can see and be moved by this fear" (*Decl.* 274). "By the public display of a naked victim at a prominent place—at a crossroads, in the theatre, on high ground, at the place of his crime—crucifixion also represented his uttermost humiliation" (Hengel 1997, 87).

Followers of Christ shared in the shame and ridicule of Jesus for honoring and worshipping a man who had undergone such a shameful death. Paul famously described his proclamation of the crucified Christ as "a stumbling block (σκάνδαλον, *skandalon*) to Jews and foolishness to Gentiles" (1 Cor 1:23). A century later, Justin Martyr could still write, "They say that our madness consists in the fact that we put a crucified man in second place after the unchangeable and eternal God, the Creator of the world" (*1 Apol.* 13.4). In the third century, the philosopher Celsus criticizes Christians for allegedly stating, "Believe that he whom I introduce to you is the Son of God, although he was shamefully bound and disgracefully punished" (*Cels.* 6.10).

THE "PERFECTION" OF CHRIST AND THE CHRISTIAN IN HEBREWS

According to Hebrews, God made Jesus "perfect (τελειόω, *teleioō*) through sufferings" (2:10). Another passage (5:7-9) gives a specific reference to this suffering: it occurred when "Jesus offered up prayers and supplications, with loud cries and tears, to the one who was able to save him from death"; commentators rightly see here a reference to Jesus' prayer in the garden of Gethsemane (Witherington 2007, 200–201). Again, this is part of the process of the "perfection" of Jesus (5:9). As Attridge notes, Jesus' perfecting "may be understood as a vocational process.... Through his suffering, Christ becomes the perfect model" who can guide others to salvation (1989, 87).

"Perfection," as we saw in James, is not to be associated with the normate standards of strength and attractiveness held by mainstream society. Rather, just as James teaches that one becomes "perfect" through accepting trials with joy and enduring them courageously (with *hypomonē*; 1:2-4), so Hebrews teaches that Jesus reached perfection through his suffering. Indeed, Hebrews uses the same endurance vocabulary found in James: Jesus "endured" (*hypomoneō*) the cross (12:2) and endured hostility (12:3). Jesus suffered and struggled in the process of being perfected; "he learned obedience through what he suffered" (5:6).

Thus Jesus can be a role model for his followers, who must also use endurance (*hypomonē*) in running the race set before them (12:1). Hebrews calls Jesus an ἀρχηγός (*archēgos*; "leader, pioneer") of salvation (2:10) and of faith (12:2): he sets the example to be followed. As in James, then, becoming "perfect" is fully compatible with courageously, and even joyfully, facing the challenges of disabling conditions.

A NORMATE READING OF JESUS' PERFECTION

Other passages in Hebrews, however, might suggest a "normate" reading of Jesus' perfection. The image of Jesus as the perfect high priest who makes the perfect sacrifice of his life on the cross in order to bring salvation to his people is central to Hebrews (developed in 4:14–10:18). A passage in Heb 7:26 describes Jesus: "It was fitting that we should have such a high priest, holy, blameless, undefiled, separated from sinners, and exalted above the heavens." Jesus, "who has been made perfect (τετελειωμένον, *teteleiōmenon*) forever" is contrasted with other high priests "who are subject to weakness" (7:28). Later, Hebrews says that Jesus "through the eternal Spirit offered himself without blemish (ἄμωμος, *amōmos*) to God" (9:14).

The language describing the high priest here belongs to the realm of sacrificial offerings. The adjective *amōmos* is used regularly to refer to the "unblemished" lambs and other animals that were offered in the sacrifices (e.g., Num 6:14, 19:2). The commandments for the Passover lamb sacrifice use the Greek *teleios*: "The lamb must be a year-old male and without blemish" (Exod 12:5).

A passage in the book of Leviticus (22:21-27), part of a section known as the Holiness Code (Lev 17–26), gives a lengthy description of animals that are unfit for sacrifice, including "anything blind, or injured, or maimed . . . An ox or a lamb that has a limb too long or too short . . . Any animal that has its testicles bruised or crushed or torn or cut, you shall not offer to the Lord" (22:22-24).

A corresponding section of the Holiness Code applies these same standards of bodily integrity to priests who offer sacrifice at the altar:

> No one of your offspring [i.e., of Aaron the high priest] throughout their generations who has a blemish [Heb: מוּם, *mum*; Gk: μῶμος, *mōmos*] may approach to offer the food of his God. For no one who has a blemish shall draw near, one who is blind or lame, or one who has a mutilated face or a limb too long, or one who has a broken foot or a broken hand, or a hunchback, or a dwarf, or a man with a blemish in his eyes or an itching disease or scabs or crushed testicles. . . . He may eat the food of his God, of the most holy as well as of the holy. But he shall not come near the curtain or approach the altar, because he has a blemish, that he may not profane my sanctuaries; for I am the Lord; I sanctify them. (Lev 21:17-23)

Yong shows how when the passages regarding Jesus as the high priest in Hebrews are read in light of the Leviticus passages, "It is natural from a normate perspective to conclude that the body of Christ was acceptable to God and able to save and sanctify because it was undefective and unblemished" (2011, 125). From such a perspective, "the perfection, purity, and beauty of Christ obviously contrasts with the imperfection, impurity, and ugliness of people with disabilities" (28).

Such a reading of Hebrews, as Yong notes, however, is not justified by the overall context. The passages describing Jesus as high priest indeed use cultic language referring to unblemished sacrifices, but the clear overall emphasis in Hebrews is on Jesus as a model for humans: a true human who himself suffered, was subject to temptation, and experienced rejection, humiliation, and death. This is a Jesus fully at home in the world of imperfection and disabilities of all types.

THEOLOGICAL IMPLICATIONS OF THE "DISABLED JESUS"

One may draw several theological conclusions from the presentation of Jesus as "disabled" in Hebrews. Since Jesus is portrayed as fully human and fully divine, it is clear that there is no inherent contradiction between the divine nature of God and the weakness and limitations of the human condition. God's nature is not one that is eternally aloof, unconcerned with the weaknesses, suffering, and disabilities of the world.

As Hebrews itself notes, "We do not have a high priest who is unable to sympathize with our weaknesses" (4:15). The divine high priest is one who is able to understand every human condition, including that of those who experience disabilities. God is thus revealed as a God of compassion who chooses to humble himself in order to be "at the margins with people with disabilities" (Eiesland 1994, 100).

The disabled Jesus shows that disability is not a consequence of sin. Eiesland (1994, 100–101) and Yong (2011, 125–30) emphasize that in gospel accounts of Jesus' resurrection appearances, Jesus still bears the wounds of hands and feet impaired in the crucifixion (e.g., Luke 24:26-39). This is a profound sign of how disabilities not only are *not* a sign of sin but in fact play a positive role in the realm of salvation beyond death. Salvation does not mean the erasure of all traces of disability but rather understanding disability in a new light.

The figure of the disabled God is a symbol that has the power to attract those people, including people with disabilities, who may have felt marginalized or alienated from churches who are often unaccommodating to their needs (Eiesland 1994, 101).

DISABILITY IN 1 PETER

AN OPPRESSED MINORITY OF CHRISTIAN EXILES

There are no clear references in 1 Peter to people with physical or cognitive disabilities.[2] If one uses the social model of disability, under which "individuals are considered disabled insofar as they experience prejudice and exclusion" (Creamer 2009, 25), however, one could make the case that 1 Peter addresses a Christian minority group that suffers prejudice and exclusion.

John H. Elliott (1982), Raymond Brown (1997, 713–14), and other scholars argue convincingly that the Christian communities addressed in the letter understood themselves as oppressed minorities in societies dominated by the mainstream Greco-Roman religions and cultures. Already the letter's opening addresses them as "exiles" (παρέπιδημοι, *parepidēmoi*); later they are called "aliens and exiles" (2:11: πάροικοι, *paroikoi* and παρεπίδημοι, *parepidēmoi*; cf. 1:17: "your exile").

Formerly members of Greco-Roman religions, the conversion of the letter's addressees to Christianity has apparently caused suspicion among their pagan neighbors. Christians were often regarded by these neighbors as secretive and immoral; they were at times accused of atheism and disloyalty because they did not take part in the public worship of the gods (Brown 1997, 713).

---

[2] A majority of scholars regard 1 Pet as pseudonymous (see Brown 1997, 719; Achtemeier 1996, 43). For convenience, I use the name "Peter" for the author with no intended implication for or against the letter's authenticity.

The letter gives evidence of attacks against the Christian "exiles": gentiles malign, slander, and blaspheme against them them as evildoers (2:12, 3:16, 4:4). The addressees are attacked specifically for their Christian beliefs and practices: they are insulted for the name of Christ (4:14) and experience suffering as Christians (4:16). Peter refers repeatedly to their suffering (3:14, 4:1, 4:19).

The specific language of "trial" (*peirasmos*) is used twice. The Christians have "had to suffer various trials" (πειρασμοί, *peirasmoi*; 1:6); indeed a "fiery ordeal" (πύρωσις, *pyrōsis*) is currently taking place to test them (πρὸς πειρασμόν, *pros peirasmon*; 4:12). As noted above, the term *peirasmos* can certainly refer to physical or cognitive disabilities, but there is no reason to suppose that this specific meaning applies in these particular cases. The trials seem to refer to slanderous attacks on Christians as a suspicious minority group.

CHRISTOLOGY IN 1 PETER

Peter emphasizes the traditional Christian belief in Christ's death as atonement for sin (cf. 1:2, 18-19), mentioning several times the suffering of Christ in his passion (1:11, 2:18-25, 3:18, 4:1, 5:1). In 1 Pet 1:19 Jesus is compared to "a lamb without defect or blemish." This traditional reference may suggest a "normate interpretation" of Jesus as physically perfect, but the strong emphasis on Jesus' suffering shows that the overall theological understanding is more in line with a "disabled Christ" paradigm.

A CRITIQUE OF "VIRTUOUS SUFFERING" (1 PET 2:18-25)

Eiesland critiques what she calls a traditional Christian "ideal of virtuous suffering" associated with images of Christ as a passive suffering servant. She argues that this ideal has been used "to promote adjustment to unjust social situations and to sanction acceptance of isolation among persons with disabilities, it has encouraged our passivity and resignation and has institutionalized depression as an appropriate response to 'divine testing'" (1994, 72).

Eiesland's critique seems to have in mind passages such as 1 Pet 2:18-25. Although Peter here addresses slaves and not people with disabilities, his message could easily be applied to the latter group as well. Peter calls on slaves to be subject to their masters, even when they are treated unjustly (2:18-20). As a justification for this passivity, the author tells his readers that Jesus himself left them an example of accepting unjust suffering without resistance (2:21-25). This passage could indeed easily be used to encourage those with disabilities to accept passively their lot in life without complaint and to avoid insisting on their rights as proactive individuals.

One must, however, understand the passage in its historical context. Slaves in the Roman Empire were in no position to demand justice for themselves. They had no legal status (e.g., slave marriages had no legal force, the children produced from such a marriage belonged to the master; only evidence obtained from slaves by torture had validity in court). If a master were murdered by slaves, all his slaves would be executed, most often by crucifixion (Achtemeier 1996, 191).

Thus Peter gives the same advice to slaves as he does to the community as a whole: be subject to the powers that govern society (including the pagan kings and governors; 2:13-14). If Christians are seen to be good, law-abiding members of society, their opponents will have no grounds to criticize them (2:15, 3:16).

In modern democratic societies, those with disabilities are in a much better position to insist on their rights, and so the advice of 1 Pet 2:18-25 will not be as relevant in this modern context.

DISABILITY IN 2 PETER AND JUDE

A strong majority of scholars see 2 Peter as pseudonymous (Brown 1997, 767). The author of 2 Peter uses in whole or in part nineteen of the Epistle of Jude's twenty-six verses (764). There is no clear discussion of people with disabilities in these two letters.

In an early passage in the letter (2 Pet 1:6-7), Peter presents a long list of Christian virtues, including godliness, knowledge, self-control, endurance, and love. Peter then makes the metaphorical comparison, "For anyone who lacks these things is nearsighted and blind" (1:8). A normate reading of the passage could easily implicitly associate vision disabilities with a lack of virtues.

The passage in 2 Pet 3:14 also admonishes readers to be found "without spot or blemish" (ἄσπιλοι, aspiloi and amōmētoi), using the exact terms used in 1 Pet 1:19 to compare Jesus to a lamb without defect or blemish. As Yong (2011) points out, such language is open to normate interpretation if read uncritically.

Echoing the values of the limits model, Peter refers to being "in the tent of his body" (1:13 NIV) and to his approaching death (1:14), clearly signifying his awareness of the brevity and fragility of human life. Indeed, he alludes to the temporary nature of the whole universe: on the day of the Lord, "the heavens will pass away with a loud noise, and the elements will be dissolved with fire" (2 Pet 3:10; cf. 3:12).

CONCLUSIONS

There is often a striking correspondence between the ethical values frequently expressed in disability studies and the Christian values expressed in the General Epistles.

Disability studies seeks to view reality through the lens of those with disabilities and thus to give voice and legitimacy to a population that is regularly ignored or devalued by the able-bodied mainstream society. In a similar way, the Christian literature found in the Epistles insists on the value of the weakest and most oppressed members of society. The Letter of James refers to this population as "the poor"—those who are without power and prestige in society. Not only are "the poor" valued, but James goes so far as to insist that God has especially chosen them and gives them an honored, exalted status (1:9, 2:5, 4:10).

Disability studies questions and challenges mainstream society's standard understandings of "ability" and "disability." Society's "ableist" standards value intelligence, physical strength, and beauty (as mainstream society defines these attributes) and thus devalue those who lack them. The Christian view expressed in the General Epistles also questions and challenges these values. James, for example, rejects these "mainstream values" as "earthly, unspiritual, devilish" (3:15) and announces God's harsh judgment on "the rich" (i.e., the wealthy, powerful, and influential members of mainstream society who oppress the poor) (see 5:1-6).

The Letter to the Hebrews completely transforms mainstream values; in fact, it stands them on their head. Hebrews presents Jesus as the paradigmatic figure who exemplifies this paradoxical transformation: he is God's chosen one who is invested with all power and wisdom—the exact image of God—while at the same time he shares in every type of human weakness and disability. Jesus' "disabilities" (his low social status, his voluntary giving up of power, his physical limitations, his suffering and shameful [in society's eyes] death) in no way detract from his divine power and glory.

Hebrews and James radically redefine concepts of "perfection" and "wholeness." These terms should not conjure up images of physical and mental strength, high social status, attractiveness, or other normate values. Rather, the "whole" person is one who has endured trials and difficulties, one who experiences and understands weakness, social marginalization and oppression—in short, one with disabilities of various sorts. This redefinition is congruent with a major aim of disability studies: to challenge and redefine normate assumptions regarding ability and disability.

Attacking the arrogant normate bias of "the rich," James reminds them of their human limitations and their utter dependence on God for any success in life. James' critique correlates well with Creamer's limits model—a model that holds that "disabilities" should not be viewed as a surprising or pitiable aspect of life but simply a normal aspect of human existence.

Disability studies and the Epistles call not only for a transformation of values at a theoretical level but for practical social changes as well. James famously writes, "Faith without works is . . . dead" (2:26). Those who ignore the needs of the vulnerable or who discriminate against the "poor" in their congregations are not true Christians. Disability studies writers similarly call for social practices that are fully inclusive of those with disabilities; Christian disability writers insist that churches must welcome those with disabilities not only in theory but also in practice.

WORKS CITED

Achtemeier, Paul J. 1996. *1 Peter: A Commentary on First Peter*. Hermeneia. Minneapolis: Fortress.

Allison, Dale C. 2013. *A Critical and Exegetical Commentary on the Epistle of James*. International Critical Commentary. New York: Bloomsbury T&T Clark.

Attridge, Harold W. 1989. *The Epistle to the Hebrews: A Commentary on the Epistle to the Hebrews*. Edited by Helmut Koester. Hermeneia. Philadelphia: Fortress.

Barton, Len, ed. 1996. *Disability in Society: Emerging Issues and Insights*. New York: Longman.

Beates, Michael S. 2012. *Disability and the Gospel: How God Uses Our Brokenness to Display His Grace*. Wheaton, Ill.: Crossway.

Brault, Matthew W. 2012. "Americans with Disabilities: 2010." https://www.census.gov/newsroom/cspan/disability/20120726_cspan_disability_slides.pdf.

Brown, Raymond E. 1997. *An Introduction to the New Testament*. Anchor Bible Reference Library. Garden City, N.Y.: Doubleday.

Creamer, Deborah Beth. 2009. *Disability and Christian Theology: Embodied Limits and Constructive Possibilities*. AAR Disability and Christian Theology Series. Oxford: Oxford University Press.

Cullmann, Oscar. 1963. *The Christology of the New Testament*. Rev. ed. Philadelphia: Westminster.

Danker, Frederick William, ed. 2000. *A Greek-English Lexicon of the New Testament and Other Early Christian Literature*. 3rd ed. Chicago: University of Chicago Press.

Davids, Peter H. 1982. *The Epistle of James: A Commentary on the Greek Text*. New International Greek Testament Commentary. Grand Rapids: Eerdmans.

Davis, Lennard J. 2013. "The End of Identity Politics and the Beginning of Dismodernism: On Disability as an Unstable Category." Pages 263–74 in *The Disability Studies Reader*. Edited by Lennard J. Davis. 4th ed. New York: Routledge.

Eiesland, Nancy L. 1994. *The Disabled God: Towards a Liberatory Theology of Disability*. Nashville: Abingdon.

Elliott, John H. 1981. *A Home for the Homeless: A Sociological Exegesis of 1 Peter: Its Situation and Strategy*. Philadelphia: Fortress.

Garland, Robert. 1995. *The Eye of the Beholder: Deformity and Disability in the Graeco-Roman World*. Ithaca, N.Y.: Cornell University Press.

Goffman, Erving. 1963. *Stigma: Notes on the Management of Spoiled Identity*. Englewood Cliffs, N.J.: Prentice Hall.

Hauerwas, Stanley.1986. *Suffering Presence: Theological Reflections on Medicine, the Mentally Handicapped, and the Church*. Notre Dame, Ind.: University of Notre Dame Press.

Hengel, Martin. 1997. *Crucifixion*. Translated by John Bowden. Philadelphia: Fortress.

Johnson, Luke Timothy. 1995. *The Letter of James: A New Translation with Introduction and Commentary*. Anchor Bible 37A. Garden City, N.Y.: Doubleday.

Kelley, Nicole. 2007. "Deformity and Disability in Greece and Rome." Pages 31–45 in *This Abled Body: Rethinking Disability in Biblical Studies*. Edited by Hector Avalos, Sarah Melcher, and Jeremy Schipper. Semeia Studies 55. Atlanta: Society of Biblical Literature.

Kloppenborg, John S. 2009. "The Reception of the Jesus Tradition in James." Pages 71–100 in *The Catholic Epistles and Apostolic Tradition*. Edited by K. W. Niebuhr and R. W. Wall. Waco, Tex.: Baylor University Press.

Lees, Janet. 2007. "Enabling the Body." Pages 161–71 in *This Abled Body: Rethinking Disability in Biblical Studies*. Edited by Hector Avalos, Sarah Melcher, and Jeremy Schipper. Semeia Studies 55. Atlanta: Society of Biblical Literature.

Lischer, J., and L. Lischer. 1985. "No Handicapped Ministers Need Apply." *Christian Century* 102: 670–71.

Mairs, Nancy. 1998. "Learning from Suffering." *Christian Century* 105: 481.

Maynard-Reid, Pedrito U. 1987. *Poverty and Wealth in James*. Maryknoll, N.Y.: Orbis.

McCartney, Dan G. 2009. *James*. Baker Exegetical Commentary on the New Testament. Grand Rapids: Baker Academic.

O'Collins, Gerald G. 1992. "Crucifixion." Pages 1207–10 in vol. 1 of *The Anchor Bible Dictionary*. Edited by David Noel Freedman. Garden City, N.Y.: Doubleday.

Shakespeare, Tom. 2013. "The Social Model of Disability." Pages 214–21 in *The Disability Studies Reader*. Edited by Lennard J. Davis. 4th ed. New York: Routledge.

Stählin, Gustav. 1964. "*astheneō*." Pages 490–93 in vol. 1 of *Theological Dictionary of the New Testament*. Edited by G. Kittel and G. Friedrich. Translated by G. Bromiley. Grand Rapids: Eerdmans.

Swinton, John. 2012. "The Importance of Being a Creature: Stanley Hauerwas on Disability." Pages 512–45 in *Disability in the Christian Tradition*. Edited by Brian Brock and John Swinton. Grand Rapids: Eerdmans.

Tada, Joni Eareckson. 1989. *Glorious Intruder: God's Presence in Life's Chaos*. Colorado Springs, Colo.: Multnomah.

———. 1993. *Diamonds in the Dust: 366 Sparkling Devotions*. Grand Rapids: Zondervan.

Tan, Amanda Shao. 1998. "The Disabled Christ." *Transformation: An International Journal of Holistic Mission Studies* 15, no. 4: 8–14.

UNICEF. 2013. "The State of the World's Children 2013: Children with Disabilities." http://www.unicef.org/sowc2013/files/SWCR2013_ENG_Lo_res_24_Apr_2013.pdf.

Vanier, Jean. 1989. *Community and Growth*. Rev. ed. London: Longman, Dartman, & Todd.

———. 1999. *Becoming Human*. London: Longman, Dartman, & Todd.

Wendell, Susan. 2006. "Toward a Feminist Theory of Disability." Pages 243–56 in *The Disability Studies Reader*. Edited by Lennard J. Davis. 2nd ed. New York: Routledge.

Witherington, Ben, III. 2007. *Letters and Homilies for Jewish Christians: A Socio-rhetorical Commentary on Hebrews, James, and Jude*. Downers Grove, Ill.: IVP Academic.

Wuellner, W. 1978. "Der Jakobusbrief im Licht der Rhetorik und Textpragmatick." *Linguistica Biblica: Interdiziplinäre Zeitschrift für Theologie und Linguistik* 43: 5–66.

Yong, Amos. 2011. *The Bible, Disability, and the Church: A New Vision of the People of God*. Grand Rapids: Eerdmans.

Contributors

MARTIN C. ALBL is Professor of Religious Studies at Presentation College in Aberdeen, South Dakota.

JAIME CLARK-SOLES is Professor of New Testament at Perkins School of Theology, Southern Methodist University in Dallas, Texas.

J. BLAKE COUEY is Associate Professor of Religion at Gustavus Adolphus College in St. Peter, Minnesota.

ARTHUR J. DEWEY is Professor of Theology at Xavier University in Cincinnati, Ohio.

JENNIFER L. KOOSED is Professor of Religious Studies at Albright College in Reading, Pennsylvania.

SARAH J. MELCHER is Professor Emeritus of Hebrew Scriptures at Xavier University in Cincinnati, Ohio.

ANNA C. MILLER is Associate Professor of New Testament at Xavier University in Cincinnati, Ohio.

CANDIDA R. MOSS is Professor of New Testament and Early Christianity at the University of Notre Dame in South Bend, Indiana.

MIKEAL C. PARSONS is Professor and Macon Chair in Religion at Baylor University in Waco, Texas.

JEREMY SCHIPPER is Professor of Religion (Hebrew Bible) at Temple University in Philadelphia, Pennsylvania.

DAVID TABB STEWART is Associate Professor of Religious Studies at California State University, Long Beach.

DAVID F. WATSON is Academic Dean and Professor of New Testament at United Theological Seminary in Dayton, Ohio.

KERRY H. WYNN teaches in the Department of Political Science, Philosophy, and Religion at Southeast Missouri State University in Cape Girardeau, Missouri.

AMOS YONG is Professor of Theology and Mission at Fuller Theological Seminary in Pasadena, California.

Scripture and Ancient Literature Index

19:3-5	178	94	197
19:4	179	96:1	192
19:9-10, 11, 12, 13-19	178	104	194
20	179–83	104:24	194
20:5-29	181	104:32	242
21:5	253	105:41	104
22	179–83	107–150	193
22:4-5	181	107:10-14	233
24:21	102	109	198
25	179–83	109:13, 15	240
28:3	225	109:25	258
29:15-16	175	115	198
29:15	73, 229	115:3-7, 5-8	198
30:16-19	175	115:5-7	235, 236
32–37	179–83	115:5	243, 249
33:26	181	115:7	243
34:10-11, 12, 13-15	181	115:8	236, 243
38–42	182	119:9	256
42:7-17	19, 172–74, 182–84	127:3	103
42:7-9	183	127:5	324
42:12-17	173	133:2	82
42:16	183	135:8	243
Psalms	19–20, 130, 189–200, 204, 235	135:16	235, 236, 243, 249
1–41	193	135:18	236
10:18	432	137	194
20	194	137:6	248
21	194	146:7-9	196
22	298	146:7–8	100, 196, 233, 268
31	130	146:8	230
31:11	258	150	193
34	194, 195	Psalms LXX	
34:10	432	9:39	432
35	198	33:19	432
38	195, 196, 197	38:8-9	432
38:14	237, 248	Proverbs	18, 159–64, 184–85
38:15	196	1:8-9	161
39	130	1:32–33	162
42–72	193	2:2	161
45:6	445	3:1-2	162
50	198	3:6	256
53:1-11	9	3:16, 17	162
58:4	228	3:35	160
73–89	193	4:10	162
74:9	223	4:11, 12	163
83	198	4:19	256
89	197, 198	4:26-27	161
89:1, 10, 13, 14	197	5:1, 13-14	161
90–106	193	7:10-11	132
91:6	225	7:26	252

Author Index

Subject Index

(in)ability to speak, 48, 50–51, 59, 61, 65, 80, 85, 87, 96, 104, 196, 198, 221, 227, 242, 243, 248, 249, 254, 294, 319–20

able-bodied, 4, 8, 9, 10, 20, 21, 61, 205, 222, 226, 227, 229, 238, 240, 255, 256, 266, 275, 279, 285, 290, 293, 294, 295, 297, 300, 335, 336, 346, 351, 352, 352n6, 354, 359, 367, 374, 390, 395, 407, 417, 419, 428, 430, 435, 440, 443, 444, 454; God/Yнwн as able-bodied, 19, 195, 197–98, 232, 235, 255, 263, 266, 371

ableism, 23, 61, 66, 85, 87, 164, 257, 276, 277, 280, 297, 299, 364, 365, 429, 436, 438, 454

ableist injustice, 364

abnormal, 217, 247, 278, 289, 313, 441

abortion, 78, 174

Abraham ibn Ezra, 151, 152

abuse, 19, 101, 176, 177, 178, 182, 220, 261, 351, 357, 382

acquired disability, 16, 17, 97, 98, 99, 101, 143, 229

ADAPT, 369

adultery, 42, 47, 59, 62, 77, 87, 277

advocacy, 155, 206, 268, 269, 328, 364

Aelius Aristides, 387

afterlife, 10, 291, 292, 293, 296

age/aging, 14, 43–47, 62, 80, 81, 83, 97, 103, 113, 114, 130, 131, 132, 162, 172, 180, 199, 257, 260, 261, 359

agency, 196, 203, 234, 237, 262, 346, 347, 348, 357, 367, 396, 406

agony, 138, 291, 297–98, 373

Americans with Disabilities Act, 369, 442

amputation, 21, 276, 373; *see also* autoamputation

animals: blemished/impure/sick, 59, 60, 67, 84, 113, 249, 261, 320–21, 449; disabled, 60, 61, 67, 68, 113, 210–11, 217, 235, 264–66

anointed, 81, 82, 85, 381, 382, 386, 387, 388, 389, 390, 391, 392, 393, 394, 395, 396, 398, 399, 400, 401, 402, 403, 404, 405, 406, 407, 408, 409, 413, 414, 415, 416, 417, 421

anthropology, 2

asceticism, 366, 416

ashamed, 253

Athanasius, 93

Augustine, 366

autism, 284, 286

autoamputation, 279–80, 291–94

Babylonian Talmud, 31, 33, 58

baldness, 67, 70, 79, 81, 82, 83, 85, 86, 88, 116

banished, 41, 251

baptism, 325, 344, 345, 348, 405

barrenness: *see* infertility

beauty, beautiful, 20, 204, 206–9, 212, 320, 440, 450, 454

benevolence, 326, 368

278–79, 283–84, 286, 289, 290, 291, 305, 306, 308, 309, 310, 325, 326, 327, 329, 330, 333, 335, 339, 341, 344, 345, 346, 350, 352, 353, 359, 385, 446; prosthesis, 23, 86, 288, 342, 357

natural: illness, 83, 126; subordination, 419

Nazirite, 15, 59, 62–63, 79, 82, 84–88, 113

negative stereotypes, 189, 191, 195, 199, 260, 312, 365, 429

neurological disability, 286

new world order, 401

nocturnal emission, 60, 70

nonnormate physicalities, 17, 124, 125–26, 138, 141, 142

nonviolent resistance, 23, 369, 374

normal, 7, 9, 18, 57, 64, 80, 88, 96, 102, 103, 104, 145, 159, 163, 172, 216, 217, 276, 279, 292, 304, 308, 309, 312, 314, 336, 336, 337, 353, 366, 428, 429, 430, 434, 436, 438, 455; bodies, 80, 88, 163, 216, 217, 292, 366, 428

normalization, 428

(non)normate, 17, 53, 124, 125, 126, 138, 141–42, 143, 144, 334, 336–37, 342–45, 345, 346, 348, 350, 353, 359, 360, 363, 365, 375, 392, 394, 428, 436, 440, 449–50, 454; gaze, 348; hermeneutic: see normate interpretation

normate: interpretation, 342, 343, 449–50, 452, 453; models, 160

obedience, 52, 61, 80, 96, 408, 409, 446, 449

obstinacy, 226

Oedipus, 292

omnipotence, 166, 232, 368

oppressed minority, 4, 25, 451–52

oppression, 25, 37, 112, 153, 156, 170, 171, 222, 225n5, 232, 268–69, 307n1, 317, 326, 333, 360, 368, 371, 373, 429, 431, 432, 433, 446, 454

ostracism, 22, 48, 150, 238, 288, 309, 322, 447

panic, 107, 262, 373

paralysis/paralyzed, 189, 248, 284, 285, 310–11, 326, 328, 340, 343, 345, 363, 431, 439

parent, 64, 143, 349

passing, 10, 17, 122, 150–53, 155, 336, 343, 353

passion narrative, 21, 283, 297–99, 335, 357–58, 363

paternal, 76, 352

pathological, 148, 286, 321, 322, 335

patience, 116, 254, 367–68, 370–71, 416, 419

patriarchal narratives, 34–47, 122

Pentecostalism, 307, 329

perfection, 292, 297, 396, 398, 448–50, 454

persecution, 370–71, 386–87, 402, 437, 446

personality disorder, 286

perspectivism, 66

pestilence, 51, 126–31, 138–39, 141, 142

physical: ability, 83, 97, 211, 262, 381, 399; autonomy, 248; capacities, 191, 243, 264; disability, 52, 99, 189, 196–98, 223, 325, 336, 337, 381, 384, 443, 446, 451, 452; healing, 19, 183, 309, 321, 322, 325, 366; idealization, 107, 110, 231; illness, 179, 185; impairment, 24, 98, 148, 163, 184, 195, 199, 262, 305, 311, 316, 317, 352, 379–80, 381, 392, 402, 431; variation, 4, 11, 49, 64, 105, 107, 116, 121, 142, 305, 398

physicality, 17, 124, 125, 126, 131, 138, 141, 142, 144, 160–64

physiognomic, 304, 319, 321, 322, 324, 327, 343, 346, 352

Pindar, 293

pistis, 284

plague, 30, 35, 51, 60, 80, 126–31, 133, 137–38, 139, 142, 317

Plato, 338

pollution/polluted, 5, 70, 74, 78, 80, 265, 308, 309, 313–14; ritual pollution, 59, 80

poor, the, 6, 25, 75–76, 161–62, 196, 226, 268, 303, 316, 327, 352n6, 362, 370, 375, 431–33, 434–35, 436, 442–43, 454–55

porosity, 13, 289–91, 313–14

porous body, 13, 21, 290–91, 314

possession, 35, 41, 44, 53, 137, 164, 168, 197, 287, 295; demon, 21, 22, 286–88, 294–95, 307–8, 312, 314, 320, 326

postcolonial criticism, 12, 345, 371, 373

postcolonialism, 21, 277, 363

postmodern, 346, 374

postresurrection, 296, 399

poverty, 25, 289, 318, 352, 362, 366, 373, 403, 432–33, 435

power hierarchies, 363, 392, 406, 408

pregnancy, 37, 245, 252, 306

pregnant woman, 35, 37, 42, 52, 245, 279, 306

procreation, 21, 33, 44, 239, 278–79, 283, 296, 410

proprioception, 280–81, 300

167, 168, 169, 170, 178, 185, 194, 358, 385, 392, 394–95, 396, 414, 435–36, 454; of God, 392–95, 414, 435–36; literature, 5, 7, 18, 159–60, 164, 184, 382; tradition, 19, 75–76, 179, 182; of the world, 392–93, 435–36
withered, 112, 113, 114, 285

womanist, 345
wounding, 126, 135, 138, 200, 212

Yhwh as able-bodied: *see* able-bodied, God/ Yhwh as able-bodied
Yhwh as abnormal, 217